I Dream a World

THE LIFE OF
LANGSTON HUGHES

Volume II: 1941–1967

I Dream a World

SECOND EDITION

Arnold Rampersad

OXFORD
UNIVERSITY PRESS
2002

OXFORD

UNIVERSITY PRESS

Oxford New York

Athens Auckland Bangkok Bogotá Buenos Aires
Cape Town Chennai Dar es Salaam Delhi Florence Hong Kong
Istanbul Karachi Kolkata Kuala Lumpur Madrid Melbourne Mexico City Mumbai
Nairobi Paris São Paulo Shanghai Singapore Taipei Tokyo Toronto Warsaw
and associated companies in
Berlin Ibadan

First published by Oxford University Press, Inc., 1988
First issued as an Oxford University Press paperback, 1989
198 Madison Avenue, New York, New York 10016

Oxford is a registered trademark of Oxford University Press

Library of Congress Cataloging-in-Publication Data is available:

ISBN 0-19-515161-5 (Cloth)
ISBN 0-19-514643-3 (Pbk.)

1 3 5 7 9 8 6 4 2

Printed in the United States of America on acid-free paper

again, to
Marvina White

CONTENTS

Politics can be the graveyard of the poet. And only poetry can be his resurrection.

LANGSTON HUGHES, 1964

THE LIFE OF LANGSTON HUGHES

1

STILL HERE
1941

I've been scarred and battered.
My hopes the wind done scattered . . .

"Still Here," 1941

O N FEBRUARY 1, 1941, his thirty-ninth birthday, Langston Hughes was released from the Peninsula Community Hospital in Monterey, California, after almost three weeks there. By this time, the disturbing illness that had forced him to seek admission—an attack of gonorrhea marked by an almost free-flowing urethral discharge, aches and pains in his legs, an excruciating locking of his left knee, and fever—was in remission. But on the day of his release he was still weak and groggy, with his temperature not quite returned to normal. He had allowed his infection to go too far before seeking treatment. Large doses of sulfathiazole and then sulfapyridine, the standard medication for venereal disease in the era before the discovery of penicillin, had left him constipated, depressed, and confused at times almost to the point of delirium—without doing much to curb the urethral flow. Finally, in a painful procedure, his physician had inserted a catheter "with tenderness & caution!!" in order to drain the discharge, which finally stopped.

The day was cool, the sky above the Monterey Peninsula murky with rain and winter mists when Langston rode from the hospital to the grounds of his friend and patron Noël Sullivan's estate, Hollow Hills Farm, some five miles away in Carmel Valley. Since September, he had been living there as a guest of Sullivan's in a one-room cottage built especially for him, where he could write and sleep free from most distractions. Now, however, he unpacked in an upstairs room in the main house where, over the next two weeks or so, he would nurse himself back to health. The room was comfortable, and soothingly decorated entirely in blue. On a side table was a gift sent from New York by his loyal friend Carl Van Vechten—a flowering plant, "a kind of glowing little tree growing out of white pebbles in a white pot," as Langston gratefully described it. "The very lovely gay and joyous plant," he wrote, "made the room seem like spring in full bloom in spite of the rain outside."

An accompanying card said simply, "Pour la vie." Nothing could have been more appropriate as a gift to Langston at this point than a symbol of life. In the middle of his own life he had stumbled and fallen so badly that he himself must have despaired at times of ever rising again. In America, the bitter saying goes, there are no second acts; would the curtain rise again for him? What weighed most on his mind now was not his illness, indelicate as it was, but something worse—the momentous step he had taken, just before entering the hospital, in repudiating one of his poems, "Goodbye Christ." A harsh attack on religious hypocrisy, the poem had been penned in the Soviet Union soon after Langston's exuberant arrival there in 1932 with a band of young black Americans summoned to make a film on American race relations, and had been published the same year without his permission, by a radical friend:

> . . . Goodbye,
> Christ Jesus Lord God Jehova,
> Beat it on away from here now.
> Make way for a new guy with no religion at all—
> A real guy named
> Marx Communist Lenin Peasant Stalin Worker ME—
>
> I said, ME! . . .

Forgotten for seven years, the piece had reappeared with almost diabolical timing the previous November when, after a number of professional setbacks, Langston had looked forward eagerly to a major address to an audience of booklovers about his freshly published autobiography *The Big Sea*. But his talk at a hotel auditorium in Pasadena, California, had been raucously sabotaged by a right-wing religious group stirred to action by the nationally known evangelist Aimee Semple McPherson. Thus McPherson had repaid Hughes—with ample interest—for a passing shot at her in the poem. Next, the powerful and widely circulated *Saturday Evening Post* reprinted the piece of verse along with Aimee McPherson's counterattack, and dispatched them both into homes across the country. (By curtly refusing one of his radical poems in 1932, "Good Morning Revolution," the *Post* had earned itself a place in "Goodbye Christ": Christ had been sold "Even to the Tzar and the Cossacks,/ Even to Rockefeller's Church, / Even to THE SATURDAY EVENING POST.")

The result was a squall of controversy with Langston Hughes at the center. "Lots of wires," a "Mountain of mail," and newspaper "Clippings by [the] ton" commenting on the poem began to descend on Hollow Hills Farm. Only a portion of this material had reached Hughes when, fearing that his entire career as a writer was in jeopardy, he took a decisive step. Bowing to his critics on the right, he drew up and circulated an explanation that dismissed "Goodbye Christ" as a regrettable error of his immature youth, an error that he would not repeat. "Having left the terrain of the 'radical at twenty' to approach the 'conservative at forty,' " and "desiring no longer to *épater le bourgeois*," he insisted that he "would not and could not write" such verse any more.

This statement amounted to a public repudiation of his alignment with radical socialism in the entire preceding decade, beginning with powerful poems in 1931 in *New Masses* against imperialism in the Caribbean and reaching its zenith with the militant verse of his Soviet year, of which "Goodbye Christ" was only the most profane. Spurning moderation in the Scottsboro Boys *cause célèbre*, when nine black young men faced the death penalty on flimsy charges of rape, he had thrown in his lot with the communist lawyers and propagandists confronting the Alabama judical system. A year in the Soviet Union had intensified the appeal of radical socialism, although he never joined the Communist Party. As a newspaper correspondent in the Spanish Civil War, he had been impartial in theory but sympathized clearly with the extreme left. As late as 1938, he had signed a statement in the communist *Daily Worker* about recent Moscow trials, a statement that asked liberals "to support the efforts of the Soviet Union to free itself from insidious internal dangers, principal menace to peace and democracy." Now he had broken with the radical left—which reacted with disdain. Citing one of his more militant pieces of verse, the San Francisco *People's World* vented its contempt. "This Hughes is a long way from the Hughes who not so many years ago wrote:
'Put one more 'S' in the USA

and make it Soviet
'Put one more 'S' in the USA,
we'll live to see it yet.'

The time had come to dismiss this traitor. "So goodbye Huges [*sic*]," the *People's World* jeered. "This is where you get off."

In the past, Langston Hughes might have shrugged off such an attack, but the acrid publicity had come after months of demoralizing failures. The previous spring, a reading tour had proved both tiring and, in the end, unprofitable. Then, after months of toil on a much touted Negro Exposition in Chicago, which was supposed to celebrate the seventy-five years since Emancipation, Langston had been left by the sponsors with shelved promises, sly evasions, and no hope of pay. "Chicago," he muttered darkly, was "certainly one of the chief abodes of the Devil in the Western Hemisphere." Anticipating not only lavish critical praise but also a financial windfall from his autobiography *The Big Sea*, he had watched in disbelief as his book failed to sell even as Richard Wright's first published novel, *Native Son*, garnered its author both a small fortune and so much acclaim that with this one bold stroke Wright displaced Hughes as the most renowned of Afro-American authors.

His troubles did not end. Several weeks of work in Los Angeles on a black musical revue organized by the putatively leftist but vacillating and almost entirely white Hollywood Theatre Alliance ended in frustration with Langston's clandestine withdrawal from the project and the city—in part because of his disgust with the Alliance, in part because of his venereal illness, which he hoped to treat quietly in Carmel. The end of the year found him "broke and remorseful as usual"—or, as he joked weakly, "broke and ruint." He was in the hospital, "moaning and groaning" and groggy from his sulfa drugs, when word came of what he himself abjectly called the "last straw." When the three subtenants—all of them his friends—negligently fell far behind on the rent at his apartment at 66 St. Nicholas Place in Harlem, the authorities formally evicted him *in absentia*. His dearest friends in New York, Toy and Emerson Harper, deposited his possessions, including many important manuscripts and books, in the basement of their apartment at 634 St. Nicholas Avenue, also in Harlem.

Twice before in his life—once in a pivotal teenage struggle with his father over his choice of poetry over profit, then later in a harrowing, protracted entanglement with his major patron Mrs. Charlotte Mason ("Godmother") over his right to choose his own path as an artist and an individual, Langston had verged on a nervous breakdown. But never before had he faced such a hostile public scrutiny of his basic beliefs and intentions, or the insinuations that he was finished as a creative artist and a moral force. At the heart of his current crisis was his act of renunciation. Although he had seldom pushed himself forward as a radical, and although his smile was ready and his laughter large, the essence of Hughes's career as a writer had been from the start an interplay between art and social conscience, with a need to defy. Instilled deep in his mentality as a child had been the example of Lewis Sheridan Leary, his maternal grandmother's first husband, who had died at Harpers Ferry fighting in John Brown's band, and whose sacrifice had been the core of Mary Langston's moral conditioning of her grandson Langston Hughes.

In his current crisis, as he sought guidance for the future, Langston must have asked himself hard questions about the grand enterprise he had made of his life—to live by his writing (as no black had ever done), and to make black America not only the major raw material of his art but also, in cunning manipulation and defiance of the white world that controlled publishing, his main audience. Was the enterprise, heroic and even sacred from one point of view, intrinsically unsound? Was it fundamentally so flawed in conception, so much an exercise in paradox, that it made his ambitions more fantasy than anything else? And why had he attempted it in the first place? Behind much of the activity of black artists in the Harlem Renaissance had been the assumption that excellence in art would alter the nation's perceptions of blacks, and lead eventually to freedom and justice. Had he subscribed too readily to this view, and then been betrayed by its falseness?

His friend the poet Countee Cullen had marvelled "at this curious thing: / To make a poet black, and bid him sing!" In spite of their sonorousness, Hughes had always disliked these lines; but had Cullen been right, and was the role of the artist an impossibility for a black in America? One thing was certain: Langston needed time to think through his crisis. In his teenage strife with his father he had retreated into violent illness, then returned to health with a determination to devote his life to the word. With his patron "Godmother," he had fled to black Haiti and the shadow of Henri Christophe's Citadel La Ferrière, then returned to America burning with radical zeal. Now he would depend on the generosity and sympathy of another white patron, Noël Sullivan.

As a committed Catholic and a major financial supporter of the Church in the Carmel area, as well as an increasingly embittered critic of communism, Sullivan had good reason to loathe "Goodbye Christ" and personally excommunicate its author. Instead, he accepted Langston's explanation of the poem, and opened his home to him as a place of refuge. The grandson of a wealthy banker and the nephew of a former mayor of San Francisco, Sullivan was well known locally both as a patron of the arts, especially music, and as a champion of liberal causes. He lived at least one part of his beliefs by employing and befriending blacks and even entertaining some—especially visiting musical stars such as Marian Anderson, Paul Robeson, Dorothy Maynor, and Roland Hayes— at home. "I don't think Mr. Sullivan had a single prejudiced bone in his body," one of his black employees later judged. Sullivan and Hughes had met in 1932 when the poet, exhausted at the end of his first cross-country reading tour, had passed several blissful days at Sullivan's mansion on Hyde Street in San Francisco. Captivated by the black poet's gentle blend of integrity, courage, and innocence, Sullivan had later subsidized a year of his writing following his return in 1933 from the Soviet Union, in a cottage in Carmel-by-the-Sea. Out of this stay had come the short story collection *The Ways of White Folks,* which Hughes dedicated to him. During some of the dreariest months of the Depression, Sullivan had sent money to Langston's mother Carrie Clark, and had made it clear, following his purchase of a small estate in Carmel Valley late in the thirties, that Langston was free to visit at any time and stay indefinitely. As for Langston's pro-socialism, Sullivan believed so strongly at the same time in his "purity of heart and goodness and kindness and intelligence" that he willingly set their ideological differences completely to the side.

Sullivan loved the life of art and pleasure that his banking fortune made possible, but also wore his nagging sense of guilt for everyone to see; in contrast to the poverty and disease of so many others (his sister Alyce, for example, was terminally ill), he viewed himself uneasily as a wretchedly fortunate man "to whom life owes nothing." To aid Langston Hughes, and have him living at Hollow Hills, was both a spiritual and psychological boon to Sullivan. "I love to know you are near Noël," one of his closest friends, the actress Elsie Arden, wrote Langston; "your serenity of spirit and manner, your gentle voice and your inviolable affection for him are of real support in his heavy and often difficult hours." No one knew better than Langston, on the other hand, how much Sullivan had done for him since 1933, and how much he was doing now. "To say what your friendship has meant to me," he would write Sullivan some months later, "would take more pages than I have ever written in any of my books. The way you stood by me last winter in my various and varied vicissitudes makes me believe in you like the early Christians must have believed in that rock on which . . . the church was founded."

On Langston's first day back at Hollow Hills, his birthday was marked by Sullivan (who fretted and worried but also passed up few chances for a celebration) with a small party that protectively included none of the Carmel arts community from beyond the Farm, excepting Robinson Jeffers and his wife Una, who had also known Langston since 1932. Too ill to attend, Langston stayed upstairs in his room. For the next few days he hardly budged from bed, although now and then he sat on a small balcony that overlooked the slopes of the Farm and the green peach orchards of the valley. Attended mainly by Mrs. Eulah Pharr, Sullivan's capable black housekeeper of a dozen years, he drank warm soup and goat's milk, swallowed his sulfa tablets, browsed through his mail—which remained swollen with letters about the controversy—and dozed. Among his birthday gifts were new record albums by Louis Armstrong and Carmen Miranda, but he made no effort to go downstairs to listen to them. As for his gifts of books, they "seem to put me to sleep," he admitted—although Isak Dinesen's *Out of Africa* was "charming." "Shame for a literary man," he concluded, "but I don't seem to be much of a reader."

The winter rains persisted. When the rain stopped, sometimes the only sounds were the bleating of Noël Sullivan's sheep and goats and the barking of his dogs, including his half-a-dozen dachshunds and two or three German Shepherds. An old bull named Julius, long past his prime but much beloved by his owner, grazed in a pasture. The sun appeared, but only fitfully. For company Langston mainly had Eulah Pharr and Noël Sullivan's close friend Leander Crowe, a handsome young Canadian who passed his days at Hollow Hills mainly writing poems and short stories, which he published from time to time in the local newspapers. On February 15, the house became even more quiet when Sullivan set out with Robinson and Una Jeffers on a pleasure trip to New York. One of his last acts was to slip Langston a loan of $150 to meet his doctor's bills.

Slowly Langston returned to health, and to a sense of what he must do, and *not* do, in the coming months to heal himself. Before settling on a plan, he carefully gauged the measure of his support in the "Mountain of mail" about "Goodbye Christ." To his relief, most of it was on his side. Typical was a letter from the black social worker Thyra Edwards of Chicago, who assured him that he was still admired and loved: "You have already given too much to the struggle of the people of the world to feel the slightest tremor of doubt now." An African Methodist Episcopal bishop, critical at first of the poem but scorning now the continuing attacks of "a few narrow minded religionists," promised his support in the wake of Hughes's statement: "I want to be among the first to assure you I appreciate and deeply sympathize with the motives that prompted you to do so." In the *Pittsburgh Courier,* a dean at Virginia Union University expressed his distaste for the poem but lauded Hughes for "his bigness of spirit." The gifted black poet Melvin B. Tolson warned Langston against despair: "You have so much fine work ahead." Support had come even from the leading black American communist, James W. Ford, who ringingly denounced the attack in the *People's World* as "a slander on the Negro people!"

Not every black was on Langston's side. In Pasadena not long afterwards, the fine novelist and folklore expert Zora Neale Hurston, a volatile character who had wreaked havoc on his mind in 1931 with her outrageous claim of sole authorship of "Mule Bone," the play they had written together, publicly dropped some scorching remarks at his expense. "They tell me Zora laid me low in Pasadena," he laughed weakly to a friend. But Hurston was almost alone among well-known blacks in taking advantage of his troubles.

Perhaps no advice was more valued by Langston than that of his best friend and look-alike Arna Bontemps, a man of quiet but granite resolve and a prolific writer who had come to Harlem from Los Angeles in 1924, married and started a family, and at the same time slowly began to build an enviable reputation as a poet and novelist. Together, Hughes and Bontemps had written the children's book *Popo and Fifina* and the play *When the Jack Hollers,* and they were in constant touch through the mail. About Langston's sharpest goad, *Native Son,* which he himself admired, Bontemps soothingly reported now on "the sudden boom and abrupt decline" of the novel; *Publishers Weekly* had concluded that "the boom was due to novelty of such a book being chosen by Book-of-the-Month and the fade-out followed discovery on part of readers (who thought they were getting a murder-thriller) that the book contained a 'political argument'." In any event, he believed, the fate of *Native Son* had little to do with Langston Hughes, who may have become suddenly too afraid of poverty. As an insider at the Rosenwald Fund in Chicago, he broke some news, then offered Langston calm advice: "Hints for recuperation: (a) Don't worry about shortage of funds; you're going to get a fellowship in a couple of months or so (b) Give up ideas of mass production writing: it puts too heavy a burden on your mind. Concentrate on two or three things that really interest you. If you can boil it down to one, so much the better. In other words, don't get frantic about making some money right away. It will only delay work on whatever serious project you may be planning. Don't get excited: wait for the worm to turn! . . . These, if followed tacitly, will restore health. Honest-to-God!"

However, the fellowship (if it came) would be in the future. Langston needed money now, since Sullivan's loan had relieved only the most extreme of his needs. Money had been at the root of so many of his troubles. Determined to devote himself solely to writing, but flatly barred by racism from many jobs, especially in radio and television, which were open to whites with talent and experience grossly inferior to his own, Hughes continued to exist on the edge of poverty. Now his need of money set up a new disaster. Arguing in the wake of the failure of *The Big Sea* with Blanche Knopf, his longtime publisher, about his forthcoming collection of poems, "Shakespeare in Harlem," he was on the defensive. From the start, her typically imperious choice of an illustrator had disturbed him. Waving away his suggestions, including the veteran *Esquire* cartoonist E. Simms Campbell, she had settled on E. McKnight Kauffer, a white American-born artist who had made a name for himself mainly in England. Ten sample sketches by Kauffer upset Langston. Kauffer seemed "not well acquainted with the American Negro types." Blacks were sensitive about their hair, and Kauffer's people all had unstraightened, "nappy" hair, which was then definitely unfashionable in the black community. The book should not give the impression that all blacks "are of the nightclub and the careless world. . . . These people work, and work hard, for a living."

Langston might have said more, but as a black and an author whose books sold indifferently, he had to be mild in voicing his objections to Mrs. Knopf. (Not long after, he phrased them more pithily to Bontemps: "I hope colored folks will like that man's drawings. I wrote to him to be sure and put some hair on their heads because nobody was nappy-headed any more! If he don't, I am ruint.") When, in the middle of the exchange over Kauffer, he requested a loan of $400, he found out that his timidity was entirely justified. An official of the firm, Joseph C. Lesser, informed him that since his first five Knopf books (*The Big Sea* had been his sixth) had earned only $111.15 the previous year, the "enormous amount of bookkeeping involved" seemed pointless "when sales are so small and books sell so slowly." Instead of a loan of $400, Knopf was prepared to pay Hughes the same sum "in lieu of all further royalties" from the five books—*The Weary Blues, Fine Clothes to the Jew, Not Without Laughter, The Dream Keeper,* and *The Ways of White Folks.*

In effect, Knopf was inviting Langston to write off his work of the previous fifteen years, and to endorse the company's judgment that the books never again would be profitable. In his financial predicament, he had no choice but to sign the letter of consent, which Lesser had thoughtfully enclosed. But Langston deeply resented the indignity. (More than three years later, he would claim that he had signed the letter under duress, while he was ill under sedation in Carmel Hospital. However, the letter from Lesser was dated February 14, two weeks after his return to Hollow Hills Farm. He was not the only person with a faulty memory of the transaction. "Blanche Knopf," he also noted, "claimed she never heard of this letter, or this February 14, 1941, proposal." The truth is that she had alluded in a letter to Langston about "the outright purchase of the earlier books" in a letter of March, 1942.)

His season of humiliation and dispossession was now complete. Behind Knopf's ploy was perhaps a sense that Langston Hughes was now utterly defenseless, ripe for the picking. Pragmatically accepting this judgment, he acted to avoid further controversy over "Goodbye Christ." Although earlier he had pressed his main legal advisor Arthur B. Spingarn about a suit against Aimee McPherson, he now lowered his voice: "Let's do no more about the poem." Next, he cancelled all of his speaking engagements. The first date to go was his participation in a program of "Negro Poetry and Song" at the plush Biltmore Hotel in Los Angeles, for which almost all of five hundred tickets had been sold. Next, he resigned from the board of the Hollywood Theatre Alliance's "Negro Revue," in spite of the news that Duke Ellington had signed to work and Paul Robeson might join the show. These sparkling names would have enthralled Langston in the past, but not now. "Me," he solemnly vowed, "I have retired from the show business and shall devote the rest of my creative life exclusively to words on paper not on the stage."

Propped up in bed, and heeding Bontemps's advice in defiance of the luke-warm sales of *The Big Sea,* Langston started the second volume of his auto-biography. "I bought a big note book and write long hand in bed," he wrote Bontemps, whose diligence he admired. "Determined to follow your example and do FOUR pages a day, rain, sun, or landslide." The heart of the new book, which would pick up the story of Hughes's life after 1931, where *The Big Sea* ended, was to be a revision of the manuscript about his year in the Soviet Union that Blanche Knopf had coldly rejected some years before. But Langston's mind soon drifted away from the Soviet Union to his own child-hood. In a fresh chapter called "No Hot Cakes For Breakfast: Cold in Bo-khara," which ostensibly was about Central Asia in winter, he fell into remin-iscing about his boyhood in Lawrence, Kansas, and exciting visits to Kansas City to see an uncle who had a barbershop there. The childhood references, out of place in a memoir of Central Asia, are telling. Stirring under the exercise in recall represented by autobiography was perhaps a more profound hope—that fetal consciousness might be reclaimed and identity reformed, so that by drifting back into the past he could move then into the future as a regenerated, indomitable human being. Perhaps the most glowing feature of his personality, both as an individual and an artist, had been his power to invoke and exude a luminously childlike sense of innocence and wonder. But the passage of years and events had contaminated this gift of innocence. In any event, in spite of his grandmother's noble lessons about resistance, he had been a lonely child. Now, for all of his striking accomplishments and thousand friends, he was a lonely man.

In *The Big Sea* the previous year, Hughes had quietly conceded all about his childhood: "I was unhappy for a long time, and very lonesome, living with my grandmother. Then it was that books began to happen to me, and I began to believe in nothing but books and the wonderful world in books—where if people suffered, they suffered in beautiful language, not in monosyllables, as we did in Kansas. . . . Nobody ever cried in my grandmother's stories. When my grandmother died, I didn't cry, either. Something about my grandmother's stories (without her ever having said so) taught me the uselessness of crying about anything." About his mother he wrote little, but the few paragraphs featured episodes in which he had twice humiliated her in public—once by refusing to recite a passage he knew by heart, and later by mugging and gri-macing on stage as she shamelessly enacted the role of the loyal mother in the Roman tale of the Gracchi family. "When the program was over and my mother found out what had happened," Langston wrote, "I got the worst whipping of my life."

With his coldly materialistic father, who scorned poetry and his fellow blacks but prized his various pieces of property in Mexico, he had created in his autobiography a veiled but memorable image of Satan tempting with untold riches an inviolable Christ. Then Langston had driven a stake of a sentence through Satan's heart: "I hated my father."

The death of Langston's grandmother in 1915 had ended his boyhood in Lawrence, Kansas. His father had died in 1934, thirteen years after Langston had last seen him, and a dozen years after Langston had calmly refused to go to his aid in Mexico, where James Hughes lived, following a paralytic stroke. After years of waywardness and poverty, and a lifetime of tension with her son mainly because he accepted penury as the price of his art, Carrie Clark had died in 1938 of breast cancer. Not long before her death, while they were living together, Langston had written a macabre playlet of one scene, "Soul Gone Home," about a dead youth sitting up on his deathbed to revile his mother, who is depicted as a heartless whore. About the same time, he had also written "Genius Child":

> This is a song for the genius child.
> Sing it softly, for the song is wild.
> Sing it softly as ever you can—
> Lest the song get out of hand.
>
> *Nobody loves a genius child.*
>
> Can you love an eagle,
> Tame or wild?
>
> Wild or tame,
> Can you love a monster
> Of frightening name?
>
> *Nobody loves a genius child.*
>
> "*Kill him*—and let his soul run
>   wild!

A brother of Langston's father lived in Los Angeles, and there were distant cousins and rumors of cousins, but essentially Langston Hughes was a man without a family to fall back on in his hour of crisis, and with a vanishing— perhaps vanished—prospect of generating one of his own. His venereal infection sadly mocked the private lovelessness that had become by now a fixed part of his life. To meet this current crisis, he had his vocation of art, and the friendships that both facilitated his vocation and were fostered by it—and he had his major audience, black people, whose gratitude and love strained to fill the void where a more intimate affection should have existed.

Three weeks passed before he finally set out to town. Faced with the challenge of hosting a lunch in Sullivan's absence, he went off to Monterey to find a black barbershop, then loitered at a popular record shop before returning to Hollow Hills. (The village of Carmel included only three or four blacks, including Al Byrd, who ran an auto service station, and his wife Fairy Lee Byrd, who laundered clothes but only for the wealthiest whites.) The next day, he was groomed but nervous and decidedly not modishly dressed—Langston no longer owned a suit—when an elegant group headed by the American-born Baroness d'Erlanger called at the Farm. In 1922, just after leaving Columbia University following his freshman year, he had worked in New York as a delivery boy for a Fifth Avenue florist, Charles Thorley. One of his regular customers had been d'Erlanger herself. "I used to take her flowers at the Ritz when I worked for Thorley," he recalled with more amusement than trepidation a few days before her arrival. "So life goes round in circles. . . . I am not sure I am up to entertaining royalty. But I will try."

The luncheon did not whet his appetite for society. Back in his cottage, he read more than he wrote. His reaction to two books, both about race and by white writers, was marked. In an unusual move, he sent a letter of congratulation to Willa Cather for her depiction of blacks, who seemed "truthfully represented" in her new novel *Sapphira and the Slave Girl*. More curiously, he also wrote to Will Alexander Percy of Greenville, Mississippi, to praise his autobiography *Lanterns on the Levee*. Undoubtedly Hughes was swayed by the memory of Percy's gallant introduction when Langston had read in Greenville in 1932, and he certainly found the book gripping: "I couldn't put it down." But *Lanterns on the Levee* was in some ways bizarre. "What he says about the Negroes he knows," Hughes wrote to a black civil rights leader, "will make the hair stand on your head straight up. (Maybe they do carry on as he depicts in the Delta, but the trouble is he generalizes from there right on out to us!)."

Hughes probably made no such objection in writing to Percy, who replied with what he called "a very nice letter." Embattled himself, Langston was now apparently more taken with Percy's and Cather's good intentions than with their success or failure as social commentators. Instead, he identified with their difficulty as artists and charitably forgave them their limitations. A little later, he would write in a similar vein to defend the late Vachel Lindsay from charges of racism. Many blacks were sensitive to the language of primitivism when invoked about them, as in Lindsay's *Congo*, but "personally, I regard him as having been a great poet." On the other hand, his tolerance had its limits. Near the end of the year, when the publisher E. P. Dutton, hoping for a blurb, sent him a novel of black life that seemed bereft of even a suspicion of black humanity, he sent back a crushing report and an icy refusal to aid the author.

He was also in touch with Richard Wright, to whom he sent thanks for a gift copy of a long essay about the genesis of *Native Son*, "How Bigger Was Born," and to explain his stay in the hospital—influenza "and general disgustedness." But Langston also had the uncomfortable task of congratulating Wright on having won the Spingarn Medal, awarded annually by the NAACP to honor "the highest and noblest achievement of an American Negro during the preceding year or years." Langston coveted the award for himself. He admired its founder, Joel Elias Spingarn, a leader of the NAACP until his death in 1939, and Spingarn's gracious wife, Amy Einstein Spingarn, who had generously loaned Langston the money to attend Lincoln University between 1926 and 1929. In 1930, he had dedicated his novel *Not Without Laughter* to them. Langston also believed that he deserved the award because of his literary service to the race, and he was convinced that his radicalism, unpalatable to the NAACP, was the main reason he had been passed over. Now Richard Wright, a Communist Party member, had won the Spingarn Prize.

Soon news came of another victory for Wright, when the play version of *Native Son,* directed by Orson Welles and starring Canada Lee, opened on Broadway to fine critical reviews and excited audiences. The news was "swell" about Wright's "triumph, isn't it?" Hughes wrote to a friend. He was both pleased for Wright, whom he liked personally, and disturbed. Some of his distress may have stemmed from envy, but Hughes had other reasons for regretting Wright's success. The great body of his own work affirmed life, and especially black life; even his radical socialist writing had been charged by a marvellously buoyant idealism. But Wright's vision, certainly in *Native Son,* seemed to Hughes the opposite. Now, as Langston sought a way to signal his return to the world and his eagerness to continue the grand fight, he attacked Wright in order to make his greater point. In his manifesto of the Harlem Renaissance published in the *Nation* in 1926, "The Negro Artist and the Racial Mountain," Hughes had demanded on behalf of the black artist an almost bohemian freedom, linked to racial pride. Now, in another essay, "The Need for Heroes," written for the *Crisis,* he emphasized not freedom but moral responsibility, once again linked to pride in the black race.

His main target was *Native Son.* But to camouflage his attack, and not through any genuine urge to punish himself, he opened by criticizing both Wright's novel and one of his own works:

> The written word is the only record we will have of this our present, or our past, to leave behind for future generations. It would be a shame if that written word in its creative form were to consist largely of defeat and death. Suppose *Native Son*'s Bigger Thomas (excellently drawn as he was) was the sole survivor on the bookshelves of tomorrow? Or my own play, *Mulatto,* whose end consists of murder, madness, and suicide? If the best of our writers continue to pour their talent into the tragedies of frustration and weakness, tomorrow will probably say, on the basis of available literary evidence, "No wonder the Negroes never amounted to anything. There were no heroes among them. Defeat and panic, moaning, groaning, and weeping were their lot. Did nobody fight? Did nobody triumph? Here is that book about Bigger. The catalogue says it sold several hundred thousand copies. A Negro wrote it. No wonder Hitler wiped the Negroes off the face of Europe."

"Negroes have a need for heroes," Hughes insisted, "now, this moment, this year." Scholarly studies abounded, and comedy, tragedy, folklore, and practical progress had been adequately served; "but where, in all these books," he asked, "is that compelling flame of spirit and passion that makes a man say,

'I, too, am a hero, because my race has produced heroes like that!'?'' Both in the past and in contemporary black life, heroes were many. "Do not say there were no living Negro heroes," he warned. "Do not say there have never been any in the past. These statements would be lies, enormously untrue." It was "the social duty of Negro writers" to take up this challenge. "We know we are not weak, ignorant, frustrated, or cowed. We know the race has its heroes whether anybody puts them into books or not. We know we are heroes ourselves and can make a better world."

Langston had used a similar argument the previous December in applying for a Rosenwald Fund fellowship to research and write a series of one-act plays on black heroes for high schools, colleges, and amateur theatrical groups. Deploring the tone of contemporary black literature, much of which was "of a protest nature depicting horror and oppression," he regretted the failure of writers to be a source of "confidence or inspiration to the Negro youth. I feel that there is a need for heroes in Negro literature, a need for achievement and triumph, a need for strength growing out of our racial past and the accomplishments of the great Negroes of yesterday and today."

With good reason, he considered himself one of the heroes who had inspired a generation of the youth of black America. Modesty prevented him from saying so, but he did not wish the future to see him mainly as a coward or backslider, with his retraction of "Goodbye Christ" waved as evidence against him. In spite of his mention of *Mulatto* as an example of defeatist literature in "The Need for Heroes," his true feelings slipped out ingenuously in writing about the essay to his friend Louise Thompson, who had led Langston and the party of young blacks to Moscow in 1932 and was still a confident radical. "To read it," he wrote her, "you would almost think *I* was a hero myself. Such is the power of literature to deceive."

In "What the Negro Wants," an essay written at about the same time but, unlike "The Need for Heroes," addressed mainly to whites, Langston was more dispassionate. Since he was black but did not "rail and sweat and frown in anger" (thus he disparaged the image of an embittered black such as Wright's Bigger Thomas), whites often wondered whether life was truly bad for blacks, and whites of good will often asked him flatly: "Just what do you want?" Hughes listed seven items. Blacks wanted "a chance to earn a decent living" and "equal educational opportunities all over America." Decent housing was essential, as well as "full participation in Government—municipal, state, and national"; also, "a fair deal before the law." Blacks wanted "public courtesy, the same courtesy that is normally accorded other citizens." Lastly, they wanted "social equality in so far as public services go. . . . We want the right to ride without Jim Crow in any conveyance carrying the traveling public. We want the right when traveling to dine in any restaurant or seek lodgings in any hotel or auto camp open to the public which our purse affords. (Any Nazi may do so.)"

If Langston's agenda for progress could hardly be faulted, his call for a literature of heroism raised questions about his evolving sense of himself as an artist and his sense of art itself. In surrendering the exuberance of "The Negro Artist and the Racial Mountain" for the prescriptions of "The Need for Heroes," he appeared to be conceding the end of his struggle to be a great writer. At least one person, Rowena Jelliffe of Karamu House in Cleveland, who had known Langston since 1915 and had staged most of his plays in the thirties, feared now for his future. In a letter to the Rosenwald Fund, she called his plan "too easy, too trivial and too unchallenging for one of his capacity." Given his remarkable talent, she argued, he had always aimed too low. "That there is danger of his passing beyond his best creative period without yielding the measure of his capacity I feel certain and it concerns me deeply."

Just as he seemed, however, to be committing himself to a literature of heroic solemnity, Langston's next professional step showed that his need for heroes might be no match for his need for cash. (In a humiliating episode just before Baroness d'Erlanger's visit, his attempt to secure a suit on credit at a local haberdashery was coldly rebuffed; yes, they may have heard of him, but did he have a job, or a steady source of income?) Thus, when a tempting request came from the producer Moe Gale for a radio series to be developed from his Harlem comedy about the numbers racket, *Little Ham,* Langston snapped to attention. (Moses Gale was the son of Sigmund Gale, the guiding spirit of the grand Savoy Ballroom on Lenox Avenue in Harlem.) He remained entranced even after his agent Maxim Lieber explained that Moe Gale wanted "a sort of Amos and Andy sequence with suspense." His reference was to the astoundingly popular radio comedy show, written and acted by whites since its start in 1929, that some blacks regarded as shameful and demeaning of the race.

Pushing aside his autobiography and, perhaps, his principles, Langston plunged into work. On March 12, he sent Lieber and Gale an outline for a series of 65 episodes called "Hamlet Jones." Built around the diminutive bootblack hero of *Little Ham,* Hamlet Hitchcock Jones, the series would "cover Harlem like a book from Sunday in the Park to Monday at the Savoy." Evidently he had been inspired. Lieber perused the outline and saw "very definite financial promise"; Gale, he reported, was "rhapsodic." The National Broadcasting Company, after requesting two sample sketches, was also delighted with Langston's work. The contract offered was more lucrative than anything he had ever contemplated. ("I don't think that Gale is a marijuana addict," Lieber joked.) For each fifteen-minute sketch, the author would receive a minimum of $75 a week; but his pay would be as much as $400 a week if Gale found a major sponsor for the series. Langston signed the document without delay. Lieber cautioned him against rash optimism, "because we've been struck so often," but could barely restrain himself: "All aboard for the Radio Special!"

In April, while he kept his ear to the rail listening for the "Radio Special," came a measure of relief from worrying about money. Just as Arna Bontemps had predicted, the Rosenwald Fund awarded Hughes a fellowship of $1500, starting in June, to write his plays about black heroes. The assurance of cash lifted his spirits. He celebrated by taking another loan from Noël Sullivan, who had returned home, against the Rosenwald sum. Then he rushed to San Francisco to buy a long-coveted brown suit with matching shoes, a shirt, shorts, belt, and tie. "Thus armoured," he proclaimed, "I return to the struggle." Effervescent in his new suit, he joined in wild applause when the latest black concert sensation Dorothy Maynor, whom he had first met in 1931 near the start of his cross-country poetry tour, electrified the San Francisco Opera House with an aria she was forced to repeat. Maynor, who rested over a weekend at Hollow Hills Farm, had grown into "a simple jolly plump little soul," he noted approvingly—besides, she was bound to succeed as a singer because she was intelligent and had "prima donna busts." He was debonair in his brown suit again when the expatriate German writer Thomas Mann, his wife, his youngest son, and a daughter whose husband had been lost at sea, lunched at the Farm. In mid-May, Langston returned to San Francisco for an interview on the CBS radio program "Of Men and Books."

By this time, Langston was almost his old self again. His confidence back, he made a definitive move to remind the world of his achievements. In June 1921, marking his first appearance in an adult magazine, the *Crisis* had published his poem "The Negro Speaks of Rivers":

> I've known rivers:
>> I've known rivers ancient as the world and older
>>> than the flow of human blood in human veins.
>
> My soul has grown deep like the rivers.
>
>> I bathed in the Euphrates when dawns were young.
>> I built my hut near the Congo and it lulled me to sleep.
>> I looked upon the Nile and raised the pyramids above it.
>> I heard the singing of the Mississippi when Abe Lincoln
>>> went down to New Orleans, and I've seen its muddy
>>> bosom turn all golden in the sunset.
>
>> I've known rivers;
>>> Ancient, dusky rivers.
>
> My soul has grown deep like the rivers.

This poem, though written at eighteen, had remained in some respects the benchmark of his genius. Seizing the moment, he ordered 250 postcards to be printed with "MY FIRST PUBLISHED POEM" and a silhouette of a black man in idyllic repose drawn by his friend Aaron Douglas, a fellow star of the Harlem Renaissance. Having signed each card, Langston distributed them as a reminder of the longevity and the noble purpose of his career—"Twenty years of Writing and Publishing—June 1921-June 1941."

Uncertain in these months exactly where he was going as an artist, Langston clearly felt the need to remind himself and the world exactly where he had been. He now launched a massive campaign of consolidation. Gathering all his poems outside of his books (or *almost* all of them, since he closed his eyes to "Goodbye Christ" and other ultra-radical poems), he divided these 343 pieces according to themes and subgenres—lyrics, ballads, protest literature, light verse, children's poems, blues, and so on. Several of the ballads, many of them written in the black vernacular, went to Frank Marshall Davis in Chicago for distribution specifically through the Associated Negro Press. (To Davis, a poet himself, most of Hughes's recent work frankly had been "more propaganda than art, but in these verses your art is foremost and your social consciousness more subtle." This judgment, he assured Hughes, was backed by Richard Wright, who had read the collection and was "quite enthused.") Maxim Lieber received a selection to offer to white journals and to the publisher of *New Directions* for consideration in its Poet of the Month series.

Langston also consigned all his skits and sketches, divided into three classes—Negro Social, Negro Non-Social, and white—to his agent, who had alerted him that Cafe Society, a novel interracial cabaret founded recently in New York by Barney Josephson, was planning a revue. He also sent twenty skits, collectively called "Run, Ghost, Run" after one of the pieces, to Powell Lindsay for possible use by the Negro Playwrights Company, in which Hughes had been nominally involved, and which was stirring again after having given every sign of a demise.

Next, he consolidated his song lyrics. Making a list of all his published songs—over a dozen in number between 1926 and 1940—he submitted it to the American Society of Composers, Authors and Publishers, or ASCAP, in order to raise his rating there and thus his remuneration. Copies of the once promising "America's Young Black Joe," written for the Hollywood Theatre Alliance and "a good Negro patriotic song of a positive nature just now," went to over two dozen black colleges and fifteen high schools. He also gave a free hand to Charles Leonard, his main collaborator on work for the Alliance, and an employee of Columbia Pictures, to sell any piece of their work to anyone who wished to buy it. When Duke Ellington evinced an interest in one song, Langston scribbled his release: "Bird in hand worth ten in bush. Better take it." To a newly formed organization of starving actors in New York, the Negro Radio Workshop, went various pieces for consideration, including his work for the ill-fated Negro Exposition in Chicago in 1940. Surprisingly, Hughes also sent the script of his 1938 radical play *Don't You Want to Be Free?*, which had been a huge success with the now-defunct Harlem Suitcase Theatre.

The wide distribution of his poems paid off, as he hoped it would, in publication in a variety of magazines, including *Poetry,* Louis Adamic's newly formed *Common Ground* (which also published his essay "What the Negro Wants"), *Span, Compass, Opportunity,* and *Crisis.* By far the greatest number, however, appeared that year in the Carmel *Pine Cone.* Lee Crowe of Hollow Hills Farm published several there in his column, "Crowe's Nest," and on July 18 the regular poetry column, edited by Dora Hagemeyer and Helen Coolidge, featured Langston's work exclusively. Although he had been virtually run out of Carmel during an upsurge of labor unrest and right-wing radicalism in 1934,

Langston was determined now not to neglect what was in effect, if only temporarily, home. Late in June, he also contributed to the *Pine Cone* an essay, "Ancient Contemporaries in the Forest Theatre," on a local production of Robinson Jeffers's version of *Clytemnestra*, with the internationally known actress Judith Anderson (who married Noël Sullivan's close friend Ben Lehman of the University of California).

These publications testified to his vitality, but if Langston could point proudly to the quantity of his publications, the quality was another matter. The seven poems in the *Pine Cone* of July 18, like most of the others that appeared there, were weak. Only one of the seven, "Young Negro Girl" ("You are like a warm dark dusk / In the middle of June-time"), touches on race, but it does so mainly in a strained, formal manner. "Refugee" bursts with emotion, but here and in other poems are revealed lapses of technique odd in a veteran poet, including clichés and archaisms of syntax and words: "the bitter broken boughs of pain"; "loneliness terrific beats on my heart"; "Though I wonder and stray / And wound her sore." Perhaps the best poem is "Big Sur," the most modest in size: "Great lonely hills, / Great mountains, / Mighty touchstones of song." He appears to have gauged his audience in Carmel—genteel, overwhelmingly white, synthetically rustic—and, like a threadbare professional wooing a monied clientele, elastically adjusted his standards. Perhaps the best that might be said for such work is that it reflects the peculiar pressures facing him as a democratic black poet seeking, paradoxically, the widest audience. In dividing his poems into groups and sending them in various directions, he showed himself aware of the instability of his audience. Rather than lapse into silence, Hughes had committed himself to adapting his voice so that its message might be heard everywhere.

Other poems showed not only the old emotive power but that his technical skill, within the bounds of his aesthetic of simplicity, was considerable. In "Merry-Go-Round," which is spoken by a "Colored Child at Carnival," he assumed the voice of a small child, then typically surpassed this diminution to project a decidedly adult authority:

> Where is the Jim Crow section
> On this merry-go-round,
> Mister, cause I want to ride?
> Down South where I come from
> White and colored
> Cannot sit side by side.
> Down South on the train
> There's a Jim Crow car.
> On the bus we're put in the back—
> But there ain't no back
> To a merry-go-round!
> Where's the horse
> For a kid that's black?

In the following decade, "Merry-Go-Round" would become one of his most effective poems read on the road, expressing at the same time the stupidity and the heartbreak of racial discrimination.

His finest poems, however, remained those saturated in blues language, the idiom of the black folk that Hughes had pioneered in literary verse in 1923 with his poem "The Weary Blues," then developed to its zenith as art in *Fine Clothes to the Jew* in 1927. Blues was a way of singing but above all a way of feeling, when the pain of circumstance is transcended by the will to survive—of which the most stylish token, aside from the blues song itself, is the impulse to laughter. Although not a classic blues, "Still Here" is in the blues idiom. With this poem, written after a crisis, Langston told the world that although he had stumbled and fallen down, he was not out. He might never prevail, but he had survived. He was "Still Here":

> I've been scarred and battered.
> My hopes the wind done scattered.
> Snow has frize me, sun has baked me.
>> Looks like between 'em
>> They done tried to make me
> Stop laughing, stop loving, stop living—
>> But I don't care!
>> I'm still here!

Spring brought magnificent weather as a stream of visitors, lured not only by the exquisite scenery of the Monterey Peninsula but also by the wealth of its inhabitants, flowed through the Farm and livened Langston's days. Among the guests were his oil-prosperous, eccentric uncle John Hughes, up from Los Angeles with his doctor for a medical convention; R. Babulal Singh of the anti-British Indian National Congress; Harold Jackman, the urbane Harlem schoolteacher and lover of the arts; the writer Henry Miller, looking around for a home in Big Sur, where he would settle; the black singer and actress Ethel Waters; Gian Carlo Menotti, whose *Amelia Goes to the Ball* was scheduled for the Metropolitan Opera House in New York, and his fellow composer Samuel Barber; the classical pianist Henri Deering, a great favorite of Noël Sullivan's. Hollow Hills Farm, Langston soon sighed, almost exactly as he had done about Carmel seven years before, "might as well be 42nd Street and Fifth Avenue—so many white folks and Negroes are always passing through."

Dining regularly with Noël Sullivan, Lee Crowe, and Langston at the Farm were prominent members of the California gentry such as Chester Arthur (the son of the former U.S. president), the actor Melvyn Douglas, and Douglas's politically prominent wife, Helen Gahagan Douglas, as well as a circle of friends better known to Langston mainly from his year-long stay in 1933 and 1934 in Carmel. It included Marie Short, who at times served informally as Noël Sullivan's hostess; her former husband Douglas Short, a lawyer; Ben Lehman of the University of California; the poet Marie de Lisle Welch; the playwright Martin Flavin and his wife Connie; the liberal activist Dorothy Erskine and her husband Morse, a physician; and Leon and Leslie Roos, of a leading San Francisco merchant family. Musicians of any note had an easy *entrée* to Hollow Hills. Over the years, in addition to his black guests like Roland Hayes and Dorothy Maynor, Sullivan welcomed stars such as the cellist Gregor Piatagorsky, and the violinists Yehudi Menuhin and Isaac Stern, who were both from the San Francisco Bay area.

Langston both enjoyed these meals and cocktail parties and found them a strain; certainly he chafed at dressing for dinner every evening. "My uncle's style of entertaining," Sullivan's niece Alice Doyle Mahoney remembered, "usually consisted of small luncheons or dinners—8 to 12 people—where conversation was the highlight (as well as delicious food!). He loved to gather people who differed radically in background and ideas and the discussions were often very exciting!" However, twenty-six guests came once to dine with Henri Deering, and fifty crowded the lunch table during the Shakespeare Festival, in which Sullivan, gaunt and sepulchral of voice, played the ghost in *Hamlet*. A buffet on the lawn "for 180!" frankly appalled Langston.

Still, Hollow Hills Farm was "a little Heaven," as he had once put it, a place largely exempt from stress and strain. The goats willingly gave up their milk, the earth seemed to breath fragrant flowers and shrubs and green grass. A crisis at Hollow Hills as often as not involved the pampered, high-strung dogs, who now and then caught and tore a skunk to pieces and stank until Sullivan had them shampooed and sprayed with *eau de cologne*. Once, the neurotic dachshunds cornered a huge snake outside the main house and playfully slaughtered it. Such events pained Langston, who from first to last was a city man with no passion for nature and no stomach for animal violence. "Langston was terribly broken up by the killing of the snake," Eulah Pharr recalled. "He kept begging us to stop the dogs, but who could stop them? I mean, who would want to? He struck me as being unusually squeamish. Most of us were glad to see the dogs take care of that snake, but not Langston. I thought at one point that he was going to faint!"

When Hollow Hills was quiet, the small but peppery black community of Carmel and its burgeoning counterpart in Monterey, augmented by the increasing number of blacks at the Fort Ord military base nearby, more than made up for it in noise. In the various intrigues and affairs among the locals, heterosexual and homosexual, Hughes took an unabated interest—as long as he was not touched personally by the paintbrush of scandal. "Langston loved to gossip," Eulah Pharr declared. "He wasn't malicious or anything like that, but he just *had* to know who was doing what, and with whom! He didn't let anything pass him that way. Maybe his curiosity had something to do with his writing—but he really enjoyed the hush-hush talk! And he found everything so funny! He could laugh at anything having to do with another human being." He knew the poolhalls and the greasy-spoon diners, the barbershops and the nightclubs, and the houses where one could always find a party going on. About one local wedding he reported: "The bride, a young lady whose mama breathed a sigh of relief because, these past months she could hardly do her work for the white folks for worrying about what the soldiers were doing to her daughter while she was on the job. Now she is safely wed and walked out of the church through an arch of former admirers on the arm of the one that mama said was responsible. Anyhow, the bugles blew and colored society turned out.''

Noël Sullivan's friend Lee Crowe, on the other hand, recalled both Hughes's love of laughter and the underlying reserve, even remoteness, that other sensitive acquaintances inevitably found in him. ''Someone would be talking softly, then you would hear this unbelievably loud laugh burst out, and you would know right away that Langston was around and was enjoying the conversation. You simply couldn't mistake his laugh; it seemed to come from deep down in him. And yet he really wasn't one of the boys. He and Noël, I guess, had that in common. They loved life, and eating and drinking; but they were grave people when you came right down to it. What was extraordinary in Langston was that he was able to be both gregarious and remote, at one and the same time. I sensed a great hurt in him that he was too proud to show, that he was determined not to show. He was determined to be happy, and if he wasn't, well, he certainly covered it up better than anybody I knew.''

Hughes himself preferred to show the world a brightly smiling face. Around this time, when he prepared a brief autobiographical note for a book about contemporary writers, he stressed his love of mainly—but not exclusively— simple virtues and values. He liked ''*Tristan,* goat's milk, short novels, lyric poems, heat, simple folk, boats, and bullfights; I dislike *Aida,* parsnips, long novels, narrative poems, cold, pretentious folk, busses, and bridge.'' As for his writing, it had been ''largely concerned with the depicting of Negro life in America.''

The passing months brought him back to health but did not eradicate completely the memory of his winter crisis. Politics and the individual conscience had been at the center of that crisis, and the war in Europe made political difference a matter of life and death. Carmel was a continent and an ocean away from the battlefields of Europe, but the war was drawing closer. One sign was the swelling number of soldiers at nearby Fort Ord. In dismay he watched as white southerners among them brought the first signs of segregation to what had been an open community. On the Fourth of July, ironically, he railed in a letter about ''the kind of Texas crackers—army officers—who are now invading Carmel and bringing their color prejudice with them.'' At first, as a continuing admirer of the Soviet Union, he had quietly backed the anti-interventionist line favored by Moscow and the U.S. Communist Party. He kept quiet on this point mainly because his host Noël Sullivan was both viscerally anti-communist and a partisan of Great Britain in its death-struggle with Hitler. Although Sullivan opposed the British over Ireland, on his recent trip to New York—as Langston coolly reported to Arna Bontemps—''he donated a pint of blood to the British.''

What Langston thought and felt about the war during this harrowing period is not perfectly clear. Unquestionably, Sullivan and most of Hollow Hills Farm had cheered on the British in the Battle of Britain, when the Nazi war machine had received its first setback since the triumphant invasion of Poland that had begun the war. Since then, Italy had attacked the British in North Africa and invaded Greece, and Hungary, Rumania, and Bulgaria had been forced into the Axis. In April, 1941, Nazi forces subjugated Yugoslavia and entered Greece. Crete fell in May, with devastating losses to the British. Having lived in Paris for several months in 1924, Langston felt the loss of France personally. He cared much less for Britain, whose record was too deeply stained by colonialism and racism for him to shed tears unreservedly over its fate. Babulal Singh, a recent visitor to the Farm, had left the United States for India and almost certainly a British jail there. But was Hughes's dislike of colonialism sufficient to make him indifferent to the outcome of the war?

In 1937, Langston had written poems in praise of Republican Spain. If, during even the most fiery battles between 1939 and the summer of 1941, he wrote a single poem about the anti-Nazi effort, it has not survived. At first, like a loyal leftist, he had stressed pacifism, as in "War and Peace," a skit depicting war as "a common hussy in death mask" and peace as "a young girl in white with dove," vying for a workingman's attention. In June, 1940, he had joined three hundred other writers in signing an anti-war statement in *New Masses* sponsored by the League of American Writers. That month, the *Crisis* had also published his "Comment on War":

> Let us kill off youth.
> For the sake of *truth*.
>
> We who are old know what truth is—
> Truth is a bundle of vicious lies
> Tied together and sterilized—
> A war-makers' bait for unwise youth
> To kill off each other
> For the sake of
> *Truth*.

These pieces had been written and the statement signed before the controversy over "Goodbye Christ." Even before the controversy and his recantation, however, his perspective on the war had begun to shift. Writing him off as a lapsed radical during the controversy, the *People's World* had certainly overstated the case in depicting him as aggressively patriotic, "bitten with the war bug," and "primping for ye imperialism." But his 1940 song "America's Young Black Joe" certainly had been in march tempo.

Six months or so after repudiating "Goodbye Christ," Langston was ready to move even further from the radical ranks. On May 26, he informed Franklin Folson of the League of American Writers (which he had long supported and had represented at an anti-fascist conference in Paris in 1938) that he would not attend the proposed Fourth Congress in June in New York. Also, he would not continue as a vice-president; perhaps Richard Wright or Ralph Ellison, among others, might take his place. Hughes's unspoken wish was to avoid being tied to a radical socialist position on the war. His statement to the Congress, "Democracy, Negroes, and Writers," ignored the war but challenged democracy as "a paradox, full of contradictions" for Afro-Americans. Mississippi was half black, but the state spent nine times as much on a white child as on a black, although its wealth was based on black labor in the cotton fields. In the North, blacks could vote but were denied jobs even in most defense factories. "We give and others take," he lamented. Should blacks defend democracy? Blacks, Hughes argued, "would very much like to have a little more democracy to defend."

His leftist audience could draw its own conclusions. Not long after, he put the matter more colorfully but far less ambiguously when the black members who made up Katherine Dunham's dance troupe discovered that most of them could not find accommodations in the Monterey area. "But at least under Democracy," he reasoned, "—even if they can't sleep in Carmel, they can still dance—and under Hitler they couldn't even do that. So I am all-out for ousting him and all his works—even though some of his works have beat him here— so we have to do a little ousting at home, too."

He was at Hollow Hills Farm when the news broke of Nazi Germany's invasion of Russia on June 22, which shattered the Nazi-U.S.S.R. pact of nonaggression with an invasion by land and air over a thousand-mile front. As with the fall of Paris, he felt personally for the Russians, whose country was not an abstraction but a place in which he had lived for a year and been treated far more humanely than at home. (The invasion, Arna Bontemps soon pointed out, "should set the stage handsomely for volume II of your autobiography, since Russia is sure to come into better favor in this country.") But he was also aware that a crisis of political belief was at hand for many people on the left and the right. Within hours of the news, Langston joined others at the Farm huddled around a crackling radio to listen to an unprecedented speech by the British prime minister, Winston Churchill. Royalist and pro-colonialist to the core, Churchill nevertheless pledged not only unceasing war on Hitler—"We shall fight him by land; we shall fight him by sea; we shall fight him in the air"—but also full support for any state at war with the Nazis, including the Soviet Union.

Overnight, the Communist Party in the United States threw out its doctrine of nonintervention and instituted a militant line. Even before the Party made its about-face, Hughes not only anticipated the indecent somersault but satirized it. "And I do declare!" he wrote Van Vechten about the invasion and Churchill's speech. "All of which will no doubt make the Communist Party change its line again. Strange bedfellows! But it's more like Ringling's flying trapezes. . . . Will the Red Cross start sponsoring Sacks for the Soviets as well as Bundles for Britain? I'm glad I'm a lyric poet."

Although Hughes had never been *only* a lyric poet, in one key respect he required no somersault to alter his position on the role of politics in art. From the start of his career he had concurrently been both a lyric and a radical poet, with a fervent militant strain in place long before the Depression. However, almost all of his radical verse consistently emphasized his romantic longing for peace and unity, and his aversion to violence. Even in besieged Madrid, his poems of the Spanish conflict had stressed the waste and tragedy of war, not the necessity of destroying others. Nowhere had he glorified war as an exalted process of cleansing, as certain leftist poets appeared to have done. "Today the deliberate increase in the chances of death," W. H. Auden had written in his poem "Spain," "The conscious acceptance of guilt in the necessary murder." Whatever Auden meant by the last words (he was denounced by George Orwell as approving of murder, and would change "the necessary murder" to "the fact of murder" in revising the poem), Hughes had bade goodbye to Christ and good morning to revolution without ever having gone so far as to defy a sense of absolute ethics and absolute morality.

As with Auden and other poets, the war (in addition to his personal circumstances) had forced Hughes to reassess the role of politics in poetry. But he was not about to become simply a "lyric poet"; he meant only to dissociate *leftist* politics from his aesthetic. The political fervor that had served radical socialism in the thirties would be rechanneled toward the greater specificity of black civil rights, and to fresh explorations of the blues idiom, which Hughes had played down in the thirties in favor of radical political verse. These concerns blended more easily with the lyric strain that he now claimed as his own, converging in a piece Langston would offer for many years to come as the concluding poem at his readings. When the National Conference of Christians and Jews invited him to contribute to a series entitled "The World We Want to Live In," he sent an article and this piece—"I Dream a World," an aria from his opera with William Grant Still, "Troubled Island."

> I dream a world where man
> No other man will scorn,
> Where love will bless the earth
> And peace its path adorn
> I dream a world where all
> Will know sweet freedom's way
> Where greed no longer saps the soul
> Nor avarice blights our day.
> A world I dream where black or white,
> Whatever race you be,
> Will *share* the bounties of the earth
> And every man is free,
> Where wretchedness will hang its head
> And joy, like pearl,
> Attends the needs of all mankind
> Of such I dream—
> Our world!

On June 1, with his bank balance down to $1.20, his Rosenwald Fund fellowship came to the rescue. But Langston made no move to leave for the East to begin his research for the plays about black heroes, as he had promised in his proposal. Although he had brought himself back from the edge, he was still not ready to return to the old life. For one thing, his writing, especially his second autobiography, was not going well; for another, he had no prospect of financial support once his fellowship ended. The "Radio Special," as Maxim Lieber jauntily called the "Amos and Andy"-style radio series for which Langston had signed a contract, had come to nothing when no sponsor was found. "After long last," Lieber reported of the producer Moe Gale, "he lays an egg." Another disappointment came after the Dramatists Guild ruled in Langston's favor in his now six-year-old dispute with Martin Jones, the producer of his Broadway play *Mulatto,* concerning not only royalties owed to Langston but also Jones's claims to co-authorship based on his changes in the script. The play had run almost two years on Broadway and then on the road, but Jones refused to honor any financial award to Hughes by an arbitrator. "Folks like that," Langston sighed, "are the kind who are waiting for Hitler." The final blow came when Maxim Lieber discovered that all of the contracts, drawn up not by his own literary agency but by another organization, were never with Martin Jones himself but with a corporation called "Marjones," now officially defunct and without assets. Collection was impossible. "That," Lieber concluded almost in awe, "is how sly Martin Jones turned out to be."

Langston's luck was not much better when, early in July, he made a quick visit to Los Angeles to see "Jump for Joy," a popular revue mounted by Duke Ellington out of the ill-fated "Negro Revue" on which Langston had worked for the Hollywood Theatre Alliance. At the gala opening, Langston was thrilled to see Marlene Dietrich, whom he adored, "in the FLESH," and to meet Mickey Rooney. However, the thrill subsided quickly. With sensational performances by Dorothy Dandridge and Ivy Anderson, the revue was "pretty good, and most beautifully set and costumed." But Langston and Charles Leonard's "Mad Scene from Woolworth's," belted out by Ivy Anderson ("The struggle is terrific! Oh! I can't make up my mind! / So I'm standing in the Ten Cent Store going mad with a dime"), was not a hit. When they inquired about royalties for the use of their words, Ellington promptly dropped the piece. "A peculiar misfortune certainly dogs your footsteps, Langston," Lieber remarked about this time, "for almost everything you get tied up with, turns sour. It's a miracle that you have been able to preserve your charming and carefree manner. I think God just left a gall out of you."

In Carmel Valley that summer, unusually cool, misty weather persisted so long that almost everyone complained about arthritis, and Langston himself developed a stiff arm. Perhaps his conscience had seized his writing arm, because he was clearly making no progress on his fellowship project, or his autobiography. He was musing about a visit to Phoenix, in the torrid Arizona desert, when news that three separate groups of blacks were about to invade Hollow Hills Farm decided the matter for him. Just before leaving on August

14, he wrote to Eleanor Roosevelt, the wife of the president and a beloved supporter of liberal causes. "I noticed with pleasure your kind mention of my name in your column a short time ago," Langston wrote. "Always you have been most gracious toward my people (and our artists) and there is a deep appreciation for you in the hearts of America's Negro citizens."

In Phoenix, where he went about as "James Hughes," he took a big front room at $3.50 a week at a black guesthouse at 1229 East Washington Street, run by Mrs. Emma Gardner. The president of the Colored Women's Clubs of Arizona, Mrs. Gardner was eminently respectable but did not insist on coat and tie for dinner. "I am delighted," Langston wrote Bontemps, "to NOT have to dress for dinner." Most of his fellow guests were black chauffeurs temporarily in town—although a group of black boxers came to stay while Hughes was there. Phoenix was charming and cheap, he reported: "WHOLE watermelons on ice are only a dime." The city was blindingly hot—"too nice and hot to stay in at all, and too nice and hot to work out of doors."

The combination of heat, anonymity, and an exotic urban culture worked for him. Along with books to read—W. C. Handy's autobiography *Father of the Blues,* written with Arna Bontemps, and *For Whom the Bell Tolls,* Ernest Hemingway's novel of the Spanish Civil War, he had brought a manuscript, his and Arna Bontemps' juvenile tale "Boy of the Border," which he had fished from the depths of his files to revise in the hope of making some quick money. Instead, relaxed but inspired, Langston did much better. As he had done in 1934 during a similar escape from Carmel to Reno, Nevada, he boldly stetched the outlines of several stories, which he would finish on his return to Hollow Hills Farm.

Loitering in bars and on the hot streets, he watched and listened to white "Okies," brown Mexicans, and blacks working together apparently without the slightest tremor of racial tension. Many of the blacks were fresh from the South, and sang the blues with gusto. As in his old transcribing days, Langston copied some down—including one with a neat twist:

> When I take you back the streets will be paved
> with gold.
> Baby, when I take you back, streets will be paved
> with gold.
> You'll do no mo' messin' around 'cause you'll be
> too goddamned old!

On long bus rides into the desert, once as far as Tucson, he took pleasure in the stark, elemental quality of Arizona, the freedom from segregation, and the low cost of living. Perhaps New York was not the place to live. "Maybe," he wrote Toy Harper (in whose basement in New York most of his possessions were stored), "that is where we should buy our house, huh?"

He was still in Phoenix on September 1, Labor Day, when he listened to one of his few successes on national radio—a half-hour adaptation on CBS radio of his script "Jubilee," written for the Negro Exposition in Chicago the previous year, and called "The Tree of Hope." The script had been cut drastically, but CBS had respected his basic intent and paid him decently. When the Dramatists Guild passed along a check from the management of the Duke Ellington revue in Los Angeles for the unauthorized use of "Mad Scene from Woolworth's," Langston was almost prosperous—if only for a moment—"so I bought a new suit, grey tweed, like the one I used to have" (but had surrendered to a Los Angeles pawnbroker in a previous cash crisis). Now he had two suits with which to face New York. Unfortunately, the revue closed and its check bounced.

With his money from CBS, he was ready to try his luck one more time in Los Angeles. Taking a room early in September at his regular hotel there, Horace Clark's Clark Hotel at the corner of South Central Avenue and Washington Boulevard, he began composing ballet scenarios for Katherine Dunham. He developed four outlines for her, of which his favorite was "Carmelita and the Cockatoo," about a colorful Mexican bird who falls in love with a maid— who gleefully unfeathers him. This was pleasant work; but Langston hoped for something more lucrative. However, the stage and the screen seemed lost to black writers and performers, as he complained to the Los Angeles *Tribune,* in spite of recent productions such as *Mamba's Daughters* and the film *Cabin in the Sky.* Visiting William Grant Still at his home, Langston heard only discouraging words about Still's ongoing effort to have their opera *Troubled Island* produced.

For all of Langston's pain over his part in the 1939 movie *Way Down South,* which had been attacked for its stereotypes of slavery and black life, the scent of Hollywood money was still alluring. He dusted off his old "Rejuvenation Through Joy" screenplay (based on a story of the same name in *The Ways of White Folks*), but he passed it around in vain. And once again, as he had done for fifteen years without any success, he sought a link with Paul Robeson and what Hughes had once lauded as "the great truth and beauty of your art." An international movie star, Robeson had acted in the 1936 Hollywood version of *Show Boat* but in no other American picture. Langston's contact was his former collaborator Charles Leonard of Columbia Pictures, who invited him to meet with two minor moguls there to discuss possible story lines for a vehicle for Robeson. A film appeared so likely that Maxim Lieber, after talking with Robeson's shrewd and decisive wife, Essie Robeson, instructed Langston to request a fee of $500 a week.

Hughes and Leonard quickly offered a tale of a low-born but famous singer suddenly moved to return to his old job as a Pullman porter. On the job, he becomes involved in various adventures, including an affair with a beautiful maid. Not surprisingly, Robeson's spine stiffened. More than "a little nervous" about the porter idea, as his wife wrote Langston, he was very fearful of what "the wolves,—that is, . . . the producers," would do with it; "the porter idea is too much of a temptation for using the same old junk, and he couldn't stomach that." Certainly Paul respected Langston. Earlier in the year, at a celebration of the International Workers Order, the giant leftist benevolent society, Robeson had recited with sure success a script based on Langston's 1931 recitation piece "The Negro Mother," adapted by Carlton Moss, with music by Alex North, and had lauded Hughes on stage. For her part, Essie Robeson liked Langston; but what she could not tell him was that she had little respect for his record as a dramatist. "All of Langston's work so far has been definitely ineffective," she had noted to Paul in June, 1939. "I saw his Mulatto, and his Don't You Want to be Free?, and felt both of them to be definitely amateur. . . . They won't do for big time. It is quite possible that he might be able to do something light and musical much better. For instance his Weary Blues are very fine. So we shall see. But DON'T make any rash promises."

"As long as the picture industry is what it is," Maxim Lieber agreed, "they'll only want negroes to act as pullman porters, and there's damn little you or I can do about it." Later, Langston and Leonard submitted "The Songs of Solomon Jones," an outline for a motion picture in which Robeson would be a young medical doctor who returns home to his Tennessee roots. When this idea fared no better, Langston gave up. "I think only a subsidized Negro Film Institute, or the revolution," he decided, "will cause any really good Negro pictures to be made in America." Ten years later he could still write accurately: "Hollywood's favorite Negro character is a grinning happy-go-lucky half-stupid servant, male or female, and usually speaking broken English."

His sortie to Los Angeles had failed. "The lamentations of Jeremiah are mild compared with yours," Lieber suggested. "Nevertheless, I must confess that yours are justified." Langston headed north to Hollow Hills. Six months had passed since his fellowship began and he had accomplished nothing on the project. He could no longer postpone his return to the East, where the research was to take place. Evading as best he could a flood of fall visitors, including Katherine Dunham's troupe, who danced once again into Carmel and then "boogied on Northward," as Langston reported in relief, he concentrated on his only important writing of the year, the stories sketched in Phoenix. Soon he had finished seven: "Banquet in Honor," "Sailor Ashore," "Mysterious Madame Shanghai," "Who's Passing for Who?," "The Bottle of Wine," "The Star Decides," and "Two at the Bar."

Although these stories did not surpass those of *The Ways of White Folks* in originality and power, they showed a definite increase in Hughes's facility as a fiction writer. Some, like "Mysterious Madame Shanghai," are only slick, but others underscore subtle alterations in his sense of self in light of what he had been through in recent months—and a determination to assert moral values in the face of extreme hardship. What is perhaps the best story, "Sailor Ashore," describes an encounter between a smooth-talking but defeatist and racially self-pitying black sailor and a black woman who picks him up but then, disgusted, boots him out of her house. She had lied about her profession and her finances and about having a son—she is a prostitute, poor and childless—but she clings to her self-respect and scorns the man's whining. "If I ever *did* have a son," she insists in the end, "and if I ever do have a job—if I wasn't what I am—I'd make something out of my son, if I had one! I swear to God I would." Self-pity is also a major theme in "The Bottle of Wine," later called "On the Way Home," in which a man drinks himself into a stupor rather than face his mother's death. The theme reappears obversely in "Banquet in Honor," where a long-neglected black artist publicly lambasts his hypocritical, bourgeois black hosts for failing to support him when he had most needed support.

Maxim Lieber found this story and "Sailor Ashore" impossible to place, until Angelo Herndon and Ralph Ellison's leftist *Negro Quarterly* took the former. Considering Hughes's essay "The Need for Heroes" and his challenging of Wright's vision of black culture and of life itself, the stories are revealing. While there is nothing conventionally heroic about any of the characters, the prostitute in "Sailor Ashore," for example, refuses to give up on herself and her people. Most of the stories are dominated by a similar spirit, in what might be called illuminations by the blues ideal, which Hughes always saw as a form of heroism. The settings are often tawdry, but in one way or another the tales repudiate all despairing judgments of black life and of human nature itself. As such, they are probably doomed to be seen as shallow. Lacking the uncompromising seriousness of Wright's typical fiction, with its constant thrusting beneath the level of civilization for signs of primitive sexuality, terror, and the will to violence, Hughes's stories emphasize humanity and the mediation of evil by humor.

Ironically, about this time Langston tried to help one of Wrights's devoted young admirers, then living in Los Angeles, by bringing his unpublished first novel to Blanche Knopf's attention. "Thanks a lot for the plug, pal," Chester Himes wrote him about the manuscript of *If He Hollers Let Him Go*, which would be the first book in a long and distinguished career.

As Langston made ready to brave the East, he received one last boost to his morale, one last confirmation that he had brought himself back from the brink, when he began work on a project started earlier in the year by Carl Van Vechten in New York. After the failure of a campaign to erect on the edge of Harlem a memorial statue of the black poet, novelist, and NAACP leader James Weldon Johnson, killed in 1938 when a train struck his car at a railroad crossing during a storm, the Library of Congress had made an offer to his widow, Grace Nail Johnson. The Library wanted to make her late husband's papers the nucleus of a new poetry room. One of the Johnsons' most trusted friends (the men had designated each other as their literary executors), Van Vechten had then countered with a proposal that she should give the papers to Yale University to start a collection that would include Van Vechten's own huge collection of Afro-Americana. He preferred the library at Yale, which he had not attended, because it was private, well run, and had almost nothing on blacks—so the university would "play this up." When the library accepted all his conditions, Van Vechten zealously sought other gifts to what was officially named "the James Weldon Johnson Memorial Collection of Negro Arts and Letters founded by Carl Van Vechten." Reminding Langston that the name was chosen to encourage others to give, he issued a challenge. "If the Schomburg collection is famous for Dunbar manuscripts," he declared, "let this one be famous for Hughes!"

"What a wonderful title you have given the Yale collection," Hughes congratulated Van Vechten on hearing the news, "and what a great compliment to Jim Johnson!" But Langston cared deeply about posterity, and the idea of Yale wanting his papers so flattered him that he needed no further encouragement to start handing them over. Coyly, however, he worried that "I will now become self-conscious and no doubt verge toward the grandiloquent" in his correspondence. He censored himself in his report on a knife fight involving blacks in a local bar, Togo's Pool Room, because "you know the Race would come out here and cut *me* if they knew I was relaying such news to posterity via the Yale Library." Later in the same letter, he slipped into gossip again. "But the very thought of Yale prevents me from going further!" Van Vechten stressed to him the importance of the Hughes papers. "As a spokesman for the Negro you are unique because you know all kinds and classes WELL and like all kinds and classes. To some extent this is also true of your relations with ofays. . . . I guess you are Garvey, Father Divine, James Weldon Johnson, and James L. Ford all rolled into ONE."

His last days passed in a flurry of packing, sorting, filing, and storing, as he prepared for yet another major move. Determined to show himself off in the East in style, Langston paid $27.50 for a double-breasted tuxedo, which he mailed directly to Arna Bontemps in Chicago in preparation for readings there together.

Early in November, about fifty black friends bade farewell to Langston. The party started in the afternoon and ended at three in the morning only after one young woman, in a fit of rage at her boyfriend, who was about to slip off with someone else, ripped every available wire from his car. Her bold act, which threatened to strand some Fort Ord soldiers past reveille, brought the festivities to a sudden halt.

Then it was time to leave Noël Sullivan and Hollow Hills Farm. To Sullivan, Langston could barely express his gratitude for the shelter he had enjoyed over the past two years, but especially in the year since his worst crisis. "If ever you need me," he pledged to his patron, "let me know, and I'll be there!"

He left Hollow Hills Farm for Chicago and the East.

2

JIM CROW'S LAST STAND
1941 to 1943

The nations they is fightin'
And the nations they done fit.
Sometimes I think that white folks
Ain't worth a little bit.
  No, m'am!
Ain't worth a little bit . . .
          "Southern Mammy Sings," 1941

A FTER A BRIEF STAY in Los Angeles, where he charmed the guests at a
League of American Writers dinner, Langston boarded the "El Capitan"
train for a pleasant ride through Arizona and snow-dusted New Mexico and on
to Kansas and eventually Illinois. On the morning of November 20 he finally
reached Chicago. Clearly he was in no hurry to return to New York; his plan
was to stay in Chicago for at least a few weeks. Although his application to
the Rosenwald Fund had mentioned only in passing the chance of theater work
there, Langston evidently had decided to make a fresh start in the Midwest,
before challenging New York. Assiduously preparing his way in Chicago was
Arna Bontemps, who had been living there for the past six years with his wife
Alberta and their five children. Knowing his friend's pinched financial state,
Bontemps had secured for him a comfortable and also free room at a large new
South Side settlement house. Alberta Bontemps promised Langston free board,
and the Rosenwald Fund agreed to make an office available to him at its headquarters, 4901 Ellis Avenue. Langston needed all the help he could get. "Tell
Horace I'll take him up on that bed, Alberta on board (you know, once in a
while) and the Rosenwalds on that office," he thanked Arna Bontemps. "But
who has an overcoat and some earmuffs to lend me?"

His office at the Rosenwald Fund proved to be spacious enough and quiet,
and his welcome was warm at the Good Shepherd Community Center, at the
corner of 51st Street and South Parkway and proud of its position as "the
World's Largest Negro Settlement House." Directing the organization was Horace
Cayton, an intense but affable black sociologist and disciple of Robert Park of
the University of Chicago, and a friend of Langston's since 1932, when they

had met in Cayton's hometown, Seattle. Under Cayton's hard-driving leadership, Good Shepherd had become, according to one newspaper, not only a center for the younger black intellectuals and artists in the area but also "the focal point for life in the south side Negro communities." He and his beautiful, intelligent wife, Irma Cayton, found Langston a genial visitor. "Langston was charming and boyish and a delightful guest," Cayton later recalled. When Cayton himself became too serious in his talk "about politics, psychoanalysis, social conditions and the like," as he recalled, "the playful poet would often join with Irma in poking fun at my intellectual talk."

"I had known Langston since I was eighteen, at Fisk," Irma Cayton remembered. "He was warm and jovial, and we became close friends. We had both been an only child, and lonely, and we used to talk about that, and just about everything else, while Horace was so intense about his political Langston didn't want to talk much about politics—although when he came to Chicago this time I was surprised how bitter he had become against the left-liberals. I guess he felt they had betrayed him. In that way, he was really a changed man. He had a nice big room near our suite and he ate with me, with us. He *loved* food! The first thing he would say whenever he came in was, 'Irma, what are we going to eat, huh?' He said he really loved my cooking. I guess he attached himself to me the way he attached himself to certain people at different times. He needed someone. He kept us in stitches with his stories and jokes, but I could see his loneliness, all the same."

By now a veteran at accepting hospitality, Langston made the most of the arrangement but looked around for something to give back to the Caytons and Good Shepherd. Almost at once he saw that the community center, which was then not quite one year old, would do nicely as the home of a theater, with actors and staff drawn from its many members. Within a few days of his arrival he had founded yet another theatrical company, as he had done in New York with the Harlem Suitcase Theatre. The new group was called the Skyloft Players.

Nervous at first about how he might be received by the larger Chicago community after his poor publicity the previous year, Langston soon relaxed. The newspapers that noted his arrival did so approvingly; none mentioned the controversy over "Goodbye Christ," and even the reactionary Hearst paper was cordial. A visit to Hull House, the historic settlement house founded by Jane Addams, brought an immediate invitation from Addams's successor for Langston to live there at any time. The radical community, considerable in Chicago, seemed in a forgiving mood. Hughes had two valuable allies there. His old Moscow and Harlem Suitcase Theatre comrade, Louise Thompson, had remained loyal to him, and he could also count on the sympathy of William L. Patterson, whom she had recently married, and who had been an influential figure among American communists ever since his heroic work on the Scottsboro case in the early thirties. Thompson had first castigated Langston for his role as a writer in the reactionary Hollywood film *Way Down South,* then reached out sympathetically to him: "In you I feel one whose whole life has been a dedication to the things you have believed in and wanted to do. And that has resulted in the high place you hold today, Lang. . . . The things you are doing I am confident are bringing to you that sort of satisfaction that can't be measured in dollars and cents." Years later she recalled her feelings for Langston Hughes: "He had done so much for all of us—blacks, the poor, people on the left—and against such great odds, that you had to forgive him if now and then he didn't live up to his own standards. For all his talent and his hard work, America had treated him like dirt. But Langston was somebody special, somebody different, and there was never really a time when we didn't recognize that fact."

When several offers arrived for him to speak, his last fears faded. Resplendent in his double-breasted tuxedo, he joined Arna Bontemps and the singer Etta Moten in a presentation sponsored by the Chicago Book and Play Club in honor of Bontemps, whose *Golden Slippers,* an anthology of poems, had just appeared. The two men also worked on a special "Bill of Rights Salute to Freedom" show, at which the actor Canada Lee, who had scored a major hit with his portrayal of Bigger Thomas in Orson Welles's recent Broadway staging of *Native Son,* read their script on black achievement to an audience that included the governor of Illinois and scores of sailors and soldiers. In particular, this implicit endorsement of his patriotism encouraged Langston. Nor did he appear to compromise much—if at all—when he spoke out on the problem of racism and segregation. In December, after he spoke to a Jewish youth group from the K. A. M. Temple of Rabbi Jacob J. Weinstein, who had met Langston on the West Coast, Weinstein praised him for exhibiting a rare mixture of courage and modesty: "You uttered all the idol-shattering truths without personal hate or self-preening and thus you removed the obstacles between you and your auditors."

Meanwhile, the appearance of his book of poems *Shakespeare in Harlem* was delayed once again. Knopf had ignored his protests about the drawings of "nappy"-headed blacks by E. McKnight Kauffer. "They keep writing me how beautiful the drawings are," Langston had complained, "and that an artist's conception must be his own emanating from what he sees in the text, etc. If such reasoning be true, then one just can't trust the average white artist to illustrate a Negro book, unless they are known to know Negroes in life—not Uncle Remus—and be sympathetic to the poetry of Negro life—and not to its (to them) humorous and grotesque, amusing and 'quaint' aspects." However, when Hughes sought help on this score from Van Vechten, who was informally supervising the production of the book as he had done with every other Knopf book of verse by Hughes, he found him also unmoved. Probably "EVERYBODY will be having nappy hair again and loving it," Van Vechten predicted. "Some few sensible persons go in for it now." Unconvinced—"*I will catch hell!!*"—Langston awaited the proofs with foreboding. His concern on this point did not spring from racial chauvinism. When his alma mater Lincoln University wrote to ask whether, breaking with custom, its next president should be black, he replied tartly that he favored choosing "the best possible man for the job regardless of race."

On December 6, the page proofs finally arrived. Whether or not he was perfectly satisfied, two days later he called the book "swell" in a letter to Knopf, praised the "big bold print," and even lauded the illustrations. In the interim, other events had put his concern in a different perspective. The nation was at war. Langston had been poring over the proofs in his room at Good Shepherd in the late afternoon when the news broke about Japan's aerial attack on Pearl Harbor and the devastation of the U.S. fleet in the Pacific. Nineteen naval vessels, including eight battleships, had gone down, almost two hundred American aircraft had been destroyed, and over two thousand sailors killed. For black Chicagoans, for black Americans everywhere, the carnage had produced a vibrant human symbol of what the war might mean for them. In one of the most extraordinary acts of heroism and resourcefulness that Sunday morning in Hawaii, Dorie Miller of Chicago, a black messman on the U.S.S. *Arizona,* had seized a machine gun and shot down four enemy planes during the attack. (Awarded the Navy Cross, Miller continued as a messman and was killed in action in the Pacific two years later. The sunken hulk of the *Arizona* became the site of a memorial to the attack on Pearl Harbor.)

Enlisting in the segregated armed forces would have been the last idea on Langston's mind. Nevertheless, his heart was certainly with the American armed forces, of whom in late 1941 almost one hundred thousand were black. Unlike many Afro-Americans obsessed by race, who emphasized the fact that the Japanese were a colored people fighting the white oppressor, he had no illusions about the Japanese government, not least of all because of his harassment by the Tokyo police in 1933. On the other hand, Langston definitely supported those black leaders, especially the editors and journalists, who did not intend to repeat the mistake made by W. E. B. Du Bois in 1918, during World War I. Facing a threat by the Department of Justice to shut down the *Crisis* magazine on a charge of sedition, the usually fearless Du Bois had knuckled under with an editorial, "Close Ranks," that urged blacks to "forget our special grievances" and join "with our own white fellow citizens and the allied nations that are fighting for democracy." From the outset of the war, Hughes was determined to link the fighting abroad to what was in effect a far longer struggle at home for justice.

He and the more perceptive leaders understood that the war with the Axis— Hitler declared war on the United States on December 11—would exert enormous pressure against segregation. That pressure would be felt importantly in the industrial sectors of the defense effort, but more so in the armed services themselves, with consequences for the entire national structure of Jim Crow. In June, months before Pearl Harbor, President Roosevelt had felt compelled to sign Executive Order 8802, which forbade discrimination in employment in government and defense industries. The NAACP vigorously protested against the War Department for requiring a higher minimum intelligence score for black recruits than for whites. Within the Army, the segregation of blacks—both officers and ordinary soldiers—had already led to violence, especially in the South, a condition that would only worsen as the war progressed; in Indiana, before Pearl Harbor, over a hundred black officers were placed in detention after entering a mess hall for white officers. While the Army trained black officers and some combat soldiers, the U.S. Navy allowed blacks to serve only as stewards and messmen. The Marines followed the Navy's lead. The Army Air Corps had allowed no black flyers until early that year, 1941, when the War Department announced the formation of the first Army Air Corps squadron for Negroes, following a lawsuit by a black university student for admission to the regular Corps. In what for many blacks would be the single most insulting, as well as ironic, act of discrimination, the Red Cross ordered that ''black'' blood be saved and administered separately from ''white'' blood—although medical experts found no difference between the two, and although a black doctor, Charles R. Drew, had set up the first blood bank, directed the British blood plasma program in 1940, and served briefly as director of blood plasma collection for the U.S. armed services. (''The Angel of Mercy's / Got her wings in mud,'' Langston mocked, ''And all because of / Negro blood.'' One of his first poems, published in the Central High School *Monthly* during World War I, had been in praise of the Red Cross nurse.) Attempts at change in the interest of the war effort, including Executive Order 8802, had met with widespread resistance. In December, General George C. Marshall warned the Secretary of War that ''the settlement of vexing racial problems cannot be permitted to complicate the tremendous task of the War Department, and thereby jeopardize discipline and morale.''

Still, Langston was sure that the war would bring change, and for the better where segregation was concerned. Before long, he was celebrating the effect of the global conflict on racism and segregation around the world. And he did so in deliberately unpoetic language, which was the kind of language he would consciously cultivate throughout the war in much of his verse, as in ''Jim Crow's Last Stand'':

> Pearl Harbor put Jim Crow on the run.
> That Crow can't fight for Democracy
> And be the same old Crow he used to be—
> Although right now, even yet today,
> He tries to act in the same old way.
> But India and China and Harlem, too,
> Have made up their minds Jim Crow is through . . .

The heroism of one black man had changed history. ''When Dorie Miller took gun in hand— / Jim Crow started his last stand.''

At first, Chicago showed only a few signs that the nation was at war. Around the corner from the Good Shepherd Community Center, the police closed down a Japanese restaurant. All Asiatics were required to wear identity badges, and many Japanese-Americans showed American flags conspicuously. The news from the West Coast was more frightening, with reports from Noël Sullivan and Eulah Pharr of blackouts and air raid sirens as the citizens watched and waited for an expected Japanese attack on the mainland, and Hollow Hills Farm steadily lost its able-bodied young men to the armed forces. Langston missed the comforts of Carmel Valley. "How I hated to leave Hollow Hills!" he wrote Sullivan. "And I hope it will not be too long before I may return." Spotting a "most amusing" dog stocking designed for a Christmas tree, he mailed it off to California as a Christmas gift to Sullivan's German Shepherd Greta and some puppies born on the Farm just before his departure.

He turned his attention to his work. Typing mainly in his office at the Rosenwald Fund headquarters on Ellis Avenue, with Arna Bontemps just down the hall, he finally started his fellowship project, or a version of it. In spite of his carefully outlined proposal, his new play would not be about a historical figure, although most often he had mentioned a play about Frederick Douglass in outlining his plans for the heroic series. Nevertheless, it certainly would be in the heroical spirit. Langston began to expand a drama called "Sold Away," about a slave couple's trials and tribulations and their eventual march with the Union Army into the Civil War, which he had once promised to prepare for the Gilpin Players at Karamu House in Cleveland. The new play would be called "The Sun Do Move," after perhaps the most celebrated sermon in the black tradition. Allegedly, it had been first preached by John Jasper of Virginia, whose ministry had lasted through much of the second half of the nineteenth century. "The Sun Do Move" would be staged by his new drama group at Good Shepherd Community Center, the Skyloft Players, with a big role for his hostess, Irma Cayton. "Langston said he wanted to write a play in which I would be a star," she recalled. "Later on, he confessed to me that what he really wanted was to guarantee a place to sleep and eat!"

On December 16, he took the final step in his return from seclusion in California when he left Chicago for New York. The first signs of the war were incongruous but gratifying: black soldiers, brought in by the thousands by the Army, guarded the bridges and tunnels into Manhattan. Back in Harlem, he felt the rush of old affection for what was, in spite of its faults and many inconveniences, his favorite place in the world. He stayed with Toy and Emerson Harper in their two-room apartment on the ground floor at 634 St. Nicholas Avenue. The accommodations were undoubtedly cramped. The two rooms served as living and sleeping quarters, as well as the sewing and fitting room for Toy Harper, still a busy modiste, and as Emerson Harper's rehearsal studio, where he practiced assiduously on his various woodwind instruments; at least for the holiday season, he had found a job in a hotel orchestra. When Toy's younger brother Robert Dudley arrived from Kansas City for the holidays, they slept in shifts. Still, with a small Christmas tree shining and pitchers of eggnog, Langston was happy to be with the Harpers in Harlem again.

In her tiny but charming apartment high in the Carnegie Hall complex, he dined with the concert singer Dorothy Maynor and reminisced about her recent stay at the Farm. More than once he visited the Van Vechtens at their home on Central Park West. The two men had been planning a book based on Van Vechten's huge accumulation of his own photographs with a text by Hughes. "It could be gay, funny, sad, glamourous, and high-hat all at the same time," Langston enthused, "and contain both pimps and professors. . . . I am dying to go to work on it." The book was never done, partly because Van Vechten was deep in his James Weldon Johnson Memorial Collection project, energetically sorting and conveying material to the Yale Library; Hughes was amazed to learn that his friend had saved programs from every black show on Broadway in the past thirty-five years. Eager to contribute, Hughes went down to the basement at 634 St. Nicholas Avenue to go through his own trunks, which had been stored there since his eviction from 66 St. Nicholas Place. To his horror, the janitor had allowed water from a broken pipe to drip on and ruin several programs and books (including, ironically, an autographed copy of James Weldon Johnson's 1927 masterpiece, *God's Trombones*). "The janitor said very calmly, Oh, water just drips down all summer!" Hughes related in a small rage. "So it goes in Harlem." Slowly he prepared the material for delivery to Van Vechten's home. Wary of Harlem janitors, he left at the Van Vechtens' perhaps his most cherished relic of the past—the bullet-ridden shawl worn by Sheridan Leary of Oberlin, Ohio, at Harpers Ferry, Virginia, and brought to Mary Langston, Hughes's grandmother, after his death in John Brown's raid. Eventually Langston gave the shawl to the Ohio Historical Society.

With the publication date of *Shakespeare in Harlem* still some time away—February 16—and Hughes in no mood for polite grinning with Blanche Knopf and her staff after the loss of his royalty rights, he put off his visit to Knopf. He was also less than pleased that the firm had reissued his novel *Not Without Laughter* without informing him; he had found out about it from a friend. However, Mrs. Knopf had alerted him to Portugese and Brazilian interest in a translation of *The Big Sea*. When at last he ventured downtown to visit his publisher, his first glance at the dust jacket of *Shakespeare in Harlem* left him stunned—it featured a wishbone and dice, among the more tawdry, as well as hackneyed, symbols of black culture. His editors, who had obviously taken pains with the design of the cover, were mystified by his response. "They think it's charming," Langston despaired to Arna Bontemps. With the publication so long delayed but finally at hand, there was no way to change it. Later in the year, he begged his editor to put out new copies of the book in a plain cover, or in "anything but dice and wishbones."

Two days before Christmas he helped to entertain black servicemen at the Harlem Defense Recreation Center; and in the new year, on January 9, he read his poems downtown on a Greenwich Village program for the Allied War Relief. He also deliberately set aside time to attend a Negro Art Show in New York that opened in mid-January at a Fifth Avenue gallery as a fundraiser for Russell and Rowena Jelliffe's Gilpin Players and Karamu House in Cleveland. He could hardly do less; Rowena Jelliffe had reported ongoing opposition in Cleveland from a section of the black middle class to "Those-Awful-Gilpins-

That-Do-Those-Awful-Langston-Hughes-Plays.'' Otherwise, he stayed at home and worked hard on ''The Sun Do Move'' (''It's going to be *good*!'') in which he had a fair amount invested—not least of all his hopes for a renewal of his Rosenwald Fund fellowship, for which he had applied. When the rattle of Toy's sewing machine and the plaint of Emerson's oboe made the Harpers' apartment at 634 St. Nicholas unbearable for his work, Langston rented a room at Harlem's most prominent hotel, the Theresa, at the corner of Seventh Avenue and 125th Street.

By this time he had become more deeply involved as a writer with the war effort. On behalf of the Department of State, Hughes agreed to broadcast to the English-speaking islands of the Caribbean, where the United States had acquired various military rights and bases as part of the Lend-Lease agreement with Great Britain. More reluctantly, because of his poor experiences with network executives, he also agreed to write a script for a Lincoln's Birthday program in a morale-boosting variety series, ''Keep 'Em Rolling,'' on the Mutual radio network, organized by the Office of Civilian Defense. When he sought payment, however, a bureaucrat flew from Washington, treated him to a whiskey sour instead, and then explained—inaccurately, he later found out—that writers were not being being paid for such opportunities to express their patriotism. Langston protested to the Office of Civilian Defense that white writers had opportunities to earn money that were closed to blacks, and (so he wrote his agent) ''that furthermore Negroes were never asked to write anything except when a segregated all-Negro program was coming up. Anyhow, I agreed to do it.''

Even more important was the question whether he would be allowed to speak his mind honestly on racism and segregation. Initially, the prospect was promising. ''I need not tell you what to write,'' an official encouraged Hughes, ''since you have always written truth, and that is what counts in all times.'' Hughes then sent the Office of Civilian Defense an eight-page script called ''Brothers,'' about a black sailor coming home from duty on a convoy, with parts for actors Rex Ingram and Canada Lee. ''Brothers'' developed President Roosevelt's recent and highly publicized pronouncements on the ''Four Freedoms'' for which the United States was fighting, but applied them to the matter of race. Hughes had written boldly, he informed the Office, because ''so far the programs seeming aimed at colored people have hedged miserably.'' To Hughes's dismay, ''Brothers'' was immediately rejected as far too controversial. Unhesitatingly, he then denounced the radio industry to the Office of Civil Defense as ''a most reactionary and difficult medium in which to put forward any decent or progressive ideas regarding Negro life.'' As for the networks, ''I, personally, have lost all interest in dealing with them.'' ''God knows we better win,'' he added sourly to Maxim Lieber, ''before Hitler comes over here to aid in the lynchings!''

Although Langston had attempted to speak loudly against racism, he made no similar effort on behalf of the far left. In fact, to confirm his move toward the political center, the day after his fortieth birthday he accepted a place on the editorial board of *Common Ground,* the quarterly magazine of the Common Council for American Unity. This was not a token move: in the decade to come, Hughes would publish more pieces in *Common Ground* than in any other magazine (thirteen originals and two reprints). *Common Ground* had already published his article "What the Negro Wants" and one of his poems, "Evenin' Air Blues," when he joined Louis Adamic, Van Wyck Brooks, Pearl Buck, Thomas Mann, and Lin Yutang on the board. Although the Council was barely a year old, it had replaced the now-dissolved Foreign Language Information Service, founded in 1918. The Council and its magazine aimed to foster unity among Americans of diverse backgrounds, "to overcome intolerance and discrimination because of foreign birth or descent, race or nationality," and to help immigrants and their children to value both "their particular cultural heritage, and share fully and constructively in American life." After a year as editor of *Common Ground,* Louis Adamic had just yielded to M. Margaret Anderson, formerly its managing editor. The cross-cultural aims of *Common Ground,* its interest in aesthetic quality rather than crude propaganda, and the prestige of most of his colleagues (Pearl Buck, for example, had won a Nobel Prize for literature) made Langston gratified to be invited to serve as an advisor. The very name of the magazine suggested the emphasis he now placed not on revolution but on reconciliation, even as he kept the faith with his race, and in spite of his continuing sympathy for the Soviet Union.

Near mid-February, after appearing on Mary Margaret McBride's popular radio interview show to talk about his latest work, Hughes returned to Chicago. He was back in time for a large book party on the afternoon of Sunday, February 15 at the Good Shepherd Community Center, on the official appearance of *Shakespeare in Harlem.* By this time, several people had already expressed their displeasure with the dust jacket. Rowena Jelliffe protested directly to Blanche Knopf about the company's use of a white artist when talented blacks were available (Mrs. Knopf had rejected Zell Ingram, who had first learned art as a child at Karamu House); the librarian L. D. Reddick of the Schomburg Collection in Harlem began planning a public protest, until Langston secured his silence. In turn, Mrs. Knopf conceded that the jacket had been "an error" and promised a new one in the second printing, if there was one. In the end, apart from the jacket, and with good reason, Hughes was happy with the look of *Shakespeare in Harlem.* "I think it is my most beautiful book," he wrote Van Vechten.

In building this book of poems on the blues, Langston had returned to the inspiration for his greatest creative period, which had culminated in 1927 in *Fine Clothes to the Jew.* Not surprisingly, then, the reaction of most black reviewers to *Shakespeare in Harlem* was very much like their reaction to *Fine Clothes;* they saw neither virtue nor virtuosity in blues poems. *Opportunity* found the volume only competent, and "concerned overmuch with the most uprooted, and hence demoralized, Negro types." In his *Journal of Negro History,* Hughes's old employer Carter G. Woodson praised him as "a soldier for human rights,'' but he also found the book added nothing to his achievement. The *Negro Quarterly,* edited by Angelo Herndon, with Ralph Ellison as managing editor, judged the book almost exclusively by its dice-and-wishbone cover. In the Chicago *Bee,* Langston's friend, the poet Frank Marshall Davis, recommended the collection only tepidly: facile, it was ''slanted particularly for the Caucasian reader.''

Other reviewers, most of them white, and better informed about poetry, saw past the lightness. ''The thing that hurts is the laughter,'' the *Christian Science Monitor* noted. ''This is a work of genuine talent and skillful artistry.'' In the *Saturday Review of Literature,* Alfred Kreymborg warned: ''The careless reader might easily fall into the error of thinking that these delicate notes are funny or gay. It is only the skillful surface that is funny or gay; the heart of the matter is tragic. Rarely in our poetry do we find this subtle blending of tragedy and comedy. It is an exquisite art and a difficult one.'' The *Herald-Tribune* spoke of ''so sure a touch and an insight so genuine'' in Hughes's brilliant gliding between exhilaration and despair. In the *New York Times Book Review,* Mary Colum made perhaps the most important comparison, but her key conclusion was unfortunate. Hughes had deliberately rowed against the most powerful current in American poetry—the ''high modernist'' tradition derived in part from the New Criticism, with its primary values of elitism, learned allusiveness, and hyper-intellectuality. Contrasting *Shakespeare in Harlem* to *The Language of Poetry* by Philip Wheelwright, Cleanth Brooks, I. A. Richards, and Wallace Stevens (also a Knopf poet), Mary Colum found faults in both works. Brooks and his colleagues were too cerebral, Hughes not cerebral enough. Hughes's emotions were strong, but ''neither his imagination nor his intelligence comes anywhere near the strength of his emotions.'' There were some impressive poems, notably in the ''Death in Harlem'' section; humorlessly, however, she saw the overall mood as ''immensely sad, even hopeless.'' Literature, she explained gratuitously, was not the Negro's forte—as if ''the Negro,'' and not Langston Hughes, had written the poems.

Although Hughes had heard this charge of shallowness before, the criticism in the *New York Times Book Review* still stung. He was a folk poet by choice, not by necessity or by chance. The deeper error was in supposing that one needs greater intelligence to write good modernist verse than to be a good folk poet. ''Various reviewers have accused me of never thinking at all,'' he wrote wryly, acting out the role of the ignorant darky in which the *Times* had cast him. ''The truth is that I do not think much, but occasionally I do think some. When I think I usually think this: Here I am in the world, poor, forty, and colored.''

In his book, Hughes had caught a not dissimilar mood in ''Me and the Mule'':

> My old mule,
> He's got a grin on his face.
> He's been a mule so long
> He's forgot about his race.

I'm like that old mule—
Black
And don't give a damn!
So you got to take me
Like I am.

Shakespeare in Harlem was emphatically, unashamedly about being black. Like *Fine Clothes to the Jew,* it was also an interior portrait, almost completely free of overt protest and self-pity, and resounding in its success as a representation of the lives and thoughts of the mass of black Americans. Blacks who failed to acknowledge this success either knew little about poetry, and thus had no way of seeing Hughes's virtuosity, or were defensively bourgeois to the extent that they considered people economically and socially "beneath" them to be unfit as poetic subjects except when treated sentimentally or ironically. No doubt, Hughes's small foreword had encouraged the sense of triviality: "A book of light verse. Afro-Americana in the blues mood. . . . Blues, ballads, and reels to be read aloud, crooned, shouted, recited, and sung. Some with gestures, some not—as you like. None with a far-away voice." From a technical and a philosophic point of view, however, there was nothing trivial about *Shakespeare in Harlem,* which represented, among other things, Hughes's repudiation of the radical socialist aesthetic that had dominated his poetry in the 1930s.

To consider the book stale because it resembles *Fine Clothes to the Jew* is shortsighted as literary history. Apart from Sterling Brown in his *Southern Road* in 1932, which itself fell undeservedly into near-oblivion, black poets had more or less ignored the challenge of Hughes's 1927 book of verse; indeed, Langston himself had ignored it in the thirties in favor of a more militant aesthetic, in which political rhetoric frequently masqueraded as poetry. Based on aesthetic and emotional truths rooted in black culture, *Fine Clothes to the Jew* had not been a mere literary stunt. Given the failure of black poets to concede the dignity of this vision of their culture, and the urgent need for them to do so in a world that continued to debase their sense of self-respect and their art, the fifteen years between the two books had been little more than a moment.

With *Shakespeare in Harlem* on the shelves, Hughes concentrated on *The Sun Do Move.* In the style of Thornton Wilder's *Our Town* and Clifford Odets's *Waiting for Lefty,* as well as, at least in some respects, his own *Don't You Want to Be Free?,* his new play aimed for the continuity of a motion picture or a radio drama, with no scenery or intermission. It told the story of a slave named Rock who, sold away from his wife Mary and their son, tries twice to return to them and lead them to freedom. Unlike Hughes's Harlem Suitcase show, where the blues ruled, the music here is mainly the spirituals, which orchestrate the black hero's relentless faith in freedom. At the end, black spirituals give way patriotically to "The Battle Hymn of the Republic," and Rock, bearing the Stars and Stripes, joins the Union army. In at least two respects, *The Sun Do Move* broke new dramatic ground for Hughes: it was his first play with a religious theme, and his first full-length musical drama (apart from his opera). Perhaps this move reflected recent stirrings of religion in him, quietly encouraged at Hollow Hills Farm by the devout Noël Sullivan's example; at least once in Chicago, at Easter, Hughes attended a Roman Catholic high mass. The religious element is mediated by a more secular history, in that the prologue shows Rock's grandparents at peace in Africa, from which slavery will rout them. In publicizing the play, however, Hughes deliberately underplayed its more solemn aspects. "You see," he laughed self-deprecatingly to a reporter for the Chicago *Sun,* "it has everything. Three death scenes, hairbreadth escapes, and, at the end, the flagwaving."

At the end of the play, Rock's wife Mary affirms her vision of hope for the race:

. . . I look ahead—and I see my race blossoming like the rose. I see schools and churches everywhere. I see love and life everywhere. I see colored men and women, fine men and women, teachers, preachers, doctors, lawyers, masons, mechanics, singers, dancers, voters, statesmen in the Congress—I see my people everywhere, all over America, all over the world taking part in the making of a new life. Folks, the sun do move! I see you, black and white together, standing with me, working with me, singing with me. Come on! Everybody! Shout! March! Sing!

At the third curtain call, according to the script, the cast was to lead the audience in singing "The Star Spangled Banner."

On the evening of Friday, April 24, *The Sun Do Move* was launched successfully by the Skyloft Players to a near-capacity audience of about 150, including many servicemen, at Good Shepherd. Thereafter, it would play every Thursday and Friday through the month of May. Unlike Hughes's plays at Karamu in the 1930s, there was little or no talk of Broadway or Hollywood, although Hughes made some breezy remarks at one point about the future of the play. Six days later, not long after speaking to a large and enthusiastic group of members of the Chicago Music Association at their headquarters, he left the city. His main reason for leaving was probably the news that the Rosenwald Fund had turned down his application for an extension of his fellowship. Although Van Vechten ("I could summon more enthusiasm for the work of Langston Hughes than I could for most other contemporary American writers") and others had backed him strongly, others were less impressed. Rowena Jelliffe of Karamu had supported his application but reiterated her earlier reservations: "There is an ever enriching of character and experience which is not, I fear, being captured or translated into creative writing. He probably underestimates his capacity and so sets tasks for himself which are not the measure of his capacity." In any case, since Langston had not lived by the terms of his first application, the outcome should not have been a surprise.

New York offered more opportunities for work, but he would have enjoyed staying longer in Chicago. He had met and made friends of virtually all the younger artists and writers on the South Side, including Robert A. Davis, Gordon Parks, Margaret Taylor Goss, Charles White, Elizabeth Catlett, Henry Blakely, Gwendolyn Brooks, and Margaret Walker, whose work (along with that of Richard Wright, the playwright Ted Ward, the musician Margaret Bonds, and others) formed a generally unacknowledged black Chicago Renaissance to match that of Harlem less than a generation before. Many of them had been known to him from previous visits, but he worked more closely with them now. His personality was magnetic. "All the women around here," one admirer wrote him after his departure, "still argue with me that you are one of the few men who have actual charm." A year later, she perhaps spoke for all of them: "Remember us young cullud writers or would-be's as yo' lil flowers, yo' lil plants what needs watering regularly." With Hughes's encouragement, Gordon Parks prepared a series of photographs based on *Shakespeare in Harlem* for a public show. Probably Langston admired most the poets Gwendolyn Brooks and Margaret Walker. As a judge in a poetry contest sponsored by the Negro Exposition in 1940, Hughes had strenuously pushed Brooks's "The Ballad of Pearl May Lee" for the main prize, but his fellow judges had considered it too militant and given Melvin Tolson the award. Although as a member of the South Side workshop led by the white writer Inez Cunningham Stark, Brooks was experimenting in high modernism, Hughes responded strongly to her work, as well as to her combination of modesty and dedication to poetry. Once, when she apologized for "my baby's destruction of the dignity of your rehearsal," Hughes gallantly autographed a book to the child. "I greatly want to discuss poetry with you," Brooks wrote him,"—the modern Negro trends, your opinions regarding them." Later she recalled his willingness to help the younger writers: "He was intent, he was careful. The young manuscript-bearing applicant never felt himself an intruder." Brooks, like Margaret Walker in New Orleans in 1932, had first presented her poems to Hughes as a teenager, after one of his readings. Later that year, 1942, when Walker won the Yale University Younger Poets Award for her volume *For My People,* she recalled their first meeting and paid tribute to Hughes: "You have never ceased to encourage and inspire me during these past ten years."

With no fellowship or other ready source of income, he had to return to New York and 634 St. Nicholas Avenue. Once there, he dug into his basement files for salable material, unearthed the manuscript of Mexican and Cuban stories he had translated in 1935 in Mexico, "Troubled Lands," and offered six pieces to Ralph Ellison at *Negro Quarterly.*

In mid-May, he passed four days working for $10 a day (a fee he himself had suggested) in New Haven, Connecticut, at the request of a senior Yale librarian, Bernhard Knollenberg. Hughes's job was to transcribe lyrics from a collection of blues records donated by Van Vechten; the regular library assistants, it seemed, could understand hardly a word. Alone in a room, Langston spun the discs and copied down the lyrics. The sometimes raunchy language of the blues seemed utterly out of place under the neo-Gothic arches of the Sterling Memorial Library—indeed, at the university itself. "Yale feels like it is ten thousand miles from Harlem," he wrote wistfully to Carl. "Everybody seems so rich up here!" he complained to Arna; "(Harlem is worlds away! Maybe isn't at all.)" Clearly he had second thoughts about his letters and manuscripts resting in perpetuity in such an alien setting. But Bernhard Knollenberg, at whose home Langston stayed, was "a splendid fellow," and if the blues and other documents of black culture were oddities at Yale, their presence also amounted to a kind of racial and cultural victory. Browsing in his correspondence, all beautifully stacked in matched blue cloth boxes with red leather labels (done by Van Vechten at his own expense), he was embarrassed to find his old letters to Wallace Thurman painfully "jejune." "I once were nuts," he conceded. Nevertheless, he had become dedicated to the collection. When Norman Holmes Pearson of Yale advised him, "Don't chuck out a thing," he took the advice literally. Previously he had chucked out very little, so strong had been his sense of his own possible importance. Now he threw away even less.

Returning to Manhattan, Langston soon found himself caught up further in the war effort when he joined Pearl Buck, Clifton Fadiman, and other well-known writers on the advisory board of the Writers' War Committee, later the Writers' War Board, the most important concerted volunteer effort of American writers during the war. As so often was the case, he was the token black. Still, the climate seemed to be improving as far as race was concerned; the Office of Facts and Figures in Washington ordered a more dignified presentation of Negroes in radio. To help the Treasury Department sell war bonds through its thrice-weekly "Treasury Star Parade" radio program, which reached over eight hundred stations, Hughes sent fifteen blues and other rhymes to the Defense Bond Drive, then two dramatic radio scripts—one on American folk heroes, the other his previously rejected "Brothers." The aim of the program was "to awaken and inspire liberty-loving Americans to rally to the common cause, to teach them what liberty, responsibility and fortitude means." To Hughes's dismay, however, while the supervisor of scripts was enthusiastic about the folk hero script, she needed to talk to him about "Brothers"; once again, it was too radical for the airwaves.

Nevertheless, he contributed his time generously. In May, he read a poem on a goodwill broadcast to the Caribbean and Latin America, where his name was hardly unknown; according to the Spanish-language journal *La Nueva Democracia* in August, Hughes and Archibald MacLeish were the most popular contemporary American poets in the Latin world. He also helped the Writers' War Committee in its efforts to propagandize Brazil, and early in June he joined the "Lidice Lives Committee," established to memorialize the Czechoslovakian village that had been obliterated in May. The Nazis had slaughtered all the men and deported most of the women and children to the death camps as punishment for the assassination by Czech patriots of Reinhard Heydrich, the ruthless Gestapo leader, infamous as "The Hangman of Europe."

Such ventures were noble but did not help him to pay the rent. He began to shift his principal focus to songwriting, with a specific goal in mind. So far, no American songwriter had succeeded in producing a hit to rival the tremendous effect of "Over There" in World War I. Langston was determined to try. His main composer was his "uncle," Emerson Harper, who had just broken the color barrier in the CBS studio orchestra through the determined efforts of the producer John Hammond, only to face unfair tests designed to dislodge him. "It seems the radio is like many of the war industries," Hughes complained, "trying their best to wriggle out of hiring Negroes, even when they pass the most difficult requirements." The men pinned much of their hopes on "Freedom Road": "Hitler, he may rant. / Mussolini, he may rave. / My boy's protecting freedom / With the bravest of the brave. . . ." Langston's longtime friend the baritone Kenneth Spencer introduced the song at Barney Josephson's Cafe Society so successfully that he decided to keep it in his program. Hughes sent the song to the "Treasury Star Parade" but also eagerly promoted it himself. He mailed copies to twenty-six black colleges and fifteen high schools and flooded black news organizations with hyperbolic press releases ("Negro Composer Has Hit with First Song") about his "triumph."

Other songs followed. With Toy and Emerson Harper, Langston wrote "That Eagle of the U.S.A." This song was introduced by Eubie Blake's protégée Rosetta LeNoire, seductive and yet patriotic in a skimpy costume of stars and stripes, at the Stage Door Canteen. With W. C. Handy and Clarence M. Jones, Langston wrote the "Go-and-Get-the-Enemy Blues," which made its debut at, of all places, the Waldorf-Astoria—"for which I once wrote an ad," he slyly noted about his 1931 parody in *New Masses* of an advertisement for the opening of the hotel.

> . . . When my gal writes a letter I can fight double-well.
> I got her in my heart that's why I can fight like hell.
> And when I get back home she will hear me tell
> > How I got those so bad,
> > Evil and most mad,
> > GO AND GET THE ENEMY BLUES.

With Elie Siegmeister, a longtime admirer of his poetry, he launched "When a Soldier Writes a Letter." When Arna Bontemps came to town early in June, they joined at Cafe Society in introducing the pianist Hazel Scott, with whom Hughes was also interested in collaborating.

In a "March of Time" radio broadcast (sponsored by Time, Inc.), on which Hughes appeared with the builder of the nation's largest flying boat and a battle-scarred general of the U.S. Armored Force in North Africa, "Freedom Road" was sung and Langston boldly endorsed the war effort. The song "tried to echo the hope of every Negro soldier, to capture his great fighting spirit. . . . We Negroes know our fate is America's fate." But if white Americans were fighting to save liberty, blacks aimed "to gain *new* freedom." At Madison Square Garden on June 16, Hughes joined eighteen thousand blacks rallying on behalf of the controversial "March on Washington" movement for black rights. A. Philip Randolph, the former editor of the radical socialist *Messenger* but now probably the most important black labor leader, entered triumphantly with an honor guard of his sleeping-car porters; Walter White and Mary McLeod Bethune both orated powerfully; and the handsome, progressive young Harlem clergyman, Adam Clayton Powell, Jr., brought the crowd to its feet with the announcement that he had decided to run for the U.S. Congress. "It was TERRIFIC!!!!" Langston wrote Arna Bontemps. The communists had opposed the march as a distraction from the war effort and the defense of the Soviet Union, but Hughes ignored them on this matter. However, he accepted a place on the advisory board of the Harlem Committee for Russian War Relief, led by Rev. Powell.

As the summer approached, and with his work yielding practically no money and the time all wrong for a lecture tour, Hughes decided to return in the autumn to his little cottage at Hollow Hills Farm, to "MI CASA," as he wrote Noël Sullivan. Only his financial plight made him consider leaving Harlem: "New York is so nice and hot now, it is WONDERFUL!!!" In spite of the war, it was the place to be, as far as he was concerned. In early July, in nearby Princeton, he attended the wedding of Dorothy Maynor and Rev. Shelby Rooks, one of his Lincoln University schoolmates, and he dined at the Van Vechtens at a glittering party that included Pearl Buck, whose outspokenness against racism impressed Langston ("She is certainly the current Harriet Beecher Stowe to the Race!"). Evenings, he frequented the integrated Cafe Society, where one night he ran into William Saroyan and George Jean Nathan, the veteran drama critic. To Langston's amusement, Nathan pulled him aside, gestured to the mixed crowd of blacks and whites, and solemnly insisted: "You know, I started all this way before C.V.V.!!!!!" On July 8, at a studio in Steinway Hall on West 57th Street, he attended the premiere of Harvey Enders's setting of his long "Frankie and Johnnie"-style poem, "Death in Harlem," which Enders himself sang. And he enjoyed working as a waiter at the Stage Door Canteen on West 44th Street, where famous artists vied with one another for the right to serve members of the armed forces in a setting that found Harold Jackman of Harlem supervising Alfred Lunt of Broadway, the sixty-two-year-old Van Vechten toiling as a head busboy, and Fania Marinoff and Toy Harper on display as hostesses.

Langston would have found it difficult to give up such lively company in New York for the goats and sheep at Hollow Hills Farm in California. Suddenly, an unexpected invitation made him change his plans. Newton Arvin, a director of the well-known Yaddo writers and artists colony in upstate New York, invited him to spend a few weeks there. With alacrity, he accepted the offer to be Yaddo's first black writer. Langston was lured above all not by that distinction but by the free room and board. On August 4, he arrived at the seven-hundred-acre estate near the town of Saratoga Springs carrying, as requested, his own sugar and his sugar rationing book, to be welcomed warmly by the executive secretary, Elizabeth Ames. His studio, set far back in the woods from the mansion, and so dark under leafy trees and summer vines that he needed to burn lights all day, seemed enchanting. There were ponds and tennis courts, croquet and a game room, a large kitchen and a fine cook who was said to have been a Hungarian countess in another life. "This is really a delightful place to work," he informed Bontemps. As usual, he quickly looked around for other blacks. The famous Saratoga Springs racetrack was close by. "I'm going down there some day," he assured Bontemps. "There seems to be lots of Negroes working around the stables." After months of sleeping on settlement house cots and on Harlem couches and in shifts, it was "wonderful" to have a big bed all to himself, as well as the assurance of three excellent meals daily.

Among the writers in residence were Arvin himself, the young novelist Carson McCullers, the poet Kenneth Fearing, and Leonard Ehrlich, who had written a sympathetic book, *God's Angry Man,* about John Brown. Hughes was pleased to discover another black in residence, the sixty-year-old musicologist Nathaniel Dett, Oberlin-trained and a former student of Nadia Boulanger's, and one of the most prominent of black arrangers and composers. Dett was at work on a series of biblical suites but was eager to collaborate on a song or two with Hughes. Happily, most of the residents seemed to be leftist. Some were refugees from Europe, with harrowing tales "forcefully bringing home to us the horrors of fascism as it spread across Europe." In the evenings, however, especially after the early August rains relented, the mood was so generally light and pleasant and yet stimulating that Yaddo reminded Langston of Carmel in the golden autumn of 1933, after his return from the Soviet Union. His best friend there became the Georgia writer Carson McCullers, whose sensitive portrait of a black doctor in *The Heart Is a Lonely Hunter* had won her many black admirers. Richard Wright, who had recommended her for a Rosenwald fellowship, had lived with his wife in the same house with McCullers and her husband in Brooklyn; she also knew Ralph Ellison well. Langston and McCullers, who breakfasted almost every morning together, sent Wright a joint postcard inviting him to visit Yaddo. Contemptuous of segregation, she liked to threaten to get a gun and go after the arch-conservative Georgia Senator Herman Talmadge; with Southerners like him, she drawled to Langston, "their hind brains don't work." When Katherine Anne Porter, another Southerner, arrived later in the summer with Malcolm Cowley, she was also friendly to Langston, comparing notes with him about music and mutual friends in Mexico City. Porter and McCullers were "two of the nicest people I ever ran into," he reported—even if they loathed one another.

For all its comforts, however, Yaddo could not give Langston what he needed most—inspiration. The lack of a deeply stimulating project to follow *Shakespeare in Harlem* had begun to bother him. He considered sending a collection of lyric poems—as opposed to blues—to Knopf as his next book, but his latest was selling poorly (because of its jacket, he insisted). Mostly he worked on songs, in a deliberate gamble that one would bring him wealth. At least once he defended his interest with what was a curious argument for a serious poet. "I've always wanted to be a songwriter," he explained; "words to music reach so many more people than mere poetry on a printed page." At the canteen in New York, "Freedom Road," sung by the dazzling young Rosetta LeNoire wrapped strategically in stars and stripes, had been greeted wildly by a group of soldiers. Unfortunately, the group was a claque, rounded up, at Langston's specific suggestion on August 20, by his song agent Levia Friedberg. For the publisher Musette, he translated his "hit" into Spanish. He penned songs about heroic aviators flying the mail, and another called "The Day of Victory," which he sent to Irving Landau of Radio City Music Hall; he sent others to Charles Leonard, his Hollywood ally. However, Hughes's ultimate aim, no doubt like that of most songwriters, was not patriotic. "The Lord has blessed me with ASCAP," he declared, grateful for the regular royalty stipends paid by the American Society of Composers, Authors, and Publishers. If one song, "Breath of a Rose" (torturously set by William Grant Still in the 1920s) earned him exactly one dollar and a penny in ten years, ASCAP paid him $400 in 1942. "I shall have four, possibly six numbers published this fall," he exulted. "Let's hope some one of them makes some money $$$$$$." When record-making was suspended as a war measure, he was crestfallen: "But my *determination* is to keep on! Just like dice, you have to pass *sometime*—if your bankroll will just hold out till 'sometime' comes!"

He also gambled at the racetrack. Ingratiating himself with the black jockeys and stable boys at the Saratoga track, he craftily drew them out on the sure bets, on which he soon lost all of his little money. By August 22, he could not afford to repair his typewriter, which had broken down, or to buy shaving cream and toothpaste. Ashamed now to mingle with his fellow residents, Hughes hid in his studio among the leafy vines and complained, when pressed, about "bursitis." When he actually developed a stiff neck, he confessed to at least one friend that it was psychologically induced. He appealed for small loans to Bontemps and Van Vechten. When five dollars came from Arna Bontemps and fifteen from Van Vechten, Hughes quickly recovered.

To his relief, he was asked to stay on at the mansion after most of the guests decamped at the end of August. He accepted at once. Pressed financially to the wall, he began to arrange a month-long lecture tour for late in the autumn.

Hughes could hardly fail to connect his poverty, in spite of his considerable reputation, to his life as a black man in America. As the war continued, and the reports piled up about devastating battles by land, sea, and air, he badly wanted to be able to stand up unequivocally for the United States in the war. Jim Crow made it impossible for him to do so. Still, he wrote his finest essay in many a year, addressed to the black community, in powerful support of the war effort. In "Negro Writers and the War," his contribution to a patriotic or "Victory" number of the *Chicago Defender,* Hughes admitted the existence of rank discrimination in parts of the country, but stressed the positive aspects of America, especially its freedom of press and speech, and the new cracks in the walls of segregation opening under the pressure of the war. He rejected as complete humbug all suggestions of sympathy for Japan. "The Axis is out to crush the little people all over the world," he warned, "to dominate by force of arms everything from labor to radio, from women in kitchens (where the Axis likes them) to jazz bands. The fact that the Japanese have slapped a few white faces in Hong Kong to the delight of American Negroes who have been maltreated by Jim Crow, does not mean that the Japanese are friends of ours. . . . Japanese militarism is a reactionary force, like the German, that respects nobody else's face, white or colored. . . . It is the duty of Negro writers to point out quite clearly that it is an error to think of World War II in terms of race." And they should not point out only the negative reasons for aiding the war effort. "The Axis represents organized gangsterism lifted to government. Against their bombs and machine guns—their frank and deadly Jim Crow—the darker millions of the world, including ourselves, could be for generations helpless."

Such an effort was mounted in the face of galling daily reminders of the power of American racism. By the end of the year, half-a-million blacks were in the Army, but not one in twenty was allowed in a combat unit. After a consuming search, the Navy at last found a black worthy of a commission—a student from the Harvard Medical School. In a major concession, Navy blacks were now allowed in its general service, but only on shore. In "The Black Man Speaks," Hughes mocked:

> . . . Jim Crow Army,
> And Navy, too—
> Is Jim Crow Freedom the *best*
> I can expect from you? . . .

When black newspapers boldly attacked segregation and racism in the military, the Department of Justice threatened their editors with charges of sedition.

For Langston, two events that year especially tested his patience, though not his loyalty. One was the widely reported beating of Roland Hayes, the gentle black interpreter of *lieder* who had been a frequent guest at Hollow Hills Farm. A white clerk had attacked Hayes after he spoke up for his wife during a dispute in a segregated shoe store in Rome, Georgia. Hughes wrote "Roland Hayes Beaten":

> Negroes,
> Sweet and docile,
> Meek, humble, and kind:
> Beware the day
> They change their minds! . . .

The other event was more serious—the lynching of two fourteen-year-old blacks, Charlie Lang and Ernest Green, beneath the Shabuta Bridge over the Chicasa-whay River in Mississippi. In "The Bitter River," Hughes mourned their deaths:

> . . . Oh, tragic bitter river
> Where the lynched boys hung,
> The gall of your bitter water
> Coats my tongue.
> The blood of your bitter river
> For me gives back no stars.
> I'm tired of the bitter river!
> Tired of the bars!

Although these and other events did not diminish his desire to see the Axis defeated, they probably made him less than exultant about Allied victories. As for the British, they put their brown colonials in jail. "Some folks think / By imprisoning Nehru / They imprison Freedom," Langston wrote; but Freedom declares: "*You'll never kill me!*" Such events also renewed his affection for the Soviet Union. The early spectacular success of Hitler's "Barbarossa" military campaign against Russia heated this renewal of interest into a revival of passion, although Hughes's passion now was not for communism, as it once had been, but for the Soviet Union and its people. On August 23, when the Nazis broke through the perimeter of Stalingrad for the first time, defeat for its defenders seemed to many observers almost certain, followed surely by the collapse of the nation itself.

Not so to Hughes. Writing in anguished response, he echoed in intensity the tones of his greatest verse written in Spain. In "Stalingrad: 1942," he predicted a Soviet triumph that would be decisive in ending the war.

> There are the inactive ones who,
> By their inaction,
> Aid in the breaking of your dreams.
> There are the ones
> Who burn to help you,
> But do not know how—
> Can only fling words in the air,
> Petition: Second Front,
> Give money,
> Beg, curse, pray,
> Bitterly care.
>
> I know,
> Those who would wreck your dream
> Wreck my dream, too,
> Reduce my heart to ashes
> As they reduce you.
>
> Stalingrad—
> Never Paradise—
> Just a city on the Volga

Trying peacefully to grow . . .

. . . .

Then out of the West the wreckers came—
Luftwaffe! Panzers! Storm Troopers!
Men with guns and an evil name: Nazis!
Invaders! Bombers! Throwers of flame!
Thieves of the common grain!
   Did we go to help?
    No.
   Did the Second Front open?
    No.
   Did the RAF arrive?
    No.
   Did the AEF get there?
    No.
   Did Stalingrad fall?
   Did Stalingrad fall?
   Did it fall?
Out of the rubble from a dead hand lifted—
Out of the rubble from a lost voice calling—
I gather instead another world is falling:
Lies and blunders and fear and greed
Are meagre feed for the people—
As quick as steel or *ersatz* swill, they kill.
But no one can kill
The dream of men
To be men again . . .

. . . .

   [Stalingrad] gives way? Oh, no!
   Though the last walls fall,
   And the last man dies,
   And the last bullets go,
   Stalingrad does not give way!
   Fight on, brave city!
   Deathless in song and story,
   Yours is the final triumph!
   VICTORY—your glory!

At *The New Republic* and the *Nation,* the editors applauded the sentiment of the poem, they said, but deplored its style. *New Masses* took it.

In late October, the war drew closer when Hughes answered a questionnaire from the Selective Service authorities and faced the military draft. A young black friend, a Juilliard-trained pianist named Jimmy Davis, had recently been on the brink of going to jail rather than submit to Jim Crow in the Armed

Forces. Langston himself offered a token of resistance. Declaring his own race as mixed—white, Negro, and Indian—he appended a statement of protest to the questionnaire: "I wish to register herewith, as a citizen of the United States, my complete disapproval of the segregating of the armed forces of the United States into White and Negro units, thus making the colored citizen the *only* American group so singled out for Jim Crow treatment, which seems to me contrary to the letter and spirit of the Constitution and damaging to the morale and well-being of not only the colored citizens of this country but millions of our darker allies as well." The draft board promptly classified him 1-A. Shaken, Hughes consulted many of his friends about his next move. Should he enlist at once, and thus be able to pick his service, or wait, and perhaps avoid being drafted at all? After a hearing on November 9 at Local Board 1560 on Amsterdam Avenue in Manhattan, he secured a sixty-day deferment on the basis of his coming lecture tour, which included appearances before several armed services organizations. But the draft board forced him to cut back on the tour.

By this time, with his spirits low and the warm weather giving way to rain and cold, and with most of the summer residents gone, Yaddo was not nearly as attractive as it had been. Langston did not like the country much "even when it is sunny," as he wrote his song agent, "let alone gloomy and dark as it has been up this way these days. . . ." He had also had more than one unpleasant brush with racism in Saratoga Springs. After Elizabeth Ames intervened on his behalf, a local proprietor declared that he would "not object to Langston Hughes, the colored writer, coming in our bar as long as he is in the company of someone else from Yaddo."

In his room in the mansion house Langston polished his old poems and sent thirty-five pieces to Maxim Lieber for sale to various magazines. He also sent an outline for a musical, "Chocolate Soldier," to Charles Leonard in Hollywood. Then he received some important news. Almost at the same time, but separately, the editors of the New York *Amsterdam News* and the *Chicago Defender* invited him to write a weekly column for their papers. At the *Defender,* his friend Metz T. P. Lochard, who had been pleased by Hughes's "magnificent piece," "Negro Writers and the War," in his "Victory" number, made the better offer: a column of a thousand words expected each Thursday (the *Amsterdam News* wanted only seven hundred), at $15 per column, dealing with "specific incidents and stories rather than abstract generalizations." "The World's Greatest Weekly" would also take care of all correspondence involving the column. On October 29, he wired his acceptance. He joined among the columnists on the *Defender* his friends Walter White of the NAACP and S. I. Hayakawa, an Illinois professor of English and a prominent semanticist and lover of the blues (and a future U.S. Senator) who had been a specially featured guest at Hughes's Good Shepherd Community Center book party for *Shakespeare in Harlem.*

Leaving Yaddo—"a grand place"—after a stay of three and a half months, he returned to New York. In Jamaica, Queens, he worked briefly with Irving Mills on songs for a Negro film planned for the West Coast, with music by

William Grant Still and Nathaniel Dett (who had set two of Hughes's songs at Yaddo). Then he set out on the road. His tour began on November 18 in St. Louis, Missouri, at Stowe Teachers' College, then drew an overflow crowd the next day at Lincoln University in Jefferson City. Among various Indiana readings was at least one to black servicemen at a U.S.O. club. Then he headed west to Kansas City, where he read under the auspices of his schoolmate at Lincoln University, Thomas A. Webster, the executive secretary of the local Urban League. In nearby Lawrence, Kansas, he fulfilled an old promise to "Auntie" Reed, Mrs. Mary Campbell, to appear at St. Luke's A.M.E. Church, which he had attended as a boy. Then he returned east by way of Chicago. Once again, he addressed Rabbi Jacob Weinstein's youth council at the K.A.M. Temple, as he had done the previous year, and he was given a rousing homecoming at the Good Shepherd Community Center. In Detroit, he read at Wayne University and at Plymouth Congregational Church. On December 15, Hughes's tour ended with an appearance in Cleveland at Karamu House.

The message he drummed on the road was that the war presented an opportunity to crush both Fascism and Jim Crow. Out of the struggle would come a better day for all. In spite of its flaws, the United States of America was "the best, the greatest, and the finest democracy in the world." The idea that blacks should sympathize with the Japanese because both were colored was "foolishness." Japan suppressed trade unions and imposed strict censorship; black America, not Japan, might provide leadership and models for emerging Africa and India. Virtually everywhere he was a success; nowhere was he picketed. At forty, the remarkable childlike charm that had won over audiences from the start of his career still shone in his face. "His personal magnetism and the boyish air of one confiding all his secrets draw the audience to him," the Kansas City *Call* noted. But he was also perceived as a veteran, an elder in the struggle; the Indiana *Recorder* dubbed him the "internationally beloved apostle of freedom." As almost always, whites were struck by his ability to talk frankly of racism and injustice and yet do so in a winning way. "You are so without bitterness, in speaking—so gentle & patient," an onlooker had written after an address at Yaddo to the senior class of nearby Skidmore College. "But not, I am glad to feel, in some of your poems! Many blaze with hot fire."

Even in his absence, through the reading of his work, Hughes could create a stir. A long piece of low comic verse, composed as a tribute to Carl Van Vechten and read at a grand testimonial dinner given in his honor by the James Weldon Johnson Literary Society at a Chinatown restaurant in New York on November 20, was a hit in an evening of hilarity. "I am heartbroken that I shall probably have to miss your dinner," Hughes had apologized to Van Vechten in telling him about his tour. However, the guest of honor was not miffed. The dinner, attended by Toy and Emerson Harper and dozens of Van Vechten's other black friends, including Alain Locke, W. C. Handy, Margaret Walker, Walter White, and Grace Nail Johnson, drew some three hundred people. They heard Langston's jovial rap-song:

Hey now!
Some skin, gate!
I can't make a speech
Cause it's getting late,
And not having heard
What's gone on before
I might be repeating
What you already know.
You're a mellow fellow
And I guess they've told you so . . .

To Van Vechten, who had never recovered, as far as some implacable blacks were concerned, from having called his best-selling 1926 novel of Harlem *Nigger Heaven* (although the title was clearly ironic), the evening "was like a Christmas tree with everything on it coming to me and when Canada Lee read your poem it was like all Christmases everywhere from the beginning of time coming to me at once."

Summoned by the draft board, Hughes returned to New York early in December. Thereafter, he had to have its specific permission to leave the city. By this time he was scheduling his weeks around the writing and delivery of his *Defender* column, "From Here to Yonder," which first appeared on November 21, while he was on tour. The first essay explained the title and the nature of the column: events happening far away affect us here, and he would write often about them. The second was a chatty tribute to W. C. Handy in honor of the sixty-ninth birthday of "the dean of popular American Negro musicians." The third reminisced humorously about his meeting in Paris in 1938 with the entertainer Josephine Baker, who had just been erroneously reported missing, and presumed killed, in the war; born and bred in America, Baker nevertheless had spoken French to Hughes, as well as English in an accent remarkably like Maurice Chevalier's. Another column assailed the extraordinary steps taken by the American Red Cross to prevent "black" blood from entering "white" bloodbanks. For Christmas, Langston wrote nostalgically about his Kansas boyhood.

By the new year, 1943, he was settling down as a columnist. The job paid little, but the little came regularly. And he was reaching directly what had almost always been, and certainly now was, his prime audience, the masses of literate blacks who read the *Chicago Defender*—as he and his grandmother had read the newspaper when he was a boy in Lawrence, Kansas. Here, as with his efforts in *Common Ground* magazine, Hughes aimed for the middle of the stream.

Two invitations in January, 1943, showed how far he had withdrawn from the far left toward the black center. He accepted an offer from Walter White to serve on the Spingarn Medal committee of the NAACP, and agreed to write a long poem or recitation piece for a special function of the National Urban League, an even less radical organization. Still, he did not entirely sever his ties to the left. At a dinner on January 12, sponsored by the leftist National Maritime Union in honor of the first black U.S. merchant marine skipper, Captain Hugh Mulzac, and the integrated crew of the *Booker T. Washington,* Hughes was the principal speaker. Mulzac's appointment was a source of deep pride in the black community, and Hughes reflected his own emotional response to its symbolism in his long poem "To Captain Mulzac" ("Dangerous / Are the western waters now, / And all the waters of the world . . ."), which he read at the dinner. More significant of his undercurrent of interest in the left was Langston's meeting later in the month with Max Yergan, the founder of the leftist Council on African Affairs, and a number of other Harlem radicals to discuss the possibility of starting a "People's Institute" there. Nevertheless, because of his fear of bad publicity, Langston was definitely more comfortable the following night attending an NAACP dance in the company of Walter White, whose fervent anti-communism, especially during the Scottsboro crisis, he had once scathingly denounced both in the Soviet press and directly to White himself. At White's request, Hughes had written a poem, "NAACP," to enliven the Association's annual convention, which was becoming a torpid affair; Hughes was also aiding White, although with far less enthusiasm, in his well-publicized efforts to censor and influence Hollywood's and Broadway's treatment of blacks. This alliance of a former radical socialist with the NAACP amused at least one old friend. "Thus do the outlaws . . . of one generation," Van Vechten teased, "become the conservatives of the next."

In February, when Hughes turned forty-one, President Roosevelt signed an order deferring the draft for men over thirty-eight. Langston's troubles with the draft board were over. The presidential order removed the last major threat to the life he had patiently rebuilt since leaving the Peninsula Hospital on his birthday two years before. With his *Defender* column and his blossoming relationship with the NAACP, he was poised to reap the rewards of his retreat from radicalism. In March, he added to his record of support for the war effort by accepting an honorary sponsorship of the Music War Committee formed by ASCAP as a counterpart to the work of the writers.

At least as significant, too, was Hughes's acceptance of the fact that from now on, barring unusual circumstances and occasional sojourns elsewhere, he would live the rest of his life among black people in Harlem, and in particular with "Aunt" Toy Harper and "Uncle" Emerson Harper in what would henceforth be his family. He had known them at least since the early 1920s, when he had come to New York to attend Columbia University; Toy Harper may have known him when he was a baby. By the early 1930s, after several years in New York married to Emerson, and with a flourishing little business in dressmaking, she had come to regard Langston, his stepbrother Gwyn "Kit" Clark, and his mother Carrie Clark, as special. "As long as I have a place to stay," she had vowed to Langston then, "you three have also." Stern and calculating in many respects—while her husband Emerson was the epitome of ease—Toy Harper loved Langston like a mother with an only son. Indeed, she loved him with far more consistent devotion than his real mother had ever shown. Since he was now living with her, she had only one remaining major desire, shared by the rootless, road-weary Langston: to own their own home, in Harlem, with space enough for them all.

In Hughes's new interest in family, his stepbrother Kit Clarke was hardly a favorable consideration, although the loyal Langston continued to preserve the fiction that Kit was a blood brother, or a half-brother. Once, Langston had sent Emerson Harper money to pay for spectacles for the errant Kit, "so he can see his way through life." "I gather that my brother is just as usual," Hughes noted resignedly after learning about Kit's latest delinquencies. Now a father, Kit had entered the Army in December, 1942.

Once Langston had wandered and roamed as a way of life and a way of making art. Now, past forty-one, the need to root himself in a family and deep within a community of black people had become his greatest priority.

His attitude to America itself was becoming more settled. When he wrote "My America," a definitive statement of his attitude to his country during the war, Hughes emphasized his permanence of place in the nation: "This is my land America. Naturally, I love it—it is home—and I am vitally concerned about its mores, its democracy, and its well-being. I try now to look at it with clear, unprejudiced eyes. My ancestry goes back at least four generations on American soil—and, through Indian blood, many centuries more. My background and training is purely American—the schools of Kansas, Ohio, and the East. I am old stock as opposed to recent immigrant blood." Yet many recent arrivals enjoyed rights and privileges denied to him. "They may repeat the Oath of Allegiance with its ringing phrase of 'liberty and justice for all,' with a deep faith in its truth. . . . I repeat the oath, too, but I know that the phrase about 'liberty and justice' does not apply fully to me. I am an American—but I am a colored American." In most places, even in their own communities, blacks could not hold even minor clerical jobs in banks, offices, and stores. "Yet America is a land where, in spite of its defects, I can write this article. Here the voice of democracy is still heard—Roosevelt, Wallace, Wilkie, Agar, Pearl Buck, Paul Robeson." America "is a land in transition. And we know it is within our power to help in its further change toward a finer and better democracy than any citizen has known before. The American Negro believes in democracy. We want to make it real, complete, workable, not only for ourselves—the thirteen million dark ones—but for all Americans all over the land."

Langston published this essay in the *Journal of Educational Sociology* in February 1943, and a year later, in amended form, in Rayford Logan's striking collection of essays by various prominent blacks, *What the Negro Wants*. (Hughes's contribution there blended "My America" with another essay, "What Shall We Do About the South?," published in the Winter 1943 issue of *Common Ground*.) He expanded again upon the idea of America when he prepared "Freedom's Plow," a long "prose poem" first requested by Lester B. Granger, executive secretary of the National Urban League in New York, then pressed on Langston by Ann Tanneyhill, another official. Tanneyhill had secured a promise to help the League from the actor Paul Muni, then a star on Broadway; would Langston write a recitation piece for him? "I do remember that Langston brought his first drafts of *Freedom's Plow* to my house," Ann Tanneyhill later recalled. Present that evening was his Lincoln schoolmate Thomas Webster of the Urban League in Kansas City, and "the three of us sat at the dinette table at my home and went over the drafts." On March 15 that year, 1943, Muni read their work movingly over the Blue Network, accompanied by the Golden Gate Quartet, with an orchestral score by the black composer and conductor Dean Dixon.

"Freedom's Plow," Langston's longest poetical piece by far, is about the building of America by black and white alike, and about the American will to prosperity, happiness, and liberty.

> When a man starts out with nothing,
> When a man starts out with his hands
> Empty, but clean,
> When a man starts out to build a world,
> He starts first with himself
> And the faith that is in his heart—
> The strength there,
> The will there to build.
>
> First in the heart is the dream.
> Then the mind starts seeking a way.
> His eyes look out on the world . . .
>
> . . . .
>
> America is a dream.
> The poet says it was promises.
> The people say it *is* promises—that will come true.
>
> . . . .
>
> America!
> Land created in common,
> Dream nourished in common,
> Keep your hand on the plow! Hold on!

The American people, black and white, must never cease to dream: "KEEP YOUR HAND ON THE PLOW! / HOLD ON!"

In its way, "Freedom's Plow" was magnificent, but it was hardly great art. Langston's songs, his *Defender* essays, his recent poems (with the exception of "Stalingrad: 1942"), and other writing, were not much more inspired. Settling down into his new life as columnist and Harlem resident, perhaps he himself had begun to doubt whether, after twenty-two years as a publishing writer, he would ever create in a truly fresh way. But he continued to try to do so. Over the previous two years or so, the main token of his continuing experimentation had been those poems—or pieces of verse—in which his persona spoke with the verbal nonchalance and semi-literacy of a putatively "typical" member of the black masses, and usually on topics of the day. These poems are distinct from the blues, in that the latter are a product of heightened moments of pleasure or pain, and thus attain levels of art that transcend the question of literacy. Hughes had been writing pieces of verse of this semi-literate, topical type for some time (in Spain, he had annoyed black members of the Abraham Lincoln Brigade, most of whom had been well educated, by taking such an approach in a series of "poems" about the war). Mainly he attempted to distribute them among black newspapers through the Associated Negro Press.

One poem, "Total War," written in October, 1942, illustrates the type.

> The reason Dixie
> Is so mean today
> Is because it wasn't licked
> In the proper way.
>
> I'm in favor of beating
> Hitler to his knees—
> Then beating him some more
> Until he hollers, *Please!*
>
> If we let our enemies
> Breathe again—
> They liable to live
> To be another pain.

To many readers, it is unclear how a poet of Hughes's ability, or a poet of any ability, could write such bad verse. His conscious aim, however (not unlike Wordsworth's in some of his own banal lines written under a similar populist pressure), was to make his persona one and the same with the masses as he heard them in the bars and on the streets.

In 1943, the main result of Hughes's efforts here was the publication by the leftist Negro Publication Society of America, which also nominally produced Ralph Ellison's *Negro Quarterly,* of his pamphlet of twenty-three poems, *Jim Crow's Last Stand.* Almost half the poems were aggressively demotic.

> I swear to the Lord
> I still can't see
> Why Democracy means
> Everybody but me.
>
> I swear to my soul
> I can't understand
> Why Freedom don't apply
> To the black man . . .

"Good Morning, Stalingrad" translated for many black readers something of the power of Hughes's "Stalingrad: 1942":

> Goodmorning, Stalingrad!
> Lots of folks who don't like you
> Had give you up for dead.
> But you ain't dead! . . .

The other poems, some in dialect but still different in approach, confirm Hughes's renewed general eagerness to speak directly to the race. At least two are from the early 1920s. One of these is "Color": "I would wear it / Like a banner for the proud— / Not like a shroud." (Almost certainly, Hughes had meant to rebuke Countee Cullen for writing about "The Shroud of Color.") Two or three pieces, such as "Blue Bayou" and "Still Here," exude genuine blues feelings and creativity of language. On the other hand, "To Captain Mulzac" and "The Bitter River," on the lynching of two black youths in Mississippi, are passionate but in formal English. At least two, including "Note on Commercial Theatre" ("You've taken my blues and gone") and "Daybreak in Alabama" ("When I get to be a colored composer") are folksy but dignified protests.

Even if *Jim Crow's Last Stand* had achieved its main purpose, Hughes could hardly have been content with it as a harbinger of his future as an artist; in some ways, the collection was a scrappy affair, perhaps best seen as a wartime measure—a fusillade of verses in the long war on Jim Crow. Semi-literate versification surely was a dead-end. And yet as a continuing token of the depth of his love of the black masses, the book bespoke renewed vitality and purpose, and was of a piece with his decison to settle down in Harlem. At the very least, Hughes had now positioned himself near the lifelong source of his finest inspiration: he had returned to a living, breathing, vibrant black community in all its colors and classes, virtues and vices, dreams and fears. He was not romantic about Harlem, which had changed dramatically since his arrival there twenty years earlier. Still relatively safe, it was not as safe as it had once been; several people he knew had been mugged at least once. In March, he himself had scampered away in terror from a man who had loomed at him on a dark street. But Harlem was home. All the sedate comforts of Yaddo or Hollow Hills Farm could not outweigh Langton's sensuous pleasure in easing his way down these familiar streets, past neighborhood barbershops, churches, shops, and bars, as he blended effortlessly with the dark flow of life on which he and his art had always depended.

That life ultimately had never failed him. If there was still a spark of artistry left within him, he would find it there. In Harlem, he waited calmly for inspiration. And, casually, inspiration came.

3

SIMPLE SPEAKS HIS MIND
1943 to 1944

Here on the edge of hell
Stands Harlem—
Remembering the old lies,
The old kicks in the back,
The old, *Be patient,*
They told us before . . .

"Puzzled," c. 1944

A S LANGSTON HUGHES himself later told the story, one night sometime in early January, 1943, he was drinking by himself at the counter in one of his favorite neighborhood taverns, Patsy's Bar and Grill, located in the heart of Harlem at 2623 Eighth Avenue, not far from his home at 634 St. Nicholas Avenue. At some point in the evening, a man he knew mainly by sight and a passing greeting—but who no doubt knew him, perhaps vaguely, by reputation as a writer—decided that Langston Hughes should not drink alone that evening. The man invited Hughes to join him and his girlfriend at a table in the rear of Patsy's Bar.

Following the man back to his table, Langston sat down and met "Mary." The man, it turned out, worked in a defense factory. He helped to make cranks.

"What kind of cranks?" Langston asked.

"Cranks," the fellow replied. "Cranks. Just cranks!"

"Mary" was not satisfied. "You been working in that war plant long enough," she drawled. "You ought to know what they crank."

"I do not know!"

How could he not know, they wondered, what kind of cranks he was helping to make?

How could *they* not know, the man countered, that white folks never tell Negroes such things? "I don't crank with those cranks. I just make 'em."

"Mary" grew exasperated, and probably not for the first time, with her friend. "You sound," she told him, "right simple."

Although hardly unusual in a Harlem bar, the quality of the exchange intrigued Hughes. He was taken by the docile and yet barbed nature of the bantering between the man and his friend, the man's sweetly relaxed but at the same time quirky personality, his way of expressing his deeply rooted social alienation in charmingly homespun language, his sometimes unpredictable blending of fatalism and aggression, of sure political insight and illogical, highly defensive racial feeling. Why Langston should have been intrigued at this particular moment is something of a mystery. After all, he had long recognized the power of uneducated speech in the mouths of people with little formal learning but with much to say. More or less, the man's voice had been that of the demotic poems Langston had been writing from time to time over the previous few years. These verses had not been composed in the hope of dignifying the semi-literate voice by introducing it into poetry. Rather, Hughes had written semi-literate verse (as opposed to his blues and jazz poetry) mainly to propagandize the black masses on issues such as the Spanish Civil War and, more recently, the gravity of the threat posed by the Nazis and the Japanese. Certainly he understood that in spite of their familiarity with the blues and spirituals, the masses of people do not speak in ballad meter. In this respect, his semi-literate compositions had rung falsely almost from the start, although they had probably conveyed at least a part of their propagandistic messages. Now, with the same basic goal in mind—that of leading the black masses to see their destiny linked to the fate of the Allies fighting against the Axis—the idea came to him that he should turn to prose, instead of verse, and use the man in Patsy's Bar as "a foil for patriotic propaganda."

On January 19, in a complete departure from the style of his column thus far, Langston drafted a piece for the *Chicago Defender* in the form of a dialogue, "Conversation at Midnight," with a man he identified only as "My Simple Minded Friend." On February 13, after weeks in which his essays touched variously on topics such as the blues, the customarily shabby and even bizarre service in many black hotels, the evils of segregation, and a benefit concert of jazz in New York on behalf of the Soviet Union, Langston casually introduced his Harlem friend to the readers of the *Defender*.

My Simple Minded Friend said, "Day time sure is a drag. I like night time a lot better."

"I do too," I said. "Day time hurts my eyes. I was born at midnight, but my mama told me I didn't start crying until morning. After that, I hollered and cried every morning straight for two years."

"I could holler and cry every morning now when I have to get up and go to work."

"That's why you don't get ahead in the world," I said. "The people who get ahead in the world are the ones who get up early."

"I get up early," said my Simple Minded Friend. "But I don't get ahead. Besides, what you say is not necessarily right. Joe Louis likes to sleep—and he got ahead."

"I'll bet he doesn't sleep in the army, though."

"I'll bet he does," said my Simple Minded Friend, "cause he's always on furlough. How come Joe Louis is always on furlough?"

"I can't answer you that," I said, "but I guess it's because he's doing Special Services."

"Naw! It's because Joe said, 'We're on God's side.' White folks like religious Negroes."

"Well, we are on God's side, aren't we? Naturally, God's against the Nazis."

"Who made the Nazis?"

"Are you trying to blame Hitler on God?"

"Who made Hitler?"

"Well, who made him?" I asked.

"God," said my Simple Minded Friend.

"Then He must have made him for some purpose."

"Sure, He did," declared my Simple Minded Friend. "God made Hitler to be a thorn in the side of our white folks."

"Aw, you're crazy!" I said. "Hitler would stick a bigger thorn in your side, if he could get hold of you."

"HE AIN'T going to get hold of me," said my Simple Minded Friend. "I'm gonna fight him. I been reclassified in 1-A."

"Good! When you hear that bugle blow in the mornings . . . you'll feel swell. The army will make you like rising early."

"Nothing can make me like rising early," said my Simple Minded Friend. "Nothing."

"Then why don't you go to bed at some decent hour a tnight?" I asked.

"Why don't you?" demanded my Simple Minded Friend in return.

"I'm a writer," I said, "and I don't have to get up until noon."

As the conversation rambles on, the men talk about Paul Robeson's performance on Broadway in Shakespeare's *Othello* (which Langston had seen and disliked, because the production seemed to emphasize black violence). Inevitably they talk about Jim Crow.

"It hurts my soul," said my Simple Minded Friend. "To be Jim Crowed hurts my soul. To have on my uniform and have to be Jim Crowed."

"If you beat Hitler, though, you'll be helping to beat Jim Crow."

"I want to beat Jim Crow first," said my Simple Minded Friend. "Hitler's over yonder, and Jim Crow is here."

"But if the Nazis ever got over here, and Hitler and Jim Crow ever got together, you would have an awful time beating the two of them. In fact, you would be hog-tied. They would have curfew laws for Negroes—just like they have curfew laws for Jews in Germany. And you couldn't stay up after nine."

"You mean I'd have to go to bed early, whether I wanted to or not?"

"That is exactly what I mean. They do let you stay up late down South, if you want to."

"They do, don't they? That is worth fighting for," said my Simple Minded Friend. "The right to stay up late! That is really worth fighting for."

"The fascists won't let Negroes stay up late."

"Then I will fight the fascists," said my Simple Minded Friend. "I will even get up early to fight for the right to stay up late. Damned if I won't!"

For three consecutive weeks, Langston's column in the *Defender* featured conversations between the educated, somewhat stuffy narrator, whom the readers could only take to be Langston Hughes himself, and his racially defensive but curiously wise and amusing "Simple Minded Friend." The basic topic remained the war and blacks. Then the man disappeared from the column for six weeks. In mid-April, without warning, he returned to "Here to Yonder," and thereafter appeared on an unpredictable but enduring basis. Soon, Langston's "Simple Minded Friend" had completely outgrown his original propagandistic purpose. Jesse B. Semple, or "Simple," as he came to be called, was too expansive to be confined to the world of war. In his first year, Simple appeared in roughly one quarter of the columns. Over the following twenty-three years, as Hughes continued to fulfill his obligation to write a column for the newspaper, this proportion only increased. Simple established himself as one of the most keenly anticipated fixtures of the *Defender,* which reached black communities across the country in its national edition, and became by far the most brilliant and beloved aspect of Langston's "Here to Yonder."

A migrant from the South, black in color (*light* black, he insists desperately, and of Indian ancestry), Simple is a sport of his youth in rural Virginia (to which he might gladly return but for Jim Crow) and his modern, Harlem destiny. Surrounding him eventually is an inspired supporting cast, almost all women, who dominate his life: Isabel, his difficult wife, from whom he dearly wishes to be finally divorced; Joyce, his attractive, likable, but too proper lady friend and later wife, who is determined to "improve" him; Zarita, his after-hours girlfriend, loud, flashy, and disreputable; his tyrannical landlady, almost always with a sharp word for "Third Floor Rear," as she prefers to call him; his importuning cousin Minnie; and others. Looming over Simple's Harlem is the grim white world, which Simple fears and detests—except for the saintly Mrs. Eleanor Roosevelt, who is above reproach. Simple's crucial setting, however, is a stool at "Paddy's Bar," as his tavern is called, and his finest moments come in his exchanges with the narrator, who is never precisely identified as Langston Hughes, and is sometimes called "Boyd."

To the narrator's pale "standard" English and colorless logic, Simple responds in language garnished with both country folk tropes and the latest Harlem hip talk. Behind his amusing, vibrant front, on the other hand, one glimpses the loneliness of the uprooted and the dispossessed. But although Simple sometimes edges toward despair, he is always saved in the end by his passion for life, laughter, and language. This conquest of loneliness and deprivation is only frugally shared with the objective, informed, but increasingly desolate narrator, a man apparently bereft of family and friends, and reduced to haunting Paddy's Bar for the solace of Simple's company and often perverse wisdom.

These men were both Langston Hughes, who once called the character of

Simple "really very simple. It is just myself talking to me. Or else me talking to myself. That has been going on for a number of years and, in my writing, has taken one form or another from poetry to prose, song lyrics to radio, newspaper columns to books." For all the humor, Simple and his questioner form a sort of colloquium of Langston's surface conflicts of belief, as well as his deeper fears and desires. The uninspired narrator is Langston Hughes without love, laughter, and poetry—the man his father had wished him to be, the man he himself feared he easily could have become. Simple, on the other hand, personifies the genius of the black folk for self-redemption in the face of adversity, a genius that Langston, with the passion of an intellectual outsider, an *aficionado,* had devoted his life to honoring. Like the publicly chaste Hughes, the narrator exudes little or no sexual feeling. Simple, on the other hand, cannot live without women. His aberrations of logic, language, and social convention indicate not so much personal weakness as the deep difficulty of the challenge haunting his race in the guise of an American identity. The distance between him and the narrator acknowledges Langston's sense of his own life as incomplete, and his art as a mere approximation of the folk genius it honors. His alternative to despair was to create tributary images in the likeness of his desire—and certainly the most creative image of his middle years, when the romantic fire of his poetry had died down, to be revived mainly in spurts, was that of Jesse B. Semple, or Simple.

With tongue in cheek, Hughes liked to pretend that there was no art whatsoever to writing the Simple columns—as if the notion of art was incompatible with the plain verities of Jesse B. Semple. Of the origins of his hero he would admit most often only that Simple "simply started talking to me one day about the war, Hitler, the draft, Shakespeare, and getting up early in the morning, so I put down on paper exactly what he said." Within a few years, however, Simple had grown into a notable, Afro-American addition, without parallel in the twentieth century, to the long line of popular fictional humorists in American literature dating back at least a hundred years. By that time he had established his claim to be recognized as a distant, dark-skinned cousin of white characters such as those in the worlds of Artemus Ward, Petroleum V. Nasby, Josh Billings, and, in the twentieth century, Finley Peter Dunne's engaging Mr. Dooley. Eventually, beginning in 1950, Hughes would winnow and edit selections from the columns and publish them as books with Jesse B. Semple as their modest but endearing hero: *Simple Speaks His Mind, Simple Takes a Wife, Simple Stakes a Claim, The Best of Simple,* and *Simple's Uncle Sam.*

From the start, Simple's excellence stood out. Arna Bontemps, pronouncing Simple "a very happy creation," sent suggestions as to how Langston might use him. To the Los Angeles intellectual and lawyer Loren Miller, one of Hughes's old traveling companions in the Soviet Union, and a stern critic, Simple was easily the best part of Langston's column. "You have a good ear for speech and a feeling for what zigs [ordinary blacks] are thinking when their guards are down," Miller wrote him shortly after Simple's debut. "You should cultivate him extensively. Never mind the political aspects of your Friend's wonderings.'' Simple's politics were indeed sometimes ludicrous, as when he announced his intention to vote for Eleanor Roosevelt, although she was running for nothing. Accusations of irresponsibility meant little to him; more than once he cantankerously insisted that he was under no obligation to be good. Simple was ''killing me,'' a black newspaperman wrote Langston; ''when he came out and asked for his 'right to be a disgrace,' I damn near keeled over.'' However, not all the *Defender* readers liked him. Many of the people who detested Hughes's blues poetry also loathed his latest creation. Undoubtedly he embarrassed quite a few, and even frightened some with his hiccoughing racial belligerence. One young black woman even suggested primly to Langston that his hero was ''much less 'simple' and much more psychopathic,'' as far as she was concerned.

Most of the letters, however, praised him. Viewing life most often through the amber haze of a glass of beer, Simple managed to convey, in the final analysis, both wisdom and dignity, as well as an unshakeable loyalty to his race. Many blacks recognized him immediately as one of them—and recognized also that never before had someone like him, with his maddeningly independent point of view and his inspired improvisations on the white man's language, gained access to a national forum from which he could pontificate on virtually any subject that crossed his mind. Before long, the *Defender* was receiving quantities of mail addressed only to Simple, as if his creator were superfluous—or a fiction himself. Gifts, including at least once a lovingly wrapped package of women's underwear, arrived for Simple.

With Simple and the weekly *Defender* column, Langston was now reaching more black people than ever before. ''Here to Yonder'' also allowed more people than ever a chance to reach him. Many readers sent Langston topics for future columns, as well as general encouragement. A few sent him gifts. The wife of a Toledo doctor, who now and then coyly signed herself ''Mrs. Hughes,'' sent over the years a typewriter, a number of ties and shorts, boxes of candy and cigarettes, cakes, and even cash. Another woman, from Mississippi, restricted herself to correspondence, but eventually wrote Hughes about 2500 letters. (For a while, he tried to answer her letters. Then he took some of them to a psychiatrist, who pronounced her probably sane, but questioned the state of mind of the man who would try to answer them.) When some correspondents offered themselves, Langston let them down as gently as possible. To one Delaware woman he protested: ''But, look here! You mustn't have too much affection for persons you don't know! It is hard enough to work out a smooth romance with someone you are near, let alone someone way off. You know, I receive dozens of letters like yours. I suppose everyone in public life does.'' On the other hand, he also had to defend himself from time to time to those who disagreed with his positions, or who accused him of disparaging fellow blacks. ''I do not recall ever in my column,'' he once responded warmly, ''making fun of or casting aspersions upon anyone's hair or complexion.''

Although Hughes's employer at the *Defender*, Metz T. P. Lochard, declared himself ''very pleased'' with the column, at least at first he found the tone too critical. "While tearing down has its values," he warned, "a little building up doesn't hurt either." Almost maternally, like the "Negro Mother" he once celebrated mainly as an adoring son, Langston criticized blacks for bad manners, excessive profanity, poor standards of service, negligent personal grooming, silly habits such as wearing dark glasses at night, and willful ignorance of their culture and its heroes. Such topics were beneath the lofty level of concern of almost all other editorial columnists but obviously struck many blacks as badly needed. A column attacking blacks for the casual use of the vile term Hughes called "moutherfouler" brought a deluge of mail. The essay "should be framed and placed in all the beer joints, pool rooms, shoe shine 'parlors' etc.,'' a Minneapolis reader wrote Langston, "so that those who have adopted this habit can read it again and again." In general, "Here to Yonder" bolstered his special place among black intellectuals. "You are a voice speaking . . . and giving form and sound to the feelings, thoughts and aspirations of inarticulate ordinary folk," one woman wrote from Texas. "Really, I feel that we can never even halfway repay you for being the truly great poet that you are."

Langston ridiculed blacks who opposed the Allied effort, but he also boldly asserted himself as a "race man" in fighting the notion that blacks should not press for civil rights because of the war. "If now is not the time," he insisted, "then there never was a time. Now is when all the conquered nations of Europe are asking for freedom. Now is when the Jews are asking for it. Now is when America is fighting to keep it. . . . How anybody can expect American Negroes not to catch the freedom fever, too, is beyond me—unless they think we are deaf, dumb, stupid and blind." The response to such appeals was often vivid. A black soldier praised Langston in recounting his initial reaction to signs for "White" and "Colored" at his training base, Camp Pickett, in Virginia: "The insides of my body seemed to do a somersault." From an army camp in segregated Texas, a private wrote on behalf of his fellow soldiers. "Continue your fight Mr. Hughes," he urged, "for yours is as great as ours and even more so as far as the negro is concerned."

Hughes's fighting spirit was also evident in his writing for M. Margaret Anderson's *Common Ground*, the magazine of the Common Council for American Unity. In the current (Winter 1943) issue, his essay "What Shall We Do About the South?" was graphic in its prediction: "The wheels of the Jim Crow car are about to come off and the walls are going to burst wide open. The wreckage of Democracy is likely to pile up behind that Jim Crow Car." The *Common Ground* readers, mainly white, were often angered by Hughes. "Why do you harp on racial equality!" a woman from Sewanee, Tennessee, sputtered; he could not have done worse "would your aim have been to cause *disunion* between the North and the South as well as between the races." Almost a year later, this essay was still drawing attention, even as another of his essays, "White Folks Do the Funniest Things," about the more farcical aspects of segregation, and "loaded with dynamite," became "the hit of the issue," in Margaret Anderson's grateful words. This essay drew more commentary than any other piece in the history of the journal. At the *Common Ground* office, Anderson read the reaction, much of it from liberals in the South, "with a kind of horrified fascination." "One smart-alect [*sic*] negro," a white man warned from North Carolina about Hughes's "purposely offensive" piece, "can do more harm to the negro cause in a community than an entire company of night riders."

Admiring his courage, Margaret Anderson praised Langston for "the way you keep hammering away" at the official treatment of Japanese-Americans, who were being shipped to "relocation centers," without any evidence of disloyalty on their part. Meanwhile, a patriotic house committee encouraged anti-Japanese hysteria, and, in the popular comic strip *Superman,* the Man of Steel discovered foul traitors in the relocation camps. In his criticism of racism, Langston did not restrict himself to the United States. He openly supported the campaign in India by the repeatedly imprisoned Gandhi, Nehru, and others in the Indian National Congress to rid their country of the British. "Millions of darker peoples are thus forced to wonder if logic is dead," Langston wrote of the repression of Indian nationalists in a formal statement for the *India News* of Los Angeles. "Freedom for India is not only a military need but a moral need to lift the fighting spirits of all who want to believe in freedom *for all.*"

As Simple settled in at Paddy's Bar and Hughes's "Here to Yonder" column took root, the winter of 1943 passed pleasantly enough at the one-bedroom apartment he shared with the Harpers. On February 7, a joint birthday dinner for Langston (six days after the fact) and Emerson Harper brought Carl Van Vechten and Fania Marinoff, Dorothy Peterson, and his Lincoln University schoolmate Thomas Webster, visiting from Kansas City. Later that month, a party for Noël Sullivan, in town from California, was also a happy affair. Langston, who turned ordinary visits into occasions, as Arna Bontemps more than once noted, had begun to indulge his gift of hospitality in a household he now regarded as his permanent home. And virtually every day brought fresh invitations to luncheons, teas, cocktails, or dinners. He was at Van Vechten's to celebrate Ethel Waters's birthday; at the Maxim Liebers', with Walt and Rose Carmon, his old friends from Moscow; at a *Common Ground* tea in honor of the folksinger Woody Guthrie; at a dinner at the Commodore Hotel to mark the twenty-fifth anniversary of the Red Army of the Soviet Union; at a Duke Ellington concert in support of the Soviet war relief effort; at a fashionable restaurant downtown, to talk over yet another project with his sometime collaborator Charles Leonard of Hollywood.

Much as he loved the food and drink, and spoke out spiritedly against segregation, Hughes also was on the watch for professional opportunities, for the chance to make some money. Past forty and still poor, he was growing more resolute than ever about making as much money as possible. "Folk know what I can do now," he wrote to Arna Bontemps after refusing two requests for free talks. "If they want ME to write for them, dig up some dough. Nobody else connected with radio or theatre works for nothing. Why should they expect the author to do so? Huh? The technicians don't, nor the directors, nor the studio executives. I WON'T NEITHER. Hell with 'em!'' In spite of this tough talk, however, he was still quick to work on speculation, such as completing a synopsis for a proposed black military musical called "Chocolate Sailor," which Charles Leonard hoped to sell to Hollywood. Or to work for nothing in a worthy cause—such as reading his Tuskegee Institute anthem, "Alabama Earth," at Columbia University on April 6, in a tribute to the black Tuskegee agricultural scientist George Washington Carver, who had died on January 5. Occasionally he turned out a short story, such as the brief "Saved from the Dogs" in March, published the following year in *Direction,* or poems. In January and February, for example, the *Saturday Evening Post,* one of his main antagonists in 1940 over "Goodbye Christ," published "Wisdom" and, perhaps inspired by the tales of Jewish European refugees at Yaddo, "Refugee in America":

> There are words like "Freedom,"
>   Sweet and wonderful to say.
> On my heartstrings freedom sings
>   All day every day.
>
> There are words like "Democracy"
>   That almost make me cry.
> If you had known what I knew,
>   You'd know why.

Such successes brought in little money. Thus, when a tax bill of $126 found Langston penniless near mid-April, he had no choice but to set out, poems in hand, to read his way back to financial solvency.

He set out confidently, but he had underestimated his opposition. The forces that had prevented him from speaking in Pasadena in the fall of 1940 were still at work, even though they had generally left him alone since then. At his first engagement, on April 14 at Wayne University in Detroit, phone calls to university officials denounced his visit. By noon, a picket line of almost one hundred supporters of the right-wing, isolationist America First Party, headed by Gerald L. K. Smith, had formed. Leaflets condemned the school for hosting "an atheistic communist, a self-confessed communist and a notorious blasphemous poet." However, with the support of a statement by the president of the university on freedom of speech—and flanked by a police escort—Langston entered an auditorium packed with students. Acknowledging the pickets, he suggested that many undoubtedly had sons fighting for democracy, some of whom would die— but not in vain, he hoped. Without recommitting himself to his radical words in the poem "Goodbye Christ," he deplored the abuse of religion in the name of patriotism. "I am for the Christianity that fights poll tax, race discrimination, lynching, injustice and inequality of the masses," he asserted. "I don't feel that religion should be used to beat down Jews [and] Negroes, and to persecute other minority groups." The students awarded him a standing ovation.

Crossing into Canada, he delivered six talks in Toronto; on April 18, he also delivered a radio lecture over the network of the Canadian Broadcasting Corporation. He spoke about the war, and especially so as a fight for "freedom— the preservation of freedom, and the extension of freedom . . . against the doctrine of Nordic supremacy, and against the theory that might makes right." He did not make the mistake of attacking the United States on foreign soil; for all its defects, his country had always had "a great tradition of democracy and freedom." Apparently he made a strong showing, or so at least one listener assured him: "You cannot imagine the great impression you made in Toronto!" Buoyed by the response of his audiences in Detroit and Canada, Langston nevertheless returned to the United States in a wary mood. However, the hostility he faced in Detroit was not repeated. Large crowds greeted him in Cleveland, Oberlin, and Youngstown in Ohio, and Pittsburgh, Harrisburg, and Philadelphia in Pennsylvania.

On May 18 at Lincoln University, his alma mater, Langston reached an important milestone in his career when he received his first honorary degree, a doctorate of letters. Delivering the commencement address was Carl Sandburg, the best-known biographer of Abraham Lincoln, and Langston's "guiding star," by his own admission, during his first unsteady years as a poet. Famously long-winded, Sandburg launched into his favorite subject, suitably updated, in an address entitled "What Lincoln Would Do Now." Apparently, Lincoln would have done a great deal. "He was timed by several watches," the official school history later marvelled, "as having spoken for three hours and fifteen minutes." (The *Lincoln University Bulletin* was more diplomatic: Sandburg turned out to be "more than anyone could expect.") "I was sitting on the platform for more than three hours," Langston reported, "and got both hungry and sleepy." Only the most perfunctory of exchanges passed between the two poets.

The visit to Lincoln was a sort of homecoming, a welcome respite from the road, where Hughes passed most of the spring. The tour was by no means a failure, in spite of the events in Detriot and the relatively low fees he commanded (in Toronto, for example, one lecture netted him only $50). Still, a major reason for the success of the tour gave him little comfort. Under pressures created by the war, several cities had been wracked by racial violence of an intensity not seen in the United States since the Red Summer of 1919. In Detroit, as in Philadelphia and elsewhere, thousands of white workers went on strike rather than work beside blacks hired because of the chronic shortage of labor; thirty-four people died there in rioting that followed. Violence rocked shipyards in Mobile, Alabama, in May when blacks were assigned to welding jobs traditionally denied them. In June, following the rape of a white woman in Beaumont, Texas, two persons died in civil disorders.

Usually ignored by white leaders and the white press, what Hughes and other black leaders had to say now suddenly seemed important. In his speeches, he struck at the obvious targets: job discrimination, especially when endorsed by trade unions; Jim Crow in travel, which he saw as the most destructive factor in race relations and feared would "explode in the face of democracy"; and the Red Cross's insistence on separate blood banks for blacks, while the blood of white felons, collected in jails, and even that of Americans of Japanese descent, in spite of the "relocation centers," was pooled with the normal white supply. "Hitler could hardly desire more," Langston angrily pointed out; the Red Cross "has failed thirteen million Negroes on the home front, and its racial policies are a blow in the face to American Negro morale." All in all, blacks "are made to feel ourselves a separate race more then ever before in this war of democracy."

In his public appearances, as often as not he offered for sale, with brisk response if only modest profit, copies of his poem *Freedom's Plow* (performed publicly with great aplomb that year by the actor Frederic March), put out by Musette Publishers of New York at ten cents a copy, and his collection of poems *Jim Crow's Last Stand,* from the Negro Publishing Society, available at only twenty five cents.

The riots and indignities at home drew him further into political activity. Perhaps his major involvement (the pay was also good) in the late spring was writing material for a dramatic spectacle about the black soldier and freedom, "For This We Fight," for a Negro Freedom Rally on June 7 in Madison Square Garden. Before a sold-out Garden, Paul Robeson sang "Joe Hill" and led a cast of two hundred persons, including Canada Lee, Robert Earl Jones (who had made his acting debut in 1938 in Hughes's *Don't You Want to Be Free?*), and the rising black concert singer Muriel Rahn; among the speakers were the Rev. Adam Clayton Powell, Jr., Ferdinand C. Smith, the black secretary of the mainly white, progressive National Maritime Union, and the popular socialist politician Representative Vito Marcantonio. At the request of Ferdinand Smith, Hughes wrote a brief piece, "Sailor Ashore" (the title taken from his unpublished short story) as a monologue for Canada Lee on behalf of the maritime union ("Don't let nobody tell you *our* union ain't no color-line buster, cause it is!"). For the Congress of Industrial Organizations (CIO), he penned another small radio play, "John Henry Hammers It Out," starring Paul Robeson, and broadcast on June 27 on station WEAF in New York.

The tour, his column, and these various smaller efforts left Langston with little time for work on longer projects. That spring, he completed a dramatization for public schools in Chicago of his and Arna Bontemps' Haitian children's story *Popo and Fifina,* which was still selling about 500 copies each year after eleven years on Macmillan's list. The dramatization was at the request of Brunetta Mouzon, a schoolteacher who had acted in *The Sun Do Move* at the Good Shepherd Community Center; it was first performed on June 12 in Chicago.

For all his disquiet over Jim Crow, Langston continued to contribute to the war effort, mainly through the Writers' War Board in Washington, D.C. Dutifully he turned out jingles and slogans for bond drives ("Blitz the Fritz"; "Invest a Dollar to Make Hitler Holler"; "Every War Bond You Buy Is a Blow in Hitler's Eye"). He read messages over the radio to Sweden and Australia, and in Spanish to the Caribbean. Would Hughes serve on a new committee to develop "message" plays for children on the war? Yes, he would. Not without reason, early in the year the Writers' War Board had sheepishly noted that Hughes probably realized by then that he was on a short list of writers "on whom we have come to depend." When the Music War Committee was formed not long afterwards, he accepted the position of an honorary sponsor. Later that year, he joined a committee judging war songs by black composers, presumably aimed especially at blacks, then also agreed to a request by Oscar Hammerstein II, of the American Theatre Wing Music War Committee, to join yet another, more general group of "top authors and composers" who would adjudicate new songs in support of the war effort.

He tried to respond affirmatively to almost all requests for appearances—and the requests came. On June 18, he read his poetry at the opening of a "Words at War" exhibition, including excerpts from President Roosevelt and T. S. Eliot and designed to illustrate the power of language, at the New York Public Library. Later in the year, he read there again in a symposium with a similar design, "The Poets Speak," organized by the poet and novelist May Sarton and including W. H. Auden, Marianne Moore, and Padraic Colum. On June 25, he rose early and unwillingly—because of the hour—to visit a Harlem school on West 113th Street and read his poetry, without a fee, to a gathering of 600 children from the fifth and sixth grades. That month, he also agreed to be a sponsor of an "Emergency Committee to Save the Jews of Europe" and to attend its first meeting, at the home of Stella Adler on West 54th Street in Manhattan.

Hoping for a stretch of time when he would be free to attempt something more ambitious, especially his long-delayed second autobiography, "I Wonder as I Wander," Langston was relieved when an invitation arrived from Yaddo for a second summer of work there. (One spur to return to "I Wonder as I Wander" was perhaps the news that Zora Neale Hurston had just won a fine prize for her own recently published autobiography, *Dust Tracks on a Road*. "The muse of black-face comedy," as Arna Bontemps called her after reading the book, which was curiously reactionary in places, had been given the Anisfield-Wolf Award for outstanding books in the field of race relations. With the award had come a check for $1000.)

Around July 1, Langston arrived at Yaddo. Unpacking his belongings in perhaps the most picturesque studio, an old stone tower reached by a footbridge and overlooking charming ponds, he soon found out that the poet Margaret Walker was also in residence, and Arna Bontemps expected (although he would be unable to come that summer). Previously, Hughes had recommended inviting Walker, Bontemps, Ralph Ellison, and the musician Margaret Bonds for a summer stay at the colony.

For Walker, the Yaddo invitation and her experience there encouraged her decision that year to give up a teaching job and become a professional writer. "Langston encouraged me but he also warned me about being a writer," she later reminisced. " 'If you send out something every day,' he told me, 'you'll get at least one check every week'.'' He was a fatalist, you know, although he wasn't a gloomy one by any means. But he was a fatalist. He said to me more than once: 'Know your state and accept your fate.' I guess he lived by that rule. He was a wonderful mixer, especially at a place like Yaddo. But I would say that his personality was more overlaid and inhibited than one would have expected from such a gregarious man. Langston had a private world that nobody entered.''

Also at Yaddo that summer was his boon companion of the previous year, Carson McCullers, as well as Afred Kantarowicz, Jean Stafford Lowell, Alfred Kazin, Morton Zabel, and a cousin of Noël Sullivan's, Kappo Phelan, who wrote short stories in the deft manner Langston associated with the *New Yorker*—although he had more than once published there in a gritty style. One newcomer, decidedly not urbane, stood out—Agnes Smedley, the American-born radical socialist author of the novel *Daughter of Earth* and of three eyewitness accounts of events in China, *Chinese Destinies, China's Red Army Marches,* and *China Fights Back.* Her *Battle Hymn of China,* already in its third printing even before its official publication, was expected in September, from Knopf. Years before, writing from China, where she had gone as the correspondent of the *Frankfurter Zeitung,* Smedley had attacked Langston in a candid personal letter for failing to offer a truly radical perspective in his novel *Not Without Laughter.* Now they struck up a friendship. Hughes always liked forceful women, and Smedley exuded force, as Margaret Walker remembered. "She looked very masculine and at the same time bohemian. At a book party she drank dry martinis and got roaring drunk. I also remember that she tried to turn me against Carson McCullers, because Carson was a Southerner, I guess. But Langston and I loved Carson—she was a little genius, she sure could write. She was a solitary drinker, though, and sick a lot of the time from drinking through the night. The next morning, her hands would be shaking and we would help her to pull herself together.''

Langston and Smedley shared not only solemn discussions of communism but also at least one visit to a local black church to deliver bushels of Yaddo-grown tomatoes and, covertly, the message of radical socialism. With Carson McCullers, however, he threw dice for money and munched on fried chicken and sipped champagne at a black-owned nightclub in Saratoga Springs. He enjoyed games of checkers with Malcolm Cowley and Katherine Ann Porter, and a weiner roast at Porter's farm nearby. Helping him prepare his taxes, Cowley pointed out—to Langston's chagrin—that he had been drastically underreporting his writing expenses throughout his entire career.

His study in the old stone tower was comfortable, but several weeks passed before Langston finally sat down to his main project, the autobiography. First, he gave his attention to less weighty but more enticing demands. He returned to sloganeering for the Department of Treasury, while he also worked on material for a big autumn revue proposed by Barney Josephson at his Cafe Society, which would star Hazel Scott, the folk dancer Pearl Primus, and other prominent black entertainers. And he spent several hours leafing through the huge manuscript of his complete poems for possible contributions to a volume of verse suggested by his first important literary rival and friend, Countee Cullen. Ideally, the volume would bring together the work of undoubtedly the three greatest poets of the Harlem Renaissance—Cullen, Hughes, and Langston's first black literary idol, Claude McKay.

Because he was the best known of the three, Langston had the least to gain from such a showing; nevertheless, he charitably agreed to take part. Charity, in fact, was at the heart of the proposal. Late in June, Claude McKay had suffered a stroke that partially paralyzed the right side of his body. He was taken to Harlem Hospital, where Langston sent him a get-well card and an inscribed copy of *Freedom's Plow*. When Cullen and his best friend, Harold Jackman, came to visit him at the hospital, McKay had asked them to read the poem to him. Out of the visit had come the idea for the book. Evidently the quarrelsome McKay had lost little of his bite over the years. "We all agreed that it was a nice poem," he assured Hughes about *Freedom's Plow*. "But we want something stronger than that for this book—a kind of reaffirmation of ourselves that we are still here and strong and nobody has really surpassed us."

Neither Cullen nor McKay was as strong as each once had been, nor as strong as Langston now was. After his dazzling start as the most acclaimed young poet in black America, Cullen had seen his career steadily dissolve. Unwilling to wander and roam, as the restless McKay and Hughes had done, he had settled for the chalky propriety of schoolteaching in Harlem and for marriage. His first marriage had ended quickly and in scandal, with his departure for Paris with his best man, Jackman, but he had married again in 1940. A Harlem novel and a brief attraction to communism in 1932 could not hide the fact that Cullen had nothing fresh to say. Unlike Langston, he had never looked hard for the muse in Harlem. In his book *The Medea*, for example, published about ten years before, he had offered a prose translation of Euripides, with the choruses as lyric poems, and a handful of other poems written mainly in France. Although McKay had fared somewhat better, his last book of verse had come in 1922, and his last book of fiction in 1932. An eloquent though not particularly artful autobiography, *A Long Way from Home*, appeared in 1937. Four years later came the provocative but indifferently researched *Harlem: Negro Metropolis*. What in McKay first had appealed to Langston was now dead; the radical who had once addressed the Fourth Congress of the Third Communist International was now only months away from baptism as a Roman Catholic.

Nevertheless, Langston was so willing to help that he offered to sacrifice all of his blues and folk pieces in favor of lyrics in standard English. "The two," he explained, "don't mix very well, and blues and such would probably throw the whole book out of key." This amputation no doubt pleased both Cullen and McKay. From the start, Cullen had regarded Langston's feverish love of the blues in poetry as almost a form of disease; McKay had set out as a dialect poet in Jamaica, but had long since given up dialect in favor of more conservative forms. The three men agreed to go ahead with their book.

This project, in addition to other efforts, further delayed work on Langston's autobiography. But even more distracting that summer was the rising tension between the races in New York, which itself reflected a nationwide unrest, garish against the backdrop of world war, as blacks and whites clashed over Jim Crow. On July 1, Fiorello La Guardia, the mayor of New York, had written to Hughes to ask his help in developing a series of radio programs, "Unity at Home—Victory Abroad," which would show "what New York is, how it came into its present being, and why there is no reason that the peace and neighborliness that does exist, should ever be disturbed." The Writers' War Board also wrote Hughes in support of the mayor's campaign, seeking programs that would stress unity, "so that there will be no danger of race riots in New York." He agreed to help the mayor and the Board, but not without a blast at radio, which had "(at least in my experience) insistently censored out any real dramatic approach to the actual problems of the Negro people. In that regard it has been almost as bad as Hollywood." Or, as he put it more bluntly a few months later, "Personally, I DO NOT LIKE RADIO, and I feel that it is almost as far from being a free medium of expression for Negro writers as Hitler's airplanes are for the Jews."

Langston's letter to the Board promising two or three scripts had barely left Yaddo when, on the first day of August, violence broke out on the overheated Harlem streets. In the lobby of a hotel, a white policeman shot and wounded a black soldier after the man intervened violently in a dispute between the officer and a black woman improbably named Margie Polite. Although the man had been only wounded, Margie Polite ran into the street screaming that he had been killed. In the uprising that followed, five persons were killed, about four hundred were injured, and the damage to property was estimated at five million dollars. Order was restored only after 8,000 New York State Guard troops, almost 7,000 city policemen and other officers, and 1,500 civilian volunteers, most of them black, had secured the streets of Harlem. About 500 persons, including about 100 women, were arrested.

The first news reports on August 2 sent Langston hurrying to telephone Toy Harper. Her reaction was almost exactly that of other middle-class blacks with whom he was soon in touch: outrage at the rioters. He found their response nothing less than amusing. A part of him longed to be on the streets. "You know I'm sorry I missed the riots," he wrote Bontemps dejectedly. "It has always been my fate never to be in one. . . . I gather the mob was most uncouth—and Sugar Hill is shamed!" Bourgeois shame did not matter. "I am dying to go to Harlem and see what it looks like after the riots," he informed Noël Sullivan. "The better class Negroes are all *mad* at the low class ones for the breaking and looting that went on. The letters I have received from the better colored people practically froth at the mouth. It seems their peace was disturbed even more than the white folks'."

Even when the looting directly affected Langston in one instance, he shrugged off his misfortune with a giggle: "I reckon I lost my watch in the riots. I left it at Herbert's opposite the Theresa to be cleaned—and they tell me the place was cleaned out!'' He was almost happy to have made this sacrifice to the rioters. ''All the best colored people declare they have been set back Fifty Years,'' he wrote Van Vechten. ''I don't exactly know from what.'' After all, he declared, civil disturbances usually brought racial progress. Following the Detroit riot earlier that year, for example, the *New York Times* had promoted its reporting about blacks from the hunting and racing section to the back page.

Neither Van Vechten nor Arna Bontemps could understand, let alone share, Langston's laughter. ''I know WHY the riots,'' Van Vechten wrote him sharply, ''and so I can understand, and they MAY have done some good locally, but the effect on the general public is extremely bad.'' ''Cullud folks, who are terribly ashamed of this riot,'' Bontemps warned, ''will find you much too tender with the rioters.'' Even black socialist leaders, including Max Yergan of the National Negro Congress and Ferdinand Smith of the National Maritime Union, who had toured Harlem with La Guardia, had spoken out against the riots. In part, Langston believed the riot to be a justified response to conditions in Harlem. In part, also, his response was conditioned by a creeping fatalism, with a slightly macabre tinge, that would only increase over the years and become his way of dealing with disaster. Beneath his fatalism and cynicism, however, was a profound sadness about the race. ''I do not know why [the looting] tickles me,'' he wrote Bontemps, ''and I am sorry in my soul. . . . NEW DAY A-COMIN' says Mr. Roi Ottley. NEW NIGHT would probably be better. (How sweetly optimistic is the cullud race!)''

Out of the riot came his bantering ''Ballad of Margie Polite'':

> If Margie Polite
> Had of been white
> She might not've cussed
> Out the cop that night.
>
> .   .   .   .
>
> A soldier took her part.
> He got shot in the back
> By a white cop—
> The soldier were black.
>
> *They killed a colored soldier!*
> Folks started to cry it—
> The cry spread over Harlem
> And turned into riot.
>
> They taken Margie to jail
> And kept her there.
> DISORDERLY CONDUCT
> The charges swear.
>
> Margie warn't nobody
> Important before—

But she ain't just *nobody*
Now no more.

She started the riots!
Harlemites say
August 1st is
MARGIE'S DAY.

.   .   .   .

They didn't kill the soldier,
A race leader cried.
Somebody hollered,
Naw! But they tried!

Margie Polite!
Margie Polite!
Kept the Mayor
And Walter White
And everybody
Up all night!

When the PD car
Taken Margie away—
It wasn't Mother's
Nor Father's—
   It were
MARGIE'S DAY!

Pressed even harder now by the mayor and the Board for pacifying material, Hughes dutifully sent the authorities some songs and two brief plays—"In the Service of My Country," inspired by pictures of blacks and whites working in harmony to build the Alaska-Canada highway, and "Private Jim Crow," about segregation in the armed forces. The Writers' War Board lauded the former as "the finest job that has been done on this subject" and promptly broadcast it on September 8 on WNYC. The latter, which exemplified, according to Langston, "only the most typical and daily kinds of incidents" that the average colored soldier faced, was deemed excellent also, but then placed on a high shelf.

He based "Private Jim Crow" on the ordinary humiliations—not the beatings and the lynchings—related to him by black soldiers, especially in the South, who were frequently denied privileges routinely granted to whites. One soldier told of being sold cigarettes and chocolate bars, but not ice cream or bottled sodas. Consuming the latter in a public place, with blacks and whites present, might be seen as breaking the Jim Crow laws that prevented the races from eating together. "Delicate nuance of the color line," Langston noted: "A chocolate bar but not an ice cream cone!"

Although he did not directly defend the riots, his approach was certainly populist, and different from that of most "race leaders," when he published "Down Under in Harlem" in *The New Republic* the following March. There were two Harlems, and he showed that he knew them both. One set, including those who were "among Dr. Du Bois's 'talented tenth'," could go "to the symphony concerts and live on that attractive rise of bluff and parkway along Edgecombe Avenue overlooking the Polo Grounds, where the plumbing really works and the ceilings are high and airy." (Langston was thinking of 409 Edgecombe Avenue, an apartment building whose tenants then included Walter and Gladys White, Aaron and Alta Douglas, and Kenneth and Dorothy Spencer, as well as the families of Thurgood Marshall, Roy Wilkins, and Elmer Carter.) There was another, larger Harlem, where in "vast sections below the hill, neighborhood amusement centers after dark are gin mills, candy stores that sell King Kong [cheap illicit liquor] (and maybe reefers), drug stores that sell geronimoes—dope tablets—to juveniles for pepping up cokes, pool halls where gambling is wide open and barbecue stands that book numbers. . . . The kids and the grown-ups are not criminal or low by nature. Poverty, however, and frustration have made some of them too desperate to be decent. Some of them don't try anymore. Slum-shocked, I reckon."

The role of Margie Polite and various other black women in the disturbances, or something, further put the creative mischief in him. At Yaddo he began work on a series of verses with an assertive, brassy Harlem heroine named Alberta K. Johnson—or *Madam* Johnson, as she insists on being called; Hughes named the entire suite "Madam to You." (Perhaps he meant to tease Arna Bontemps' wife, whose maiden name had been Alberta Johnson, although she was nothing at all like his creation.) The first two "Madam to You" pieces had been composed the previous year, but now he raced through more than a dozen toward the end of August. "Madam and the Phone Bill":

> You say I O.K.ed
> LONG DISTANCE?
> O.K.ed it when?
> My goodness, Central,
> That was *then*!
>
> I'm mad and disgusted
> With that Negro now.
> I don't pay no REVERSED
> CHARGES nohow.
>
> You say, I will pay it—
> Else you'll take out my phone?
> You better let
> My phone alone.
>
> I didn't ask him
> To telephone me.

Roscoe knows darn well
LONG DISTANCE
Ain't free . . .

. . . .
Un-humm-m! . . . Yes!
You say I gave my O.K.?
Well, that O.K. you may keep—

But I *sure* ain't gonna pay!

Madam Alberta K. Johnson was a fitting and memorable, though much less developed, feminine counterpart to Hughes's Jesse B. Semple. The first four pieces ("Madam's Past History," "Madam and her Madam," "Madam and the Army," and "Madam and the Movies") were quickly taken by *Common Ground* and published together in the Summer, 1943 number. At Yaddo, one of the composers in residence, no doubt prodded by Langston, worked at setting some.

The "Madam" poems and "The Ballad of Margie Polite" were probably his only interesting work done at Yaddo that summer, although he often labored in his study. As in his previous stay, much of his effort went to songwriting, as he tried to hit upon "THE lyric for THE war song!" One after another, various compositions seemed to hit the mark ("It's got all the boys of all the branches, mama, papa, love, tears, and prayers in it! So that ought to be it! . . . . It has almost made me cry. Also feel noble. Also buy War Bonds!") before flopping short of the golden target. At least twice that summer the music publisher Edward B. Marks rejected songs by Hughes, including "One Day Nearer to Victory" and "America's Young Black Joe," in which Langston had invested much hope. Suitable neither for dancing nor the concert hall, Marks decided, the latter had no commercial possibilities. Resignedly, Arna Bontemps diagnosed Langston's compulsion to write songs as his substitute for a family: "It's almost exactly like a fellow who has a wife to fight with comfortably, while having no inclination to leave home." In any event, the summer was almost over when he at last sent word out that he had started work again on his second autobiography. For once, Bontemps did not bother to conceal his impatience. "I'm walking on air," he exulted; "the assurance that I WONDER is under way is the news I've been waiting for these past months!" Bontemps was not in the air long before Langston's work on his second autobiography came once again to a halt.

Since Yaddo was unable to afford to heat its mansion, he did not linger there deep into the fall as he had done in 1942. Besides, he was sick of fresh air. "Back in town, thank God!" he alerted Van Vechten near the first day of October. On October 10, he was the keynote speaker at a citywide cultural conference, with the emphasis on folk groups, organized by the International Workers Order. A week later, he was at a black church in Newark for a benefit, then off to Philadelphia at the invitation of the record producer John Hammond for a preview of the all-black musical play *Carmen Jones,* based on Georges Bizet's opera *Carmen.* He found the show handsome to look at but gallingly inappropriate—Paris gowns on gorgeous bodies, but *"dis-and-dat* dialect to speak and sing . . . 'You's a drip, you is, sho you is!' Which simply sounds stupid and not the least quaint or funny.''

At a showing of *Stormy Weather,* the all-black film released by Twentieth-Century Fox, he enjoyed Bill "Bojangles" Robinson tap dancing to a musical rendition of his 1923 poem "Danse Africaine" set by Clarence Muse and Connie Bemis. However, *Stormy Weather* was essentially in the same class as *Cabin in the Sky* (with Ethel Waters, Lena Horne, Louis Armstrong, Duke Ellington, Butterfly McQueen, and other black stars displaying their musical and comic talents), which Hughes had seen and dismissed the previous February. About his own latest hope for Hollywood, "Chocolate Sailor," his collaborator Charles Leonard was nothing but gloomy. On Labor Day that year, Leonard sent word from Hollywood that the studios were fearful of doing black films, because both *Stormy Weather* and *Cabin in the Sky* had precipitated racial trouble in the South, a major market for the industry. Besides, "with colored boys in the Navy taboo anyway, our screen treatment seems doomed to oblivion.''

Langston settled for less ambitious ways of exhibiting his talents, and less munificent rewards than those possible from Hollywood. On October 27, for the second time that year, he gave a reading at Columbia University. Near Yaddo, at a meeting of the Saratoga Springs Historical Society, he read a dozen of his poems and hammered at Jim Crow (he was followed on the platform by Agnes Smedley). Jim Crow retreated another inch that October. After efforts by Edwin Embree, Agnes Smedley, and Malcolm Cowley, Langston became probably the first black, certainly the first in the United States, to be admitted to the prestigious international writers organization, PEN. Apparently, Richard Wright once had been mentioned as a possible member before the idea was allowed to die. "I am personally not interested in the least in belonging to it," Langston declared to Arna Bontemps, who had first raised the question, "but I suppose since the American branch poses as a liberal organization, it should be faced with the Problem!'' Years afterwards, he would recall being admitted at a special moment in American history, "when a wave of democracy swept over our hitherto lily white institutions.'' Evidently the wave was still sweeping in May 1944, seven months after his admittance, when he was elected to the executive board of the group.

Invited to Washington, D.C., for a meeting in mid-November of the Writers' War Board, he seized the chance to make some money on a small speaking tour. At Frankfort, Kentucky, he earned a good fee of $125. Then he headed south to visit Arna Bontemps in Nashville, Tennessee. After completing a master's degree in library science at the University of Chicago, Bontemps had moved there with his family early in September to become librarian of Fisk University. He was so pleased with his proximity to the library stacks ("I like this environment of books. They intoxicate me.") that he had hinted as broadly as he could to Hughes about a job in publicity just opening at Fisk at $300 a month. As much as he loved his friend and admired Fisk, which he had first visited in 1927, Langston ignored the chance. He was in Harlem to stay. Still, he was in splendid form when he appeared before the students, who welcomed him as a veteran warrior in the struggle. He dominated his audience, which included many people from the adjacent Meharry Medical College, from the start. "You left Fisk and Meharry humming like violin strings," Bontemps marvelled. "I think I can guarantee you'll never make a so-so appearance here again. Did yourself brown this time!"

Langston was still in his best form on November 27, when he was back in the North for a major appearance in Manhattan at the 33rd annual convention of the National Council of Teachers of English at the Hotel Pennsylvania. Other engagements took him to Scranton, Pennsylvania, and southwards again to Howard University in Washington, the Raleigh-Durham area, where he spent a week reading in various black schools and colleges, and to Hampton Institute in Virginia.

Everywhere, his copies of *Freedom's Plow* and *Jim Crow's Last Stand,* pamphlets of inspiration for the burgeoning Civil Rights Movement, sold briskly. Unlike his great tour of 1931–32, when he had first probed the South with his posters, pamphlets, and cheap editions, bringing poetry to the people, Langston now found blacks far less passive, in brave response to the transformation of the world by war. Even at high-toned Fisk, for example, the students had become bolder in facing up to Jim Crow, in testing segregated lunch counters here, baring their teeth at other insults there. "They groan aloud in school when the Red Cross is mentioned," Bontemps wrote Hughes, "—or anything else identified with discrimination and Jim Crow and indignity. They are constantly nipping at the color line. . . . It's quite a place, this Dixie." The bitter past of the South, and its future, seemed to hang in potentially explosive balance. The explosion was likely to come, Langston was sure, over Jim Crow transportation: "The Jim Crow car seems to me the most antiquated and barbarous thing on this continent. And should be broken up RIGHT NOW!"

Back in New York on December 12 for an NBC program, "Lands of the Free," when he spoke for three minutes following a drama on the slave trade, he stressed the moral urgency of the moment. "You and I, living today," Hughes insisted, "can blame nobody for history." But no one else was to be blamed if history were repeated.

He had another, more personal opportunity to expand on this theme when he wrote a letter of rebuke late in December to the editor of the University of North Carolina Press, William T. Couch. Having commissioned a book of essays by prominent blacks, including Hughes, Du Bois, A. Philip Randolph, Roy Wilkins, and Mary McLeod Bethune, edited by Langston's friend Rayford W. Logan, a prominent historian at Howard University and the author of a book on diplomatic relations between the U.S. and Haiti, Couch now balked at publishing it. If the authors were right about the Negro's wants, Couch suggested, "then what he [the Negro] needs, and needs most urgently, is to revise his wants." The contributors should accept as a fact that segregation would last at least fifty or even a hundred years more in some form; Roland Hayes should have behaved with docility during the incident in 1942 in which he was insulted and struck in a Georgia shoe store. Couch's view of the incident appalled Langston, who had specifically denounced it in "My America," his contribution to the volume. Diplomatically mailing Couch a gift copy of *Freedom's Plow,* he also made it clear that he did not agree with the editor "at all! I do not understand how one can expect any Americans to ask merely for half-democracy, half-equality (or whatever word you want to use)," he insisted. "We, too, are citizens, soldiers, human beings—and we certainly don't like Jim Crow cars! Would you?" (Couch eventually published the book, *What the Negro Wants*—but included in it a reactionary personal preface.)

Langston's relatively brief but lucrative venture on the road encouraged him now to think not only of planning a much longer tour, but also of going boldly after white audiences, who could afford to pay handsomely for his services. This was a daring move. No black had ever broken into the top level of the lecture market among whites. Accordingly, he asked his literary agent Maxim Lieber to find out what he could about Langston's chances. On his own, however, he began to put together a winter-spring tour aimed at his oldest constituency—blacks in their churches and schools.

While he organized this tour, the first few days of 1944 found him working, for excellent pay, on the first draft of "The Ballad of the Man Who Went to War," a sort of black ballad opera of blues, lullabies, and other songs, commissioned by D. Geoffrey Bridson of the British Broadcasting Corporation, to be recorded in New York and broadcast as a morale-boosting salute to war-ravaged Britain from "your Negro allies in the U.S.A.—by Americans, in other words, Americans of color." The performers would include Paul Robeson, Canada Lee, Ethel Waters, Josh White, the bluesmen Sonny Terry and Brownie McGhee, and the Hall Johnson choir.

He set aside this work temporarily to fly to Fort Sill, Oklahoma, where sixteen thousand black soldiers had voted to invite him as their special guest; the previous year, Joe Louis had been so honored. Langston thoroughly enjoyed his foray among the military. At the base, he was chauffeured about in a staff car and almost mobbed by the soldiers, who kept asking about his friend Simple. Later, he read his poems at Langston University, Oklahoma (named after his grandfather's brother, John Mercer Langston) and rode in a jeep in a gala War Bond parade in Oklahoma City. He went to Montreal for two readings, then was a featured guest in Manhattan at a folklore evening at the Young Men's Hebrew Association at Lexington Avenue and 92nd Street. He also appeared on the "March of Time" radio program, on which he spoke a few words about music and the war.

Just before his YMHA reading, he had a nasty experience in Harlem. A man loomed out of the night, pulled out a razor, and ordered Langston: "Come here!'' Langston was startled but defiant. ''Come here, hell!'' he replied (or so he recalled). He grabbed at the mugger's hand. They struggled for a moment, then the man broke away. He left Langston bleeding from a slight cut—but ''me remaining triumphant with weapon!'' Proud of his victory, Hughes looked forward to donating the razor to the James Weldon Johnson Collection at Yale—but the police seized it as evidence.

Shortly afterward, a different, but in its way almost equally dangerous test came when he took part in the live, nationally popular NBC radio debate program, ''America's Town Meeting of the Air.'' The title of the program on Thursday, February 17, was ''Let's Face the Race Question,'' the underlying question being whether or not the Federal government should intervene to end segregation. On his side was Carey McWilliams, a former Commissioner of Immigration and Housing in California and the author of a pro-integrationist work, *Brothers Under the Skin.* Against them were the well-known white Southerner John Temple Graves II, author of the elegantly written pro-segregationist *The Fighting South,* and a conservative black college president, James E. Shepherd, of North Carolina College for Negroes.

An argument over race on a national network, bringing together black and white speakers, was an extraordinary event. Nervous about extemporizing—Langston considered himself a relatively slow thinker, hesitant in debate—he prepared himself diligently. ''Just be yourself at Town Hall,'' Bontemps advised. ''No more, no less than in your humblest lecture, and you'll do yourself brown!'' From the *Common Ground* offices, Margaret Anderson sent material for him to show ''how bankrupt southern white leaders are of any program for action.'' More pragmatically—and Langston certainly needed no reminder here—Maxim Lieber saw an unusual chance for a big publicity break, perhaps the biggest of his life, especially in light of his client's ambitions to make his way onto the white lecture circuit.

In his prepared opening statement, delivered in a voice that at first quavered with tension, Langston attacked the idea of segregation: ''Some people bring up the dog-gonest arguments against doing something concrete towards solving the Negro question! Even some liberals declare the South would rather fight another Civil War than abolish the Jim Crow car and its attendant indecencies. Others profess a profound fear of intermarriage—as if permitting Negroes to vote in the poll tax states would immediately cause whites and Negroes to rush together to the altar. Others . . . say there is *no* solving of the race problem at all—evidently forgetting the examples of Brazil and the Soviet Union.'' How could America find the courage and the will to bear down on the Nazis and the Japanese, he asked, but balk at compelling changes in the South? As for the momentous question that raised the hideous specter of interracial sex, ''Would you want your daughter to marry a Negro?''—a Negro might not want to marry your daughter. ''Or, suppose the Negro did? All the daughter has to say is, 'No'.'' Blacks did not want to rob whites of their rights: ''We merely wish, as Americans of long standing, those same rights.'' A federal order had opened war industries to blacks and furthered the war effort; "an over-all Federal program protecting the rights of all minorities, and educating all Americans to that effect, should be evolved."

In the impromptu portion of the one-hour program, Hughes and McWilliams, helped by a partisan studio audience, threw Graves and Shepherd onto the defensive. To the consternation of all, including his white ally, the Negro president declared that blacks certainly did not want unqualified freedom. By this time, Langston seemed completely at ease. Questioned from the audience about notoriously bad manners among blacks, he replied that all of one group should not be held accountable for the weakness of a few. Definitely there were good whites living in the South, he went on—"Mr. Graves, for instance. He's one of the nicest men I've ever met." Graves, who carefully had refrained from calling either his ally or Hughes "Mister," blushed in confusion as the audience applauded wildly.

A deluge of praise for Langston followed the program. Essie Robeson, listening at home in Enfield, Connecticut, thought him beautifully natural: "I could hear your shy little stammer, and could see in my mind your disarming innocent smile!!" In the *Baltimore Afro-American,* the columnist J. Saunders Redding of Hampton Institute marvelled at Hughes's "truly genuine simplicity," how he was shy "without being difficult . . . gracious without condescending . . . courageous without being bold." A Houston, Texas educator lauded "the excellent manner you represented the cause of Negroes"; Hughes had done so "with fine manners but without compromise." To a Spelman College woman in Atlanta, Hughes's words "—and the way that you said them—penetrated to my very soul!" "*God bless you!!!*" wrote a listener in Danville, Illinois. And a Chicagoan summed up the almost universal response of blacks: "You deserve the thanks of the entire Negro race in America."

Not all of Langston's listeners were charmed. "Go on back to Russia," one advised, "if that's your idea of Utopia." And he should take all the other blacks with him, since they certainly were not wanted here. "Dear old hunk of Asafoetida," an Atlantan saluted Hughes, who should depart at once, after "that smelly program," for Africa, where one might find "little Langston with his . . . cloth around his loins, rings in his ears and nose, bracelets around his ankles, trotting around knawing [*sic*] on the boiled arm of some fellow creature."

Out of Langston's triumph on the program came his breakthrough into the white lecture market. A few days later, Maxim Lieber reported on a most encouraging conversation with William B. Feakins of Feakins, Inc., probably the most prestigious speakers' bureau in the country. Not long afterward, Hughes was accepted as the firm's first black offering. And he had brilliantly advertised his own coming tour. Three days after the radio show an overflow crowd welcomed him in Chicago at the Woodlawn A.M.E. church, and again at a reading for the American Jewish Congress. Between late February and mid-May, he made at least fifty appearances, sweeping from Chicago through Cleveland into West Virginia, and then back through Columbus, Ohio, to Chicago, where he appeared before a chapter of the National Conference of Christians and Jews. He passed a week in Kansas, then headed to the Southwest and black colleges in various Texas towns. In Wylie, Texas, he visited his admirer and fellow poet Melvin B. Tolson, whose accomplished first volume of verse, *Rendezvous with America,* was scheduled to appear later that year from Dodd, Mead.

On March 25, Langston made a major stop at Fort Huachuca, Arizona. The fort was proud of itself as the largest black army post in the world—even if all the top officers were white and a high voltage electrified fence surrounded dormitories housing white civilian women (the fence was to keep the white women from getting to them, the black men confided to Langston). A special moment was his reunion with his good friend Lt. Irma Cayton (later a captain), who had boldly said goodbye to her husband and the Good Shepherd Community Center in Chicago in order to join the initial class of the Women's Army Corps, or WACs. Following an excellent training record, she had been banished to the desert after Ovetta Culp Hobby, the head of the WACs, discovered that she was sending information about the mistreatment of blacks to the press through Horace Cayton. But she loved Fort Huachuca and the Army. "Langston had strongly opposed my going into the WACs," she later remembered. "He had told me that it wasn't our war, it wasn't our business, there was too much Jim Crow. But he had changed his mind about all that. He was very very proud when he saw us there at Fort Huachuca. And the men and women couldn't get enough of him. They *loved* Langston!"

Impressed by the discipline and polish of the black men and women there, Langston made Fort Huachuca the subject of long articles published in the *Defender.* In turn, his listeners were clearly impressed by him. In Tucson, seven hundred people attended one reading. As before, the Arizona landscape—the desert blooming with poppies, gray-green cacti, purple sage, century plants, amid misty smoke trees; the sky blue and wide, under a scintillant sun—touched something tender in him. "I wonder why anybody lives anywhere except where it is warm and bright and beautiful?" he mused in the *Defender.* "I wonder why I live in Harlem? I don't know. But I do."

The tour exacted its toll on him, but there were many moments to prize. At Salt Lake City, for example, a white Unitarian church astonished Langston by taking up a collection for him, as if he were a missionary—about $100 ("To help me with my work!"). In Grinnell, Iowa, he was allowed to stay at a prominent hotel, the Monroe, where the contralto Marian Anderson had been turned away the previous year because of her race. "I reckon the war has done some good," he reflected. And when the Flint representatives of the reactionary Gerald L.K. Smith group threatened to picket his Urban League talk at the Institute of Arts, support for Langston grew so strong that his program was moved to an auditorium twice as large.

On the other hand, after a pleasant evening with a chapter of the American Jewish Congress in Glencoe, near Chicago, a human relations group bowed to conservative pressure and cancelled his visit. The local Urban League executive secretary also wrote bitterly to him about life as a black in Glencoe. The black president of a college in Texas dourly refused to have such a radical person speak on his campus. And in a Chinese restaurant on East Kearsley Street in Flint, Michigan, he was refused a seat for dinner, an episode that hurt Langston so deeply he wrote a long letter to the owner. The man claimed to be protecting his business with whites, but down the street Langston ate in another Chinese restaurant filled with whites who obviously did not mind his presence there. "As I told you that night," Hughes wrote the owner, "I have been in China and I have seen there white English and American people who have set up the same kind of discrimination against you. I very much regret that you in this country contribute to the further humiliation of your colored brothers."

As he collected his fees at one stop after another on the tour, and hawked his copies of *Freedom's Plow* and *Jim Crow's Last Stand,* Langston understood he was paying a price himself. He was in no position to create effectively. Nevertheless, his financial need was real, and the compensation hardly negligible. In late April, 1944, in fact, he passed a major milestone in his life: "My first one thousand dollars!" Two checks from the *Defender,* one from *Esquire* for a piece of fiction taken for a special "bedside" edition of the magazine, and a fourth check from a reading put his bank account in New York at $1010.26—"the most I have ever had at once in life!" He had achieved this milestone after twenty-three years of publishing. Nevertheless, Langston was so excited that he sent word of the momentous event to Toy Harper, Carl Van Vechten, and Noel Sullivan—and perhaps to others.

By this time he had passed from Arizona into California. In Los Angeles, he visited his uncle John Hughes and his cousin Flora Coates, and just missed meeting Emerson Harper, who himself had been on the road for a while playing in Fletcher Henderson's orchestra. Then he headed north to Hollow Hills Farm and a blissful ten-day visit with Noël Sullivan, Eulah Pharr, and his other friends there. One presence was gone from the Farm—Greta, the intelligent, affectionate German Shepherd that had kept Langston company at "Ennesfree" and romped on the beach with him in Carmel-by-the-Sea during his stay there between 1933 and 1934. Greta had died in January, aged fourteen, mourned by Langston as "the most loved of any of the animals I have ever known."

In mid-May, exhausted and overweight—he had put on twelve pounds on the road—but definitely satisfied with the financial results of his tour, he returned to 634 St. Nicholas Avenue in Harlem. Almost at once he became involved in a few projects that promised to continue his run of prosperity. For the American Film Center, in cooperation with the Rosenwald Fund, he worked on a film script based on his poem "The Negro Speaks of Rivers." For NBC, he sketched a program of songs and stories by Paul Laurence Dunbar for Josh White, Canada Lee, and the Hall Johnson Choir, for a network series, "Ever See a Song?" And a major recording company, Decca, bought twelve of his blues for a proposed album. Capping Langston's sense of satisfaction and accomplishment in the late spring of 1944 was the appearance of *13 Against the Odds,* a superficial but benevolent and widely noticed biographical study of prominent figures by Edwin Embree, the director of the Rosenwald Fund. "He's had some bad bumps, as every Negro must who lives in America," Embree informed the world in "Shakespeare in Harlem," his essay on Hughes. "He pours out his wrath at injustices. . . . But for the most part he is having too good a time dancing in the street carnival of life to brood bitterly over his hurts." ("The good qualities he attributes to me are as I wish they were," Langston scribbled privately in amusement, as he savored the fine publicity, "—and am glad he thinks they are!")

As much as he cherished his freshly accumulated pile of dollars, Langston was willing to spend it all, if necessary, on one goal in particular. He was determined to recover the rights taken from him by Knopf in February, 1941, in return for a lump sum of $400, which he had desperately needed then. If Knopf wanted him to return the money, in exchange for his right to royalties, he was ready to do so. He was probably also ready to fight. Certainly he consulted his lawyer, Arthur Spingarn, about his position in the matter, which was that he had signed the waiver while he was groggy with "sulfa drugs— which makes a person doppy anyhow," in the hospital in Carmel, after approaching Knopf with only a simple loan in mind. Spingarn evidently advised him that his case was strong.

(Possibly, Langston had still been using some form of sulfa medication when the Knopf offer arrived fourteen days after his discharge from the hospital. Within a week of giving his consent, however, Langston was sufficiently recovered to have his hair cut in a Monterey barbershop, and to dawdle on his way home in a local record store, where he listened to a new recording of "The Last Time I Saw Paris." Despite the conflicting dates, when Hughes finally broached the matter with Blanche Knopf, he encountered no resistance. Curiously, Mrs. Knopf claimed that she had never seen the correspondence between him and Lesser and had never heard of his surrender. But in a letter of March, 1942, she had alluded to it quite clearly.)

She telephoned Langston to inform him that the matter was now resolved, and in his favor. His offer to repay the sum of $400 was declined, but Knopf would not have to pay him royalties on the sales since 1941 of the five books in question: *The Weary Blues, Fine Clothes to the Jew, Not Without Laughter, The Ways of White Folks,* and *The Dream Keeper.* A new letter from Joseph Lesser, still secretary of Knopf, confirmed the reinstatement of contracts as of May 1, 1944—"and without payment of any further sums between us." A typically chill covering note from Mrs. Knopf to Langston closed the matter: "I told you on the phone I had gone into the matter which you discussed with me regarding the reinstatement of your contracts, and the enclosed letter covers it."

For Langston, this was one of the more fulfilling moments of his life. With his rights recovered, his weekly column in the *Defender* solidly established, his readings in great demand, and a coming lecture tour promising new heights of success, he seemed to have every reason, in the summer of 1944, to think of himself as on the brink, at long last, of something like settled prosperity.

4

THIRD DEGREE
1944 to 1945

Hit me! Jab me!
Make me say I did it.
Blood on my sport shirt
And my tan suede shoes . . .
"Third Degree," 1949

F OR THE FIRST TIME in three years, Langston saw the summer approach without an invitation to Yaddo. For various reasons, not least of all the exigencies of the war, the writers' colony did relatively little in the summer of 1944. Instead, Langston planned to stay at home as much as possible, work on his various small projects, and save his strength for a challenging autumn and winter, with two demanding speaking tours. The first would take him to a variety of high schools around New York for Read Lewis's Common Council for American Unity. The second, under the expert management of the Feakins lecture bureau, would take him further afield, and last for several months. Both would require a rested, physically fit Langston Hughes.

A brief excursion far from New York early in the summer presented virtually no demands at all. On July 8, Langston breezily mounted a stage at the White Sox Baseball Park in Chicago as master of ceremonies of the Fifth Annual American Negro Music Festival; two days later he and the festival moved in a caravan to the Sportsman's Ball Park in St. Louis, Missouri; then, on July 12, they ended their tour at Briggs Stadium in Detroit. This extravaganza was organized as part of the *Chicago Defender*'s contribution to the war effort, with the *Defender* executives W. Louis Davis and John Sengstacke serving as president-director and vice-president of the festival, and with all profits going to the Army and Navy Relief Fund. Despite driving summer rain in Chicago, the festival was a success, as thousands of people turned out for what Langston called admiringly "an ALL STAR million dollar show!" The attractions included a bevy of preening beauty queens, a mass choir led by the gospel composer Thomas A. Dorsey, an orchestra led by Noble Sissle, the trumpet playing of W. C. Handy, and the concert singers Lillian Evanti of the National Negro

Opera Company, the young black Canadian Portia White, and Richard Bonelli. Hollywood offered two movie stars, Don Ameche and Pat O'Brien.

Remembering all too vividly his financial disaster in 1940 working in Chicago on the Negro Exposition, Langston did not hesitate this time to collect the sum of $300, plus expenses, promised for his efforts. He was able to report to Arna Bontemps, his partner in the Exposition fiasco, that this time "the Negroes are paying and I am getting mine after *each* performance." Under such circumstances, he had no trouble enjoying his prominent role in the festival, which included at least one truly moving moment—in St. Louis, when blind old W. C. Handy, accompanied by Noble Sissle's orchestra featuring staccato piano and muffled drums, played his "St. Louis Blues." (Apparently Langston looked out for Handy, who was now past seventy, on the tour. At the end of the Detroit performance, just before the group broke up, the old man slipped $50 into Langston's hand—for "all the fine little things" Langston had done for him.) Less moving were the parades of soldiers and sailors at each venue, and definitely humdrum, if not hypocritical, were several speeches about the urgent need for racial harmony. That year, the *Defender* festival had received every encouragement from the local—white—authorities, no doubt because of the ugly riots of 1943.

Returning to New York, Langston passed the rest of the summer uneventfully but none too pleasantly. A summer cold struck, then held on; and a stream of visitors, which would only swell over the coming years as he remained fixed in Harlem, found its way to his front door. Many of the visitors were from the Caribbean, and seeking his help in some way. The Trinidadian dancer Beryl McBurnie, or "La Belle Rosette," as she called herself on the stage, wanted to establish herself professionally in New York; the future Jamaican novelist Roger Mais ("I am a colored West Indian & have never been to university") sought help to go to drama school in the United States. Still generous to other artists, Langston helped where he could. A cocktail party that summer brought a host of musical people, including Nora Holt, Dean Dixon, and Dan Burley, by invitation to the small apartment. As for work, Langston turned out a song or two—notably "Let My People Go—Now!," a campaign ditty for Adam Clayton Powell, Jr., who was campaigning for a seat in the U.S. Congress.

As the summer came to an end, he turned his attention to the tour of high schools first suggested on May 25 by Margaret Anderson of *Common Ground*. On behalf of the Common Council for American Unity, it was scheduled to bring him, between mid-October and mid-November, before two or three dozen student convocations within commuting range of Manhattan, mainly in New Jersey and Philadelphia. Anderson's idea was that Hughes would not only read his poems but also visit a class or two at each school and eat lunch with students informally in the cafeteria. As much as Langston disliked rising early, he had no difficulty deciding to take on this essentially missionary assignment. He believed in the work of the Council and the magazine, and the general aims of the tour. These were, according to Langston, to instill pride in black students by his presence and bearing as a lecturer (in schools where often there was not a single black teacher and no black had lectured before) and to "interpret Negroes as human beings to white students," who would be in the majority almost everywhere. He blamed much of American racial tension on the glaring ignorance of Negro history ordinarily shown by blacks and whites alike.

The plan was noble, but it almost collapsed. As if in direct response, on October 3 and 5, in Washington, D.C., the House of Representatives' Special Committee on Un-American Activities heard its director of research, J. B. Matthews, denounce Langston Hughes as a dangerous radical. He was "an avowed Communist," who had been "a leading member of the Communist Party in this country for approximately 20 years."

This was not the first attack on Hughes by the Special Committee on Un-American Activities, which was charged with investigating the "extent, character, and objects of un-American propaganda activities" in the U.S., the spread of propaganda, either foreign or domestic in origin, that "attacks the principle of the form of government as guaranteed by our Constitution," and also "all other questions in relation thereto that would aid Congress in any necessary remedial legislation." In December, 1938, the Committee had heard Dr. Theodore Graebner of Concordia Seminary in St. Louis, Missouri, during a general attack on radicals in the universities, testify that Langston was "a Communist poet." Graebner also recited into the record a stanza from his "Good Morning Revolution" and from "One More 'S' in the U.S.A.," which he indeed had written in 1934 as an anthem for the Eighth Convention of the U.S. Communist Party. In 1941, J. B. Matthews himself had testified not only that Hughes was an acknowledged member of the Communist Party but that he had "run for office on the Communist Party ticket."

Now, however, Langston figured far more prominently in the Committee's deliberations. Specifically under attack was the recently formed National Citizens' Political Action Committee, which had been organized by the CIO with Sidney Hillman of the Amalgamated Clothing Workers Union as its chairman. Its 141 members represented a fairly wide spectrum of progressive political opinion. Among the black members, for example, were Hughes, Mary McLeod Bethune, Canada Lee, Judge William Hastie, Dr. Robert C. Weaver, Captain Hugh Mulzac, and Paul Robeson. Among the whites were Dr. Will Alexander of the Rosenwald Fund, Bruce Bliven of *The New Republic,* Freda Kirchwey of the *Nation,* the theologian Reinhold Niebuhr, Edwin Embree of the Rosenwald Fund, Katherine Anne Porter, Professor Arthur M. Schlesinger of Harvard, and Louis Adamic. In the face of Sidney Hillman's vehement denial that he was a Communist or encouraged communism, the purpose of the investigation was to demonstrate, as one HUAC member put it, that the National Citizens' Political Action Committee was "the leading Communist front organization in the United States," with its membership virtually determined by the Communist Party.

Matthews traced the 141 members to 25 groups designated as "subversive and Communist" by the Attorney General of the United States. Of the 141 members, only one was affiliated, or had been affiliated, with more of these "subversive and Communist" groups than Langston, who was linked to twelve. They included the American League Against War and Fascism, American Peace Mobilization, the Communist Party (Hughes was the only person so designated), the *Daily Worker,* the International Workers Order, the *Labor Defender,* League of American Writers, the National Committee for Defense of Political Prisoners, National Committee for People's Rights, National Federation for Constitutional Liberties, and *New Masses* magazine.

Equally dramatic was Matthews's list of Hughes's affiliations, past and present, with forty-nine allegedly communist and communist front organizations and publications. In fact, he had "a perfect score," in that he figured in each of eleven categories established by Matthews. Among 119 persons mentioned by name, no one belonged to more organizations than did Hughes. In fact, only two other members were connected to thirty or more such organizations and publications. "His name is so well known," Matthews insisted of Langston, "that there can be no doubt whatever that Mr. Hillman is acquainted with him, if not personally, certainly by reputation, and must know him as an avowed Communist."

Into the official record again went excerpts from "One More 'S' " and "Good Morning Revolution," as well as a longer excerpt from "Goodbye Christ." Asked about Hughes and the publication of these poems, Matthews was erroneous and damaging: "He has written a number of volumes of poetry beginning, I think the first was published in 1928. Most of—in fact, all of these have appeared in Communist publications, such as the Daily Worker and New Masses. . . . His occupation, so far as I know, is that of a writer. He has written novels as well as poetry, and again, as I say, he makes his living as a writer. He is still an avowed Communist, a member of the Communist Party of public record as late as the beginning of the present year, and presumably was transferred to the Communist Political Association with all the other members of the Communist Party when the party went underground." (That year, 1944, apparently in support of the war effort, the Communist Party of the United States, under the leadership of Earl Browder, declared itself disbanded and reconstituted as the Communist Political Association. The following year, however, Browder's leadership was denounced by other communists.)

The response to this testimony was immediate, and damaging. On October 23, in his syndicated column in the New York *Sun* and other papers, the conservative columnist George Sokolsky set upon Langston. (Ironically, Sokolsky had once been at the very least a progressive, with past connections to a number of the people now under attack; he had known Agnes Smedley quite well in Shanghai between 1926 and 1931.) Within a day or so, the principals of several high schools scheduled for the *Common Ground* tour hastily cancelled their engagements. Dismayed, Langston rushed in with his patented explanation of "Goodbye Christ." The poem had been "meant to be a kind of ironic satire on religious racketeering," but was also "one of my less expert verses" and thus misleading. Langston did not, however, consider the poem to be the real cause of the attacks on him. To Anderson he noted indignantly how people who opposed him on religious grounds never picketed to open factories to black workers, or to force anti-lynching legislation: "So I figure it isn't just the poem they don't like. It's Negroes, too. And liberals." He would also begin to notice a pattern to the expression of hostility by the right wing, which emerged almost exclusively when he spoke to white or heavily integrated audiences, but showed little interest in his appearances before blacks.

Although Langston was probably unaware of its involvement, behind the Special Committee on Un-American Activities, and especially some of its false information, stood the Federal Bureau of Investigation. The interest of the FBI had begun officially in November, 1940, immediately following the luncheon disaster in Pasadena, California, when Hughes's speech had been prevented by truculent members of the Four-Square Gospel Church and the Angelus Bible College, organized by the evangelist Aimee Semple McPherson. The local police had backed Langston, but the FBI saw him as a target. Proud of its reputation as the world's foremost police agency, the Bureau had swiftly gathered information about Langston. Most of its "facts" were egregious errors—that he was 5 feet 8 inches tall (he was four inches shorter); was an avowed Communist Party member; had run for public office; had called for a race war in which the darker peoples would subjugate the Caucasians; was married to one June Croll, a white woman, and had a child by her; had gone to Russia to study communism; and supported a group called the "International Association for the Preservation of Colored People."

Diligently pursuing their investigation, agents had checked his draft records and rifled his mailbox, reported on his friends, including Noël Sullivan and William Patterson and Louise Thompson Patterson, quietly interrogated the building superintendant at 634 St. Nicholas Avenue about Langston and the Harpers, and scrutinized the provisions in their apartment lease. Whatever they learned did not impress them very much. The FBI did not consider Hughes a major subject of inquiry, demanding constant surveillance, but it routinely revived its interest every six months according to Bureau policy. However, his appearance at Youngstown, Ohio, in April, 1943, was closely watched, with information gathered on local white communists and on Langston's private, informal meeting with some black community leaders after his reading. In formally refusing to honor private requests for information on him, the FBI customarily cited a ruling by the Attorney General on the confidentiality of its files. Whether members of the Bureau itself spread information surreptitiously is unclear.

Although Langston had become a target of organized right-wing interest at least as early as 1940, recent events had made him an increasing focus of that interest in 1944. As he reestablished himself as a prominent writer through his books of verse, his *Defender* column, and his war work, he found himself courted afresh by the left. No doubt, many radical socialists continued to regard him, in spite of his repudiation of "Goodbye Christ" and his evasions of opportunities to identify publicly with the left, as a radical at heart. There were good reasons for them to think so. The more acclaimed and confident he became, the more he tended to forget the troubles that radicalism had brought him and to respond warmly to the revived charisma of radicalism in America.

The magnificent military sacrifice of the Soviet Union had overcome the ignominy of the Soviet-Nazi pact of 1939 and done much throughout the U.S. to restore the luster of communism, which further repaired its reputation by disbanding as a party in 1944 in the name of national unity. Moreover, the enemies of radical socialism were often heavy-handed. Many of the men and women stigmatized as "subversive" by the Attorney General had attempted to subvert only the worst of capitalistic excesses and racism. Attacks on the left such as Elizabeth Dilling's widely quoted *Red Network,* in which Hughes was denounced as a communist, often cast aspersions on the patriotism of citizens of unimpeachable loyalty to their country and of essentially conservative integrity. Perhaps no one better exemplified this victimization than Mary McLeod Bethune, the black educator, women's leader, and presidential advisor who had long personified for Langston the greatness of the black race. Bethune was linked to nineteen "subversive" organizations by the Un-American Activities Committee and crudely smeared by even less discreet right-wing opponents of her civil rights goals.

Even as he feared the power of the right to harm and perhaps to destroy his career, covertly and openly Langston sent signals of his continuing affection for the left. The odd mixture of caution and commitment was there, for example, in his dedication in 1942 of his book of poems *Shakespeare in Harlem* "to Louise." Of his six Knopf books, this was the first dedicatee who could not readily be identified. Only a few close friends would know "Louise" to be Louise Thompson Patterson, a socialist now married to one of the best-known Communist Party leaders in the United States, William L. Patterson. Langston's relationship to the Pattersons epitomized his dilemma as an artist who loved the left but dared not speak, out of fear that his tongue might be cut out altogether. Repeatedly he solicited their opinions, obviously valued them, but could not, or would not, bring himself to follow them.

The Pattersons tried to bolster his radical consciousness. "You are the leading poet of your people," William Patterson once reminded Langston, "a leading poet of America, a leading poet of humanity." When Patterson, who perhaps was more easily satisfied than his wife by Hughes's work—or was more forgiving—read "To Captain Mulzac," he applauded Langston: "So often I have tried to make myself clear to you, now you have made it clear that you saw the course, only you were slow to embark upon it." Louise Patterson, however, saw the equivocation in Langston's recent work. She expressed this sense strongly when she criticized one of his poems—perhaps "Freedom's Plow": "What I think is missing from your poem is that grim, stern note of hate which we must feel toward Hitler and Hitlerism abroad and at home. We must destroy or be destroyed!"

Hatred had never been a significant theme in Langston's poetry, and he could hardly express it easily at this point in his life. In spite of his deliberate turn to the center, he continued to offer some of his work to progressive journals but was careful about what he sent. For him, the perfect subject combined his pro-Soviet feeling with anti-Hitlerism, so that the work might be considered by the casual reader to be principally for the Allies. The previous September, for example, *New Masses* published his "To the Underground," followed in February by another poem, "Salute to Soviet Armies." "To the Red Army" appeared in the July 1944 issue of *Soviet Russia Today.* The revival of Hughes's leftist identification was also signalled that month when he became a contributing editor of the progressive journal *Span,* edited by Joseph Hoffman. He allowed himself to be included in such politically radical anthologies as Thomas Yoseloff's *Seven Poets in Search of an Answer,* Joy Davidman's *War Poems of the United Nations* (sponsored by the League of American Writers, and including his "Stalingrad: 1942"), and *Lament for Dark Peoples.*

To other invitations from the left, he responded in various ways. In few cases did Langston aggressively refuse to help. In some, he actually became involved—but only to the extent of attending a meeting or two, or supplying a little material for propagandistic purposes. In most instances, it seems clear, he simply allowed his name to be invoked without actually doing anything. In some ways, indeed, he seemed anxious to help everyone. About this time, his name appeared in connection with Yugoslavian relief efforts (no doubt through the influence of Yugoslavian-born Louis Adamic of the *Common Ground* circle) and with the American Palestine Committee, chaired by Senators Robert F. Wagner and Charles L. McNary.

Nevertheless, the renewal of his interest in the left became discernible during the war, although it was conspicuous only to the most eagle-eyed patriots on the right. He attended at least one meeting of the National Negro Congress with Max Yergan to discuss yet another socialist initiative in Harlem ("a people's institute in our community," Yergan wrote, "to provide lectures and classes on current questions and problems which we face"). His acceptance of an invitation to deliver the keynote address at the IWO city-wide conference in October, 1943, did not pass unnoticed; nor did his work for the National Maritime Union, as well as at least two appearances in support of the financially strapped *New Masses.* Although quite possibly he did not take part in any of its activities, early in 1944 Hughes became a sponsor of the progressive American Youth for Democracy, which later became a prime target of the right. That summer, he helped to sponsor a nominally pro-Roosevelt event put on by the progressive Independent Voters Committee of the Arts and Sciences. (Later that year it became the Independent Citizens Committee of the Arts, Sciences and Professions, of which Langston was an initiating sponsor.) In fact, his early membership in the National Citizens' Political Action Committee, denounced by one critic as the most revolutionary threat to American politics since the evolution of the party system, was the immediate cause of J. B. Matthews's attack on him before the Committee on Un-American Activities.

Without a doubt, Langston belonged to many committees and groups because he had been asked to join by members who wanted a token black presence, and perhaps *only* a token black presence, among their number. He understood this point, although he did not often use it as a reason to decline. One group "got hot because I wouldn't be on a Conference Committee they're planning," he laughed to Arna Bontemps. "Said they *had* to have Negro. I told them I certainly wasn't the *only* one. 14 million more around."

The list of his links to the left, certainly to the left as identified by organizations such as the Committee on Un-American Activities, grew apace. A sponsor of the Joint Anti-Fascist Committee, Langston supported the Spanish Refugee Appeal, the Veterans of the Abraham Lincoln Brigade, and the Friends of the Spanish Republic, which had launched a drive to break diplomatic relations between the U.S. and Franco-ruled Spain. In this respect he was like certain spectacular renunciators of communism, such as Arthur Koestler, who upheld at the same time the correctness of their old faith in the Republican cause in Spain. So, too, with his unflagging love of the Soviet Union—whatever his opinion of its government as opposed to its people. He needed no encouragement to accept election to the National Council of American-Soviet Friendship, or to sponsor at least one effort of the American Russian Institute.

In 1944, Langston's clearest gesture to the left was made in early August, when Louis Burnham of the radical Southern Negro Youth Congress asked him for a poem to be set as an anthem by the jazz pianist Mary Lou Williams. He sent "Lenin," which, like his "Ballads of Lenin" written in the 1930s and published in *A New Song,* proclaimed his continuing admiration for the founder of the Soviet state:

> Lenin walks around the world.
> Frontiers cannot bar him.
> Neither barracks nor barricades impede.
> Nor does barbed wire scar him.
>
> Lenin walks around the world.
> Black, brown, and white receive him.
> Language is no barrier.
> The strangest tongues believe him.
>
> Lenin walks around the world.
> The sun sets like a scar.
> Between the darkness and the dawn
> There rises a red star.

As an anthem, this was fairly inspired work. At its heart is Hughes's desire for a genuine internationalism, which would admit on an equal footing all people of all races. Lenin embodies this idea in the poem. Communism is unquestionably endorsed. (Yet within a few weeks, Hughes would distance himself from the poem.)

What made such a gesture by Langston even more telling was the sensational appearance in the *Atlantic Monthly* that summer of Richard Wright's essay, "I Tried to Be a Communist," a highly personal attack on the authoritarianism and insensitivity of many of the men with whom Wright had once been ideologically intimate. From Chicago came reports of hurt and confusion among the younger black writers, several of whom insisted on thinking of themselves as radical, although they had done little or nothing to deserve the term. At least one saw the contrast between Hughes and Wright immediately. "You are re-elected as the People's artist," Margaret Goss wrote Hughes. And the dramatist Ted Ward, who once had been extremely close to Wright, now denounced him to Langston as "a ruthless egomaniac, utterly unscrupulous in his bent for exploiting others." Apparently, with Wright's defection from communism, Hughes had reclaimed his place of preeminence among progressive black American writers. The fact that there was now more shadow than substance to his socialism escaped almost everyone, including his enemies, who would hold him accountable both for shadow and act. In one respect, on the other hand, Langston Hughes was radically distinct from Richard Wright. In turning away from communism, Wright was on his way to exile from his native country, including his fellow blacks. In having drawn away from the far left, Langston had recommitted himself to expressing in his art his love of the black masses, and his determination to be wherever they were.

Faced by the hostility spawned by George Sokolsky's articles in the New York *Sun,* he offered at once to withdraw from the *Common Ground* tour. However, Read Lewis, head of the Common Council for American Unity, brushed aside his proposal. After a rebuttal was issued, some of the school principals who had cancelled his visit called to reinstate him. As scheduled, Langston began the tour on the morning of October 16 at Gratz High School in Philadelphia. Thereafter, undoubtedly nervous about what to expect at each stop, but determined to succeed, he spent virtually every weekday until November 17 beaming down brownly on assemblies, laughing and talking energetically in classrooms and across dining tables in high school cafeterias. In Philadelphia during the first week alone, almost ten thousand students heard him speak and read his poems.

In Pennsylvania, most of the schools were clustered around Philadelphia, but his itinerary took him through many New Jersey towns, including Montclair, Jersey City, Camden, Elizabeth, Hoboken, New Brunswick, Newark, and Englewood, as well as Kingston and White Plains in New York. He played the role of ambassador of the race, and most of the administrators seemed glad to receive him. In addition to never having hosted a colored speaker before, many of the schools were in the first tense stages of a racial transition from exclusively white to predominantly black, in the wake of the dramatic shifts in population and industry generated or accelerated by the war. And if the students needed education about race, their parents almost certainly needed it more. In some places, the chance to present a cultivated black man to an adult audience of whites was seized. In Camden, New Jersey, for example, where two hundred local blacks were also invited to attend, a few were seated on the stage and formally introduced. In Paterson, a white principal was so dazzled by the visitor that he pressed him into service, with practically no warning, as a speaker at a Rotary luncheon.

Langston needed to perform no emotional somersaults to appear before these audiences. After all, except for Lincoln University, all of his education had been in overwhelmingly white schools. Some of the high schools on the tour must have reminded him of Central High in Cleveland. He told the audiences more or less what he told everyone else on his tours. Always he tried to relate the topic of segregation to the war, and to affirm before the young the promise of a bright future. When the war ended, would skin color be again used against black Americans? Possibly, but not necessarily. "We have a fight on our hands if we are to preserve democracy," the New Brunswick *Daily Home News* reported him as asserting. "I do believe we are going to preserve and extend it."

Later, Langston would complain theatrically about the hardships of the tour and about its terrible demands on his body and soul. A late sleeper, he had been forced to rise at "ungodly morning hours, and I was no good for six weeks thereafter. . . . It is not easy to appear spiritual and poetic before a thousand children at the crack of dawn." At the Common Council office, however, Read Lewis and Margaret Anderson were "delighted and thrilled" by his success on the road, especially in the face of opposition. Years later, Anderson remembered going with him to his program at Frank Sinatra's old high school in Hoboken. "Hughes had a fantastic time," she remembered. "The principal was so nervous that his hands trembled when he introduced Langston and he dropped his watch on the stage. But Langston seemed completely at home and relaxed. He won over all the boys in no time at all during his reading, and he was grand in the cafeteria afterwards. He had time for everyone. But that was Langston—he made time for everyone."

Letters from school principals, at least one of whom, in Burlington, New Jersey, was visited after Hughes's departure by officials of both the FBI and the Army, and "put 'on the rack'," almost unanimously praised him in glowing terms. "It is impossible to estimate how deeply he has enriched our lives and stirred our souls to action." "His day with us did more for inter-racial understanding than we could have done ourselves in many months." "It is too bad you do not have at least three men of his type to give their full time talking throughout the schools of the nation. Here is the real hope for racial understanding." "A better lesson in true American democracy could never have been taught in a more interesting and human way." "The question now is, when can we have him back." "Not in years have we had a speaker received with such enthusiasm."

Obviously, Langston had brought almost all of his considerable diplomatic skills to bear on the tour. But while he never struck back openly, he had nothing but scorn for the vacillating types who pretended to be liberals but quaked before attacks such as George Sokolsky's. After reviewing the performance of one timid principal, who went so far as to consult the FBI and almost everyone else about whether or not to allow Hughes to speak, he bared his contempt to Arna Bontemps: "The whole business made me a bit sore at folks who strain at gnats and daily swallow all the camels of discrimination we have to put up with year in and year out. My personal feeling is TO HELL WITH THEM! I do not care whether they like me or my poems or not. They certainly do us as a race very little good—Christian though they may be.''

Nevertheless, to counter the attack on him in October by the Committee on Un-American Activities, Langston quickly took such steps as he could to establish an image of orthodoxy. Although he had freely sent his poem ''Lenin'' to the Southern Negro Youth Conference, he now begged off from attending the group's major convention in the fall, then curtly refused even to send a public greeting to the participants. In a sense, his campaign for absolution in direct response to the Committee would culminate the following June, when in the *Defender* pages Simple announced to the readers that he had just joined the NAACP—or ''the National Organization for the Association of Colored Folks,'' as he thinks it is called—''and, Jack, it is FINE.'' Led by Walter White, the NAACP was a bastion of anti-communism. Not even W. E. B. Du Bois, who that year returned to the service of the organization after having edited its magazine the *Crisis* between 1910 and 1934, would be able to sway it even slightly toward the left; four years later he would be summarily booted out mainly because of his determined pro-communism. The NAACP was, in a sense, Hughes's counterpart to Claude McKay's Roman Catholicism. Or perhaps it would be more accurate to say that the black masses were Hughes's counterpart, and the NAACP their convenient if inappropriate symbol.

Possibly for the first time in his life, he voted in November. Apparently he favored the Democratic Party slate—certainly Franklin Delano Roosevelt and Adam Clayton Powell, Jr., whose campaign song he had written with Chappie Willett of Philadelphia. He was delighted when the strikingly handsome, articulate, and independent Powell, who also had been endorsed by the Republicans and the Communists, was elected to Congress.

That fall, still tottering under the attacks by Sokolsky and the Committee on Un-American Activities, Langston's prestige received a welcome boost when Leopold Stokowski, among the most glamorous conductors in the United States, announced his determination to perform *Troubled Island,* Langston's opera with William Grant Still. Stokowski, who promised to stage it the following spring at the New York City Center, evidently was intent on challenging racism. In November, conducting the NBC Orchestra in Beethoven's Ninth Symphony, he astonished observers by using two black principal singers in the last movement. Staging *Troubled Island* would be an even more historic event, since most prominent American opera stages barred black performers. William Still, who had written four operas without seeing one performed, was ecstatic: ''It will be the biggest thing that has ever been done for the Negro culturally.'' Stokowski had assured him that he was making the move ''not only to prove that Negroes can sing opera, but that Negroes can create it. Nothing like it has ever been done before, and nobody but Stokowski is big enough to do it.'' On

November 27, backstage after attending a symphony concert, Hughes met Sto-kowski, who talked excitedly about employing not only black soloists in *Troubled Island* but also a black choir led by Eva Jessye and a troupe of black dancers led by Pearl Primus. "I had a very pleasant visit with Mr. Stokowski," Langston wrote Still about the opera; "they have very interesting plans for its production."

Before long, these plans had to be postponed while a search began for $30,000 for the production, which the City Center had no intention of financing out of its normal budget, the wishes of the maestro notwithstanding. However, Sto-kowski repeated his determination to stage the opera, perhaps the following fall. A fund-raising committee was set up, with Eleanor Roosevelt as its honorary leader. The name Langston Hughes was not unknown to Mrs. Roosevelt. After mentioning him in passing in one of her newspaper columns in 1941, she had received a letter of fulsome praise from him. He shared the strong perception among blacks of Eleanor Roosevelt as a matchless force for liberalism and justice in the White House.

Whatever his misgivings earlier in the autumn, Langston obviously felt satisfied and self-assured as the Christmas season of 1944 approached. On December 10, aided by Toy Harper, who had definite ideas about how such things were to be done, he gave the most ambitious party of his life at the Harpers' apartment. To honor Loren and Juanita Miller, visiting from Los Angeles, and his old Cuban friend and champion José Antonio Fernández de Castro, then on leave from the Cuban diplomatic legation in Moscow, the guest list was a roll call of cultural stars from the black world, including Du Bois, Richard and Ellen Wright, Ralph and Fanny Ellison, Chester Himes, Owen Dodson, Henry and Mollie Moon, Alta Douglas, Nora Holt, and Hughes's Haitian biographer, René Piquion. Although Langston loved casual parties, this affair clearly aimed high. At some point he read from his poems, the Canadian contralto Portia White, a member of the *Defender* touring company in the summer, sang classical airs; and Toy Harper theatrically moaned the blues.

Financially, the previous year had been his best in a long time. His income before taxes, according to his filed statement, had been just over $6,000, or more than three times as much as in certain past years. A little more than $2,000 had come from speaking engagements; the *Defender* column had brought in $1,235; and ASCAP had paid him $623 for his songs. However, his expenses were also high. He had purchased more books ($1,303) than he had sold ($909); and travelling had cost him $1,271. After taxes, he was left with $1,815.

Nervously awaiting the start of his unprecedented, four-month tour under the Feakins management, Langston clung close to home through Christmas and the first few days of 1945. On January 9, however, he was in Cambridge, Massachusetts to read his poems in Agassiz Theatre at Radcliffe College. The next day, he joined the actor Canada Lee to discuss the portrayal of blacks on stage and screen at a luncheon at the Harvard Faculty Club that attracted several socialist-minded professors, including F. O. Matthiessen, Ralph Barton Perry, Julian Coolidge, and Gordon Allport. Then he returned to New York to continue his preparation for the road.

Mainly Langston spent his time corresponding with various sponsors around the country and with preparing as many *Defender* columns as possible. But he also found time for a story, "Saratoga Rain," not two pages in length, about a man and a woman lying in bed. She has been repeatedly unfaithful to him, he has been a gambler and probably a crook. Yet the bad deeds and bad times are less important than the years they have spent together, loyal to one another in their fashion: "The room is pleasantly dark and warm, the house safe, and though neither of them will ever be angels with wings, at the moment they have each other." The thinness of the effort revealed the current state of Hughes's art. On the other hand, he, like each character in the tale, was holding on to essences more vital than sin or error—life itself, self-knowledge, and a subdued but still breathing spirit of hope.

On January 29, rested and ready for the challenge, he opened his tour at the State Teachers College in Eau Claire, Wisconsin. He was still in high spirits a few days later on February 1, his forty-third birthday, when he gave four readings in Kalamazoo, Michigan, for a total fee of $175. In one place, he cut a two-foot high birthday cake and grinned bashfully as his audience of three hundred persons sang their congratulations. In five days in Milwaukee, hampered by blizzards and drifting snow but meeting all his engagements, he appeared at no fewer than eight high schools. Then he boarded a swift train to Boston for a program at Symphony Hall to mark Negro History Week. After Boston, Langston returned to New York to get ready for what he advertised, in spite of his recent appearances in the South, as his first Southern tour in twelve years.

He faced this part of the tour with serious misgivings. "*I do not wish under any circumstances, to travel by bus in the South,*" he had instructed the Feakins employee in charge of arranging his transportation (he also did not want any public dinners before his readings, since such meals usually proved to be "a BOTHER and a BORE and NO honor!"). The back of the bus, where blacks had to sit by law even if other seats were empty, could be the most humiliating place in the world; he preferred the Jim Crow car on the train— and he loathed the Jim Crow car. "It's a savage country!" he explained to Feakins. "No kidding!" Jim Crow was not restricted to the South. When he visited Milwaukee for four days in February for the National Conference of Christians and Jews, the Hotel Schroeder agreed to let him stay there but drew the line at admitting him to its dining room. However, he was told, "you will have no difficulties whatsoever in the coffee shop." Jim Crow was all over America, and with a maddening lack of logic. Some nightclubs, like the Zanzibar in New York, still hired all-black bands, then segregated black customers. Insurance companies, such as Metropolitan Life, hustled to sell policies to blacks but would not hire one for their offices. Many branches of the Young Men's Christian Association fervently barred blacks from their front door. In Kansas,

Hughes noted with exasperation, whites would sell a young black a Coke "but won't let him drink it inside the store." In Delaware, they would sell a black man a hamburger, "but in a sack to eat outside. Yet this is America! Yes, it is, too!"

The week of February 14 passed in swift train rides and brief stops throughout Tennessee, Alabama, and Georgia. At the Tuskegee Army Air Base, home of the first black flying unit, the 99th Pursuit Squadron, which had already flown over five hundred combat missions in Europe, Langston declined to accept payment for speaking. With occasional quick returns to New York or Chicago, he continued on through Louisiana, then completed a dozen readings over a huge territory in Texas before he headed north to Ohio in May. By this time he unquestionably had become bolder in confronting Jim Crow. Always now he entered the dining car at the first call, instead of shrinking back and waiting for the last as blacks were supposed to do.

Picking a center table, he usually tried to brazen it out before incredulous but discreetly supportive black waiters and often indignant, but often yielding, white stewards. "Are you a Puerto Rican?" a steward demanded in Alabama. "No, hungry!" The man handed over a menu. "Are you Cuban?" a curious white Navy officer then asked. "No, American," Langston coolly replied. "Are you Cuban?" On a train in Alabama, a Filipino steward offered menus to everyone at a table except him.

"Chef want to see you in kitchen," he mumbled.
I said, "What?"
He repeated, "Chef want see you in kitchen."
"I have nothing to do with the kitchen!" I said. "Tell the chef to come here."

The man scurried into the kitchen, then returned with a menu for him. "I would advise Negro travellers in the South," Hughes wrote in the *Defender,* "to use the diners more. In fact, I wish we would use the diners in droves— so that whites may get used to seeing us in diners."

Wherever possible, he preferred to use the commercial airlines, which usually cost more than the train but were free of Jim Crow even in the South. "Have spent my life buying tickets all month," he once complained to Bontemps. "Five minutes for 3 plane tickets. 5 weeks for 3 or 4 Pullman reservations. (And they mark 'Colored' on the orders even here in New York! May the Lord smite them down!)" On one occasion, however, he was thankful to be on a Jim Crow train and not on an airplane. Early in March, leaving Savannah, Georgia, after a program at the site of reputedly the oldest black church in North America, the First African Baptist Church, Langston took a flight out on "a very bad, rainy, foggy afternoon." At Raleigh, North Carolina, the plane was grounded because of the weather, and he continued his trip in a Jim Crow train carriage. Later that day, a few miles north of Raleigh, the plane crashed. Nineteen people were killed.

Except for an engagement in Texas, which he missed because he had been informed about it too late, he met all his speaking obligations. In fourteen years of touring, this was only his second miss—the first had been caused by extremely bad weather. Little had changed in his presentations over the years. Sometimes he offered "Poems of Negro Life," as he had mostly done in 1931-32; at other times, he offered "Race Around the World," which allowed him to explore "the nuances of color in Europe, Soviet Asia, Russia, Japan, and China as compared to our own country." Even deep in the South, Hughes kept up his attack on racism, praised the Soviet Union for its treatment of minorities, and stressed the need for jobs, the right to vote, and equal education. At Clark College in Atlanta early in April, he called on black schools to help meet the industrial needs of their areas and to offer courses on labor unions and labor organization. "Pay attention to the labor field," he admonished the academics. Always he warned, too, that the practice of Jim Crow in transportation would "explode in the face of democracy." As other blacks had done for many years, he even recommended instituting the European system of first, second, and third class cars on trains to smooth the way out of segregation.

Various engagements in Ohio and Michigan, a special convocation address at Indiana University, where he was introduced by the jazz scholar Marshall Stearns, a reading before an audience of five hundred at Worcester, Massachusetts, for the local interracial council, and a June 7 high school appearance in Summit, New Jersey, brought the gruelling tour to a close.

From several points of view, his venture under the Feakins banner had been a triumph. His sponsors had paid well, attendance in general had been excellent, and Langston had sold over a thousand dollars worth of his books after his readings. By the end, however, and possibly earlier, he was emotionally depleted and physically worn. One reporter in Detroit, taken aback by his sing-song voice and clearly exhausted manner, suggested that he might benefit from having "a dramatic or interpretative reader present the program. His readings did not move the audience as much as is usually expected of a poet of such eminence." Arna Bontemps, scanning Hughes's columns in the *Defender* and conscious of the work *not* being done while his friend rode on trains from one town to another, voiced a grave warning quietly. "I don't think a tour provides the material for your most arresting column style," he wrote Langston. "You do your best when you're sitting around Harlem or in the Grand in Chicago, not when you are being entertained by sweet people in small towns." What was true of Hughes's columns was equally true of his general literary career. How long could it endure four-month tours across the United States? Nor was the tour, which left him flabby, good for his health. Melvin Tolson, who had watched Langston read in Texas, teased him about the weighty impression made by "your increased stature, physically and poetically!"

On the other hand, he had gone on the road to make money, and he had made money. He was better off than he had been in a long time. Langston had become a little sensitive about his poverty since a remark ridiculing his shabby dress and possession of only one suit, attributed to the poet and Howard University professor Sterling Brown, had appeared in the July issue of Frederick W. Bond's *The Negro*. (Brown denied having made the remark, and Langston pretended not to care.) Now he was able, at long last, not only to dress better but also to repay at least two extraordinary debts.

On June 26, after attending mass at Our Lady of Lourdes church in Manhattan, he sat down to write certain checks. To Carl Van Vechten ("Dear Carlo") he sent a check for $200, the exact sum he had borrowed on May 26, 1930, after Langston's dramatic expulsion from Park Avenue luxury by his patron Mrs. Mason. "The interest," he admitted to Van Vechten, "will have to be my gratitude for your friendship all these years, and your kindnesses not only to me, but to many artists and writers, and to the Negro people." To Noël Sullivan he sent $150, which Sullivan had lent him during his depressing stay in the hospital in California in January, 1941. (Sullivan quickly returned the check: "From most relatives, some of my friends, many acquaintances and most every stranger I am willing . . . to accept payment; but you are in a class all by yourself.")

The end of the Feakins tour virtually coincided with the end of the war in Europe. On May 8, the unconditional surrender of Germany was ratified in Berlin. In the Pacific, the United States moved inexorably towards the shores of Japan and victory. The war had not brought an end to segregation. Indeed, the day that Berlin fell, as Hughes told his *Defender* readers, "I was riding in a Jim Crow car through Oklahoma, separated and segregated from the rest of my fellow Americans because I happen to be colored." Only one coach, next to the baggage car, was for blacks. The conductor and the brakeman, both white, claimed two sets of double seats, leaving eight for all the blacks. Black men and women shared one toilet, and there was no separate smoking compartment. "It is right and fitting," Hughes declared, "that Berlin should be captured for the Allies by Moscow, rather than by the armies of London or Washington. Berlin was the capitol of all the race-haters in the world, the apex city of white supremacy, the center of the Hitler-Aryan blood theory that influenced even our American Red Cross. . . . Moscow has no colonies, no voteless citizens, and no Jim Crow cars. Moscow will support NONE of Hitler's policies in Berlin."

On August 14, after atomic bombs had been dropped on Hiroshima and Nagasaki, Japan surrendered. World War II was finally over. As Harlemites joined, though not as enthusiastically as did the white folks downtown, in the celebration of V-J Day, Langston reflected on the ultimate meaning of the Allied victory: "Plenty of people are dead and cannot shoot any more, and the atom bomb has terrified the heart of man. Death has beaten death, force has beaten force. Those of us triumphant . . . have now the urgent duty of winning the war in our own lands and our own hearts. . . . This war will be won only when EVERYBODY can celebrate being alive on a basis of equality with everyone else alive, when there is education and economic security for everyone, and our billions of dollars are spent on life, NOT death, on human well-being, NOT atom bombs.''

In the *Defender,* Simple had nothing amusing to say about nuclear war. Any politician, black or white, ''running on any Atom Bomb Ticket, they will not get my vote. Them atom bombs make me sick to my stomach!''

Death by warfare had touched Langston personally twice, if from a great distance. A youth named Jimmy Holmes, the shy, handsome grandchild of Mr. and Mrs. J. V. Peoples, in whose home Hughes had lived in Westfield, New Jersey, in 1930, had been killed in the Allied landing at Anzio the previous year. Langston was also moved by the death of a cousin he had never met, Lt. Carroll N. Langston, Jr., a former Harvard University student and the great-grandson of the illustrious John Mercer Langston. Carroll Langston had perished as an airman in the Pacific.

In a column in the *Defender,* Hughes wrote quietly about these losses, and about an evening passed in the home of a black college president whose son had been killed on the Italian front. The president and his wife had calmly showed him the Purple Heart their son had received posthumously ''for wounds received in action.'' Earlier in the day, at stops on the railway, from the Jim Crow car, Langston had watched weeping whites send off their sons, most of them poor and countrified, to the armed forces. He had thought about how these young white men would not have saved him from a lynch mob, and yet might soon die in a war that was being waged partly in his defense. Just so, the young black son of the college president had died in *their* defense. ''They will die for me, I thought, just as the Negro son from this home died for them. There is no color line in death. In spite of each other, we die for each other—poor whites—Negroes—soldiers—sons—heroes of the Purple Heart 'for wounds received in action.' Eligible for medals, eligible for tears at death—as at departure. Eligible to shake hands tomorrow—when we grow big enough to know how to live for each other. Eligible for friendship then—not hate.''

America had not learned what it should have learned from the war. ''As an American I am deeply sorry this is so. I would have my country know that what we have here of Hitler should have gone long ago. I would have my country know that there is no truth in the false differences of blood, and no democracy in the false limitation of opportunities because of race, and no justice in segregated buses and trains, and no decency in a separate Army and Navy. I regret my country did not learn more quickly, but I never really expected bullets and bombs three thousand miles away to be good teachers. The dead never know what hit them, and the wounded seldom realize that their own collective failings at home helped make the bullets that struck them down.''

Yet Jim Crow had been dealt some serious setbacks at home by the war. And abroad, if in a different way, colonialism had received critical blows. With the Japanese driven from the formerly all-white enclaves of power in Manila, Hong Kong, Singapore, and other cities in the Pacific, white Americans and British would be returning to reclaim their ''possessions.'' But those cities would never be the same again. The yellow and brown people who lived there would remember that a colored race, the Japanese, had once held them. "That is the thought that will eventually shake the British Empire down to the dust," Hughes predicted. "That thought will shake Dixie's teeth loose, too, and crack the joints of Jim Crow South Africa. The colored peoples of the world are getting very tired of white hotels and white apartment houses and white governors and white viceroys and white generals set down in the midst of their own colored communities, arrogantly demanding respect and special privileges and white rights."

Most of all, however, war was horror and waste. In "World War," published four years later, he jeered sardonically at those who pretended otherwise.

> What a grand time was the war!
>   Oh, my, my!
> What a grand time was the war!
>   My, my, my!
> In war time we had fun,
> Sorry that old war is done!
> What a grand time was the war,
>   My, my!
>
> Echo:
>   Did
>   Somebody
>   Die?

In July, the Writers' War Board alerted him that it was "preparing to close up." On behalf of the Board, Rex Stout assured him, and no doubt others, that the "memory of this association with you will be a lasting one." With the carnage over, the future seemed strangely bright, if more with challenge than with promise. Prosperous for the first summer in many years, Langston thought of going to Haiti but decided that he had travelled enough for the year. Besides, there were continuing demands on his time and talent. With Howard Fast and Norman Corwin, he worked on a script, "Carry on America, Victory Is What You Make It," for a dramatic pageant that would be part of a Negro Freedom Rally to be held on June 25 at Madison Square Garden, in which Paul Robeson, Fredric March, and Canada Lee would take part. For a Harlem civic committee he at last achieved a collaboration he had long wanted when he penned a song, "Heart of Harlem," with Duke Ellington.

Then, ironically, Haiti came to Hughes. He agreed to work on a translation of Jacques Roumain's posthumously published novel *Gouverneurs de la Rosée,* or "Masters of the Dew." In August, 1944, at the age of thirty-eight, after a life of turmoil in which he had rejected his privileged past in favor of the international communist movement, enduring imprisonment and threats of banishment and murder, Roumain had died in Haiti. Various chilling reports of his funeral during a tremendous tropical downpour in Port-au-Prince had reached Langston, who more than once had spoken out fiercely in defense of Roumain's rights. Ignoring the rain and the disapproval of the local authorities, hundreds of Haitians had turned out for the funeral. Soon afterward, Hughes was approached by one of the leading Afro-American professors of French language and culture, Mercer Cook, who was then teaching in Haiti, with an offer from Roumain's widow, Nicole Roumain. She asked Hughes to translate the novel into English, because her husband had often expressed this wish himself.

Langston had not read *Gouverneurs de la Rosée,* but Cook assured him that it was "the finest Haitian novel yet published." Although he knew that the translation would bring little or no money, he agreed to take on the project if Cook would provide a first draft. Fascinated by Hughes's racial feeling and his wanderlust, Roumain had once written a brilliantly evocative poem, "Langston Hughes." After Roumain's death, Hughes had finally replied, in a sense, with his terse "Poem for Jacques Roumain," which Canada Lee read in May at a memorial for Roumain in New York organized by the Association Democratique Haïtienne, at which the U.S. Communist Party leader Earl Browder had spoken. In his poem, Langston asked a troubling question, fraught with self-reference, of the former Haitian aristocrat turned revolutionary: "When did you learn to say / Without fear or shame, / *Je suis communiste?"*

Suddenly, Langston's talents as a translator seemed in great demand. In July, Mercer Cook's draft of "Masters of the Dew" arrived. In mid-August, in Havana, Cuba, Nicolás Guillén signed formal authorization for Hughes and Ben Frederic Carruthers, a leading Afro-American scholar of Spanish, to translate a volume of his poems, to be called *Cuba Libre,* into English. And Miguel Covarrubias, discovering Langston's 1937 translations of Federico García Lorca's *Gypsy Ballads* (a few pieces had appeared in *New Directions* and *New Masses*), approached Knopf about bringing them out in a volume which he would illustrate.

Langston even "translated" one of his own short stories, when Whit Burnett, editor of *Story* magazine, insisted that the tale "On the Way Home," written in 1941 as "A Bottle of Wine," be changed to identify the characters as black, although the story originally had nothing to do with race. Hughes was annoyed by the request. "It just seems to me," he protested wryly to Arna Bontemps, "to illustrate the curious psychology that our white folks have that everything written by a Negro has to be definitely colored colored." He also noted his objection on a copy of the manuscript: "I am afraid many American white people have a color complex, even editors." Nevertheless, he changed the story as requested. (For Bontemps, coloring the story was less important than the fact that Langston was working on fiction: "Glad you colored up the story for *Story.* You should do more fiction. Also autobiography!")

Early in the summer Langston was pleased to mail to his close friends complimentary copies of *The Poems of Langston Hughes,* four ten-inch discs issued by Moses Asch of the Asch Recording Company, which had previously made its reputation recording American folklore. Hughes's selection of some thirty poems included almost the entire range of his verse, from blues to pure lyrics, but slighted his radical socialist verse. "Good Morning, Stalingrad" was included, but not "Stalingrad: 1942." The discs were well received. One reviewer praised Hughes's "simple, vigorous and friendly" manner, as well as his "successful fusion" of social concern and poetic art in the pieces.

With the translations and other assignments facing him, Langston used the Feakins tour money again to hire a secretary who would serve him at least on a half-time basis—the first such hired help he had been able to afford since he employed Roy Blackburn in Carmel in 1934. Ironically, his new secretary was also a figure from his Carmel past. A regular visitor to Hollow Hills Farm, where he had sometimes worked as a typist during Langston's most recent year under Noël Sullivan's roof, young Nathaniel V. White of Monterey was a son of the affable Mrs. Willa Black White, one of the few blacks Langston had met in Carmel in 1932. Another son, Cliff, was a professional guitarist currently touring with the popular singing group the Mills Brothers. Nate's ambition was to be a writer. "I was fresh out of the Army," Nate White recalled, "and wanted to stay in New York. I was tired of Monterey and Carmel. Besides, I wanted to be a writer and I thought that one way to start would be to work for one. Also, I needed the money. And you could hardly ask for a nicer guy to work for than Langston Hughes." Now and then White reported to Langston at 634 St. Nicholas. "More often, I met him at the studio he had rented not far away, near 141st Street. It was a small place, but he had room to write, and just about all the quiet and privacy he needed to compose. And we worked hard from the start."

With his secretary and his concealed studio, Langston was ready to toil, and to accept the rewards of toil. The big break, the windfall that would give him financial security as he moved steadily into his mid-forties, still eluded him. But he had carefully restored himself and was ready to capitalize on such opportunities as peace would bring.

One hot day in the last week of August, a telegram arrived at 634 St. Nicholas from the well-known playwright Elmer Rice. "THERE IS SOMETHING I WOULD LIKE VERY MUCH TO TALK TO YOU ABOUT. WOULD APPRECIATE YOUR CALLING ME CIRCLE FIVE 7930 AT YOUR EARLIEST CONVENIENCE."

5

STREET SCENE
1945 to 1947

Sometimes a few scraps fall
From the tables of joy.
Sometimes a bone
Is flung.

"Luck," 1946

IN RESPONSE TO his telegram, a phone call to Elmer Rice brought Langston
Hughes a proposition as fascinating as it was utterly unexpected. Walking
away together from a meeting in Manhattan of the Dramatists Guild, Rice and
the German-born composer Kurt Weill had started to talk about the possibility
of collaborating on an opera based on one of Rice's plays. The work in question was *Street Scene,* a pungent drama of Manhattan tenement-house life that
had won Rice a Pulitzer Prize in 1929. Having seen the play in Europe, Weill
later claimed, he "had thought of it many times as a perfect vehicle for a
musical play. . . . It was a simple story of everyday life in a big city, a story
of love and passion and greed and death. I saw great musical possibilities in
its theatrical device—life in a tenement house between one evening and the
next afternoon. And it seemed like a great challenge to me to find the inherent
poetry in these people and to blend my music with the stark realism of the
play." Within a few days of the Guild meeting, Elmer Rice and Weill decided
that the time was right for such an effort. What Rice wanted to know now was
whether or not Langston Hughes would be interested in joining their team as a
lyricist.

Although Langston barely knew Rice, he had seen and enjoyed not only the
first production of *Street Scene* in 1929 but also the motion picture of the play,
starring Estelle Taylor and Sylvia Sidney. In 1933, Rice had responded swiftly
and generously to Langston's appeals for help to defend the Scottsboro Boys
by sending not only money but, ironically, the original handwritten draft of the
germinal idea of *Street Scene.* The following year, when Langston had organized his Scottsboro auction in San Francisco, with James Cagney wielding the
hammer as auctioneer, the draft had been sold quickly. Yet Langston's knowledge of Rice's generosity did not make the present invitation any less surpris-

ing. That two highly successful white artists, with scores of veteran white lyricists at their command, had asked a black writer to join their work on a drama dealing almost exclusively with white people was so remarkable as to be virtually without parallel in recent decades. When Langston was a child, James Weldon Johnson, Paul Laurence Dunbar, Will Marion Cook, and other lyricists and composers had written for Broadway musicals. Then blacks had been steadily pushed off the stage by their white competitors, in spite of the periodic triumphs of all-black shows and the widespread exploitation of black music and dance. Now, breaking with racist custom, Elmer Rice and Kurt Weill had turned to Hughes and offered him a place in their plans for *Street Scene*.

Ten years later, a sense of wonder still lingered in Langston's recollection of their choice. "That I, an American Negro, should be chosen to write the lyrics of *Street Scene* did not seem odd or strange to Kurt Weill and Elmer Rice," he wrote. "They wanted someone who understood the problems of the common people. . . . They wanted someone who wrote simply. . . . I did not need to ask them why they thought of me for the task. I knew." The two men wanted someone who knew all aspects of the city but empathized most with its working poor, whose humanity *Street Scene* would attempt to honor. The ideal songwriter for the show should be clever without being facile, inventive but not vulgar or faddish, simple and yet capable of genuine poetic flight. The lyrics, Weill declared, "should attempt to lift the everyday language of the people into a simple, unsophisticated poetry." "We asked Langston Hughes to come in," Rice remembered, "because we didn't want any slick, wise-cracking lyrics."

Rice later claimed the credit for suggesting Langston's name to Kurt Weill. Certainly the move was in keeping with the playwright's reputation as an iconoclast at war with Broadway conventions. Once he had blasted the Broadway critics as "men without intellect, perception, sensitivity or background," and Broadway theater as "a trivial pastime, devised by grown-up children for the delectation of the mentally and emotionally immature." Nevertheless, Rice was unquestionably one of America's most admired dramatists. Before the success of *Street Scene* he had been praised for his expressionist play *The Adding Machine;* after the triumph of *Street Scene,* in the early years of the Depression, *Counsellor-at-Law, We, the People,* and *Between Two Worlds* had all been well received. In 1943, with twenty-four plays behind him, and determined to work in opposition to the dominant Broadway producers, Rice had helped to found the Playwrights Producing Company (of which Kurt Weill would soon become a member).

No doubt, Weill himself approved enthusiastically of the invitation to Langston Hughes. Mainly because of its Afro-American jazz and blues influences, his music had been condemned by the Nazis as decadent. In working with Langston on *Street Scene,* Weill would be deepening his involvement with a culture that had helped to nourish him, even at a great distance. And Hughes's radical background, although largely a thing of the past, must have revived Weill's memories of his greatest collaborator, the revolutionary Bertolt Brecht.

After substantial successes in his native Germany with various operas, including *The Protagonist,* Weill had achieved international fame in 1928 with his and Brecht's *The Threepenny Opera.* Later, fearing for his life as a Jew in Germany, he had fled to France following the burning of the Reichstag, then emigrated in 1935 to the United States. Encouraged by George Gershwin, he had his first American production the following year with *Johnny Johnson.* Two years later, collaborating with Maxwell Anderson, he enjoyed a major triumph with *Knickerbocker Holiday.* Weill failed now and then, but critics praised his music in *Lady in the Dark,* on which he worked with Moss Hart, and in S. J. Perelman's *One Touch of Venus,* with lyrics by Ogden Nash. Now, with *Street Scene,* he hoped to take a decisive step toward his often professed goal of bringing to Broadway—which he often praised as a native, democratic institution that rivalled European high culture in musical drama—the equivalent of grand opera. He would draw on American themes and situations, on American folk traditions and music, and aim to please the masses of people.

Within a few days of the first phone call, Rice and Weill met Hughes in the offices of the Playwrights Company in Rockefeller Center in mid-Manhattan to explain their goals in adapting *Street Scene.* A burly fellow, the fifty-three-year-old Rice was open and friendly. Weill, however, looked forbidding. Only two years older than Langston and about the same height, he nevertheless seemed much older. His eyes bulged behind thick lenses, and his glance was intense, even severe. To Langston's relief, nevertheless, the composer soon showed himself to be as gentle and quiet as he was obviously determined and ambitious. The meeting went well. Taking pains to cover his excitement, Langston left Rockefeller Center with a verbal agreement that he would try out for the position as lyricist on *Street Scene.*

So eager was he to succeed in this extraordinary venture that he kept the news a secret even from Arna Bontemps. None of his friends would know about his good luck until the first press release about the proposed musical version of *Street Scene* appeared in mid-October in the *New York Times.*

On Labor Day, September 3, a copy of the original play reached him. Without waiting for Rice to start his book, Langston finished two songs the next day. To his relief, Weill and Rice found them, according to the playwright, "fine in quality and very right in mood." On October 10 Langston signed an agreement with the Playwrights Company and accepted $500 for further trial work. If his lyrics proved unsuitable, he would receive another $250 and be dismissed by November 15. Otherwise, he would thereafter be entitled to two percent of the gross weekly box-office receipts (Weill and Rice each received four percent), in addition to twenty percent of the motion picture rights, and other income.

Within a week of signing he submitted about a dozen lyrics, all of which were praised. A few days later, just before leaving New York on a brief tour, he sent fourteen lyrics, although his schedule called for only nine. He was determined to win the job. Seeking inspiration, he visited the house on West 65th Street on which Rice had based his play. It seemed a polyglot mixture of old and immigrant America, a place where Jews, Italians, Swedes, Anglo-Saxons, and blacks lived in apparent harmony. Langston's enthusiasm and confidence grew. "I am delighted, of course, at the prospect of working on a play that I remember as one of my great evenings in the theatre," he flattered Rice. "I think it will make a terrific music-drama in a form quite new to the American stage."

Although he wanted to stay in New York to be close to Weill and Rice, on October 29 he began a new reading tour at Northern Michigan College on remote Lake Superior. In the following two and a half weeks, anxious about *Street Scene* but bound by his other commitments, he faced crowds in Illinois, Indiana, and Ohio. With the war finally over, and perhaps also elated by his *Street Scene* opportunity, Langston emphasized the positive aspects of America. In spite of drawbacks, he insisted, "our democracy is so big and flexible and has such fine qualities that the American Negroes are the outstanding group of their race in the world. Democracy is growing all the time, and people of good will can help it grow bigger and better and correct defects." And indeed he found, here and there, a few signs of racial progress. In Anderson, Indiana, Langston was allowed to pay for a room at the Hotel Anderson, the best hotel "in this former Klan territory! The sun do move!" Nevertheless, the tour was bleak and discouraging. Coming down with a bad cold, he was soon counting the days before his return to New York. The Midwest was "raw, cold, and prejudiced, trains crowded and smoky and travel the worst I've seen it so far, soldiers going home and mad, and an air like pre-cyclone weather in Kansas used to feel, with open and under-cover gusts of fascism blowing through forlorn streets in towns where desperate little groups of interracial Negroes and whites are struggling to keep things half way decent."

He lived with a sense of the futility of poetry in the face of such racism. As he wrote in the *Defender,* "Art must be like religion—both can cross physical color lines with ease, but neither seems to have much effect on most white people's hearts and souls—at least not in this rude American country of ours. Or can it be that most American white folks have no hearts and no souls? I am really puzzled about this, ours being a Christian country, but with so many people who are not Christ-like toward their darker brothers." Were race relations improving? "To tell the truth," he wrote in another column, "I do not know. . . . Race relations look like a see-saw to me—up on one end and down on the other, up here and down there, up and down." The Midwest had once been tolerable. Now parts were as bad as the South.

One undoubtedly pleasant moment came on November 2 at the Ward Chapel A.M.E. church in Peoria. Langston had "a wonderful surprise" when his audience included his eighth grade English teacher from Lincoln, Illinois, Ethel Welch. In *The Big Sea,* he had credited her and others at his Lincoln school with inspiring his first poem. Also memorable was his visit to Springfield, Illinois, where he met and stayed one night with the recently widowed Olive Lindsay Wakefield, the sister of his "discoverer" in 1925, Vachel Lindsay.

After thirty-five years away—twenty in China and fifteen in New England—she had returned to live in the now ramshackle old Lindsay home where she and Vachel had grown up. Almost seventy years old and obsessively idealistic, Mrs. Wakefield was determined to carry on her dead brother's ecstatic moral crusade in recalcitrant Springfield. "I must make this a city of dreamers," he had once written, "or die trying." The first house guest since her return, Langston was the center of attraction at a dinner party for nine, including two other blacks, served amidst tattered walls, unopened packing crates, and cracked floor boards. As Olive Wakefield cooked chop suey and rice on a single-burner electric hot plate, Langston did his best to keep the party alive with droll tales "about his travels over most of the countries of the globe, when he, as a young person fired by a desire to see for himself the whole world, had worked his way through all the 'seven seas'." Staying the night, he slept in a hastily erected four-poster bed that had once belonged to Mrs. Wakefield's great grandmother. "Come again soon, won't you?" she pleaded with Langston. "You can consider this one of your many homes."

Olive Lindsay Wakefield's kindness only emphasized for him the hurt of the racism found abundantly elsewhere. "I was never so glad to get back to New York in my life!" he confided to Arna Bontemps when he returned in mid-November. "Cold seemed to disappear the minute I got back to Penn Station!"

On November 15, to his great satisfaction, his efforts to impress Elmer Rice and Kurt Weill paid off. Langston became an official member of the *Street Scene* project. This success, with its dazzling promise of a small fortune to come, more than made up for a string of reverses. Mercer Cook's translation of Jacques Roumain's novel "Masters of the Dew," which awaited Langston's polishing, was rejected by Doubleday as too slight to interest American readers. Doubleday also declined to publish "Cuba Libre," the proposed volume of Nicolás Guillén's poetry to be translated by Hughes and Ben Carruthers. The firm published little poetry, its editors explained, and in any event Guillén's work was unpromising. An impulsively prepared anthology of poems by Walt Whitman about blacks and Indians, "Walt Whitman's Darker Brothers," met a similar fate first at Doubleday, then at Oxford University Press. The anthology had emerged from Hughes's work on an introduction, "The Ceaseless Rings of Walt Whitman," written in November for a Whitman anthology published by Young World Books, intended mainly for children. Appropriately, given both his audience and the scant pay, Langston had stressed Whitman's humanitarian sacrifice. Although he was "one of the greatest 'I' poets of all time, Whitman's 'I' is not the 'I' of the introspective versifiers who write always and only about themselves. . . . In this atomic age of ours, when the ceaseless rings are multiplied a millionfold, the Whitman spiral is upward and outward toward a freer, better life for all, not narrowing downward toward death and destruction. Singing the greatness of the individual, Whitman also sings the greatness of unity, cooperation, and understanding." A year later, Whitman was the subject of another introduction and another anthology by Hughes, published by the left-wing International Publishers of New York. (In addition, Whitman's grand elegy on the death of Lincoln, "When Lilacs Last in the Dooryard Bloom'd," was also a part of the original play and the revised musical version of *Street Scene.*)

The *Chicago Defender* raised Langston's weekly pay by $10, but only when he threatened to resign after discovering that he was earning less than the other columnists on the staff. And yet the popularity of Jesse B. Semple, or Simple, in the column had grown so much that Ira de A. Reid, editor of the scholarly journal *Phylon,* founded by W. E. B. Du Bois at Atlanta University, requested an essay by Langston on this "amazing character." To Arna Bontemps, Jesse B. Semple was "the only new humorous creation in black flesh in a very long time"; more than a comic character, he was also "the very hipped, race-conscious, fighting-back, city-bred greatgrandson of Uncle Remus." To *Phylon,* Langston sent the essay "Simple and Me," which appeared in the Winter 1945 number. The most perplexing puzzle for him was how to capitalize on Simple's fame. For a while he toyed with the notion of making a comic strip out of the character. Then he turned his attention to an idea of Carl Van Vechten's, for a cheap, paperback selection of the sketches. John H. Johnson, the ambitious and capable owner of the magazines *Negro Digest* and *Ebony* (the first issue appeared that November), suggested a pocketsized volume with illustrations by Ollie Harrington, famous in the black community for his "Bootsie" newspaper cartoons. The idea of a black publisher and illustrator appealed to Hughes. "I personally like this idea very much," he wrote his agent, Maxim Lieber, who sent Johnson a contract and a request for an advance of $100. Unfortunately, nothing more was heard of the plan.

Continuing uncertainties in Langston's career asserted themselves in the face of his growing international reputation. Belatedly but proudly he received copies of an anthology of his poems published during the war by the Dutch resistance in Holland. Copies—along with only token royalties—also arrived of a Spanish translation of *The Big Sea* (*El Inmenso Mar*) and a Portugese version (*O Imenso Mar*), published in Argentina and in Brazil the previous year, 1944. An Italian translation of *The Big Sea* (*Nel Mare Della Vita*) would appear in 1948. Before the end of the decade, Hughes's autobiography would also be published in German (*Ich Werfe Meine Netze Aus*), French (*Les Grandes Profondeurs*), and Polish (*Wielkie Morze*). Everyone, it seemed, wanted to read the story of his life—and yet, except for the profits from his tiring, often humiliating tours, Langston lived close to poverty.

He pinned his hopes on *Street Scene.* However, working with Rice and Weill was both intriguing and an almost constant reminder of his own lack of means. After Rice's wife's severe nervous illness so curtailed the playwright's travels that he thought of leaving the project, Rice converted a cottage on his estate near Stamford, Connecticut, into a studio, complete with a piano, where the three men could work. Weill himself owned a lovely farm in New City, New York, through which a trout stream flowed and where he lived with his wife Lotte Lenya, who had starred in several of his plays, including *The Threepenny Opera.* Sometimes the collaborators met there to work. In either case, after each session Langston made his way back to Harlem. He accepted the situation, as he had to. "I have bought two fine suits with the *Street Scene* check," he wrote jauntily to Arna Bontemps, "and intend to see some fine shows, and it don't worry my mind!"

In the inevitable clash of wills between playwright and composer, the lyricist had little room to maneuver. Rice was so emotionally attached to the original *Street Scene* that he repeatedly resisted suggestions for changes in the text, and often flatly refused to allow the dramatic emphasis to shift from the text towards the music, which was necessary in operatic composition. Weill, on the other hand, could not conceal completely his nostalgia for his greatest collaborator, Bertolt Brecht. Once, when Langston mentioned cockroaches in one line of the sadly beautiful song, "Lonely House," Rice stamped his foot. There must be no cockroaches in such a haunting lyric! Weill sighed his disapproval. *Street Scene* would be no *Threepenny Opera,* he confided to Langston. "Brecht would have left the cockroaches in." Langston mainly kept his counsel. "I had no theatrical precedents to hark back to," he later conceded tersely, "so I was caught in the middle."

He liked both men, but found Kurt Weill the more admirable. Weill was "a swell guy to work with," Langston confided to Arna Bontemps. Later he would write of him as "a great folk artist"; Weill was "one who would capture in his art the least common denominator uniting all humanity." To write "A Marble and a Star," a song for the black janitor (converted by Rice from the original Swede, who was later reinstated and joined the black), the composer and the lyricist dropped in together at several Harlem cabarets. For a "Children's Games" sequence, the two men spied on children at play on typical New York streets and attended a session of the Folklore Society devoted to the subject. The result of Weill's efforts at authenticity, Langston later argued, was "music in an American Negro national idiom—but which a German might sing, or anyone else, and without seeming affected or strange." Weill amazed Hughes by his tirelessness in making changes until "music matched words, and words matched music, and the whole was just what it should be in terms of emotional expressiveness, character-true and situation-true, as well as communicative in theatrical terms."

On New Year's Eve, just after finishing the lyrics for the first act, Langston left New York on his most ambitious reading tour in recent years, organized once again by the Feakins agency. A Trans World Airlines flight took him across the country to California, where his tour opened on January 6, 1946, before a thousand people at Los Angeles City College. Exactly a week later, after the first of two pleasant visits to Noël Sullivan at Hollow Hills Farm, Langston was preparing for a radio interview in Los Angeles when the news came that Countee Cullen was dead at the age of forty-two.

Beleaguered by high blood pressure, Cullen had succumbed finally to uremic poisoning of the kidneys. He had not been helped by fierce criticism by blacks, led by Walter White of the NAACP, of his play with Arna Bontemps, *St. Louis*

Woman (which Langston had converted into a musical for Clarence Muse some years before, but which had been redone by the white artists Johnny Mercer and Harold Arlen). In the name of race pride, White had taken upon himself the task of censuring books and plays about blacks. He invited Langston to join the effort, but Langston had done so only half-heartedly. One day in Harlem the previous summer, he had come upon a distressed Cullen, who literally trembled with rage as he showed Hughes a private letter of praise for *St. Louis Woman* from the former actress Fredi Washington. Under pressure from White, however, Washington had become a harsh critic of the show. Ironically, Cullen had died while his play was about to start rehearsals for Broadway, with Pearl Bailey in a major role.

Langston read a memorial poem to Cullen on the radio. Later that day, in his program at Bowen Memorial Church, he eulogized his one-time close friend and his greatest poetic rival in the Harlem Renaissance. In Harlem, after a service in the same church, Cullen's father's Salem Methodist, where he had married Yolande Du Bois, with Langston in the wedding party, he was buried in a muddy cemetery, under a gray sky. Sadly befitting a poet so gifted and yet so uncertain of his relationship to folk and other popular black art, Cullen's two-hour funeral was a stuffy affair. No one sang a spiritual, Van Vechten regretted. Arna Bontemps, who had gone to New York from Nashville for the funeral, heard little of Cullen's verse, and no other black poetry: "Instead (nigger-like), they quoted Tennyson and Tagore."

To Langston, his quarrel with Cullen in the 1920s about the distinction between proudly black poets, like Langston himself, and poets who happen to be black, as Countee wished to be seen, was no longer important. "We do not have any other poet quite like Countee Cullen," he wrote in opening a column in the *Defender* devoted entirely to him. Cullen was black America's "finest lyric poet. From Phyllis Wheatley to Paul Laurence Dunbar to Gwendolyn Brooks, no other of our poets, if they sought expression in the lyric forms, had his magic and his music." His death was "a loss not only to American letters or contemporary Negro culture, but to the poetry of mankind and its readers everywhere."

With the death of Cullen, his good friend until their bond of affection snapped mysteriously late in 1924, a part of Langston's life had vanished forever. Another part, also from the 1920s, passed a few months later, on April 15, 1946, when Charlotte Mason, or "Godmother," died at the New York Hospital on the Upper East Side of Manhattan. She was ninety-two years old. Thirteen years before, on February 22, 1933, Mrs. Mason had had a bad fall and entered the hospital for treatment. After recovering sufficiently to begin to enjoy her room, which had a fine view of the East River, she gave up her apartment at 399 Park Avenue (the scene of many of Langston's happiest hours, and of his banishment by her). She had lived in the hospital the rest of her life.

Langston returned to Hollow Hills Farm for another brief stay, then journeyed to Oakland to read to four hundred people at a church program organized by Roy Blackburn. On January 21 he resumed his travels in earnest, venturing north to Oregon and Washington. Many of the blacks he met seemed furtive and demoralized. In Portland, Oregon, where Langston saw "Whites Only" signs, Negroes were so hungry for inspiration that eighteen hundred came out for his Urban League reading. Seattle was more liberal, but jobs for blacks were hard to find. In Walla Walla, no hotel would accept him or any other black; only six of the local thirty-eight restaurants served Negroes. He was almost pleased to move on to where there were fewer blacks, and fewer confused and unhappy black faces. Wonderfully clear, dry weather welcomed him in Utah, especially in the spectacular Bryce Canyon region, where many Westerns were filmed. Deep in the southwestern corner of the state he read in Cedar City ("Not a Negro in town!"), at Brigham Young University in Provo, and at Weber College in Ogden before reaching more familiar ground at Salt Lake City.

He spent his forty-fourth birthday hustling between high schools in Logan City, Utah. Then he headed south across Colorado, gave a major reading at the University of Colorado in Boulder, and crossed into New Mexico for his first visit to Albuquerque. The pace left him a little dizzy. "I have lectured more lectures this season," he joked to Arna Bontemps, "than any other living Negro of mixed blood." His trail led through Dallas, St. Joseph in Missouri, Memphis, and a number of black high schools in small Mississippi towns. In Tupelo, Mississippi, the hometown of the notoriously anti-black congressman John Rankin, a local reporter questioned him cordially and many whites attended his talk, which did not fail to attack segregation. From Jackson, where Richard Wright had lived as a boy, he sent Wright a cordial postcard. At last, after two readings in Nashville, Langston returned to New York and *Street Scene*.

Things were "getting pretty hot" with the show, Kurt Weill had alerted him. Best of all, Paramount Pictures was definitely interested. Hollywood involvement would boost the budget for the show, which was now set at about $150,000, well below the sensible amount for a Broadway musical. A major producer had been signed—Dwight Deere Wiman, a veteran of over fifty shows, who had spent most of the war in charge of Red Cross shows in Britain. Charles Friedman, who had scored a hit recently with an updated version of Bizet's *Carmen*, would direct. In Langston's absence, Weill and Rice had made a multitude of revisions: "You see there is quite a lot of work waiting for you."

Immediately he postponed an appointment he had accepted as a visiting professor of English and Creative Writing for a semester at Atlanta University. Cutting all other engagements to a minimum, he took the train almost every day to work with Weill and Rice at Rice's home in Connecticut. With a healthy share of the film rights guaranteed by his contract, he assured Arna Bontemps, "I cannot be worried with anything else." In a long nighttime session on March 1, Hughes and Weill finally revised the lyrics for Act I. Six days later, Rice joined them to assemble the entire act, pruning and rewriting until they agreed finally on its shape. Rehearsals were set for the fall. *Street Scene* was scheduled to open on Broadway in December.

In spite of the demands of the show, however, Langston could not afford to give up the road entirely. In March, he read and lectured in a variety of cities, including Boston, Toledo, Pittsburgh, Cleveland, and Chicago, where he gave two programs for Jewish organizations and another for the National Conference of Christians and Jews. He took part in an interracial "experiment" in Montclair, New Jersey, where twenty white couples sat down with twenty black couples at a church supper, with the well-intentioned white minister beaming with pleasure that the blacks seemed perfectly at ease. On May 9, attending the centenary celebration of Central High School in Cleveland, he was hailed as Central's best known alumnus, and read a long, trite piece of verse, "Centennial," in praise of education and his alma mater. At least one of his classmates, reminiscing about the Latin instructor Helen Chesnutt (who was present) and dances at her home with her Garden Club, found Langston wonderfully unchanged—"most of all—you were just you—despite the years that have passed you were still just the high school boy I used to know."

On May 17 a measure of critical recognition came mixed, as Langston no doubt would have it, with cold cash. At the joint annual ceremony of the American Academy of Arts and Letters and the National Institute of Arts and Letters in the Academy's auditorium at West 156th Street in Manhattan, he accepted an "Arts and Letters" grant of $1000, as well as a medal of merit. Hughes (who apparently had been recommended by the playwright Ridgeley Torrence) was one of twenty-three nonmembers, including fellow blacks Gwendolyn Brooks and the sculptor Richmond Barthé, Marianne Moore, Malcolm Cowley, Marc Blitzstein, Kenneth Burke, and Arthur M. Schlesinger, Jr., to receive grants. Wallace Stevens, Lillian Hellman, and Charles Ives, among others, became members of the Institute; and Robinson Jeffers of Carmel was inducted into the Academy, the elite inner circle drawn from members of the Institute. As his guests on the occasion, Langston formally invited Noël Sullivan, Richard Wright, and Amy Spingarn, who did not attend, as well as Carl Van Vechten and Ralph Ellison, who were present. Ellison slipped away before the close to take the train out to a Long Island retreat where he was hard at work on a novel.

The recognition of young Gwendolyn Brooks, in particular, seemed to Langston to confirm his optimistic sense of a coming resurgence in Afro-American literature. In California, he had talked boldly of a new Renaissance to match the vanished era of Harlem in the 1920s, when he had emerged as its most brilliant poet. Now, in the 1940s, Melvin Tolson and Gwendolyn Brooks, whose first collection, *A Street in Bronzeville,* had appeared in the previous year, 1945, to excellent reviews, seemed to be harbingers of the new day. Langston had helped to publicize both writers. To Brooks's delight ("YOU ARE A VERY GENEROUS MAN"), he had pushed *A Street in Bronzeville* at length in a column in the *Defender:* "This book is just about the BIGGEST little two dollars worth of intriguing reading to be found in the bookshops these atomic days. It will give you something to talk about from now until Christmas." In her absence, he had also talked her up at a reading in Chicago, where she lived. "You can imagine how happy I was," she thanked him. "That was such a *kind* thing for an established author to do. I'll work mighty hard to be continually deserving of it." Hughes had even reviewed *A Street in Bronzeville* in *Opportunity*. He disliked writing reviews. "I do not consider myself a good critic," he had conceded, "since often I cannot analyze clearly why I like or dislike a book." Nevertheless, *A Street in Bronzeville* seemed to him outstanding work. In his California address, he had once again called for black writers to stress the brighter, less sordid and defeatist side of their culture. And once again, a book by Richard Wright—his brilliant, embittered, and best-selling autobiography, *Black Boy*, published the previous year but read belatedly by Hughes—was behind this call.

If Langston's involvement with *Street Scene* favorably impressed many people, it sat weakly with those writers who had a more lofty concept of the function of the artist, especially the black artist, in the modern world. To Wright and Ralph Ellison, in particular, he had declined in recent years as a writer, perhaps fatally so. Wright had made himself almost inaccessible to Langston, who nevertheless from time to time would send notes of gentle inquiry about his whereabouts and plans. As for Ellison, Hughes's respect for him had only grown over the years. In November, 1944, for example, writing a small essay about Southern and Midwestern black writers, he had marked Ellison as the most promising of all the younger artists. Recently Langston had recommended him as a lecturer at the New School, and as a book reviewer for the *Saturday Review of Literature*. More than once, Ellison's gracious wife, the former Fanny McConnell, had written to acknowledge Langston's generosity. Always welcome at the Harpers' home, the Ellisons had shared Thanksgiving dinner there the previous year. About Ellison's almost monastic devotion to his first novel, which he doggedly refused to rush into print in spite of bubbling praise by various editors, Langston was sympathetic—although Ellison's zeal for perfection was in contrast to his own more casual standards.

Ellison, on the other hand, had distinct reservations, which he did not express to Langston, about the older writer's approach to a literary career. Perhaps he believed that until he himself had published substantially, he had no authority to show Hughes these reservations, which were becoming too serious to ignore. A year later, for example, when Hughes neglected to comment on a dazzling piece of fiction Ellison had sent him (probably the "Battle Royal" scene that would form one of the most memorable parts of *Invisible Man*) but insensitively then asked for help on the Simple book, Ellison complained to Wright about having his work ignored by Hughes—"which would be ok with me if he hadn't while knowing how busy I am called up to ask me to edit a potboiler he's getting together from his Chicago Defender columns offering of course to pay me. . . . What does one do with people like that?"

The gulf between Hughes, on one hand, and Wright and Ellison, on the other, would only widen. In May, 1946, when Langston was awarded his "Arts and Letters" grant, Wright, his wife Ellen, and their daughter Julia left the United States for France, where they would eventually settle. On May 22, as if in direct response to the news of Wright's departure, Hughes wrote an essay implicitly attacking the autobiography *Black Boy,* which excoriated black American culture, as well as the novel *If He Hollers Let Him Go* by Wright's young admirer Chester Himes. Pointedly Hughes called for "a good novel about *good* Negroes who do *not* come to a bad end." There were millions of blacks "who never murder anyone, or rape or get raped or want to rape, who never lust after white bodies, or cringe before white stupidity, or Uncle Tom, or go crazy with race, or off-balance with frustration."

To Langston, his work on both *Street Scene* and the Simple book was demanded by the professionalism he had maintained almost from the start of his career, and which he saw as perfectly consistent with his populist and democratic identity as a writer. (Years later, defending Kurt Weill from the charge of commercialism, he probably also defended himself: "Some people contend that when Kurt Weill worked in the vein of the popular theatre he became 'commercial.' I contend instead that he became universal.") If Langston did not want to pay the price of Wright's success—exile—why should he not have that of Frank Yerby, whose new historical romance, set in the South, would have a first printing of one hundred thousand copies?

Hughes's commercial sense, nevertheless, was clearly growing tougher. It showed itself somewhat unpleasantly when the firm of Reynal and Hitchcock accepted his and Mercer Cook's translation of Jacques Roumain's *Masters of the Dew.* Of the advance of $750, Roumain's widow received $500, and Langston the rest. Only after these sums were earned in royalties (requiring the sale of three thousand copies—a most unlikely event) would Mercer Cook begin to earn his share, which was twenty-five percent of royalties up to $500. Maxim Lieber, who had nothing to do with setting these terms, was annoyed by the treatment of Cook: "This is indeed a labor of love!" (Mercer Cook, an affable man and an academic with a regular salary—unlike Hughes or Nicole Roumain—had raised no objections.) The worst was yet to come. Working diligently with his Haitian biographer, René Piquion, Langston scanned every line of both the original novel and Cook's draft in order to achieve Roumain's folk-poetic rhythms and to avoid a long glossary of foreign terms; "I have also tried to simplify a bit the peasant language, keeping at the same time its archaic and folk quality." Then he floated the idea to Lieber that the title page might carry only his name. Scandalized, Lieber reminded him that Mercer Cook had completed his first draft in good faith, and with unquestioned competence. Langston dropped the matter. At his suggestion, Cook wrote a foreword; at Cook's suggestion, they both signed it.

Overconfidence sparked in large part by *Street Scene* also showed in an approach to Knopf by Hughes that was in contrast to his defensiveness and diffidence of recent years. He boldly proposed a series of books, including his translation of Lorca's poems, a collection of the Simple stories, a "Selected Poems" of Langston Hughes, and a new volume of his verse. (He was not so overconfident as to offer Knopf poetry by the radical socialist Guillén). In Blanche Knopf's absence, Alfred A. Knopf himself, advised by a senior editor, flatly rejected the Lorca book, without offering much of an explanation. Except for the proposal for a new collection of Hughes's recent verse, he shelved the other projects. His curt rejection of the Lorca book was telling. In spite of Knopf's continuing association with Hughes, the firm almost certainly regarded a translation of Lorca as out of his depth. To some extent, this attitude was based on their "objective" assessment of his ability; to some extent—and Langston certainly felt so, in spite of his smiling stoicism—this attitude was racist and patronizing. The fact is that Knopf looked upon Hughes with scarcely hidden condescension. "When Wallace Stevens visited the office, people were in awe of him," a Knopf official later recalled. "We treated him like a lord. Hardly anybody cared about Hughes. As far as I am concerned, he wrote baby poetry, poor stuff. If we had to go out to lunch with him, say to a French restaurant in mid-town, it was kind of embarrassing. He was a nice enough guy, but you couldn't get around the race thing. This was the nineteen forties, mind you."

Certainly it was an age of confusion in race and politics, and Langston himself seemed to some people confused. His proposed new book of verse was a case in point. Inspired, according to him, by his work on the *Street Scene* lyrics, the new collection would be called "Fields of Wonder" and contain only "lyric" poems—verse without reference to race and politics. Although Langston temporarily dropped the word "lyric" when Carl Van Vechten strongly objected to it as confusing, he continued to think of the volume as "my first more or less completely lyric book." And the word later appeared on the dust jacket of the volume. Almost certainly, the new book was part of Langston's strategy for political rehabilitation, a program perhaps vaguely conceived but also now thinly disguised. In July of the previous year, 1945 (as if in delayed response to Louise Thompson Patterson's earlier call for poems that showed a burning hatred of Fascism) he had magisterially defended his lack of bitterness: "I do not believe there were ever any beautiful 'hate' poems. I think the dreams in my poems are basically everybody's dreams. But sometimes, on the surface, their complexion is colored by the shadows and the darkness of the race to which I belong. The darkness has its beauty and the shadows have their troubles—but shadows disappear in the sun of understanding."

What is reasonably clear is that Langston was engaged now not simply in hustling for gain but in once more reassessing the role of politics in art. While in California, he had talked for a long while with perhaps the most intellectually gifted of his black travelling companions in the Soviet Union, Loren Miller. Once a doctrinaire Marxist, Miller had given up dialectical materialism: "Dictatorship of the Proletariat is too rigid a concept and it may, even does, permit and encourage stifling of many things that are too valuable to lose." Langston's renunciation of his poem "Goodbye Christ" was, in Miller's words, "lucid and valid." On October 20, 1945, the *Defender* had published Hughes's own statement on art and integrity. In politics, he argued, it is sometimes expedient to lie; in art, as in science, lying is never expedient. Sometimes, "an acquired surface knowledge may lead an artist to think that the surface is all there is to a subject.'' Sometimes, an artist lies unconsciously; like the good scientist, however, the good artist probes and probes "far beneath surface phenomena. It is the conscious liar who becomes a shoddy and utterly unworthy artist.''

For every artist the old moral problem of truth and compromise frequently comes to the fore. Compromise often brings food and drink. Truth alone glorifies the spirit. Guile permits a lion to stalk a deer for food, or a Hitler to close in on a new country and therefore gain more food. But guile will never create a single book or a single picture or a single stained glass window that any human animal can contemplate with pride and say, 'I, when not eating, made that.'

The things of which man can be proud, the beauty that he can really enjoy, are born only of truth, or the attempt to attain truth. That is why art in its essence is a path to truth. Propaganda is a path toward more to eat. That the two may be inextricably mixed is not to be denied. That they may often be one and the same is certainly true. But that the greatest art is also the greatest truth—and at the same time therefore the greatest propaganda for a good life for everybody—is beyond the possibility of sane denial.

Those who wish to be good artists must face the problem and make a choice—with the knowledge that it is often a hungry choice if you choose the great side: *truth* whether there is food or not, *beauty* if there is temporal success or not, *your creation* if it is expedient or not. Taking the long view (which is the only view art can take) integrity is the sole expedient.

For all this high and yet obviously heartfelt sentence, his dealings with the left continued to be puzzling. Sometimes he lent his name to black leftist groups but increasingly denied it to mainly white organizations, because he saw clearly now that his involvement with white groups, whether liberal or radical, antagonized his enemies, who cared little or nothing about what blacks did by themselves. But even with black groups he was cautious. The previous November, he was a sponsor of a "Conference on Puerto Rico's Right to Self-Determination" organized by Max Yergan, who now associated with Paul Robeson in leading the radical Council on African Affairs. In March, however, he had declined membership in the Council itself, because "I already belong to more Committees than I can keep track of." The same month, he shunned an invitation from the cultural division of the National Negro Congress to be the keynote speaker at a conference on free expression in the American arts. And in April, he frankly declared himself to be too busy to write a salute to Paul Robeson requested by William L. Patterson. On May 30, 1947, he seemed to have taken a bold new step toward the Afro-American left when he was guest of honor at a banquet of the Miami branch of the Southern Negro Youth Congress, the same group he had refused to greet publicly during their last convention. On the other hand, for speaking at this dinner, he was paid $250.

Towards *New Masses,* in which he had long published, his attitude was similar. His poem "Lenin" (written years before) appeared in *New Masses* in January, 1946, as did another radical poem, "Projection of a Day." Nevertheless, a request the following winter to speak in aid of the struggling journal elicited only silence, then a whimsical and perhaps fatuous reply by Langston about how dull life would be without something to fight about. Obviously the Soviet Union still meant much to him. On May 17, he had been barely able to sit still at the "Arts and Letters" ceremony when the principal speaker, Senator J. William Fulbright of Arkansas, had used the occasion to launch an attack on Russia in which he declared America's willingness to go to war against the U.S.S.R. in defense of freedom—"As if such freedom existed in Arkansas," Hughes jeered in the *Defender* on June 1, when he announced a series of columns on the Soviet Union. "I am tremendously impressed by the fact that this country, comprising one-sixth of the earth's surface and almost two hundred different nationalities of varying colors, has NO Jim Crow, NO anti-semitism, and NO racial prejudice. That alone is enough to attract toward the Soviet the sympathies of colored people the world over." He kept his promise with a series of six columns in which he reminisced about Russia, which he insisted was neither perfect nor paradisaical but was a vast improvement in certain ways over capitalist countries. He continued to praise its racial policies, and he once or twice attended cocktail parties at the Soviet Consulate in New York.

His affection was reciprocated, apparently. On November 2, 1946, the *Saturday Review of Literature* reported him as one of the most popular American authors in Russia. On the other hand, Langston evaded any association with a welcoming rally for three major Soviet journalists, including Ilya Ehrenburg, scheduled for Madison Square Garden in New York.

For an auction organized in support of the Progressive Citizens of America, he sent a few books to Howard Fast (who would be sentenced to jail the following year for contempt of the House Committee on Un-American Activities). However, Langston declared himself too busy to serve with Mark Van Doren, William Rose Benét, and others on the executive board of the literary division of the Independent Citizens Committee of the Arts, Sciences and Professions. When, against his will, he was elected to the board in March, 1946, he demanded to be removed from it. After Maxim Lieber, still a radical socialist and a member of the group, personally renewed the invitation, Langston again refused it. Indignant, Lieber directly voiced the opinion of many on the left about Hughes's commitment. Langston belonged to several committees with "fine sounding names," but was he *doing* anything to fight for peace and security? Scathingly, Lieber cited Lenin on the wish of many people in the revolution to reach it by express train, taking no action themselves, but waiting "for the conductor to ring the bell and shout—'All out, last stop—Revolution!' "

Undaunted by such criticism, Langston waltzed away from the embrace of the left. He kept his eyes mainly on the opportunity that was *Street Scene,* and

Street Scene, for its part, seldom allowed his attention to stray. Almost every week certain songs were abandoned and new songs requested in their place; practically every line of every lyric was revised at least once over the course of the summer. Just when the script seemed set to Langston, Weill and Rice decided to revise it from top to bottom. Their demands, and especially Weill's perfectionism, taxed his patience. "Wrapped in a Ribbon and Tied in a Bow," written for a graduation scene, so teased Weill that he spent almost as much time on this song as on the entire act to which it belonged. Langston's major single success as a lyricist was almost an accident. Desperate for a lyric for the only dance number—a jitterbug—in the show, he was leafing through his files of old songs and ideas for lyrics when he found one several years old, in almost perfect thirty-two-bar form, called "Moon Faced, Starry Eyed." Set overnight, the song required virtually no changes and eventually won praise as the best lyric of the Broadway season. Rice and Weill seemed to value his work. "All of us think you have done a magnificent job on the lyrics," Rice assured Langston. Weill later remarked that Hughes, for someone who was musically untrained, had "the most musical sense of anybody I have ever known." Still, there were many discouraging moments. After Langston lovingly wrote three songs for the black janitor, all were denied him; in the end, one was reinstated. "The only way for colored to do much down on that street without outside influences diluting their product," he complained quietly about Broadway, "will be for the race to open a theatre of its own." The pressures of Broadway were almost too heavy. "Shows, I do believe," he mourned, "were designed to bring authors to an early grave!"

Over the summer, a fine company was assembled. The single set would be designed by Jo Mielziner, whose work on the original *Street Scene* had been an early triumph in an illustrious career that included sets for *Annie Get Your Gun* and *Carousel.* Weill's friend of his youth, Maurice Abravanel, who had conducted every Weill musical since *Knickerbocker Holiday,* joined him again for *Street Scene.* To sing the challenging music, the sixty-member cast included the accomplished Polyna Stoska of the Civic Opera, making her Broadway debut; Norman Cordon, a majestic, drawling Southern veteran of the Metropolitan Opera, who charmed Langston by singing spirituals for his audition; and Hollywood star Anne Jeffreys, whose thirty-three pictures in four years had earned her the title "Queen of the B's." She had recently sung *Tosca* at the Brooklyn Academy of Music. (Jeffreys "looks like a junior Mae West instead of ROSE of the tenements," Hughes noted privately, but added that she was good for the box office and intelligent.) Personally chosen by Rice, Richard Manning would sing the leading role as the young law student Sam Kaplan, taken by many to be a self-portrait of the dramatist. A black baritone, Creighton Thompson, lately of *St. Louis Woman,* won a janitor's role, and Juanita Hall, hailed later in the musical *South Pacific,* earned herself a small part.

Langston was ready to respond in mid-September when Kurt Weill, after a flurry of conferences in Connecticut and New York, sounded the call for a mighty effort before rehearsals started. Everyone agreed on the major problem facing Street Scene: how to effect a balance between the grandeur of opera and the demands of entertainment on Broadway. The word "opera" was declared anathema. Although they used it privately, no one must even mention the term in publicity for the show. (Langston himself knew a great deal about the cost of opera; in spite of many promises, Troubled Island still had not made it to the City Center stage.) Kurt Weill, on the other hand, was determined to lift the music of Street Scene as high as possible. Only time and the critics would tell whether he had lifted it over the listeners' heads on Broadway. Cautiously, the opening there was postponed to January, with a brief tryout in December in Philadelphia.

Once rehearsals started, Langston was able to slip out of town for talks and readings in New Jersey, Pennsylvania, Virginia, and Massachusetts ("Are We Solving Our Own Race Problems?"), now and then stirring up opposition. In Trenton, New Jersey, a group of Catholic war veterans protested the visit of "an outspoken, militant, and atheistic communist whose blasphemous, scurrilous diatribes" appeared regularly in the Communist newspaper the Daily Worker (for which Hughes never wrote). However, he gave his talk and collected his fee. After such harassment, he had a striking surprise on December 12 at Lynchburg College in Virginia. The first colored assembly speaker in the white school's history, Langston was treated with courtesy and even some warmth. Breaking with Jim Crow, his hosts lunched with him in the campus dining room.

From Lynchburg, he hurried to Philadelphia for the opening there of Street Scene. He found the company nervous and fearful almost to the point of panic. On December 16, at the Shubert Theatre, the show at last had its debut. The next morning, almost all the worst fears were realized. Apart from complete enthusiasm in one newspaper ("an extraordinary and engrossing evening," with "imaginative and vivid lyrics"), the critics found the production wanting. It was too long, too dense. Weill's music, especially as conducted by Abravanel, was too heavy—"grotesquely disproportionate" to the action, the Philadelphia Inquirer judged; Hughes's lyrics were quite remarkable—but "remarkable in the wrong way." To the Daily News, they were decidedly "something else." Billboard magazine, warning of "an avalanche of Langston Hughes poetry," a "monumental" score, including twenty-five songs in a score replete with "boring and annoying" musical detail, and "rather horrible" acting, offered its advice: "A gargantuan task of scissoring is needed." To Variety, the play showed its age; the lyrics were "uneven and sometimes silly and banal." Street Scene was neither "fish, flesh nor fowl . . . As it stands it is definitely on the tedious side, sometimes painfully so."

Gloom swept over the company. The Philadelphia run was "cataclysmic," Elmer Rice later recalled, "the three longest weeks I have ever lived through." With much "changing and re-changing, yowling and howling," Langston wrote, Rice and Weill contended for influence but then hesitated before the enormity of the task. His influence was limited. Humiliatingly, he could not stay, or even dine, with his white colleagues in their luxurious hotel downtown, but was forced to find a room "miles away," as Rice remembered. Once, at the posh Warwick Hotel, a group led by Rice and including Langston barged into a dining room one step ahead of an indignant maître d'hôtel and commandeered a table. "We were served without comment," Rice recalled. Such events could hardly boost Hughes's confidence, or help him to work better. He did what he could. Drawing up a memorandum, he outlined his response to the problems facing them. He wanted more unsung dialogue to move the action along, as he later complained, but the musicians "were all bent, bound, and determined to sing for about an hour and a half of the two-hour length of the show." *Street Scene* was basically fine, he wrote to Arna Bontemps, but needed leadership. "As yet nobody is big and bad and bold enough to put a foot down flat and say it will be this or that OR ELSE," he declared. "I wish I were running it. It would be one thing or another in a week. As it is now it sways back and forth between musical comedy, drama, and opera. (Which only a Meyerhold could make a unity—or ME!) (Maybe!)."

With the weather cold and snow coming early, both Weill and Rice went down with influenza. A contingent of show doctors, including Moss Hart, Marc Connelly, and Oscar Hammerstein, descended on the Shubert Theatre. All recommended amputations. In the second act alone, three songs were abandoned altogether; almost all the others, such as the important opening number "Ain't It Awful the Heat," were severely trimmed, and at one performance, the singers and orchestra faced nineteen musical changes. Within a few nights, thirty minutes had fallen away from the show. Also lost was one lead, Richard Manning; in his place came Brian Sullivan, a veteran performer in musical theater.

In its three weeks in Philadelphia, *Street Scene* lost over $50,000. Going to Broadway seemed more and more an act of folly; for most performances, the audiences were sparse. A droll moment came at a champagne supper bravely put on by the producer, Dwight Deere Wiman, after the sold-out performance on New Year's Eve (when, as Rice wrote later, "every play sells out"). Wiman's sister, unaware of its troubles, had come to Philadelphia to see *Street Scene* and enjoyed it. "I loved the show so much, I'd like to see it again at the matinée," she announced to the champagne supper. "Do you think I can get a ticket?" The pained silence was broken by Wiman's business manager: "Could you use a couple of hundred seats?" At the end of the Philadelphia run, *Street Scene* was $170,000 in debt. By this time, Langston had just about given up all hopes of its success. "Me, I am resolved NOT to die of theateritis—nor even to have a stiff knee!"

On January 9, in vile weather, *Street Scene* opened at the Adelphi Theater on Broadway. Elmer Rice later remembered going to the theater "as though I were on my way to the scaffold." However, the Adelphi was packed. Langston himself did not lack support at this crucial moment; twenty-five telegrams wished him luck, and in the audience was a host of friends. Augustus Granville Dill, once of the *Crisis,* and Hughes's first true Manhattan friend after his arrival in 1921, was present, as well as Carl Van Vechten and Fania Marinoff, Toy and

Emerson Harper, Maxim and Minna Lieber, Amy Spingarn, Eulah Pharr (visiting from Carmel), Langston's stepbrother Gwyn Clark, Dorothy Peterson, Walt and Rose Carmon, Zell Ingram and his wife Garnett, and Henri and Elie Cartier-Bresson. (In California, as Langston found out later, his old Hollywood collaborator Clarence Muse appealed to God: "Believe it or not I even prayed that this would be it for you. You have tried so hard for years and they wouldn't let you in.") *Street Scene* started stiffly. Then it crackled into life with Polyna Stoska's rendition of "Somehow I Never Could Believe." No applause had been expected after Norman Cordon's "Let Things Be Like They Always Was," but the audience erupted spontaneously. From that point on, the house was enthusiastic and warm. The final curtain fell to thunderous applause.

The next morning, Brooks Atkinson's review in the *New York Times* opened with a reverberating sentence about a musical play "of magnificence and glory" and a score "fresh and eloquent." The cast was "superb." As for Langston Hughes, his lyrics "communicate in simple and honest rhymes the homely familiarities of New York people and the warmth and beauty of humanity"; "Moon Faced, Starry Eyed" surpassed any other song on Broadway. In the *Journal-American,* George Jean Nathan reported "an approach to American folk opera without the slightest pretentiousness, with an affecting book resolutely handled, with simple and appropriate lyrics." If other reviews were not quite as enthusiastic about *Street Scene,* the critics' general response was fine. Hughes's lyrics—essentially unchanged from the Philadelphia run—were highly praised, and the production seen as historic. Olin Downes, the major music critic of the *New York Times,* called *Street Scene* "the most important step toward significantly American opera that the writer has yet encountered in musical theater."

In spite of these notices, however, *Street Scene* was not assured of financial success. Several critics had used the dreaded word "opera." Perhaps the average theater patron would take the hint and stay away. Langston badly needed and wanted a success, but he had little reason to hope for one. "The Lord," he was sure, "does not intend for me ever to roll in even pocket change!"

Uncertain about the fate of the show, he left town four days after the opening on yet another exhausting tour. This time, it had been organized by the firm of W. Colston Leigh, to which Langston had gone following the sudden death of the head of the Feakins agency. His itinerary took him as far west as St. Joseph's, Missouri, but kept him mainly in Illinois and Ohio. At Kenyon College, in Gambier, Ohio, the poet John Crowe Ransom, whose verse Langston claimed to "have long known and admired," apparently spent a class session discussing Hughes's work before his arrival. Ransom then missed the reading because of illness, but spent the late evening chatting with Langston at Alumni House, where the visitor stayed—far more consideration than Hughes might have expected of a former "Fugitive" poet. Evidently times had changed. Ransom even solicited some of Langston's poems for a little magazine of verse, where he, Robert Lowell, Randall Jarrell, and other prominent poets sometimes published.

As concerned as Hughes was about *Street Scene,* he made no effort on the road to find out its fate. When he was finished with his round of visits, he returned to Manhattan. There he found a letter awaiting him from Elmer Rice. "The customers are rolling in and making loud noises, indicating approval," Rice joked happily, "and you should be getting a very pleasant weekly check for quite a while." With its large cast and orchestra, *Street Scene* was by no means a financial bonanza. Nevertheless, Langston's two percent of the weekly gross, which hovered tantalizingly for a while just above the necessary $30,000, in addition to subsidiary sums from his work on the show, was far more money than he had ever earned in his life—and without an end in sight.

After almost thirty years of publishing, the prospect of financial solvency—though hardly of financial independence—was at last at hand. Langston had no intention of frittering away money that had taken so long to arrive. Already he knew precisely how he would spend at least a part of his new wealth. After a lifetime of rented houses and rented rooms, he was determined to own a home, and in Harlem. Cautiously he waited for his weekly royalty payments to accumulate. Then he posed a blissful question, such as he had never posed to anyone before, to Carl Van Vechten. "Into what slow, safe, solid depression-proof securities," Langston inquired, "can one put a couple of thousand a month? Where moths will not corrupt nor thieves break in and steal? I would very much appreciate your advice."

6

HEART ON THE WALL
1947 to 1948

The circles spin round
And the circles spin round
And meet their own tail . . .
    "Circles," 1948

O N FEBRUARY 9, about two weeks after his arrival in town, the Atlanta
Daily World announced the presence of "the troubador, the people's poet,
the bard of the streets, Langston Hughes," who would serve that semester as
Visiting Professor of Creative Writing at the predominantly black Atlanta University. For his first venture into teaching, Langston offered two courses—one
in "creative writing," the other on "The Negro in American Poetry." Eagerly
awaiting the arrival of a glamorous figure whose poetry probably had been a
part of their childhood, the students in the creative writing class saw instead
(as one, Griffith J. Davis, soon confessed in a class paper) "a roly-poly guy
with slick hair and a brief case walk in and pull out a dozen books. He propped
himself casually on a chair, lit a cigarette and started class." Langston Hughes
"seems to be pretty regular." Another student, "there to observe the star shine,"
was quickly won by the instructor's "simple, informal, and direct manner."

If his style was informal, he was also well prepared. The creative writing
students faced a four-page reading list that included works by Carl Sandburg,
Paul Laurence Dunbar, Federico García Lorca, Richard Wright (*Twelve Million
Black Voices,* Wright's only admiring portrait of blacks), Walt Whitman, and
James Weldon Johnson. Speaking to the class at Hughes's request at one time
or another were Arna Bontemps, the cartoonist E. Simms Campbell, a white
journalist, Stetson Kennedy, whose *Southern Exposure* had criticized racism,
and a professional photographer, Marian Palfi, who had been befriended by
Hughes and other blacks after her arrival after the war as a refugee from Europe. Boldly, Langston also invited to his classroom the most celebrated writer
in Atlanta, Margaret Mitchell, author of *Gone With the Wind;* she declined the
honor.

Given the use of a huge apartment ("It would be occupied by at least seven families in Chicago,'' he joked), he lived in comfort. His apartment, located in the new Atlanta University dormitory, looked out on ''a rolling green sloping down to the quarter-mile track where, every day, dark athletes work out . . . and young couples sit on the green grass watching them.'' Once he had settled in, students and faculty alike were free to visit. The sociologist Mozell Hill and Nathaniel P. Tillman, the chairman of the English Department, invited him to their interdisciplinary seminar, where he lectured three times on the social force of literature and on ''My Adventures as a Social Poet,'' an essay published in the fall in *Phylon*, the journal of race and culture published at the university. (Hughes was soon appointed a contributing editor.) Over the course of the semester, at N. P. ''Tick'' Tillman's regular poker game, an after-hours faculty institution, Langston regularly lost a little money.

Younger people also found him congenial. Harry Murphy, whose mother Mrs. Josephine Murphy ran the dormitory for the university and often had Hughes to dinner, found the visiting professor amazingly unaffected. He was always ''playing records from his collection,'' Murphy recalled, ''telling stories and impishly discussing people he *knew* who, to me, were larger than life.'' Murphy was twenty and Hughes forty-five, but they laughed like boys together when Langston told about his shock at first seeing a nude man on a beach whose pubic hair had all gone gray. One Sunday, at a solemn classical concert by the rising opera star Camilla Williams in the Wheat Street Baptist Church, Murphy whispered a question to Hughes in the middle of an Italian aria: ''What's she singing about?'' Langston's whispered reply almost cost Murphy his composure: ''She's singing, 'Baby, baby, why do you do me like you do, do, do!' ''

In his first week, over a meal at the local James' Cafe, he gave up an hour to a student reporter for the *Maroon Tiger* of Morehouse College, who watched him eat and noted with awe that Langston Hughes ''not only has a soul that grows 'deep like the rivers,' but he has also a digestive tract deeper than a river, for he can really put away food.'' To this reporter, Hughes was both expansive and modest. Everything was an influence on him as a writer—''the people I have met, the books I have read, the food I've eaten, the sleep I don't get—or the sleep I do get; everything has influenced me as a writer.'' Did he awake to find himself prominent, ''or was your arrival at prominence gradual?'' ''Gradual,'' Langston assured the student, ''—very gradual—quite long, slow and gradual. In fact, it was so gradual that I got tired.'' How did it feel to achieve prominence? ''Well, it was so gradual that I didn't know that I had achieved it. I'm not quite sure yet how I feel.''

Away from the university, life was less pleasant. Atlanta was a city of contrasts—thriving black businesses but not a single black policeman; more black colleges than any other city, but with black public school students taught only half the hours allotted to whites; a black bank that closed annually to honor Jefferson Davis, the slave-owning president of the Confederacy. ''I am continually amazed at some of the things that go on here,'' Hughes wrote a friend, "which seem to me beyond the pale of civilized living." His worst single experience was being stranded for hours at the Atlanta airport, cold and hungry, because no taxi would accept a black, and the lunch counter would not serve him; he recalled the humiliation for a story published on April 10 in the *New York Post* ("Jim Crow Can't Keep a Poet Down"). The campus was pleasant, "but the rest of Georgia I would be willing to give to the British Empire if they wanted it." With mingled feelings of delight and disgust he sat through a concert given by Marian Anderson before a segregated audience. Anderson and her white accompanist held hands when they took their bows, but "if a white person and a colored person in the audience had held hands across the dividing aisle, evidently it would have been against Georgia law, and they could be put in jail." To the recently formed President's Commission on Civil Rights he denounced, yet again, "the discourteous and uncivilized treatment" of blacks on buses and trains, a situation "absurd, antiquated and stupid."

On the other hand, the pay was good—$2,000 for the semester—and, since his classes met at night, and never on Friday, he was able to read and lecture not only locally but outside the state. The highlight of his reading season came in late April at Fisk University in Nashville when Hughes attended the gala opening of the George Gershwin Memorial Collection of Music and Musical Literature. The collection was a gift to the university from Carl Van Vechten, who was present with his wife Fania Marinoff; also there was George Schuyler, whose daughter Philippa Duke Schuyler, a piano prodigy, performed as part of Fisk's annual music and arts festival. With Arna Bontemps and young Robert Hayden of Detroit, who had published a collection of poems, *Heart-Shape in the Dust*, in 1940, and who recently had joined the Fisk faculty, Hughes took part in a seminar on contemporary writing. For Langston's taste, Hayden was too quick to point to the dangers of politics as an influence on poetry, but he was a deeply serious, gifted writer. Later that year, recommending Hayden for a fellowship, Langston hailed him as "a poet of great promise whose work has a genuine individuality."

Near the middle of the semester, when the azaleas and dogwood bloomed bountifully on the Atlanta campus, Langston's *Fields of Wonder* appeared, dedicated to Arna and Alberta Bontemps. Black reviewers, who in general had never approved of either his blues or his radical verse, liked the "lyric" style. The most influential of them, J. Saunders Redding, who published a column in the *Baltimore Afro-American*, declared that Hughes had "rediscovered himself." He had "come back to the importance of emotional insight" and the power of "simple, colloquial idiom." The New York *Amsterdam News* reported that the poet Hughes had "matured in his talents." Other reviewers were less enchanted, although the *Christian Science Monitor* also saw a mature Hughes—"penetrating, compassionate, mellow in his cynicism," with "the most skillful and practised hand, and an unerring poetic insight." On the other hand, the *New York Times*, relishing "the brevity and leanness" of many poems, nevertheless found the collection monotonous, and the *Herald-Tribune* called the simplicity apparently "shallow, or false and contrived." The left was also hostile. The communist *People's World* scorned "the empty lyricisms of a man who is fugitive from his origins and his sources of strength," and *New Masses,* finding too many poems about nature, hoped that "the poet's deep sense of reality will lead him to more passionate fields of wonder."

Critics who saw in *Fields of Wonder* evidence of a new maturity were wrong. The volume contains several poems from Hughes's early years as a poet, when at Jones Point up the Hudson River, in Paris, and in Washington, D.C., he had scribbled and revised his way to his first book of verse. "Heart" and "For Dead Mimes," for example (about Pierrot and Pierrette), were written in 1922 or 1923, and "A House in Taos" in 1925. Only a few pieces were new. The emphasis on lyricism at the expense of politics represented not something novel but the assertion of a poetic strain that had been present, although at times subdued, in Hughes's work from the start of his career.

Although the two concluding sections, "Stars Over Harlem" and "Words Like Freedom," gesture towards political and social conditions (the poem "When the Armies Passed" is even a tribute to the Red Army), the volume holds generally to the "lyric" form planned by Hughes. As such, it is a reliable guide to Hughes's consciousness isolated—to the extent that such isolation is possible—from his concern with race and politics. He celebrates the "fields of wonder" out of which not only stars and sun and moon are born but "me as well":

> Like stroke
> Of lightning
> In the night
> Some mark
> To make
> Some word
> To tell.

Many of the poems are fragmentary tributes to nature—to the snail and the snake, the wind and the rain, the "Great mountains" at Big Sur, California, and the commanding waves on the beach at Carmel. And yet the most memorable "word" of the poet in this volume probably is the sometimes deeply pessimistic, even nihilistic sections "Border Line," "Desire," and "Tearless," which emphasize the inherent loneliness of life.

> There are
> No clocks on the wall,
> And no time,
> No shadows that move
> From dawn to dusk
> Across the floor.

> There is neither light
> Nor dark
> Outside the door.
>
> There is no door!

This surreal anxiety is hardly relieved by Hughes's reflections on nature. The anxiety has penetrated all aspects of his poetry, and is in fact reinforced by wind and rain, mountain and ocean, so that an expansive "lyric" utterance is itself impossible.

> I used to wonder
> About living and dying—
> I think the difference lies
> Between tears and crying.
>
> I used to wonder
> About here and there—
> I think the distance
> Is nowhere.

Only when this primitive anxiety is objectified and channeled into race and politics, when it is turned outward through a sense of social obligation, does a genuinely "lyric" language emerge. Then, at its best, the lyricism is sometimes that of the "sorrow songs" or spirituals: "Rocks and the firm roots of trees. / The rising shafts of mountains. / Something strong to put my hands on.

> Sing, O Lord Jesus!
> Song is a strong thing.
> I heard my mother singing
> When life hurt her:
>
> *Gonna ride in my chariot some day!* . . .

Or, perhaps more appropriately for an urban, secular poet, the lyricism is that of the blues and jazz, as in the more recently composed "Trumpet Player: 52nd Street":

> . . . The Negro
> With the trumpet at his lips
> Whose jacket
> Has a *fine* one-button roll,
> Does not know
> Upon what riff the music slips
> Its hypodermic needle
> To his soul—

But softly
As the tune comes from his throat
Trouble
Mellows to a golden note.

In spite of its lyric ambitions, *Fields of Wonder* negatively endorses the poetic power of Hughes's racial and political sense, which endowed him with almost his entire distinction as a poet. Nevertheless, the volume is valuable in that it illuminates the gloomy, brackish pool out of which this poetic power emerges, and which it aims mightily to transcend.

While in Nashville, Hughes and Arna Bontemps discussed various proposals for joint literary projects. Although they had first collaborated some fifteen years previously, the men now seemed to view such work with fresh eagerness. More important, no doubt because of *St. Louis Woman* and *Street Scene*, they seemed to have reached an agreement on the desirability of capitalizing on their literary talent. In fact, Bontemps had reached this point in his own career long before Hughes. "I think that with the publication of Wright's *Native Son*," one of his children later suggested, "my father understood that he was never again even going to attempt to write literature of such quality. He would continue to be a writer, but the sense of high purpose he had started out with was now largely gone. What he would try to do now would be valuable, but I think he understood that it would never compete with what he knew to be literature of the first rank."

Although Langston did not share this pessimism about his own future work, he now seemed more eager than ever to establish himself as a commercial writer. The result for both men would be a measure of financial success, but also a chilling sense of obligation to the marketplace. "This week I'm hog-tied again," Bontemps had complained two years before. "A play, a juvenile, a novel, several articles! Ho-hum. I love to sign contracts." In this love he would soon be matched by his best friend, and a similar refrain would run through his and Langston's letters to each other for the rest of their lives. Every literary success on a race theme, or by another black writer, stirred them to think of new ways to make money by their pens. Usually this meant taking an advance, but "once you contract in advance," Bontemps had discovered (and as Hughes soon would find out), "you're in slavery. They'll press you to the limit for the few hundred dollars they've baited you with." The advances, by and large, were paltry sums, but neither Bontemps nor Hughes was in a position to dictate to publishers.

In Nashville, they explored the possibility of writing a play about Booker T. Washington; a hint of an interracial affair might add just the right amount of spice to the plot. Then they decided to focus their attention on preparing a definitive anthology of black American poetry to supersede James Weldon Johnson's *Book of American Negro Poetry*, first published in 1922 and revised in 1931, and Countee Cullen's 1927 *Carolling Dusk*, which was now in its ninth printing. Langston had first proposed the book to Blanche Knopf. When she hesitated, a senior editor at Doubleday seized on the idea and offered an advance of $1000—far more than Blanche Knopf had ever offered him. He himself was looking for a chance to reprimand Mrs. Knopf, who recently had turned down not only his volume of poetry by Nicolás Guillén but, more annoyingly, had coldly dismissed his offer of a collection of Simple stories: "I think that there is little chance of our being interested in such a column and do not advise you to consider it at all for a book. . . . I do not believe, also, that there is anything in the poems by Nicolás Guillén for us." When the Doubleday offer came, Hughes quickly informed her that his friend Arna Bontemps had just received an invitation from another publisher to do the anthology. "If he wishes," Langston smoothly wrote, "I will help him with it." On May 12, he signed the agreement with Doubleday. Mrs. Knopf, who was not fooled, became "apparently kinder mad" at losing the book, he told Bontemps, "but I DO NOT CARE about that."

Hughes and Mrs. Knopf fenced again later in the year when he flatly refused her request for a blurb for Chester Himes's latest novel, *Lonely Crusade*. "Most of the people in it just do not seem to me to have good sense or be in their right minds, they behave so badly," he explained, "which makes it difficult to care very much what happens to any of them." Increasingly, Hughes abhorred fiction that stressed violence, insanity, and "aberrant" sexuality; specifically, he hated to see blacks treated as murderous, crazed, or inflamed with lust for white bodies. In addition—although he never mentioned this objection to his publisher—the novel was a strongly anti-communist *roman à clef*, in which he recognized at least one of his friends, a veteran of the Soviet movie trip, unsympathetically and thinly disguised. "I am sorry that you feel as you do about Chester Himes," Blanche Knopf responded, "but I rather expected it. It is a good book even though you do not agree."

He stood his ground again with a publisher when the genial Bernard Perry of Current Books offered him his biggest advance ever to publish the Simple book but suggested adding chapters with Simple in Turkish baths, at the opera, and other highly unlikely settings for the black everyman hero. Hughes angrily let his agent know that signing the contract was "just about the *last* thing I would like to do." "I do not see why a firm that does not understand Simple should be publishing him," he fumed in March to Bontemps. "He does not understand it either and he told me not to bother with them, and I do not blame him." After reconsidering the matter, Perry concluded that the Simple collection, as it stood, was unpublishable.

One reason for Langston's resistance to Knopf and Perry was the flow of income from *Street Scene*. Then attendance faltered in early spring. A proposal to save the show by cutting the combined royalties of Hughes, Rice, and Weill from ten to six percent brought Hughes into conflict with his collaborators when his agent, Maxim Lieber, tried to renegotiate Langston's share of the royalties. In a sharp letter to Langston, Weill denied that he was cheating him. No one had said so, but Lieber evidently had offended the composer and Rice, who both threatened to close the show rather than renegotiate. (Weill was under great pressure, heading towards a nervous breakdown provoked by the sudden death of his favorite brother.) *"Don't* be mad at ME,"* Langston begged Weill from Atlanta, "because at this distance I haven't the least idea what is going on up there." In any event, the show could not be saved. On May 17, after two long ovations broken by the playing of Auld Lang Syne, *Street Scene* closed after 148 performances. In his tax statement at the end of the year, Langston reported his various earnings from the show at $10,298.66.

Prosperity also allowed him to show his disgust with the rigors and humiliations of the speaking tours on which he had long depended. "Like Pearl Bailey in *St. Louis Woman,*" he breezily informed his lecture bureau, "I'm *TI-ARD!*" A little later: *"I DO NOT* want any speaking engagements whatsoever this summer or this fall. I may go to California, I may go to Mexico, I may go to the West Indies, or I may remain in Harlem which is just as full of color as any place else."

On June 3, Langston donned his Lincoln University doctoral robes and marched in the commencement ceremony at Atlanta University. Then, after showering eighteen A's and nine B's on his students, he left Atlanta after "one of the richest and most interesting experiences of my life"—or so he assured the university president about his semester. After a week in Chicago, with a book party for *Fields of Wonder* at Horace Cayton's Parkway Community House (formerly Good Shepherd), he was back in Manhattan for the official appearance on June 16 from Reynal and Hitchcock of his and Mercer Cook's translation, *Masters of the Dew*. Pleasant reviews appeared in most journals, and glowing ones greeted the novel by Haiti's most famous communist writer, Jacques Roumain, in the leftist organs. Only Edmund Wilson demurred; he dismissed the story of black Manuel and Annaise and their heroic attempt to unify their people as typical communist proletarian propaganda. Virtually all reviewers agreed that the translation was excellent. The *New York Times Book Review* reported "a vivid, simple, lyric English that seems right for the peculiar excellences of Roumain's work." In the *Herald-Tribune,* Bertram Wolfe praised "a marvellously close rendering of primitive yet formal speech rhythms and the poetic essence of the book." For a while there was talk of filming the novel with the help of the Haitian government; later, an option was purchased to convert it into a musical. However, the talk and the option led nowhere.

In Manhattan, with the aid of three part-time secretaries, Langston faced his steadily mounting mail and his new projects. (He tried to answer each letter sent to him; in April alone, according to his own count, he answered 313 pieces of mail, including 43 letters from fans.) In addition to preliminary work on the anthology of poetry with Arna Bontemps, he began to prepare a new collection of verse—although Mrs. Knopf did not care for his timing: "Is it not a little soon for us to have a book of poetry?" Unperturbed, Langston began to prepare a collection "of my more racial poems," including the "Madam to You" poems written in 1943. He first called the manuscript "Projection of a Day," after the poem published in *New Masses,* then "To Me It's Here," and finally "One-Way Ticket." For the first time in preparing his books of poetry, the manuscript went first for scrutiny not to Carl Van Vechten or Blanche Knopf, but to Arna Bontemps.

Finishing an essay for *Ebony* magazine on the contrast between Atlanta's genuinely cultured black bourgeoisie and its desperate ghettos, Langston then quickly wrote a long poem in response to an outrage that offended him and many other blacks. With a fanfare of publicity, the American Heritage Foundation had announced its plan, using a special train, to send the Declaration of Independence and other historic national documents on a grand inspirational tour of the United States. In response to inquiries, however, the Foundation flatly refused to guarantee that its exhibitions would not be segregated. At the request of the editor of *Our World* magazine, John P. Davis, a friend of Hughes since the 1920s, Langston swiftly finished "The Ballad of the Freedom Train":

> . . . Who's the engineer on the Freedom Train?
> Can a coal black man drive the Freedom Train?
> Or am I still a porter on the Freedom Train?
> Is there ballot boxes on the Freedom Train?
> Do colored folks vote on the Freedom Train?
> When it stops in Mississippi will it be made plain
> Everybody's got a right to board the Freedom Train?
>
> Somebody tell me about this Freedom Train!

This poem, the essay on Atlanta, and even his new manuscript of verse were tasks he finished rather easily. What concerned Langston more in the summer of 1947 was finding a project to match *Street Scene* not only in intensity but also in financial promise. His *Street Scene* work should have led to other opportunities on Broadway. In fact, although four inquiries came, they all died quickly and quietly. Then, on June 30, a thirty-four-year-old German-Jewish composer, Jan Meyerowitz, only one year in the United States, wrote to tell Langston that he had just set two of his blues poems, and wanted to meet him. Perhaps with visions of championing a new Kurt Weill, Hughes agreed to a meeting. Born in Breslau, Germany, Jan Meyerowitz had attended the Hochschule für Musik in Berlin and the Academy of Saint Cecilia in Rome. He had arrived virtually unknown in the United States with his wife Marguerite, a French-born concert singer. Cosmopolitan in outlook (he had converted to Roman Catholicism, perhaps under the influence of his wife), the ebullient composer had been befriended by a number of blacks, including Langston's friends the dancer Avon Long and the poet Waring Cuney.

"I was wonderfully welcomed by Emerson Harper," Meyerowitz recalled, "pleasantly received by Langston, and given the cold shoulder by Aunt Toy. Later she became my great friend, but she kept yawning during this first meeting. She was a tough lady, until she decided she liked you." Suggesting that he and Langston should write an opera, Meyerowitz mentioned the short story "Father and Son" from *The Ways of White Folks*. "Before Langston could open his mouth, Emerson told me all about the play *Mulatto,* and how it had been on Broadway for more than a year. So that was settled." (Already that year *Mulatto* had been staged in Milan, Rio de Janiero, and Marshall, Texas.) Later, the composer claimed to have had no trouble as a foreigner responding to Hughes's tragic tale of race in the South. "I had been very German in thought and every other way, and I had been forced out, rejected by my country. I knew what *Mulatto* was about. And perhaps it had even wider symbolic implication." To him, the connection between the story and his own Jewishness was clear: "Musically it is my and my people's story too."

After Langston agreed to adapt his play, Meyerowitz wasted no time. Early in September, he and his wife Marguerite arrived at 20 East 127th Street with the first act. "Aunt Toy looked at the pages," he remembered, "and sort of sneered. She said, you know, lots of people have written the first acts of operas. She was quite discouraging." He and his wife then played and sang the entire first act for Hughes and the Harpers. The composer's thick German accent combined with his modern music to puzzle and yet fascinate them all—including Toy Harper. "I like what you've done on *Mulatto* immensely," Langston wrote Meyerowitz shortly afterwards, "and think it will make an exciting show." Alerting Maxim Lieber, he ventured the opinion that the score was "quite good and genuinely moving in places." To Van Vechten he confessed that "the opera sounds like nothing I have ever heard before." Whether there was money in it was another matter, but Langston raised no questions about pay in spite of his new commercial zeal.

As one new opera slowly and improbably came into being, trouble flared over another, *Street Scene,* long after the end of its Broadway run. By August, with royalties going to Hughes and Weill alone, according to the contract, Columbia Records had sold over thirteen thousand boxes of their six-disc recording of the show. On the strength of the recordings, Weill and Hughes were hailed as the best musical team of the year; the New York *News* declared the set of records the best of the Broadway season. In addition, Hughes's "Moon Faced, Starry Eyed," recorded by Benny Goodman, Freddy Martin, Johnny Mercer, and Teddy Wilson, had become something of a hit. Suddenly, to Hughes's stupefaction, Elmer Rice demanded half of Langston's record royalties and half of his royalties from sales of the sheet music, published by Chappell and Co. The previous summer, mentioning only his interest in an ASCAP rating—and not a percentage of the income—Rice had asked for partial credit as a lyricist, since he had sometimes helped Langston, and since the lyrics were often close to the words of the original play. "While many of the lyrics—and the best!—are wholly and indubitably yours," he had written Hughes, he himself deserved credit for others. "But please don't worry about any of this. I assure you that whatever agreement we reach will be satisfactory to me."

Langston did not dispute Rice's contention, but he had tried in vain to raise the matter during the rehearsals. Rice was always too exhausted or too preoccupied to discuss it (he had missed several rehearsals because of illness). Now Langston offered him co-credit on seven numbers, and one-third of his record royalties; on the Chappell and Co. text, Rice could have two-thirds of all royalties. Rejecting the offer, Rice insisted on forty percent of the recording revenue. At lunch with Hughes, Kurt Weill confirmed his understanding about the division of royalties and—apparently fearing an attack by Rice on his own sole right to revenues from the piano score—urged him not to give in. Hughes was ready to fight. At the Chappell office, where the two men found Rice's name added to the manuscript as co-author, Langston insisted that it be erased at once. "*CERTAINLY* we stick by our guns," he instructed Maxim Lieber. Then Rice returned with new demands, including exclusive credit for one number and a share of credit on another for the director, Charles Friedman. "Do you think Elmer has lost his mind?" Hughes asked Maxim Lieber. " 'There is no business like show business,' according to Annie Get Your Gun! It's so dramatic! I am delighted that I do not live by it—I fear my perspective would be warped and I wouldn't be able to enjoy it so much."

This squabble over money sealed his decision to take a vacation. Turning the *Street Scene* matter over to his lawyer, Arthur Spingarn, he left New York on the cold, rainy night of September 29. The following afternoon, Langston alighted from an airplane at Palisadoes Airport in Jamaica. For the first time since 1931, he was under the blazing tropical sun. Then, lean and hungry, he had travelled to Cuba and Haiti to recover from his fall from grace with Godmother, Mrs. Mason. Seventeen years later, he returned to the West Indies as a middle-aged, plump American tourist. Instead of being greeted by radical young writers, he was met by a grinning brownskinned hostess with a tall, "free" glass of Jamaican rum punch. In Kingston, although his travel agent had warned him, with good reason, to expect problems as a black at the better hotels, he checked in smoothly at the fashionable Myrtle Bank. Soon he was entirely at ease, dining on papaya and crushed pumpkin, yams and guava ice cream, and bantering with waiters who elegantly poured Blue Mountain coffee while murmuring in charming Jamaican English. Sipping rum and coconut water ("it no drunk me yet," he assured Toy Harper), he loafed under the sun by the large pool.

After a trip by car around the island, Langston returned to Kingston, moved into a boarding house on Elletson Street, and released his cover. Soon a man from the Jamaican *Gleaner* came around to interview him. In the next few days—and with an eye towards including them in his anthology with Arna Bontemps—Hughes met virtually all the important writers and artists, including the folklorist Louise Bennett; the talented United Kingdom-born sculptor Edna Manley, wife of the lawyer, politician, and future prime minister Norman Manley; Vivian Virtue, who was married to Claude McKay's daughter, Hope; ex-R.A.F officer Basil McFarlane and his father, J. E. Clare McFarlane, the president of the Poetry League of Jamaica; Roger Mais, with whom Hughes had corresponded briefly; Vic Reid, a part of whose first novel was at Rinehart in

New York (Knopf would publish it the following year); and the scholar Philip Sherlock, who invited Hughes to lecture under the auspices of the University College of the West Indies. On October 25, Langston was the guest of honor at a luncheon given by the Poetry League. At a press club luncheon chaired by the journalist and novelist Walter Adolfe Roberts, where Hughes read his "Ballad of the Freedom Train," he stressed the importance of racial consciousness in uniting colored peoples of the Caribbean and the United States—just as he had done in his visits to the Caribbean in 1930 and 1931.

Edna Manley, who had been trying to convince Jamaican artists of the wisdom of depicting local scenes and people, remembered trying to blow a breath of freedom into the stuffy League lunch, while Langston sat at ease "with a strongly repressed twinkle—being so genuinely kind & sweet to all of us." Among the Jamaican writers, Hughes was undoubtedly received with a mixture of condescension, confusion, and pride: condescension because of their "superior" British colonial background; confusion in some quarters because of his radical Afro-American race consciousness, so unlike their West Indian sensitivity to nuances of skin color; and pride among the few who were inclined to feel as he did about blacks and folk culture. Almost everyone, however, wanted to be included in the proposed anthology; sixteen Jamaican poets later appeared in it. And whatever its limitations, Jamaica was a reassuring example of a predominantly black community that was orderly, efficient, and purposeful—a vivid argument against the paranoia among American whites about trusting blacks with power.

"MY NEW LOVE IS JAMAICA!," Hughes cheerfully confessed in the *Chicago Defender* on November 29, in the first of nine columns devoted to the people and customs of the island. "She is dressed in green, and her face is as dark and as beautiful as any in the world. Her skies are clear, her sun is warm, her moon is bright, her fruits are luscious and rich, and the clean blue sea is all around her, kissing her chocolate feet."

On November 3, after more than a month away, Langston returned in a driving rainstorm to the United States. Visiting Fisk in Nashville, he attended the presidential inauguration of Charles S. Johnson, who as editor of *Opportunity* had championed him in the 1920s. Back in Manhattan, his bags were hardly unpacked when Jan Meyerowitz called excitedly to report that he had not only finished the score for *Mulatto* but had also secured a firm promise of publication. "I believe it's gigantic," Meyerowitz insisted; "Mr. Lieber heard it, too—and some other people and all agree that it is gigantic." (Lieber, who cared little for modern music, reported mainly his bewilderment to Langston.) When Hughes tried to warn him about the theater and about the difficulty of finding a publisher for material concerning miscegenation, the composer exploded: "We _must_ do efficient and urgent work. We've got *something,* a big something. No timidity or hesitation, is allowed!!"

Langston escaped to Cleveland for a lecture at the Public Library. Then, on Thanksgiving Day, at the Hotel Stevens in Chicago, he delivered the keynote address before three thousand delegates attending the first postwar convention of the American Education Fellowship, the leading progressive teachers' association in the country. Although Langston spoke optimistically about the flexibility and strength of American democracy in dealing with its problems, his appearance was attacked on November 28 in a New York *Journal-American* front page story (''Leftist Poet Opens Education Parley''), which identified him as a Communist Party member. Soon after, he was attacked again by a popular radio commentator, Henry J. Taylor, on his Mutual Network show sponsored by General Motors. Another attack, by an even more powerful personality, did not come to light until later. Invited to speak before a conference of Methodist ministers in Evanston, Illinois, but unable to attend himself, J. Edgar Hoover, the director of the F.B.I., had sent an emissary to deliver a speech entitled ''Secularism—Breeder of Crime.'' In it, Hoover quoted ''Goodbye Christ'' in its entirety, in order to expose ''the blasphemous utterances of one who sought public office on the ticket of the Communist Party.''

A major offensive was under way against Langston and his right to speak. In November, 1945, two years before, the FBI had removed him from the New York ''Key Figures'' list because ''his Communist activities'' were not important enough to keep him there. However, after a call from U.S. Senator Joseph H. Ball of Minnesota for information about Hughes, Hoover requested from his agents a summary report of information ''of a legally admissible character as will tend to prove, directly or circumstantially, membership in or affiliation with the Communist Party.'' This report, a farrago of newspaper stories, misinformation about Langston's alleged marriage and party membership, and the text of ''Goodbye Christ,'' was submitted in June, 1947. It formed the basis of Hoover's epistle to the Methodists. In addition, Hoover received from Senator Ball certain handbills about Hughes that had been disseminated by the right-wing Gerald L. K. Smith organization.

Ignorant of Hoover's attack, Langston took a special pleasure in the holiday season. His income that year had totalled almost $20,000. He and Elmer Rice had reached a compromise on their disagreement and repaired their friendship. On January 15 in Montreal, he confidently opened a new season of lectures, arranged by Colston Leigh. According to the plan, some forty engagements would take him out to the Pacific by the end of spring. Within days, however, he was thrown on the defensive. In a broadcast repeatedly mentioned in black newspapers, the well-known radio commentator Fulton Lewis, Jr., attacked him for ''Goodbye Christ.'' At every stop, Hughes faced the old charges. ''I am not a member of the Communist Party and do not advocate Communism here,'' he assured an audience in Sayville, Long Island; he admired only the Soviet Union's treatment of its sixty million nonwhite citizens; as for black civil rights—if Poles deserved to vote in Poland, as the United States constantly trumpeted to the Soviet Union, why shouldn't black Americans vote in America? ''I am a writer,'' he insisted in Florida, ''subject to no political discipline.'' He had never written for the *Daily Worker,* nor belonged to over eighty front organizations. He was not dangerous. "If I were a loud speaking gentleman—like Adam Powell—delivering some world-shaking message," he reasoned, "or a politician running for office, it would throw a different light on the matter. But all this worriation over a poet!"

For a while, Langston craftily expected to turn the latest round of attacks to his advantage. "Publicity is what has made me what I am today!" he admitted breezily to a friend. In this instance, however, he had underestimated his opposition. As his lectures in Illinois, Indiana, and Ohio drew near, various people and groups there, including an Urban League sponsor and an American Legion opponent, appealed to the FBI for information on his politics. Almost always, Hoover invoked the rule of Bureau confidentiality, but he sent the Urban League several documents, including the pamphlets "How to Fight Communism" and "Red Fascism," and his own anti-Hughes speech, "Secularism—Breeder of Crime." Hoover also mentioned that FBI files contained "several references reflecting Hughes to be a Communist." When a local minister protested that the director was smearing Hughes's name while declining to give facts, Hoover hotly denied the accusation but refused to elaborate on his knowledge of Hughes. When an agent informed Hoover that violence might erupt if Hughes spoke, he was instructed to inform the local police, but to be careful not to suggest that the meeting be prevented. Hoover clearly was attempting to damage Hughes by spreading information, much of it false, which had been obtained ineptly by a bureau whose main business was investigation.

Opposition to Hughes seemed to spread in a concerted way, with Akron, Ohio, and Springfield and Winnetka, Illinois, apparently chosen for a protracted showdown between March 10 and 12. A seemingly unified campaign by the Gerald L. K. Smith group, the American Legion, and the Knights of Columbus attempted to block his appearances (a similar alliance had sparked an attack on Paul Robeson in Peoria the previous year). Racism became a distinct feature of the opposition's campaign: the Smith forces issued a graphic circular bearing the text of "Goodbye Christ" and a picture of Langston Hughes—"one of the most notorious propagandists for the lovers of Stalin," and a frequenter of upper-class white circles, "mongrelizers and race mixers." On March 8, the commentator Henry J. Taylor again inveighed against Hughes, and read from his poem "Good Morning Revolution."

Under heavy attack, the Springfield lecture committee, including the NAACP, the Urban League, the YWCA, the Council of Churches, and the Vachel Lindsay Association (led by Olive Lindsay Wakefield) decided that it had no choice but to cancel the talk. That the real issue was white supremacy and black subordination was clear to many people. "It is definitely a race war," Olive Wakefield wrote to a friend, "and there are too many people in Springfield who would just love to have an excuse for a mob attack on any Negro to risk giving them an excuse." Hughes, in turn, tried to bolster the morale of his few vocal supporters in these areas. "It is heart-warming to know," he wrote Wakefield, "that I have real friends in your city, and that faith and understanding are bigger than bigotry. I have never doubted that and I believe, like your dear brother, in the basic goodness that will eventually make our America the land we dream about in our hearts.''

Although he stressed the need to ''stand up for the traditional American right of freedom of speech and press—if we want any of that right to be left to us at all,'' other groups also found the pressure too intense. ''Red-Tinged Poet To Speak at Winnetka Private School,'' the powerful Chicago *Tribune* announced on its front page on March 1. Mortified and humiliated, as he admitted to Langston, the longtime headmaster of the exclusive North Shore Country Day School cancelled his talk. At Kankakee, Illinois, an interracial committee led by two women, one black, the other white, trying to raise funds for a community center for ostracized young blacks by selling tickets to a benefit reading, was denied a hall. As punishment for backing Langston's right to speak, the Urban League in Akron lost the support of the Community Chest. Various booksellers were forced to take his books off the shelves. The Akron *Beacon Journal,* denouncing him as ''really an agent of a foreign power because of his pro-Communist writings,'' opposed his right to speak. Too late, the newspaper altered its position, and backed freedom of speech. After Langston arrived in Akron, every hall was denied him, including the Jewish Community Center, the black Mt. Olive Baptist Church, and the local CIO union hall.

Resistance to right-wing groups by the Social Workers Club and by a Methodist group in Detroit cheered him. And in Salt Lake City, Utah, when he was barred by the Hotel Utah, its objection was at least old-fashioned; according to the management, the only socially acceptable blacks were Paul Robeson and Marian Anderson. In Arizona and southern California, most of his engagements were allowed to take place, but conservative opposition forced a cancellation at the state university in Tempe, Arizona, and at Occidental College in Los Angeles.

On April 1, as if in keeping with a plan, he was denounced on the floor of the U.S. Senate by Albert W. Hawkes of New Jersey. In a church in Montclair, New Jersey, the senator complained, ''I was amazed to see a Communist [Langston Hughes] stand up in the pulpit and to hear him, without ever making a reference to the life of Christ or to the fact that we have a Bible, berate the United States, tear it down for 55 minutes, and eulogize Russia.'' Hawkes then entered into the Senate record the texts of ''One More 'S' in the U.S.A'' and ''Goodbye Christ.'' When the news reached Langston, he was furious. The senator, he informed the black educator Horace Mann Bond, was ''an unmitigated liar'' and a ''dope.'' But opposition to him stiffened. In Vallejo, a community near San Francisco dominated by the navy and openly racist, the few local liberals put up no fight at all, and Langston was barred. On the other hand, when the Palo Alto High School denied him space for a reading, members of the local chapter of the Council for Civic Unity (a liberal organization drawn into the controversy in several places) condemned it as ''a direct attack on the Negro people and the organizations which support their civil rights.'' After a threat of legal action, the ban was lifted and Hughes spoke at the school on April 21. In Oakland, however, an intimidated black minister would not budge on his decision to deny Hughes the use of his church.

To a reporter in Palo Alto, the ever smiling, ever gracious Langston Hughes appeared untouched by the controversies, "a twinkling, goodhumored man in his early forties" (he was forty-six). Nevertheless, the ordeal had left its mark. Sipping tea at Hollow Hills Farm, with Noël Sullivan's dachshunds spread sympathetically at his feet, he seemed to another reporter "a very bewildered man at the moment . . . puzzled, embarrassed and worried over having become a 'cause célèbre'." "I'm the same man I have always been," Langston pleaded, "and my lectures are very much the same—really very mild—all about how poetry is made from the experiences of life." He refused, however, to be silent about what he saw as anti-Soviet hysteria: "If the elderly radio commentators, middle-aged thinking newspaper editors, antiquated politicians, and gray-haired generals who are now calling so loudly for war" actually had to fight, they would speak much more softly. Nor was he silent about the racism underlying his opposition: "I don't think it is I or my poems that are the target, but these groups working for civic unity." In any case, he was really harmless. "Certainly I have no especially timely or world-shaking message that needs to be presented—only the same simple poems I have been reading for years."

Although many admirers, such as Noël Sullivan, who offered to build a permanent refuge for him and the Harpers at Hollow Hills, rallied to his side, some gestures misfired. Roger Baldwin of the American Civil Liberties Union, sending Langston a copy of "Goodbye Christ," offered a curious vote of confidence: "I am sure you could not have done it." The Tuskegee-based *Negro Year Book* exasperatingly lauded him, along with A. Philip Randolph, Richard Wright, and Angelo Herndon, for having given up his membership in the Communist Party. A more humorous, if macabre, note was struck on April 9 at the Los Angeles Philharmonic Hall when he attended a lecture by Arthur Koestler, his travelling companion in Soviet Central Asia in 1932 and now a strident anti-communist. With a tremor in his voice, Koestler suddenly alluded to Langston Hughes, "that great Negro poet whom I met in Soviet Asia, a Party member as I was then, but who is now dead." Easing himself backstage after the lecture, Langston laughed loud and long when Koestler's mouth dropped open in disbelief (Koestler rushed to alert newspapers and wire services about his twin errors). Over drinks in Beverly Hills, Koestler told dark tales of villainous Soviet officials. Did Langston know they had put mercury pellets in Maxim Gorky's coffee?

"My LAST engagement—Thank God A-Mighty!" Langston wrote home to Toy Harper after a reading on May 16 at a Methodist church in San Francisco. He withdrew at once to New York.

In fact, against his best efforts, he had been driven from the field. In the *Defender* he had been defiant: "Gerald L. K. Smith, the Klan and others who think like them, evidently want me to retire from the American lecture platform—but they have another want coming." He had continued to attack racism and aspects of foreign policy he saw as ludicrous—such as government leaders giving away billions of dollars to foreign countries, including those of Eastern Europe, in defense of freedom, while saying and doing nothing about injustice against blacks at home. However, noting that no new requests had come for his services, the Colston Leigh lecture agency suggested strongly that Langston should take at least a year off from lecturing. He conceded defeat. "Certainly I agree with you about next season," he answered. "I would not mind staying put for a year or two."

To secure another source of income, he met in Chicago with Warren Seyfert, the head of the much admired Laboratory School of the University of Chicago. Dining at Seyfert's home the previous Thanksgiving, Hughes had so charmed Seyfert's three young daughters that their father proposed a visiting appointment for him as an instructor. Langston accepted the invitation for early in the following year, 1949. Also in Chicago he delivered a brief speech on "Human Relations in the Twentieth Century" at the ceremonial farewell dinner for past and present fellows and staff of the Julius Rosenwald Fund, which had twice awarded him fellowships, and which was liquidating itself according to its plan after twenty-five years of work.

Over the gathering was a pall of sadness. At fifty-eight, Claude McKay had just died in Chicago. Later, in New York, a funeral mass at the Church of the Resurrection on West 151st Street marked the passing of one of the finest black writers of his age, and the principal influence among blacks on Langston as a young writer. The one-time radical had died in the arms of the Roman Catholic Church. Illness, poverty, and isolation had driven him there. McKay had even died without ever meeting his own daughter, Hope, whom Langston had encountered in Jamaica.

Of the triumvirate who had once planned a joint commemorative collection of verse, two were now dead. If Langston reflected on this unfortunate fact, his return to New York on the weekend of June 12, 1948, was nevertheless joyful and momentous. On December 23 the previous year, Emerson Harper had purchased a house at 20 East 127th Street in Harlem. Evidently Emerson Harper had been mainly a front for Langston Hughes, whose name almost certainly would have pushed up the price, but whose *Street Scene* income must have made the deal possible. (The piece of property apparently cost $12,500, with a mortgage of $5,800 carried by the sellers.) Three days later, the deed was conveyed into joint ownership by the two men. A few months later, Toy Harper legally joined the ownership of the property.

Firmly resisting one effort by Mrs. Harper to convince him to take a place further north, near 150th Street on genteel Sugar Hill, Langston had insisted on a place flush in black Harlem. At last they had found a brownstone rowhouse, between Fifth and Madison Avenue, only three blocks from the heart of Harlem at Lenox Avenue and 125th Street. Designed by the architect Alexander Wilson, and constructed in 1869 as part of the post-Civil War building boom in the district by two real estate developers James Meagher and Thomas Hanson, the rowhouse eventually had passed into the hands of a couple, Eino and Alina Lehto, among the last survivors of what had once been a thriving

Finnish community in this section of Manhattan. On a nearby corner was a Finnish settlement house, but the neighborhood would soon be all black.

In the last week of July, 1948, after a few last days at 634 St. Nicholas Avenue and his studio, which would not be needed anymore, Langston moved into the house at 20 East 127th Street. Six months past his forty-sixth birthday, he was finally living in his own home. He would stay there for the rest of his life.

7

ON SOLID GROUND
1948 to 1950

. . . Too many years
Climbing up the hill—
About out of breath,
I got my fill.

I'm gonna plant my feet
On solid ground
If you want to see me,
Buddy, *come down!*
"Down Where I Am," 1949

"I WOULD RATHER have a kitchenette in Harlem," Langston insisted with feeling, "than a mansion in Westchester." In the summer of 1948, his days of studios, of borrowed beds and shared rooms, ended once and for all as he joined Toy and Emerson Harper at 20 East 127th Street—"Aunt Toy's house," as he discreetly told one and all. In the preceding weeks, the indefatigable Mrs. Harper had transformed the old property by supervising the painting and repapering of its aging walls, and freshly resodding the yard—"there is even a beautiful lawn in the back garden under tall trees," Langston wrote a friend, "cool and restful, sort of like some of the gardens in Greenwich Village."

Since she intended to make the property pay for itself by housing roomers, Mrs. Harper had allocated the space precisely. At street level, in the "English" basement (there was also a "sub-basement") was their living room, complete with a piano; the kitchen and a spacious dining area were on that floor. On the level above, reached also by a flight of steps from the street, she had set up a bedroom for herself and Emerson. Up another flight was a nondescript suite of rooms. Then, on the third floor above the "English" basement, where bright windows faced the tops of the cool, green trees, was Langston's two-room suite: Jesse B. Semple's own "third floor rear." Here, at last, Langston had ample space for his growing library of books, his manuscripts, clippings, photographs, memorabilia, and correspondence, and work tables for himself and his helpers.

Langston had no particular interest in elegance, but Mrs. Harper knew exactly how they should live. Since no one had money to support the grasping furniture retailers on 125th Street, the new owners made do with what they had, with Langston leaving virtually all decisions about decor in the hands of Mrs. Harper. Eventually, a living room of excellent, if antiquated, neo-Victorian furnishings, most of which had done veteran duty at 634 St. Nicholas Avenue, welcomed guests. A large formal mirror and an elegant fireplace, in addition to pieces of original art, heavy velvet draperies, an overstuffed sofa, a thick, soft carpet, and a baby grand piano, created a striking impression. The rest of the house was pleasantly but cheaply furnished. Framed photographs, mainly from Langston's and Emerson's varied careers, added a splash of glamour to the walls. Above all, the house was neat and clean, because Mrs. Harper resented clutter and abhorred dirt. "She was almost fanatical about cleanliness," one person later judged "She stayed up late into the night taking care of the house; she was relentless about washing floors and walls. The furnishing may have been shabby in places, but the house was clean and neat."

Less ostentatiously, in his two rooms on the third floor facing the trees, Langston also insisted on order. Visitors who climbed the flights of stairs to his study expecting to encounter some sort of poetic chaos were often startled to find instead a casual neatness. Books and papers were abundant, but each piece more or less knew its place. Comfort was secondary to efficiency; Langston's only major addition to the floor was a shower installed the following year. The suite showed few signs of the presence of women; his world was wide, but his bed was narrow. "Langston's suite was pleasant, but it was more a place to work than to live," one secretary later recalled. "It was, above all, a kind of business office, where he earned his livelihood. And he had a good head for details and for management; in some ways, he was definitely his father's son. What he did not keep track of, he often did not *want* to keep track of. Whatever anyone else thought, he was definitely in control of the way he lived."

By the fall, the first roomers—all as intensely respectable as Mrs. Harper could find—were installed at 20 East 127th Street. The photographer Griffith J. Davis, one of Langston's former students at Atlanta University, now enrolled in the journalism program at Columbia University (at Hughes's suggestion), shared a room on the third floor with John Howard, an art professor from Arkansas State A. and M. who was taking a degree at New York University. On the first floor, behind the Harpers' bedroom, two rooms were occupied separately by a bachelor in his thirties and a young woman who was learning the embalming business. On the floor above were an older single woman and a married couple. The husband drove a city bus and was an avid ham radio operator. "No children lived in the house," Griffith Davis remembered (none ever lived at 20 East 127th Street in Hughes's twenty years there). Every room was taken, but under Mrs. Harper's firm control "there was not much confusion. Everybody in the house knew each other. There was a family atmosphere. Sometimes on special occasions Aunt Toy would have us down in the basement, usually the large kitchen, for a drink usually—not much food."

The tendencies into which Langston had slipped over the years settled now into certain enduring patterns of life. Usually his day began around noon. Then, after much hacking and coughing brought on by over a decade of chain-smoking pungent cigarettes such as Camels and Lucky Strikes, Langston pushed open the heavy velvet curtains to let in the light, took his first cup of coffee, showered and shaved, and settled down to a generous breakfast of whatever Aunt Toy chose to offer. Even as he shaved, he listened as his secretary Nate White read portions of the morning mail. He reached out, in dressing for a day at home, for more or less whatever was at hand, with a blind eye to fineness of material or fashion. When he stepped out, on the other hand, he showed quiet good taste. Throughout the afternoon, if he had no appointment downtown, he worked on his correspondence, met with visitors who had survived Mrs. Harper's inquisition at the front door, or kept his appointments outside the house. "Langston generally hit the streets late," according to Griffith Davis, "—after 10 or 11 p.m. We were all asleep when he came in after the bars closed around 1 or 2 a.m." At last, when the old house was quiet and Harlem itself relatively subdued, he finally settled down to write. Working steadily until just after dawn, he ended his day by going out for the morning newspapers. Then, as the rest of Harlem struggled to rise, he took to his bed.

Increasingly, the narrowness of his bed—his enduring bachelorhood—intrigued some people. More than a few women saw in him a perfectly fine prospective husband going to waste. "Dear Mr. Hughes," one lady wrote from New Jersey, "I seen your picture in the Ebony magazine if you want a wife I am for you. You are not getting any younger and I am not to. so why not take me for your love?" Langston set her down, but gently. "Thank you so much for your nice note," he answered nine months later. "I know that by now you have found somebody . . . who suits you just fine." He himself had found the life that suited him just fine, a home where he was not only admired for his books but adored as a son, and fiercely so by Mrs. Harper.

"Toy was like a tigress with a cub as far as Langston was concerned," one friend recalled. "You could say absolutely nothing critical of him. She always wanted him as a son and once she had him she did not intend to lose him." Butler Henderson, a Morehouse graduate who had known Langston and the Harpers since coming to study at New York University around 1945, remembered Toy as loving but dominant. "Once we were at the table having a meal when a ball sailed over the wall and landed on the grass. Some kids were playing in the next yard. Langston immediately jumped up to return it. 'Sit down, Langston,' Toy said. 'Sit down!' He sat down. Of course, as soon as he got a chance, he went after that ball. Mrs. Harper was about the *bossiest* person you would want to know, and he was like a child around her. But there was love there. I remember that Langston always said grace, and he always ended by saying, 'Bless the precious hand that prepared this food.' He meant it."

Not so fiercely but perhaps as well, Emerson Harper also loved Langston. Long subjugated by his wife, in their home he was sweet and complacent, even passive. Since she had forbidden him to play his woodwinds in the house, he kept up with his music mainly by playing the piano. Its notes became familiar to children who played on the street outside. "Emerson was full of fun, great fun," according to Henderson, "and he was a real student of music, not just a performer. They were all very good people."

By this time, marriage was a dead issue for Langston. In some notes for a long profile by Arna Bontemps in *Ebony* magazine, he tossed off the bare facts of his connubial history, such as it was: "Never married, but once reported engaged to Elsie Roxborough in public press"—Elsie Roxborough from Detroit, who had tried to pass for white and then apparently had killed herself in despair. Now and then Langston stepped out with single women, but he did not try to mislead them about his intentions. On the other hand, he gave his acquaintances no reason, other than his increasing age and relentless bachelorhood, to suppose that he was homosexual. Undoubtedly some people, like his young friend from Atlanta, Harry Murphy, who also visited Hughes in New York, wondered about him. "He was certainly very friendly with the ladies I would see in his presence," Murphy recalled later, "but I never saw any gesture by him even remotely sensual toward any of them. And yet I never detected anything on his part that could be construed as indicative of homosexuality, either. I concluded that Lang was either a person who screened from view his personal relationships or, for whatever reason, had simply excluded from his being that part of life." Openly gay, Bruce Nugent remembered sitting in a particular bar in Harlem favored by homosexuals. One day, Langston passed by when the front door was open. Nugent invited him in; he laughed but only peered inside. "He was definitely curious about what might have been going on," Nugent declared. "But that kind of curiousness is more a sign of a basic lack of real interest than of anything else. In any event, I never saw him inside."

One pretty young woman who had known Langston since about 1938, first as a part-time secretary, then as a close friend into the early forties, and who went out from time to time with him to parties and other functions, was firm about one aspect of his sexuality: "Langston may have been bisexual, but I'm willing to take an oath of God that he was not homosexual. I knew other women who had gone out with him and they could not have been deluded, since they were—most of them—healthy, intelligent people."

Obviously he now wanted not so much his freedom as the sweet, familial confinement that life with the Harpers brought. Highly conventional in many ways, Toy Harper allowed her roomers little or no latitude where the honor of the house was concerned, as she conceived it. One night, years later, she watched unseen as a virile young roomer known only as Mr. Poole tried to smuggle a young woman upstairs on his back. When he reached the top of the stairs, she spoke up: "Mr. Poole, I see that you got her up there on your back. Now bring her down the same way, if you please!" Langston had his run of the house, but Mrs. Harper was his mother and he played the role for which he had pined throughout his youth—that of the loving, dutiful son in a complete family. He surrendered to the purer pleasures of home, which definitely included fun. To show off the house, he planned its first party—a gala summer affair held in honor of the Texas poet Melvin Tolson. Tolson himself failed to show up, but the guests devoured the rattlesnake meat impishly ordered as a tribute to Texas by Hughes. A dog arrived—a wire-haired terrier—as a gift to Langston from Aunt Toy, to round out the domestic scene. Unfortunately, the animal had been owned and trained by whites. One day, after two or three weeks padding nervously among the blacks, it espied an open door. "The little hound lit out," Langston reported not altogether unsympathetically, "turned the corner at a thousand miles an hour, headed straight downtown, and was heard to bark as he crossed 110th Street, 'No More Niggers!' "

Later in the year, as befitting a settled man of property, Langston made a will—his first since 1937, just before leaving for the Spanish Civil War. If they survived him, the Harpers would receive income from his estate as long as they lived. Whether or not he was still employed by Hughes, his excellent secretary, Nate White, would receive a bequest of $2,500. (*One-Way Ticket*, his new collection of poems expected shortly from Knopf, was dedicated to White and his wife Geraldine.) Provision was made for a trust fund to take care of the educational expenses of Gwyn "Kit" Clark's children. Yale University would receive the rest of his papers for the James Weldon Johnson Collection. His ultimate legatee, however, would be his alma mater, Lincoln University. Maxim Lieber was to serve as his literary executor, the lawyer Arthur Spingarn as his general executor.

He attempted to help Gwyn Clark's children, but Gwyn himself was almost past help. Over the years, Gwyn had gone from bad to worse. The previous year he had entered Bellevue Hospital in Manhattan; "I needed treatments for alcoholism," he explained. Having fallen asleep while smoking, he had set his mattress on fire and narrowly escaped death. When Gwyn's bouts of alcoholism prevented him from working, or attending embalming school—his latest venture in education—Langston sent gifts of money. He got little in return. "Kit was often drunk and very ugly in those days," Nate White recalled. "He would work himself up into horrible rages, and reproach and abuse Langston in the worst kind of language. I had no idea what he was reproaching him for, except maybe for being a success when Kit was a total failure. But Langston just took it all, quietly, without ever protesting. And, no matter what Kit said or did, he did not stop sending money. I guess he was being loyal."

In this first summer at 20 East 127th Street, little could dull Langston's enjoyment of his new home; as casually as he presented himself to the world, he was deeply satisfied with what he had accomplished with his life, where others had allowed themselves to fail.

> . . . You may see me holler,
> You may see me cry—

But I'll be dogged, sweet baby,
If you gonna see me die.

Life is fine.
Fine as wine!
Life is fine!

And yet, with his hyperactive conscience and his uncompromising love of the black masses, he could not be totally contented with a merely personal victory. While his own dream of solid, professional success and a home had apparently come true, the hopes that had brought black folk north by the millions remained either largely unrealized or so tainted by racism, poverty, crime, and vice that the dream had turned bitter for many. Their plight haunted him.

Just as he had pioneered the literary appropriation of the blues and jazz in the twenties, so now, in the new transformations of serious black music—to which Langston listened in the bars and jazz joints as no other black writer listened—he heard the unmistakable sounds of cultural change. Nowhere was this change more apparent or portentous than in the "be-bop" jazz developed in the previous decade by musicians such as Dizzy Gillespie, Charlie Christian, Thelonius Monk, and Kenny Clarke, and especially at Minton's Playhouse on West 118th Street in Harlem. A new musical idiom, tortured in comparison to past harmonies, with faster harmonic and rhythmic changes then ever before, now rebuffed the sweetened, whitened strains of swing—the dominant popular music of the war years—and epitomized the new fragmentation of black cultural consciousness. Traditional lyrics had been replaced most spectacularly by a language of sound often without apparent sense, or "nonsense." In this new style Hughes saw the growing fissures in Afro-American culture, the myth of integration and American social harmony jarred by a message of deep discord. Out of his return to Harlem late in 1941, after almost two years in California, had come the birth of a new kind of black hero, Jesse B. Semple. Now, six years later, Langston felt again the depth of his emotional dependency on the black masses, as well as his painful detachment from them both as an artist endowed with second sight and, suddenly, as a bourgeois property owner. Once again, the result was a surge of art.

On September 14, he exultantly announced his breakthrough. "I have completed a new book I wrote last week!" he informed Arna Bontemps. "No kidding—a full book-length poem in five sections called *Montage of a Dream Deferred*. Want to see it? . . . The new poem," he added in an excited postscript, "is what you might call a precedent shattering opus—also could be known as a *tour de force*." In quick succession one poem had expanded into a suite of verse on Harlem, then divided itself into five parts (later six), each designed to be autonomous, all intended however to form a diverse unity. Believing that the crucial medium of the twentieth century was probably the montage (the composite, swiftly changing picture) or the collage (the inspired arrangement of still fragments), he sought to catch in verse the variety of Harlem life. The idea for the new book probably came during the composition of *One-Way Ticket,* one section of which is called simply "Montage."

From the start of his career, the dream had been perhaps the central motif of his poetry. In his grandest artistic guise, when he assumed the mantle of poet of his people, Langston Hughes was the Dream Keeper, who urged others to "Hold fast to dreams"; "I Dream a World," an aria from *Troubled Island,* had become the amen-piece at his lectures and readings. Now, ironically, the personal realization of his dream of owning a home apparently triggered in him a heightened sense of the futility of Harlem dreams—not completely futile, perhaps, but delayed so persistently that it amounted to a denial. In the music of the jazz musicians revolting against the dishonor of swing he heard both resignation and rage, despair and defiance, and the faint persistence of the dream.

So, in his new book of poems, the dominant image or idea became the dream deferred. Isolated vignettes of Harlem life, discrete and sometimes clashing fragments of the culture, were unified thematically by the notion of the dream denied; and unified technically, in Hughes's art, by a centripetal appeal to the rhythms of the new, "be-bop" jazz.

> Good morning daddy!
> Ain't you heard
> The boogie-woogie rumble
> Of a dream deferred?
>
> Listen closely:
> You'll hear their feet
> Beating out and beating out a—
>
> *You think*
> *It's a happy beat?*
>
> Listen to it closely:
> Ain't you heard
> something underneath
> like a—
>
> *What did I say?*
>
> Sure,
> I'm happy!
> Take it away!
>
> *Hey, pop!*
> *Re-bop!*
> *Mop!*
>
> *Y-e-a-h!*

At varying, unpredictable times witty, sardonic, ironic, expository, whimsical, documentary, and tragic, "Montage of a Dream Deferred" is an expansive poetic statement on the fate of blacks in the modern, urban world. The manuscript was Hughes's answer in 1948 to the overwhelming question of the day in Harlem and communities like it, and possibly, prophetically, of the Afro-American future: "What happens to a dream deferred? / Does it dry up / like a raisin in the sun?" "This poem on contemporary Harlem," Langston wrote as a preface, "is marked by conflicting changes, sudden nuances, sharp and impudent interjections, broken rhythms, and passages sometimes in the manner of the jam session, sometimes the popular song, punctuated by the riffs, runs, breaks, and disc-tortions of the music of a community in transition." The poet's love for the community is paramount, but his brooding intelligence is such that the wooden phrase "community in transition" is really portentous. In the *Defender*, Simple soon spoke eloquently to his obtuse friend on the meaning of "be bop" music. "That is where Bop comes from," Simple explains—"out of them dark days we have seen. That is why Be-bop is so mad, wild, frantic, crazy. And not to be dug unless you have seen dark days, too. That's why folks who ain't suffered much cannot play Bop, and do not understaind it. They think it's nonsense—like you. They think it's just crazy crazy. They do not know it is also MAD crazy, SAD crazy, FRANTIC WILD CRAZY—beat right out of some bloody black head! That's what Bop is. These young kids who play it best, they know."

Langston's excitement about *Montage of a Dream Deferred* was matched at once by that of his oldest friends. "With mounting excitement and interest," Carl Van Vechten raced through the manuscript. To Arna Bontemps, it was "super—perhaps your strongest, most sustained creative expression in a long, long time." At a Fisk University party, the artist Aaron Douglas, who had come to Harlem in 1924, recited parts of the manuscript and mistily compared it to "a re-flowering of the Renaissance. Like the silver tree, the shining rivers, the sobbing jazz band, the long-headed dancers and the shameless gals"—all emblems from the poetry of Langston's and his own thrilling youth.

With *One-Way Ticket*, his latest collection, about to appear from Knopf, Langston made no attempt to offer the new manuscript to his publisher. Instead, he moved to develop it on his own. He sent a copy to the artist Jacob Lawrence, who, at Langston's expense, had provided drawings for *One-Way Ticket* after Knopf had refused to pay $600 for them. Another copy went to the black composer Howard Swanson, a possible collaborator. Hughes also envisioned a ballet libretto and a recording of spoken verse based on "Montage." Not everyone, however, shared his enthusiasm for this ode to Harlem. Five magazines, including *Esquire* and *Mademoiselle,* rejected a suite of the be-bop poems.

If "Montage of a Dream Deferred" was a gratifying triumph of the spirit, Langston looked elsewhere for a financial return on the scale of *Street Scene*. For a while, his prospects seemed bright. In June, he had barely unpacked his bags after his major tour when the National Broadcasting Company, in an emergency, hired him to rewrite an expensive black variety show called "Modern Minstrels," intended for that summer. On August 7, three different inquiries came about his availability as a librettist on musicals. Certainly he was available. However, he insisted on a business arrangement, including some sort of advance. As the librettist of a landmark show in the American musical tradition, according to the best critics, Hughes believed he was entitled to nothing less. He was again firm on this point when John Houseman, who had worked brilliantly as a producer in the Federal Theatre Project in Harlem in the 1930s, and with Orson Welles in the Broadway version of *Native Son* in 1941, asked about making a musical play of *Masters of the Dew*. The various inquiries led nowhere.

With NBC, money was not a problem. Protests against the minstrel format, led by Walter White of the NAACP, the self-appointed and vigilant censor of the image of blacks in the American arts, had almost forced the network to cancel the show. For a fat fee, Langston stepped in to lift its tone—although, with blacks involved, NBC did not want it lifted too high. He was prepared to cooperate. "Looks kinder hopeless," he confessed to Bontemps about the show, which was "now at the usual nobody-knows-what-they-want stage. All I want is my CASH which Ah intends to git. They're not doing anything with the racial taboos surrounding either Hollywood or the radio." The talent included the bandleader Lucius "Lucky" Millinder, the humorist Jackie "Moms" Mabley, the King Odum Quartet, Ella Fitzgerald, her husband the bassist Ray Brown, W. C. Handy, Count Basie, and Billie Holiday. Abandoning minstrelsy, Langston organized instead "Swing Time at the Savoy" ("Home of happy feet! / Harlem's Hall of Joy"); both Millinder and Fitzgerald had starred at Sigmund Gale's Savoy Ballroom early in their careers. The series, which was broadcast on five consecutive Wednesday evenings, was quite successful. However, it did not lead to other major assignments. The Columbia Broadcasting System hired him to help write an Emancipation Day program, for which he and another writer, Arnold Perl, each received $250. For black writers—even those as well known as Hughes—the doors to the radio networks were as tightly guarded as ever.

If there was no shortage of work for him on various books, inevitably the pay was shabby or worse, to his increasing disappointment. One such venture was with the publishing firm of Anderson and Ritchie, which offered to publish an illustrated edition of "Cuba Libre," Langston's translation, with the Howard University professor Ben Frederic Carruthers, of a selection of poetry by Nicolás Guillén. Impressed by the young Cuban, Langston had started translating his work almost from their first meeting in 1930 in Havana. Around 1944, he had begun discussions with Carruthers, a professor of Spanish who had also visited Cuba, and who had translated some of Guillén's verse, about a book of their translations. According to Carruthers, "there were many which I had finished which Langston thought good enough to stand as they were and many others which Langston had completed without my having touched them. We collaborated completely on the final editing and polishing and Langston secured the publisher and the artist, Gar Gilbert." The size of the proposed edition—five hundred copies—discouraged Langston. The venture would be "a labor of art and love," he judged. But he was eager to honor Guillén, and accepted the terms. The fifty poems came from Guillén's early books—*Motivos de Son* (1930), his breakthrough into Afro-Cuban language and rhythms, largely inspired by Langston's visit to Havana that year; *Sóngoro Cosongo* (1931); and *Sones para turistas y cantos para soldados* (1937).

Meanwhile, his Simple manuscript was compiling the worst record of any major manuscript in his career. White publishers seemed impervious to the charms that had captured readers of the Chicago *Defender,* and black publishers were impotent. "We ought to be smart and make use of this material before other people use it all up for nothing," Langston prodded the *Defender* after hearing reports that certain nightclub comedians were pirating the Simple sketches in their routines. Nothing came of his prodding. Later in the fall, after yet another editor stalled, then suggested that he turn the book into a novel, Langston practically snapped at Maxim Lieber: "My temperament at this moment will not permit me to make it into a novel. I am more inclined to making it into a radio program which I think it will become—that is, if radio can grow up enough to take a little controversial comedy."

Another manuscript that demanded his attention that summer was his anthology with Arna Bontemps, *The Poetry of the Negro.* Langston's share of the advance had long since been spent when he wailed out a complaint: "I DO NOT BELIEVE THIS HERE ANTHOLOGY WILL EVER END." The anthology would survey not only black American poetry from its beginnings but also poetry by whites about blacks and by blacks outside the United States, notably in the Caribbean. Securing biographical notes and formal permissions proved to be a monumental task in itself. Most annoying was the attitude of various color-conscious West Indians, "whom one drop of white blood makes white," Hughes noted tartly, "and not the other way around as it is here." Afraid of being mistaken for a Negro, Frank Collymore of Barbados, the editor of *Bim* magazine, first refused to have his work included, then relented. Louis Simpson, a U.S. citizen apparently done with his place of birth, Jamaica, and wary of racial themes, worried in a letter to Langston that the book would be, "in short, exclusive." An English-born Jamaican woman, Lettice King, agreed to be included, then wrote the Jamaican *Gleaner,* as Langston jibed, "setting forth very clearly that she is not cullud!" Then she changed her mind again. When other West Indians protested directly to Doubleday that they were not Negroes, Hughes testily suggested to Bontemps that they be notified that "neither are we and that we are using plenty of white folks in the book!"

Not all the West Indians were difficult. It was "thrilling to receive mail from you," one Trinidadian poet wrote Langston. "You have inspired me without knowing it." White Americans gave no trouble at all. Deferentially approached by Hughes ("you are my favorite American contemporary poet"), Carl Sandburg approved changing the word "nigger" in a poem in order not to hurt sales to schools. "Your letter," he wrote Hughes, who had apologized as a poet for making the request, "shows that there can be complete understanding between two former spitoon polishers."

Nevertheless, anthologies must have seemed a good way of making quick money, since Langston agreed to another collaboration proposed by Arna Bontemps. In October, they drafted an outline called "So This Is Harlem." Unfortunately, both Doubleday and John Farrar of Farrar and Straus, whose firm published a series of books on individual American states and cities, yawned in response. Then Hughes and Bontemps decided to attempt an anthology of comic Negro verse. The first draft had Maxim Lieber "flabbergasted and amazed at the richness and extent of this material," Langston reported, and guffawing mightily. However, no publisher smiled approval. Another project was abandoned.

As the fall deepened, his income fell off alarmingly. For his various projects he needed extensive secretarial help, and about this time employed (in addition to Nate White) Butler Henderson of Morehouse College and New York University, who was a roomer at 20 East 127th Street, and Hugh Smythe, an Atlanta University graduate (and later U.S. Ambassador to Syria). But Langston had trouble paying his help. "We are all so broke here," he lamented, "it is a cullud shame. I am looking diligently for my two War Bonds that I hid from myself so they could mature. But almost nothing matures in Harlem soil. (And if I find these they will never mature in my hands.)" His income for the year would be about $13,000—a superb figure, but most of it was earned before September. To retain his contractual interest in the movie rights to *Street Scene,* which Hollywood had once found so appealing, Langston needed to pay $300 before Christmas. He tossed off a children's story, "A Dog and Cat Tale," but could not sell it. Then he decided to try his hand at journalistic assignments for *Ebony* magazine. Working with the photographer Griffith Davis, he hoped to complete one article each month, sometimes about entertainers such as Dizzy Gillespie and Lena Horne but also on less glittering subjects. The men completed "Silently They Worship God," about the integrated St. Ann's Church for the Deaf on West 148th Street in Harlem. The series soon foundered when both Hughes and *Ebony* lost interest in the arrangement.

Just before mid-November, anxious to avoid controversy but in need of cash, he took to the road with a deliberately quiet one-week tour—for decidedly modest fees—before black audiences in the South. When he returned home, his luck appeared to change: the producers of one of the musical shows broached the previous August were ready with a contract. Langston formally joined the writers Abby Mann and Bernard Drew and a composer, Joe Sherman, in the preparation of a play variously called "The Happiest Days," "Happiest Holiday," and finally "Just Around the Corner." Set mainly in Greenwich Village during the Depression, the play related the adventures of three insouciant young men recently arrived by boxcar in New York City, who are confident that prosperity is just around the corner. Mann, Drew, and Sherman had written the show with a friend, Charles Bick, when all were students and members of the Dramatic Society at New York University in the Village. After the decision was made to try for a Broadway production, Bick was dropped as the lyricist and the others turned to Hughes because of his success with *Street Scene.*

"We all admired Kurt Weill," the composer Joe Sherman later recalled, "but we hoped for something a little less operatic, a little more commercial than *Street Scene.* Once Langston Hughes came in, the whole enterprise became more serious, sensitive, meaningful, because we had a poet's mind at work now. He and I worked a great deal of the time at his home on East 127th Street, and it was a pleasure to know him. I was very young—only twenty-two—and I don't think I realized at the time exactly who I was working with, what a great man he was. He certainly didn't carry himself in any special way. I never found Langston egotistical in any sense of the word. He was by nature easygoing, a beautiful guy to work with—an extremely sweet, wonderful, loving person. If anything, he was a little *too* soft in giving in to others."

Accepting this job was indeed a concession in itself. Most of the music had already been written to suit Charles Dick's lyrics, for much of the way, therefore, Langston would have to compose words for a finished score. Mainly to secure an advance, he accepted this challenge, but he was not insensitive to the discomfort of working under such terms. "I WARN YOU ONE MORE TIME ABOUT FOOLING AROUND WITH THE THEATRE," he counselled Arna Bontemps. "It does more than cripple your legs. It cripples your soul."

When financial backing was slow in coming, Langston and the others suspended work on their show. Soon, however, two other musical projects were progressing nicely. More than ten years after Langston had begun work on the libretto of *Troubled Island* for William Grant Still (who recently had been hailed by *Time* magazine as "the U.S.'s leading Negro composer"), their opera about the Haitian Revolution was about to be staged. Leopold Stokowski's bold announcement in 1944 of his determination to mount the piece at the New York City Center, where he was musical director, had come to nothing. After marrying the young heiress Gloria Vanderbilt, the maestro had resigned to devote himself to travel and rest. Freed of his enthusiasms, the Center leadership decided not to fund the opera from its yearly budget. A public appeal for donations, in spite of the entreaties of Mrs. Roosevelt and Mayor La Guardia, drew only $2,000 of the $30,000 needed. The project languished until early in 1947, when the Center announced that it would produce two new operas, both by foreigners. This news enraged William Grant Still, who had written operas since he was a child without seeing even one produced (although his symphonies and tone poems had been played by Stokowski, Artur Rodzinski, and Pierre Monteux). "The recognized opera companies in America," Still fumed, "can *always* find enough money to produce operas by foreign composers, even by enemy composers, while when an opera by an American is under consideration, they have to ask the public for charity funds."

Early in June, after the Center once again declined to commit itself to produce his opera without donations, Still issued a statement withdrawing the opera and demanding that donations be returned. By November, the embarrassed Center had given back the money. Throughout the controversy Langston tried to remain inconspicuous; in a letter to the Center, however, he dissociated himself from Still's position. He wanted *Troubled Island* produced. A black opera had been one of his goals since 1926, and he had been sincere in 1937 when he had pledged to Still his full cooperation: "It must, of course, be as integrated as possible, libretto and music, and I am beginning to wish we were one person, like Wagner, so that our creativeness would be a single powerful force, indissoluble in its beauty and strength." In 1947, when his own *Street Scene* was approaching Broadway, and City Center had appealed for $15,000 to produce *Troubled Island,* he had written Still that "this seems a very *small* sum to me, and if STREET SCENE is a success I may be able to put it on myself!"

Troubled Island fared no better when it was offered next to the most prestigious of American opera companies, the Metropolitan. Perversely citing the absence of blacks in its company, the Met declared itself unable to mount the production. "They never heard of make-up, I guess," Still mused sarcastically in *Time* magazine. At last, the City Center agreed to mount the production. Prickly under normal circumstances, the composer now bristled in almost all his dealings with the Center. He also reserved a few quills for Langston, whose selflessness he used to praise ("Really, you are unique among collaborators"). Now Still demanded—"I am not prepared to compromise"—that Langston yield ten percent of his half of the royalties to Verna Arvey, Still's wife. A talented pianist, Arvey indeed had written some lyrics for *Troubled Island* in 1937, during Langston's absence in Spain, and had also worked hard over the years to promote the opera. "As I remember," Hughes agreed, "most of one of the love arias where you had left a vacant lyric spot when I was in Europe [in 1937] is Verna's. But I don't recall what else. So please let me know." Still obliged him: unless Hughes gave in, he would drop the opera altogether. Langston sent a soothing telegram in reply, but also consulted his lawyer Arthur Spingarn. Conceding that sixty-five lines in three arias were Verna Arvey's work, he yielded on the percentage of royalties but flatly refused co-authorship. "This problem is further evidence to my mind," he told his agent, "that show business, even opera, is born of the Devil."

(Almost forty years later, a documentary film on Still would credit Verna Arvey with having done most of the work on the libretto. In 1938, however, she herself had accurately stated the facts in the *New York Times:* "Before Langston Hughes left for war-torn Madrid he finished the libretto of an opera for the composer William Grant Still. Today that opera is well on its way toward completion." And in her autobiography, *In One Lifetime,* she mentioned—accurately—only that "a major change had to be made at the end of the second act. New lines had to be written to fit the music and the new turn in the drama." At Hughes's suggestion, she had filled in the lines, and with such skill that she became her husband's major lyricist.)

Langston's relationship with Jan Meyerowitz, who had completed "The Barrier," the opera based on *Mulatto,* was also ruffled. For the two composers, opera was their first love and their whole existence; Langston's affections were invested widely. Still and Meyerowitz—and, apparently, every other serious composer—regarded their own talent with a solemnity that amazed the affable Hughes. Once, after hearing a beautiful aria from ''The Barrier'' for the first time, Langston mischievously remarked: ''It is the most beautiful aria ever written on these shores.'' Meyerowitz's response was immediate: ''That's right.'' Thrashing about for a way to get *The Barrier* on stage, he found Langston's and Maxim Lieber's caution exasperating. One angry telephone conversation ended with Meyerowitz suggesting to an appalled Lieber: ''Max, why don't you take your foreskin and make an umbrella out of it?'' ''Langston laughed and laughed for days when he heard that one,'' Meyerowitz said. ''He laughed until he coughed, and he kept repeating the remark, which I didn't think was so extreme. He would never have said something like that. I could never understand his attitude to certain people. Sometimes he allowed them to treat him very badly, and he only smiled and smiled and took it. I tried to get him to fight, but he smiled at me, too. I guess he must have thought that his way was best. Well, it was not my way.''

''Both of my opera people,'' Hughes informed Arna Bontemps, ''are behaving as though they smoked reefers between every note. Since I do not indulge in such habits myself, I am not given to displaying temperament. I just sit calmly and let them blow their tops.''

At 20 East 127th Street, all was calm and bright as 1948 ended. A mighty snowfall that whitened New York brought a measure of enchantment to his first Christmas in his new home. A deluge of gifts also arrived—holly from Seattle, fruitcake from Florida, maple candy from Vermont, cakes and candy from Sweden, ashtrays and cigarettes, and prints by Käthe Kollwitz. Best of all, a brace of new books gleamed on his coffee table: *One-Way Ticket,* with six illustrations by Jacob Lawrence (''a very beautiful job of bookmaking indeed''); *The Poetry of the Negro 1746–1949,* his anthology with Arna Bontemps (''a very fine looking book with a stunning jacket''); and perhaps the most handsome of all, from Anderson and Ritchie, *Cuba Libre: Poems by Nicolás Guillén,* translated with Ben Frederic Carruthers, illustrated by Gar Gilbert, and set by hand on fine Early American paper. Visiting New York a few weeks later, Guillén thanked Langston for ''una edición espléndida.'' *Cuba Libre* won general praise, except in the communist *Daily Worker,* which deemed the translation inadequate—without elaboration—and complained about the elitist size (five hundred copies) of this edition of a communist poet's work.

Poetry of the Negro stirred more controversy. Although the *New York Times* hailed the anthology as ''a fine and rewarding anthology and a magnificent choir of many voices,'' and most other reviewers recommended the book highly, certain objections recurred. The dates in the title were misleading; after a dozen or so pages, the book entered the 1920s. Some reviewers, all white, objected to the inclusion of West Indians; several West Indian critics objected to the presence of whites; *The New Yorker* regretted that folklore had been ignored; a Dutchman bitterly attacked Hughes for omitting Africa almost entirely. Perversely, as Langston saw it, some whites objected to the involvement of white poets: "My feeling is that they are still for strict segregation when it comes to poetry—as most of the 'white' anthologies attest—since they leave us out entirely." In the *Saturday Review of Literature,* Jean Starr Untermeyer attacked the inclusion of whites ("one wonders if this was a gesture of humility or bravado"), the political mildness of the preface, and the shunning of folk material. That she should attack them for espousing an integrated and a liberal view of culture, or tell them what was or was not demeaning to blacks, struck Langston as ridiculous: "I think Jean Starr 'has done lost her mind!' " Bontemps, too, responded with some heat to her objections, but his real desire, and Hughes's, was for publicity. Langston should encourage people to write letters to the *Saturday Review* "whether for or against us. I'd like to see a big hoopla break out."

Poetry of the Negro, which sold briskly from the start, was a historic anthology that would not become outmoded in the lifetime of its editors, who had shown an internationalist understanding of blackness, and a deep pride in their race without a limiting chauvinism. They were the first editors to bring to the attention of North Americans the new Caribbean writing that would flower in the work of V. S. Naipaul and Derek Walcott. (Before the end of the year Walcott's first volume, *25 Poems,* had been published, Edgar Mittelholzer's first novel had been accepted by Hogarth in London, and both Frank Collymore's *Bim* in Barbados and A. J. Seymour's *Kyk-over-al* in British Guiana, the landmark magazines, were flourishing.) "Never before," Seymour later recalled, "had literature been so alive in the West Indies."

Poetry of the Negro also boosted the morale of black American poets. Touched to be remembered at all, the aging Effie Lee Newsome chided its editors: "It is a waste of postage for you or Mr. Bontemps to ask permission to use verse of mine, to say nothing of trimming off some of its Victorianism." Jessie Fauset, on the other hand, was pleased but also offended by Arna Bontemps's failure to treat her adequately in her biographical note. "I've suffered a good deal from colored men writers from Locke down to Bontemps—you know," Fauset wrote Langston. "Only you and [the scholar Hugh M.] Gloster have been fair." And some young writers were delighted to be discovered. One of them, Bruce McM. Wright, an alumnus of Lincoln University studying law at Fordham, and a veteran of World War II who had published a volume of verse in Europe, saluted him: "You have been the Dean of Negro Literature since I passed my first reading exam." Not all the youths were responsive. A letter from Hughes to a twenty-one-year-old who had just created a sensation in *Commentary* with a stunning article on Harlem, brought no reply. "I wasn't writing poetry anymore," James Baldwin recalled later. "I sort of stopped after one of my high school teachers told me my poetry sounded too much like Langston Hughes's. My teacher was Countee Cullen. As for not writing to him, I just didn't know what to say. So I didn't say anything."

As it was intended to do, *Poetry of the Negro* brought black poets to the attention of a wider audience. Early in February, Harold Vinal, editor-in-chief of the New York-based poetry journal *Voices,* which previously had accepted some of Hughes's poems, asked him to edit a special number, preferably on black writers, for the summer. "With so many fine poets among your race," Vinal wrote, "this strikes me as being a fine thing to do." Langston accepted the proposal, but for the following winter.

One-Way Ticket, however, was not well received. Once again, as with other blues and jazz-based volumes, and those of social protest, black critics were the most hostile. In the *Baltimore Afro-American,* J. Saunders Redding, who had lavished praise on the "lyric" volume *Fields of Wonder,* pronounced the new book "stale, flat and spiritless"; by this time, Hughes should have outgrown the folk idiom, especially since he "not now, nor ever really was one of the 'common' folk." Deploring this "so-called poetry," the Pittsburgh *Courier* claimed to have known always "that Hughes lacked about everything one expects in a poet"; in the 1930s, he had written "incredible trash." Many white reviewers also found faults, if more graciously. "I for one should like to see," Rolphe Humphries wrote in recognizing his "studied artlessness," "what Mr. Hughes could do if he would try his hand on work more elaborate, involved, complex." "Mr. Hughes is a highly sophisticated individual," *The New Yorker* teased, "and, like all imitation folk artists, he often sounds thin and artificial." To David Daiches, Hughes was a "documentary" poet—a term Langston liked at once and began to use about himself. "The ultimate meaning, the subtler vision of reality, the oblique insight into man's fate are not for him," Daiches judged; Hughes had "a more urgent and immediate problem, to project the living American Negro onto the page. And he does so, on the whole, with success." Langston himself did not claim that his poetry was flawless. Writing to the Chicago poet Frank Marshall Davis to congratulate him on a new volume, he mentioned that he saw in the book certain "faults same as mine at times—just wanting to make damn sure—for the sake of the social message—that folks understand what is being said."

In the *New York Times,* Herbert Creekmore was closest to the mark in assessing *One-Way Ticket:* Hughes's folk verse showed evidence of change and growth, in that it had become more stripped and bare in resisting sentimentality; and the best poems, spurning poetic fashion, affirmed joy, love, courage, and plain fun. Few reviewers seemed capable of accepting Hughes's aim as an artist to reflect a passionate saturation in his culture, and to write not only about but also *for* blacks, in language they would understand and cherish; or recognized his unstated conviction that their sense of ultimate meaning, reality, and man's fate—to use David Daiches's terms—might not necessarily be the same as that of whites or of fashionable poets of either race. Although it did not sound any radically new notes within his own writing, *One-Way Ticket* was another significant step, with appropriate variety and range, in Hughes's highly original and continuing addition to American poetry. The twelve poems in the opening "Madam to You" suite, about Alberta K. Johnson, formed a minor comic masterpiece; a poem such as "The Ballad of Margie Polite" exemplified Hughes's brilliant fusion of protest and the vernacular; a tossed-off piece, such as "Bad Morning," showed the ease in Hughes's relationship to the muse:

> Here I sit
> With my shoes mismated.
> Lawdy-mercy!
> I's frustrated!

Steeped in the authentic sounds and sights of the urban black community, the poetic voice slips from formal English into the inspired shufflings of illiterate speech and then back again into—sometimes—a studied, elegiac language, as in "Song for Billie Holiday":

> Who can purge my heart
>   Of the song
>   And the sadness?
> Who can purge my heart
>   But the song
>   Of the sadness?
> What can purge my heart
>   Of the sadness
>   Of the song?
>
> Do not speak of sorrow
> With dust in her hair,
> Or bits of dust in eyes
> A chance wind blows there.
> The sorrow that I speak of
> Is dusted with despair.
>
> Voice of muted trumpet.
> Cold brass in warm air.
> Bitter television blurred
> By song that shimmers—
>   Where?

Here, a sense of tragedy dominates. But while an element of tragedy haunts *One-Way Ticket,* and poems about loneliness and death abound, the transcendent blues spirit brings the culture through in the end:

> . . . I could've died for love—
> But for livin' I was born.
>
> You may see me holler,
> You may see me cry—

But I'll be dogged, sweet baby,
If you gonna see me die.

Life is fine!
Fine as wine!
Life is fine!

Tepid reviews of *One-Way Ticket* notwithstanding, 1949 opened brightly for Langston. A festive round of seasonal parties was capped on January 7 by an elegant evening affair at the Schomburg Library in Harlem. With Langston reading from *Poetry of the Negro* and *One-Way Ticket,* and the Cuban actress Eusebia Cosme chanting in Spanish from Guillén's work, the soirée became something of an adventure in nostalgia, "a flashback to the twenties," because of the evocative presence of such stalwarts of that decade as the playwright Ridgely Torrence, the editor and poet William Stanley Braithwaite, Carl Van Vechten, Arthur Spingarn, and the debonair Harold Jackman. The following Monday, Knopf and Doubleday combined their forces to throw a huge book party for Hughes. And on Feburary 1, Nate and Gerry White poured champagne and joined Ralph and Fanny Ellison and the Harpers in toasting him on his forty-seventh birthday.

Soon he was off to North Carolina for a Negro History Week tour that included an appearance at Joseph Albers's experimental Black Mountain College ("just about the most amazing campus I have ever seen in my natural life—and interracial, too!"). In Washington, D.C., after reading at a luncheon of the black Capital Press Club, he joined Arna Bontemps at Howard University for a gala Poets' Festival, organized partly in honor of their *Poetry of the Negro,* which once again sparked memories of the glorious days of the Harlem Renaissance.

When Langston returned to Manhattan, he was met with news of a sourly ironic twist of events for one of the major figures of that age. Zora Neale Hurston, whom he had not seen since their friendship ended in 1931, after she had claimed sole authorship of their play, "Mule Bone", had been arrested the previous September at a room where she lived at 140 West 122 Street in Manhattan. The charge was "sodomy" with a ten-year-old boy, the son of a woman who had rented a room to Hurston in Harlem in the winter of 1947. Believing that the boy was emotionally disturbed, Hurston had apparently antagonized the woman by suggesting that she seek psychiatric help for him. To Hurston's profound sorrow, the black press had reported her arrest and indictment gleefully. Langston himself had giggled to Arna Bontemps about her predicament, though without naming her: "Have you heard the awful story going around about one of [our] leading lady writers of color (not a poet, thank the Lord) getting in jail, to stand trial next week, on a charge that should hardly be written down?"

Now a subpoena ordered Langston to appear in Manhattan Municipal Court, 10th district, in the case of Richard D. Rochester vs. Zora Neale Hurston.

Incredibly—since they had never been reconciled—Hurston wanted Hughes to testify to her good character. Considering her past behavior, Langston marvelled to a friend, "I was amazed." Still, he agreed to testify. In March, before he could do so, the palpably false case was dropped by the district attorney. The move could not save Hurston from despair. She never recovered fully from this humiliation. "All that I have ever tried to do," she had written Carl Van Vechten and his wife, "has proved useless. All that I have believed in has failed me. I have resolved to die. . . . No acquittal will persuade some people that I am innocent. I feel hurled down a filthy privy hole."

Near the end of February, just after learning that Simon and Schuster had agreed to publish his often-rejected book of Simple sketches, Langston left town to take up a three-month teaching position, with a stipend of $2,000, at the Laboratory School of the University of Chicago. After a brief stay in the black South Side, he moved closer to the school, to a room on the seventh floor of the International House of the university, at 1414 East 59th Street, in the mainly white Hyde Park district. Even at this point, it was not altogether clear how Langston would fit in. The Lab School, which taught children from kindergarten through high school, was hardly a typical institution. Founded in 1903 in a merger of three schools controlled by the University of Chicago, and first headed by John Dewey, it offered an innovative curriculum that tried to stimulate a love of knowledge among the students by emphasizing Dewey's dictum about "learning by doing." Fluidly conceived, the arts were central to its methods and goals. As "Visiting Lecturer on Poetry," Hughes would work mainly not in the Department of English but in the Department of Unified Arts, founded in 1941.

On his first official day, March 1, the forty-seven-year-old poet found himself sitting on the floor of a room at 5835 Kimbark Avenue, serving as secretary in a colloquium with six students. Each child was four years old. As the students developed a story called "She Found Her Coat Again," about Princess Maleef, who keeps losing her things, Langston listened carefully and scribbled on a pad. Dutifully he recorded the narrative and sometimes—discreetly—nudged it along. Later, the children developed the somewhat happier story of "The Bad Lion." Restless in his zoo, the big beast runs away. He eats everybody in sight. Then he decides to drive a car. Since it has no steering wheel, he drives it with his nose. Then he goes into the jungle to tell the other animals a lie about his adventures.

Langston enjoyed these kindergarten sessions, but was soon in demand all over the school. "He was a hit," one teacher later remembered. "I am not sure what the principal had in mind exactly when Langston was hired, but the school certainly got its money's worth." His three months at the Lab School called for far more work than his term at Atlanta University, but he was prepared to toil. Certainly the students found him ready. "Mr. Hughes seemed perfectly at ease and put his audience at ease," one girl wrote later in evaluating him. "He spoke very plainly and loud enough and had his material ready.

He didn't fumble around looking for material, his papers were organized and so were his lectures, although he did seem to wander sometimes. His friendliness and pleasant manner soon won him the friendship of his audience.'' His teaching was ''an experience I will not forget.''

Upper grade students wanted classes in creative writing and help in publishing a literary supplement to *Midway,* the school magazine. On Fridays, he taught poetry recitation to a group of eighth grade students (one of his pet hates was ''people who recite poetry in a far-away voice''). A ninth grade group was interested in autobiography; he also offered a short course, ''The Negro in American Poetry,'' to the upper grades. Responding to impromptu requests, he gave lectures on Mexico in a geography class, prepared an ''America in Song'' program for a school choir, and helped teach folk ballads and drama; one class had its own orchestra and planned to write a musical with him. In addition, he gave two formal readings of his own poetry to the university community. At his invitation, Gwendolyn Brooks, much admired by Langston, gave a thoroughly successful lecture on one of her poems to a group of students. In these months, she also had perhaps her best chance to take the measure of Langston Hughes. ''He was an easy man,'' she recalled later. ''You could rest in his company. No one possessed a more serious understanding of life's immensities. No one was firmer in recognition of the horrors man imposes on man, in hardy insistence on reckonings. But when those who knew him remember him the memory inevitably will include laughter of an unusually warm and tender kind.''

''Children are not nearly so resistant to poetry as are grown-ups,'' Langston believed; ''in fact, small children are not resistant at all.'' About writing and adolescents he had still another theory; he saw ''a psycho-therapeutic value in that, unconsciously and by indirection, they may get down on paper some of the things that trouble them—and thus relieved, live better, freer, less confused lives.'' At the Lab School, where he had a chance to test his theories, he came away convinced more than ever about their soundness. The fact that he was a black instructor among children almost all of whom were white seemed not to matter. Loving children, and eager to please, he made friends easily. His favorite student, and the one he thought most talented, was a handicapped white boy from Arkansas. As for his colleagues, he warmed especially to Bob Ericson, an artist and a musician trained in trumpet and voice, who owned about three hundred jazz and blues records and taught jazz classes; Hughes joined him in offering a course in jazz. Ericson and his wife, Cathline Iatser Ericson, a kindergarten teacher, remembered Langston as intelligent and shrewd but also gentle and spontaneous. ''He must have been nearly fifty by this time,'' she recalled, ''but he seemed almost miraculously young, fresh, open, unaware. He came to our little attic apartment at 5611 Blackstone and made himself at home, without any show or pretense. He spent lots of time just watching Bob paint his pictures. When we cooked okra as a special treat for him, he just loved it and wouldn't stop talking about it. He was just tremendous fun, always with a sparkle in his eyes, a chuckle, a smile, a laugh. And although he really couldn't sing or play an instrument, he refused to keep still when we played. He clapped his hands and tapped his feet along with the blues and jazz records.''

About his Lab School months, the late-rising Langston had only one plaintive reservation: "Seven o'clock in the morning lower-school teaching is too much for me at my advanced age. Since I did not do it in my youth and was never on time for school myself when I was a pupil, I see no need to start straining my ego now just to improve race relations.''

On March 30, he flew to New York to attend the premiere at the City Center of *Troubled Island*. For Hughes and Still, the evening was the realization of a personal dream long deferred; it was also a historic event in race relations—the first opera written by blacks to be produced by a major American company. Although the major roles were sung by whites, with the illustrious Robert Weede in the central role of Dessalines, nine blacks had places in the chorus; eight others danced to the choreography of George Balanchine and Jean Leon Destiné of Haiti; and Weede's understudy, Lawrence Winters—the former Larry Whisonant—would sing the role of Dessalines at the second performance. "The race is a-rising!" Langston quipped. (He was also able at last to open a bottle of Barbancourt rum from Haiti that he had been saving for this occasion.)

The audience applauded madly, but the premiere was a failure with most of the critics, who were impressed least of all by the music. Listening in vain for "an idiom personal to the composer, or the subject," Irving Kolodin heard instead "a turgid, confused mishap called Troubled Island"; a "Still-born opera," his newspaper mocked. In the *New York Times,* Olin Downes was kinder but also found nothing fresh. Reviewers reported strains of Gershwin, Sigmund Romberg, Delius, Puccini, and Massenet, but little of William Grant Still. Evidently the costumes and the dancing could have been better. Prowling the lobby at intermission, his ears cocked for candid reactions, Hughes's secretary Nate White overheard a complaint about the quality of the emperor's cloak. "When I saw that bathrobe," someone jibed, "I was damn sure the taxes hadn't been paid." To Langston, White likened the dancing on stage to "a bad evening at Small's Paradise" in Harlem.

With the weak reviews, Still saw no reason to overlook his problems with Hughes. Thereafter he declined to answer any letters from Langston, who patiently kept writing in hope of a thaw. Finally, he gave up. "Composers and librettists usually fall out by the time any show opens," he philosophized. "Still and I are no exceptions.''

What Langston did not know, and perhaps never found out, was that Still, a profoundly religious man and a dedicated anti-communist who later supported Senator Joseph McCarthy to the end, blamed at least part of the failure of *Troubled Island* on Langston and his friends on the left. As far as Still was concerned, the production had been "a great success . . . but the New York critics reported it as a failure." To another of his heroes, Richard Nixon, Still explained that his collaboration with Hughes, "a man listed in 'Red Channels' " (which published the names of leftists in radio and television), was "definitely a thing of the past" as early as 1939, much less in 1949. "It is significant," Still informed Nixon, "that as 'Troubled Island' came near to production, he opposed me at every turn, as did other people who are also listed in 'Red Channels'."

Adding to Still's sensitivity to the danger of the left was the opening at the Waldorf-Astoria Hotel in Manhattan, in the same week as the premiere of his opera, of an international Cultural and Scientific Conference organized by the radical National Council of the Arts, Sciences and Professions. Both the National Council and the conference were major initiatives of the left in America in the years following World War II. The National Council, denounced as a communist-front organization by the House Committee on Un-American Activities, had emerged out of the Independent Citizens Committee of the Arts, Sciences and Professions (of which Hughes had been a sponsor), which in 1946 had been repudiated by its own chairman as a communist force. As for the Waldorf Astoria conference, it was a clear successor to the pro-Marxist World Congress of Intellectuals held in Wroclaw, Poland, the previous August, 1948, at which the United States repeatedly had been attacked, and the Soviet Union extolled.

Attracting delegates from all over the world (although the State Department barred about two dozen representatives), the conference nevertheless featured mainly Soviet-bloc countries. The star of the most controversial group, from the U.S.S.R., was unquestionably the renowned composer Dmitri Shostakovich, who was reportedly on domestic probation after his "bourgeois tendencies" had been unmasked and condemned by the Central Committee of the Communist Party in Moscow. Also present, if outside the hotel, were hundreds of pickets vehemently protesting Soviet aims and actions in Eastern Europe and Germany. A few well-known American anti-communists, such as Robert Lowell, attended sessions of the conference, but their influence was offset easily by progressive writers such as W. E. B. Du Bois, Norman Cousins, Norman Mailer, Lillian Hellman, F. O. Matthiessen, Agnes Smedley, Mary McCarthy, and Dwight MacDonald. Langston Hughes, in addition to being a member-at-large of the National Council, was one of the sponsors of the conference; but if he spoke one word at any session of the conference his name went unmentioned in the lively and comprehensive reports of speeches and events in the national newspapers. Nevertheless, in a burst of publicity he must have deplored, the April 4 issue of *Life* magazine—clearly designed to counter the influence of the Conference—included his portrait among fifty pictures of politically misguided Americans in a story on the conference headlined "RED VISITORS CAUSE RUMPUS: DUPES AND FELLOW TRAVELERS DRESS UP COMMUNIST FRONTS." Among the other dupes and fellow travellers were Albert Einstein, Paul Robeson, Leonard Bernstein, Dorothy Parker, Lillian Hellman, Arthur Miller, Susan B. Anthony II, Norman Mailer, and Adam Clayton Powell, Jr.

The condemnation in *Life* magazine, with its huge national and international circulation, capped a period of hostility to Hughes from the right wing even as he carefully stayed away from the lecture circuit and savored the pleasures of his new home. "I am a bit weary of six months of red-baiting," he had confessed to Olive Lindsay Wakefield the previous July, after his battering tour; he was determined to get on with his work rather than "wear out typewriter ribbons on people of no integrity whatsoever." That month, however, the powerful *Reader's Digest* had jarred him by publishing an excerpt from the anti-Hughes broadcast by Henry J. Taylor earlier in the year, in which Taylor had not only denounced Langston as a professed communist but also quoted five inciting lines from the poem "Goodbye Christ." Once again Hughes denied vehemently that he was a communist, or had ever been one. Once again, his denials were ignored. Deploring the "anti-Negro, anti-Jewish, anti-labor sources of such attacks, that have lately been taken up by slightly more 'respectable' and official, but no less ill-intentioned groups," Langston talked menacingly of taking legal action. When he was advised, however, that lawsuits would be costly and drawn out, he lowered his voice.

In September, the New York *Journal-American* again had called him a Communist Party member. Now, according to a fresh count by the House Committee on Un-American Activities, Hughes either belonged or had once belonged to ninety-one communist-front organizations, far more than any other American it had investigated. And, as anti-communist feeling continued to build across the nation, and new targets were identified, his name began to be invoked in campaigns against others. When the Guggenheim Foundation was attacked for an allegedly leftist bias, Hughes's name on a list of past winners of fellowships was offered as damning evidence. The presence of some of his books on a bibliography in a YWCA publication drew fire in an anti-communist pamphlet, *Behind the Lace Curtains of the YWCA,* attacking the Association. Langston warned the YWCA that the right-wing groups were mainly interested "in breaking up the growing unity and decency between Negroes and whites, Jews and Gentiles, and in keeping labor weak and divided, and wages low—not in truth or democracy."

J. Edgar Hoover, the director of the FBI, now had a deeper personal interest in the case of Langston Hughes. In May of 1948, Hughes had refused permission to a Methodist group to reprint "Goodbye Christ," which had been cited in the course of Hoover's essay "Secularism—Breeder of Crime," in which he had attacked Hughes by name. This essay was scheduled for publication in a volume, *Secularism and the Christian Faith,* by the Abingdon-Cokesbury Press. When Langston curtly refused his permission, the editors deleted the text of the poem without consulting Hoover. He took the news badly. One of his deputies, Louis B. Nichols, who had read the speech in the director's absence on November 26, 1947, denounced the publisher's decision as an insult to his leader. Keeping behind the scenes, but obviously angry and vengeful, the director instructed: "Make certain we furnish this outfit no more material for publication. They are too squeamish about offending the commies." The FBI then set out once again to find hard evidence of Hughes's place in the Communist Party. Finding none, Hoover nevertheless signed an order on December 7 calling for a "new report" on Hughes "in view of the tense international situation at the present time."

Hoover was referring to the blockade of Berlin by the Soviet Union, and the dramatic U.S. effort to supply the city by air. To many observers, the major powers seemed to be heading inevitably to World War III. Against this backdrop, the presidental elections of 1948 had acquired an acute significance. Clearly Langston had vested his hopes not in Harry Truman or Thomas Dewey but in Henry A. Wallace, the former Vice President of the United States and Secretary of Commerce who had broken with President Truman over foreign policy. The candidate of the Progressive Party, Wallace enjoyed the enthusiastic support of the National Committee of the Arts, Sciences and Professions and the leftist community in general. Hughes did not hide his enthusiasm. The previous year, one column in the *Defender* had completely endorsed a speech by Wallace at a rally in Madison Square Garden. "I got a good view of the man," Langston assured his readers. "He looks like a good man with a simple honest midwestern face. And he makes a good speech. He touched upon a number of subjects that interested me greatly because they affect me personally." Wallace was against imperialism, universal military training, and the House Committee on Un-American Activities. He was for a conciliatory attitude to the Soviet Union, full employment, and the implementation of the U.S. Constitution and other documents pertaining to freedom.

As the presidential elections of 1948 drew near, Langston made another gesture or two in favor of Wallace. On September 10, he attended a tumultuous fund-raising "Yankee Doodle" rally for the candidate at Yankee Stadium, sponsored by the American Labor Party. A crowd of fifty thousand paid over $78,000 to hear Paul Robeson render "Old Man River" and "Let My People Go," Avon Long sing an anti-Truman parody based on Gershwin's "It Ain't Necessarily So," and Representative Vito Marcantonio and Wallace himself deliver stirring speeches. Later, Hughes helped sponsor a Council dinner for Wallace. Otherwise, he had deflected its requests for help for the candidate; at a time when he was trying to consolidate his finances, and had just acquired his house, he could not afford to jeopardize his means of livelihood. In fact, the attack in the *Reader's Digest* had almost cost him the lucrative radio job with NBC the previous summer. He kept his distance from the campaign, which ended in disaster. Wallace received slightly more than a million popular votes, and no Electoral College votes.

Still, Langston wanted to help the radical cause. In the *Defender,* he took the measure of liberals and found them wanting. The liberal "is a nice man who acts decently toward people, talks democratically, and often is democratic in his personal life, but does not stand up very well in action when some real social issue like Jim Crow comes up." On the other hand, he would not step forward eagerly to be counted. In the new year, 1949, a call by Harlow Shapley, the Harvard University astronomer and leftist leader, for a Cultural and Scientific Conference for World Peace went unheeded at 20 East 127th Street.

Hughes was not one of the two hundred distinguished persons responding to Shapley even though the director of the Council pressed him hard: "I cannot conceive of a Conference of this nature which is not endorsed by you." By this time, his unreliability evidently was well known to the Council. "I've always admired your inaccessibility to a telephone call," she added tartly. "I wish I had the same strength of character." He had backed up this inaccessibility with strict orders to his secretaries. In response to a telegram of entreaty ("KNOW YOU ARE WITH US BUT UNWILLING TO PROCEED WITHOUT YOUR SPECIFIC AUTHORIZATION"), Nate White instructed the Council on Hughes's behalf—and perhaps in Hughes's presence: "KINDLY DO NOT USE HIS NAME WITHOUT PERMISSION." Later, citing his writing schedule, Langston flatly declined to accept almost all engagements as a member.

Yet the times were too extraordinary for him to be entirely unresponsive. Just before the peace conference, he had answered a telegram for help from the friends of the executive director of Yaddo, Elizabeth Ames, who had been accused of abetting a communist plot to subvert the institution because of her support of the radical Agnes Smedley. This telegram had been followed by a mimeographed letter of explanation from a committee of her supporters, including Alfred Kazin, Noël Sullivan's distant cousin Kappo Phelan, and John Cheever, all of whom declared themselves to be anti-Stalinist but affronted by the charge against Ames. Her main accusers were Robert Lowell and Elizabeth Hardwick; the volatile Lowell had reportedly threatened to ruin the colony's reputation unless Ames resigned. Since February, when General Douglas MacArthur had made serious charges of disloyalty against Agnes Smedley based on her years in China, the FBI had been gathering information about Ames, Smedley, and a possible communist connection at Yaddo. A trusted secretary at Yaddo, it turned out, had been an informant for the FBI. In her four years there (including 1943, when Langston had also been in residence), Smedley had advertised her communist sympathies; Elizabeth Ames, uncomfortable with this aspect of her friend's life, finally had sent her away. Grateful to Ames for twice admitting him to Yaddo and for favoring his advice about prospective black residents, Langston responded promptly to Kappo Phelan's telegram with a plan of action that evidently worked. "Your help was invaluable," Hughes heard after the Yaddo directors rejected Lowell's charge. "*Everyone* you suggested came through in time." Elizabeth Ames and Yaddo were saved—but not Agnes Smedley, who died the following May in England, embittered and defeated. "The strangest things are happening these days," Langston wrote Ames in consolation.

This help followed hard on his boldest political act in some years. In the *Chicago Defender* of February 5, Hughes stoutly defended twelve communists (one defendant was separated later) on trial in Manhattan for allegedly advocating the overthrow of the United States government. Identified by the *New York Times* as "members of the American Politburo or national board" of the Communist Party, the group included Benjamin Davis, Jr., the black Amherst and Harvard Law School graduate who had defended Angelo Herndon in 1933 and was now a popular New York City councilman. Almost coyly ("my feelings being more emotional than scientific"), Langston had refused an appeal from Davis to testify at the trial, along with other noncommunist notables, about Marxist theory. He was weak in debate, and the prosecutors would trip him up; his enemies had been "hammering at me tooth and nail" for two years. With the start of the trial on January 17, however, he joined the fight. Calling the trial "the most important thing happening in America today," he warned his readers that it was "your trial—all who question the status quo—who question things as they are—all poor people, Negroes, Jews, un-white Americans, un-rich Americans are on trial." The situation was exactly like Hitler's Germany, where first communists, then Jews, were slaughtered. Blacks were second on the American list of hate, behind communists; Jews were not far behind. "If the 12 Communists are sent to jail—I am no prophet and was born with no veil over my face, but mark my words—if the twelve Communists are sent to jail, in a little while they will send Negroes to jail simply for being Negroes and to concentration camps just for being colored. Maybe you don't like Reds, but you had better be interested in what happens to the 12 Reds in New York City—because it is only a sign of what can happen to you."

Praising this "very moving and splendid column," the Communist Party of New York asked permission to reprint it. Langston gave permission, then retreated into intermittent silence. He had fired his guns, but in a black arena, where reports would not carry far—or so he probably hoped. When Olin Downes begged him to take a seat on the dais at the annual dinner of a Spanish Civil War organization ("Your support of the Spanish Refugee Appeal has been constant"), he in turn begged off. Although he agreed to be listed as a sponsor (along with W. E. B. Du Bois, among blacks) of the China Welfare Relief, in support of the fledgling People's Republic of China, he did nothing else to help it. Invited to visit the Soviet Union for the 150th anniversary of Pushkin's birth, he refused. Once the most radical black artist outside of the party, Langston Hughes had faded from the scene. Preeminence had passed to the dynamic Paul Robeson, who, four years older than Hughes, had moved slowly but steadily to the far left just as Hughes was shifting in the opposite direction. In the fall, after Robeson's ordeal at Peekskill, Hughes devoted an entire *Defender* column to defending the right of "the greatest concert attraction in the world today to speak out" on political issues.

A part of Langston still wished to be at the barricades, but only his powerful verse, such as "The Ballad of the Freedom Train" (which Robeson, with his resonant voice, loved to recite), spoke for him there. When *Ebony* magazine wrote to ask about the person he admired most, Langston chose in the field of "literary-race relations" W. E. B. Du Bois, to whom he had sent a ringing telegram the previous year, 1948, on his eightieth birthday: "TO ME AS TO MILLIONS OF OTHERS YOU HAVE BEEN A GUIDE AND INSPIRATION SO WITH GRATITUDE AND AFFECTION HERE IS WISHING YOU MANY HAPPY RETURNS." Thrown out of his NAACP job later that year for radical activity, Du Bois was intensifying his involvement with the predominantly white left that he had once scorned mainly on racial grounds, and from which Hughes, who had once embraced it, was in retreat.

Late in May, he wound up his affairs at the Lab School in Chicago after three enjoyable months. With many people sorry to see him leave, Gwendolyn Brooks threw a farewell party in his honor at her home at 623 East 63rd Street. "We squeezed perhaps a hundred people into our Langston Hughes two-room kitchenette party," she recalled. "Langston was the merriest and the most colloquial of them all. '*Best* party I've ever been given!' He enjoyed everyone; he enjoyed all the talk, all the phonograph blues, all the festivity in the crowded air." Then, near the last day of May, after drafting a fourteen-page report, "Three Months at the Lab School," and an anthology of writing by members of the various grades, he left Chicago.

Offers to teach again at Atlanta University and at Hampton Institute soon arrived, but he preferred to stay home in Harlem. (He never again accepted a teaching position.) Assured of a new contract and an advance of $1000, Langston returned home to work on the musical play of the Depression, "Just Around the Corner," with Abby Mann, Bernard Drew, and Joe Sherman. The work did not go easily. "Meshing Langston's lyric, poetic style to music I had already composed was troublesome for all concerned," Sherman remembered. "The first few months were really arduous. But he did everything to help—he would write copious lyrics for me to set, and without any complaint. And he never regarded anything he wrote as precious and unchangeable. It was a pleasure and an honor to work with him."

Then, although "Just Around the Corner" required a full-time effort, Langston took the kind of step he would increasingly take, and increasingly come to regret: he accepted yet another job. The new task was to write a libretto for the highly regarded young American musician Elie Siegmeister, who had studied composition with the influential Nadia Boulanger in France, and whose *American Holiday, Western Suite,* and *Sunday in Brooklyn* all showed his love of blues, jazz, and American folklore. In the late thirties, Siegmeister had set his first poem by Langston; eventually he would set over fifty (and include one, Hughes's "A New Wind A-Blowing" in *A Treasury of American Song,* which he edited with Olin Downes). "To my mind," Siegmeister later asserted, "Langston Hughes was the most musical poet of the twentieth century. No one else comes even close to him in this respect. His verse practically begs to be set to music." When the American Opera Company of Philadelphia and the Pennsylvania Federation of Music Clubs commissioned him to compose an opera, with the sole stipulation that the work should be set in Pennsylvania, he turned to Hughes. The provision did not dismay Langston, who had lived in the state for three years, 1926 to 1929, while at Lincoln University. He accepted the commission—and an advance of $500.

Putting together the "Negro Poets Issue" of *Voices,* he earned at least one compliment from a young poet: while it would have been easy for Hughes "to enjoy your eminence in solitary splendor . . . you share it selflessly.'' Langston made room for the entire range of black poets, from veterans like Effie Lee Newsome and Georgia Douglas Johnson to at least half-a-dozen neophytes. With growing discomfort, he faced certain new approaches by black writers. Melvin Tolson, for one, had committed himself to a high modernist style that Langston found exciting but, in places, excessively elitist. In challenging one of Tolson's rhymes—"china" and "orchestrina"—Langston slipped in some further criticism. "Nobody knows what an *orchestrina* is," he wrote Tolson, "(that is, nobody of the Race)." Nevertheless, he accepted the poem. Bent on giving the number *cachet,* and honoring Gwendolyn Brooks as a master craftsman, he asked Richard Wright in Paris to review her new volume of poetry, *Annie Allen.* When Wright did not reply, he wrote it himself. By August 25, the number was complete except for the reviews (the first one to arrive, he judged sternly, was "God awful!").

Of all his proliferating projects in the summer of 1949, however, Langston probably worked hardest on the manuscript carved from his almost two hundred Simple sketches, first called "Listen Fluently," then finally "Simple Speaks His Mind." At Simon and Schuster he had found an editor, Maria Leiper, who seemed to understand Simple perfectly. Ironically—given Simple's ghetto proletarianism—Maria Leiper was an American blueblood. Thomas Jefferson had drawn up the Declaration of Independence in the home of her ancestor Thomas Leiper, and John Paul Jones was also in her family tree. Urging Langston to consider using a rigorously anonymous narrator, instead of the "Boyd" of the original pieces, she also wanted more emphasis on Simple's womenfolk. The result was a more sympathetic and humane hero, and a lonelier, more compelling narrator. Langston praised her suggestions as "most intelligent and very helpful," and Simon and Schuster as "a really fine office to deal with . . . most careful and cooperative about everything." She, in turn, lauded him: "You are a model among authors."

Late in August, he delivered the final manuscript of "Simple Speaks His Mind"—typed neatly by his talented secretary Nate White, who had also helped here and there with its composition. "Some of the Simple touches," Hughes admitted, "may be laid at his door." White himself recalled that "Langston was very relaxed about such things. I would make suggestions or add something to his column and show it to him and he hardly ever changed a line. I never dared to change his poetry, but he didn't mind it at all when I edited his prose. In fact, he pretty much gave me a free hand."

His first full summer in his home was a delight—albeit sometimes noisy, with music resounding from his collaborations or from Emerson and Aunt Toy enjoying themselves at the piano. (Mrs. Harper herself had recovered nicely from a misadventure in June, when a nearsighted neighbor, mistaking her for his wife, who had smashed his glasses in a fight, knocked her out on the street.) The house on 127th Street was now a magnet. Visitors arrived from all over the United States, as well as from Jamaica, Haiti, Argentina, Germany, and France. "It seems to me," Langston wrote wearily early in September, as he braced himself for a visitor from Trinidad, "we have had a house full of people for the last month of varying nationalities at all hours of the day and night." Soon the phone company sent a man around to soften the bells and, more important, to allow Langston to unplug his telephone altogether.

In spite of his many projects, money continued to be a problem. Between 1947 (the year of *Street Scene*) and 1949, Hughes's income had dropped each year by about one third. Half of his 1949 income of $8,800 came from the Lab School job in Chicago and the *Defender* columns. Almost a third of this money went to pay his full-time secretary, Nate White, without whose services Langston could hardly do. Even when a book did well, he seemed to be the last to profit from it. Although *Poetry of the Negro* had sold briskly, Doubleday informed the editors that the high cost of permissions still prevented any payment beyond the advance. "It's all so familiar," a skeptical Hughes wrote Lieber about the claim, "I did not bat an eye nor turn a hair." A long reading tour was effectively closed to him. When he inquired about the winter season, the Colston Leigh agency reported only three lectures booked for Langston Hughes by the end of November; other sponsors had found it impossible to secure halls. "I would be delighted to remain off the lecture platform for the rest of my natural life," he responded bravely, "if I can get along without it—and I am doing all right at the moment. It is not an easy life." By mutual agreement, his name was dropped from the roll. In November, broke, he wrote to his uncle John Hughes, who lived in comfort and prosperity in Los Angeles, for a loan of $100. The money came.

More eagerly, and in spite of his other commitments, Langston looked for projects that paid at once. To this end, on Sunday, September 18, he visited one of the most remarkable men in Harlem, the sixty-six-year-old retired Parole Commissioner of New York City, Samuel Jesse Battle. Having passed the police force entrance examination in 1910, the North Carolina-born Battle initially was turned away in his quest for an appointment, then became the first black policeman in the history of the city. In the summer of 1911, trolleys stopped in their tracks to allow riders to gape at the unbelievable sight of a black man on patrol. Shunned and "silenced" by the white, largely Irish rank and file until he heroically led a squadron of reserves through showers of bricks and stones in the infamous San Juan Hill riots in Manhattan in 1912, Battle won a reputation as a tough, fair-minded policeman and led the way for other blacks on the force. Now he wanted someone to write the story of his life. Although a Hollywood screenwriter was enthusiastic about the chance of a film, Battle wanted a book first, preferably by a black writer. From Hollywood, Clarence Muse had recommended Langston, who saw at once that Samuel Battle's story was in many respects the story of black Harlem. Hollywood, Hughes heard, suddenly was " 'hot' for stories with Negro or race relations themes."

Leafing through the commissioner's many scrapbooks, and thinking of the film money, Langston warmed to the idea of either writing a biography or of "ghostwriting" an autobiography. With Maria Leiper at Simon and Schuster professing "our keen—and unanimous—interest in such a book" (Blanche Knopf wanted no part of it) he committed himself to write "Battle of Harlem." Soon a screenplay contract was signed between Battle and the Hollywood screenwriter, Leo Katcher, with Hughes and Battle to share equally the book, serial, and film revenue. A few months later, Langston accepted $1500 from Battle and started work on his life.

He approached Mrs. Knopf once again to offer her the manuscript of "Montage of a Dream Deferred" (his "first full-length sustained poem") and new outlines of another autobiography and a volume of "Selected Poems." With his package went a breezy request for an advance of $1000. "Now that we've settled in a big house of our own with a third floor of peace and quiet for working," he explained (with no mention of his other jobs), the money would free him to write. But he had again miscalculated in approaching his publisher. "I don't think we should do the poetry," she decided. The autobiography also seemed "weighted," by which she almost certainly meant that it devoted too much attention to the Soviet Union, a taboo at the moment—unless treated with hostility. "If this means that you feel you should take it elsewhere, I think I will have to free you to do it with great regret." She was writing "with great difficulty—we are old friends and have had a great deal of fun publishing together."

He had now reached a decisive point in his career. That his publisher of over twenty years had refused a book of his verse was not in itself crucial. She had done so before, with his radical writing in the 1930s, then published him again when he had changed his tune. This time, she had not even complained about the tune, only—as far as he could guess—about his singing. Nor was it decisive that Knopf had a large stock of unsold copies of his books, including over a thousand copies each of the slow-selling *Fields of Wonder* and *One-Way Ticket*. The true difficulty was his deepening entanglement in a web of projects that appeared to signal, both by their quality and quantity, the end of his sense of self as a serious artist. The peril was evident to some people. In the *Baltimore Afro-American*, J. Saunders Redding soon called on Hughes to stop lecturing (Redding did not know the half of Langston's various involvements) "and devote himself to writing the great poetry that is still in him."

Pushed on, nevertheless, by happy memories of his income from *Street Scene,* Langston soon took on yet another musical project. For the folksinger Burl Ives and the Golden Gate Quartet, he finished an outline called "Swinging to the Golden Gate," set in the Gold Rush days of 1849 in California. Although that project quickly collapsed, musical plays remained on Langston's mind as the quick fix for his financial problems. Two months later, when Arna Bontemps visited New York, the two men discussed another musical venture, based on the life of the jazz pioneer Jelly Roll Morton but tailored as a vehicle for Pearl Bailey, the former star of *St. Louis Woman*. This venture also died.

A third musical venture, however, was showing signs of life. Joel Spector, a young musician who had worked as an assistant stage director at the Metropolitan Opera and in televising opera in England, hoped to bring Langston's opera based on *Mulatto,* with music by Jan Meyerowitz, to Broadway. As a way station, the Theatre Associates of Columbia University, which had staged workshop productions of operas by Gian Carlo Menotti, Ralph Vaughan-Williams, and other contemporary composers, agreed to stage a ten-day run in late January at the Brander Matthews Theatre on the campus. The Columbia faculty member Felix Brentano would direct, his colleague Willard Rhodes would conduct, and the sets would be designed by the accomplished H. A. Condell; the dynamic Roger Stevens would help with all aspects of the production. Anxious not to link the opera in publicity to *Mulatto,* which had been hardly "an 'artistic' success" on Broadway, Hughes explained, but had been "slanted for box office by the producers and staged as a 'sex-melodrama'," he and Meyerowitz changed its name to "The Barrier," a title suggested by Felix Brentano.

When the first act proved to be too short, he quickly wrote a prologue, which Meyerowitz hastened to set. Unfortunately, Brentano rejected the new music. Agitated, Meyerowitz tried again. The result was pleasing, but it did not blend with the old overture. Brentano needed a new one. All this pressure proved almost too much for the excitable composer, and Langston. When the new overture was finally played and accepted, he took to bed for a whole day—to recover his wits, he claimed.

On November 30, rehearsals began with an excellent cast that included two black leads. Muriel Rahn, a graduate of Tuskegee who had been the original Carmen in the Broadway show *Carmen Jones,* and young Mattiwilda Dobbs of Atlanta were cast as the mother and sister of the doomed young hero, who was played by the experienced Robert Goss. Paul Elmer, seasoned in both light and grand opera, was his father. Broadway began to seem more and more a possiblity when the tickets went on sale; before the first curtain rose, all ten performances sold out. In the *New York Times* on January 15, Hughes praised the sacrifices of all concerned—including his own. "I had sworn never to have anything more to do with non-commercial theatre," he admitted, "since lecturing and teaching, I had found, met the demands of the landlord so much better." But Meyerowitz had made him change his mind. " 'What? Another opera!' " his lawyer (Arthur Spingarn, "who very kindly never accepts a penny") had groaned. "And in his voice was not delight but despair. I said, 'But this will be a very exciting one'."

January, 1950, was a month of success that started with the formal opening at Yale University of the James Weldon Johnson Memorial Collection of Negro Arts and Letters founded by Carl Van Vechten, of which Langston's own burgeoning store of papers was not the least part. With approval, Langston listened as the Fisk University president Charles S. Johnson lauded Van Vechten as "the first white American to interpret objectively, with deftness and charm, the external features of the American Negro in a new age and setting." Later in the month, the New York *Herald-Tribune* saluted the appearance of the special number of *Voices* by reprinting six poems, including two by Hughes.

The highlight of the young year, however, was undoubtedly the premiere of *The Barrier* on January 18 at Columbia University, when the opera scored a stunning success. The *New York Times* hailed the libretto as "one of the strongest" in a long time, while the *Post* pronounced the show the best in the splendid history of the Theatre Associates. To Virgil Thomson, it was "a distinguished production"; and *The New Yorker* thought "it would be difficult to imagine a more brilliant one."

After attending a performance, Kurt Weill made a long telephone call to Langston praising the show but warning against a Broadway run. "Langston told me," Meyerowitz remembered, "that Weill said that there were not in New York thirty thousand people who would even be theoretically interested in such a production." But the backers had other ideas. Not long afterwards, Langston accepted an advance of $250 from Joel Spector and Michael Meyerberg, a more experienced producer who had joined forces with Spector, towards that goal.

Almost from the start, working on *The Barrier* had brought Meyerowitz hostile reactions from some quarters. "There were people who called me and insulted me about the fact that I was working with Langston Hughes. *How* can you work with Langston Hughes? What's this now?" The first person for whom he had played part of the opera told him flatly, "People are going to say you are crazy." After the Columbia success, the criticism seemed to intensify. "So I called Virgil Thomson, with whom I was very friendly, and he told me, '*Of course,* Jan! Why are you astonished? He is a homosexual and he is a communist.' Virgil was not being critical. He was just trying to explain to me what was going on." Undismayed by the political charge, Meyerowitz was sure that the anti-communist hysteria would die down. As for the accusation that Langston was a homosexual, "I believe that he was. I remember he had a picture on his desk of some black men in a chain gang, and one of the men was so unbelievably beautiful. Very beautiful. And Langston told me, 'I *love* him!' Now this man in the chain gang was very beautiful, and I would have loved him too. But the way Langston said it, it was too profound, too profound. I knew he was a homosexual." In any event, Meyerowitz had no intention of ending their collaboration.

The Broadway advance was not nearly enough to cover Langston's expenses. As in other times of need, he gambled on songs—for which there was no shortage of willing collaborators. Recently, composers as different as Edward Ballantine ("In Time of Silver Rain," for example) and Eubie Blake ("Life Is Fine") had set his verse. A Carmel composer had sent a setting of "Merry Go Round," which Langston pressed in person—without success—on a sulking Billie Holiday after one of her appearances at the Apollo Theatre in Harlem. Sammy Heyward set his "Ballad of the Freedom Train," and Gene Bone and Howard Fenton collaborated on "White Magnolias." With his good friend Juanita Hall, who had made a name for herself in Rodgers and Hammerstein's *South Pacific,* he wrote a blues, "Love Can Hurt You"; with Aunt Toy Harper, he penned the patriotic "This Is My Land." Nate White, his secretary, collaborated with Langston on a revue, "Hot Cinnamon." Not one became popular.

Success appeared mainly in the form of implied critical esteem, as when Olin Downes praised Marian Anderson's rendition of Howard Swanson's setting of "The Negro Speaks of Rivers" in a concert at Carnegie Hall. The latest Dwight Deere Wyman revue featured a number by Langston, "Dorothy's Name Is Mud," but paid him only $10.70 in royalties.

His winter of songwriting, as he called it, was followed by "my record spring!" Recordings of his songs featured Nellie Lutcher ("Baby, What's Your Alibi"), Juanita Hall ("Love Can Hurt You"), Burl Ives ("I Got the World by the Tail," with Albert Hague), and a singing group called the Striders ("Cool Saturday Night" and "Five O'Clock Blues"). Hoping for recordings, he took some gospel songs around to tempt the majestic Mahalia Jackson, and sent three pieces, probably more secular, to Lena Horne at her luxury hotel. But the winter-spring campaign in songwriting and recording would fail to result in the kind of rewards Hughes wanted and needed.

That spring, however, even before the official publication of *Simple Speaks His Mind* on April 14, a financial bonanza from the book seemed likely. "You've written a masterpiece," Van Vechten flatly declared; Arna Bontemps called the revision of the *Defender* columns "a miracle." What Langston wanted now was a best-seller. To this end, he showered complimentary copies on a long, sometimes incongruous list of writers, actors, comedians, folklorists, songwriters, and politicians, including John Foster Dulles, Robert Taft, and Harold Stassen. Although Simple was often militant, Langston tried to soften the tone of the advertisements. "Our difficulty has been," Maria Leiper once summed up, "to give something of the flavor of the book, and, at the same time, not to frighten prospective readers away by indicating that it is, in any sense, a tract." When frivolous advertisements brought a complaint from Hughes, Leiper reminded him of his role in shaping them: "We have been entirely convinced by you that the light-hearted approach is best." The light-hearted approach, at the expense of racial protest, seemed to be working. By its publication day, *Simple Speaks His Mind* had already sold almost fourteen thousand copies—more than any of Hughes's previous books. Unfortunately for his royalties, on the other hand, two-thirds of the sales were in cheap paperbacks. In a decision that pleased Langston, Simon and Schuster had taken the step, common in Europe but rare in America, of bringing out the book simultaneously both in cloth and inexpensive paperback printings.

Simple Speaks His Mind was the best received of all the books Hughes had ever published. Typical was Van Vechten's remark in his *New York Times* review that it was "better than a dozen vast and weighty and piously pompous studies in race relations"; and favorable comparisons were made between Hughes's Simple and Finley Peter Dunne's classic Mr. Dooley, as well as Artemus Ward and Josh Billings. Many readers marvelled at the balance between humane wit and racial assertion. "I don't know anything that is so candid & reasonable," Prentiss Taylor (Langston's collaborator on *Scottsboro Limited* in 1932) wrote privately, "& yet with such a core of militance." The brilliance of this loving portrait of a Harlem philosopher struck many black readers as unprecedented; to the novelist William Gardner Smith, Simple was "the voice of the American Negro as few have heard him speak." Not altogether inaccurately, another man suggested that black literature, until Simple, had been mainly "a literature of ideas, and ideals . . . but without human love for the people themselves as a group or as individuals." Overseas, the book fared very well. British reviewers seemed to enjoy its offbeat humor, and Mondadori of Italy bought the translation rights on unusually good terms. Proud of his success, Hughes let his *Defender* readers know—with several excerpts from the glowing reviews—that Simple, "this gentleman of color, who can't get a cup of coffee in a public place in the towns and cities where most of our American book reviewers live (unless it is a 'colored' place) is, nevertheless, being most warmly received by white critics from Texas to Maine."

His best-seller, however, did not come. Redoubling his efforts, Langston convinced Simon and Schuster to add $1500 to its advertising budget and insisted on advertising in at least one black newspaper. Sales did not increase. A link to a social affair at a Harlem nightclub, the Baby Grand, netted an order for one book. He mailed eighty-five letters about the work to various presidents of black colleges and related institutions; not one person replied. Free copies went to the *American Journal of Psychiatry,* presumably for use with black patients, but no new market developed there. Moreover, curious errors in delivery plagued the sale. Time and time again, as Maria Leiper noted in a house memorandum, copies were imperfect, failed to arrive on time, "—or at all"; in fact, the page proofs had disappeared after leaving the printer. By November, the problem had become so serious that a "terribly disturbed" Leiper insisted that all orders for *Simple Speaks His Mind* be delivered to her desk to be personally handled by the head of the shipping department. The mystery, and the question of sabotage, was never resolved.

Eventually the sale of the book crested near thirty thousand copies—a remarkable performance for Langston Hughes, but no *Native Son.* And the critical sensation of the spring in the publishing world, as far as black writers were concerned, was not Langston Hughes. "WONDERFUL about Gwendolyn Brooks getting Pulitzer Prize!" Hughes wrote with genuine enthusiasm to Arna Bontemps, as he reminisced about how he had helped to place her first published poem in the *Negro Quarterly* when Ralph Ellison was its managing editor. No such honor had ever come Langston's way; he must have wondered, given the kind of jobs he had taken on, whether such a prize would ever be possible. But he did not envy Brooks her triumph, nor question her portrayal of black culture as he had done with Richard Wright and *Native Son.* Reviewing the book in *Voices,* he had written of her as "a very accomplished poet indeed. . . . The people and the poems in Gwendolyn Brooks' book are alive, reaching, and very much of today." He sent Brooks a telegram of congratulations, then penned a "glowing tribute," as she judged it, in the *Defender:* "For almost ten years now, I have been hailing Miss Brooks as one of the most important literary talents in America. Naturally, I am delighted to see my own contentions vindicated."

Instead, he consoled himself with the appearance of the first scholarly essay on his work, John W. Parker's "Tomorrow in the Writings of Langston Hughes," which appeared in *College English* in May, 1949. "You did a fine job here," he praised Parker, a professor of English at Fayetteville State Teachers College in North Carolina, in requesting a dozen reprints of the essay. And foreign publication of his work, especially in Europe, continued. He was proud of Italian translations of *The Big Sea* (*Nel Mare Della Vita*, with a superb cover by Pablo Picasso) and his novel *Not Without Laughter* (*Piccola America Negra*), which also had previously appeared in France (*Sandy*), in Holland (*Niet Zonder Lachen*), and Argentina (*Pero Con Risas*). A Swiss house contracted to publish as a little book (*Vatur und Sohn*) the fertile short story "Father and Son," from which had come *Mulatto* and *The Barrier*. Never pressing for better pay, Langston urged his agent and Knopf to accept foreign offers even on unfavorable terms, as in the case of a Czechoslovakian offer to translate *The Big Sea* ("I'd rather like to see the book come out there"). His eagerness to help anyone who showed interest in his work led to the publication of translations by Herbert Roch of some of Langston's poems in the German magazines *Das Lot* and *Ulenspiegel,* and several poems were broadcast on Radio Berlin. Encouraged by his kindness and thoughtfulness, a Swedish correspondent in the United States, Eugenie Soderberg, helped to place his writing in Scandinavia, where a Swedish translation of *Not Without Laughter* (*Tant Hagers Barn*) appeared, along with an anthology of Negro poetry, *Mork Sang*, in which his work was featured.

In the spring of 1950, however, editions abroad could not lessen the sense of entrapment Langston was beginning to feel as he faced his various uninspiring projects. Badly wanting release from them, if only for a while, he applied to a foundation (Arna Bontemps had recently won a Guggenheim fellowship) for support to study the literature of black communities in the Caribbean and adjacent parts of South America. The foundation was not fooled.

Darkening the spring in April was the death at only fifty of Kurt Weill, which shocked Langston, who had been advising him in his attempts to cast *Lost in the Stars,* his opera with Maxwell Anderson based on Alan Paton's *Cry the Beloved Country.* "ALL MY LOVE AND SYMPATHY AND ASTONISHMENT AND GRIEF ARE WITH YOU TONIGHT," he wired Lotte Lenya. "IF THERE IS ANYTHING I CAN DO LET ME KNOW." A few days later, Carter G. Woodson, his stern but caring employer in Washington, D.C., in 1925, and the founder of the Association for the Study of Negro Life and History, as well as Negro History Week, also died.

Another loss came in April when M. Margaret Anderson's *Common Ground,* the journal to which he had retreated from the organs of radicalism, and in which he had published more pieces than in any other magazine in the forties, collapsed. "There is money for hate," Anderson regretted, "little for love." Thanking him for his support in its early days, almost ten years before, she remembered "the stature it gave the magazine and the stiffening it gave the spine of this unknown editor."

Now, as anti-communist hostility increased across the nation, Hughes's support stiffened few spines. After months of dodging the National Council of the Arts, Sciences and Professions, he finally agreed to join the playwright Arthur Miller on a radio broadcast protesting the jailing of two of ten Hollywood writers who had been cited for contempt by the House Committee on Un-American Activities for refusing to answer questions about membership in the Communist Party. Langston could not ignore the implications of the first imprisonment of an American writer for his beliefs in the 152-year history of the Alien and Sedition Acts. But when the radio networks all refused to carry the broadcast, he avoided further calls to protest the jailing or to work with the National Council. Both Hughes and the networks themselves had come under fresh attack, notably in *Red Channels: The Report of Communist Influence in Radio and Television,* published by a right-wing group, which devoted four pages to a list of Hughes's leftist sins. He remained a member-at-large of the National Council, but only in name. While other blacks, such as the sociologist E. Franklin Frazier, Paul Robeson, W. E. B. Du Bois (who that year, 1950, ran unsuccessfully for the U.S. Senate on the American Labor Party ticket), the novelist Willard Motley, author of the bestselling *Knock on Any Door,* and the composer-conductor Dean Dixon had become active in the counsels of the left, Langston kept his distance. Although he may have felt outrage at the official harassment of Robeson, especially the restrictions on his travel overseas, he declined to join any protest.

Uncontroversially, he himself travelled in the spring. Near the end of May, he joined Arna Bontemps, Melvin Tolson, Sterling Brown, and S. I. Hayakawa at the dedication of a new library at Lincoln University in Jefferson City, Missouri. (To Langston's sorrow, as he reported in the *Defender,* fewer than five whites came to hear them read and speak—in this, the capital of his native state.) Passing through Chicago, he joined Gwendolyn Brooks at a public celebration of her Pulitzer Prize on the South Side. Then he visited Ann Arbor, Michigan, for a week of performances, excellently received, of *The Barrier,* with Jan and Marguerite Meyerowitz accompanying the singers on two pianos at the Lydia Mendelssohn Theatre of the University of Michigan. He then returned home, via a quiet engagement in Pittsburgh, to begin a summer that promised mostly hard work at his typewriter.

Four projects dominated his study: the biography "Battle of Harlem"; the planned Broadway production, preceded by trial runs in Washington and Baltimore, of *The Barrier,* which demanded further changes in the libretto; the musical play "Just Around the Corner," which was booked for a tryout soon at a Maine playhouse; and the Pennsylvania opera with Elie Siegmeister. Pressed on all sides, Langston maneuvered to keep his collaborators at bay. To pacify Samuel Battle, whose biography was still unwritten, although the $1500 advance had long been spent, he left Harlem on June 12 for Greenwood Lake, New York, a favorite resort for prosperous blacks from nearby New York City. Working deep into the warm nights in a rented cottage near Mr. Battle's vacation home, he pushed forward for two weeks on the biography and—when

Mr. Battle was not looking—his other projects. That summer, respites were few—a birthday party at Carl Van Vechten's, a memorial concert for Kurt Weill, and a concert by the pianist Philippa Duke Schuyler at Lewisohn Stadium in Harlem, where Langston sat with Van Vechten and the determined young curator in American Literature at Yale, Donald Gallup, who had descended to the sub-basement at 20 East 127th Street to view his manuscript treasures. "The social high spot of my summer" came at Greenwood Lake on July 16, when Dr. and Mrs. Ernest Alexander, old friends and members of Harlem's elite, gave a catered buffet dinner for fifty, complete with engraved invitations, in his honor (Hughes had given some papers to a collection at Fisk that bore their name). Otherwise, he toiled virtually around the clock. One day, he staggered into the Harlem streets at dawn after a fifteen-hour stint at his typewriter only to be "THUNDERSTRUCK" to realize that it was Saturday— and that he, who prized reliability, had completely forgotten a radio appointment for the New York *Amsterdam News*.

Near the end of July, he reached the resort town of Ogunquit, Maine, to join Abby Mann, Joe Sherman, and Bernard Drew for the opening of their *Just Around the Corner*. At the Ogunquit Playhouse, he found the company in high spirits, with an able corps of singers and dancers led jointly by Fred Kelly, a brother of the Hollywood star Gene Kelly, and Langston's friend Avon Long, whose vivid career had included a triumphant portrayal of Sportin' Life in a 1942 production of *Porgy and Bess*. Liska March Cracovaner, who was co-producer ("in the sense that I was looking for a producer"), remembered pleasant days in Ogunquit, especially after the wealthy, exuberant producer Mike Todd, in town with another play, took out an option on *Just Around the Corner*. On July 29, the first-night crowd, drawn mainly from New Yorkers on vacation, reacted with enthusiasm. The critics were more reserved. *Variety* magazine praised Joe Sherman's "sock" score and Langston Hughes's "thoughtful lyrics," but joined other journals in finding little else of distinction in the show. "We had a meeting—Abby Mann and I—with Mike Todd in New York," Liska March Cracovaner recalled. "Mike Todd insisted on a new book, and Abby was very contrary about the matter. Todd threw us out of his office." Not long after, Todd filed for bankruptcy on debts of a million dollars.

"Just Around the Corner" quietly died, and with it went yet another of Langston's hopes for a windfall. "We were sometimes together in those days, he and I," Liska Cracovaner said. "One topic that came up often was money— I guess because I was nominally the producer, and had to worry about it. He would always say that he wanted to be financially secure, he really wanted that. But he never had any money. He was shy and private, and if I pressed him too much there was a very discreet veil that would descend when we talked. He was a very gentle man, with a great sadness behind his eyes, and you often wondered what was there after he took off all his onion skins. I don't think many people ever found out."

Back in Harlem, Langston turned again to the libretto of the Pennsylvania opera with Elie Siegmeister. They decided on a light rather than tragic opera,

Cocktails at Hollow Hills Farm, 1941. Third from left, Robinson Jeffers; at right, Noël Sullivan and Una Jeffers.

Noël Sullivan, 1941. *Photo by Carl Van Vechten. Courtesy of Bruce Kellner.*

Richard Wright and Carl Van Vechten, c. 1941. *Photo by Carl Van Vechten. Courtesy of Bruce Kellner.*

A busboy at the Stage Door Canteen 1943. *Photo by Carl Van Vechten.*

Yaddo, 1943. Back row, Carson McCullers; front row, center, Katherine Anne Porter.

With Ralph and Fanny Ellison, at a
tennis court in Harlem, c. 1943.
*Courtesy of Ralph and
Fanny Ellison.*

With Ethel Dudley "Toy" Harper, 1946. *Photo by Marian Palfi.*

Kurt Weill, c. 1946. *Photo by Karsh of Ottawa. Billy Rose Collection, New York Public Library.*

Blanche Knopf, 1932. *Photo by Carl Van Vechten. Courtesy of Bruce Kellner.*

Negro History Week, Atlanta, 1947. *Photo by Griffith J. Davis.*

Teaching class at Atlanta University, 1947. *Photo by Griffith J. Davis.*

At Fisk University, 1947: Arna Bontemps, Helen Pollock, Alberta Bontemps, Arna Alexander Bontemps, and Fania Marinoff (Van Vechten). *Photo by Carl Van Vechten.*

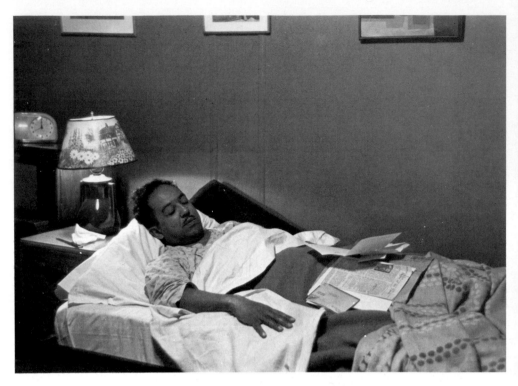

About noon one day in 1949. *Photo by Griffith J. Davis.*

Later that day. *Photo by Griffith J. Davis.*

William Grant Still, c. 1949. *William Grant Still Papers, University of Arkansas Libraries, Fayetteville.*

With Gwendolyn Brooks, Hall Branch Library, Chicago, 1949.

(*Above*) With Dizzy Gillespie, backstage at the Apollo, Harlem, 1949.
Photo by Griffith J. Davis.

With Jan Meyerowitz, c. 1949.

(*Above*) With Muriel Rahn and Lawrence Tibbett of *The Barrier*, 1950.

Working on *Just Around the Corner*, Ogunquit, Maine, 1950. *Courtesy of Joe Sherman.*

Book party for *Laughing to Keep from Crying*, 1952. Ellen Tarry, Roberta Bosley Hubert, Charles S. Johnson, and Grace Nail Johnson (Mrs. James Weldon Johnson).

The Sweet Flypaper of Life, 1955. With editor Maria Leiper; in background, Roy DeCarava. *By Maynard Frank Wolfe*.

With lawyer Frank Reeves, before Senator Joseph McCarthy's committee, U.S. Senate Building, March 1953. *AP/Wide World Photos*.

"Our Block's Children's Garden," 1955. *Photo by Don Hunstein.*

With Eartha Kitt, Henry Armstrong, and Pauli Murray, 1956. *A. Hansen Studio.*

"For a treasured Friend—Langston Hughes." Raoul Abdul, c. 1955.

In a neighborhood bar, c. 1955. *Photo by Roy DeCarava.*

At home, c. 1955.

first called "Pennsylvania Stars," then "The Princess of Altoona," and at last "The Wizard of Altoona" (after a Pennsylvania town). At the heart of the libretto would be a love story set in the western Pennsylvania coal fields, with Siegmeister drawing on the folk music of the region. But Langston had made little progress on "The Wizard of Altoona" when *The Barrier* summoned him to Broadway. By this time, with Samuel Battle growing daily more impatient to see his biography written, he was aware of the pressures he had brought on himself. "One show is enough!" he admitted. "But three . . . ."

Still, a success with *The Barrier* would make many things possible. Heading the cast, as the white father, was the fading but still renowned Lawrence Tibbett of the Metropolitan Opera, who had taken a leave of absence and personally invested $3,000 in the show. Opposite him, and with equal billing at his gallant insistence, was Muriel Rahn of the Columbia University production. Wilton Clary, who had gained admirers with his singing in *Oklahoma!*, would portray the troubled son. Before the first curtain in September, however, controversy struck. Protesting the plan to play the Ford Theatre in Baltimore, where blacks were forced to sit only in the "Buzzard's Roost," the back seats of the most remote balcony, the local branch of the NAACP questioned the propriety of Jewish producers, a Jewish theater-owner, Negro singers, and a famous Negro author all agreeing to segregation—especially since no law required it in Baltimore. Stung by the charge, Langston (who had once pilloried the producers and the cast of *Cabin in the Sky* for condoning segregated audiences) pointed defensively to his record: "My whole creative output has been devoted to fighting the color line in all of its forms." Since neither he nor the cast had any say in the bookings, "all we can do is bring moral pressure and persuasion to bear."

In fact, he and the producers saw a chance for free publicity. When Muriel Rahn declared that she would both sing (honoring her contract) and, when not on stage, picket the production, Langston declared that he would join her there. Moral pressure failed. The theater-owner refused to budge, and the Baltimore run was cancelled. Hughes then sent a wire to the local NAACP office: "FOR NEGRO ACTORS TO PERFORM IN THEATRES WHERE THEIR OWN FRIENDS AND RELATIVES MAY NOT PURCHASE SEATS AS DESIRED CAUSES BOTH THE ARTIST AND THE NEGRO PEOPLE HUMILIATION, SHAME, AND IRRITATION AT A DEMOCRACY WHICH PERMITS THIS CONDITION TO EXIST IN PLACES OF PUBLIC ENTERTAINMENT. . . . I AM HAPPY THAT MY PLAY IS NOT BEING PERFORMED UNDER EXISTING JIM CROW CONDITIONS."

This publicity backfired badly in Washington, D.C., a stronghold of racism that had nominally desegregated its theaters the year before only in order to end a boycott instituted by the "legitimate" drama guilds. Advance sales for *The Barrier* were slight. Evidently the theme of miscegenation repelled many white theatergoers, and an *opera* on the subject repelled others—and blacks as well, in spite of a sensational story by the Associated Negro Press (probably instigated by Hughes himself) that promised a "BOMB SHELL OPERA TO

EXPLODE IN WASHINGTON.'' No reservations were needed when *The Barrier* opened on Tuesday, September 26, at the New Gayety Theatre, a former burlesque house in a seedy area downtown.

The critics were almost uniformly hostile. In a typical response, the Washington *Post* reviewer called the show "altogether disappointing. . . . I don't believe such a story in the least"; the play made for "a sordid, depressing evening." Milton Berliner of the *Daily News* dissented. Noting the depth of critical hostility, he later argued that only a powerful production on a disturbing subject could have driven his colleagues to such extremes. Indeed, other critics had alluded to the stark, Greek-like tragic tone, the overwhelming sense of hopelessness in the end. In any event, *The Barrier* closed after five performances. In a memorandum to the producers, Hughes himself blamed not racism but a tendency as old as the original Broadway production of *Mulatto*. Although the current production was stronger and more beautiful in some respects than the previous stagings, something of its "simplicity and directness" had been lost, replaced by "a kind of bombastic melodrama" in which brutality and even sadism, "rather than a tragic self-defense," dominated the stage.

Later, Meyerowitz (who conducted the orchestra) blamed the fiasco on the shabby group of musicians assembled by Michael Meyerberg, and on Lawrence Tibbett. "Musically it was very bad. Meyerberg wouldn't spend any money, so we got these hacks who simply couldn't play the music. As for Tibbett, the poor man was past his prime and had no voice left. Once he had been one of the greatest baritones of the century, but now he sounded more like a drain pipe. He was also drunk a lot of the time. He wasn't nasty, but he just instinctively tried to take over, and dragged out his part. We should never have had him in the show. That Washington run was the worst experience of my life."

Muriel Rahn's husband, the veteran producer and singer Dick Campbell, later weighed the matter differently. "Muriel and I thought Tibbett fine, although the role had been sung better at Columbia. He was quite nice and affable to everyone in the cast, and everyone liked him. The problem was the music. The critics just didn't go for the music."

His Washington visit gave Langston a chance for a long delayed visit to the most controversial poet living in the city—in fact, in the United States. At St. Elizabeth's Hospital for the Criminally Insane, to which he had previously been invited by Prentiss Taylor, who worked as an art therapist there, Hughes read to an assembly and later met the hospital's most famous inmate, Ezra Pound, to whom Prentiss Taylor had given a copy of Langston's *Fields of Wonder*. For four years, or since being judged permanently and incurably insane by a government psychiatrist after his arrest on a charge of treason for pro-fascist, anti-American speeches in Italy during the war, Pound had been confined to the hospital. To Arna Bontemps, as to many liberals, he and his supporters for the Bollingen Poetry Prize of the Library of Congress—awarded to Pound the previous year—were "a sick lot." However, in addition to mere curiosity, Langston perhaps also remembered that Pound had written to him from Italy in 1931 in an effort to promote a greater knowledge of African art and culture, and later had responded favorably (unlike, for example, the Afro-American writer Jean Toomer) to Hughes's appeals for the Scottsboro Boys. He met Pound willingly.

Pound seemed anxious to make one thing clear to Hughes. In spite of reports to the contrary in East German radio reports, he had never denounced or vilified blacks. The two men exchanged books, with Langston offering a copy of *Simple Speaks His Mind.* A few days later, when the "insane" Pound wrote to thank Hughes for the gift, he showed at the very least that he had lost little of his critical ability. One of Simple's spoken phrases, "on which to lean" ("I can lean on this bar, but I ain't got another thing in the U.S.A. on which to lean") was all wrong for the character. "Dazz L. H.'s musical sense buttin' in," Pound perceptively admonished Hughes in his typical dialect style. Moreover, in developing Simple, Langston should try to employ more ideas taken directly from African folklore.

In New York, weighed down by misfortune, *The Barrier* staggered toward its planned opening at the Mansfield Theatre. Instead, when CBS offered Michael Meyerberg, who owned the house, a fabulous amount for its use, he insisted that the contract be broken. While the opera waited for another theater to become free, it toured the "subway circuit" in Brooklyn and the Bronx. Unfortunately, Lawrence Tibbett missed several performances. Meanwhile, to pay his bills, Langston left for a reading tour in Virginia, North Carolina, and Maryland, cramming about twenty-five readings into nine days, for fees that never exceeded $100. For extra money, he also took with him two hundred copies of *Simple Speaks His Mind.* He sold all. The idea that blacks didn't buy books was nonsense—almost. "I have found through many years of lecturing," he declared sagely, "that Negroes will buy books if they are brought directly to them." (Within five months of its appearance, he personally sold 647 copies of *Simple Speaks His Mind.*)

On November 2, he was back in Manhattan for the opening of *The Barrier* at the Broadhurst Theatre, which had suddenly become available when John Steinbeck's tedious drama *Burning Bright* flopped. *The Barrier,* which by this time had cost its investors about $63,000, fared no better. Meyerowitz's music was damned by Brooks Atkinson (who had reviewed *Mulatto* with sympathy in 1935) as "overcivilized and as remote from lynching and the blood lust as anything could be; and it is European in its artistic derivation"; Hughes's libretto was "hardly distinguished enough to sustain the complicated texture" of the score. In the *Daily News,* John Chapman praised the libretto, but found "little poignancy, little heartbreak, in the music." A few reviewers admired the show. "There is magnificence in it," Arthur Pollack claimed in praising the plain honesty of Hughes and Meyerowitz; "the season's hits look like nonsense compared with 'The Barrier'." He was decidedly in the minority, and the opera lasted only three days at the Broadhurst. "Such is show business," Langston gloomily concluded after his latest failure to recapture the glory of *Street Scene.*

To Meyerowitz, the reasons for the failure were clear. "These Broadway producers are born blackmailers," he confided many years later. "I advise you to have nothing to do with them, if you can help it. If we had had the Mansfield Theatre, as in our contract, we could have made a go of it. But the CBS money was too big. As for my music, well, I think maybe it was too Jewish. I listen to it now and it sounds awfully Jewish to me. It is also Negro, but maybe not enough for the show."

Ironically, when a stage success finally came Langston's way, he could claim neither profit nor satisfaction as a playwright from it—even though his own Jesse B. Semple, or Simple, was at center-stage. Alice Childress, born in South Carolina but raised in Harlem, and a versatile alumna of the Broadway run of *Anna Lucasta,* had adapted a small portion of *Simple Speaks His Mind* to the stage as part of a bill of one-act plays at the Club Baron on Lenox Avenue. Modestly offered, and smartly acted by a cast that included Kenneth Manigault, Clarice Taylor, and Maxwell Glanville, "Just a Little Simple" had caught on at once. One downtown reviewer reported "a charming little thing of a sort neither Harlem nor Broadway has ever seen before, . . . warm and wise and very friendly, played softly and affectionately."

This was not Simple's debut on stage. In May of the previous year, 1949, a rough-cut but effective little musical show based on the character had opened in Chicago at the Du Sable Community House. A few months later, Hughes had met with the experienced Harlem composer Dave Martin and the dancer-singer Avon Long to discuss Simple's future on the musical stage. Then Alice Childress, urged on by the Committee for the Negro in the Arts (a group of young Harlemites, including Ruth Jett and the playwright Loften Mitchell, who hoped to improve the place of blacks in the arts world), had begun her own adaptation. The success of her Simple, casually and modestly built, in contrast to the storm and stress of *The Barrier,* or the glitter of *Just Around the Corner,* encouraged his creator.

The last weeks of 1950 found him nevertheless in a melancholy mood, his spirits sinking lower as he again became a target of red-baiting, this time in New York City itself. On the powerful radio station WINS in Manhattan, Joe Rosenfield, the host of a program called "Big Joe's Happiness Exchange," accused Hughes of having been a member of the Communist Party for over twenty years. For several nights, Rosenfield regaled his listeners with testimony from the Committee on Un-American Activities about Hughes's subversive connections. What seemed to have provoked this attack was the announcement that Langston had been hired to write material for an exhibition at the New York Public Library on 42nd Street marking the twenty-fifth anniversary of the Schomburg Collection of Negro Literature and History, for which he had composed a poem, "Prelude to Our Age: A Negro History Poem." Although he did not allow the attacks to overwhelm him—he appeared prominently that month on a forum on censorship organized by the National Council of the Arts,

Sciences and Professions, at a Quaker luncheon, and at an NAACP party at Columbia University—unquestionably they threatened his morale.

Keeping close to home, he toiled mainly on the Battle book and his Pennsylvania light opera. Both, however, had begun to bore him. When Samuel Battle called with complaints that Hughes was ruining their chances for a movie, Langston turned a stony ear to the telephone. Elie Siegmeister, too, was clearly disappointed by Hughes's work. The composer's marginal notes on the second draft of the libretto called the first act "too 'atmospheric' " and like an oratorio; the hero was "too mamby-pamby." "I can see now," Siegmeister reasoned more than thirty years later, "that it simply wasn't Langston's kind of story, and maybe it was my fault for getting him involved in it. He was trying very hard to keep his end of the bargain, but the inspiration just wasn't there. He struggled with the show, and he wasn't very forthcoming when he fell behind. He didn't return calls, and so on, and that led to a little friction between us, although he was a wonderful guy otherwise."

Pressed by his collaborators, Langston responded by taking another job—an educational children's book for the publisher Franklin Watts, Inc. The manuscript could be done in about a week's time—or so Hughes deluded himself in accepting yet another advance. About this time, the firm of Henry Holt took "Montage of a Dream Deferred" on terms superior to those Hughes usually received from Knopf for his books of poetry.

"I am a literary sharecropper," he wailed to Arna Bontemps as the year came to an end. Often subsisting in a dreary kind of neo-slavery, black sharecroppers toiled on land not their own. In the old days, Hughes had lived like a valiant runaway slave, owning nothing, wanting little besides freedom. Now, slavery apparently over, he had forty acres—but he was the mule.

He first wrote of himself as a literary sharecropper—a term he would use again and again—a few minutes after a telephone conversation on December 27 with Ralph Ellison. Striving mightily for years to make his first novel a brilliant achievement, Ellison still had not finished it. Although some people had begun to snicker at his delays, Ellison continued to toil. "If he can take that long," Langston querulously wrote Arna Bontemps, with more self-pity than indignation, "why can't I—and he has been several years. I do not understand why my people all want their work delivered within the year, contracts not withstanding. They must be simple, and do not seem to know that creation needs to germinate." Ralph Ellison, however, was not dissipating his energy on popular songs, vapid Broadway shows, or the biography of a policeman. Setting a singular, grand goal for himself as an artist, he allowed little to deflect his effort. For which, in fact, Langston Hughes respected him above all the other younger black writers. *Montage of a Dream Deferred,* for which page proofs had just arrived from the publisher Henry Holt, was dedicated to Ralph and Fanny Ellison.

Sorrowfully, Langston knew that in spite of the burst of creativity that had led to "Montage," in many ways he was not working as a serious artist. And

Arna Bontemps, despite their partnership, understood that Hughes was paying a price and yet did not know exactly how to advise him. When he read a reprint of Hughes's old tale "On the Way Home" in Whit Burnett's anthology *Story: The Fiction of the Forties,* he asked Langston to reflect on its quality: "Do some more like that—strong, human, with race in the background, almost out of sight." Perhaps the downplaying of race was not the answer to Hughes's problems. But certainly he needed to improve the quality of his work, to make it stronger, more human, even as he looked for money.

Langston's Christmas postcards alluded to his financial plight.

> This Here
> Is a Lean Year,
> But, Anyhow,
> Christmas Cheer!

To which came a gently mocking reply from a poet with problems somewhat greater than his own:

> Langston's Lamenting
> Loud an' Long
> hope he gits cash
> fer his New Year song.

This was from "Ez" Pound, at "S. Liz."

On Christmas day, 1950, Nate White's wife Geraldine cooked a wonderful goose stuffed with wild rice. For a day or two, all at 20 East 127th Street were contented and sleepy. Weighed down by the projects hanging over his head, Langston remained in bed through the day after Christmas with what he said was a terrible cold. Shutting out the world and its deadlines, he snuggled warmly under his favorite Christmas present, an electric blanket.

"I hope I'm not electrocuted," he wrote Arna Bontemps. "I send you all my good wishes for a Happy New Year to you all!"

8

IN WARM MANURE
1951 to 1953

Hit me! Jab me!
Make me say I did it.
Blood on my sport shirt
And my tan suede shoes.

Faces like jack-o-lanterns
In gray slouch hats . . .
          "Third Degree," 1949

A S 1951 OPENED, Langston Hughes felt less than ever the glamour of authorship. The sheer drudgery of many of his labors was bad enough, but
boredom came attended by a nagging feeling of guilt about promises made and
contracts taken in the face of deadlines that loomed and then passed unmet.
Little relief was in sight, and little relief came. On January 28, after he and
Elie Siegmeister met at the latter's home to listen to the prologue and the first
scene of "The Wizard of Altoona," Langston left behind him a solemn promise to work soon on the libretto, which was far from completion. The promise
was genuine, but his attention soon wandered. A year later, he still groaned
under his burden. "I'm still a literary sharecropper," he confessed to Arna
Bontemps, "with deadlines from past larcenies to meet."

Needing not only cash but a vacation of sorts, and one preferably in warm
weather, he capitalized on Negro History Week and set off early in February
on a reading tour that took him first to New Orleans. There he loitered awhile
as the city prepared for Mardi Gras, then moved on to Baton Rouge, Jackson,
and Nashville, before working his way back to the North via Georgia, Alabama, Kentucky, and Maryland. On February 23, he ended his tour in Baltimore; for a fee of $40, he drew on his teaching experience at Atlanta Univer-
sity and the Lab School in Chicago when he addressed the annual convention
of the College Language Association, the major predominantly black organization of literary academics, on "Ten Ways to Use Poetry in Teaching." Although his ten ways were somewhat pedestrian, his definition of poetry was
generally inspired: "Poetry is rhythm—and, through rhythm, has its roots deep
in the nature of the universe; the rhythms of the stars, the rhythm of the earth

moving around the sun, of day, night, of the seasons, of the sowing and the harvest, of fecundity and birth. The rhythms of poetry give continuity and pattern to words, to thoughts, strengthening them, adding the qualities of permanence, and relating the written word to the vast rhythms of life.''

Except for a late cancellation by the president of West Virginia State College, who cited as his reason "certain unfortunate state wide publicity," the tour had gone off without conservative opposition. One national black leader, however, was not so lucky; his fate brought the possibility of trouble forcibly home to Hughes in the middle of his tour. In Washington, D.C., the venerable W. E. B. Du Bois and four white associates in the Peace Information Center, which was responsible for circulating the international anti-nuclear Stockholm Peace Pledge in the United States, and which had been widely attacked as a tool of the Soviet Union and international communism, were indicted on the charge of being the unregistered agents of a foreign principal. Du Bois and his colleagues faced a maximum sentence of five years in prison and a fine of five thousand dollars. To the consternation of many people, not least of all Langston, the eighty-three-year-old Du Bois was briefly handcuffed before being released on bail. When a public banquet in New York, arranged in defiance of the indictment, celebrated Du Bois's birthday on February 23, Langston bravely sent a telegram: "YOUR BOOK DARKWATER GREATLY INFLUENCED MY YOUTH. I GREW UP ON YOUR EDITORIALS. AS EDITOR OF THE CRISIS YOU PUBLISHED MY FIRST POEM. IN GRATITUDE ON YOUR EIGHTY THIRD BIRTHDAY I SALUTE YOU AS ONE OF AMERICAS GREAT MEN AND THE DEAN OF NEGRO WRITERS AND SCHOLARS.''

Nevertheless, this indictment strengthened his determination to avoid the left. Unlike Du Bois, he did not dare risk the ostracism by a large part of the black leadership that followed Du Bois's indictment, a banishment that deprived the old scholar-crusader of many speaking engagements in black communities, and led him later to mourn this period of his life as the time when "the colored children ceased to hear my name." Psychologically dependent on the regard of blacks to an extent matched by few other blacks, and by no other major black writer, Langston would have found such a loss virtually unbearable. Accordingly, pleading overwork, he turned down an invitation to speak at the end of April on a writers' panel at a cultural conference organized by the Philadelphia branch of the National Council of the Arts, Sciences and Professions and featuring a banquet in honor of Du Bois. On March 16, he rejected a nomination to serve as a member-at-large in a division of the New York branch of the Council—''since I do not like to assume responsibilities I cannot fulfill or be responsible for activities in which I cannot myself take an active part." On April 7, he declined a nomination to serve on the board of directors of the National Council—he was too often out of New York, and would not be active in the position. And he excused himself from an April 12 meeting of the National Council, where he was wanted on a public platform with John Howard Lawson, Dalton Trumbo, and Albert Maltz of the celebrated "Hollywood Ten" jailed and blackballed leftist screenwriters, who had just emerged from prison.

A personal reminder about the dangers of identification with the left came on the heels of the news about Du Bois. Along with the author John Hersey and the president of Twentieth Century-Fox, Spyros Skouros, Langston had been scheduled to receive an award for contributions to the arts at a banquet on March 1 in Philadelphia sponsored by an interracial group, the Philadelphia Fellowship Commission. At the last minute, however, Skouros, whose fame as a liberal came from having produced *Pinky* and *Gentleman's Agreement,* two movies purporting to address the racial issue from a liberal perspective, discovered Hughes's socialist record. Skouros then refused to accept an award with him unless Hughes specifically denounced communism. Quickly reaching Langston on the telephone, the executive secretary of the Commission demanded an impromptu denunciation for release to the public. The request appalled Langston, who denied that he was a communist but flatly refused to give such a statement under duress. The award was withdrawn. The black writer William Gardner Smith, who served as librarian of the Commission, and had nominated Hughes for the award, sent his apologies. "I am ashamed that it was my letter which dragged you into this idiotic mess," he wrote. "Even more, I regret the insanity of the national climate."

Faced with such evidence of the national insanity, Langston moved to defend his major means of livelihood. In a statement requested by Franklin and Helen Watts of Franklin Watts Inc., for whom he had finished a children's book, he denied any personal identification with the views of the persona of the poem "Goodbye Christ." Denying past or present membership in the Communist Party, however, he also conceded that his goal as a writer was to effect social change in a free, harmonious America: "If my little book, *The First Book of Negroes,* can help to that end, I'll be grateful." Both Hughes and the company, which clearly pressed him to make his book as inoffensive to conservatives as possible, asking for various revisions along this line, freely circulated the statement. Eventually, a copy went to Noël Sullivan at Hollow Hills Farm in California, who personified perhaps better than any of Langston's close friends the radical deterioration in the national attitude to the Soviet Union. "That we have merited the scourge and punishment that they represent," Sullivan wrote Langston, "I have little or no doubt, nor do I question that they, as the uncompromising allies of satanic falsehood and destruction, have evolved an almost fool-proof strategy for our doom."

In April, just after his accomplished secretary Nate White left him to pursue his own writing career, and in spite of other projects, Langston nevertheless began a second book based on the Simple columns ("I will NEVER take another advance," he solemnly vowed, "—unless it is BIG enough!"). He launched the project buoyed by the news of a fresh printing of *Simple Speaks His Mind* and by magnificent reviews of Victor Gollancz's London edition. "A piece of the pure gold of literature," the *British Weekly* hailed it. The authoritative *Times Literary Supplement* concurred: the book "enlists sympathy for the whole coloured race, and indeed all suffering humanity, through a shiftless ignorant drinker''; although a weak fellow, Simple nevertheless develops into ''a monumental representative of the outcast and oppressed'' through the revelation in the book of ''a deeper stratum still, a poetic stratum''; Hughes was one of those American writers who made British prose style ''seem anemic and insipid.'' Soon, Simple would make an impact in Germany, when the Berlin newspaper *Der Tagenspiel* started to publish a column about ''Kugelfang,'' a middle-aged city laborer admittedly based on Hughes's hero by the writer Rudolf Reymer, who had visited Langston in Harlem.

Citing the London reviews, on April 18 Hughes sent Maria Leiper at Simon and Schuster one hundred pages of the new book, which he called ''Simply Heavenly: A Conversational Novel,'' and which he proposed ''should really be a novel in overall form, telling more of a connected story than before. . . . And perhaps dealing a little less with purely racial situations.'' To Maxim Lieber, he wrote of ''the new novel—and NOVEL it will be,'' in projecting an eventual trilogy to be called ''The Saga of Simple.'' Although he had once spurned the idea of making the columns into a novel, he was now all eager to do so. One reason was his competitive anticipation of some news that Ralph Ellison, who had long endured Langston's teasing about his tardiness as a writer, brought triumphantly and in person on May 1 to 20 East 127th Street. As Langston immediately informed Arna Bontemps, Ellison announced that he ''has FINISHED his novel!''

For the moment, however, Langston had center-stage with the appearance from Henry Holt of his book-length poem *Montage of a Dream Deferred*. At a Sunday evening book party at the Afro-Arts Gallery at 7 West 125th Street, owned by the singer Etta Moten, Ida Cullen (the widow of Countee Cullen), and Estelle Osborn, a prominent figure in Harlem civic affairs, two hundred guests toasted its success with champagne; a few days later, in Greenwich Village, a New York University book club added its hurrahs. The critical response, however, was generally cool. J. Saunders Redding equivocated about Hughes as a poet: ''His images are again quick, vibrant and probing, but they no longer educate. They probe into old emotions and experiences with fine sensitiveness . . . but they reveal nothing new.'' Hostile as almost always, the *Pittsburgh Courier* reported ''a melange of self-pity, grief and defeatism.'' And in the *New York Times*, the poet Babette Deutsch delivered the harshest review Hughes had ever received there. Attacking his alledged tendency to lapse ''into a facile sentimentality that stifles real feeling as with cheap scent,'' she deplored the musty, nineteenth century quality she found in his repeated use of the word ''dream.'' In a work that demonstrated ''the limitations of folk art,'' Hughes's verse ''suffers from a kind of cultivated naiveté, or from a will to shock the reader, who is apt to respond coldly to such obvious devices.''

Hurrying to his defense, Maxim Lieber assured Langston that Babette Deutsch's own poetry ''will be as dead as the Egyptian mummies at the museum while yours will be sung the world over.'' And from his madhouse, Ezra Pound applied the balm of a simple criterion: ''Am glad to git some po'try I can read.'' Nevertheless, the severity of the criticism undoubtedly rattled Langston.

One year after Gwendolyn Brooks's Pulitzer Prize for poetry, he faced the judgment, broadly based, that he was utterly washed up in the genre. The tide of Modernism had apparently swept him out to sea—as it had swept to oblivion, apparently, all poets of social purpose, including the "guiding star" of his youth, Carl Sandburg. Later that year, in *Poetry* magazine, William Carlos Williams launched a crushing attack on the quality of Sandburg's work ("*The Collected Poems* make a dune-like mass; no matter where you dig into them it is sand"). Ominously for Hughes and his place even among black poets, the same number brandished a fifteen-page poem, "E. & O.E.," complete with scholarly notes in the manner of T. S. Eliot's *The Waste Land,* by Melvin B. Tolson, who had completely gentrified his aesthetic into High Modernism. With its myriad arcane allusions, the poem was basically unintelligible except to some scholars. Ironically, Tolson's champion at *Poetry* magazine was Karl Shapiro, who earlier in the year had summarily rejected some of Hughes's verse as being much too weak for the journal.

Faced with such criticism, Langston nevertheless was not about to cease writing verse. Indeed, his central creative identity, in spite of his plays, fiction, and essays, remained that of a poet. "Your dedication to poetry," Arna Bontemps wrote him encouragingly, "translated or written, even in periods of shortage, is something to be commended." Langston was thus especially pleased when the American Inter-Collegiate Poetry Association invited him to join his fellow Missouri-born poet Marianne Moore, of whom he was fond (because, "though we meet seldom, you have the gift of creating friendship and affection"), as an honored guest at a festival of poetry in Brooklyn. He was even more gratified when Robert Glauber, editor of the *Beloit Poetry Journal,* which had acquired his old translation of García Lorca's *Romancero Gitano,* or "Gypsy Ballads," proposed an edition of a thousand copies in chapbook form. Quickly endorsing the project, on June 7 Langston spent hours with García Lorca's brother, Francisco García Lorca, at the Columbia University professor's home at 448 Riverside Drive. Approving the publication, García Lorca pored over Langston's translations, most of which had been done in Madrid in 1937, and compared them to existing English, French, and Italian versions. The beauty and power of the original verse struck Hughes almost as forcefully as when he had begun the translations in Madrid fourteen years before. "The poems are really beautiful," he wrote wistfully to Arna Bontemps. "Wish I had written them myself, not just translated them."

In the fall, the first number of the *Beloit Poetry Chapbook* was devoted to *Gypsy Ballads,* Hughes's translations of fifteen of the original eighteen ballads in García Lorca's text.

Early in June, also most encouragingly, Maria Leiper sent her report on the Simple manuscript: "Your hero is as charming as ever, and as revealing to his readers of all kinds of facets of life." Not long afterwards, a contract followed for what Leiper had deftly renamed "Simple Takes a Wife," since the book would end with Simple's second marriage, to his loyal girlfriend Joyce.

The summer passed mainly in hard work at the typewriter, as Langston tossed off quick efforts for quick pay, or whittled away at his store of long-delayed projects. On June 24, he sent *Negro Digest* in Chicago an essay, "Do Big Negroes Keep Little Negroes Down?" about snobbishness within the race and the proverbial rudeness of many upper-income blacks. When he completed a one-act libretto, "Swamp-Town Outlaws," or "Wide Wide River," promised four years before to the white Southern composer Granville English, he was tickled by the man's astonishment: "Why, Ah can not believe ma ears!" The heart of the summer went, however, to the Simple book, the Pennsylvania light opera, and a new draft of "Battle of Harlem." For the last two projects, Langston made a sacrifice. Giving up the hot summer days in the city, which he loved, he made several visits to the country, which he detested. He joined Siegmeister at Lake Candlewood, near Danbury, Connecticut, and then Battle at Greenwood Lake, New York.

He did so reluctantly. "I am as happy in the city in August as I am in the wilds—indeed happier," he admitted in the *Defender*. "I like wild people much better than I do wild animals. And domestic animals, while pleasant to contemplate, never say anything interesting. A horse, a cow, a sheep, a goat, are amusing for a moment, providing you have not seen such for a long time. But animals are not much company after the novelty wears off. And I never miss them when I get back to New York." "I know the poem says, 'Only God can make a tree'," Langston later added. "But I am delighted that He has permitted men to make neon signs. Forgive me if I say I like neon signs just as much, if not better, than I do trees."

Among the neon signs were engagements high and low—PEN cocktail parties and visits to neighborhood Harlem bars, lunches with publishers and dinners with wealthy and poorer friends, and the stream of visitors from overseas that summer usually brought to his home in Harlem. Being in town also meant last-minute requests for lectures and readings in the metropolitan area that sometimes brought a little money and sometimes did not. At least once that summer, Langston read his poems, for a fee, at the International House at Columbia University, and once he spoke, but without pay, at the United Home for Aged Hebrews in New Rochelle. His various skirmishes with conservative forces had scarcely dulled his appeal to the newspapers and other media. Journalists, especially foreign, dropped by with fair regularity; his voice was heard on various radio shows, where he avoided politics but was eager to talk about his recent writing; and in August, at Columbia University, CBS-TV interviewed him as part of its popular magazine program, "All Around the Town."

He was careful not to speak about international affairs. The summer had also brought an uneasy peace to Korea, broken by bloody fighting, and the start in July of two years of rancorous negotiations between South Korea, the United States, and other forces under the United Nations umbrella and the alliance of North Korea and the People's Republic of China. By this time, more than 50,000 Americans had died and over 100,000 been wounded. In his column and other writings and in his speeches Hughes made virtually no reference to the conflict—except obliquely in a *Defender* column in which he contrasted the fate of General Douglas MacArthur, who now lived in the height of luxury at the Waldorf-Astoria Hotel in Manhattan after being dismissed for insubordination by President Truman, with the fate of certain individual black men who had been harshly sentenced for far less serious offenses. Otherwise, Langston was silent about almost all political and military affairs.

A ten-day "Book Week" tour of South Carolina, where at least once he shared a platform with Arna Bontemps, enlivened the fall. However, the change of season and the stimulation of the road brought no exciting new projects, no respite from the professional grind. Although Bontemps had joined Hughes "in renouncing literary sharecropping," mainly because "too many cullud have been bought too cheaply," they soon were ready to hitch up their plough for another scheme—an illustrated "juvenile" of 10,000 words about a black Philadelphia caterer who, according to his daughter, had brought the first recipe for ice-cream to the United States from France. When Bontemps suggested asking for an advance of $500, Hughes fairly leaped at this shadow: "I'd love to do it with you." Unfortunately, their plan collapsed when they discovered half-a-dozen accounts, all conflicting, of this momentous event.

At about the same time, the heat of right-wing indignation singed Langston even as it consumed his literary agent, Maxim Lieber. Fearing arrest after being identified as an underground communist operative by Whittaker Chambers in his autobiography, *Witness,* the Polish-born Lieber fled the United States for Cuernavaca, Mexico. His agency, which had served Langston with integrity and skill since 1933, was closing down; Lieber's wife, Minna, stayed behind briefly in New York to wind up its affairs. On October 19, she and Langston met with Ivan von Auw, Jr., of Harold Ober Associates of Manhattan to work out some of the details of Hughes's switch to the latter agency. Langston felt the loss of Lieber, and the circumstances surrounding it, keenly. In return for Lieber's service, and in recognition of his plight, he was determined to assure him continued revenue ("The contracts Max got for me are so much better than any I ever signed myself that I think he deserves this").

In Ivan von Auw, Langston had acquired another seasoned, successful agent. An Ober official since 1939, he had worked with the literary properties of F. Scott Fitzgerald, Faulkner, Pearl Buck, and other world-famous writers; that year, 1951, he had enjoyed a major success with the publication of J. D. Salinger's *Catcher in the Rye.* "Langston and I got along well from the start," he later said. "He would kid himself all the time. I never forgot his laugh—and when he wasn't laughing, he seemed to end every sentence with a chuckle. We had certain things in common. I sympathized with him in his left-wing ties, because I had some myself. I had never met Maxim Lieber, but Van Vechten I knew. And I had once been a very serious music student, playing the piano, and I had heard a lot of the old musicians, people like Bessie Smith and Eubie Blake. I found Langston a jolly, amusing guy, very sharp and witty. He was a man of intellect and principle who worked hard but didn't take himself too seriously. We had no trouble establishing a solid relationship. If I had been his manager, though, some things would have been different. He didn't concentrate enough on just one project. Instead, he seemed easily distracted, always running all over the place. He honestly believed that the way to get ahead was to take on everything offered. I think he was wrong; but perhaps he had no choice, really.''

The routing of Lieber from the United States made Langston keep an even greater distance from political controversy. Still, he watched closely, with a mingled sense of apprehension and outrage, as the trial drew near of Du Bois and his co-defendants in the Peace Information Center. In August, he had ignored separate calls by Du Bois himself and by William L. Patterson, among the leading voices in the radical ranks, to support W. Alphaeus Hunton, Frederick V. Field, Dashiell Hammett, and Abner Green, who had been arrested and jailed for their political activities. He had also ignored the National Council of the Arts, Sciences and Professions when it requested his signature on a statement by writers in support of world peace. And at the end of the summer, Langston was also deaf to an invitation from the writer Shirley Graham, who had married Du Bois soon after his indictment, to at least one meeting planned by the National Council to protest her husband's indictment.

Consistent with his approach to the trial of the twelve communist leaders the previous year, he held his fire until the last moment; when at last he spoke his mind, he again did so in his weekly column in the black *Chicago Defender*. On October 6, under a disclaimer by the *Defender* management, he broke his silence with an impassioned essay that opened by calling the threat of imprisonment to Du Bois an affront to world opinion and closed on an almost incantatory note: ''Somebody in Washington wants to put Dr. Du Bois in jail. Somebody in France wanted to put Voltaire in jail. Somebody in Franco's Spain sent Lorca, their greatest poet, to death before a firing squad. Somebody in Germany under Hitler burned the books, drove Thomas Mann into exile, and led their leading Jewish scholars to the gas chamber. Somebody in Greece long ago gave Socrates the hemlock to drink. Somebody at Golgotha erected a cross and somebody drove the nails into the hands of Christ. Somebody spat upon His garments. No one remembers their names.''

This gesture did not go unacknowledged. Not long after the column appeared, the presiding judge ended the trial by allowing a motion by the defense for a directed acquittal. Du Bois's key supporters thanked Hughes for his ''magnificent'' essay: ''It was of the stuff that contributed to the vindication of Dr. Du Bois.''

In spite of his courageous essay, however, Langston was no more eager than before to stand up to the wave of anti-communist emotion sweeping the nation, which now seemed to be generated by Senator Joseph McCarthy and his staff on the Senate Sub-Committee on Permanent Investigations. But his gestures of conciliation, or of timidity, were often in vain. Seeking an engagement at black Texas Southern University, he was asked to sign an oath of loyalty as required by state law; after he complied, the president of the school banned him anyway. Langston practically begged the publisher E. P. Dutton not to quote "Goodbye Christ" in the forthcoming book *Shanghai Conspiracy* by General Charles A. Willoughby, who had been chief of intelligence for Douglas MacArthur for a decade. The poem, Willoughby argued, was evidence of the "traitorous and corrosive quality" of the League of American Writers ("this poisonous outfit"), to which Hughes had belonged, and of other allegedly communist front organizations. Langston countered that the poem had been used unfairly by racist right-wing groups to foment hatred. "Since it is an ironic poem (and irony is apparently a quality not readily understood in poetry by unliterary minds) it has been widely misinterpreted as an anti-religious poem. This I did not mean it to be." Beneath the utterances of the persona, who sees all religion as bad, "is a pity and a sorrow that this should be felt to be true." Any other interpretation of the poem comes from "a failing of craftsmanship on my part." The publisher was not swayed. "Goodbye Christ" appeared in its entirety.

With the new year, 1952, Langston developed a "sty" on one of his eyes. His doctor warned about extreme fatigue, but Hughes was also suffering from mounting nervous tension. February 1 should have been a momentous date—his fiftieth birthday—but he did not draw attention to this milestone. The quiet at 20 East 127th Street was broken only by a party in honor of Arna Bontemps, the Columbian writer Jorge Artel, and Jan Carew, a tall, handsome actor and intellectual from British Guiana, and a celebrity as a member of Laurence Olivier's Old Vic company then visiting New York. Otherwise that month, Langston kept to his various writing tasks, venturing only occasionally into the limelight.

In Cleveland, he read poems and lectured about black music in a program that included the pianist-composer Margaret Bonds and the baritone Daniel Andrews, a former soloist with the Tuskegee Institute choir. Managed by the experienced promoter Dick Campbell, Langston and his colleagues hoped to make money by performing on a regular basis. From Cleveland, he left for a Negro History Week tour of North Carolina and points south. In Texas, he ran into trouble. Predictably, an invitation from a white group, the Business and Professional Women's Club of Fort Worth, which wanted to raise money for a water-cooling system for a poor local black school, incited opposition. In San Antonio, local conservative forces, including the American Heritage Protective Association, attacked his sponsor. A local "Minute Woman" refreshed the city council's memory about the violent mob of five thousand protestors who had stormed the library auditorium when alleged communists had attempted to speak there in 1939. In both Fort Worth and San Antonio, Hughes's engagements were cancelled. Pearl Buck, the liberal Southern author Lillian Smith, and the presidents of Atlanta University and Morehouse College recently had endured similar setbacks with interracial efforts. "It looks as if reactionary whites are out to destroy interracial good will in so far as audiences and speakers go, especially in the South,'' Hughes regretted to his Fort Worth sponsors; ''the kind of 'democracy' they claim to be protecting is the kind that keeps the FOR WHITE signs up all along the line, and not just in the South.''

Defiant as his words were about interracial efforts, his acts were more cautious. When in May he resigned from the National Council of American-Soviet Friendship, Hughes stated his reason flatly: ''A major portion of my income is derived from lecturing in the Negro schools and colleges of the South. . . . Negro speakers do not have the vast area of white women's clubs (with their teas and other social aspects) from which to secure engagements. So our fees must come almost entirely from Negro institutions,'' which, he explained, too often had to submit to conservative pressures. Langston justified his inaction in another way when he replied testily, even bitterly, to a questionnaire from the Authors League of America, a major professional group, on the effects of right-wing hostility on its members. Naturally he was unaffected by political censorship in radio and television: ''Negro writers, being black, have always been blacklisted in radio and TV.'' In twenty-five years of writing, he had been asked to work commercially on radio or television no more than four or five times. White racism, not conservative political ideology, kept NBC from hiring black writers even for ''black'' shows—''the better to preserve the stereotypes, I imagine.''

Angry or not at racism, he refused invitations from the radical American Labor Party and one from the U.S.S.R. Writers' Union to visit Russia to celebrate the centenary of the death of Nikolai Gogol. His secretary—or he himself—replied to a request from the World Council of Peace in Prague that Hughes was out of town and not expected back for several weeks (in fact, he was due back in New York City within a few days). Fresh requests from Du Bois, whose leftward march had only accelerated with his trial, were ignored. A wire asking for a short statement backing clemency for the Rosenbergs, who had been sentenced to die for treason after allegedly passing atomic secrets to the Soviet Union, and in whose support Du Bois was conspicuous, went unanswered. Yet in the *Defender* Langston unambiguously praised Du Bois's latest book, *In Battle for Peace,* about his indictment and trial, and recommended it to his readers.

He was prepared, on the other hand, to work openly for black civil rights, especially through the NAACP and the Urban League, as he testified in the *Defender:* ''I would like to see every Negro belong to both the NAACP and the Urban League, since these organizations have proven over the years their great social value to American democracy.'' When he returned to New York from Texas, he set aside other projects to work for an NAACP fund-raising rally on March 6 at Madison Square Garden, which featured a variety of top artists and entertainers, including Henry Fonda, Yul Brynner, Canada Lee, Steve Allen, and Tallulah Bankhead. Working with the musicians Josh White, Margaret Bonds, and Sammy Heywood, he composed ''The Ballad of Harry Moore'' in honor of an NAACP state organizer who had been killed with his wife the previous Christmas Eve when his home in Mims, Florida, was bombed—a crime for which no one had been punished. In particular, the NAACP commanded his respect; his distaste for the organization in the nineteen thirties was far behind him. "What the NAACP is doing benefits not just colored people but the whole U.S.A.," he would write at the end of the year, after a dazzling series of victories by the legal branch of the oganization headed by his Lincoln University schoolmate Thurgood Marshall. "Certainly the NAACP is currently washing democracy's ears with legal wash cloths that are getting rid of some of the dirt that has been clogged there for a long, long time. It's also removing some of the scales from democracy's eyes."

Segregation was under steady legal attack, but most of the old racist divisions endured. Looking for a cup of coffee in a Houston train station, Langston was directed by a helpful white woman at an information desk to the kitchen of a café. "When I said that I was not used to eating in the kitchen in public restaurants," he recalled, "she simply turned her head away. Had I been a citizen of Houston directing a stranger in a railroad station to the kitchen to eat, I would have been ashamed, but not this Southern white woman. She did not even blush."

A few months later, on the other hand, in a dining car on a train in Mississippi, he received the most courteous treatment he had ever received in the South. The usual screen preserving the "Negro" table from the vision of whites had been removed, and the white steward, as well as the black waiters, was the soul of solicitude. The South was certainly changing, Langston mused almost mistily. At the end of the meal a waiter thanked him. "We are delighted to have you on this train, Mr. Marshall."

"Mr. Marshall?" I asked. "Which Mr. Marshall?"

"Thurgood Marshall," said the waiter.

Within the black world, however, there were also trends and portents in the early years of the ninteen fifties that more and more disturbed Hughes. In reponse to the comparatively few concessions to blacks in the postwar years, and in spite of the bitter counterattacks of die-hard segregationists, racial pride seemed to be dramatically on the wane; the whispered promise of integration was lulling many members of the black middle class to sleep.

Clear signs of the trend were noticeable. The attack on his *Montage of a Dream Deferred* by certain black critics, although it sounded notes heard since the nineteen twenties, had been part of this revival of a mood that seemed to Langston almost like racial shame. In Cleveland, the Karamu Theatre, which once had spurned black plays altogether, then had accepted them, now refused to stage a play—Hughes's *Mulatto*—because it ended with a lynching. Basking in the new "progress," middle-class black audiences were demanding more optimistic dramas; once again, as in days of old, they seemed to prefer dramas that avoided race altogether. In the *Defender,* he protested that young blacks were rushing through doors barely cracked in white colleges while black instructors, who were not being hired by these schools, were being laid off as a result. On January 13, 1952, speaking at Club Baron in Harlem with the veteran actresses Fredi Washington and Abbie Mitchell on the possibility of a local community theater, he lashed out at the virtual refusal of black groups to stage plays by or even about blacks. "Every colored college I visited," he lamented a few weeks later, "had just done some 'white' play, with nary a Negro authored or Negro subject-matter play on the list this year! Not one! Which *do* seem strange to me." He had made the same point in the *Defender:* "There is nothing wrong in Negro groups presenting plays about other people's lives. But . . . we will never develop a theatre of our own based on the plays of other races." On February 8, when he served as master of ceremonies at an annual black folk festival in Cleveland, Langston made a similar point. "We have a rich folk heritage in our country, and much of it has come out of the Negro people," he declared; but some people were "ashamed" of that heritage.

Early in 1952 Langston's morale was boosted by the appearance of *Laughing to Keep from Crying,* his first book of short stories in almost twenty years. Brought out by Henry Holt, the volume collected twenty-four stories, most of which had been published previously in a wide range of magazines, including *American Spectator, The New Yorker, Esquire, Stag, Story, Negro Story, Scribner's,* and *Crisis.* The oldest probably had been written in 1934 in Reno, Nevada, near the end of the turbulent year in Carmel that had produced *The Ways of White Folks,* Hughes's highly praised first collection. While often lauding him for his technical facility, however, reviewers now as often as not commented also on the uneven quality of the book. Certain stories flashed with illuminations, but others were allegedly passé because of changes in the racial climate. Bucklin Moon, who had edited *The Poetry of the Negro* at Doubleday, praised Hughes's sharpness of imagery, his fine ear, and above all his "economy of words." The *Nation,* on the other hand, found Hughes "very very good" when he was good, "and when he is bad he is either insincere or superficial." Other reviewers were less kind. J. Saunders Redding, now firmly established as the grey eminence of Hughes's reviewers, looked in vain for "something more, something deeper and darker that he could tell us if he would."

But the voices of the reviewers of *Laughing to Keep from Crying* were soon drowned in the rolling thunder of praise that greeted the appearance in April, 1952, of Ralph Ellison's *Invisible Man.* Almost universally, the long-awaited novel was hailed as a magnificent work of American fiction—certainly the finest accomplishment in the Afro-American novel since the appearance of *Native Son* in 1940. After his long friendship with Ellison, which dated from the latter's first star-struck days in New York City in 1936, Langston felt an almost proprietary interest in the book; Ellison was "a protégé of mine, so naturally I'm delighted." In turn, the Ellisons unquestionably saw him as someone special. "We feel these days," Fanny Ellison wrote Langston, "as if we are about to be catapulted into something unknown—of which we are both hopeful and afraid." With her husband's triumph at last in view, she thanked Hughes for his help to them over the years: "You are a much loved person, Langston, and your generosity and friendliness have touched and helped many people. But we feel you have invested in us a very special generosity, a very special faith, and a selflessness even.''

Touched, Langston sent a telegram in reply. "DEAR FANNY (AND RALPH—YOU MUST GONNA BE GREAT BECAUSE I CANNOT READ YOUR NAME) THAT WAS ABOUT THE MOST WONDERFUL LETTER I EVER RECEIVED.'' If this reply was slightly barbed, perhaps it was because Langston may have sensed that Ralph had not subscribed fully to his wife's unequivocal statement of gratitude. Certainly Hughes was happy for Ellison. "I've given it some thought," he had written privately only a few months before, "and think of no young Negro writer who seems to me more talented." Nevertheless, the appearance of *Invisible Man* marked the beginning of the end of the warm relationship between the two men. Critical and financial success now freed Ellison to develop a course independent of the Harlem literati and intellectuals, such as they were; he had become uncomfortable in the very circles in which Langston revelled. Appearing less and less frequently at book parties and cocktail hours, he eventually became a stranger at 20 East 127th Street, where he had once come and gone freely. At least at first, Ellison made a careful distinction between Hughes and Hughes's friends. Langston undoubtedly admired and liked him, he wrote to Richard Wright—"but few of his friends do.'' Toy Harper regularly invited him to her home but then tried to bait him into tiresome disputations on politics and other affairs for which, Ellison believed, she was ill equipped. "I have no time for such foolishness," he informed Wright.

Although Langston initially was happy for Ellison, the astonishing success of *Invisible Man*, coupled with the growing privacy of the younger writer, slowly antagonized him. A year after its publication he confided to a friend that he had not been able to read past page 90 of the book—"but it is my determination to keep on." Unlike *Native Son*, however, nothing in *Invisible Man* offended Hughes—unless he was taken aback by its complexity. Indeed, its life-affirming essence, in spite of Ellison's modernist virtuosity, seemed to support Hughes's belief that the artistic and social vision of black Midwesterners, such as Ellison and himself, was fundamentally different from that of Southerners, such as Wright, in that the latter were more conditioned by racism, violence, and gloom. In choking on the novel, Langston to some extent was simply envious of its author. On the other hand, he did not act on his envy. Before the book appeared—before, apparently, he had read it—he plugged *Invisible Man* in the *Defender* as a novel "that will make you shake in your boots and see the race problem anew from twelve different angles according to your line of vision." A year later, after Ellison's triumph had been established, Hughes was still attentive: *Invisible Man* was "deep, beautifully written, provocative and moving."

From this point, however, Ellison would scarcely need the help of someone he had come to see as intellectually and creatively almost irresponsible. Years later, he would look back on Langston Hughes as someone who, early in his career, had made fateful, even fatal decisions about the life of the Afro-American artist. In the late thirties, there had been no question of the young man from Tuskegee becoming his disciple. "Langston was a lot of fun to be with," Ellison allowed, "and a warm and very gracious man; but as far as being impressed by his intellectuality is concerned, how could I be? There were people at Tuskegee who were far more intellectual." In 1940, Ellison had reviewed the autobiography *The Big Sea* without enthusiasm; it was a "chit-chat book," he later judged, unworthy of a man who had known intellectuals around the world. Langston had responded to the review in a fashion Ellison found "rather appalling": "Langston said to me, 'If I wrote the book you wanted me to write, people wouldn't buy it, and I would have to take a job'." As for Hughes's dedication of *Montage of a Dream Deferred* to him and his wife, Ellison guessed that the gesture probably stemmed from the fact that "I had called his attention to what was happening in the vernacular—be-bop and so on." To Ellison, Hughes as an artist "used his emotions and sensibility more than his intellect." Langston Hughes "was very easy-going. He would not think, and during that period I was trying very hard to deal consciously both with writing and with politics." The paths of the two writers diverged forever.

Feeling more than ever the ignominy of his role as literary sharecropper, Langston packed his typewriter and his dog-eared files on Jesse Battle and set out in early May for Greenwood Lake, determined to rid himself at last of the biography "Battle of Harlem." His mood was not leavened by conditions there. His borrowed cottage proved to be cold and damp, in spite of June; as he pecked at his typewriter, a fire snickered at his back. Once he went out to the training camp of the brilliant boxer Sugar Ray Robinson, whose popular bar in Harlem he liked to visit; but mostly he worked. Without the slightest inspiration or any encouragement beyond an aching desire to be rid of the task, he pushed on. He still had one chapter to go when the owners of the cottage arrived with a grandchild, a dog, and a passion for the Brooklyn Dodgers baseball games on the radio. Langston quit Greenwood Lake for Harlem. There he found awaiting him not peace, as he noted impatiently, but a mound of importuning letters from "folks who want a parole, immediate cash help, lyrics for music, and such time taking and thought consuming things."

Overworked, he reluctantly turned down a producer's invitation, approved by Katherine Anne Porter, for him to dramatize her story "María Concepción" from the *Flowering Judas* collection. His only fresh and yet mature work was the relatively brief libretto of an Easter cantata, "The Glory Around His Head," to be set by Jan Meyerowitz. Then, in time stolen from the Battle book, to his own mystification Langston sank suddenly into writing for children. "Where, whence, and how come all the juveniles for me all of a sudden," he wondered, "I don't know!" He needed the advances. Having successfully completed the *First Book of Negroes* for Franklin Watts Inc., he quickly agreed to do another book—on rhythms—in its "First Book" series. For Dodd, Mead, Hughes had composed earlier that year an introduction to a special edition of Harriet Beecher

Stowe's *Uncle Tom's Cabin* ("the most cussed and discussed book of its time," "a moral battle cry," but also "a good story, exciting in incident, sharp in characterization, and threaded with humor"). Admiring the easy charm of the essay, Edward Dodd, Jr., commissioned a thirty-thousand-word effort in juvenile biography to be called *Famous American Negroes*. In addition, fishing out of his files an ancient, often-rejected effort for young children, "The Sweet and Sour Animal Book," Langston attempted again to peddle it to various publishers.

On August 9, at twelve minutes to midnight—as he noted with relief and exasperation—he at last finished the sixth and final draft of "Battle of Harlem." By this time, the Hollywood movie agreements, on which he had once banked heavily, had lapsed. Nor was Jesse Battle the only man disappointed, even disillusioned, by Langston and his habits of work. "I am terribly distressed about what is happening to our show," Elie Siegmeister had warned Langston in January. His distress had brought few results. Finally, on July 17, under increasing pressure from his sponsors, and with most of his telephone messages and letters to 20 East 127th Street unanswered, the hitherto patient Siegmeister lashed out. "Apparently," he accused Langston, "you are quite content to walk out and leave me holding the bag." Siegmeister then delivered an ultimatum: Hughes should either send a libretto within one month—it was more than two years overdue—or return the $500 advance.

The money was not returned, and the libretto was not delivered within a month. Instead, Langston made peace with Siegmeister with a promise to meet an interim demand of the sponsors for a one-act version of "The Wizard of Altoona" within a few months. Keeping his public appearances, especially those that took him out of town, down to a minimum, he made time, however, for a concert at Carnegie Hall with Margaret Bonds and William Marshall, who had sung and acted in *Lost in the Stars, Green Pastures,* and other major shows; Langston Hughes "triumphed in his portion of the program," a reporter noted, "speaking from notes with the skill born of years on the lecture platform." But Langston also had to work on another manuscript on which he was behind schedule—the second collection of his Simple stories. When Maria Leiper of Simon and Schuster returned from vacation in Europe, on her desk were gifts from him: a bouquet of pink roses, a copy of the special edition of *Uncle Tom's Cabin,* his "Battle of Harlem" biography ("a kind of Negro success story"), and the dulcet promise of the second Simple manuscript soon. In fact, it took a tremendous effort in one week in September before he finished it. When he presented the manuscript to Maria Leiper at lunch on September 26, Langston congratulated himself. "White folks (and Ralph)," he boasted genially to Bontemps, "would take at least two years on such."

Throughout the preparation of his second Simple book, Ellison's work had remained on Langston's mind. Aware that the greatest material and critical successes in black fiction in his time—*Native Son* and *Invisible Man*—had been achieved in the novel, he wondered elaborately to Maria Leiper and to his new agent whether the Simple book might not be marketed in that form. "I wish it was a novel!'' he grumbled to Ivan von Auw of Harold Ober. ''(Why don't I write one, huh?)'' Simon and Schuster accepted the manuscript, but for what it was—a skillful stitching of work two thirds new, the rest from the *Defender*—but not a novel.

Now he was free to start work on his one-act version, called ''Princess of Altoona,'' of the libretto ''The Wizard of Altoona.'' In mid-October, he had made some gratifying progress when he broke off to travel to Jackson, Mississippi, for the Diamond Jubilee celebrations of Jackson College (later Jackson State University). There he joined a stellar cast of black writers, including Margaret Walker, now a professor at the college, Arna Bontemps, Robert Hayden, Sterling Brown, Melvin Tolson, Owen Dodson, J. Saunders Redding, and Era Bell Thompson, the managing editor of *Ebony* magazine, for several days of readings, discussions, and debates on literature and culture. Here at least—in spite of the high-toned objections of the poet Robert Hayden, in particular—he found a refreshing, even exhilarating appreciation of folk and other forms of vernacular black culture. Although the event was perhaps too drawn out for his liking, Langston was gratified to see people come from miles away to listen to and applaud the speakers—''the largest and most appreciative week-long audiences I've ever seen for writers and writing.''

At Fisk University in Nashville, where he read on November 3, an alliance of the local post of the American Legion, a unit of the American Federation of Labor, and a group of ministers attempted to block his appearance. However, unlike certain weak-kneed college presidents, Charles S. Johnson stood fast. He even forbade the tape-recording of the reading by the conservatives as a violation of freedom of assembly and academic expression. Spurred by the presence of the unwanted visitors, the International Center of the university rocked to one of the most wildly applauded programs of his career. Then Langston caught an airplane for New York to be in time to vote in the presidential elections. Unlike in 1948, when he had publicly praised Henry Wallace, nowhere did he give any indication of his choice among the candidates.

The Christmas season found him with exactly $9.04 in his bank account. Near December 25, to his premature relief, he sent off ''Princess of Altoona,'' the one-act version of ''The Wizard of Altoona.'' About a month later, he finished what he now called ''Pennsylvania Spring,'' after overhauling the entire project; it acquired a new plot and characters but preserved some of the old songs. Soon, *The First Book of Negroes* appeared from Franklin Watts to excellent reviews—''truly the finest book of its kind,'' one fellow author lauded him—but with little promise of much financial reward. His agent, Ivan von Auw, like Maxim Lieber before him, thought Langston's Watts contracts ''rather appalling in some respects.'' Langston agreed—but he needed the cash.

Meanwhile, although he made relatively little money from them, the many translations of his works testified to growing interest in him abroad. A Japanese version of selections from *Poetry of the Negro* appeared, as well as a translation by the Argentian writer Julio Galer of eighty-one Hughes poems, published by Editorial Lautaro in Buenos Aires. Additional Argentinian editions came of *Laughing to Keep from Crying* (which also appeared in Czech) and *Mulatto*. From Paris, the progressive publisher Pierre Seghers inquired about a volume in his *Poètes d'Aujourd'hui* series, to be translated by Léon Damas of French Guiana. A Chinese book of black American poetry, translated by Tsow Chiang, prominently featured his verse. Langston also assisted the Dutch-born scholar Rosey Poole, soon a major promoter of black writing in Europe, in preparing a selection of poetry for the BBC in London. And he continued as always to champion foreign writers, especially those of Latin America and the Caribbean, even after a senior editor at Knopf warned him that "the sad fact is that for most people in this country, Latin America and its history simply do not exist."

Such consolation as came from foreign editions of his work probably amounted to little when the aging literary sharecropper looked disconsolately on the harvests of certain younger men. On January 29, 1953, Ellison's triumph with *Invisible Man* was crowned when he accepted the National Book Award in fiction. Present at the ceremony but obviously alienated in spirit, Langston reported to Arna Bontemps that the proceedings were "mildly interesting," dull really, with all the speeches stuffily delivered from prepared texts. Not long afterwards, at a cocktail party at the Algonquin Hotel in mid-Manhattan to welcome Ellison as a new member of PEN, he begged the new star of Afro-American writing not to read a long, dull paper when he visited Fisk University soon—long papers were so dull. As he had with Wright almost fifteen years before, Langston was feeling the chill of his own eclipse.

He shivered again early in February when an advance copy reached him of the latest sensation in black literature, James Baldwin's dramatic first novel *Go Tell It on the Mountain,* about a black boy's troubled passage to manhood in the face of raw conflicts with his domineering father and the terrifying pressures of black "storefront" religious fundamentalism. Worse yet, from Hughes's point of view, the book was being published by Knopf, who for all practical purposes had dropped him (the reception of *Montage of a Dream Deferred* had gutted its interest in his volume of selected poems). Criticizing Baldwin's sometimes unstable blending of gritty realism and refined rhetoric in the novel, Hughes judged that if Zora Neale Hurston, "with her feeling for the folk idiom," had been its author, "it would probably be a *quite* wonderful book." Baldwin, however, "over-writes and over-poeticizes in images way over the heads of the folks supposedly thinking them," in what finally was "an 'art' book about folks who aren't 'art' folks'." *Go Tell It on the Mountain,* he concluded, was "a low-down story in a velvet bag—and a Knopf binding."

In spite of this criticism, Langston dutifully mailed a blurb for the novel to Knopf. His racial loyalty and his desire to help younger writers overcame his dismay at being superseded by them. If the ground was shifting under his feet, he would go down gracefully. However, racial loyalty and professional indebtedness meant less to Baldwin, who was far more concerned (as Ellison was) with meeting what he then saw as absolute standards of literary quality, and (much more so than Ellison) with establishing his personal superiority in the field. Nowhere was this clearer than in the current issue, edited by the scholar-critic Lionel Trilling, of the magazine *Perspectives USA* (intended mainly for foreign distribution), which included a two-essay piece, "Two Protests Against Protest," by Baldwin and Richard Gibson, another young black writer. The piece had first appeared in *Partisan Review;* Baldwin's essay was included later in his *Notes of a Native Son.*

Stressing his "disgust for the black hands, black faces, black Christs leering up at him from those sordid pages" of most anthologies of Negro literature—such as, presumably, *Poetry of the Negro* and Hughes's special number of *Voices*—Gibson knew exactly what had to be done. The young black writer must turn to the work of Joyce, Proust, Mann, Gide, and Kafka, "and not merely that of Chester B. Himes. The young writer might do well to impress upon himself the fact that he is a contemporary of Eliot, Valéry, Pound, Rilke, Auden and not merely of Langston Hughes." Baldwin, in his essay "Everybody's Protest Novel," attacked Stowe's *Uncle Tom's Cabin* (which Langston himself had praised in his introduction to the Dodd, Mead edition, as Baldwin probably knew) as a "very bad novel." Baldwin's major target, however, was Richard Wright (the two essays formed a pincer movement), whom he perhaps wished to punish for the older writer's sundry acts of kindness to him when Baldwin had been struggling in Paris. Stowe's book is "activated by what might be called a theological terror, the terror of damnation," to which Wright's *Native Son* is complementary in that Bigger Thomas—and Richard Wright—accepts an inhuman view of himself and acts accordingly. "The failure of the protest novel," he declared, "lies in its rejection of life, the human being, the denial of his beauty, dread, power, in its insistence that it is his categorization alone which is real and which cannot be transcended."

Langston was not taken in by this flight of rhetoric with which Baldwin, in whom tenderness coexisted uneasily with a chronic need to assert independence, tried to wound Wright professionally while suggesting that their main quarrel was over a significant difference of artistic and philosophic vision. On the other hand, Baldwin's words echoed some of Hughes's own original misgivings in 1940 about *Native Son*—but also, ironically, Hughes's current misgivings about Baldwin's *Go Tell It on the Mountain,* "which must be one of the books he is protesting against." In light of the *Perspectives USA* essay, he soon let Baldwin know, "I didn't expect you to write such a colored book." To Arna Bontemps, he wrote with bewilderment about the new black writers, including Baldwin, who commendably were "trying to leap fences and get out of pens—even if they do fall into lily ponds." "Lily ponds" was his term for New Criticism, art that evaded its social context, and black snobbishness based on the absorption of the more flaccid white artistic values. Lily ponds were beautiful but often stinking. Arna Bontemps, who had a superior sense of literary history, reminded Hughes that New Critical standards were tied to the Fugitive tradition and its Bible, *I'll Take My Stand,* in which Allen Tate and John Crowe Ransom, in their unregenerate days, had been prominent.

Langston's misgivings about the new black writing mainly concerned its emphasis on black criminality and on profanity. In "How to Be a Bad Writer (in Ten Easy Lessons)," published in *Harlem Quarterly* the previous year, the second lesson was: "If you are a Negro, try very hard to write with an eye dead on the white market—use modern stereotypes of older stereotypes—big burly Negroes, criminals, low-lifers, and prostitutes." The third lesson was: "Put in a lot of profanity and . . . near-pornography and you will be so modern you pre-date Pompeii in your lonely crusade toward the best seller lists. By all means be misunderstood, unappreciated, and ahead of your own time in print and out, then you can be felt-sorry-for by your own self, if not the public." His reference to a "lonely crusade" was a shot at Chester Himes, who had published a novel by that name. The point about self-pity might have referred to any one of a number of the younger writers, who, unlike more quietly proud men like Hughes, Wright, or Bontemps, seemed eager to advertise their plight and their self-absorption. To some extent, these writers were drawing on the new freedom of the "confessional" approach to literature, increasingly in vogue, and on certain militant aspects of the Afro-American autobiographical tradition; to some extent, they were exploiting the guilt of the white liberal community. If Hughes intended criticism of Baldwin here, as almost certainly he did, his words were only a faint echo of Richard Wright's. "This man disgusts," Wright had remarked indignantly, "there is a kind of shameful weeping in what he writes." In any event, an unfortunate and unbridgeable gap had opened between Langston and the most gifted new black writer.

Increasingly, Langston was caught between two fields of fire. To younger blacks like Gibson and Baldwin, he was something of an outmoded racial chauvinist (at that time, Baldwin seemed sure that the conditions that had produced Bigger Thomas were long gone). Hughes's harping on blues and jazz and the beauty of black folks was an archaic position many were eager to repudiate in the dawn of integration, whose glorious sun would be the Supreme Court's 1954 decision, in *Brown vs. the Board of Education of Topeka, Kansas,* that "separate but equal" facilities were a violation of the U.S. Constitution—itself a reversal of Supreme Court decisions in the 1890s endorsing Jim Crow. To the left, on the other hand, Hughes was exactly the opposite: as a radical force, as a believer, he was spent. From both perspectives, however, he was finished. On a podium in February at Brandeis University in Waltham, Massachusetts, the former black lion of the left opened his mouth to roar but showed empty gums to at least one student. For all his reputation for controversy, Langston Hughes seemed more like "an average, successful business man" than a radical poet. Many students believed that he "should have presented a more forceful crusading speech about the need for social action."

Certain professional failures now threatened to reinforce his sense of being left behind. First Simon and Schuster, then Henry Holt, and finally John Day rejected "Battle of Harlem"; each firm politely called the work a bore. Also unhappy were the Pennsylvania sponsors of his opera with Siegmeister: his one-act libretto, "Princess of Altoona," was distressingly like trite Broadway fare. Langston took the news stolidly. He seemed completely calm, even fatalistic, about these failures in collaboration.

The fate of the Battle book and the Pennsylvania musical mattered less than the fact that they were now more or less behind him. He seemed to relax and enjoy the winter pleasures of 1953 in Manhattan as he had not done in some time. He saw Tennessee Williams's *A Streetcar Named Desire* and *Camino Real;* a revival of Gershwin's *Porgy and Bess* at the Ziegfeld; and Gian Carlo Menotti's *Amahl and the Night Visitors*. His opera with Jan Meyerowitz, *The Barrier* (which had been produced in Italy on excellent financial terms), was revived in Greenwich Village, where it shared the Circle-in-the-Square Theatre with Tennessee Williams's *Summer and Smoke*.

Throughout the winter, as he contemplated his clouded future, the past was very much with him. Down in the basement of 20 East 127th Street, young Bill Delany, the nephew of Hubert Delany, a friend of Langston's from the Harlem Renaissance who had gone on to an influential New York judgeship, was helping to sort letters and manuscripts for the James Weldon Johnson collection at Yale. Over lunch at the Yale Club in New York City, Donald Gallup, curator of the collection in American literature there, had asked Langston to begin transferring the bulk of his papers to New Haven after three leaks and a flood in his basement had threatened to ruin the material. A Yale grant to him of $300 for an assistant had quickly vanished, but the archaeological work continued. Treasures were unearthed—a letter in the black bibliophile Arthur Schomburg's own hand; two dozen touchy, touching letters from the late Claude McKay; the entire bizarre history of Langston's fight in 1931 with Zora Neale Hurston over *Mule Bone;* ghostly drafts of letters to "Godmother," Mrs. Rufus Osgood Mason; early correspondence with Arna Bontemps, when he and Langston were bright young men.

However, Hughes now needed no special reminders of the past. Despite his resignations and refusals, his words of twenty years before continued to haunt him. The internationally known gossip columnist Walter Winchell several times denounced him as a disguised communist. At the last moment, NBC cancelled a broadcast of an interview about his writing recorded some months before. His name was invoked publicly again in renewed attacks on the Guggenheim Foundation, with threats to its tax-exempt status; the longtime secretary, Henry Allen Moe, testified that awarding a fellowship to Langston Hughes indeed had been a mistake. In December, testifying about foundation grants, Louis Budenz, formerly a member of the National Committee of the Communist Party and an editor of the *Daily Worker,* and now a professor at Fordham University and a voluble informant on American communist matters, identified Hughes among twenty-three alleged Communist Party members to have won such awards.

Feeling himself more and more under scrutiny even as he backed away from the fray, Langston retreated yet again in a step that he could not have taken without a sense of guilt. When *Ebony* magazine made ready to print a feature,

"The Person I Admire Most," prepared in 1949 but delayed for routine reasons, he took one look at his choice "in the field of literary-race relations" and insisted on a change. He had selected Du Bois, whose *The Souls of Black Folk* had been "the first book to awaken in me a love of literature." Revoking his selection now, he named instead William C. Chance, a minor black North Carolina educator who had appealed against Jim Crow laws up to the U.S. Supreme Court, and won. "The victory is not his alone," Langston explained. "It is Democracy's."

If he hoped that such moves would keep him safe from censure, he hoped in vain. On Saturday, March 21, he was in his third-floor study putting the final touches to his latest Franklin Watts children's book when a visitor was announced downstairs. Descending, Langston found waiting for him a United States marshall, who politely served him with what he had been dreading—a subpoena to appear in Washington, D.C., before an investigating committee.

The document demanded his appearance, at two o'clock on Monday afternoon, before the Senate Permanent Sub-Committee on Investigations, led by Senator Joseph McCarthy. It specified no reason for the summons; the relevant space was blank. No reason was necessary.

Badly shaken, Langston quickly called Arthur Spingarn, his lawyer-without-fee of over twenty-five years. Not long afterwards, he hurried downtown to the office of another attorney and prominent NAACP official, Lloyd K. Garrison, a senior partner in the highly respected law firm of Paul, Weiss, Rifkind, Wharton, and Garrison, and a great-grandson of the Abolitionist hero William Lloyd Garrison. Although his specialty was corporate law, Garrison had some experience in counseling clients faced with anti-communist reprisals by the government. With the Washington, D.C. attorney Joseph Rauh, he had represented the playwright Arthur Miller in his own controversial struggle with the House Committee on Un-American Activies. Miller, who was indicted for contempt of Congress when he refused to provide the names of communists he had known, was tried and convicted on the charge. Later, after an appeal, the conviction was overturned on a technicality.

"After I talked with Langston for a few minutes," Garrison later recalled, "and we both agreed that he did not want to plead the Fifth Amendment, I called up Roy Cohn in Washington, asking for a postponement. Cohn was his typical rude, arrogant self: 'What does he need an adjournment for? He's going to plead the Fifth, isn't he?' I said, 'No, he's going to tell the full story.' Cohn was shocked. 'Oh for God's sake!' he said."

Garrison and Langston went over the latter's record. "We made notes. I saw nothing really serious in his record, but I warned him that Cohn would push hard for names of any Communist writers he had known, and that if he refused to answer he could be held in contempt of Congress and might have to face penalties in court. That did not seem to faze him in the least. He was calm. Langston said that he really thought he couldn't remember any names, that they had slipped out of his mind, but that he wasn't going to make any effort to remember them, or to consult his files—and he would tell the committee that.''

Borrowing money to pay for his airfare and a hotel room, Langston made a reservation to fly to Washington to be present there as demanded. Garrison could not travel with him, but, as he advised Hughes, his presence there would not be necessary. "My judgment was that he was so delightful, so full of charm and humor that he could win the committee over. He was a most unusual person, and his statement of belief in democratic values was eloquent and obviously sincere. He had a serious interest in the betterment of life for the underprivileged and the poor and he had thought that Marxism might offer the way out. But he grew out of that idea and had a good, robust faith that people could work things out without a revolution. In any case, a lawyer really couldn't help him much in that spot.''

On Sunday, on Garrison's advice, Langston sent a long wire to Senator McCarthy: "AS AN AMERICAN CITIZEN WHO BELIEVES IN DEMOCRACY AS A WAY OF LIFE FOR THE AMERICAN PEOPLE I DESIRE AT ALL TIMES TO COOPERATE WITH ANY AGENT OF OUR CONSTITUTED GOVERNMENT.'' However, he needed time to secure a lawyer and prepare himself; he wanted a one-week extension "SO THAT I MIGHT NOT BE CONSIDERED AS TECHNICALLY IN CONTEMPT OF A DULY CONSTITUTED AGENCY OF GOVERNMENT.'' On Monday, a rude answer came from Roy Cohn, chief counsel of the subcommittee: "YOU ARE DIRECTED TO APPEAR BEFORE THIS COMMITTEE AS SPECIFIED IN YOUR SUBPOENA AT 2PM TODAY. IF YOU FAIL TO DO SO CONTEMPT ACTION WILL BE RECOMMENDED.''

Langston was actually at La Guardia Airport on Monday when word came that he had been granted a delay of twenty-four hours. On Tuesday, he rode through sheets of dreary rain to the airport. An hour and a half passed before American Airlines Flight No. 331 rose from the tarmac.

At National Airport to meet him was Frank D. Reeves, a black lawyer from the firm of Reeves, Mitchell, and Harris of 1901 11th Street, N.W. Reeves, who had firm ties to the NAACP, was known to both Arthur Spingarn and Lloyd Garrison. He would guide Langston through the coming ordeal. In New York, as Garrison later recalled, Langston had been his normal self—"unusually relaxed and natural, spontaneous, at home with himself and the world, with a delightful sense of humor.'' But he obviously had become more and more agitated as he approached his encounter with Joseph McCarthy in Washington. In the past, as in the South in 1931-32, and in Japan in 1933, Langston had been almost reckless in the face of force. Now the reflex of courage had grown dull; his nerves were frayed by a high-tensioned anxiety that reduced him at times, to his dismay, to actual trembling. A week later, when he wrote to thank Reeves for his help, he did not bother to conceal the fears that had ripened in Washington. "No words—and certainly no money (even were it a million dollars),'' he confessed, "could in any sense express to you my gratitude or from me repay you for what you have done for me in a time of emergency. Without your able help and kind, considerate, patient, and wise counsel, I would have been a lost ball in the high weeds or, to mix metaphors, a dead duck among the cherry blossoms!''

He had come to Washington not to fight but—if possible—to negotiate an honorable surrender. Others had attempted to defy McCarthy's Permanent Sub-Committee on Investigations and his chief counsel Roy Cohn, but none had done so with success, much less impunity. McCarthy had crushed men of far greater prestige and importance than Langston Hughes. In fact, the current proceedings against Hughes and other writers was an incidental and almost negligible portion of McCarthy's campaign against the left. Since assuming the chairmanship of the subcommittee the previous January, when he had launched the most unrelenting attack on American radicalism and its sympathizers real and imagined in the history of American anti-communism, his major target—barely camouflaged at first as a probe of the U.S. Foreign Aid program—had been the U.S. Department of State and the undesirable elements it allegedly harbored.

Early in February, after sparring with John Foster Dulles, the new secretary of state in the Eisenhower administration, McCarthy had opposed the appointment of a former president of Harvard University, James B. Conant, as U.S. High Commissioner for West Germany, because of Conant's alleged softness on Communism in resisting an investigation of subversive activities at the university. Next, with the meetings televised to maximize publicity, McCarthy had shifted his focus to the Voice of America network and the entire overseas propaganda effort of the U.S. government administered by the State Department. This inquiry led to an examination of materials in over one hundred and fifty libraries, in sixty-three countries, maintained by the State Department through its Information Centers. Under humiliating pressure from the subcommittee, the Department of State formally banned books, music, and art by suspect authors and artists from its libraries and from the Voice of America. Estimating that thirty thousand volumes were tainted by the left, McCarthy saw to it that several hundred books were removed. Many were reduced to pulp, and eleven were actually burned; various programs were eliminated, and several libraries closed altogether. (The danger posed by the removed books was debatable. Two, for example, were Hughes's novel *Not Without Laughter,* which contained hardly a trace of propaganda, and *Fields of Wonder,* his "lyric," or least racial and political, volume of verse.)

The human cost of the McCarthy investigation was already high—if only by democratic standards—when Langston arrived in Washington in late March. Eventually, hundreds of employees of the Department of State would be fired, sometimes with disastrous personal and professional consequences, and usually after testimony from fellow workers that further poisoned morale within the State Department. Certain individual victims, of whom Langston was well aware through the newspapers, stood out. Earlier that month, a veteran New York schoolteacher, Czechoslovakian by birth, was forced into invoking the Fifth

Amendment—and thus into being automatically dismissed from the city school system—because of an innocuous broadcast, from a script prepared by the Voice of America, to his native land. The editor of the anti-Communist but liberal New York *Post,* after hearing McCarthy liken his paper to the Communist Party *Worker,* was forced to name activists he had known in his long-repudiated radical youth. Various heads of sections of the Voice of America were publicly accused of atheism, free love, and insubordination, all construed as forms of disloyalty to the nation and the anti-Communist cause; at least one high-ranking officer resigned after being harrassed by the subcommittee. Early in March, in the wake of accusations that the sites of key transmitters had been deliberately chosen to weaken their effectiveness, a Voice of America engineer who had been involved in selecting sites committed suicide by throwing himself in the path of a truck. "You see," he had written his family, "once the dogs are set on you, everything you have done since the beginning of time is suspect."

Intimidated, Langston had brought with him a five-page typed statement, prepared over the weekend but based heavily on the political apologia Franklin Watts, Inc., had circulated about his relationship to the left, especially as represented in his poems. This document would be at the heart of his defense and his negotiations. When he drove with his attorney Frank Reeves from the Washington airport to the U.S. Senate Office Building, the terms he hoped to secure had already been decided in New York in his meetings with Spingarn and Garrison.

In two closed executive sessions, these matters were negotiated with Roy Cohn, McCarthy's chief counsel, G. David Schine, the Sub-Committee's "chief consultant," and other members of the group, including the courtly Senator Everett Dirksen of Illinois. Langston found Dirksen gracious and helpful, but chief counsel Roy Cohn was a different man. Brainy, ill-tempered, and vindictive, he was a formidable adversary and the spearhead of McCarthy's far-reaching drive for power; he would also be Hughes's main questioner in the public part of the proceedings. In a real sense, the inner circle of Langston's political enemies over the recent years was now complete. Cohn, who had issued the subpoena sent to him, was a close friend of the nationally known columnists Walter Winchell and George Sokolsky, both of whom consistently had attacked Langston in the newspapers as a communist. Sokolsky was himself an intimate of J. Edgar Hoover of the F.B.I. And years later, Cohn would dedicate *McCarthy,* his sympathetic study of his former employer, to Sokolsky. As a member of the U.S. Attorney's office in New York, Cohn had assisted in the prosecution of Julius and Ethel Rosenberg, and in the mass trial of Communist Party leaders against which Hughes had protested in one of his few forthright statements in recent years in defense of the left.

Presenting the subcommittee with his five-page personal statement, Hughes and Reeves also offered sixteen other documents, mainly letters and newspaper reports, designed to establish Langston's anti-communism. After some rough questioning by Cohn and Schine, a deal was struck. In a week of public interrogations of leftist writers, Langston Hughes would appear before the Senate Permanent Sub-Committee on Investigations as a cooperating witness, one ready to explain and deprecate his radical past. In return, Hughes's most inflammatory poems would not be read aloud—unlike the work of other authors who dared to resist the subcommittee.

Although he had a reservation at the Statler Hotel, Langston quickly accepted Reeves's invitation to stay with him and his mother at their home on New Hampshire Avenue at 7th Street. In Langston's agitated state, he much preferred the reassuring presence of the lawyer to the chill efficiency of a hotel room. After dinner at home, he and Reeves settled down into a long evening session of mock questions and answers. Methodically they isolated the weak points in their case. The weakest points were the content of certain incendiary pieces of verse and prose, as well as the absence of any evidence of a clean break with the left. Then, or earlier, Langston nervously doodled on sheets of paper curious variations on the Fifth Amendment, which nevertheless he was determined not to invoke: "I refuse to answer on the grounds that it might tend to degrade or incriminate me." And: "I am sworn to tell the truth, the *whole* truth, and nothing but the truth, and I do not intend to tell half the truth, I have no recollection as to yes or no. I will not lie."

At 10:30 a.m. on Thursday, March 26, two days after his arrival, the subcommittee met in the glare and the heat of television lights in Room 357 of the Senate Office Building to interrogate writers whose books tainted the overseas libraries of the State Department. Senator McCarthy was present, as well as Roy Cohn and David Schine, assistant council Daniel G. Buckley, and Senator John L. McClellan of Arkansas. The first witness was the novelist Edwin Seaver, who had helped to found *New Masses* and had been editor-in-chief of *Soviet Russia Today* and a literary editor of the *Daily Worker*. At least as cooperative as Hughes, Seaver appeared without the benefit of a lawyer, as McCarthy noted approvingly.

After Langston was sworn in, and his lawyer identified, his prepared statement was formally accepted:

Poets who write mostly about love, roses and moonlight, sunsets and snow must lead a very quiet life. Seldom, does their poetry get them into difficulties. Beauty and lyricism are really related to another world, to ivory towers, to your head in the clouds, feet floating off the earth.

Unfortunately, having been born poor—and also colored—in Missouri, I was stuck in the mud from the beginning. Try as I might to float off into the clouds, poverty and Jim Crow would grab me by the heels, and right back on earth I would land. A third-floor furnished room is the nearest thing I have ever had to an ivory tower.

Some of my earliest poems were social poems in that they were about people's problems—whole groups of people's problems—rather than my own personal difficulties, but when one writes poems of social content there is always the danger of being misunderstood. As Mr. Archibald MacLeish, Pulitzer prize winner, formerly Librarian of Congress, said before the senators, "One of the occupational hazards of writing poetry is running the risk of being misunderstood."

I have written many poems characterizing many different kinds of people and expressing many varied ideas, some seriously, some satirically, some ironically. For instance, in my book of poems, *Shakespeare in Harlem,* there is a poem called "Ku Klux" in which a Klansman speaks. But I am not a Klansman. In *The Weary Blues* there is a poem called "Mother to Son" in which an aged mother speaks. But I am not an aged mother. In *Shakespeare in Harlem* there is a poem called "Widow Woman" in which a woman laments the loss of her husband. But I am not myself a widow-woman, although I used the pronoun "I" to characterize the woman, and it is my poem.

Perhaps the most misunderstood of my poems was "Goodbye Christ." Since it is an ironic poem (and irony is apparently a quality not readily understood in poetry by unliterary minds) it has been widely misinterpreted as an anti-religious poem. This I did not mean it to be, but rather a poem against racketeering, profiteering, racial segregation, and showmanship in religion which, at the time, I felt was undermining the foundations of the great and decent ideals for which Christ himself stood. And behind the poem is a pity and a sorrow that this should be taken by some as meaning to them that Christianity and religion in general has no value. Because of the publication of this poem—which more than fifteen years ago I withdrew from publication and which has since been used entirely without my permission by groups interested in fomenting racial and social discord, I have been termed on occasion, a Communist or an atheist.

I am not now an atheist, and have never been an atheist. On page 55 of my book, *The Dream Keeper,* I write:

"MA LORD"

Ma Lord aint no stuck-up man.
Ma Lord, He ain't proud.
When He goes a'walkin'
He gives me His hand.
"You ma friend," He 'lowed

Ma Lord knowed what it was to work.
He knowed how to pray.
Ma Lord's life was trouble, too,
Trouble ever' day.

Ma Lord ain't no stuck-up man.
He's a friend o' mine.
When He went to heaben,
His soul on fire,
He tole me I was gwine.
He said, "Sho you'll come wid Me
An be ma friend through eternity."

I have personally the greatest respect for sincere religionists, but none whatsoever for professional racketeers in religion, nor for those who use religion as an anti-Negro, anti-democratic weapon for thwarting the progress of the common man.

I am not a member of the Communist Party now and have never been a member of the Communist Party. I have, in the past, belonged to the "John Reed Club," the "American League Against War and Fascism," and the "League of American Writers," none of which are now in existence. But many other American writers have belonged to one or all of those organizations, including such distinguished persons as Ernest Hemingway, Dorothy Parker, Vincent Sheean, and the late Heywood Broun. They appear to me to belong to that true American stream of criticism and of libertarianism which has enriched American life since its very beginning. I do not believe in a static America. I believe in an America that changes as Americans want it to change. I do not believe that the desire for change, and working toward it, is necessarily un-American. In our country great changes have been achieved through the democratic process, and I believe they will so continue to be achieved. I have frequently over the years affirmed my beliefs in democracy, as in the radio poem written for the National Urban League, "Freedom's Plow," or my short story "One Friday Morning," in *Laughing to Keep from Crying,* and many speeches and poems. Also through my various Writers War Board scripts.

I concede the right to anyone to read me or not, as he may choose, to publish me or not, to invite me to speak or not, as desired. I also feel (and especially since one of the Four Freedoms is Freedom of Speech) that I have the right to oppose in speech or writing those who would make of democracy, or religion, a reactionary, evil, and harmful mask for anti-Negro, and anti-American activities.

I would like to see an America where people of any race, color, or creed may live on a plane of cultural and material well-being, cooperating together unhindered by sectarian, racial, or factional prejudices and harmful intolerances that do nobody any good, an America proud of its tradition, capable of facing the future without the necessary pitting of people against people and without the disease of personal distrust and suspicion of one's neighbor.

In my opera based on the life of Dessalines and the Haitian struggle for freedom, as produced at the New York City Center, there is an aria so placed as to express opposition to violence and killing as a solution to men's problems. This aria expresses also my own personal feeling in regard to social and political relations.

The text of the aria "I Dream a World" ended the statement. Opening the interrogation, Roy Cohn informed the gathering that "approximately" sixteen different books by Hughes were to be found in "approximately" fifty-one different State Department libraries around the world—a total of about two hundred copies.

Cohn: [Was there] ever a period of time in your life when you believed in the Soviet form of government?
Hughes: There was such a period.

Cohn: And when did that period end?

Hughes: There was no abrupt ending, but I would say, that roughly the beginnings of my sympathies with the Soviet ideology were coincident with the Scottsboro case, the American Depression, and that they ran through for some ten or twelve years or more, certainly up to the Nazi-Soviet Pact, and perhaps, in relation to some aspects of the Soviet ideology, further, because we were allies, you know, with the Soviet Union during the war. So some aspects of my writing would reflect that relationship, that war relationship.

Cohn: And, as a matter of fact, when would you say you completely broke with the Soviet ideology?

Hughes: I would say a complete reorientation of my thinking and emotional feelings occurred roughly four or five years ago.

Cohn: . . . In 1949 you made a statement in defense of the Communist leaders who were on trial, which was published in the Daily Worker. Would you say that your complete break came thereafter?

Hughes: I would say that whatever quotation you are referring to, sir, might have been made in a spirit of wishing to preserve our civil liberties for everyone, and in a kind of remembrance of the happenings in Germany and what it had led to for minority peoples there, and a fear on my part that possibly, if we disregarded civil liberties, it might lead to that in relation to the Negro people.

Cohn: Now, you have changed your views in regard to that? . . .

Hughes: Well, I have certainly changed my views in regard to the fact that one may not get a fair trial in America. I believe that one can and one does.

Cohn: You now believe that one can and one does get a fair trial in this country?

Hughes: Speaking by and large. Of course, we have our judicial defects, as does every system or country.

Cohn: Would you say what you call your complete change in ideology came about 1950?

Hughes: I would say certainly by 1950. Yes.

Cohn: . . . Just what . . . made you change your thinking from a belief over a period of years to the effect that the Soviet form of government was best for this country, to the present day, when you no longer believe that, and when you are a believer in the American form of government?

Hughes: Well, there would be two aspects, and I would say, sir, that I have always been a believer in the American form of government in any case, but interested in certain aspects of other forms of government, and I would like to give two interpretations of my feeling about my reorientation and change. The Nazi-Soviet Pact was, of course, very disillusioning and shook up a great many people, and then further evidences of, shall we say, spreading imperialist aggression. My own observations in 1931–32 [he meant 1932–33], as a writer, which remained with me all the time, of the lack of freedom of expression in the Soviet Union for writers, which I never agreed with before I went there or afterwards—those things gradually began to sink in deeper and deeper. And then, in our own country, there has been, within the last ten years, certainly within the war period, a very great increase in the rate of acceleration of improvement in race relations. There has been a very distinct step forward in race relations . . . a greater understanding of the need for greater democracy for the Negro people, and then the recent Supreme Court decisions, which bolstered up the right to vote, the right to travel, and so on, have given me great heart and great confidence in the potentialities of what we can do here.

Cohn: Have you received any disillusionment recently, concerning the treatment of minorities by the Soviet Union?

Hughes: Well, the evidence in the press—I have not been there, of course, myself—indicating persecution and terror against the Jewish people, has been very appalling to me.

Roy Cohn then mentioned the revolutionary poems of the thirties, especially "One More 'S' in the U.S.A." Langston conceded that he had written them. When a passage from *Simple Speaks His Mind*—from the chapter "Something to Lean On"—was identified by Cohn as "a takeoff on an imaginary hearing" of the House Committee on Un-American Activities, Langston disagreed that the passage "thoroughly ridicules" the committee and its anti-Communist goals. The chapter had been written after "the incident as reported in the papers, which, I think, occurred in the Un-American Committee, where one of the counsel, or one of the members of the committee, if I remember correctly, called a Negro witness a very ugly name. And that went throughout the Negro press and shocked the Negro people very deeply."

(" 'Your honery'," Simple elsewhere had threatened to testify, if called, " 'I wish to inform you that I was born in America, I live in America, and long as I have been black, I been an American. Also I was a Democrat—but I didn't know Roosevelt was going to die.' Then I would ask them, 'How come you don't have any Negroes on your Un-American Committee?' And old Chairman Georgia would say, 'Because that is un-American'.")

Joining the questioning, McCarthy then asked Langston whether such a book, in a library on foreign soil, "would be an effective way of fighting communism? Or would that tend to put us in a bad light as compared to the Communist nation?" Langston replied that, on one hand, the dialect might confuse the foreign reader—a good argument against offering the book; on the other hand, its criticism of a branch of the government would show foreigners that freedom of the press was a reality in America.

McCarthy: . . . You appear to be very frank in your answers, and while I may disagree with some of your conclusions, do I understand that your testimony is that sixteen different books of yours which were purchased by the information program did largely follow the Communist line?

Hughes: Some of those books very largely followed at times some aspects of the Communist line, reflecting my sympathy with them. But not all of them, sir.

McCarthy: . . . Do you feel that those books should be on our shelves throughout the world, with the apparent stamp of approval of the United States Government?

Hughes: I was certainly amazed to hear that they were. I was surprised, and I would certainly say "No."

Pressed by McCarthy, Langston confirmed again that he had never been a party member, and that he was now, in McCarthy's words, "neither a member of the party nor a sympathizer with the cause." As for books in the libraries, "I have more recent books which I would much prefer, if any books of mine are kept on the shelves." Asked by Senator McClellan for proof of his change of heart, Langston again offered documents such as his poem "Freedom's Plow" and the last lines of *The First Book of Negroes,* about the promise of American democracy. "Goodbye Christ" was mentioned, but McCarthy placed the poem into the record without reading it; Langston dismissed it as "a very young, awkward poem." (Earlier, Roy Cohn had made a special point, "in deference to Mr. Hughes," of avoiding the public reading of controversial poems—"We went into them with Mr. Hughes in executive session.")

McCarthy then closed out the meeting.

McCarthy: May I ask you just one question, Mr. Hughes? We've had so much screaming by certain elements of the press that witnesses have been misused. . . . Do you feel that you were in any way mistreated by the staff or by the Committee?

Hughes: I must say that I was agreeably surprised at the courtesy and friendliness with which I was received.

McCarthy: In other words, from reading some of the press you thought you'd find the Senators might have horns and you discovered that the staff didn't have any horns at all, eh?

Hughes: Well, Senator Dirksen, is that his name? . . . He was most, I thought, most gracious, and in a sense helpful in defining for me the areas of this investigation. And the young men who had to interrogate me—of course, had to interrogate me. Am I excused now?

McCarthy: Thank you very much. You're excused.

At this point, something happened that startled Hughes. "When he got back to New York, Langston told me and other people," a young friend recalled years later, "that after McCarthy's last words, after he excused him, he looked at Langston and winked. There was no mistaking it. He winked. He was telling Langston in no uncertain terms, 'You got yours, and I got mine. Now we are even'."

If this was indeed McCarthy's perception of the hearing, he was perhaps to some extent in error. In its quiet way, Langston's testimony had been a rhetorical *tour de force* that must have been less than McCarthy and Cohn and Schine had hoped for. Not once had he unequivocally attacked communism. Deftly avoiding the leads of the questioners when they challenged his deeper sense of intellectual and ethical decorum, he had disarmed their hostility and preserved something of his dignity.

On the other hand, Hughes's dignity had been largely passive, perhaps supine. His triumph of rhetoric may have been at the expense of a victory of the spirit. In the final analysis, he had given in to brutish strength, not to moral or even constitutional authority, for such authority was clearly being abused. To cooperate with McCarthy, even given the integrity of Langston's change of political heart, was to appear to endorse his cruelties. Hughes had come to his decision by recognizing that his choice was between two imperfections. He could defy the body and destroy much of his effectiveness in the black world. Or he could cooperate, draw the disapproval, even the contempt, of the white left, but keep more or less intact the special place he had painstakingly carved out within the black community.

The decision was relatively easy for him to make, but seemed to contrast weakly with the spirited resistance of other prominent blacks such as Paul Robeson, who in the coming years would be virtually martyred to the international socialist cause, and Doxey Wilkerson, formerly a professor at Howard University, who earlier that week flatly refused to admit that he had been a communist and a leader of a Communist Party cell at Howard, and accused the committee of trying to intimidate Negro educators as a group. And in the afternoon following Langston's testimony had come Dashiell Hammett, the tall, white-haired, celebrated writer of detective stories, who had been jailed for six months in 1951 for refusing to testify in a similar investigation, and who still defied his questioners; and Helen Goldfrank, the author of several children's books as "Helen Kay," who gently taunted the subcommittee and pleaded the Fifth Amendment "and every other amendment of our lovely constitution." Elsewhere that day, at a different government hearing, the broadcaster Edward R. Murrow, who would lead the successful counterattack on McCarthy, demanded the independence from the State Department of the Voice of America and related bodies. Other witnesses in this phase of McCarthy's campaign included the former head of the Communist Party of the United States, Earl Browder, and William Marx Mandel, who answered questions by shouting, "I am a Jew," and who accused Senator McCarthy of murdering the Voice of America engineer who had committed suicide.

Still, certain questions about Langston's true feelings toward radical socialism remained unanswered. He had moved from near-membership in the Communist Party to his hour of cooperation with McCarthy's subcommittee. There is evidence that he had come to a new understanding of the relationship between art and propaganda, as had many other writers; that he was so psychologically mortgaged to his race that he could not risk being excluded from its loving regard; that he was perhaps dissatisfied with the subsidiary place of race in communist reckonings, since the special problems of black Americans seemed to be inadequately treated; that the great goal of his life had always been to live by his writings, and that he did not wish to imperil that goal. But the fact is that, with the weekly *Defender* column and countless other opportunities to speak out at his disposal, Hughes never once—apart from his testimony before McCarthy and his retraction of "Goodbye Christ" years before—attempted to explain his position on these crucial matters. Nowhere did he attempt in an essay or a speech to fuse his admiration of the left with his love of the race— and thus possibly to remain loyal to both. Nowhere did he criticize the left for anything at all—until, suddenly, he implicitly repudiated it. Indeed, he never explicitly repudiated the left.

Instead, as in the case of his sexuality, he had allowed the expression of his radical political zeal to wither, to atrophy, to evaporate. And yet he could no more genuinely kill his political indignation than he altogether could destroy his sexual drive. Both became sublimated into work and more work, whose saving grace would be its service to and saturation in his race. Still, the magma of political indignation in Hughes remained, below the placid surface, red-hot. In his posthumously published *The Panther and the Lash* appeared a poem which, written probably before his Senate appearance, recorded nevertheless what would be his loathing of, and his enduring rage against, the tyranny of the right and its public humiliation of him.

UN-AMERICAN INVESTIGATORS

The committee's fat,
Smug, almost secure
Co-religionists
Shiver with delight
In warm manure
As those investigated—
Too brave to name a name—
Have pseudonyms revealed
In Gentile game
  Of who,
  Born Jew,
  Is who?
Is not your name Lipshitz?
  Yes.
Did you not change it
For subversive purposes?
  No.
For nefarious gain?
  Not so.
Are you sure?
The committee shivers
With delight in
Its warm manure.

As soon as his session ended, Langston returned to New York, where at midnight he tape-recorded his testimony rebroadcast on the radio. The next day, at cocktails with Lloyd Garrison and dinner with Walter White, he spun his tape for them. Both assured him that he had done well. "Your handling of yourself before McCarthy," Garrison soon concluded, "and your whole attitude throughout gave me a great lift of the spirit." On Sunday he sent Frank Reeves a check and a letter overflowing with gratitude. Soon the tape was transcribed and 500 copies prepared. Sending the transcript to about 155 publishers, educators, journalists, acquaintances, and friends, he anxiously hoped for their support.

Under the headline "Someone in Washington Fears 'Jess B. Simple'," the communist *Worker* calmly censured Hughes for ignoring his own words about Du Bois's prosecutors in facing his inquisitors: that no one would remember their names; "their purpose in such a discussion is to turn Hughes against himself and to put him under the threat of 'contempt' and 'perjury' prosecution." The black press, however, was friendly. The *Amsterdam News* noted with pleasure that Simple of Harlem "managed to speak something of his mind" before the mighty committee. Stridently anti-socialist, *Time* magazine noted approvingly that Hughes had been "a more cooperative witness" than some others. Maria Leiper pledged Simon and Schuster's support: "We want to help in any way we can, with the American Legion or any group or any person, at any time." Franklin and Helen Hoke Watts of Franklin Watts, Inc. were also satisfied; Langston could continue to write for them—if he remained careful. To Charles S. Johnson of Fisk University, his testimony had been "clear cut and convincing." Significantly, the NAACP assumed Langston's expenses for the hearing, in return for the extensive work he had done for the organization in the past. His most dependable rich friend, Amy Spingarn, who had helped him in financial emergencies since 1926, when she supported his attendance at Lincoln University, sent two checks, including one for $300, to aid "your gallant fight."

In consultation with Garrison and Arthur Spingarn, he moved to finish the job started by the subcommittee. Relying on a long list of "subversive" organizations drawn up by the Attorney-General in 1950, Langston made sure that he belonged to none. Thereafter, he was vigilant about any connection between his name and the left. Months later, for example (just after the FBI questioned him about the American-Soviet Friendship group on December 10), he wrote the Spanish Refugee Appeal of the Joint Anti-Fascist Committee about being listed as a national sponsor with Paul Robeson, Pablo Picasso, Orson Welles, Eugene O'Neill, Dorothy Parker, and others, on its stationery: "I would appreciate it very much if my name were removed from your letterhead and membership lists."

Incredibly, his appearance before the Senate subcommittee did not end hostility from the right. Indeed, within a month, the columnist George Sokolsky attacked Hughes on the same old score. But the Senate ordeal seemed to lift from Hughes the burden of obligation to contest the legendary charges against him. In January of the following year, when the American Legion in New York accused him of being a communist, he wrote wearily but defiantly to an inquirer: "I have been accused of such membership so often, that I have gotten used to it, know that the accusers pay no attention to denials, and therefore I pay no attention to their accusations."

His intention indeed had shifted. For Langston, the long, rugged public road away from radical socialism had at last come to an end.

9

OUT FROM UNDER
1953 to 1956

Well, the poor old Negro's
Had a hard, hard time——
But he still ain't bowed his head.
Yes, the poor old Negro's
Had a hard, hard time——
Yet he *sure* ain't dead. . . .

"Here to Stay," 1953

I N THE WEEKS following his appearance before Joseph McCarthy's committee, Langston looked anxiously for signs of public disapproval. None of any
consequence came. Somewhat reassured, but feeling the strain of his ordeal,
he looked for a vacation. A train ride across the continent to California, with
two or three weeks passed pleasantly on the Pacific coast among old friends,
including Noël Sullivan at Hollow Hills Farm, seemed his best bet. "I'm
homesick for your valley," he had sighed to Sullivan at Christmas. Only the
usual grim state of his finances barred Langston from leaving at once.

Hoping for a windfall with the heralded appearance in May of *Simple Takes
a Wife* from Simon and Schuster, Langston was teased by the news that the
Book-of-the-Month Club might offer the work as a main choice to its many
members. With Henry Seidel Canby, a selector, championing it as "an informal masterpiece worthy with a little compression of a long life in American
literature," *Simple Takes a Wife* was among the final three works considered.
To Langston's disappointment, however, it was passed over in the end.

Nevertheless, praise of the book verged on the extravagant. In the *New York
Times Book Review,* Carl Van Vechten, in hailing the second Simple volume
as "more brilliant, more skillfully written, funnier, and perhaps a shade more
tragic than its predecessor," dubbed him "the Molière of Harlem." The veteran literary critic Ben Lehman of the University of California saw Hughes's
art in Simple as remarkably like that of Mark Twain. ("I'd not thought of it
before myself," Langston offered. "But am glad if there's something of the
same quality there, naturally.") In Oklahoma, the Tulsa *World* compared him
favorably to Damon Runyon. To the Virginia Kirkus review service, Langston

Hughes was the O. Henry of Harlem. "The relaxed, witty prose of a matured and wizard-like Langston Hughes," the *St. Louis Post-Dispatch* declared, "artfully conceals a profound sociological treatise." This view was echoed privately by Mozell C. Hill, the editor of *Phylon* magazine at Atlanta University: "I know of no anthropological monograph that is more accurate of life and thought among Negroes on the American scene than that found in 'Simple'." Even the left-wing *Masses and Mainstream* praised the book, if mainly in condemning "the 'arty' degeneracy of writers like Richard Wright and Ralph Ellison," whose recent novels *Invisible Man* and *The Outsider* had derided communism. Hughes's new book was "a vivid picture of Negro life and its richness," and "a pleasant relief" from Ellison and Wright (later that year, praising Gwendolyn Brooks's novel *Maud Martha*, Langston called it charming—"and it is about time for a little charm in Negro novels!"). To other readers, especially blacks, *Simple Takes a Wife* was pure fun. "My stomach is actually aching from laughing," the young playwright Loften Mitchell swore to Langston. "I've had tears in my eyes."

In spite of such reviews, *Simple Takes a Wife* did not flourish. Whereas the first Simple volume had sold thirty thousand copies, sales of the second barely reached five thousand by the end of the year. A Hollywood studio wired a request for copies of the book, but "from long experience" Langston expected nothing of the American film industry—and nothing came. His literary agent Ivan von Auw of Harold Ober Associates warned him flatly that although Ober's Hollywood representative loved the book, "most studios won't touch it." Victor Gollancz snapped up the British rights, but paid only seventy-five pounds for them. Unquestionably, the book had been damaged by Hughes's radical reputation. "I only wish it weren't as controversial a book as Hughes [*sic*]," a San Francisco bookseller lamented to Richard Simon of Simon and Schuster; "were it not, we would really go all out to promote it in every possible way." And a similar attitude almost certainly was behind the swift rejection of excerpts by *Collier's, Woman's Home Companion, Ladies Home Journal, McCall's,* and *Today's Woman.*

On the other hand, the publicity—or the notoriety—surrounding Langston moved the publishing firm of Rinehart to gamble on the success of his second autobiography, at which he had scratched from time to time over the preceding years. Without seeing a line, Theodore Amussen of Rinehart offered him $2,500, by far his largest advance ever. He accepted the terms at once and quickly borrowed some money against the expected check. On May 15, a few days after a cocktail party at the Waldorf-Astoria Hotel which Langston hosted on behalf of PEN for the flamboyant Welsh poet Dylan Thomas, who failed to appear, he was on his way by train to California. Soothed by the rhythm of the wheels, he rested, and read poetry. Mainly he read Walt Whitman, but he also found himself drawn to the verse of Emily Dickinson. Why he turned at this particular moment to the reclusive and often cryptic Dickinson is unclear, but for a considerable time to come he would be fond of quoting three of her lines that deftly caught his own freshly ironic sense of the treachery of fame: "How public—like a Frog— / To tell your name—the livelong June— / To an admiring Bog!'' At least one of his poems, "Peace," written about this time, reflected to some extent certain of her more mournful cadences:

> We passed their graves:
> The dead men there,
> Winners and losers,
> Did not care.
>
> In the dark
> They could not see
> Who had gained
> The victory.

Walt Whitman was an older, more exuberant attraction, one that dated back to Central High School in Cleveland and Langston's beginnings as a poet. To Whitman he returned now as to some personal fount of inspiration and justification as an artist—almost certainly with his compromise before Joseph McCarthy in mind. Soon he would devote an entire *Chicago Defender* column to Whitman, whose *Leaves of Grass* "contains the greatest poetic statements of the real meaning of democracy ever made on our shores." When a black literary scholar, Lorenzo Dow Turner of Roosevelt College in Chicago, wrote to protest that Whitman, in spite of his liberal effusions in *Leaves of Grass,* hypocritically had been pro-slavery and anti-Negro, Langston declared his ignorance of these aspects of Whitman's life and scrupulously printed Turner's criticism. (In fact, Turner cited Whitman's early writings but ignored his later vigorous championing of the anti-slavery movement in the years leading to the first edition of *Leaves of Grass.*)

In yet another column, however, Langston defended Whitman—and, obliquely, himself in the aftermath of charges that he had betrayed his trust as a radical and a truth-telling poet. "Whitman wrote, 'Not till the sun denies you, will I deny you,' and I believe it, for his poems—his greatest work—came out of the greatest of the man himself. It is by Whitman's poems that the whole world knows him." If Whitman's newspaper editorials sometimes contradicted his ideals, "it is the best of him that we choose to keep and cherish, not his worst." Without invoking Whitman's celebrated defense of contradiction—"Do I contradict myself? / Very well then I contradict myself, (I am large, I contain multitudes)"—Langston deliberately drew a distinction for his readers between the personal failings of an individual and the integrity of his or her best work. Mentioning figures as diverse as Mary Magdalene, Isadora Duncan, Charlie Chaplin, Ethel Waters, Billie Holiday, Edgar Allan Poe, François Villon, and Dmitri Shostakovitch—all of whom could be both strongly admired and strongly criticized—he argued that "if we let temporary human failings destroy for us the timeless values of the best of their work, we will have only their sins to contemplate." The sins of the famous were "no more beautiful than the sins of the rest of us,'' except that, as was true of Mary Magdalene (with whom Langston now clearly identified), their sins were redeemed by their virtues. To the rest of the world it might be said, as Christ said to the critics of Mary Magdalene, '' 'My head with oil thou didst not anoint: but this woman hath anointed my feet with ointment. Wherefore I say unto thee, Her sins, which are many, are forgiven, for she loved much.' Out of the best of his love, Whitman created the best of his poems. For these, all may be thankful.''

About this time, he also wrote ''Old Walt'':

> Old Walt Whitman
> Went finding and seeking,
> Finding less than sought
> Seeking more than found,
> Every detail minding
> Of the seeking or the finding.
>
> Pleasured equally
> In seeking as in finding,
> Each detail minding,
> Old Walt went seeking
> And finding.

Between the wisdom of the two nineteenth-century American poets and the therapy of a train ride westward across the American continent, Langston reached California in a benign mood. There, the warmth of his reception confirmed that he was still wanted and admired and loved. To Matt and Evelyn Crawford and their daughter Nebby Lou, now a teenager, Langston was essentially undamaged by his Senate appearance. ''I know what had gone on with him under the tyranny of McCarthy,'' Matt Crawford later recalled, ''but it didn't matter at all. I was not changed in my views about the left, which I believed in then as I believe in it now, but I certainly wasn't changed in my views about Langston either. He had been through too much for any of us to turn our backs on him. He was still a hero to us, still the old Langston. We were happy to see him then. We would always be happy to see him.'' In the ornate Venetian Room of the Fairmont Hotel on Nob Hill, where Langston stayed, he watched his old friend Katherine Dunham and her dancers perform, and promised to compose a ballet libretto for the troupe. He also visited with Roy Blackburn, his secretary in 1934 when they had lived together at ''Ennesfree'' in Carmel, and Roy's wife, Marie. Then he headed south to Carmel Valley to stay at Hollow Hills Farm as Noël Sullivan's guest. The visit was a complete success—though not as restful as Langston had hoped it would be: ''I've been to more concerts, shows, and dinners in the three days I've been here than I attend in a month (sometimes) in New York.'' The large Sullivan circle welcomed him almost as a returning son. Una Jeffers was now dead, but at Tor House, Robinson Jeffers greeted Langston warmly when he paid a call. In ''a wonderful ten days at

Hollow Hills,'' he estimated that he met more artists and writers than in ten months in New York.

His way back East, broken by several stops to see friends, was smoothed by "the very good publicity you have been getting," as one man referred to several positive newspaper stories on Hughes in the wake of his Senate visit and the appearance of *Simple Takes a Wife*. "After this anointing by the press you could not be good copy for the local paper except to praise you for your late 'conversion'.'' In Phoenix, Langston felt more than ever the old attraction of Arizona as a place to retire—if he could ever bring himself to retire. A grove of orange trees glittered and green leaves crowded to the window of his room when he stayed for a few days "of real summer sun" at the home of a niece of Noël Sullivan's, Alice Doyle Mahoney, whose husband, William Mahoney, had just been elected County Attorney with strong support from local blacks and Mexican-Americans. On a small ranch within the city limits, the Mahoneys and their lively young children lived what seemed to Langston a blissfully idyllic life, with a brood of Arabian horses and playful dogs and an open, generous approach to life—"such *gone* (be-bop) Mahoneys!" he wrote in admiration. "I love them." Across town, in less favored but still pleasant surroundings, he visited the fine black artist Eugene Grigsby and his wife, Thomasena. At El Paso, Texas, he crossed the border into Juarez, Mexico, to see his first bullfight in years. And on June 16, from New Orleans, Langston paused to wire birthday greetings to Sullivan: "MY HAPPINESS IN HAVING KNOWN YOU MAKES ME WISH YOU EVER ALL THE HAPPINESS IN THE WORLD ON EACH OF YOUR VARIOUS BIRTHDAYS."

His passage through the South was not without incident. In steamy Louisiana, while a perspiring Langston argued in vain with a white brakeman about the lack of air-conditioning in the crowded Jim Crow car, an old black lady quietly listened to him. Then, embarrassed for them both, she lowered her eyes, took out her lunch box, sighed, and began to eat. As the train rolled on, Langston penned a bitter little poem about Jim Crow:

> Get out the lunch-box of your dreams
> And bite into the sandwich of your heart,
> And ride the Jim Crow car until it screams
> And, like an atom bomb, bursts apart.

On the last day of spring, after five weeks away, Langston was once again in Harlem. He found Mrs. Harper in a stormy mood. While she had been out of town visiting relatives, her husband Emerson had allowed the grass in the back garden to wilt by neglecting to water it; now he himself wilted under her glare in his "upholstered doghouse," as Mr. Harper sorrowfully dubbed his favorite armchair. Soon, a flood of visitors arrived. A truck rattled in from Kansas City bearing Mrs. Harper's eighty-four-year-old mother, a brother, his wife, and two aggressive children. Not long after, a niece from Los Angeles dropped in for the summer, then a nephew, his wife, and four amusing little boys. Later in the summer came a distant cousin of Langston's who was studying for the Roman Catholic priesthood. Keeping an eye on the stairs to the third floor, Hughes tried to be sociable but also to keep working. Nevertheless, he broke off with pleasure late in August to organize a party for Arna Bontemps, up from Nashville, and the folklorist-comedienne Louise Bennett of Jamaica.

The Harlem streets had lost nothing of their particular charm. Within a few days of his return from California, he witnessed two robberies. One occurred on teeming 125th Street itself, as he related incredulously: "Me standing at hot dog stand in front of station on Saturday A.M. as bars let out reading my *NY Times,* street full of people, stand crowded, busses passing and lights ablaze. Next to me fat Jewish gentleman. Notice cullud boy pacing around behind us. Thinking he wants to get to counter I look at him. He smiles and motions for me to keep quiet. Thinking he meant to play joke on someone, I kept on reading. Next thing I know, he snatches Jewish guy's pocket-button off with one hand, seizes wallet with other, and flees. Not a pickpocket, just boldly and brazenly grabbed it openly. Man yelled bloody murder—such a scream you never heard. Gave chase. No results. Must have had a lot of money in it. Oh!''

For all the distractions at home and the thrills of the street, Langston was obliged to keep his mind on work. Fortunately, with the arrival of the check from Rinehart for $2500 he could increase his secretarial help. Unable to guarantee a steady income, much less a salary, he had found it hard to hire and keep skilled secretaries. Recently he had employed a young white man, Robert Heeney, and Wesley Collier, who was black, but both had moved on. Now, after hearing from the actress Rosalind Russell, who took an interest in Asian affairs, that Chinese foreign students often could not find summer jobs, he called Asia House at Columbia University to seek a helper. The person sent turned out to be a Chinese-American graduate of Stanford University in California, Zeppelin Wong. "I was in New York for the summer only," Wong later remembered, "and was definitely committed to go home to San Francisco to attend law school in the fall. A friend of mine answered the phone at Columbia and she knew I wanted a job—so she sent me. By the time Langston discovered that I could not type, and knew nothing about short-hand, I had started giving lessons in Chinese cooking to Mrs. Harper. He threatened to fire me, but she warned him: if Zep goes, you go." Zeppelin Wong—"a wonderful fellow," Langston soon agreed—stayed. By the time he left New York late in September, Wong, like most of Hughes's helpers, had gained a deep respect for his employer. Later he would write nostalgically to Langston about "the wonderful summer I spent with you," as well as admiringly of "the cause that has made you so noble in my sight."

Thus supported, Langston threw himself into his various projects. To mark the coming centennial of his alma mater, Lincoln University, he agreed to help his old friend Waring Cuney (who in 1925 had led him to apply for admission) and Bruce McM. Wright publish a volume of poetry by its most talented alumni. For his operatic collaborator Jan Meyerowitz, who recently had supervised the recording of their opera *The Barrier* with a full orchestra and chorus at Radio VARA, Hilversum, in the Netherlands, Langston composed another libretto. Five pages in length, the text was for an oratorio, "The Five Foolish Virgins," based on Matthew 25:1-13, about the five wise virgins who watched and waited for the bridegroom, and the five who did not ("Watch therefore, for ye know neither the day nor the hour wherein the Son of Man cometh"). "Langston laughed and told me," Meyerowitz said, "that he liked that episode because he assumed that those five foolish virgins just had to be Negro. I asked him why, and he said because they weren't ever on time!" The composer was also thinking seriously of an opera based on Hughes's comedy of 1937, *Joy to My Soul;* Langston was amenable to work on this libretto, but it was never done.

For the dancer-choreographer Katherine Dunham he worked on "Two Brothers: Dos Hermanos," a libretto in English and Spanish for which he provided lyrics—and was paid ("Miracle before God to come from show business, Katherine Dunham sent me a CHECK for the ballet libretto I did for her! The only time a libretto ever paid off—a-tall! I mean, a-tall!") And near the end of the summer, he began an active association with the Institute of Jazz Studies, an organization founded by the jazz scholar Marshall Stearns, a professor of music, and Philip and Stephanie Barber's Music Inn in Lenox, Massachusetts. Operating in the shadow of the internationally famous Tanglewood Festival of classical music, the Music Inn had offered every summer since 1950 scholarly panel discussions of jazz and folk music led by Marshall Stearns. That summer, as part of a plan to broaden the appeal of the summer panels, Langston joined the board of advisors of the Institute.

The main task of the summer of 1953, however, was probably to complete the collection of biographical essays "Famous American Negroes," which Langston presented to Dodd, Mead early in September. What started as a routine "juvenile" job became a source of pain and distress when his editors there suggested—indeed, demanded—several cuts. The excisions removed almost all accounts of incidents of overt racism from the text. Three lines were cut in one place from the story of Paul Laurence Dunbar. Also dropped was an incident (one cut of nineteen lines) in which the entrepreneur Charles C. Spaulding of North Carolina, then an old man, was struck in the face by a white drugstore clerk in a building owned by Spaulding's bank, because Spaulding had sipped a beverage on the premises. A cut of ten lines reduced the essay on the newspaperman Robert Abbott. Two cuts, totalling twenty-three lines, removed references to the fact that young George Washington Carver had been sickened to see some of his white schoolmates and their parents cheering the lynching of a black man. Cut also (five sections adding up to thirty-nine lines) were allusions to encounters with discrimination in Washington, D.C. by Ralph Bunche, who had received the Nobel Prize for Peace in 1950 for his work with the United Nations in Palestine. Three cuts (fourteen lines) were made in the essay on the labor leader A. Philip Randolph. Similar cuts were demanded in at least six biographies, and a six-page chapter on the blond, blue-eyed, but "black" Walter White of the NAACP was dropped altogether.

These excisions of "references to racial discrimination" were carefully noted by Hughes. But the unkindest cut in his book, and one about which he should have felt a degree of agony, although he never referred to it publicly, was the omission altogether of any reference to the greatest of black intellectuals, W. E. B. Du Bois. In fact, Langston managed to write a chapter about the accommodationist Booker T. Washington without once mentioning his most celebrated antagonist. Undoubtedly, it was taken for granted by his various publishers that even brief references to Du Bois and other radicals were out of the question in a text aimed at children. Such books were virtually indefensible when attacked by the right wing. The first edition of Hughes's *First Book of Negroes* had contained a picture of Josephine Baker, but after a New York columnist threatened to attack the book unless all references to her were removed (he accused her of being a communist), she vanished from the text in the next printing. Nor were only children's books vulnerable. Just about everyone at the firm of Henry Holt who had been involved in publishing Hughes's *Montage of a Dream Deferred* in 1951 and *Laughing to Keep from Crying* in 1952 had been summarily fired and various contracts cancelled. Stock of the books, including *Montage*, was sold off cheaply—all because of pressure, Langston was told, from reactionary groups backed by oil-rich conservatives. "That Texas oil money suddenly found them on *their* list!" Hughes joked desperately about the fired editors. "All due to a few little poetries."

Langston himself had steered almost completely clear of radical politics or international affairs in the aftermath of his McCarthy appearance. In the Chicago *Defender,* only one column since then had addressed such issues, when Langston called for an enlightened attitude on the part of the U.S. government towards the emerging nations of Asia. The anti-colonialist military zeal of Asians must be heeded. "Certainly Japan shook the white world to its very roots at Pearl Harbor," he wrote. "The Dutch were no military match for the Indonesians. Red China told everybody to kiss her unbound feet." The U.S. forces failed to reach the Yalu River in Korea. "Almost anybody could see, just by reading the papers, that modern Asia does not mind fighting and dying to achieve its independence, or to keep it once it is achieved." Plans by the Pentagon, recently revealed, to drop atomic bombs on Korea were signs of madness on the part of the white world. "I think it would only step up the beginning of that world's end . . . in so far as military or moral power goes. Of course, the white world might HAVE to drop an atom bomb in Asia to find this out, since a sense of reality and reason seems alien to a large portion of our officialdom."

Other than in this column, Langston was virtually silent on such matters. In his books, to preserve his career and certain sources of income, he had compromised his principles in a way that would distress many of his friends and admirers, and not only on the left. Ten years later, in 1965, he would quietly defend privately—never publicly—his part in these excisions, starting with *The First Book of Negroes,* published in 1952. "It was at the height of the McCarthy Red baiting era," he wrote an inquirer, "and publishers had to go out of their way to keep books, particularly children's books, from being attacked, as well as schools and libraries that might purchase books. . . . It was impossible at that time to get anything into children's books about either Dr. Du Bois or Paul Robeson.'' By 1965, to Langston's satisfaction, the anti-communist scare had died down: ''I am glad times have changed.''

In 1953, however, he apparently never considered taking a stand on the matter, even to the extent of struggling with his publishers before giving in to their wishes. If writing *Famous American Negroes* and leaving out Du Bois caused him any pain, Langston admitted none to his publisher, Edward Dodd, Jr., when he thanked him for having had the chance to write the book: ''It was fun.''

This message was to his white publisher. To Arna Bontemps he sent the fifth draft of a new poem, ''Here to Stay,'' in tribute to the blacks in the book (''Those Negroes *were* tough''):

> . . . They done beat me and mistreat me,
> Barrel-staved me and enslaved me,
> Lynched me, run me, and Jim Crowed me,
> Acted like they never knowed me.
>
> But I'm here, still here——
> And I intend to be!
> It'll never be *that* easy, white folks,
> To get rid of me. . . .

Langston's compromises were not designed to make him rich, only to allow him to survive on acceptable terms as a writer and continue his lifelong service as an artist to his race. That year, 1953, his income amounted to just under $9,000, a decent sum; but almost half went to pay various secretaries. ''Another year of starvation,'' he mourned to Arna Bontemps at Christmas. ''My art costs me more than I make . . . . . . Precious Lord, take my hand!'' With his projects accumulating, the literary sharecropper was forced to switch his basic metaphor of self-description. ''I am running a literary factory right now,'' he confessed late in the fall, ''with three assembly lines going.'' Where other writers, under similar conditions, might have collapsed into total confusion, Hughes's factory system by this time was streamlined. ''Langston bought boxes of paper in different colors,'' Alice Childress recalled. ''He had a different color for each project. When you came into his study, you saw this Jacob's Coat of a work table, with neat stacks of different-colored paper around the edges. He laughed and explained to me that when he was tired of working on one project, he only had to shift his chair to another color, and picked up where he had left off. If all the paper on the table fell on the floor, he told me— laughing all the time—he could keep on working. Oh, the man knew what he was doing, all right!''

The year closed with a rush of activity. Aside from revisions of the new play, Langston mailed five hundred Christmas cards, scanned the proofs of two juvenile texts, drew up an outline for another children's book, and composed promotional material for his various publishers. With the poets Waring Cuney and Bruce McM. Wright, he also finished work on the Lincoln University Centennial poetry volume, then personally arranged with an expert New York printer, Fine Editions Press, for a run of one thousand copies. (The volume appeared in 1954 with an introduction by J. Saunders Redding.) And at last following the lead of Alice Childress, whose "Just a Little Simple" he had enjoyed in 1950, he also started work on a play about his Harlem hero Jesse B. Semple. Just before Christmas, he finished the first draft of "Simply Heavenly" (the original title of *Simple Takes a Wife*).

With his unrelenting guidance, his assembly lines rattled efficiently into the new year, 1954. He loved to complain to his friends about his demanding schedule, but he obviously was finding a measure of satisfaction in his work and its results, including his books for small children. He was pleased when his *First Book of Rhythms,* a "deceptively profound little book," one scholar judged, appeared early in the year from Franklin Watts. Not long after, Langston briskly started work on, then abandoned, a "First Book of Gypsies." Another failure was "The Train that Took Wings and Flew," which Helen Hoke Watts rejected as "too abstract." However, he later entered readily into writing his *First Book of Jazz,* published by Watts the following year. This book was "just about the toughest *little* job I've ever done" but would bring the music he loved best to the attention of children of all races. Since "what I really know about Jazz would fill a thimble!" Hughes carefully had this text scrutinized by Dave Martin, Marshall Stearns, John Hammond, and other jazz experts. Not the least of his troubles with the book on jazz came from his squeamish editors. "Have to be SO careful, no risqué titles or lyrics," he wrote Arna Bontemps. "These children's editors! Much more naive than the children! (If they knew where the word *jazz* came from. . . .")

Next he finished *First Book of the West Indies,* which Franklin Watts would release in August, 1956. The last of these essays for Watts, *The First Book of Africa,* appeared in 1960.

In spite of his efforts, these books for children made Langston little money. Accordingly, he also saved time for work on his Simple play, for which he now had a sponsor—Arnold Perl of Rachel Productions, who had developed the highly successful drama *The World of Sholom Aleichem,* which Langston had enjoyed on Broadway (it was "really different and human and though half fantasy, doesn't seem contrived"). *The World of Sholom Aleichem* was based on the writings, mainly in Yiddish, of the Russian-born writer Solomon Rabinowitz, who had helped to found the Yiddish Art Theatre in New York. But the inspiration for the play may have come from the world of Langston Hughes—or rather, from Alice Childress's *Just a Little Simple.* Ruth Jett, its producer, worked for Rachel Productions. "Arnold Perl had seen the show and thoroughly enjoyed it," she said. "I'm sure it helped to inspire his own work on Sholom Aleichem." Now Perl offered Hughes a contract for a play about Simple and even an advance—the first he had ever received for a drama. A few weeks later, Perl was "very excited" about a new outline submitted by Hughes.

A more high-toned venture by Hughes on the stage, one in collaboration with Jan Meyerowitz, reached the public on February 11, 1954, when their oratorio "The Five Foolish Virgins" was presented at the Town Hall in New York by a choir conducted by Margaret Hillis. The critics commented only in passing on the libretto but were harsh on the music. The piece, according to one writer, was "full of the clichés of twentieth-century instrumentation and amateurishly clumsy vocal writing." Hurt and indignant, but defiant as usual and buoyed by the news that he had been awarded a Guggenheim Fellowship, Meyerowitz asked Langston to expand the libretto for conversion to an opera. Cheerfully Hughes agreed to begin work on a new "Five Foolish Virgins." But the project did not mature. "We produced some fragments," according to Meyerowitz, "but the thing fizzled. Neither of us knew how to go ahead with it, and nobody encouraged us."

By this time, Hughes's finances were such that he could no longer avoid the road. When Negro History Week brought, as usual, several invitations for him to lecture, he travelled to Norfolk, Virginia, to hold forth to the Federation of Colored Women's Clubs on "Dark Beauty in America." Then, after returning home to speak at an Urban League convention at the Hotel Theresa in Harlem, he was soon off again on his first planned tour since his Senate appearance one year before. As with his more informal cross-country jaunt the previous year, he met virtually no opposition. Indeed, in St. Louis, Missouri, long a stronghold of segregation, one sign of progress astounded Langston. "The sun do move!" he marvelled to Carl Van Vechten; "I'm staying at a 'white' hotel in St. Louis!" Responding to the first tremors of court-imposed desegregation, the Hotel Statler at St. Charles and 9th Street had agreed to rent him a room. However, not every stronghold was surrendering without a struggle. In Cairo, Illinois, Langston ventured out to see a new landmark—an electric sign conveniently pointing to the home of David Lansden, an embattled local lawyer for the NAACP. Just as he arrived at the house, a car pulled up to the curb and a white man jumped out and threw a rock through a window of the house. Storming out with gun in hand, the lawyer, also white, was ready to do battle with—Langston Hughes? "No lie! I'm telling you, something happens everywhere I go," Langston laughed. "But I'm still here!"

At Bethune-Cookman College in Daytona Beach, Florida, he joined Ralph Bunche as honored guests when the school, still headed by its indomitable founder and President-Emeritus Mrs. Mary McLeod Bethune, a friend and admirer since 1931, celebrated its fiftieth anniversary. In 1931, urging him to take his poetry to the people, Mrs. Bethune in a sense had sent him out on the road, starting with his cross-country tour begun that year. Now, at fifty-two, he had far less energy for such a venture. The road now tired him quickly, and cut decisively into his time for writing. Thus he was elated on his return to Harlem, after a few days of rest in Nassau—"a kind of West Indian-British

Carmel''—in the Bahamas to find a check for $1000 awaiting him. Along with a work on Africa, *Simple Takes a Wife* had won the 1953 Anisfield-Wolf Book Award in Race Relations. The prize had been founded in 1934 by the Cleveland civic leader and poet Edith Anisfield Wolf in memory of her father and her husband, both of whom had been prominent leaders in Jewish and interracial philanthropy and social service. (Among the distinguished list of previous winners was Zora Neale Hurston, for her autobiography *Dust Tracks on a Road*.)

He knew exactly what he would do with the money, which he saw as "fortifying my resolution to accept no lectures or time-taking outside activities for next season." Now he could concentrate, at least for a while, on a mature literary project. About this time he started work on at least two short stories, "Thank You M'am" and "Dialogue at Dawn," both strikingly adult in setting and tone—the latter about a tryst between a man and his lover, who must leave his bed before the man's wife comes home with a baby. As committed as he was to his children's books and his Simple play, on this matter Langston had suddenly become sensitive. He believed that he needed such a project, and quickly. Additional evidence had come that his work was falling into disrepute among the most respected critics, whose judgment mattered to him in spite of his proletarian sympathies and his contempt for snobbishness. On almost all sides, younger writers were being anointed as his superiors. Sarcastically he giggled—"We's rising plus!"—at the news that Ralph Ellison that summer would add his voice to the polished deliberations at the Harvard Seminars in Salzburg, then proceed to Rome under a fellowship from the American Academy. ("Langston had traveled more than anyone I knew," Ellison later remarked with a laugh, "—except maybe for some Pullman car porters. So why shouldn't I go to Salzburg?")

Somewhat harder for Langston to take, however, was the sudden elevation by the critical establishment of Melvin B. Tolson to the position of the principal black poet—finer than Gwendolyn Brooks, in spite of her Pulitzer Prize, and finer certainly than the old warhorse, Langston Hughes. In matters of poetry, the genial Melvin Tolson had always approached Hughes far more as a pupil than as a fellow master. Suddenly, having overhauled his craft according to the most complex tenets of high modernism, and having also renounced the militant pro-Marxism of his first volume, *Rendezvous with America*, Tolson was now sporting laurels of a quality never before conceded by white critics to a black writer. Langston did not wish to deny Tolson his honors. On May 2, he gamely joined John Ciardi, an accomplished poet and translator who wrote frequently for the *New York Times*, in toasting Tolson at a book party for five hundred people in Harlem hosted by the American Friends of Liberia. Nevertheless, Langston had a difficult time sorting through the ironies of the hour. The book in question, Tolson's *Libretto for the Republic of Liberia*, which had been commissioned by the Friends of Liberia to mark the centenary of the African republic, glowed with a preface by the former Fugitive reactionary Allen Tate, who in 1932 had refused to attend a party in Nashville for Hughes and James Weldon Johnson because of their race. Now Tate was championing

Tolson as the first Negro poet who "has assimilated completely the full poetic language of his time and, by implication, the language of the Anglo-American poetic tradition." Langston Hughes and Gwendolyn Brooks had done "interesting and even distinguished work" in the folk and the high modernist idioms, Tate noted, but their work was fatally flawed because "the distinguishing Negro quality" appeared not in their language but only in their severely limited general theme, racial hurt. (In a preface to a later volume, the poet Karl Shapiro would make essentially this same point in asserting—extraordinarily, given Tolson's love of arcana—that *"Tolson writes in Negro."*)

Such judgments dumbfounded Langston. He had always liked and admired Tolson, a dashing if sometimes erratic professor of drama and debate, a dazzling public speaker, and a gifted poet who did not take himself too seriously. "More power to tongue-in-cheek Tolson!" Hughes wrote to Bontemps. "He told me he was going to write so many foreign words and footnotes that they would *have* to pay him some mind!" Just before Kurt Weill's death, Langston had tried to convince him to cast Tolson in the leading role in *Lost in the Stars*. Above all, his friend had nerve. "Nobody but Tolson could talk his way into being Poet Laureate of Liberia," Hughes wrote in admiration; Tolson was "a very talented fellow." However, the poet laureate of an African country had written probably the most hyper-European, unpopulist poem ever penned by a black writer. Did it not matter that very few of the American Friends of Liberia, and even fewer Liberians themselves, could understand the poem, which was supposed to commemorate the centenary of the founding of the republic in 1847? And yet Tolson's poem, gritty with allusions in sundry languages, had been acclaimed as a masterpiece in the *New York Times* by the white poet and art critic Selden Rodman. The previous year, ironically, Langston had written to Rodman protesting against his total exclusion of American blacks from various of his anthologies even as Rodman elsewhere fervently praised the daubings of various Haitian "masters." Rodman had not bothered to answer Hughes; perhaps his review of Tolson, echoing Tate, was his reply. Until Tolson, Rodman explained, the black poet had locked himself in a prison first of "resigned pathos," then of "tragic aggressiveness," both of which assured artistic mediocrity. But Tolson's poem, comparable in quality to T. S. Eliot's *The Waste Land,* Hart Crane's *The Bridge,* and William Carlos Williams's *Paterson,* "bids fair to put an end to all that."

Although Arna Bontemps saw malice ("Nasty boy!") in Rodman's "overpraising Tolson at the same time slapping all other Negro poets," Langston declined to be drawn into this controversy. And neither Hughes nor Bontemps wished to find fault with Tolson—even if Tolson himself now began to address Hughes with more than a hint of majesty. "I've read all your latest," he assured Langston about this time. "You're doing a great job for the general public in these disjointed times." Praising the white critics—"the greatest group of critics ever"—Tolson regretted that no Negro poets had risen "to carry on in the new idiom imaged in Negro life."

Wondering at this somewhat crazy turn of events, Langston received some encouragement from the sage of St. Elizabeth's Hospital in Washington, D.C., Ezra Pound. In happier days, Pound had presided over the development of modernist poetry in the English language, as Eliot himself had attested in dedicating *The Waste Land* to him as *"il miglior fabbro,"* the greater craftsman. From his cell in Washington, Pound wrote Langston to dismiss the "iggurance like A. Tate's when he compliments whazzis name on having riz to level of immitating Hart Crane."

If "the greatest group of critics ever" now belittled his voice, he would make what he could of a diminished thing. He would continue to sing, when he could do so, on behalf of younger writers. As he had done with Tolson himself in 1931, when he had patiently gone over the fledgling poet's verses with him in Harlem, Langston was open to practically any young person seeking encouragement. About a dozen envelopes of material came every month, almost invariably unsolicited and unwanted ("most of it is bad, illiterate, or dull," he flatly judged). But when talent surprised him, he encouraged it at once, as in the case of Ray Durem of San Francisco, or the Jamaican writer Andrew Salkey, who wrote from England offering an epic poem for criticism by Hughes—"your articles influenced me a great deal." In May, on the appearance of the promising Afro-American writer John O. Killens's first novel, *Youngblood,* Langston dispatched a telegram of congratulations; and he encouraged Sarah E. Wright, a young Philadelphia writer, on the appearance of her *Give Me a Child.* Nor was Langston's generosity restricted to blacks. After a young Dutchman, Paul Breman, a free-lance writer and a sometime student at the University of Amsterdam, slapped him with a letter condemning *Poetry of the Negro* for its only token inclusion of Africa, Langston replied with the other cheek and a large parcel of books. "Now if you will just get on a plane and fly over here some weekend," he assured Breman, "you could sit down in my studio and read to your heart's content. And then we could go downstairs and eat some good old pig feet and sauerkraut with cornbread. . . . I would also make you a nice highball, and play you some of my records." This sweet answer fairly reduced Breman, who sheepishly conceded: "I hardly expected a reply." Langston Hughes "turned out to be very much unlike the man who, asked for a 'robe of love,' gave a fur-coat. He's done something rather miraculous—like the prophets—he's turned the fur-coat into that robe of love."

And if, as his critics averred, he was finished in America, perhaps another country would have him—Africa. A world not new, but old and neglected, reopened quietly before him in 1954, when from Johannesburg, South Africa, a request arrived from Henry W. Nxumalo, assistant editor of *Drum: Africa's Leading Magazine,* for help in judging its third international short story competition. He accepted the invitation at once. Then the president of Lincoln University, Horace Mann Bond, just back from Africa, where he had visited his school's most famous African alumnus and the continent's leading black political leader, Kwame Nkrumah of the Gold Coast, informed Langston that Nkrumah wanted him to write his official biography. No doubt mindful of his biographical debacle with "Battle of Harlem," he declined this honor. However, he sent two large parcels of his books as a gift to Nkrumah in Accra. In return came a sentimental note of thanks, with some challenging words from the leader about the fact that "Africa on the whole, and the Gold Coast in particular, are in the world news these days."

Four years before, Langston had confessed to an inquiring publisher that he had no contacts with Africa, no reliable, fresh knowledge of the land he had visited in the summer of 1923 as a messman on the *West Hesseltine*. In 1953, he modestly had declined to attempt a translation of a Francophone black poet for Indiana University Press. However, the name Langston Hughes was hardly unknown in Africa. His evocative poems on the beauty of blackness had gained him readers there, and among Africans in Europe, since the 1920s. Drawing up plans in the late 1940s for the magazine *Présence Africaine*, which would soon be the most influential journal of African cultural debate, Alioune Diop had solicited Langston's advice and counsel. From Paris, the poet Leopold Sédar Senghor of Senegal, long an admirer, had also corresponded with him on similar matters. From Africans of a humbler sort had come other signals. Once, the startling arrival of a gift of a monkey skin from an admirer in Accra, Ghana, had created a Christmas sensation at 20 East 127th Street. Above all, many African writers were grateful to Hughes for having composed so many poems that defied the myths of black ugliness and inferiority. A young Gold Coast poet, citing certain sonorous lines from "The Negro"—"Black as the night is black, / Black like the depths of Africa"—admitted to worshipping the author of the poem. Similarly, a black woman from Johannesburg, South Africa, told simply of her pride in knowing that the celebrated author Langston Hughes actually was a man of color.

Thus, in the wake of the Senate hearings and with his apparent eclipse by Wright, Ellison, Brooks, Baldwin, Tolson, and others, he took increasing comfort in his tie to Africa—which then and later would mean less to the others, even to the "poet laureate" of Liberia, Melvin Tolson. In a book published that year, *Black Power: A Record of Reactions in a Land of Pathos*, about a visit to West Africa, Wright betrayed an impatience with the alleged limitations of the African "mentality" that might have embarrassed a typical British *bwana*. Hughes, on the other hand, was open and hospitable to the land and its various peoples. At a party at Henry and Molly Moon's, he enjoyed meeting Alan Paton, South Africa's most famous writer, and he sent greetings and words of admiration to another white South African, Nadine Gordimer, admired by young black compatriots. In May, Langston responded enthusiastically to a letter from Lincoln University's other major black African leader, Benjamin Nnamdi "Zik" Azikiwe of Nigeria, informing him that Zik would attend the Lincoln University Centennial celebrations (Hughes had included one of Azikiwe's student poems in the Lincoln Centennial volume). The same month, Hughes wrote a genuinely felt blurb for Peter Abrahams's autobiography *Tell Freedom* ("a very good book indeed," he judged privately), in which the South African "colored" writer testified to the impact of Langston Hughes's writing on his youth.

Helping to judge the *Drum* magazine short story competition led Langston to a new project. He was determined to have the new voices of Africa heard in the United States. Just as he had done with Mexican writers some twenty years before, he began to assemble an anthology of short stories by Africans (probably the first such venture in the history of American publishing), and he was undeterred when Simon and Schuster rejected the first six stories he submitted as a sample. Carefully he wrote to virtually every young writer whose name had come to him, including Amos Tutuola, Efua Sutherland, John Mbiti, Gabriel Okara, Davidson Nicol, Cyprian Ekwensi, Peter (Kumalo) Clark, Richard Rive, and Ezekiel Mphahlele. The response was frequently moving. Richard Rive, a "Cape Colored" like Peter Abrahams, wrote to Langston about the powerful impact on him in his youth of *The Ways of White Folks,* and of "a spirit of 'New Africa' awakening in the Dark Continent, in conformity with the rise of colonial masses in the rest of the world." Ezekiel Mphahlele, out of work for two years after being banned from teaching by the South African authorities for opposing the Bantu Education Act ("which is calculated to enslave the African child's mind"), was certainly touched by the attention from Langston: "It is indeed very flattering to me to have such warm complimentary comment from a great writer like you on my amateurish attempt (as I regard it)—for that matter, from a Negro to another. Believe me, we at this end are starved for Negro literature."

Some of these young writers first addressed Hughes obsequiously. One man had wondered "what great fellow would be writing to a little dot like me." Quickly Langston brought the relationships down to earth and encouraged the Africans to see him mainly as a fellow writer and a friend. In March of the following year, 1955, following much work and personal expense, he would send two manuscripts to various publishers for inspection. One included fifty-four short stories by twenty-eight authors from seven African countries. In spite of Langston's best efforts, this collection would never be published. The other collection in 1955 was "Big Ghost and Little Ghost," also made up of African short stories but intended for teenagers. This collection, too, was never taken by a publisher. Few American publishers were then interested in foreign literature, and almost none in that of Africa. Carl Murphy of the Baltimore *Afro-American* rejected without comment a selection of stories offered by Hughes. However, Langston persisted in the following years in his efforts on behalf of Africa, which culminated in his publication in 1960 of *An African Treasury: Articles, Essays, Stories, Poems by Black Africans.*

Within months of his renewal of communication with Africa, as Langston put it, he was "dreaming Nigeria in my sleep." In fact, the dream for Langston at this time was perhaps more complicated. Nigeria most likely was only a token of a deeper fantasy of self-fullfilment as he approached his mid-fifties, a wish that involved both inclusion and repudiation as he looked toward an ideal, harmonious rounding of his life. Peering toward his end, his death, he began to dream more and more of paternity. Actual paternity was by now impractical for him, but a symbolic paternity, properly designed, was not. His wish for such a symbol surely was driven by his sense that his record had become stained by political compromise. He needed now, toward his end, to reassert the original, best values by which he had lived. Another influence prompting Langston to dwell now on paternity could have been the arrival in the fall of 1954 of Paul Bontemps, Arna's handsome, athletic son, in his mid-twenties, to study at Columbia University. "Paul dines with us ever so often, and has a GOOD appetite," Langston wrote Arna. "Aunt Toy loves him because he helps wash dishes. Real nice boy! Tell Alberta we're glad to have him around." Paul Bontemps stayed for a few months, then left to get married.

Bontemps did not remember Langston as fatherly or even avuncular. "Nobody would have called Langston 'uncle'," he asserted, "because Langston, regardless of his chronological age, never seemed to be in a posture of elder-to-young. He treated you as if you were the same age. He was just your friend." With the Harpers, he was like a son, "close, very close. They acted like his parents. They took care of him, they were interested in his friends, they protected and shielded him from unwanted intrusions." Bontemps recalled how Hughes seemed to dominate any gathering, black or white, with his charm and friendliness, which ran deep. "Psychologically, he was not an extreme anything. He seemed to me a whole person. You just weren't worried about Langston as a person." As for later rumors of Langston's homosexuality, "I have no evidence of that at all. The people that I knew who knew Langston would be as surprised as I am to hear the charge. I have wracked my memory and I can find no incident to support the idea in any way."

Langston was fascinated by young people named after him, especially those named Langston Hughes. "What I would really like to know," he wrote a friend on hearing of one such person, "is how my namesake came to be named after me, how old he is and where is he from and what does he look like?" Youth was the key. Dreaming of a child, perhaps of a son, he found himself opening more and more to those who were young and black, and whose faces were turned optimistically to the future. And almost as if by magic in its timeliness, one of his poems, reprinted in Nnamdi Azikiwe's *West African Pilot*, brought him the apparent embodiment of his fantasy of self-fullfilment—an African son. From Funtua, Nigeria, an enterprising young man, allegedly fifteen years old (subsequent letters suggested, however, that he was older), wrote to Langston declaring his filial devotion. "Your thoughtful poem infused a new life in me," Chuba Nweke claimed, "and made me determined to seek friendship with you." After reading the poem, he had written a piece of fiction and five poems, which had languished until recently. Then, the young African declared, "remembering, I have a (Father) over the Mighty Seas (YOU) though you do not know me, I thought of begging you a fatherly help—to read the unworthy story and raise it to a worthy base, and if possible to write a forward to it." The letter was signed "Your son, Chuba Nweke."

At fifty-two, Langston was hardly an innocent. Moreover, as he reached lovingly towards Africans, he saw at least two or three of them reach lovingly towards his pocket. One self-described poet had practically demanded of Langston not help in shaping his verse but a scholarship to an automobile engineering school in the U.S., as well as cash. "I know you are a big man," he assured Hughes. "My mind tells me that." This fellow got nothing, but Chuba Nweke touched a more tender nerve. "Dear son Chuba," Hughes soon replied. "Since you've adopted me—and thus become my one and only son (and I'm very happy that you have) you will have to send me a photograph (just a Kodak snapshot will do, it needn't be an expensive one) so that I can see how you look. Certainly I am very proud and flattered to be taken as a father by so ambitious a boy as yourself, already working on a novel, and only 15 years old!" Langston closed: "With all my love and good wishes to my Nigerian son."

This "fatherly missive," as Nweke called it, was swiftly answered by one from Africa to "My dear dad." Over the following months, Hughes remained intrigued as young Nweke stoked the fires of paternal affection: "May God endorse our dear dreams then Dad you'll one day be more proud of me: your son who is very far beyond the seas—your son who have not even seen your portrait!" Cagily, Langston neglected to send Nweke his picture, even as he accepted Nweke's. After a while, as Nweke overplayed his hand by asking too much of Langston, his replies became infrequent—to his son's chagrin ("My anxiety turns to madness as I rush to the mailbox every day. . . . Dad!"). Eventually the two men met, but no friendship developed between them. However, Langston was in no way disillusioned by Nweke's failure to live up to his hopes in this regard. The idea of an African son took root. A few years later, on a visit to Lagos, after meeting a polite young black policeman, he would quietly enter into another adoptive, paternal relationship. Tactfully nurtured on both sides, and quite above suspicion, this "kinship" would result in the young African being named as a major beneficiary in Hughes's last will. In this way, Langston emulated (though only weakly) W. E. B. Du Bois's own dramatic design of his last years. In 1961, Du Bois left the United States for good and moved to the Republic of Ghana, where he would renounce his American allegiance and die as a Ghanaian citizen in 1963.

Though Langston's sense of himself as a wandering, wondering child could never be eradicated, it had steadily eroded under the sheer pressure of years and circumstance. Surfacing now perhaps, at last, was the obverse self-image, which had been latent in him from the start—his sense of himself, in his most intimate role as a poet, as mother (hardly father) to the race, rather than its princely child. Early poems such as "Mother to Son" and "The Negro Mother" had indicated the presence of this essential capacity, even if it had been only sparingly invoked. Now, as an object of his own will, he was moving irrevocably from confidence that Langston Hughes heroically, epically, could determine the future—that is, save and deliver his race—toward the tender hope that his "children," nurtured by him, would do so. His commitment to writing juveniles, mysterious even to himself, and constant even when the writing of such books led him to compromise, was probably as significant. "I'm becoming a children's writer these days,'' he noted once with quiet wonder. His books were becoming "simpler and simpler! And younger and younger.''

To the black writer Ellen Tarry, who had first met him in the 1930s, and whose devout Roman Catholicism appealed to Langston, "his affection for and kindness to children was remarkable, and it showed in his writing for them. He was simple, but he also knew that every word has to count for ten when you arc writing for young people.'' To her daughter, as to a number of children, Langston sent postcards and other tokens of affection with a diligence that was as touching and delightful as it was surprising. "There was something deep about his feeling for children,'' Ellen Tarry concluded. "I think he remained a child at heart, in spite of everything else.''

On May 27 that year, 1954, when he watched a group of young actors, former members of the Karamu Theatre in Cleveland, perform a two-hour program at the Countee Cullen library on the history of Negro playwrights, he felt poignantly the difference between his age and their own. The stars of the show were "an amazing new talent," twenty-four-year-old Clayton Smeltz (later Clayton Corbin), and the self-possessed narrator ("cullud in spite of his name''), Raoul Abdul, only a year older. To Langston, sitting bashfully in the shadows at the back of the room, the evening brought bittersweet memories of "the old library days of the '20's,'' during his first years in Harlem. He saw his youthful self reborn in the performers, and his adult self watching the promise of black youth as some older patron—the bibliophile Arthur Schomburg, or Dr. Du Bois, or even Alain Locke (who died less than two weeks later)—might have done way back then. It seemed to him "really one of the most interesting evenings I've had in Harlcm in ycars.'' Afterwards, he sent a note of appreciation to Raoul Abdul, who had also written and directed the show, and suggested that it might do well on tour. Late in July, he published a *Defender* column in praise of Clayton Smeltz's talent.

Years after Hughes's death, the Harlem-reared writer Toni Cade Bambara would recall another tie between Langston and children. "I loved the library as a child,'' she remembered, "and I was often there. Langston Hughes would come in, and the amazing thing to me now is that instead of sitting in the adult section, he would almost always sit with us children. He didn't talk to us, or try to draw anyone out; he just liked to do his reading with the children, it seemed. Some of us knew who he was, because his books were on the shelves and the librarians were proud of him. But he always behaved as if he was one of us. He seemed completely at ease in the children's section.'' In the 1960s, growing up on the block, David Givens (later a community leader) knew the poet as friendly to all the children around. "In those days Yellow Cabs still came up regularly to Harlem,'' he reminisced, "and we would see him getting in and out, smiling and friendly, just a regular guy—although everybody knew he was famous and had visitors from all over the world all the time. We loved it when he sent us on errands, because Mr. Hughes was definitely the biggest tipper among all the adults on the block. You had to like him. Everyone did, young or old. And when you walked by the house, as often as not you heard the piano playing—Mr. Harper or Mrs. Harper, most likely—and the sound of music from their parlor.''

In the backyard at 20 East 127th Street, where the lawn in the summer of 1954 was dense and green, a gardener named Mr. Sacred Heart, a follower of the evangelist Father Divine, planted some flowering shrubs. In front of the house, at Langston's request, someone later planted Boston Ivy that crept up the walls and eventually luxuriated, so that everyone knew in which house on the street had lived the poet Langston Hughes. But most of the patch of earth beside the front steps, about six feet square, was barren from years of trampling by neighborhood children, who had little time for flowers. Langston decided to rescue it, and teach the children a tender lesson at the same time. He named the plot their garden. From Amy Spingarn's home upstate in Dutchess County came nasturtiums, asters, and marigolds. Under his supervision, aided by Mr. Sacred Heart, each child chose a plant, set it, and assumed partial responsibility for weeding and watering the garden. On a picket beside each plant was posted a child's name. Proud of the garden, which flourished, and prouder still of his children, Langston was photographed at least once beaming in their midst. On August 27, 1954, readers of Meyer Berger's ''Around New York'' column in the *New York Times* learned about the tiny garden planted by neighborhood children in front of the home of the writer Langston Hughes in Harlem. ''The garden's in full bloom now, mostly with nasturtium, marigolds and asters, not one of which has been stolen or torn. Mr. Hughes wishes he'd thought of the name stakes two years ago.''

Another chance to help a younger person came in July, even as he anxiously faced a deadline for his second autobiography, when Roy DeCarava, a thirty-five-year-old photographer and a native of New York, impulsively telephoned Hughes and made an appointment to show him some of his work. In 1952, DeCarava had accumulated more than two thousand pictures of Harlem after taking a Guggenheim Fellowship for a pictorial study of the community. Trained as a painter at the Harlem Art Center early in the forties, DeCarava had turned to photography in 1947. After a period at the Cooper Union Institute in New York and impressive small exhibitions, he had been recommended for the fellowship by Edward Steichen, who would include his work in his landmark show *The Family of Man* in 1955. The fellowship year had resulted in a magnificent collection of photographs. ''What to do with them was another matter,'' DeCarava later recalled. ''I had simply shelved them, put them away for good, I was sure, until one day I started to think about Langston Hughes—we had met only once, I think, just after the war—and his Simple sketches. I thought, if anyone would like to see my pictures, and understand them, it would be the author of those sketches, which really captured Harlem life in words. I telephoned him. He didn't hesitate at all. 'Come on over!' I chose about three hundred and went over to show them. Langston looked and looked and when I was finished showing them he said, 'We have to get these published!' I was amazed. I hadn't gone there with anything like that in mind at all. I had simply wanted him to look at them. But he asked me to leave fifty or so, and give him a little time. I was embarrassed. Anybody could see that he was busy, very busy with his own work. But he insisted.''

He was indeed busy. A few days later, at four o'clock on Saturday, July 17, with various of DeCarava's pictures propped up around his study as inspiration, he began his second autobiography, "I Wonder as I Wander." His start was both unpromising and inspired. Having neglected to sift through his files in the basement for raw material, as he should have done, he was now forced to "write it from memory," as he had composed *The Big Sea* in 1939. Only if he had time later would he bother to check the facts. "If publishers want a really documented book," he insisted self-righteously, "they ought to advance some documented money—enough to do nothing else for two or three years. I refuses to sharecrop long for short rations!" But the words flowed. By three o'clock the following morning, he had typed thirty pages. "I hope it reads as easily as it writes," he informed Arna Bontemps. At this rate, within a month he would have three hundred pages, which would become, when typed strategically, with wide margins, about four hundred—"which is just about a book."

By August 8, however, the autobiography was stalled. Since he was broke, as he explained, he had turned to another juvenile, *The First Book of the Caribbean*. Then deadlines on other projects jammed the assembly line, and the autobiography was set aside altogether. "New York," Langston wailed, "is impossible for long-term effort. I need a BIG staff!" The former literary sharecropper turned factory manager now sketched himself as a poolplayer in deep trouble: "I am currently behind a three-way dead-line 8-ball." In addition to the book about the Caribbean, he was working on two albums for Moses Asch's Folkways record company—*The Story of Jazz*, to complement his *First Book of Jazz*, and *The Glory of Negro History*, a documentary narrative that included the voices of Ralph Bunche and Mary McLeod Bethune, with narration by the young Karamu actor Clayton (Smeltz) Corbin and the actress Hilda Haynes. For the composer Ulysses Kay, Langston quickly revised his sardonic mother-son play of the 1930s, *Soul Gone Home*. Another brief libretto, "Love from a Tall Building," about a would-be suicide saved at the last minute, was offered to the composer-conductor Leonard Bernstein, who cited a hectic schedule of his own in declining it. For Margaret Bonds, Langston wrote a Christmas piece "The Ballad of the Brown King," and for Jan Meyerowitz he wrote another, "On a Pallet of Straw."

He also lectured in the Berkshires at Marshall Stearns's Institute of Jazz Studies panel at the Music Inn, and visited Chicago for a revival in late October of his 1936 play *Emperor of Haiti* (then called *Troubled Island*). In the meantime, he did not forget his promise to help the photographer Roy DeCarava. First, he had written to his friend the artist Aaron Douglass, a professor at Fisk University, to suggest an exhibition of the "quite marvellous" photographs. Douglass was moved by the pictures but could do nothing there. (Later, another of Langston's artist friends, Eugene Grigsby of Phoenix, would mount an exhibition of the Harlem photographs.) Hughes then tried his contacts among the publishers in New York. One by one, each admitted the brilliance of the pictures but refused the book. Calling DeCarava "a Rembrandt of the camera" and "a master of the darkroom," the editor-in-chief of Doubleday saw no way not to lose vast amounts of his firm's money on "the work of this genius." Langston would not give up. Trying "one more long shot," he sent the pictures to Simon and Schuster, which recently had published Henri Cartier-Bresson's *The Decisive Moment,* including a portrait of a Harlem girl in her Easter hat. But Richard Simon called it "really heartbreaking" that DeCarava's pictures were "unpublishable in book form."

Because DeCarava's work captured not simply Harlem's poverty but also its joy and humanity, Langston believed the photographs needed to be seen by as many people as possible. "We've had so many books about how bad life is," he argued, "that it would seem to me to do no harm to have one along about *now* affirming its value." Then Richard Simon had an idea. If Hughes himself would write a narrative of some sort, a story based on the pictures, and if Simon and Schuster held down its costs by printing a small clothbound edition and at the same time a much larger paperback edition, both on relatively cheap paper and pages of small size, a book just might be feasible. "We agreed to a contract at once," DeCarava remembered. "I was happy beyond words to have a book coming out, when I had never expected to have one. As for his story, Langston did not want to know any facts about the persons I had photographed on the streets. He told me he knew them already, although he had never met them. And of course he did! He said he would simply meditate on the pictures, and write what came into his head." The result was a loose and spicy but inspired little tale that matched the images almost perfectly.

With his autobiography still stalled, but money still an issue, he typed up a fresh cover sheet for his old "Anthology of Harlem" and offered the manuscript to Ted Amussen at Rinehart. Amussen quickly rejected the proposal but set a new date of delivery for the autobiography. Langston marked his reprieve, however, by securing another contract from Franklin Watts, this time for a *First Book of Africa* (which would appear in 1960). For Moses Asch of Folkways he developed the texts for two new recordings—one, "The Rhythms of the World," to accompany his *First Book of Rhythms,* another based on *The Dream Keeper,* his beautiful book of poems for older children published by Knopf in 1934. And on December 6, after a furious effort, he was able to send to his sponsor Arnold Perl of Rachel Productions a revised version of the Simple play for which he had taken an advance.

In spite of missed deadlines and accumulating projects, the Christmas season was pleasant, and 1954 ended on a successful note. A week before Christmas, Langston not only had already mailed one thousand specially printed cards but had finished wrapping all of his many presents "in spite of visiting foreigners and Africans, West Indians, et al., in town by the dozens." On the radio, he heard two of his songs with flattering frequency: "Sail! Sail! Sail!" sung by the Mitch Miller Chorus, and "Lonely House," from *Street Scene*, sung by June Christie. If neither was a hit, Langston could still look forward to a rise in his royalties from ASCAP. Taking his pick of more than a dozen seasonal invitations, he dined with Amy Spingarn and with his dentist and longtime friend Dr. Frost Wilkinson and his wife, Anne, at their apartment at 706 Riverside Drive in Harlem. At home, he helped organize the second so-called "Yard Dog" party—"where we got together and howled for our own amusement"—on December 27, with the informal guest of honor Mrs. Harper's old friend from Kentucky, Edith Wilson, who had portrayed "Aunt Jemima" in radio advertisements of the pancake mixture. The guest list did not lack prominent names. Eubie Blake and Noble Sissle were asked, as well as W. C. Handy, Ethel Waters, Carl and Fania Van Vechten, Leonard Feather, Juanita Hall, Inez Cavanaugh, Franklin and Helen Watts, Maxine Sullivan, Mary Lou Williams, and Margaret Bonds.

Two days later, Langston and Edith Wilson went off to the Berkshires for another jazz program at the Music Inn. But entertainment of a more historic order claimed his attention on January 7, 1955, when he escorted the actress and writer Cornelia Otis Skinner (at her invitation after he expressed interest in what was "bound to be an historical evening") to Marian Anderson's debut with the Metropolitan Opera. The performance, which broke the unspoken barrier excluding blacks from the most prominent operatic company in the United States, had sold out swiftly with the announcement that the contralto, then fifty-two years old, would sing the role of the sorceress Ulrica in Verdi's *Un Ballo in Maschera*, with Richard Tucker, Roberta Peters, and Zinka Milanov. The fact that Anderson was now clearly past her prime only added to the pathos of the evening. A tremendous ovation greeted her appearance in the second scene of the opera, and another rewarded her at the end of the act. When Milanov embraced and kissed her, the house responded wildly, and some members of the audience brushed away tears. Elated in spite of the cold, blustery weather, Langston returned with Miss Skinner to her home on East 66th Street for supper with her husband and a few friends. The evening, Hughes later wrote her, had been "one of the most memorable of my now rather long life."

Anderson's belated appearance at the Met was yet another bittersweet occasion marking the decline and fall of Jim Crow. Soon Langston would note mordantly another. When the revolutionary jazz musician Charlie Parker and the veteran NAACP leader Walter White died within days of one another near the end of March, both men left behind white widows. (Walter White had divorced his first wife Gladys, who was black, to marry Poppy Cannon.) "Social equality," the ancient euphemism for miscegenation, especially the dreaded union of black men and white women, apparently was the order of the new day of integration—at least for prominent black men. Langston's attitude to this trend was perhaps not unlike his view of Marian Anderson's triumph. Opera was hardly his favorite genre, but he was proud to see a black step through a gilded door once shut to the race. He did not favor intermarriage, but he was glad to see the taboo against miscegenation shattered. "So, you see," he punned to a friend in Europe, "we're integreating!"

Scrupulously written and edited, with handsome designs by Clifford H. Roberts, Langston's *First Book of Jazz* appeared to superb reviews, with more than one critic noting that the book was not only the first of its kind for children, but would also appeal to adults. For Dodd, Mead, he completed a second book, *Famous Negro Music Makers,* so quickly—within ten days—that even he was appalled by his speed ("don't tell anybody," he begged a friend). In generating income, speed and versatility were of the essence. Digging in his extensive files he once again came up with "Bon Bon Buddy" and "Boy of the Border," two oft-rejected efforts written with Arna Bontemps about twenty years before, and another, hardly younger children's tale, "The Train that Took Wings and Flew." Once again, he needed money desperately. In particular, the cost of postage and typing as he gathered over two hundred manuscripts of short stories from Africa drained his bank account. After a check to a stenographer bounced, he turned one more time, as he had turned so often since 1925, to Carl Van Vechten. If his friend was also broke, fine, "but if you aren't, and want to help ART and the RACE through the rainy months of April," a loan of a hundred dollars would be nice. Van Vechten sent the money.

In spite of the jaunty phrasing of his request, Langston unquestionably was more than a little ashamed to be still borrowing money at such an advanced stage of his career, indeed, of his life. On the other hand, as much as he resisted feelings of bitterness, and even more its public expression, he also found it hard to avoid thinking that, as a black artist, he was still being treated unfairly. He had few complaints against publishers. "There is practically no race prejudice in book publishing," he more than once asserted even as he noted with exasperation that "I am continually trying to make publishers aware of Negro reviewers and Negro publications, and prove to them that we are 'on the ball' literarily." But Hollywood, Broadway, radio, and television were different stories. With mixed emotions Langston watched as the once-struggling immigrant Albert Hague, who had collaborated with him on some songs, successfully brought a musical play, *Plain and Fancy,* to Broadway while he himself met the usual indifference from producers. Indignantly he eyed a limousine dispatched by MGM to ferry Hague to his premiere ("See what happens to white! In US about as long as Meyerowitz. Cullud here all their days and—!"). Langston knew that no colored writer received such treatment from Hollywood.

Even without discrimination, his path in the theater was almost always trying. After receiving the latest draft of Hughes's Simple play, Arnold Perl had decided that he wanted not a straight comedy but a show with music. Again, Langston would have to start over. Inviting the veteran Harlem musician Dave Martin, who had played the piano for years at Cafe Society in New York and toured Europe extensively with Eddie South's orchestra, to join him in the venture, he reluctantly began his rewriting. "After this one," he vowed as he started the latest draft, "I retire. (If not before)."

His successes, when they came, seemed inevitably to be successes not in cash but in prestige, as when after severe drubbings in the press, he and Jan Meyerowitz scored an authentic hit on April 14 with their Easter cantata *The Glory Around His Head,* performed at Carnegie Hall by the New York Philharmonic Orchestra, conducted by Dimitri Mitropoulos, and sung by the Westminster Choir led by Margaret Hillis. Olin Downes praised "an arresting score, packed with tell-tale flashes of originality and a driving attraction for the folk-like incantations of Langston Hughes's poetic text," while another reviewer touched on the "poignant, childlike simplicity" of Hughes's words. "This was probably the most important thing we ever did together," the composer later judged.

Thus encouraged, Langston completed his ill-fated "Five Foolish Virgins" libretto for Meyerowitz, then fended off a request by his collaborator for a libretto based on the fall of Adolph Hitler (he would need $1000 for a special research assistant for such a venture). He thought of a proposal for a libretto based on *Uncle Tom's Cabin* ("I've always loved the book. So, maybe"). For the actress Hilda Haynes, he fashioned a narrative called "All About Women: A Sequence of Monologues, Poems, and Songs," drawing on his "Madam to You" poems, his ballads, and historic speeches by Harriet Tubman, Sojourner Truth, and other black heroines. And for Dorothy Maynor, no longer a concert star but a lively cultural leader in Harlem, he wrote a little drama with songs, "St. James: Sixty Years Young," for performance at the prominent Presbyterian church where her husband Rev. Dr. Shelby Rooks was pastor.

Finally, in May, 1955, Langston returned to his autobiography. He did so just after coming across Arthur Koestler's *Invisible Writing,* in which Koestler recounted in detail his impressions of Central Asia in the 1930s, including his travels there with Langston Hughes. Certain inaccuracies about their meeting (for example, that Langston had been playing on his victrola a Sophie Tucker recording) amused him: "I *never* owned a Sophie Tucker record!" But he was less charmed by Koestler's hostile retrospection on the Soviet Union. Koestler's backward glances were "all with a jaundiced eye." Since the Soviet Union would occupy a large part in his own text, *Invisible Writing* presented a definite challenge. A manuscript of four hundred pages, especially one hammered out without research, suddenly seemed inappropriate.

The task would take him into the fall, because early in the summer he took on yet another project—the text for a pictorial history of black America already under contract with Crown Publishers, but from which Arna Bontemps wished to withdraw because of his own full schedule. One glance at the "absolutely thrilling" photographs, compiled after relentness hunting by Milton Meltzer, a former education student at Columbia University who worked in public relations for a chemical company but was determined to publish a book, convinced

Langston to take over the job. "I don't see how you can bear to give it up," he wrote frankly to Bontemps. Surveying the collection, an "awestruck" Mrs. Harper paid Meltzer a backhanded compliment: "Now, why didn't some Negro do that?" On this score, Langston himself had no difficulty. "My feeling is," he reasoned, "why be selfish about culture?"

"I was overjoyed when Arna Bontemps—I had approached him first—suggested Langston Hughes," Meltzer later recalled, "but I went to meet Langston with real trepidation. After all, he was the most famous author I had ever met. Ten minutes later, I was completely relaxed. He was so down to earth, disarming, relaxing, I felt I could do or say anything I wanted and he simply wouldn't mind. And he was very quick and attentive in working on the book." Finding a publisher, however, proved frustrating. At least ten firms turned down the project. "Most of them replied simply that no one was interested in black history," Meltzer remembered. "Two or three even said that blacks don't read, so why bother with them? And a few suggested going to a foundation, since no normal publisher would take on such a pointless task. But Langston and I refused to do this." Then, one night at a dinner party in Ossining, where he lived, Meltzer impulsively went on for ten minutes about the project to a man next to him whose name he had not caught. "The man listened to me. Then he said, 'I'll publish it.' I said, 'You'll do what?' He turned out to be Robert Simon, one of two partners at Crown Publishers. I told him that a dozen houses had already said no. He said, 'They are fools. They just don't know what is happening in this country.' And that was that."

Langston jealously guarded his time through the summer—although dashing young foreigners such as George Lamming of Barbados, whose first novel *In the Castle of My Skin* had just appeared, and Peter Abrahams of South Africa were welcomed to his suite. Most of the time he toiled, sometimes for eighteen hours a day. Moving around his many-colored table, he also found time to put together "How to Integrate Without Danger of Intermarriage," a manuscript culled from his over seven hundred *Defender* columns, intended to "provoke, shock, amuse, or otherwise intrigue" more people into thinking of the race issue. He found no takers. Simon and Schuster declared flatly that the Simple books better accomplished the same objectives.

Leaving town as seldom as possible, he was happier in Harlem, and happiest at his typewriter. "Nicest thing about going away," he wrote Arna Bontemps, "is to get back to Harlem again." Near Labor Day, he lectured on gospel music at the Music Inn and enjoyed a concert by the high priestess of gospel, Mahalia Jackson. Not long after, finishing a ballet libretto, "The St. Louis Blues," based on Handy's music, he dispatched it to various performers, including the dancer-choreographer Alvin Ailey. In October, he spent a peaceful day or two with Amy Spingarn in the crisp air at Amenia, where she still had a home, although "Troutbeck," the splendid estate that Langston had first visited in 1926, had been sold. In Manhattan, he attended a performance of *La Bohème* with Adele Addison, a rising black singer, and enjoyed cocktails with Lotte Lenya just before she left for the European premiere of *Street Scene* at the Dusseldorf Opera House in Germany, from which her late husband Kurt Weill had fled the Nazis. Invited to attend, Langston sent instead an essay in sincere tribute to "My Collaborator Kurt Weill." At a reading of the play *Mr. Johnson,* organized by Cheryl Crawford for potential backers, he met Marilyn Monroe, for whom he had once professed, in a flippant aside in the *Chicago Defender,* a passion. In person, Monroe was "awfully pretty and awfully nice, too, seemingly."

On November 1, over drinks in the Rinehart office in mid-Manhattan, Langston finally delivered the manuscript, amounting to 789 pages, of "I Wonder as I Wander." He had weighed it as carefully as if it were his newborn baby—seven pounds, eight ounces. His contentment in a job well done was further boosted later that month when the first copy of his book with Roy DeCarava, *The Sweet Flypaper of Life,* appeared from Simon and Schuster. DeCarava, on the other hand, looked at their book and almost burst into tears. "I knew that it was not supposed to be as large as the usual book of photographs," he would recall, "but somehow I still expected a big, glossy book, with my photographs lavishly laid out. Instead, there was this puny little book that you actually could put into your back pocket. I was very disappointed." But the critical reception of *The Sweet Flypaper of Life* soon brought him around. No book by Hughes was ever greeted so rhapsodically. Lewis Gannett hailed "a harmony which is more than poetry or photography alone, but its own kind of art." Calling it "a delicate and lovely fiction-document of life in Harlem," the *New York Times* praised its "astonishing verisimilitude." *Image,* an authoritative journal of photography, noted "the subtle, the almost exquisite interplay of text and photographs." The *Village Voice* wrote of "a mixture of the warm and the stark, the tender and the slightly terrifying—in short, very like life itself." And from Paris, Henri Cartier-Bresson saluted "the sensitivity of the photographs and the excellent blending of the pictures with the text that gives all Lang's warmth. Bravo!"

Unfortunately, although the first printing of 3,000 clothbound and 22,000 paperback copies sold out quickly, and a second printing of 10,000 was ordered, Hughes and DeCarava made little money from the book. At a dollar a copy, the paperback sales yielded slight royalties. Then a lawsuit devoured most of the authors' profits. In the laborious process of gathering signed releases from everyone photographed in the book who was also mentioned in Langston's tale, DeCarava had allowed one man to sign for his sister, an elusive person, without her consent. Her enterprising lawsuit for $10,000 was settled out of court—exclusively from the authors' royalties—for $500.

Nevertheless, the critical success of *The Sweet Flypaper of Life,* and its wide circulation, cast a rosy glow over the end of 1955. On December 10, he gave a party at home for the South African writer Peter Abrahams, whose *Mine Boy* had just appeared, and two days after Christmas, he attended the wedding reception of Joe Louis and his bride Rose Morgan. To crown the season, a major new project with Jan Meyerowitz came Langston's way—an opera commissioned by the Fromm Foundation, which promoted projects in music, to celebrate the feast of Purim, marking the ancient deliverance of Persian Jews from a threatened massacre. The opera, "Esther," would be based on the biblical story of the beautiful Esther and her cousin Mordecai in their dealings with her husband Ahasuerus, King of Persia. Ahasuerus does not know that Esther is a Jew. After his evil minister, Haman, who has steadily fed the king's distrust of the Jews, plots their destruction, Esther risks all by revealing that she is Jewish. Ahasuerus's love for her triumphs over prejudice.

Langston undertook this latest effort with Jan Meyerowitz in spite of his growing concern about their own relationship, which was then almost ten years old but had bred little financial or artistic success. In fact, failure had been frequent. Langston's continued link to the world of opera was itself something of a puzzle, since he was no passionate lover of the form. He had enjoyed opera almost from childhood, but, although several blacks had achieved distinction in the field, opera as an art form was even more alien to the black community than it was to American culture in general. While Walt Whitman had declared that *Leaves of Grass* could not have been written without the inspiration of opera, for Langston it was blues and jazz that had been indispensable. Blues and jazz, however, enjoyed nothing of the refined social prestige of opera in the United States. Perhaps because of this prestige, and because he insisted on seeing his art as a liberal, even ecumenical mission, he remained involved in operatic composition. He did not seek out Meyerowitz, but responded to his requests as he tried to respond to all requests—compliantly, generously. In the case of "Esther," an opera based in Jewish history and religion was particularly appealing to him, since he had admired Jewish culture from his high school days in Cleveland.

On the other hand, Meyerowitz's music often left him cold. "He swoons each time he plays it!" Langston confided to Bontemps about the composer's ecstasy over his latest setting. "Not having heard a note, I swoon to think how operatic it probably sounds." Langston was even less enchanted by Meyerowitz's temper, which could be now sweet, now so explosive that one drama agent, Leah Salisbury, dropped Langston as a client in 1952 because she wanted nothing more to do with his impetuous collaborator, who despised agents as a thieving lot. But Langston could not bring himself to drop Meyerowitz. On only one point was he growing truly resentful. He detested the fact that the composer's settings often smothered his carefully chosen words under thick sheets of sound. "I beg of you," he wrote despairingly to Meyerowitz once, "that the librettist himself might understand something here and there, kindly please por favor s'il vous plait per favore pajalsta as a favor to me, *do* have a few arias ariettas recitatives and songs in the clear once in a while obscured by nothing but lutes or harps." To which Meyerowitz, hardly chastened, irrepressibly replied: "Your threateningly witty letter worries in the wrong direction. I *does* believe that I'm skillful enough to make an opera listenable and understandable."

Before "Esther" was fairly begun, Meyerowitz began to press Langston about seeing parts of the first draft of the libretto. Unwillingly, Langston gave in: "I trust you realize that this is *not* the ideal way to work—piecemeal like this.'' When a clash came, it was precipitated by Meyerowitz who, in his rage against agents, also violated one of Hughes's most cherished rights: the right to undisturbed sleep. One morning, after Langston had just written to his collaborator naming Ivan von Auw of Harold Ober Associates as his agent for "Esther," a call shattered the quiet of his bedroom.

> *Hughes:* Hello.
> *Meyerowitz:* Langston?
> *Hughes:* Yes?
> *Meyerowitz:* You have fouled up my whole morning with that lousy letter of yours. I cannot write a note!
> *Hughes:* Why?
> *Meyerowitz:* I will not sign a letter with any name of any lousy agent in it.
> *Hughes:* But why must you waken me out of my sleep [to] tell me that? You know I work at night.
> *Meyerowitz:* You and your lousy agent have fouled up *The Barrier*. And I will not sign anything with an agent in it. I will not—
> *Hughes:* Very well, then don't! Do whatever you like! (BAM!)

Unplugging his phone, Langston wrote down the exchange, then went back to sleep. His uncharacteristic outburst worked. Later that day, a letter arrived, special delivery, from Creskill, New Jersey. "The finest living American author should have so little comprehension for the mind of his fellow," Meyerowitz humbly complained. "I'm under great strain and you upset me so horribly!" To which Langston, drawing on the story of Esther and her Persian king, replied in kind: "Art thou Ahasuerus? A mere piece of paper on my part does not constitute a decree. . . . " He had forgotten, he explained sweetly, to unplug his phone—"so kindly forgive me for unplugging it then." The next day, Meyerowitz apologetically wrote again: "The stuff I received this morning is of course, *marvellous*." Langston ended the episode with a calming word to Meyerowtiz—the hope that "you will not permit art to become art-hritis. It's not worth it. Better your health, strength, and sanity than all the operas or collaboration agreements in the world. Compare poor unbalanced aching Ahasuerus with healthy little, wise little, well-fed little, clever little, perfumed little, triumphant little, still living little, artistic little, non-arthritic little Esther who never let her blood pressure or her temper rise. . . . Sweet Hadassah!"

In large part, what had happened was of a piece with the world of the stage, which Hughes persisted in seeing as almost lunatic. "If you want to die, be disturbed, maladjusted, neurotic, and psychotic, disappointed and disjointed," he once warned James Baldwin, "just write plays! Go ahead!" He continued as a friend to Meyerowitz, whom he respected, and who in turn also liked and respected him. But Langston quietly despised and feared the world of the theater, which seemed to breed or attract aggression and egotism. "I remember once being with him just before a meeting he was to have with some important theater people," the playwright Alice Childress later recalled. "I was about to leave the room when he stopped me. 'Don't leave me here to face them alone,' he practically pleaded. I was amazed that he, Langston Hughes, should be so scared of anyone. But he hated the tricks and the egotism of so many theater people. He simply wasn't prepared to act that way, and it hurt him to see it in others."

With such pressure, he was happy when a fifty-fourth birthday present arrived from Noël Sullivan in California: a round-trip airline ticket for him to visit Hollow Hills Farm. Setting aside "Esther," as well as his notes for an anthology of popular black songs from minstrel days to the present, on the cold, drab, winter morning of January 31, 1956, he left New York ("Left, oh, left me!" Meyerowitz mourned). Within hours, after checking into the luxurious Fairmont Hotel, he was dining on shrimp at Fisherman's Wharf and watching the fishing boats rock outside a restaurant window on San Francisco Bay. The next day, he flew down to Monterey for a reunion with Sullivan and a birthday party that included their old friends Marie Short and Robinson Jeffers. In spite of the festivity, a sense of an imminent ending—Noël Sullivan's— hung in the air. "My 65 year old heart," he had confessed after a series of medical tests, "is wearing out." On several occasions recently he had blacked out. "If you need me," Langston replied, "I'll get on a plane and come out there. . . . This *quite seriously,* as I'm sure you know—so you have only to let me know."

After a week in which he rested but also went over with Sullivan his account in "I Wonder as I Wander" of his stay in 1933 and 1934 in Carmel, he left Hollow Hills Farm. "I hadn't had a leisurely quiet non-working week for almost two years," he later thanked Sullivan, for whom the visit was evidently also a tonic. "I think you were the best 'medicine' Noël could have had," Marie Short wrote Langston; "he felt quite lonely when you left." Returning to San Francisco, Langston took a room at the black-owned Booker T. Washington Hotel. A stay at a black hotel was usually amusing, and he was not disappointed. When he sat down in an armchair in the lobby, he and the chair collapsed to the floor—to the vast amusement of members of the staff and other idlers. He sat in another, and an arm fell off. In Oakland he dined with Roy and Marie Blackburn, and in Berkeley with Matt and Evelyn Crawford and their daughter Nebby Lou. In nightclubs on both sides of San Francisco Bay he heard Earl "Fatha" Hines and a locally popular young singer named John Mathis.

For his two weeks of loafing in California, he paid dearly. "I'm dying!" he groaned. "I get back to Harlem from California to find two years of unfinished commitments clouding the Eastern skies with gloom—ranging from books to operas for which nobody has given enough to cover working time adequately— and dreaming time and creative time NOT AT ALL. (Colored are supposed to do in two months what white folks take 2 years for, or more.)" Nevertheless, he took on another task. Quickly he finished the notes for a recording, *A Night at the Apollo,* about the celebrated Harlem music hall, for Vanguard Records. A more substantial task came Langston's way when Bernard Perry, now the director of Indiana University Press, asked him to consider making a translation of between sixty and eighty poems by the Nobel Prizewinning poet of Chile, Lucila Godoy Alcayaga, better known as Gabriela Mistral. Langston promised to try a translation only "if there are enough poems in which maintaining the music might happen, not just the meaning," or "if I feel I can, with justice." On a train trip out to Bucknell University in Pennsylvania, he browsed in two books of her poems and found "some very beautiful indeed." Three months later, he signed a contract with the University of Indiana Press for the book.

By this time the libretto of "Esther" was finished. " 'Esther' reads better than I'd thought," he confessed, "and is most compact, concise, and unified. She comes through like a Tiffany diamond." Evidently, all was forgiven between Hughes and Meyerowitz. Again avoiding Meyerowitz's revived interest in an opera about Hitler, Langston hinted about their joint work on "a heroic and *very* American historical subject that is sure fire,—and *so beautiful* I doubt if you can stand it!" What he had in mind is uncertain, but perhaps he was thinking of an opera based on *Uncle Tom's Cabin.* Later that year, he started work—but quickly stopped—on this libretto. However, he also was in touch with a physician and amateur composer, Dr. Vincent T. Williams of Kansas City, who had expressed an interest in collaborating with Hughes, about a sort of cantata (as Langston put it) "or composition with orchestra, singers, and perhaps a Narrator, perhaps to be called MISSOURI after my native state. . . . It could have history in it, and Mark Twain, and the rivers, and a bit of folk lore."

In fact, his next major "libretto" was even closer to the most commanding artistic interest of his life outside of literature—black music. How he turned from opera to a musical play based on gospel music is not altogether clear. What seems certain is that his attendance around the Fourth of July at the annual jazz festival at Newport, which he had never visited, had a great deal to do with this move. In 1954, in an incongruous setting given the humble origins of jazz, Elaine Guthrie Lorillard had founded the first jazz festival in the United States, with the help of her husband Louis Lorillard, a tobacco millionaire. The historic New England naval town of Newport had long been world famous as a resort for the very rich, with their yatchs and tennis courts and noble mansions (quaintly called "cottages") on Bellevue Avenue. Acknowledged as the leaders of the younger set, the Lorillards had turned to jazz after an earlier festival of classical music, featuring the New York Philharmonic Orchestra, had proved a flop. With the aid of George Wein, a skilled Boston jazz promoter, they had launched their jazz festival at the old Newport Casino.

When jazz succeeded where the classics failed, the Lorillards found themselves and their festival opposed by many members of the old guard at Newport, to whom jazz, especially jazz played by black musicians, was beneath the dignity of the town. Once, according to Wein, a Newporter asked him to invite guests to a jazz party but to be careful not to invite any "Africans." The man was stunned when no one showed up. "You told me to be careful," Wein explained. "I was very careful—I didn't invite anybody." But the Lorillards had the means to carry on. When they were denied the use of the Newport Casino, they responded by purchasing Belcourt Castle, a fifty-room "cottage," and by pressing on with the festival. In the summer of 1956, despite driving summer rain, jazz proved once again to be a powerful draw. Record crowds totalling over 25,000, almost all white, gathered at Freebody Park to hear performances by Count Basie, Charles Mingus, Louis Armstrong, Sarah Vaughn, Dave Brubeck, Toshiko Akiyoshi, Ella Fitzgerald, the Modern Jazz Quartet, Teddy Wilson, Bud Shank, and Duke Ellington and their various aggregations. Above all, the audience's spontaneous response to jazz amazed some observers. Near the conclusion of the festival, when the tenor saxophonist Paul Gonsalves of the Duke Ellington Orchestra launched into a marathon solo of twenty-seven choruses, a blond woman leaped up in a private box and began to gyrate to the music, and the audience of seven thousand was soon moving almost as one. As the baffled members of a contingent of police stirred uneasily, Ellington regally declined to heed a signal to stop the performance. "Duke made the cool night hot," Langston reported. "His solid beat brought the crowd to its feet. And the Festival ended with jazz at its jazziest [wailing] its way toward midnight."

Perhaps no one was more fascinated than Langston by the strikingly emotional response to black music by this supposedly sophisticated audience of whites. On July 6, when he held forth on "Jazz as Communication" on a panel with Marshall Stearns and other speakers at the Newport Casino Theater, he stressed the importance of this visceral, rather than cerebral reaction. He emphasized this side of jazz again at the end of the month at the Music Inn in Lenox, Massachusetts, where jazz continued to form the dark underbelly to the Tanglewood classical season, and jazz concerts were held only when the symphony orchestra was not playing. There, to his satisfaction, for the first time since the founding of the summer panels on folk and jazz in 1950, round-table discussions of jazz included a variety of professional jazz musicians, from traditionalists like Pee Wee Russell and Willie the Lion Smith to more progressive artists such as Quincy Jones, John Lewis of the Modern Jazz Quartet, and the visionary Charles Mingus.

The American Jazz Festival at Newport probably led to Langston's next major creative move. Since 1947, he had tried and failed to duplicate the artistic and financial success of *Street Scene*. His latest effort, *Simply Heavenly*, with Dave Martin, had not excited any producer. These failures all had one element in common. Even when the composer and the setting were black, the basic form had been essentially foreign to his own best inspiration, which had always come from black mass culture. When the social setting was mainly white, Langston virtually eliminated his chances of creating striking theater. In working on *Simply Heavenly* with Dave Martin as composer, he had consciously followed the loose format of the innovative *Pal Joey*—a play with a few songs added—to produce a work squarely in the Broadway tradition. Now, with an inspired, unprecedented fusion of black music, evangelical religion, and Harlem melodrama, his new venture in musical theater would take him closer to the black masses.

On July 14, 1956, he began "Tambourines to Glory: A Play with Songs" (soon, "A Play with Spirituals, Jubilees, and Gospel Songs"). The piece, he explained, was "an urban-folk-Harlem-*genre*-melodrama" based squarely on the black gospel tradition. He had long loved black gospel music. The form had been developed most brilliantly in the 1920s by the composer Thomas Dorsey, whose best compositions, such as his "Precious Lord, Take My Hand," fused traditional Christian hymns and spirituals with the blues, of which Dorsey had been a master before repenting. Alert to every significant shift in black musical styles, Langston had devoted an entire *Defender* column almost ten years before to the arrival of the highly paid gospel singer as a phenomenon in black entertainment. By 1956, the gospel singer had become a spectacle on the musical scene. Cynically, Langston noted how many of the performers, with barely a nod to the Lord, now were taking on the trappings of secular entertainers. "Some gospel singers these days are making so much money," Simple had jeered in the *Defender,* "when you hear them crying, 'I Cannot Bear My Burden Alone,' what they really mean is 'Help me get my cross to my Cadillac'."

Attracted by the soaring concert fees, hustling white business managers had become common in the black gospel world. On stage, the lowly tambourine and the piano were now often backed by drums and other instruments more easily associated with the nightclub, where indeed some gospel singers would soon perform. Unwilling to set foot in that devilish place, but eager to capitalize on her success, Mahalia Jackson had taken her music to the equally secular if high-toned Carnegie Hall—where Langston had heard her enthusiastically at least once. Nevertheless, commercialism could not obscure the power of the music, which was capable at its best of wrenching the emotions and sweeping the most hardened sinner to ecstatic heights and depths. In a culture tragically cut off from its Southern roots, gospel had become, Langston judged, "about the last refuge of Negro folk music."

Within ten days, he had finished his play. "It's a singing, shouting, wailing drama," he excitedly explained, "of the old conflict between blatant Evil and quiet Good, with the Devil driving a Cadillac." On August 2, he met to discuss it with the veteran producer Oscar Hammerstein II and the playwright Paul Peters, a friend since 1930, when they had met through the John Reed Club of New York. Two days later, Langston dispatched the script to Jobe Huntley, Jr., a talented Harlem singer and composer who enjoyed a solid local reputation as a skilled maker of gospel, blues, and love songs.

Born in Monroe, North Carolina, the son of a Baptist minister, Huntley had been musically precocious. As a boy, he had directed a church choir. In World War II, he had done duty as a member of the Army Special Service Unit, formed a vocal quartet, and conducted the all-male G.I. Glee Club. In 1948,

Huntley had met Langston after a gospel concert by Mahalia Jackson at the Golden Gate Ballroom, and so impressed him with his knowledge of music and the church that Langston had asked him to set some of his poems to gospel music. Over the years, Huntley wrote more settings for him. "His lyrics were so easy to set to music," Huntley later remembered. "I could take his poems and sit at the piano and play it through the very first time. That was just how musical his writings were to me. I kept writing song after song. It was fun working with the beautiful lyrics."

Soon Huntley had written over a dozen. "So now I had some gospel songs," Langston told a reporter some years later. "It seemed a pity to waste them, so I sat down and wrote a play around them." In 1956, however, he was much more excited about what he had done. Fantasizing to his agent, Ivan von Auw, about an ideal cast for his "urban-folk-Harlem-*genre*-melodrama," Langston saw the pious Mahalia Jackson as the heroine and the insouciant Pearl Bailey as her sinful sister in the ministry. As the young lovers needing to be saved from Satan, Langston envisaged the dazzling young folksinger Harry Belafonte and the sultry beauty Dorothy Dandridge admirably filling these roles.

Even as he waited eagerly for Huntley's music, Langston wasted little time in exploiting his new property. With an opportunism that matched that of the gospel singers, between August 24 and September 12 he deftly converted *Tambourines to Glory* into a novel of the same name—"thus killing two birds with one stone." Next, to be ready for a quick sale to a magazine, he trimmed the novel down to a novella of some seventy pages. But his main hopes rested on the musical version. Suddenly, good news arrived about another of his musical dramas. The tiny but purposeful Greenwich Mews Theatre in Manhattan agreed to stage a production of *Simply Heavenly* early in the next year, 1957. At long last, Langston's fortunes as a playwright seemed to be on the rise.

Behind his almost unseemly conversions of *Tambourines to Glory* was an urgent need for cash. Terrific rainstorms in August had opened two holes in the rotting roof of his brownstone and flooded part of his suite on the third floor. Not long afterwards, two hefty bills arrived for books Langston had bought through his publishers. He owed $1079 to Simon and Schuster and about $700 to Franklin Watts. Lectures at the University of Michigan on the contributions of blacks to America and at the Music Inn on blues and jazz brought a little cash, but when he spoke on "the Importance of African Culture" to a Harlem cultural group, the Afro-Arts Theatre, he probably did so for nothing, since he was nominally its chairman.

His *First Book of the West Indies* appeared from Franklin Watts in September, and a similar volume on Africa was overdue ("so I reckon I have to explore that continent directly"); but those advances were long gone. Once again casting around for unpublished material to lure an advance, he chanced upon the manuscript of Negro humor he and Arna Bontemps had compiled around 1949, which had been spurned by various publishers. Adapting part of the work into a book of Negro folklore, he tried the editors at Dodd, Mead.

To his relief, the manuscript was promptly accepted. But a moldy children's story, "A Dog and Cat Tale," was rejected by the juvenile department of Knopf as "a little thin for our list." "Bon Bon Buddy" and "Boy of the Border," written with Arna Bontemps over twenty years before, also impressed no one.

On Sunday, September 16, Langston had just returned from an afternoon visit on Long Island when he found a telegram from San Francisco: "GOD CALLED NOEL SULLIVAN TO HIMSELF AT 7:30 THIS SATURDAY AFTER A CORONARY OCCLUSION." Shortly afterwards, Eulah Pharr, Sullivan's housekeeper of almost thirty years, telephoned the house with the news that Sullivan had been fatally struck down on his way from the Bohemian Club in San Francisco to the opera. This had been his second heart attack in a few days. He had died at the Stanford University Hospital.

Broke, Langston made no attempt to attend the funeral. Nevertheless, Sullivan's death, though not unexpected, was a blow. With his passing, Langston had lost a haven he had perhaps outgrown, but one which had served him in times of personal crisis ever since his return from his year in the Soviet Union in August, 1933. "California (indeed the whole world) is not quite the same with Noël gone," he wrote to Sullivan's niece Alice Doyle Mahoney in Phoenix. A Carmel newspaper published his eulogy, taken in large part from a private letter to Marie Short: "We who had the good fortune to share his friendship knew that he lived so beautifully he had no fear of going and he leaves in our hearts memories that will glow always although we cannot help but miss him greatly. I wish I were there to sorrow with those close to him in Carmel."

Throughout the fall, he did his best to push forward the various versions of *Tambourines to Glory.* To Rinehart he sent the novel for consideration. The play itself went to his old *Street Scene* collaborator Elmer Rice at the Playwrights Company, along with a quietly spoken reminder that black actors were complaining bitterly about the lack of roles for them on Broadway. Rice was sympathetic but asked the crucial question: "Are there enough people who would be interested in a whole evening of spirituals?" No one asked openly whether the traditional Broadway audience, which typically included many Jews, should be asked to tolerate, much less enjoy, an evening of Christian religious songs. Langston was sure only that people were hungry for *something,* and that black music seemed to be at least part of the answer. The Newport Jazz Festival that summer had demonstrated this fact. And in September, when Langston and the pianist-composer Dave Martin staged a jazz demonstration lecture, "A History of American Jazz," at the new Donnell Library across from the Museum of Modern Art in mid-Manhattan, a capacity audience had cheered mightily, while about two hundred persons were turned away. Langston could only hope that gospel music, like jazz, would prove to be widely alluring.

On November 6, after voting in the presidential election, he watched and listened to the returns at an election night party, complete with six radios and two television sets, at the apartment of Franklin and Helen Watts on East 66th Street in Manhattan. Solidly Democratic and almost all devoted to the fortunes of Adlai Stevenson, the gathering had very little to cheer about that night. Instead, they drank a great deal and mourned the defeat of their hero and the prospect of four more years of Dwight D. Eisenhower. Whether Langston had voted for Stevenson is unclear. Earlier in the year, Simple had derided Stevenson in the *Defender* after the self-professed liberal had vacillated badly on the question of civil rights for blacks.

Langston, however, was himself on the brink of twin victories. November brought the almost simultaneous appearance of *I Wonder as I Wander* from Rinehart (his twenty-first book, he noted proudly in the *Defender*) and, with Milton Meltzer, *A Pictorial History of the Negro in America* from Crown Publishers. And from Paris, as lagniappe, came the first copies of François Dodat's translations of his poems, published by Pierre Seghers ("depuis bien longtemps j'aime votre poésie, votre travail, votre présence") in his *Poètes d'Aujourd'hui* series. As the publication dates drew near, his efforts to advertise the books astonished his new publishers. "If all authors," Franklin Watts attested, "were a. as competent, b. as good guys, and c. as zealous in promoting their books as you are, all of us would make more money." Now, however, as Langston sensed the approach of triumphs that might crown his return from the depths to which he had sunk before Senator McCarthy three years before, he outdid himself as a self-publicist. His biggest book party, shared with three other authors—the lawyer-activist Pauli Murray, the singer Eartha Kitt, and the former boxer Henry Armstrong—was held at Lewis Michaux's National Memorial Bookstore on 125th Street in Harlem. Eartha Kitt, then at the height of her stardom, created a stir, but Langston also shone. "It was really *your* party," a friend assured him. "Crowds and crowds of people continued to surround you. . . . Your name was the one I constantly heard." In fact, invitations to the party were based on Langston's private list of potential book-buyers, which now numbered over three thousand, and was "kept right up to date," as he proudly noted, down "to the last fan letter in today's mail."

Critics hailed *A Pictorial History of the Negro in America* as a landmark. George Schuyler of the *Pittsburgh Courier* "had hardly expected to live to see the day when such a startlingly superlative book . . . should be researched, planned, written and published. Its publication in itself is an event in Negro history." Almost everywhere, Hughes and Meltzer were lauded for giving, as the New York *Herald-Tribune* put it, "a kind of majestic sweep to a story . . . usually made niggling and constrained." "Few of its pages can be read with pride by any white person," the *Saturday Review* judged, "and most call forth a sense of shame and a corresponding awe that human beings can so well endure what has been the lot of the Negro in America." The book also sold very well. Twenty-five years later, it was still in print.

I Wonder as I Wander drew a more divided response but was by far the more important book for Langston as he looked towards the future. The two main points of critical disagreement were the quality of genial detachment that

was central to the narrative and—what for many critics was a related issue—
his treatment of radicalism. Although several reviewers found the text insuffi-
ciently reflective (J. Saunders Redding allowed himself to jibe that Langston
Hughes apparently had done "more wandering than wondering"), others were
happy with his unwillingness to preach. "Your own buoyant heart emerges all
through the book," Nancy Cunard applauded him, "and power of vivid description." The gentle and yet heroic suppression of pain by laughter that had
made *The Big Sea* something of a classic blues narrative was again in evidence,
but an older, tougher Langston had much less pain to report in his account of
the years from 1931 to 1938. He could tell of no conflict as wrenching as that
with his mother, no hatred as intense and yet as germinal as what he had felt
for his father, no clash as apocalyptic as his break with "Godmother," no
humiliation as intense as that visited on him by Zora Neale Hurston. Detached
amusement, on the other hand, is not allowed to obscure completely the perils
of his tour of the South in 1931, the disappointments of the movie-making
venture in the Soviet Union, his prolonged mistreatment by the producer of
Mulatto, the bombs and bullets of Madrid in 1937, or the grinding poverty he
had endured even as his fame grew.

Asserting laughter and life over his individual suffering, although he documented the latter, both autobiographies celebrate a triumph of the human spirit
over circumstance. Despite Redding's sneering, Langston's choice of the title
I Wonder as I Wander was inspired. Mirroring the fundamental sense of innocence and awe with which he had met the world, it accurately suggested an
imaginative spirit unsullied by bitterness, rancor, fatalism, or dogma, as well
as a philosophic acceptance of the changes through which he had passed in the
years between his banishment by "Godmother" and the terrifying moment of
stillness in Europe before the start of World War II. Or *almost* all the changes.
"I've now cut out all the impersonal stuff," he had written in the course of
revising the book for Rinehart, "down to a running narrative with *me* in the
middle of every page . . . the kind of intense condensation that, of course,
keeps an autobiography from being entirely true, in that nobody's life is pure
essence without pulp, waste matter, and rind—which art, of course, throws in
the trash can."

Although Senator Joseph McCarthy fell outside the chronology of the book,
Langston's appearance before him in 1953 cast a long shadow over *I Wonder
as I Wander*. From the start, Hughes aimed to hide the figure of the radical
black poet who, early in the 1930s, had bade an insolent goodbye to Christ and
a rousing good morning to revolution (just as *The Big Sea*, written mainly in
1939, had also hidden his radicalism, which was even then in decline). Langston Hughes as a radical socialist simply was left out of the book, just as Du
Bois had been left out of *Famous American Negroes* and Paul Robeson left out
of Langston's *Famous Negro Music Makers*. (Earlier that year, 1956, Robeson
had boldly denounced the House Committee on Un-American Activities to its
face. Angered by Robeson's exclusion, one reader of *Famous Negro Music
Makers* demanded of Langston how he could "in a sense betray your race" in

this way. Another called his act "both disgusting and cowardly.") His Carmel friend Marie Short was shocked to see no mention in *I Wonder as I Wander* of their radical John Reed Club and of the strikes and demonstrations and right-wing threats of 1934—"but you are a *wise* person," she offered, "and I am not." She was sure that his exclusions had a noble purpose, one that concerned Langston's race: "I know you *never never* ignore a chance to help your people—and I love you more for that."

Yet, in spite of his omissions and his public record of apostasy, leftist reviewers generally applauded *I Wonder as I Wander*. Far more readily than liberals and conservatives, they saw at once how Hughes's easygoing account of the Soviet Union as a nation that was normal and functional rather than alien and aberrant, one with many annoying inconveniences but no innate horrors (as Arthur Koestler, for example, had drawn it), refuted the cold-war American vision of an evil empire. In fact, Langston's approach to the Soviet Union in *I Wonder as I Wander* was consistent with his testimony before Senator Joseph McCarthy. He had used neither occasion as a chance to distort the facts of Soviet Russia as he saw them, or to slander or denounce the Soviet people. For this not inconsiderable favor, in a time of anti-Soviet hysteria, the American left was generally grateful. The *Daily Worker* commended the book as "not only a readable tale of one man's journeyings," but as "a reminder of both what America had gained from great talents like his own and and lost in others crushed beneath the weight of racism."

His second autobiography was the last significant statement he would ever make on radicalism and his own historic part in it. Unquestionably he regretted some of the hurt he had inflicted in redefining his political position. Earlier in the year, for instance, he had made an oblique gesture of contrition to Du Bois. In a brief note to him, Langston praised Du Bois's epochal *The Souls of Black Folk*, which he had read as a child and had just read again "for perhaps the tenth time. . . . Its beauty and passion and power are as moving and as meaningful as ever." More than once, Langston also mentioned Du Bois admiringly—if briefly—in the *Chicago Defender*. Du Bois ignored these gestures, which were certainly insufficient. Two years later, in April, 1958, at a public sixtieth birthday celebration for Robeson, he replied to Hughes, in a sense, by denouncing Robeson's detractors, including those among his own people—"even men like Langston Hughes, who wrote of Negro musicians and deliberately omitted Robeson's name."

Even so, Langston's affection and regard for Du Bois never flagged. A year later, he made sure that his regard was known. When, during a drive to collect books to donate to Ghana, he received from Du Bois himself a copy of his recent novel *The Ordeal of Mansart*, his hand-written note of thanks was effusive: "Personally, I found the book fascinating—so vivid, so graphically true! What a motion-picture it will make—when such films are made. (As we know they will be!)." He ended with "Cordial regards and affection" but added a postscript: "You're the most!"

The happy publication of *I Wonder as I Wander,* aided by the triumphant reception of texts such as *The Sweet Flypaper of Life* and the *Pictorial History,* seemed to lift a staggering burden from Langston's shoulders. They freed him at last to move on as a man, almost justified in the difficult decisions he had made to preserve his career and his prominence as an interpreter of the American scene. The lingering criticism of his compromises he would live with; as one of his more humorously defiant poems went, he was "still here." In contrast, the previous December, 1955, Joseph McCarthy had been officially condemned by his peers in the U.S. Senate on a motion of censure for his contempt of an investigating subcommittee, as well as for abuse of certain senators and of the U.S. Senate itself. Two months before *I Wonder as I Wander* appeared, Langston read reports in the newspapers that McCarthy was gravely ill and had lost over forty pounds. He would die the following year, 1957, not fifty years old. By this time, his name had become an ignominious byword for the right-wing abuse of power through innuendo and slander.

Jauntily, Langston now promised to deal with his persecutor in his next autobiography. According to him, McCarthy had asked for his approval of television coverage of his Senate appearance. "Delighted!" Langston had replied (or so he now insisted). "I figured I photographed as well as he did." McCarthy, Roy Cohn, and David Schine had pulled various of his volumes from U.S. libraries overseas, but almost on the exact day that Langston had delivered the manuscript of *I Wonder* to his publishers, the United States Information Service had purchased the right to translate *Famous American Negroes* "into 50-11 languages," as he jubilantly put it. If "Goodbye Christ" still surfaced from time to time to tax him with charges of atheism, his Easter cantata, "The Glory Around His Head," had been solicited, along with others of "your great verses," by Albert Christ-Janer, the respected editor of the American Hymnbook.

For Langston and most black Americans, the cold war was a dead issue. Another, mightier matter was at hand—the struggle for civil rights in the troubled wake of the victory on May 17, 1954, when the Supreme Court had ruled against segregation in *Brown vs. the Board of Education of Topeka, Kansas.* (Ironically, it was the Topeka Board of Education that Langston's mother had challenged and overcome on his behalf in 1908, thus allowing the six-year-old Langston Hughes to start his schooling in an integrated classroom.) Jim Crow was dying, but violently. The following May, the first black to register at the polls in Belzoni, Mississippi, since Reconstruction, a minister, had been shot to death from ambush. Later that year, 1955, fourteen-year-old Emmett Till had been lynched in Mississippi after whistling at a white woman. Then, on December 1, Rosa Parks, a former secretary of the Montgomery, Alabama, branch of the NAACP, refused to give up her seat on a bus to a white man, thus beginning the struggle between segregationist forces and the supporters of black civil rights led by a young minister from Atlanta, Rev. Martin Luther King, Jr. A year later, on December 21, 1956, after bombings and beatings that drove the local struggle into national and international headlines, blacks in

Montgomery ended their boycott of public transportation when the once intransigent white city government voted finally to comply with a Supreme Court ruling of the previous month declaring segregated buses unconstitutional.

Langston himself did not go to Alabama. Instead, he avidly followed the white journalist Murray Kempton's detailed accounts of events there in the New York *Post*—''just about the most moving pieces of American reportage I've ever read.'' A fighter for black rights all his life, he would not become physically involved in this, the climactic phase of the legal aspect of the struggle. But he was still capable of standing up, as when he fired off a night letter to the mayor of Houston, Roy Hofheinz, after Hofheinz claimed, incredibly, that Houston was free of racial discrimination. Langston recounted his recent personal humiliation in Houston, when he was sent to the kitchen at the railroad station to get a sandwich. ''Have these things been changed within the last few weeks?'' he demanded. ''Kindly enlarge upon your statement. . . . '' Anticipating a coming rift between the relatively timid black leadership and the determined masses, he noted a difference between what the diplomatic Roy Wilkins and the bolder Thurgood Marshall, on one hand, were urging publicly on behalf of the NAACP, and what, on the other, ''the guys in the corner bars are saying, which is why, I suppose, so few leaders ever catch up with the people.'' If Harlem blacks were to award the annual Spingarn Medal of the NAACP, he thought, they would give it to the two black youths who had beaten a white man in Tuscaloosa '' 'just to get even for Miss Lucy'.'' (Autherine Lucy, daring to integrate the University of Alabama, had been forced to withdraw in the face of civil disorder, then was expelled by the university when she sued for reinstatement. ''If Miss Lucy wanted to go to bed with a white man instead of to college with one,'' he wrote in the *Defender,* ''nobody at the University of Alabama would throw stones at her, nor defy the Supreme Court.'')

''Which means,'' Langston reckoned about the two black youths, ''that the Civil War has started all over again, but the Union troops this time are lonely cullud kids who 'just want to get even'.'' But at Christmas, 1956, he was thinking less of the civil war he saw coming than of the relative peace he had recovered for himself since his Senate appearance in 1953. An unexpected gift of money, the last from a beloved source, sweetened the days leading to the new year, 1957. This was Noël Sullivan's bequest to Langston of the sum of $2000, plus a little interest, as executed by the Crocker-Anglo National Bank of California.

10

MAKING HAY
1957 to 1958

I play it cool
And dig all jive
That's the reason
I stay alive.

My motto,
As I live and learn,
        is:
*Dig And Be Dug
In Return.*

"Motto," 1951

B EAMING WITH CONFIDENCE about his future, Hughes rang in the new year
by attending so many celebrations—three "white" gatherings downtown,
two "cullud" parties uptown in Harlem, capped by a lively visit at six o'clock
in the morning to his favorite Harlem nightclub, the Baby Grand—that even he
was amazed by his carousing. Certainly there were tasks at hand, and he was
eager to accomplish them. Yet he was also determined to enjoy his success. "I
am ready to retire to an ivory tower," he wrote to his friend Arna Bontemps,
"but have never yet spotted one in Harlem." By "ivory tower" he did not
mean a place for pure contemplation. At most, he wanted only a quiet room
apart from the worst distractions, some place where he could take advantage,
without fear of constant interruption, of the bonanza of professional opportunities that he saw on almost every side, now that his political rehabilitation was
apparently complete. He wanted to exploit these opportunities and through them
secure a measure of financial prosperity; he also wanted to enjoy himself. Only
after the last New Year's toast was drunk did Langston plunge readily into a
year he soon called, with good reason, "about the busiest of my life."

In his public appearances he veered away from the controversies that had
once almost silenced him. Faced with the news of increasing turmoil in the
South over civil rights, he emphasized humor and good cheer. On January 10,
as the main speaker at a gala luncheon in Chicago when the predominantly
black Windy City Press Club gave its first Man-of-the-Year award to the hero

of Birmingham, Alabama, Rev. Martin Luther King, Jr., Langston talked not about the civil rights struggle but about "Humor and the Negro Press." The Negro press, he explained, with its volatile journalistic mixture of solemnity on civil rights and scandal, of stodginess and sensationalism, was "my favorite reading"—the main thing he missed (along with American ice cream) when he was overseas. On the whole, the black press was too solemn—a point he emphasized when he allowed his *Chicago Defender* stalwart, Jesse B. Semple, to explicate each letter in the hated word "Mississippi," starting with "Murders" and ending with "Infidels." Simple made "a double entendre out of P-P over Mississippi," Langston reported, "which Simple will do when he gets to be an angel, hoping the Dixiecrats don't have time to get their umbrellas up as he wets all over Mississippi."

As for Martin Luther King, Jr.—he should run for President of the United States, Simple argued later that year in the *Defender*. The fact that King wasn't thirty-five years old meant nothing. "What Rev. King lacks in years," Simple asserted, "he makes up in guts. He did not run away from Montgomery when they put a bomb under his house, did he? What he lacks in years he also makes up in being wise. That minister is a wise man."

Langston spoke again through Simple on the question of civil rights—this time more comprehensively—when he quickly finished work on his third collection of columns, "Simple Stakes a Claim." Unlike the earlier volumes, this would be "essentially a topical book," as he explained to Carl Van Vechten, with less emphasis on his hero's personal adventures, especially his love affairs, and more on his claim to democracy. Langston then turned to an entirely different literary task. On the day of his humorous Chicago lecture, and before he could meet her, Gabriela Mistral died of cancer at a hospital on Long Island. Now he moved in earnest to attempt the translation of her poems promised to the Indiana University Press. With Mistral's executor and literary agent approving his concentration on poems about love, women, and children, to give the book a consistency of "mood and meaning," Langston seemed to welcome the chance to speak, if only as translator, with the voice of a woman and mother. He pushed ahead with the task—although he was certainly not flattered when Mistral's friends suggested that his translation should be printed with a foreword by Archibald MacLeish, "an American poet."

Once again, however, he could not give an important project his complete attention. As usual, the distraction was money, or the relative lack of it even with his newfound "prosperity." "Trying to run a major career on a minor income," he would complain, "is something!" He could expect scant financial returns from the Gabriela Mistral volume. To subsidize it and the other important work that inevitably would capture his attention, he seized on an advance of $2000 from Dodd, Mead, to be shared with Arna Bontemps, for the adaptation of part of their collection of Negro humor into a "Book of Negro Folklore." This commission emphasized the extent to which the nation was changing under the pressure of the civil rights campaign in the South. To Langston's amazement, the editors at Dodd, Mead asked him to ensure "a *socially slanted* book.'' Needing the money, he himself had been ready to produce a more innocuous volume. ''If I had proposed it,'' he noted wryly about the request, ''they would have thought me a leftist!''

Glad to shift his emphasis, he nevertheless remained wary about following too eagerly any progressive turn by an American publisher, or mistaking an editorial whim for a sign of a substantive change in the social conscience of the nation. On the project most promising financially to him at the moment, Stella Holt's forthcoming production of *Simply Heavenly,* with songs by Dave Martin (''a wonderful collaborator''), he was emphasizing not politics but entertainment, which had a far greater chance of succeeding with the public. Since the producer Stella Holt was doing her part, against the odds, to make the show possible, he would do his. The forty-year-old Holt, blind since the age of seventeen, was something of a crusader. In 1952, giving up her job as a social worker (''I felt there was so little I could really do for people in ordinary social work''), she had become managing director of the Greenwich Mews, which was sponsored by the Village Presbyterian Church and the Brotherhood Synagogue. To make money was not her goal: ''We try for an artistic success, and follow the concept of the author in a straightforward way.'' She was accustomed to working with small budgets and expected to launch *Simply Heavenly* with only $4200. Partial to ''plays of serious content, poetic quality,'' she had been working for some time with the gifted black playwright Loften Mitchell on his *A Land Beyond the River,* which depicted the fight of a black country minister on behalf of black children. In 1954, she had staged William Branch's play about Frederick Douglass, *In Splendid Error;* in 1955, Alice Childress's *Trouble in Mind.*

''Stella Holt was very important to us,'' Loften Mitchell later judged. ''We used to have plays in Harlem, but the theater audience in Harlem was vanishing to Queens and Westchester and the other suburbs, with integration. The Greenwich Mews had been used mainly by progressive types, with interracial casting. It began to fill the void for those of us who wanted to put on plays about us. It was a time of tremendous energy and hope and expectations. We felt like, tomorrow we will own the world! She helped us in a very basic way.'' As he remembered her, ''Stella was a lovely, lovely woman, a bundle of dynamite. She came up to Harlem to see our shows and she asked to do *A Land Beyond the River* when I hadn't even typed up the script! She said, 'Give it to me. I'll produce it.' And she did just that!''

When the church and synagogue which housed the Mews objected to having a play about blacks that was set in a bar, Holt found the 85th Street Playhouse. She did not mind the lack of an overt political message, and Langston himself had no doubt what he wanted. ''What Broadway needs,'' he decided after the first musical auditions for the show (and after squirming through what he called a monumentally tedious all-black version of Samuel Beckett's *Waiting for Godot*), is ''a real good old-time colored singing and dancing *HAPPY* show, instead of all these sleepy white-orientated problems and half integrated watered down white-scored musicals—like frozen string beans, or canned phalarops.''

As for racial watchdogs, such as those from the NAACP who sourly scanned theater productions for evidence of black racial "progress," Langston for some time had been almost openly contemptuous. "I do believe cullud liberals and white liberals both are related to ostriches," he had jeered after attending a fatally gentrified revival of a Paul Green play about blacks. "Or am I prejudiced?"

On his fifty-fifth birthday, contented and evidently at ease with himself, Langston celebrated at home with lobster and champagne and the company of the Harpers and two friends from Paris, Henri and Eli Cartier-Bresson. There was no public notice of the milestone, but from the Van Vechtens came gift boxes of wine jellies, and an admirer from the Midwest had birthday cakes delivered to his home on three consecutive days. The approach of Negro History Week brought a cascade of invitations, from which he chose carefully. At Hunter College in Manhattan he shared the stage uneasily with Mahalia Jackson, whose prestige was then at its peak (she had opened and closed the Democratic Party convention the previous year); Langston loved Jackson's magnificent voice but found her almost unpardonably tight-fisted with money. He also staged a jazz program with Dave Martin at a Jewish Center on Long Island and took part in a "Musical Tribute to Negro History Week" at Town Hall in Manhattan, sponsored by the local chapter of the American Federation of Musicians. Avoiding other engagements in order to remain at his desk, in mid-March he turned down an offer to teach short-story writing during the summer at the prestigious Bread Loaf writers' colony. He was simply too busy, he pleaded.

As usual, he kept several projects going at one time. For Jan Meyerowitz, who was planning a concert at Carnegie Hall, he composed a cycle of five "Songs for Ruth," intended for the Atlanta soprano Mattiwilda Dobbs, and a hymn, "The Lord Has a Child," for the American composer William Schuman. Langston's main concern, however, was not the classical stage. Indeed, when he offered manuscripts of various concert settings of his poems to the Fisk University Library, he dismissed them almost testily: "I neither sing, play— nor care much for—concert music." He had much more fun writing calypsoes, which were then in vogue in New York—especially as sung by Harry Belafonte—and Langston even tried his hand at rock 'n roll. In 1957, the greatest revolution in the history of American popular music had just begun, first with white performers such as Elvis Presley, Pat Boone, and Jerry Lee Lewis "covering" or exploiting the recordings of black musicians, then with black musicians sharing the stage, and finally with the progression of the form into an all-American and worldwide musical idiom. "You've taken my blues and gone," Langston had once mourned accusingly in a poem about the white exploitation of various black cultural forms. Now, well aware of the roots of the rock revolution in the black "rhythm and blues" of the South, he tried to swivel his hips with his "Plymouth Rock and Roll":

> . . . Made in U.S.A.—
> And it rocks from pole to pole!
> Aw, it's high octane grade A—
> I mean Plymouth Rock-and-Roll!
> Plymouth Rock-and-Roll!
>
> Rock! Rock! Rock—
> And Roll!

"I see no reason," he informed Dave Martin in dispatching these lyrics to him, "why we shouldn't get in on the tail-end of Rhythm and Blues Rock and Roll. Do you? So set this here—and get somebody to rock and roll it."

In spite of his disparaging words about concert music, Langston remained proud of his ventures in opera. On Sunday, March 17, on the Feast of Purim in the Jewish calendar, he was in the audience at the Lincoln Hall Theater of the University of Illinois in Champaign-Urbana for the world premiere of his and Meyerowitz's three-act opera *Esther*. The ironies of the production amused him: "Jewish theme, Gentile cast, cullud lyrics! American! By a Hebrew Catholic." *Esther* was a definite success. The *Daily Illini* heard "a powerful libretto," one that added "immeasurably" to the music; another journal called Langston's words "intelligent and beautiful." Coming bashfully to the stage, he helped the triumphant Meyerowitz accept wave after wave of applause. Their success with the opera was not, however, untainted. When Langston suggested some small changes for a future performance, the temperamental Meyerowitz sharply rebuffed him. As usual, Langston did not strike back. "I note you are *just like a composer*," he quietly remonstrated; "you will accept no suggestions at all. No doubt the Lord made you that way, so I trust He will accept the responsibility. . . . Maybe someday you will explain to me *why* composers expect lyricists and librettists to make ALL the changes a composer wants, but maestros are seldom, if ever, willing to change a NOTE. Even those with less talent than yourself are equally adamant. May God help you all!"

The men clashed again over his traveling expenses. Assured by Meyerowitz that funds for his attendance had been guaranteed by Paul Fromm, head of the Fromm Foundation, which had commissioned the opera, Langston had spent $113 to travel to Illinois. When he appealed to Meyerowitz for help after the Fromm office failed to respond to his request for reimbursement, the composer curtly dismissed him with the remark that he, Meyerowitz, was no babysitter. After Paul Fromm denied ever having promised the reimbursement, Meyerowitz wrote Langston a scathing denunciation of "Frommochai, the Jew" and his "obscene" denial: "I tell you, in a hurry, and UNDER OATH, if you wish,—that his epistle does not contain one word of truth." Eventually Langston recovered his expenses from Fromm, but he clearly found Meyerowitz's behavior appalling.

He himself faced others in a different way. With prosperity, his standards of courtesy, as well as the aura of benevolence and love about him, only intensified. Kindness had become a kind of compulsion. His little deeds of generosity, heartfelt but also a part of his calculation, astonished strangers and friends alike. "He claimed the whole black race as his family," one of his secretaries later asserted; but in truth, Langston opened his arms to the whole world. That April, for example, he made time in his crowded schedule to serve cider and cake at home to a group of thirteen freshmen students and two professors from Sarah Lawrence College at the conclusion of their social-science expedition into Harlem. Almost any kindness to him triggered an act of gratitude. Easily recalling names and faces, he overwhelmed the bashful with the exuberance of his greetings; and his gift-giving, especially of copies of his books, was prodigious. "He's walking down the street," the same secretary recalled, "and he meets you, and you invite him to have a beer, he would take down your name and your address, and . . . he would send you a book. And if you had a wife and children, he would send a book for your wife and each one of your children. Autographed personally to each of you."

His book of birthdays and Christmas card list, ever expanding, had become crucial. Preparing birthday cards in advance of each month, he inscribed the precise date of mailing in a corner of the envelopes, where the stamp would be affixed, and gave firm instructions: "They must not be mailed too soon, and they must not be mailed too late. They must be mailed on the date that he has written in the corner." Two gestures, both made in the 1960s, illustrate the premium he placed on thoughtfulness. The young writer John A. Williams, who had sent Hughes a story for an anthology, was on board ship, sailing quietly off to Europe with his bride, Lori Williams, when a loudspeaker summoned him to the purser's office. There he was handed a telegram: "THANK YOU FOR THE NEW STORY FOR ANTHOLOGY AND ALL GOOD WISHES FOR HAPPY SAILING HAPPY LANDING AND HAPPY WRITING OVERSEAS." "Langston had sent it," Williams recalled. "I had never met him, and I don't know for sure how he knew I was going away, and on which ship, and when. But there it was, this telegram. We were touched." To an inquiring graduate student, Doris Abramson, Langston sent a warm and detailed letter concerning her prospectus for a study of black drama, and an invitation to visit his home so she could have access to his files. "I had never met him, and yet it is a whole page, single-spaced, typed. He had gone to all this trouble to answer a request I had just made through a mutual friend. . . . This just to somebody who has been introduced to him over a telephone!"

A visit to Washington, D.C., to deliver the Charles Eaton Burch Memorial Lecture at Howard University, where he dined with Clarice and Arthur P. Davis, a professor of English there and the author of the first scholarly essay on Langston's Simple, "Jesse B. Semple: Negro American," was pleasant. And when his aged uncle in Los Angeles, John Hughes, who had been seriously ill, asked him to visit, Langston flew without delay to California—where he found the old man much improved, and back on his staple diet of whiskey and cigars, which his continuing income from his oil wells in Oklahoma assured. Sure that his end nevertheless was at hand, John Hughes begged Langston to promise him that he would be buried near his parents in a cemetery close to the Indiana farm on which he had grown up in the late nineteenth century. Langston duti-fully promised to see to the matter, and also to hunt in the Midwest for mem-bers of the long-scattered Hughes clan. To his cousin Flora D. Coates, who looked after John Hughes in Los Angeles, Langston was entirely admirable. "Each time we are together," she wrote after one of his visits, "I love you more because you are always so sweet and understanding."

He could not linger in Los Angeles, because rehearsals for *Simply Heavenly* were about to begin in New York. Directed by Joshua Shelley, the cast was now anchored to everyone's satisfaction by the gifted Claudia McNeill ("the Marian Anderson of the Night Clubs," Langston ventured to a reporter), a former protégée of Eubie Blake who had performed in New York cabarets for over twenty years but was still relatively unknown. McNeill would play Miss Mamie, a colorful regular patron in Simple's favorite bar. Ethel Ayler, pretty and sinuous, would play Zarita, Simple's after-hours girlfriend; Marilyn Berry, also lovely, would be the proper Joyce. The casting of Simple was more of a problem. Langston was present early in April when a young, inexperienced actor named Melvin Stewart tried out.

Stewart, who went on to a solid acting career on the stage and in television, remembered his audition. "I dressed casually and loosened my tie, as I thought Simple would, and read for Joshua Shelley. Looking in the corner—I just hap-pened to glance that way—I saw this Santa Claus of a little brown man with these myopic-looking, huge lenses and this perennial—I came to know it as perennial—cigarette dangling from his lips, with a smile that *never* went away. I very seldom saw this man *not* smile; it was the strangest thing." Shelley asked Stewart to sing. "I can't sing, but I had to. So I tried 'How Deep is the Ocean,' which I thought I might be able to handle, and just mangled it, with Josh Shelley feeding me lines and my voice falling apart. And this roly poly little man in the corner, Langston Hughes, just cracking up."

Joshua Shelley gave Stewart the role of Simple. Although Langston and the young actor soon became good friends, the choice at first disturbed Hughes, who definitely wanted instead Nipsey Russell, the veteran comedian and star of the Baby Grand nightclub, and a man much closer than Stewart to Simple's age and background. "We are skating on thin ice with the currently chosen Simple," he warned Stella Holt and Shelley. Nevertheless, Stewart was on stage at noon on April 15, when rehearsals started. Behind Langston's objec-tions to the casting of Stewart were certain reservations about Shelley's ap-proach. While Shelley worked quickly and solidly in achieving broad effects, Langston saw little subtlety in his work in this play, and little sense of the poetry underlying the black man Simple. As almost always, however, he would not raise a direct protest. In facing white producers and directors and compos-ers, in spite of his fame and fifty-five years, he was almost fatalistic. "You know show business in the U.S.A. as well as I do," he wrote Claudia McNeill at one point. "For us the dice are loaded and usually throw craps. On the other hand, sometimes even the dice have more integrity than the housemen. So let's hope!"

Just after attending his first seder at Passover, a high-toned affair on Central Park West that included the Israeli Ambassador to the United Nations, Langston slipped out of town in order to concentrate for a while on his Gabriela Mistral volume. At the secluded hill-top home of his friends Wesley Potter and his wife Charlie not far from Princeton, he worked on the poems assisted by two Latin-American students from the university. He then ventured to Morgan State College in Baltimore, where he was guest of honor at a luncheon hosted by Irene Diggs, a professor of sociology and a former secretary to Dr. Du Bois, and to Worcester, Massachusetts, where he addressed the local Interracial Council. Back in Manhattan, he did his best to stir up support for *Simply Heavenly* and his latest books. Early in May he made a successful appearance on the CBS television show, "Night Beat," where he smoothly fielded questions by the probing journalist Mike Wallace. To at least one viewer Langston seemed "calm, collected, reasonable; yes, and wise and witty and entertaining, too."

He was not so much witty and entertaining as blunt on May 7 at the Alvin Theater in Manhattan when he addressed the first national assembly in the forty-five-year history of the Authors League of America, the parent body of the Authors' Guild and the Dramatists' Guild, which together represented 3,500 American writers. The only black on a panel on "The Writer's Position in America," which was to focus on the question of political censorship, he boldly redefined the term to make it properly applicable to blacks: "Negro writers, just by being black, have been on the blacklist all our lives." He hit at the historic bias against blacks in motion pictures, radio, and television, on lecture circuits, in publishing and reviewing, and even in certain libraries "that will not stock a book by a Negro writer, NOT EVEN AS A GIFT." Censorship for blacks, he insisted, "begins at the color line." Why did half of the top black American writers live abroad, "far away from their people, their problems, and the sources of their material? . . . Because the stones thrown at Autherine Lucy at the University of Alabama are thrown at them, too. Because the shadow of Montgomery and the bombs under Rev. King's house, shadow them and shatter them, too. Because the body of little Emmett Till drowned in a Mississippi river and no one brought to justice, haunts them, too. Because Jim Crow schools from New York to New Orleans, Jim Crow them, too."

Ending with some lines of poetry and the subject of children, Langston concluded his address with a reading of "Merry-Go-Round," one of his most touching poems from the nineteen forties. In the audience, the playwright Alice Childress looked on as one white woman "wept unashamedly" while he recited his lines about prejudice and the baffled black child.

As the opening of *Simply Heavenly* drew near, he remained unhappy about the basic interpretation of his play. He had designed it as a flexible vehicle, to be played in a relatively light spirit. But the director and the actors, as if unable to conceive of a dignified comedy of black life, seemed eager to push it toward farce, to drown its undertone of tenderness and natural dignity in raucous laughter. Just before the first preview, in a private letter to Melvin Stewart and Marilyn Berry, Hughes pleaded for a humane vision of their characters:

> What I suggest now is that you hold them very *closely* to your heart and play them out of *love* for all the little ordinary guys in the world who are lost and lonely—and loud-talking and boastful because they are lost and lonely—and all the girls who are desperately seeking a rock on which to build a castle that won't sink into the sand. If you *love* deeply enough this simple man and the simple woman you are playing, such men and women in the audience—and who isn't simple?—will love you . . . Simple and Joyce—and the wonder of [recognition] will reach from stage to audience, and back again to you. And between you and all the people in the audience—and in the world—there will be the beauty of affection and understanding that finds no barrier in footlights . . . or color lines, or images in the mind, for the mind (and its often ugly images) will no longer matter—since the heartbeat in all of us is the same.

On May 21, *Simply Heavenly* opened at the 85th Street Playhouse, between Columbus and Amsterdam Avenues in Manhattan, a makeshift affair of 299 seats on the first floor of the United Order of True Sisters building. Although at one point a breakdown of the lighting system threatened the performance, the audience closed ranks and cheered the cast through to a rousing final ovation. Claudia McNeill, brilliant in her singing and acting, was the star of the evening; for all his youth and inexperience, Melvin Stewart was excellent as Simple. The critics, too, enjoyed the show. While *Simply Heavenly* was not tightly written ("a trifle ramshackle in structure," the *Post* warned), and Dave Martin's music was conventional, reviewers appreciated the unpretentiousness of the play, its "unhackneyed freshness and cheeriness of spirit." "Mr. Hughes loves Harlem," Brooks Atkinson wrote in the *Times*. "He loves the humor, the quarrels, the intrigues, the crises and the native shrewdness that makes life possible from day to day. He has written 'Simply Heavenly' like a Harlem man. If it were a tidier show, it probably would be a good deal less enjoyable." Atkinson judged that "Melvin Stewart could hardly be better as Simple." To Walter Kerr, the production was a "rambling, sometimes ramshackle, but always utterly delightful salute to Lenox Avenue."

At least two critics noted that blacks in the audience seemed to enjoy the play, its jokes and allusions and situations, more than their white fellow patrons did. But some blacks did not care at all for Simple in this theatrical guise. Alice Childress, who had declined Langston's invitation to direct the show, was openly "disturbed and bewildered" by aspects of *Simply Heavenly*, especially its apparent scorn of the middle class and its contempt for integration; the play "did not ring true as a real reflection of Negro life." Still a major leader in the Communist Party, William L. Patterson, who saw the play with his equally committed wife, Louise Thompson Patterson, was blunt: "I cannot say that I liked it." Dismayed at the hedonism of Langston's characters, who seemed to live only for food, dance, and sex, he quietly chastised the author: "To me, Lang, the play was political. But the politics suited my enemy's—Simple's enemy's—aims and purposes in describing the Negro."

These were serious charges, but Langston did not hide behind the argument that the director and actors had distorted his play. To "Pat" Patterson he replied that "it's the old story—and the problem I've been wrestling with for years—how to get everything to suit everybody into one piece. When it comes to plays, it is a miracle to end up with anything at all one wishes left in the play." To another disappointed viewer, he made a more sweeping and significant defense of his view of life: "Bitterness is not a part of me and so I cannot spew it. I see myself, I see the Negro people as, first of all human beings . . . aspiring for all the things that other Westerners aspire, but conditioned by the outside pressures of prejudice and discrimination. Some of these situations are tragic, many of them humorous, all of them are wonderful to write about. If we human beings were not the resilient animals that nature has made of us, perhaps our species would not have survived. . . . But the universality which is common to all men, makes of us all, basically, brothers."

Simply Heavenly quickly recovered its initial investment, and his checks came promptly from Stella Holt. Still, the production was in financial trouble almost from the start. The musicians' union, unhappy about the treatment of its members, wanted higher salaries for them. By June 1, the lack of an air-cooling system in the hall was a problem, by mid-month a crisis. At one performance three people fainted, including one determined fellow who passed out in the first act but staggered to his seat for the second. At another showing, the famed comedians Jack Benny, Gracie Allen, and George Burns fled the steamy hall after the first act, promising to return when it was cooler. "Always something, as Simple says," Langston grumbled, "when a man is colored!" Feverishly he worked to keep the show going, swiftly making changes in the script, preparing understudies, promoting it at every opportunity. *Simply Heavenly* held on at the 85th Street Playhouse.

If his efforts to keep the play alive consumed much of his time, there were other, more pleasant distractions. On June 1, for example, he gladly attended a barbecue lawn party hosted by the gregarious Adam Clayton Powell, Jr., the pastor of Abyssinian Baptist Church in Harlem and one of the most controversial members of the U.S. House of Representatives. On June 15, two days before the actual event, Langston helped celebrate Carl Van Vechten's seventy-seventh birthday at a party at Van Vechten's home on Central Park West, then went further downtown afterwards to a Greenwich Village jazz concert to hear Billie Holiday and Charles Mingus. The next day, he took a leading role in a tribute to the "father" of the blues and his friend since the 1920s, W. C. Handy, at Rev. Powell's church. Soon after, he talked about and read some of his verse on a Sunday radio program, "The Enjoyment of Poetry," on WEVD, a New York radio station.

Such outings, as much as he enjoyed them, made him despair at least once about his writing: "God, when will I ever get my work done?" Langston's work remained as varied as ever. Completing jacket notes for a recording, *Song of Haiti,* by Jean Vincent, a Haitian who had sung with the New York City Opera and Katherine Dunham's dance troupe, he also kept at his translation of Gabriela Mistral's work, which he still admired ("such beautiful poems!"). His first draft of the book drew nothing but praise from his editor at Indiana University Press: "You have made Miss Mistral's poetry sound like a woman's work." The response of the audience was also encouraging when he devoted a thirty-minute reading exclusively to Mistral at a function of the Poetry Society of America. Weeks later, after an enormous effort capped by two consecutive all-night sessions, he finished the manuscript with a sigh of relief—"Gracias a dios! Although it was a real pleasure to work on such lovely poetry."

By this time, *Simply Heavenly* had expired on 85th Street. Just as Langston was planning a party to mark the fiftieth performance, the Fire Department visited the theater. Curiously zealous marshalls found twelve violations of fire regulations, including inadequate exits, poor wiring, and inflammable scenery; a water tank with a capacity of 10,000 gallons had to be installed on the roof. Moreover, Stella Holt's theater lacked a permit to operate. An occasional cabaret was permissible, but not a regular playhouse. They ordered the show stopped—although plays with mainly white casts and audiences had been using the hall for years. The cast was devastated. "The gloom was so thick," Langston remembered, "you could have cut it." He decided to proceed with his party, but on June 3, when the cast and crew gathered at 20 East 127th Street, the mood was more like that of a wake. Then Stella Holt, who had vowed to revive the show, entered with exhilarating news. *Simply Heavenly* would reopen on August 1—and on Broadway itself, at the 48th Street Playhouse, with a budget of $30,000. The ensuing celebration lasted late into the night. "Something is always happening to a man, especially if he is colored," Langston soon drawled to a reporter. "In Simple's case, the Fire Department kicked him right square into Broadway."

Determined to see Simple succeed there, he begged Holt not to make too many changes and repeat the mistakes that had turned his opera *The Barrier,* a success at Columbia University, into a "bore and a flop" when brought to Broadway: "Let's not allow an angel to end as a man." Yet he made another try, again in vain, to have Nipsey Russell play Simple. And he looked forward to having an orchestra and a new set, as well as a hall with 996 seats instead of just under 300. His optimism about the show swelled further when Samuel Goldwyn of Hollywood ("his *own* self") telephoned him to request a copy of the script. Soon the *Amsterdam News* carried a breathless story, probably planted by the playwright himself, that the author of *Simply Heavenly* might soon receive $75,000 for the movie rights to the play.

A day or two after Goldwyn's call, Jack Hylton, a prominent British producer, telephoned from London with a similar request. The actor Laurence Harvey, who had attended the show twice in New York, had just recommended it for a London production in which he was prepared to invest. Harvey's recommendation meant a great deal. Born in Lithuania but raised in South Africabefore emigrating to Britain, he had survived notoriety as a flamboyant Edwardian-style dandy, then earned the respect of his peers as an actor and a businessman. A favorable notice in the Paris edition of the *Herald-Tribune* sealed Jack Hylton's interest in *Simply Heavenly.* "So we're internationally known!" Langston concluded happily, after reaching an informal agreement on a London production.

On August 20, after a postponement, *Simply Heavenly* opened at the 48th Street Playhouse. The production now included the famed blues singer and guitarist Brownie McGhee, an eight-piece orchestra, and a sparkling—and presumably fireproof—new set. The audience was packed with Langston's admirers and friends, including Arna and Alberta Bontemps from Nashville, who had come determined to cheer the first Broadway musical play of black life by a black author in more than twenty years—or since the glory days of the Harlem Renaissance. Once again the reviews were good, with the best notices going once more to Claudia McNeill. But they were not quite as good as before. One reviewer thought "the amiable little show . . . rather frail in the harsh glare of Broadway." Another saw its effect as "warming but not overwhelming; it offers affection and asks for it." *Variety* magazine endorsed the show, but tentatively. With its small budget and early start, *Simply Heavenly* might survive its major fall competition.

By the second week, the show was playing at about sixty percent of capacity, or uncomfortably near its break-even point. Nevertheless, with his play royalties flowing again, Langston indulged himself with a trip to Los Angeles around Labor Day. He went mainly to see a show in which he had more than a passing interest—*A Part of the Blues,* written by the young white actor Walter Brough, and produced on weekends in Hollywood by the Stage Society, a professional but nonprofit actors' organization which offered for the most part neglected classics but also some original works. In a tribute to the achievement of Langston Hughes, *A Part of the Blues* wove together excerpts from *The Big Sea* and *I Wonder as I Wander,* as well as his poems, blues, and songs. As Brough explained to him, *A Part of the Blues* sought to "capture you as an alert, pleasant, intelligent, very human person who lived in the first half of the twentieth century in America, who earns his living as a writer and who happens to be a Negro."

Flattered by the prospect of such a play, he had agreed to accept a royalty of only $5 each for a dozen performances, plus a percentage of the receipts. He attended two performances of the show and was moved by what he heard and saw, what it offered as his essence as an artist and a man. With a narrator and nineteen musicians and actors who never left the stage, *A Part of the Blues* sped along swiftly and lyrically to its conclusion. "One of the things which still brightens my life," he assured Brough later from New York, in promising to support a production in the East, "is my memory of my two evenings at 'A Part of the Blues' in Hollywood."

He returned to New York just in time for the recording on Sunday, September 8, of the cast album of *Simply Heavenly* by Columbia Records. However tenuous, the continuing run on Broadway also made bright publicity for his latest book, *Simple Stakes A Claim,* which appeared early in the fall as the first selection of the Negro Book Society, an organization founded by Langston's close friend and sometime secretary Adele Glasgow, to whom the work itself was gratefully dedicated. By this time, few reviewers could fail to recognize Jesse B. Semple's power. Even J. Saunders Redding suspended his habitual quibbling: Simple "looms in and over the life of colored Americans with indisputable authority . . . because he is more real than thought, more vital than a birth cry, and more true than knowledge. He is Experience's very self." The *New York Times* reviewer predicted that Simple, whose range of reference had broadened in this volume with his commentary on the civil rights struggle, would become one of those fictional characters "who cease being fictional and become historical." At least one Southern newspaper admired the book as a significant tract for the times.

The times had become so turbulent in the South that Langston had feared for the safety of Arna Bontemps and his family in Nashville during the battle for the desegregation of grade schools there. Joan Bontemps, Arna and Alberta's eldest daughter, was married to Avon Williams, a partner in the law firm of the leading black lawyer in the local struggle, Z. Alexander Looby. In one frightening incident, a white man with a rope had harangued a crowd, demanding Looby's lynching. In Little Rock, Arkansas, after National Guardsmen and angry white mobs prevented black students from entering Central High School, President Eisenhower ordered a thousand paratroopers of the 101st Airborne Division into the city and placed ten thousand National Guardsmen under Federal control. In Montgomery, Alabama, violence marred the end of segregated public transportation. Rev. Martin Luther King Jr.'s home was fired on, and an attempt made to bomb it. A sniper shot a black woman riding in a bus. Four black churches in Montgomery were bombed.

Graphic reports in newspapers and on radio and television of these and other acts of violence brought the Southern struggle into homes all over the nation, including 20 East 127th Street in Harlem. Although he read and watched and listened, Langston gave no thought to venturing as a warrior into the South. Clearly he considered himself too old to don armor—despite the New York *Post* profile of his character that invited its readers to see "a plump pixy of a man who looks nowhere like his 55 years." On the other hand, he did not counsel silence at such a time. In the *Defender,* especially through Simple, he struck consistently at segregation. On a radio show, he defended the right of the trumpeter Louis Armstrong, who had long faced the white world with a broad grin, to vent his racial anger. In their legal and more directly confrontational challenges to Jim Crow, he backed the NAACP and other civil rights groups. Two years later, in 1959, he would personally endorse the fiftieth anniversary celebration of the NAACP: "For most of my life I have been a member of the NAACP, but sometimes when funds were low, or when I was out of the country, my membership lapsed. However, as soon as I have had a dollar or two, I renewed my membership in one branch or another throughout the country.''

Still, he would not join the struggle in person. In late September, he spent a stimulating afternoon with the poet Bruce M. Wright and other friends at the home in Mamaroneck, New York, of perhaps the most defiant of the crusading civil rights attorneys, William M. Kunstler. ''Langston forgot his tie and I wore it throughout the South as an attorney for Dr. Martin Luther King, Jr.,'' Kunstler later recalled. ''I once wrote Langston and told him that one of the ironies of life was that his tie had gone to places which were closed to him. He wrote back and said that it was a shame that ties had more rights than people!''

A prolonged hot spell that thinned theater audiences put *Simply Heavenly* to a test it could not pass. On October 12, after sixty-two performances at the 48th Street Playhouse, the show closed. By this point, Langston was ready to abandon it altogether (''me, I'm somewhat weary of it—and show biz in general''). But once again the resourceful Stella Holt found another house, the small but ''very comfortable and pretty'' Renata Theater at 144 Bleecker Street in Greenwich Village. A half-dozen investors, including Count Basie, John Hammond of Columbia Records, and Oscar Hammerstein II, contributed $5000 towards the move. On Friday, November 8, trimmed back to close to its original lean form, *Simply Heavenly* opened once again. And again the show was soon in trouble. Equity, the main professional organization of Broadway actors, was at war with the rival Off-Broadway Association. Ignoring the reduced capacity and the location of the Renata, Equity officials demanded that the producers of *Simply Heavenly* return the entire cast to the salary scale paid on Broadway. While Langston kept his distance from the ''feudin' and fightin','' the dispute turned ugly. Stella Holt was struck by two heart attacks, brought on in part—so Langston judged—by a reckless black Equity deputy who accused her of racism (her thanks for producing the only black plays either on or off Broadway that year—*Simply Heavenly* and Loften Mitchell's *A Land Across the River*). There were ''charges and countercharges,'' a tired Langston reported, ''of which I can't make head or tail, and am not trying since, besides being busy, I've got a stiff neck, too, plus holidayitis.''

Working hard in the days before Christmas, partly in order to clear the way for the season's parties, he delivered the manuscript of a book for young readers, *Famous Negro Heroes of America,* to Dodd, Mead, and then quickly drafted a collection of original poems, ''Year Round,'' for an even younger audience. Although he would find no publisher for this venture, the year 1957, like 1956, ended on solid professional notes. Under a contract with the enterprising publisher George Braziller, he began selecting material for a *Langston Hughes Reader*. Better still, in Langston's opinion, Alfred A. Knopf, Inc., finally agreed to publish his ''Selected Poems.'' (He was also pleased and flattered when the New York chapter of his college fraternity, Omega Psi Phi, marked his thirty years of membership by naming him its local Man-of-the-Year.)

For years, citing its large stock of unsold Hughes volumes, Knopf had resisted his call for a selection of his poems. Then Langston, better off now than
ever before in his career, had applied some pressure to the firm, which had not
published a book by him since *One-Way Ticket* in 1949. With his *Simply Heavenly* income, he offered to buy out the remaining books at reduced prices. At
the same time, he also approached Rinehart, the publisher of *Simple Stakes a
Claim*, about bringing out his "Selected Poems." Rinehart's eagerness finally
moved Knopf. Choosing between the two, Langston decided to return to the
latter, in part because of its greater prestige and his long association with the
firm, in part because of its remarkable dedication to making beautiful, durable
books. With the cheaply produced *Simple Stakes a Claim* obviously in mind,
Langston had warned Rinehart that he wanted a book of "good paper that will
not turn yellow and crackle away within a few years."

Deeply pleased by Knopf's decision to publish the volume, he made a sentimental gesture to Carl Van Vechten, his friend and supporter of over thirty
years—although the men were not nearly as close as they had been in Langston's youth: "I guess you know *who* I would want to do the Foreword or
Introduction—*most much want* if such should be my honor." He repeated his
invitation, "so we would have come full circle together, poetically speaking!"
But a senior Knopf editor killed the idea of any introduction, including one by
Van Vechten: "I certainly do not think that at this time it would be a good
idea to ask Carl Van Vechten to write one." Unlike Hughes's stock, Van
Vechten's had fallen in the literary world since the spring of 1925, when a
word from him had virtually assured the publication of Langston's *The Weary
Blues*. In his gesture, Hughes meant both to thank Van Vechten and to bolster
his flagging sense of purpose. Most of Van Vechten's time was now devoted
to the James Weldon Johnson Memorial Collection he had founded at Yale for
the "perpetuation of the fame of the Negro." But, as he more than once complained to Langston, "it saddens me to realize how few Negroes realize this
and how still fewer make any attempt to assist the collection." Young blacks
especially, ignorant of his background and suspicious of his enthusiasm, sometimes balked at being photographed by him. Sidney Poitier had been "exceptionally" rude to him. Ralph Ellison had rebuffed his entreaties. ("I despised
his photography," the writer recalled. "In fact, I didn't care for the whole Van
Vechten influence. It introduced a note of decadence into Afro-American literary matters which was not needed. The literature had not earned its decadence.") Loyal to Van Vechten as to most of his old friends, Langston placated, encouraged, and humored him, as the moment demanded, and kept to
his promise to send his papers to Yale.

Bitterly cold weather in Buffalo, New York, where Langston read early in
January, sent him with a severe attack of influenza into Mt. Morris Hospital in
Manhattan. Once there, he decided to rest for ten days before going home
to oversee the final preparation of his biggest manuscript ever, twelve pounds
in weight and eighteen inches tall, "The Book of Negro Folklore," edited with

Arna Bontemps. On January 29, chuckling with delight at the commotion stirred by the large parcel, he delivered it in person to Dodd, Mead. His typists on the massive project had been the reliable Adele Glasgow, who still worked from time to time for Langston, and Raoul Abdul, the young man whose narration and directorship of a program on the history of black theater at the Countee Cullen library had so impressed Langston in May, 1954.

His prosperity allowed him now to retain Abdul as a full-time secretary. Born in Cleveland of an Indian father and a Canadian mother, Abdul had trained from the age of six as a singer and actor at the semi-professional Cleveland Playhouse, where he was the only colored child, then at the integrated Karamu Theatre with Langston's oldest friends, Russell and Rowena Jelliffe. After a stint as a journalist and helping in the Karamu box office, in 1952 he had come to New York, where he worked as a clerk and also studied voice. A summer scholarship to the Marlboro Festival, followed by roles in Karamu productions of Mozart and Menotti, cost him his Manhattan job. When he returned to New York early in 1957, Abdul worked with Langston first as an occasional typist, then in a full-time capacity by the start of 1958. He would serve in this way until just after the middle of 1960, then again return to Hughes's employ later.

Abdul found his new job absorbing. A formal element persisted in their relationship, but he and Langston also became close friends. The working day for Abdul, who never lived at 20 East 127th Street, normally began near noon. "Usually, Mr. Hughes was still sleeping or waking up slowly—very slowly—when I arrived," he later recalled, "so I had a good hour to open up all the letters and sort them out." As part of their often comic starting routine, his employer sometimes saluted him from his bed, through the closed door, with a melodramatically loud, mock-derisive accusation: "I know you're there Abdul, I can hear you, you're reading my mail. I know you're reading all my private mail." In fact, Langston did not discriminate much between his private and public mail, but saw himself as a man with little to hide. "As he had his breakfast, which was usually huge," Raoul Abdul remembered of most days, "I would read some of his mail to him out loud. I would pick important letters, or very funny letters, anything special. . . . I learned very quickly not to read any bad reviews that came from a clipping service early in the morning, or anything else that might upset him. You had to save those for later. Only the happy, bright things first."

A pile of material to be typed, the result of Langston's own labor the previous night, would be awaiting Abdul. Otherwise, Langston made no attempt to set Abdul apart as an employee. "I'd like to feel that we had a very, very special relationship," Abdul believed more than twenty years later. "Langston, I think, found in me the son that he wanted," although he also "may have found that in other people at different times." On the other hand, their relationship was too unguarded to be quite like that between a father and son: "It was very difficult for me to think of him in terms of being considerably older than I was. I just felt he was like an older brother, but there was hardly anything that we didn't say to each other, at times.'' Mainly Abdul saw Langston's gentle side, but he also witnessed his not infrequent betrayals of a sardonic temper, and his rare fits of anger when he felt he had been wronged. To some extent Langston was a vulnerable man, but at a deeper level ''he had a wonderful sense of self. . . . Everyone wants to be admired, and Langston was a people-pleaser, I think. But, on the other hand, if he failed to please someone, I don't think that he really cared that much. I think he was very aware of his own position in the whole scheme of literature and life.''

For all the familiarity, Abdul found it hard to call Langston anything other than ''Mr. Hughes.'' ''I thought that a person of Langston's stature,'' he remembered, ''deserved to be called Mr. Hughes. . . . But then late at night when we were finished work, of course, we'd have gin and ginger beer—Seagram's gin, the golden bottle, and then we would start talking, and we would just talk about whatever we wanted to. Especially the latest gossip of the literary world and friends, and then I would slip into 'Langston.' But I never thought that I, or anyone else, ever saw all of Mr. Hughes. There was a part of himself that he allowed no one to enter, that he kept gently but firmly to himself in reserve. That part always had to be respected, and I never lost respect for him—who he was, what he had done and gone through, the difference he had made as an artist and a human being in the world.''

In February, with no particular desire to travel, Langston accepted only two engagements for Negro History Week, including one to speak to students at his alma mater, Lincoln University. Near the end of the month he spoke on a panel at New York University sponsored by PEN, to whose executive board he had returned. And some of his time went to conferences in Harlem with a celebrity from London, Laurence Harvey, who now owned one-third of Jack Hylton's proposed London production of *Simply Heavenly*. Apparently in agreement with Langston on all important production questions, Harvey moved decisively to hire a company. In mid-March, Langston saw off to London the nucleus of the *Simply Heavenly* company, composed mainly of veterans of the New York productions—but not including their star, Claudia McNeill, who did not wish to travel.

He himself stepped further than ever on stage as a performer the first Sunday in March when, at the Village Vanguard nightclub in Greenwich Village, in what the black New York *Age* saluted as ''a memorable evening,'' he read his poetry to the jazz accompaniment of the bassist Charlie Mingus and the pianist Phineas Newborn. As a novel part of the eccentric but flourishing ''Beat'' movement, the recitation of poetry to jazz was definitely in vogue, as a jeering *Daily News* columnist satirically told his readers: ''You cats know what the big thing is in jazz these nights? Poetry, man.'' For Langston, the reverse had long been true. Not only was jazz ''the big thing'' in much of his poetry; he had first included blues and instrumental jazz on his reading program in 1926, more than forty years earlier. Looking with a mixture of amusement and disdain on the largely white ''Beat'' movement, which in many ways only parodied aspects of modern black urban culture, Langston nevertheless wanted to have his primacy in the field acknowledged. He begged Knopf to call him the "original jazz poet" on the cover of his coming *Selected Poems*. (Soon, the poetic "guiding star" of his youth, Carl Sandburg, a showman himself, hustled to point out that his 1919 poem "Jazz Fantasia" gave *him* primacy in the field.)

In spite of his poetry-to-jazz sessions, Langston generally dissociated himself from the "Beat" culture, just as he had questioned the Bohemian culture of Greenwich Village as early as 1923. "I don't know the beatniks," he insisted to a reporter. "They all seem to be down in the Village and I practically never go there. I stay up in Harlem." Finally, he was pragmatic about poetry-to-jazz as a trend. "Jazz gives poetry a much wider following and poetry brings jazz that greater respectability people seem to think it needs," he told the Toronto *Star;* "I don't think jazz needs it, but most people seem to." But his performances went so well that Langston, first with Mingus and Newborn, and later with Ben Webster's group, read to capacity houses at the Village Vanguard on several Sundays that spring.

The following year he was still at it, playing the Village Gate with a quintet led by an inventive, intelligent young jazz pianist from Brooklyn, Randy Weston, whose playing, developed out of admiration for Count Basie, Nat Cole, and Thelonious Monk, Langston particularly admired—as he declared at least once in the *Defender*. Langston also recorded a poetry-to-jazz album, *The Weary Blues with Langston Hughes*, produced by the jazz scholar Leonard Feather for MGM, and featuring on one side the master jazz trumpeter Henry "Red" Allen, whose first recording had been with Jelly Roll Morton, and, on the other, the Charles Mingus Quintet. He preferred Mingus's group to either Dixieland jazz or more cerebral outfits such as the Modern Jazz Quartet. Mingus was also a modernist, "but with more beat to my ear."

Whether poetry-to-jazz was an important fusion of cultural forms or only a fad was a matter of opinion. In the spring of 1958, it was mainly a diversion for Langston as, with Raoul Abdul's assistance, he cleared his desk of its backlog of literary projects and readied himself for some major new effort. For a while, no big challenge loomed, although he had committed himself to such a task the previous September, when he had signed an agreement with a Hollywood producer to begin work on a proposed epic, "Let My People Go," and accepted an advance of $1500. Charting the fortunes over three generations of a black and a neighboring white family, the screenplay would delve into the history of the race since Emancipation. The time seemed right for such a grand story about black Americans, their roots, and their struggle for civil rights. But Langston never delivered the script. A year later, in fact, when he agreed without argument to return the money advanced, he apparently had not even started it. Why he backed away from such a potentially lucrative effort is unclear—although his suspicion of Hollywood and the media networks was by now deeply ingrained.

Instead, he contented himself with smaller projects, such as providing the introduction to a book of cartoons by his old friend Ollie "Bootsie" Harrington, who was well known in the black community for his amusing drawings. (The following October, Harrington illustrated "Speak Well of the Dead," a droll article by Langston in *Ebony* magazine about funerals.) Longer projects, especially collaborations, were less appealing. Langston was willing to work with his good friend Adele Glasgow on a book about the English-speaking Caribbean, but he rejected a proposal to collaborate on a book, perhaps an autobiography or a memoir of the civil rights struggle, with Rev. Martin Luther King, Jr. As he informed Arna Bontemps at the time: "Me, no more do nothing with anybody but ME (or you)." Although it would have fetched a fine advance, a book with Dr. King would be both demanding as a task in itself and also eagerly anticipated by too many people. At this point in his life, Langston seemed determined not to accept such a burden.

If his future projects seemed uncertain, his past seemed more than merely admirable when, late in March, the five-hundred-page *Langston Hughes Reader* appeared from George Braziller. Offered as a main selection by the Book Find Club, the volume was thus assured of initial sales of eight thousand copies and a second printing. Langston leafed through the thick volume of selections from his work since 1921 with a genuine sense of amazement at the scope of his imagination in his younger days. "Some of those *Ways of White Folks* stories are hair-raising—for real!" he marvelled about work done in the early 1930s. "How did I ever think of such?"

Well aware of the prestige involved in having a "reader" appear in his own lifetime, he stirred himself to help in its publicity. Not long afterwards, however, the reception of his *Selected Poems of Gabriela Mistral* brought him down to earth. Although at least one reviewer thought his translations "excellent," and Paul Engle in the Chicago *Sun* called the book "useful and moving," two widely respected critics differed emphatically. Calling Hughes's temperament unsuited to the task, which demanded a woman, Dudley Fitts dismissed the book in the *New York Times* as "a *fracaso* of good intentions." In the *Saturday Review of Literature,* Edwin Honig of Brown University also questioned Langston's qualifications as a translator, deplored the absence of a Spanish text alongside the English, criticized the range of the selections, and regretted Hughes's decision to omit three celebrated sonnets ("*Sonetas de la muerte*") because of the admitted difficulty of translating them: "Shouldn't Mr. Hughes have called in some collaborator? Shouldn't he have worked harder and used more devices for rendering the poetry more exactly?"

This harsh response, with its insinuation of laziness and irresponsibility on his part, stung him. In it he obviously saw something more than objective, professional judgment. To Langston, it ignored his efforts over thirty years— met largely with the cold indifference of publishers—to bring Spanish writers to the attention of North American readers. Also ignored was the related fact that this was the first book of translations into English of Mistral's work. In reply to Honig, he sent a public rebuttal—virtually unprecedented for him—to the *Saturday Review:* "I can say only that—since no one else *at all,* over a period of more than thirty years, tried to make a volume of Mistral poems in our language—as humbly, sincerely, and honestly as I knew how, I tried. I would be the last to claim perfection for my translations, but my hope is that they might perhaps stimulate other more competent translators to render the same poems into our tongue. . . . So fine a poet as she was deserves many translations.''

Langston did not condescend to raise the one point—race—that some of his friends saw as central. For a black American to dare to translate a work by a white writer, or to review a book by a white writer not on a racial theme, was clearly considered in many quarters an indignity and possibly an affront. White editors virtually never employed black writers for such purposes; Langston must have forgotten his place in presuming to be able to speak for a white writer, let alone a white woman. On the other hand, he knew Fitts and Honig were men of liberal associations and sympathies. In the end, he had one consolation. Almost at once, the entire printing of the *Selected Poems of Gabriela Mistral* sold out.

In April, the arrival of proofs of his *Selected Poems* moved him to plan a major fall reading tour arranged around its coming appearance. He also moved to exploit the steady swell in requests for his appearance, especially before wealthier audiences, encouraged by the civil rights cause. A day or two after serving as a pallbearer at W. C. Handy's funeral in Harlem, he flew to Los Angeles for a series of poetry-to-jazz concerts accompanied by the bassist Ralph Pena. At one particularly glittering session there the audience included Joanne Woodward, Beatrice Lillie, and Sidney Poitier, the first black Hollywood matinee idol, who had been an acquaintance of Langston's since Poitier's early days as a struggling actor from the Bahamas in New York. Returning by way of Nashville and the annual arts festival at Fisk University, Langston took a prominent part in festivities surrounding the inauguration of Stephen J. Wright as its president. At lunch, he enjoyed meeting the excellent black historian John Hope Franklin, whose landmark study *From Slavery to Freedom* he had mined several times for his children's books. At Fisk, he also gave his first poetry-to-jazz program before blacks. The high-spirited students "almost stomped down the chapel," Langston noted with pleasure. "I had fun." (However, when later he ventured poetry-to-jazz at a Harlem nightclub, one black woman protested. "What are you reading about Negroes for and there are white folks present?" he reported her asking. "I started to say, 'How dare you be so dark in the midst of a white culture?' Only I thought of it too late!'')

Back in New York, he was honored by a concert made up exclusively of his songs, organized largely by the pianist-composer Margaret Bonds, an old friend, and sponsored by the Women's Association of the Community Church on East 35th Street, where Langston was introduced by the novelist Fannie Hurst. Then he was off to Boston for the successful regional premiere at Jordan Hall of his and Jan Meyerowitz's opera *Esther*, directed by Boris Goldovsky for the New England Conservatory of Music. *Esther* was "not a sensation or presumptuous novelty," according to *Opera News*, which praised the libretto, "but an unselfconscious, eloquent statement evolving naturally out of nineteenth-century grand opera.'' Once again, however, Hughes and Meyerowitz exchanged sharp words. Langston's complaint was his oldest in their collaboration: the words of his libretto often could not be heard above the music. One witty reviewer suggested that, on the whole, Esther herself might just as well have sung in Hebrew. Again, Meyerowitz seemed entirely indifferent to the complaint. Once more keeping to himself the full extent of his displeasure, Langston promised Meyerowitz another libretto.

Meanwhile, glowing reports about *Simply Heavenly* in Great Britain were coming from the composer-conductor Dave Martin and Melvin Stewart, who still held the role of Simple. Laurence Harvey was wonderful to work with as a producer. After arranging for the stage curtain to depict a typical darky devouring a watermelon, Harvey had cheerfully abandoned this touch when the Americans grumbled. In the provinces, all the reviews had been smashing, with the *Daily Mail* correspondent predicting that the show would rival *My Fair Lady*. Although the absence of a progressive political message in a contemporary play by a black author bothered one or two observers, Dave Martin rudely dismissed this objection. ''To hell with the message,'' he wrote Langston just before the show opened at the Adelphi Theatre in the Strand: ''Let's entertain and make these pounds.''

Three sorry weeks later, *Simply Heavenly* had lost more than 15,000 pounds. In mid-June, the show closed. A metropolitan bus strike hurt attendance, but the London reviewers had been caustic. Kenneth Tynan despaired of ''a score that harks back to the thirties and lyrics that hark back to the ark.'' The London *Evening News* first dismissed Dave Martin's music as ''the most undistinguished score we have slept through since the war,'' then deplored the entire ''raucous, tasteless, humorless hotch-potch.'' From various sources, Langston deduced that the enormous potential danger in dramatizing the Simple character—the tendency of the cast to lapse into farce and even burlesque, rather than offer a comic but dignified human being—had been realized. Apparently, ''in being restaged, Simple's original simplicity must have become real simple, and the accent shifted from a character study to entertainment—which doesn't quite come off.''

Langston took his London drubbing in full stride. Almost everything else overseas tied to his name was going splendidly. Encouraged no doubt by the worldwide fascination with the civil rights campaign, interest around the globe in black America suddenly revived. Victor Gollancz published the British edition of *Simple Stakes a Claim* to reviews even more flattering than in America. A contract with the United States Information Agency of the Department of State for *Famous American Negroes* bore its first fruit: a translation into Hindi—to be followed by translations into Bengali, Marathi, French, Portuguese, and Arabic. In June of that year, 1958, Langston readily pledged support for an edition of some of his poems in the Soviet Union, where he was assured that ''your name and books are known to our readers.'' The previous year, a Czechoslovakian edition of selected Langston Hughes poems, *The Songbook of*

Harlem, translated by Jiri Valja, appeared from the State Publishing House of Literature in Prague, with sales of 11,000 copies reported by 1963.

Responding briskly to their requests, Langston treated his translators with every courtesy, including the yielding of royalties when necessary. He wanted his work, and the culture of black Americans, known overseas. To the German writers Paridem von dem Knesebeck and Eva Hesse (she had included a generous share of Hughes poems in an important recent anthology of black poetry, *Meine Dunkle Hande*), he was "most grateful . . . for introducing my work to the German people." An edition of his and DeCarava's *Sweet Flypaper of Life,* translated by Knesebeck, and printed far more handsomely than the almost makeshift original American edition, had been published in 1957, and plans were set for Simple's German debut, *Simpel Spricht Sich Aus* in 1960, as well as a combined edition, abridged, of Langston's two autobiographies. In 1954, the Free Academy of the Arts in Hamburg had awarded Hughes a plaque, one of two selections that year, "in the name of Humanity and Democracy." That year also, he was invited to Poland by the Union of Polish Writers, but declined.

In Japan, Hughes and Meyerowitz's *The Barrier* was staged, and his children's tale with Arna Bontemps, *Popo and Fifina,* translated and issued successfully by Iwanami-Shoten, a major publisher. Next, *The First Book of Jazz* was in demand. "Japanese people, especially teen-agers, are enjoying Jazz fervently," the poet and translator Shozo Kojima assured Langston, "but do not know who made it, or how it developed. So your book will enlighten Japanese people, I think."

At home, in spite of the occasional setback, his prestige and popularity mounted steadily. Locally, early in May, he made a featured appearance at an Intercollegiate Poetry Reading at Adelphi College on Long Island, then joined the soprano Betty Allen and Ida Cullen Cooper in a program of songs and speeches at a Harlem library. A vast audience, spread over forty cities, saw and heard him read poetry on NBC backed by the jazz pianist Billy Taylor and followed by discussions with the critics Gilbert Seldes and Harold Taylor. This television appearance sparked so many requests for readings that Langston at one point simply unplugged his telephone. His projected fall lecture tour blossomed into a transcontinental affair, for which he confidently ordered two hundred copies of his old Knopf books both to help reduce the stocks and turn a profit for himself.

This soaring of his popularity he viewed almost with amusement. He pretended to see a link between his many invitations and the sharp economic recession seizing the nation in 1958: "When headed for the pit, I guess folks seek knowledge—or at least poetry." On the other hand, in the midst of the controversies over integration, and the transition from Jim Crow, he was sure that black writers could perform a significant service. "Colored literature in these days of integration," he told a Washington, D.C. gathering marking the start of the latest black book club—even as he lamented the paucity of bookstores in black communities—"will help whites understand the transition; help them learn that colored Americans are like any other people; help our children to know our contribution to the struggle and development of America, and help white children gain respect for colored people.'' The task of liberation was not over: ''The sun has moved over Washington but not over Mississippi.''

Whatever the reasons—the turmoil concerning integration and civil rights was certainly prominent among them—Langston Hughes was now definitely in vogue. On June 5, photographers from *Life* magazine arrived to take his portrait for a forthcoming article. In Nashville, Arna Bontemps read the various press notices on his friend and was impressed. ''You are, as the expression used to be, *smoking!*'' he congratulated him. ''So make hay!'' Late in June, Langston led a workshop in literature for high school teachers at Atlanta University, then was off to Rhode Island for the annual Newport Jazz Festival, of which he was still a director. A week later in Lenox, Massachusetts, a poetry and jazz concert with the clarinetist Tony Scott and his quintet at the Berkshire Music Barn left a *Berkshire Eagle* reporter praising their efforts as ''extraordinary on every one of the numbers.'' On July 22 and 23, after surviving a demand by a conservative senator from Nova Scotia that the Canadian government ban this ''blasphemous creature,'' he read with a jazz group including Henry ''Red'' Allen, J. C. Higginbotham, and Cozy Cole, at the Stratford, Ontario, Shakespeare Festival.

Even doubling the amount of his lecture fee did not stem the tide of requests for his program, which themselves increased with each new recognition. Previously honored by the New York chapter of Omega Psi Phi, he was nominated now as the organization's national Man-of-the-Year. The Library of Congress asked him to make a special recording of some of his poems. And the *Life* magazine story, which ran in its *Life International* and *Life en Español* editions, lauded Langston Hughes as one of the blacks who brought honor to the United States. ''How times do change!'' he marvelled, thinking no doubt not only of the historic indifference of such a magazine to blacks but also of his place, in an issue of *Life* only a few years before, on a lavishly illustrated list of communist ''dupes'' and ''fellow travellers'' who brought dishonor to the nation.

Digging into his files, he had little difficulty now in selling the little novel *Tambourines to Glory*, which previously had been rejected as too slight by Simon and Schuster and other publishers, to the John Day Company. For Franklin Watts, Inc., he tossed off what turned out to be his last manuscript for the firm, ''The First Book of Africa.'' Encouraged by the prospect of large sales, he spent much time that summer cutting and revising the ''Book of Negro Folklore'' manuscript for Dodd, Mead to make it as commercially attractive as possible. Not every effort met with success. When, with an eye to a gift book in December, he strung together ''A Christmas Sampler'' of his work for young people, he found no publisher. And he proposed but then left undeveloped a plan for a short novel, ''The Nine O'Clock Bell,'' on the civil rights question in the South, intended ''for Adults or Teenagers (Or anyone of any age if written simply).''

He was hardly ignorant of, or altogether untroubled by, the price he was paying as an artist for exploiting his swelling popularity. Certainly he needed and wanted the money generated by his appearances and his ventures into musical comedy and juvenile writing, but he understood well that there was another, more ascetic approach to art. When the deeply serious poet Robert Hayden wrote him once from Fisk University to complain about the stultifying effects of a university schedule, Langston was unsympathetic. "I could tell you about writing for a *living*," he told Hayden. "It makes nothing but a literary sharecropper out of a man." Offering to swap his chattering typewriter for Hayden's classroom of quiet students, Langston presented himself as "perfectly willing to let them relax and sleep while I lectured"—and, presumably, later enjoyed the calm of his academic study.

The previous summer, on the other hand, at the Newport Jazz Festival, he had crossed paths with an old friend whose studious avoidance of the lecture circuit and conspicuous dedication to "serious" art seemed particularly to irk Langston. "Ralphie is getting real baldheaded," he had joked unhappily to Arna Bontemps about Ralph Ellison, "—further proof that he is an intellectual." Far from rushing to capitalize on the prestige won with *Invisible Man* in 1952, Ellison had published only a few short stories and essays since then. Supporting himself with a teaching job at Bard College, he had begun what he anticipated would be yet another taxing effort in writing fiction, to produce a worthy successor to *Invisible Man*. Essential to Ellison's sense of self as an artist was a relentless brooding on cultural and artistic matters, a continual refinement of his intellectual positions, a laborious questing after excellence in his fiction and his critical pronouncements. But Hughes seemed now to distrust such brooding, and also to be incapable of sustained labor on a single, epic enterprise.

"Langston was always genial to me," Ellison would recall, "but I remember once blowing my top at him, over drinks. He was still emphasizing race as a source of everything, and I was saying, 'For God's sake, I wish you would stop this and begin to see other dimensions of our particular problem, because you just can't resolve everything on the basis of race. To me, it was simply lazy-mindedness on Langston's part." Refusing to grow as an artist, Langston kept invoking "the excuse of racism. Every period of history is reflected in a metamorphosis of poetic forms and the techniques that produce them. It's the only way the poet gets into the game, so to speak. But Langston had stopped thinking. He had cut himself off from what was really important in art and the intellectual life."

Of another artist encountered at Newport the past summer, Langston had a different but germane complaint. Dismissing as "not very good" the performance of Duke Ellington, who had ventured with his orchestra to accompany the gospel singer Mahalia Jackson, Hughes offered an opinion ironical in light of his own wide dispersal of his talents in recent years: "It must be hard to keep from falling between so many stools." Since his orchestra's magnificent performance at Newport in 1956 (with Hughes in the audience), Ellington's fame and popularity had—like Langston's—surged dramatically. The album of his 1956 Newport music had been the first long-playing record to become a best-seller in his remarkable thirty-year career. After a decade of struggle following his earlier vogue, his band was now in such demand all over the United States and Europe that *Time* magazine had featured him on its celebrated cover. Like Langston, Ellington now seemed determined to accept every invitation to perform. But even as he won honor after honor not only in popularity polls but also in the assessment of critics, some listeners, including Langston himself, believed that Ellington was sacrificing his genius in an understandable but sometimes indiscriminate pursuit of the money and prestige denied him in the past.

Privately, Langston could make such a judgment of Ellington. He would not have done so publicly. And apparently he could not do so, privately or publicly, of himself.

As the fall of 1958 began, in fact, he prepared to make more hay, and to do so on the sweetest ground possible—by returning in triumph to Lawrence, Kansas, where he had lived as a boy until the age of thirteen, and to Joplin, Missouri, where he had been born in 1902 but had not visited since his infancy.

11

YOU ARE THE WORLD
1958 to 1960

Go slow, they say—
While the bite
Of the dog is fast.
Go slow, I hear—
While they tell me
You can't eat here!
You can't live here!
You can't work here!
Don't demonstrate! Wait!—
While they lock the gate. . . .

"Go Slow," c. 1960

EARLY IN October, 1958, Langston opened his fall reading season with a journey into his most distant past. Splendid Indian summer weather swept the Midwest as he arrived to be publicly honored in his childhood home of Lawrence, Kansas. Although he had visited the town more than once since his departure in 1915, this visit was clearly different. The previous year, after a brief inquiry by Donald Dickinson, an acquisitions librarian, he had eagerly begun donating copies of his books and manuscripts to the University of Kansas to start a Langston Hughes Collection there. His aim, he said, was to honor the memory of his mother, who had taken courses at the university—but Langston himself clearly wanted a place in Lawrence. He wanted honor, as he saw it, in his own country.

Welcomed not only by the university but by the few remaining childhood friends who still lived in Lawrence, he thoroughly enjoyed his visit. On Thursday, October 7, after lecturing informally to various classes in English and the theater, he drew almost a thousand students, according to the university newspaper, to the ballroom of the Student Union. There, backed by a group from the university jazz club, he was the star of a poetry-to-jazz performance. The program was evidently a hit. "Mr. Hughes conveyed not merely poetry," one reporter judged, "but the true essence of that form of writing; the feeling, the mood, the atmosphere. When he spoke, he embodied the feeling he was talking about."

The next day, he drove south to Parsons, Kansas, with the director of university libraries, Robert Vospar, for another honor—an appearance as the main speaker at a banquet of the Kansas Library Association. There, still bubbling with good spirits after his triumphant return to Lawrence, he treated his listeners to stories about his Kansas childhood, read some of his poems, then sold dozens of his books at an autograph party afterwards.

On Saturday afternoon, with the weather still magnificent and his spirits still high, Langston made a deliberate detour on his way to New York when he flew southwest on Ozark Airlines for a four-hour stay in his birthplace, Joplin, Missouri. His first visit to Joplin since his departure as an infant had been encouraged by a stranger, Max Baird, a professor of English at the University of Missouri at Columbia. Born in Joplin, but with some experience in New York as an editor at the *Times* and at Doubleday, Baird had started an exchange of letters with Langston about his Missouri roots. If the professor's research was correct, a nameless older son of James and Carrie Hughes was buried in the local Fairview Cemetery. For Langston, this was something of a revelation. His mother had only hinted from time to time that she had lost an older child in Joplin at the dawn of the century, but she had died without ever confirming the loss. Her hinting, like Joplin itself, was too buried in Langston's past to mean much to him now, but it clearly meant something. He decided that the Fairview Cemetery, and Joplin, were finally worth a detour on his long way home.

Although Max Baird could not be in Joplin when Langston arrived, his brother Ralph, a local lawyer, met his airplane. At the old burial ground out on Maiden Lane they stood briefly at the site, located through cemetery records, of the unmarked grave. Perhaps Langston felt some surge of emotion about what might have been in his life, about how different his life might have been had he been brought up with understanding parents and an older, loving brother; if so, he kept his feelings to himself. After a brief tour of the city, including a stop on which he quietly insisted—to meet some local blacks at the Negro Service Council Center on Main Street—they hurried to Baird's office for a small cocktail party. The few guests included his wife, Virginia, representatives from the George Washington Carver National Monument nearby (Carver had grown up in the region), and a reporter for the Joplin *Globe*.

In his homecoming, Langston understood that a party mixing the races, even a party for a "world-renowned poet and author" and "literary giant," as the *Globe* called him, was hardly commonplace in Joplin, Missouri. He made the most of the occasion: "They even had an *interracial* cocktail party for me in that way-down-home town!" But at least one guest, a Welsh-born engineer named Philip Jones, could scarcely believe that, instead of being publicly feted by the city, Langston Hughes was "stuck in a corner" at a party in a law office on Saturday afternoon. To Jones, thinking about how "horrible" Anglo-Saxon prejudice could be, Langston Hughes seemed both at home in Joplin and garishly out of place. Rather than take offense, the guest-of-honor was "extraordinarily charming and gracious." In the warm, humid room, his brown skin glowed as he sipped his drink or dribbled cigarette ash from his lips and spoke volubly about his life in Harlem and his travels around the world. He was genuinely sorry he couldn't stay longer, "the mild-mannered, soft-spoken poet-author" assured the *Globe* reporter, to whom he also "expressed a desire to make a lengthier sojourn in the city of his birth in the near future." Then, at the end of a visit that marked not so much an indulgence of nostalgia on Langston's part as the confirmation of a sense of achievement, of having described a full circle in his life, he left with more graciousness than his welcoming by the town deserved. "I now have a warm spot in my heart for Joplin," he later thanked Max Baird, "and will never forget the friendly reception given me."

Returning briefly to New York, Langston soon paid another visit to California. Again, his invitations were first-class. On October 31, he read poetry to Ralph Pena's music at the sixtieth anniversary conference of the California Library Association in Long Beach. A week or so later, when he read with Buddy Collette's group in Los Angeles at the Screen Directors' Theater, a scroll was formally presented to Sidney Poitier and Tony Curtis for their acting in the controversial integrationist film *The Defiant Ones*. Making more use of airplanes than on any tour in his career, Langston returned east for readings at Antioch College in Ohio and Haverford College in Pennsylvania. Home on November 23, just before Thanksgiving, he was the star at a book party for his new novel *Tambourines to Glory* at the Market Place Gallery, an arts shop and cultural center founded by Adele Glasgow and her friends Ramona Lowe and Marguerite Moorman on Seventh Avenue near 135th Street in Harlem. Not long after, his and Bontemps's *The Book of Negro Folklore* appeared.

Both volumes only added to Langston's soaring reputation. Unsure exactly what a folk poet was, the *Saturday Review of Literature* still saluted him as "one of the greatest folk poets our country has produced"; and a *New York Times* writer was certain that "the consistently high quality" of his work over the years, given its great quantity, formed "a remarkable phenomenon and the mark of an exuberant professionalism." Although elsewhere its lack of scholarly notation was regretted, *The Book of Negro Folklore* was widely praised. The scholar Ray B. Browne declared it perhaps the most significant volume of the year in the entire field, while in *The New Republic,* a reviewer saluted the book as "one of the best anthologies it has been my pleasure to see." *Tambourines to Glory,* spawned opportunistically from the musical play, was also well received—though not unanimously so. But in spite of "a limp and pallid recommendation for those who must have Hughes" from the *Library Journal,* the novel won praise widely for its humor, simplicity of line, and liquid rhythms. To the *New York Post,* it was "a wonderfully funny yet touching book, a blend of comedy and fantasy in Langston Hughes's poetic style"; and at least one writer made a flattering comparison of the novel to Sinclair Lewis's *Elmer Gantry,* in its acerbic treatment of religious hypocrisy. Soon, the Folkways recording company issued an album of music, also called *Tambourines to Glory,* of eleven gospel songs by Hughes and Jobe Huntley, sung by the Porter Singers and recorded at the Second Canaan Baptist Church in Harlem.

Still in demand and still determined to "make hay," Langston crossed the continent again in December. This time he passed up the airlines for a comfortable seat in a "Vistadome" tourist car on the Canadian railroads. After a poetry-to-jazz performance in Vancouver at the University of British Columbia and a half-hour recording session for CBC-TV, he continued south to San Francisco. Although he had been visiting the San Francisco Bay area since 1933, he was received now as a true celebrity. His readings in San Francisco, Berkeley, Oakland, and Palo Alto were newsworthy events to the leading radio and television stations, which all sent reporters to interview him. In Palo Alto, where Hughes had once encountered trouble as a speaker, his way was well paved this time by the regional legal counsel of the NAACP Franklin Williams and his wife Shirley, and the vigorous local liberal leader Rachelle Marshall. "We raised lots of money for the NAACP!" Marshall recalled. He was featured on the "Books and Authors" show on KQED-TV, the major educational television station in the region. When the blues expert S. I. Hayakawa, now a professor at San Francisco State College, asked the jazz pianist-bandleader Earl "Fatha" Hines to join Langston in a poetry-to-jazz program on December 5 at the Museum of Art in the Civic Center, Hines was so overwhelmed by the honor that he brought along his entire orchestra.

Langston's tour of Northern California ended with his first visit to Carmel since the death of Noël Sullivan two years before. In Carmel Valley, the goats and sheep and yelping dogs had vanished. Hollow Hills Farm was no more. Eventually the gentle slopes would become the site of a nursing home. In Carmel, Langston passed the time as a house guest of his old friend Marie Short, and visited the widowed Robinson Jeffers. He delivered one reading at the Monterey Peninsula College, then drove with Marie Short one day down the sublime Big Sur coast, where he had picnicked on his thirty-second birthday in 1934 with Noël Sullivan and Robinson and Una Jeffers. In Big Sur, he recited his poems at Nepenthe Restaurant, overlooking the Pacific Ocean.

In Carmel, with Noël Sullivan gone, the sense of the vanished past was almost palpable. Early in the new year, 1959, another death touched Langston. At the funeral of Alta Douglas on January 2 at the Grace Congregational Church on West 139th Street in Harlem, he read in her honor what her grieving husband, the artist Aaron Douglas, called "your masterful poem." To Langston and others who had arrived in the 1920s, Alta Douglas's death had a special meaning. Over the previous years, many friends from that magical decade had died. Some, such as Wallace Thurman, Rudolph Fisher, and Countee Cullen, had gone prematurely. Others, including Walter White, Charles S. Johnson, and W. C. Handy, had been, or had seemed to be, of another generation. But Alta Douglas was very much of Langston's and Arna Bontemps's generation. In the breathtaking summer of 1926, she and Aaron Douglas had often formed the warm human center of the group of gifted black young men and women who had come together for the first time in New York in a world that was, if only for a moment, brave and new and almost at their feet. To Arna Bontemps, in a sentiment that Langston felt and understood, her passing marked definitively "the closing of the ring" on the Harlem Renaissance.

For some time, above the din of his own earned applause, Hughes had begun to hear the strains of his own looming closure. Spooked by the lavender-purple and gray colors chosen for the jacket of his coming *Selected Poems,* he demanded that Knopf use less sepulchral tones. "It looks like your last will and testament," two friends had said (or so he claimed). If the end was near, however, he wanted to leave in glory. A proffered contract for a long-playing record of his songs, with music from W. C. Handy to Kurt Weill, was another step "to crown my career." Boldly, Langston also went after one honor that had long eluded him, the annual award of the Spingarn Medal by the NAACP to the black American "who shall have made the highest achievement during the preceding year or years in any honorable field of endeavor." Quietly but firmly he solicited nominations and other help from Arna Bontemps, Van Vechten, Knopf, Dorothy Peterson, and other friends. To assist them, he drew up a convenient list of his various achievements—of which one seemed supremely important as he enumerated them to Bontemps: "Have lived longer than any other known Negro *solely* on writing—from 1925 to now without a regular job!!!!! (Besides fighting the Race Problem)!!!!" He was also proud that, virtually alone of the major black writers, he still lived within a bona fide black community (in Chicago, he noted, Gwendolyn Brooks had moved from the South Side; and Ralph Ellison aristocratically surveyed the Hudson River from an apartment uptown but on Riverside Drive, which Langston insisted was *not* Harlem). Bontemps received a stack of publicity material "so you might send it on to the Spingarn Award Selection Committee if you deem it now the moment to make that nomination. (It is about the month, I believe)." When Dorothy Peterson wrote the NAACP to urge them to select Langston, she sent a copy of her letter to him: "Was this what you wanted? Good luck!"

All his efforts were in vain. In recent years, the medal had gone to current heroes of the civil rights struggle, not to its aging literary veterans. Langston was ready to try again—but definitely not at the price of a freedom ride into the South. His efforts on behalf of the race were more genteel. In January, for example, he recorded a one-minute radio announcement for the United Negro College Fund. He also helped to launch a project that reflected his genuine pride in the steady march of various African nations to independence. To send a gift of books, art, and other objects to Ghana on its second anniversary, he joined a group called the Afro-American Committee for Gifts of Art and Literature to Ghana. "Pride rose within me," he rather sententiously assured Kwame Nkrumah, the prime minister, "that you had been chosen to carve the path of African independence." Although he shared the credit for the project with Ida Cullen Cooper, the leading Harlem librarian Jean Hutson, Aaron Douglas, Adele Glasgow, Louise Thompson Patterson, and other prominent blacks, his role was major, in that gifts of books were received at his home.

About this time, stirred also by events in Africa, he revived work on an anthology of African writing he had started in 1954, then suspended because of the lack of publishing interest. Now publishers were definitely interested in Africa, whose leaders were being received on their visits to the United States by high-ranking government, banking, and business officials. When Crown, which had published his and Milton Meltzer's *Pictorial History of the Negro,* agreed to take the manuscript, Langston redoubled his efforts to make the anthology representative of the new Africa. Called "An African Treasury," the anthology would include poetry, fiction, and brief articles on African life, culture, and politics. Among its main aims, as he saw it, would be to inform black America about the continent of its ancestry, about which there had been much confusion, doubt, and shame. Not, however, where Hughes's Jesse B. Semple was concerned. "If I could find out what it were," Simple announced now in the *Defender,* "I would take my African name back. . . . I mean my family names from way back, when I were an Afro, not an American. . . . There never was an African named Semple. My great-great-greatest grandfather's name was probably Abdula Wazit or maybe Damri Itsme, or something simple like So Wat. But it were my name, my very own name, before the white folks got to handing out Smiths, Johnsons and Jones." Simple had some ludicrous ideas about Africa, but he instinctively knew also that he had lost something irreplaceable in surrendering his African identity.

By February, after his hectic schedule of the preceding year, making hay far from home held few pleasures for Langston. Snow and sleet in Chicago during Negro History Week wreaked further havoc on his disposition. His appearance at Orchestra Hall on a musical program, "From Spirituals to Gospel Songs," was a disaster, as last-minute changes left him stranded on the vast stage "with an *integrated* (God help us) threesome that one critic said 'must have been lent by the Salvation Army'." ("I am afraid I am not only anti-white," an exasperated Langston concluded, "but anti-Negro.") He had better luck with a radio interview with the sympathetic journalist Studs Terkel and a television appearance with Mahalia Jackson, Sidney Poitier, and others on a program of blues, gospel, and jazz. And in Cleveland, his three shows of poetry-to-jazz netted $1200 as a benefit for Karamu House.

After a reading at Tuskegee Institute, where he declined an offer to teach for a semester, he returned to New York for a "Conference of Negro Writers" late in February, organized by the recently formed American Society for African Culture (AMSAC) and including John O. Killens, Arna Bontemps, Arthur P. Davis, Loften Mitchell, and J. Saunders Redding. He also made a light-hearted appearance at New York University on a "Writers on Writing" panel with the comic authors Steve Allen and Margaret Halsey. The AMSAC gathering was by far the more important for Langston. He used the occasion to deliver an address, "On Selling Writing," which seemed curious in light of his ancient racial emphasis, but which he also saw as largely ironic (although he thought he should avoid irony, "it being hard to make irony clear to most earnest people.'') The full significance of the speech, however, would become apparent within a few weeks.

"Even to sell *bad* writing," Langston advised, "you have to be good. There was a time when, if you were colored, you might sell passably bad writing a little easier than if you were white. But no more." Today, race in itself would not get a writer far: "To sell writing you have to be consistent, professional, a continuing writer." Urging a strict professionalism on aspiring black authors, he asked them to look past color: "Color has nothing to do with writing as such. So I would say, don't be a *colored* writer—even when dealing in racial material. Be a *writer* first. Like an egg—first *egg*, then an Easter egg. The color you apply. To write about yourself, you should first be outside yourself—objective." Blacks might even try to see themselves as whites viewed them—"then the better will you see how distinctive we are. Sometimes I think whites are more appreciative of our *uniqueness* than we are ourselves." No wonder, then, that whites had made far more money writing about blacks, than blacks themselves had made.

"Langston's speech just tore up the place," according to Loften Mitchell years later. "He just tore up the place. It was a hell of a session." Unquestionably, however, the spotlight at the AMSAC gathering was not on Langston but on twenty nine-year-old, dramatically shy Lorraine Hansberry, who delivered the closing address. Her heralded play *A Raisin in the Sun*, with its evocative title taken from Hughes's poem "Harlem" ("What happens to a dream deferred?") was to open in a few days on Broadway. The previous year, she had written almost demurely to introduce herself ("I am the author of a three act dramatic play on Negro family life") and to ask permission to use the title. Langston had another interest in the production. Prominent in the cast of *A Raisin in the Sun*, with Sidney Poitier, Ruby Dee, Louis Gossett, Ivan Dixon, and Diana Sands, was Claudia McNeill, regarded by him as "my discovery" because he had put her on Broadway in *Simply Heavenly*. Having enjoyed the play during its trial run at the Blackstone Theater in Chicago, he had set out in high spirits for the New York premiere on March 11: "I intend to holler REAL loud!" Soon he alerted his *Defender* readers that *A Raisin in the Sun* "bids fair to become a milestone in Negro dramatic art."

The tremendous commercial and critical success of *A Raisin in the Sun*, which won the New York Drama Critics Award and a lucrative Hollywood film contract, seemed to please Langston and leave him not at all envious. But once again, a younger writer had reaped enormous rewards in a field where he himself had been sharecropping with scant financial success for decades—a fact of which Langston was reminded repeatedly when various people kept insisting that the play was his because of its title. As usual, his own successes paid little. In April, for example, the month after the *Raisin* premiere, he had four different plays in four cities—*Street Scene*, revived by the City Center in New York; *Il Mulato* (*The Barrier*) in Rome; *Simply Heavenly* in Cleveland and in Washington, D.C. at Howard University; and *Emperor of Haiti*, staged by the Manhattan Art Players. But he had no Broadway bonanza, no Hollywood contract, and no award from a prestigious circle of metropolitan critics.

On March 23, however, Knopf officially published his *Selected Poems,* dedicated to Flora D. Coates, Langston's cousin, with a smiling cover portrait by his friend Henri Cartier-Bresson and deft sketches by E. McKnight Kauffer, who had illustrated his 1942 volume of verse, *Shakespeare in Harlem.* Hughes's long career as a poet had come full circle, an event he honored by sending the first copy to Carl Van Vechten "because you were the first one to lead me to my *first* book." Clearly Langston had labored over the arrangement of the poems. Echoing perhaps Walt Whitman's evolving attempt at organic harmony in the several editions of his *Leaves of Grass,* he had ignored chronology in favor of thematic and chromatic clusters, organizing his poems into groups according to theme and mood—"Afro-American Fragments," "Feet of Jesus," "Sea and Land," "Distance Nowhere," "After Hours," "Lament over Love," and so on. Apparently without prompting from Knopf, he had omitted any example of his radical socialist verse. Undoubtedly Langston hoped thus to propose a single transcendent song of himself as a major American singer, and to confirm his standing as the central poet of the black condition in America. (Although Hughes revised many of his earlier poems, his changes on the whole were modest. He included, without revision, the entire text of *Montage of a Dream Deferred.*)

A rapturous early private response from Ben Lehman of the University of California praised "familiar poems and new-to-me ones; pure lyrics and swift raw opening of the vein & artery of the world; revelation by arrangement as well as by word." Later, most reviewers, although regretting Hughes's lapses of quality, chose to emphasize instead his innate talent as a lyric poet whose chanting of the Afro-American and the human condition deserved respect and admiration. One writer stressed the "voice of pain and isolation, of a deeply felt contemporary anguish" in Hughes's verse. Another found "some of the saddest, most humorous and beautiful insights ever given into the heart of a race."

The most influential review, however, that in the *New York Times Book Review* on March 29, 1959, shocked Langston to the core. "Every time I read Langston Hughes," the appraisal began, "I am amazed all over again by his genuine gifts—and depressed that he has done so little with them. . . . This book contains a great deal which a more disciplined poet would have thrown into the waste-basket." There were "poems which almost succeed but which do not succeed, poems which take refuge, finally, in a fake simplicity in order to avoid the very difficult simplicity of the experience!" Hughes had Negro speech, music, and other forms "working for him" in his verse, but although he "knows the bitter truth behind these hieroglyphics . . . he has not forced them into the realm of art where their meaning would become clear and overwhelming. . . . Hughes is an American Negro poet and has no choice but to be acutely aware of it. He is not the first American Negro to find the war between his social and artistic responsibilities all but irreconcilable."

The reviewer was James Baldwin. His tone of nonchalant dismissal, diffused throughout his essay, was perhaps its most devastating aspect. As in his unrepented public attacks (notably the essay "Everybody's Protest Novel") on his former friend and mentor Richard Wright late in the late 1940s, Baldwin apparently had felt an almost Oedipal need to slay the paternal figure in the field of black poetry, Langston Hughes. But he was also repaying Hughes, with abundant interest, for a review in 1956, published also in the *New York Times,* of his collection of essays *Notes of a Native Son.* There, Hughes had depicted Baldwin as a gifted but still immature writer. As an essayist, Baldwin was "thought-provoking, tantalizing, irritating, abusing, and amusing," but his American and Afro-American viewpoints, incompletely fused, formed a "hurdle which Baldwin himself realizes he still has to surmount. When he does, there will be a straight-from-the-shoulder writer, writing about the troubled problems of this troubled earth with an illuminating intensity."

Behind Baldwin's review were issues somewhat deeper than his desire for revenge. Two, above all, were at stake in the exchange: Langston's status as an intellectual and, more important, his disagreement with Baldwin about the proper attitude of black writers toward race in the age of integration—or, for that matter, at any time. On the first issue, Langston knew flatly how he was perceived in certain quarters, and he resented it. The previous summer, coming upon Baldwin in the company of Ralph Ellison at Newport, he was sure that he had caught more than a whiff of hauteur from the younger writers. To Langston, however, conspicuous intellectualism at the expense of human warmth was a kind of neurosis—certainly for a black American, who should share in a more communal sense of values. Ellison, he quipped after another meeting, looked "fat, fine, and worried (about the Hungarians and such) as usual." A black American writer should be at least as concerned with black Americans, and with Africa, as with the latest crisis between the white superpowers. Ellison, to Langston, seemed unconcerned by the former, and affectedly obsessed by the latter.

("With all this talking about the Free World," Simple said not long after the Soviet invasion of Hungary, "and ain't-it-a-shame about the Hungarians, there is nary a word about ain't-it-a-shame about the Negroes that cannot vote in Mississippi." The crisis of 1960 was not much different. Apparently, "our white folks will never get through talking about that U-2, Khrushchev, Eisenhowser [*sic*], and the Summit. I wish I was at the summit—I would do a little talking myself. . . . But what would be different about me is I would be black. I would take my black face, black hands, and black aspirations [right] up there to the top." Food for the hungry would come first, then civil rights, and peace and justice among all nations.)

Why, then, did Langston urge the black writers at the AMSAC conference to see color as less important than the art of writing itself, which he stressed as being beyond color? His attitude spoke, paradoxically, for the depth of his identification with the race, which freed him not only to understand that the profession of writing was distinct from its "subject," but also to see his race in a rounded, humane way, rather than mainly as a deformed product of white racism. To Langston, Baldwin was tortured by a sense of an "all but irreconcilable" tension (in Baldwin's words) between race and art because he lacked confidence in his own people and certainly did not love them, as Langston did. To Hughes, only a deep confidence in blacks and a love of them (two qualities that could not be divorced) would allow a black writer to reach the objectivity toward art that Hughes saw as indispensable. Baldwin was undoubtedly more *troubled* by race than he was, but Langston was far more what blacks regarded approvingly as a race man, far more involved with other blacks on a daily basis as a citizen and an artist, far less willing to estrange or exile himself from the culture as Baldwin had done in going to live abroad.

Between Hughes, on one hand, and Baldwin and Ellison, on the other, was one difference far greater than any between the latter writers. While Langston psychologically needed the race in order to survive and flourish, their deepest needs as artists and human beings were evidently elsewhere. He wanted young black writers to be objective about the race, but not to scorn or to flee it. And all around him he saw young blacks confused by the rhetoric of integration and preparing to flee the race even when they made excoriating cries as exquisitely as Baldwin did in his essays. Baldwin's second novel had contained no black characters; his third would include blacks, but as characters secondary to his hero, a white American writer. To some extent, Baldwin was much more concerned with the mighty and dangerous challenge of illuminating—as a virtual pioneer in modern American fiction—the homosexual condition than with the challenge of writing about race, which by contrast had been exhaustively treated.

Although Langston did not dispute the right of black authors to tell any story they chose, a black writer's place was at home, which in Manhattan was Harlem—a perfectly fine place if not deserted by its human talent. At the end of the following year, 1960, when he spoke on the WABC television program "Expedition: New York," he stressed the positive. Harlem a congested area? "It is. Congested with people. All kinds. And I'm lucky enough to call a great many of them my friends." This cheerful, uncritical acceptance of Harlem was anathema to the tortured James Baldwin, whose "Fifth Avenue Uptown," his portrait of the Harlem community in *Esquire* magazine the previous July, had showed warts and only warts: poverty, degradation, filth, and "the silent, accumulating contempt and hatred of a people."

In the half-decade of integration since 1954, and despite stirring essays on race by Baldwin and other blacks, Langston was one of the few black writers of any consequence to champion racial consciousness as a source of inspiration for black artists. No such call came from Richard Wright, Gwendolyn Brooks, Melvin Tolson, Robert Hayden, Ralph Ellison, Chester Himes, or—to be sure—Frank Yerby, by far the most financially successful Afro-American author, as a writer of avidly read Southern romances. And, as the youngest writers began slowly to perceive an emptiness in their art and lives in spite of the afflated rhetoric of integration, they would turn to Hughes more than to any other living author. "Oh if the muse would let me travel through Harlem with you as the guide," Conrad Kent Rivers wrote to him, "I, too could sing of black America." "The Negro Speaks of Rivers," Rivers admitted, "changed my outlook toward myself as a Negro." Lorraine Hansberry, writing to Langston to dissociate herself from an *Esquire* attack on him by Baldwin which she allegedly had sanctioned, confirmed her regard for him "not only as my mentor but the poet laureate of our people." (As for Baldwin's attack on Langston, she told a journalist, "Jimmy shows Langston no *respect*. . . . He refers to Langston in public the way we niggers usually talk in private to each other.")

At least one older poet also seemed, at least for the moment, to be learning from Langston's example. Robert Hayden found himself marvelling at some poems by Hughes "because they were *about* something—not merely a display of technique. Poetry is becoming so damned *arty* these days—slick poems about fountains and statues. Too much Richard Wilbur elegance and not enough of the old-time guttiness. I see this clearly now that I have gotten past my own arty-elegant period of a few years back."

Baldwin's review of *Selected Poems* deeply offended Langston. In the right company, the mere mention of the younger writer's name would set Hughes to making sardonic remarks about his physical features. "Some things in his deepest nature came out, I guess," Raoul Abdul said later of his employer, who was "downright angry" at Baldwin for the review and "wanted somehow to get back." He devised at least one punishment. "For about a year," according to Abdul, "any time we received a request from a school or an organization for a free personal appearance by Langston—we got them all the time—he made me answer with the suggestion that the wonderful Negro author Mr. James Baldwin be contacted instead. Of course we made sure they had Baldwin's home address, so it would be easy for them to write to him."

Baldwin himself was probably unaware of the pain he had inflicted on Langston. But the pain was real, and would not be forgotten. Since Baldwin was now only infrequently in New York, years passed before he and Langston met by chance, at the popular Ginger Man restaurant near the newly opened Lincoln Center complex in Manhattan. Perhaps two versions of the meeting exist. "Langston and I were sitting there, eating," Raoul Abdul recalled, "when who should walk in but Jimmy Baldwin, his coat slung over his shoulder. He was genuinely glad to see Mr. Hughes. 'Langston!' he said out loud, and he kissed him on each cheek. I bent over and whispered to Mr. Hughes: 'The kiss of Judas.' Langston smiled and smiled. They were very nice to one another." The journalist William J. Weatherby remembered sitting in the Ginger Man once with Baldwin and a drunk young white friend of Baldwin's who had been causing trouble. "Baldwin, who was usually relaxed and philosophical about such occasions, was strangely embarrassed," Weatherby recalled, "and when I asked him what was bothering him, I was informed that Langston Hughes was sitting at a nearby table. It was as though his father had caught him in bad company; it at least reflected great respect. When we left, Baldwin went over to Langston Hughes and the two men, one black, one brown, one so slightly built, the other as round as an apple, shook hands and exchanged a few polite remarks. They both seemed extra courteous, in the way you are when you're uneasy with each other. Both extraordinary men, both eloquent spokesmen for the black experience in their totally different ways, they really had nothing to say to each other that night.''

Years later, Baldwin would think back to his review of *Selected Poems* with some misgiving: ''I hadn't really read the book, to tell the truth. I wrote the review without fully understanding what I was doing and saying.'' Some time later, in an interview with the writer Clayton Riley, he conceded the authenticity of Langston's voice: ''I suppose it's not too much to say that reading Langston made me understand something about my father's rages, and my mother's seeming passivity, and the people on the streets, the people in the church, the deacons, sisters and brothers. When I read Langston, it was like I was reading a book and looking up and what was on the page was in a sense right before my eyes. But he helped me to see it, you know. He helped me to locate myself in it.''

In spite of Baldwin's review, three days after it appeared the Countee Cullen Library was packed with Langston's Harlem admirers when he signed copies of his *Selected Poems*. The following night, he dashed from a revival of *Street Scene* to make a flight to St. Louis for another appearance before the kind of race audience he loved—a convention of the National Council of Negro Women. Readings followed in Nashville, Toronto, Toledo, and Ann Arbor before Langston returned to help celebrate African Freedom Day at Carnegie Hall on April 15 (the date set by the conference of independent African states in Accra, Ghana, that had called for the observance). There he recited his poetry to the sound of African percussion on a program that included the Nigerian drummer Olatunji, the Kenyan trade unionist and politician Tom Mboya, who was the chairman of the All-African People's Conference, Governor G. Mennen Williams of Michigan, who was regarded as an expert on Africa, and Harry Belafonte. (In the coming summer, Langston would devote almost a dozen of his *Defender* columns to Africa.) A week later, he joined Ralph Bunche and other prominent black and white leaders at a dinner downtown on Madison Avenue at which Samuel D. Proctor, the president of Virginia Union University, presented a confidential progress report on school desegregation in the South.

The cheerful picture of Harlem that Langston painted on television and elsewhere was not insincere. For all its crime and poverty, the Manhattan ghetto was his home. He loved its brashness and noise, its raucous gaiety and offbeat humor. To the extent that it knew him, Harlem returned his love. The local cultural institutions definitely could count on his support; he was not ''above'' any of them. He gave a lively reading at the Afro Arts Cultural Center on 126th Street in April, and in May the Manhattan Arts Theatre of Harlem presented him with an award of appreciation. On the street, too, he was known and loved. Raoul Abdul, who lived downtown, sometimes feared the Harlem streets, but Langston did not. ''He made so many friends up and down the block, everyone knew he was Langston Hughes,'' Abdul remembered. ''He could go to any of the bars he wanted to. People had a protective attitude toward him.'' He knew the good people and many of the bad. Once, he was stopped on 125th Street by ''a pick-pocket thug'' (as Langston remembered him), whom he had not seen in some time. The fellow explained that he had been serving time in the Tombs, a city jail. ''I had plenty time to read your book with the yellow pages,'' he assured Langston about an old copy of his first autobiography, ''—The Deep Sea—they got it in the library down there. It were fine!''

On the other hand, Langston was no fool about the worst changes sweeping through Harlem, especially as heroin and cocaine, long available in the community, began to devastate it. ''It was almost a sudden kind of thing,'' the jazz pianist Randy Weston recalled thirty years later. ''In the mid and late fifties, drugs just suddenly got out of hand. Places you could have gone easily before were now a battle zone, and you took your life into your hands going there. People you had grown up with and had known as good people were suddenly nodding off right out in public on stoops, and ripping other people off for drugs. It was something very sad and very frightening to watch, because it all happened so quickly, and it struck so deep.'' Hughes's sense of a possible rift between himself and the latest generation of the race was heightened by a visit from a young, distant cousin from the Midwest, ''a basically nice kid, but with some WILD Chicago ways,'' as Langston characterized them, whose comings and goings so fascinated Langston that he kept a carefully typed schedule of his erratic, irresponsible movements over a period of two weeks. The teenager's almost complete lack of moral sense and inhibition dismayed him, but Langston declined to moralize to his cousin, who cheerfully confided his escapades, including the deflowering of a virgin in Langston's bed while he was out of the house.

Hughes saw a similar fatalism and irresponsibility spreading among an entire generation of the race—its youth. Certainly the new black writers were doing well, he knew; ''but young ones who can't make art out of their derelictions, where are they going? 'Montage of a dream deferred—daddy, ain't you heard? . . . . Lenox Avenue headed toward the Park—faster, faster, faster after dark. . . . . ' '' Still, he could not bring himself to denounce or rebuke or criticize an entire generation of his own people. As for his wild Chicago cousin, he not only forgave him his trespasses, but dedicated one of his ''juvenile'' books to him.

Measuring other places against Harlem, Langston found most wanting. In May, following a visit to Washington, D.C., and Cleveland to record poems at the Library of Congress and to see productions of *Simply Heavenly,* he flew to Bermuda at the invitation of the women's auxiliary of the local chapter of the Alpha Phi Alpha fraternity. ''Folks treated me so nice . . . I ought to love their Island, too—but NOT I. Nay!'' With dull music, duller dance, and no lilting dialects as in the other islands, Bermuda was not sufficiently African and tropical for his taste—although he did not want his opinion known. As green as North Carolina, it was ''almost as segregated, full of British crackers.'' He was glad to come home. ''HOW BEAUTIFUL Idlewild Airport this afternoon!!!!'' he rejoiced to Arna Bontemps. ''How nice this New York heat in nice noisy Harlem!''

Others could flee the race, or worry about the Hungarians and such; he would worry about blacks, and love them, and do what was necessary (while certain other black writers kept their distance) in order to allow blacks to be seen and heard. For the CBS television network's religious series ''Lamp Unto My Feet,'' he prepared a script, including songs for the deep-voiced folksinger Odetta and a black church choir. When CBS asked him to tone down his text because he had stressed the political role of religion during slavery, Langston quickly touched it up with whitewash to allow ''the lack of bitterness, no desire for revenge, in the spirituals'' to come through. Approved, the show was recorded later that summer in a black church in Montclair, New Jersey. With pleasure, and for $400, he wrote an introduction to a Bantam Books edition of *The Tragedy of Pudd'nhead Wilson,* Mark Twain's ''ironic little novel'' of miscegenation. Long an admirer of Mark Twain (Cyril Clemens, the president of the International Mark Twain Society, had nominated Langston as an honorary member in 1950, and as a ''Knight'' in 1952), Hughes saw him standing ''head and shoulders above the other Southern writers of his time'' in his depiction of blacks as neither pure heroes nor horrible villains but plain ''human beings.''

In his allusion, Langston may also have had in mind a more recent Southern writer, William Faulkner, as well as the revival of the old literary tendency, as Langston saw it, to depict blacks as vile. In January, he had endured the Broadway premiere of Faulkner's *Requiem for a Nun,* with Bertice Reading (from the London production of *Simply Heavenly*) as ''the cullud dope-taking servant-whore,'' as he identified her in a letter. ''The best critic there,'' he judged sourly, ''was a member of the Race who sat just behind me and snored real loud for *long* stretches at a time.'' Langston's hostility to Faulkner was doubtless colored by reports (misleading, according to Faulkner, who indeed had been on record in favor of racial equality) of an interview in February, 1956, in which Faulkner seemed to endorse shooting down blacks in the streets if they threatened the security of the white South. *Requiem for a Nun* only confirmed Langston's suspicions about Faulkner's social vision. Langston was far more tolerant of comic distortions of black life, as when on August 30 he published a favorable review in the New York *Herald-Tribune* of Avery E. Kolb's *Jigger Whitchet's War,* a book which to some observers was a vulgar burlesque of black life and culture.

That summer, Langston said goodbye to Raoul Abdul, who left after two years as his secretary to study lieder and oratorio at the Academy of Music in Vienna. His loyal friend of many years Adele Glasgow still helped him on occasion, but up from Nashville to train as a replacement, on Arna Bontemps's recommendation, came George Houston Bass, a ''quiet and unconspicuous'' new graduate of Fisk University in mathematics, bound for business school at Columbia University. On Langston's side, he hoped only that Bass would be "not TOO energetic. Some secretaries will work a writer to death." As for being quiet, "I wouldn't care if he was a Mau Mau," as long as he could type accurately. By June that year, 1959, young Bass was living at 20 East 127th Street. He would remain Langston's secretary until July, 1964. "By that time," Bass later recalled, "I had long given up thoughts of business school. Columbia had been a harsh and unhappy experience, for some reasons having to do with racism and some that were my own fault, not knowing who I was and what I really wanted to do. Living and working with Langston Hughes revolutionized my life. He steeped me in black American culture, when I had thought I knew it well; and he showed me what could be done as an artist, what needed to be done. Before I understood what was happening, I was in some ways completely different from the youth who had come up from the South."

In the South that summer, the various drives by black and white civil rights workers to register black voters were countered by the rise of White Citizens Councils. Attempts at federally mandated school desegregation were met not only by white civil unrest but also by legislation, in Georgia for example, designed to bolster the declining power of Jim Crow. Ominously, the first lynching of a black in four years was reported in Mississippi. Also ominously, but virtually without modern precedent, an NAACP official in North Carolina, Robert Williams, advocated the use of violence against violence, lynching against lynching. Although he was immediately suspended by the Association, the notion of a coming racial conflagration began to gather strength as the summer arrived. The increase in tension in the black communities of the North was also noticeable, although as yet they had been largely exempt from the kind of strife common in the South. One result of the deterioration of mood in the North was that Langston found himself in even greater demand. Early in August, a crew from CBS television came to his house to film part of a documentary. Later that month, he watched himself on the program, "Harlem: A Self-Portrait," as he tried to explain Harlem's attitudes and hopes, its chronic problems and their possible solutions.

In fact, his summer passed peacefully. After composing liner notes for *My Lord, What a Mornin'*, a recording of spirituals by Harry Belafonte, Langston attended the annual Newport Jazz Festival over the Fourth of July holiday. However, the weather there was damp and chilly, and the festival something of a bore, perhaps because too many "pop" musicians, notably the "Four Freshmen" vocal group, had been invited. On July 19, he played only a minor role in an uneventful NAACP rally at the Polo Grounds uptown in Manhattan. One evening, he donned black tie for a gala reception given by Nnamdi Azikiwe, now the Governor-General of Nigeria, in the Empire Room at the Waldorf-Astoria, and was rewarded with the pleasant task of escorting home Eartha Kitt (whose praises he had sung in an entire *Defender* column in April, 1957). As for writing, Langston did little that summer of much consequence. At the request of a little-known composer, he finished the libretto for a one-act opera, "Adam and Eve and the Apple" (which was probably never set to music); and he wrote one of his now infrequent short stories, "Sorrow for a Midget," which went eventually to a literary magazine at Fairleigh Dickinson University.

Unquestionably the most entertaining evening that summer for Langston was at Lucille Lortel's innovative White Barn Theater in Westport, Connecticut, on the last Saturday of August, when he attended the first of two productions of *Shakespeare in Harlem*, a one-act play "by" Langston Hughes, "adapted" by Robert Glenn. An amalgam of vignettes from Langston's works, the little play had been entirely put together by Glenn, a young white dramatist and director who had first staged the show at the Little Theatre in Dallas, Texas. The effect, in general, was stunning, with one young actor stopping the show with a moving rendition of the poem "Theme for English B" from *Montage of a Dream Deferred*. The mellow beauty of *Shakespeare in Harlem* so charmed Langston that he returned the following day with Stella Holt to see what he would recall as "about the loveliest show I ever had." With enthusiastic audiences and praise from *Variety* magazine as "a lusty Harlem sideshow set to the imaginative cadences" of Hughes's poetry, Lucille Lortel decided to make *Shakespeare in Harlem* part of a special matinee series of the American National Theatre and Academy—she was artistic director of its New York chapter—to be presented at her Theatre de Lys in Greenwich Village. Not long afterwards, for use as a prelude to *Shakespeare in Harlem*, Langston wrote "Mister Jazz," a brief, dramatic panorama of the history of black dancing.

At long last, also, *Tambourines to Glory*, Hughes's gospel musical play with Jobe Huntley, began to move. The English edition of the novel had just emerged to superb reviews. *Tambourines to Glory* was "a small masterpiece" and "a minor classic of its kind," and Langston Hughes was William Saroyan, J. D. Salinger, and Damon Runyon rolled into one in a tale "brilliantly executed, excruciatingly funny." Earlier in the year, Langston had sent the veteran producer Lawrence Langner of the Theatre Guild the script of the play—and a pointed reminder: "There has not been a bang-up good Negro *singing* show on Broadway for a long time. And, so far as I know, this new genre, the gospel song, has not been used in the theatre at all." Admitting that tight play construction was not his forte, Langston bowed to Langner, "a top-notch playdoctor," and made several suggested changes that "immensely improved" the script. Although Langner could not guarantee a production, which would require a budget of $150,000, he had sent out the script to prospective directors.

In October, to Langston's joy, the Theatre Guild announced that it would make *Tambourines to Glory* its third production that year. The first two had done poorly, but Langston hoped for the best. Herbert Machiz, who had directed the City Center revival of *Street Scene*, as well as important productions of dramas by Tennessee Williams, would stage the musical play. But when Langston eagerly set about the business of securing stars for the various roles, he met unexpected resistance. Few seemed interested in this pioneering gospel entertainment. Citing her doctor's orders, Pearl Bailey declined a part. After a long, tantalizing talk with Langston, Mahalia Jackson stuck by her determination, as a devout member of the National Baptist Convention, never to sing the gospel in a theater. In vain, Langston approached the former boxing champion Sugar Ray Robinson first as a potential backer, then as an actor. Soon he was after Della Reese, Leontyne Price, William Warfield, Nipsey Russell, and—or so it seemed—every prominent black star with whom he had the slightest contact. To his growing surprise, none jumped at the chance to star in his gospel show.

Puzzled and disappointed, Langston left the United States for his first visit to the Caribbean since 1947. In the first week of November, after "a glittering affair" at the Waldorf Astoria—a dinner by the American Society for African Culture in honor of Sékou Touré, the president of Guinea—Langston flew to Trinidad in the West Indies to deliver a series of readings and lectures. One person in particular looked forward to his coming: Anne Marie Coussey Wooding, his girlfriend "Mary" of Paris in 1924 in *The Big Sea*. "Mary" was now the wife of perhaps the most prominent black lawyer in Trinidad, H. O. B. Wooding. She had "a wonderful husband" of whom she was "very proud, and four grown up children who make me feel very old, at times." Thirty-five years before, she had wondered openly whether her young American friend, this dabbler in poetry who was wasting his time as a dishwasher in a vile Place Pigalle nightclub, would ever amount to anything. "Through the years," she wrote now, "I have caught glimpses of you in many ways through your talent. I am so happy that you have been such an outstanding success, and have reached the top." She recalled "those carefree days" in Paris, which "I have always treasured."

In eleven days in Trinidad, Langston made four appearances to read poems and lecture on black American poetry and race relations in America to audiences caught up in the heady march of the British West Indies towards independence, which would come three years later to Trinidad and Tobago. Since Langston's visit to Jamaica in 1947, the predominantly black populations of the British Caribbean had taken brave strides away from colonialism. At a dinner before the opening of Parliament, Langston renewed his acquaintance, made on that visit, with Edna Manley and her husband Norman Manley, the Jamaican leader. He was also entertained by the premier of Trinidad and Tobago, the Oxford-trained historian Eric Williams, who had taught for some years as a professor at Howard University in Washington, D.C. The Trotskyite intellectual C. L. R. James, who served as the main propagandist of Williams's party, the People's National Movement, introduced the visitor in his lectures at the Public Library in Port-of-Spain. There, Langston met "the very good poet" Derek Walcott of St. Lucia, still almost unknown outside of the Caribbean. ("What I remember most about Langston," Walcott judged many years later, "is his hearty, immediate laughter. There was a sense of fun in it, fun that had come from experience. It was very refreshing.") He also met Walcott's fiancée Margaret Maillard, a cousin of Sylvia Chen, Langston's Moscow sweetheart of 1933. A poetry-to-jazz reading filled the Little Carib Theatre run by Beryl McBurnie, known to him during her days in New York as the dancer "La

Belle Rosette." Dining at "Woodhurst," the handsome home of Anne and Hugh Wooding, he talked with her about Paris and about their mutual friend Rayford Logan, who had brought them together, and who was now an eminent historian at Howard University. A long, dusty drive to an asphalt lake, of which Trinidadians were inordinately proud, left him weary and irritated. But to the *Trinidad Guardian* Langston diplomatically expressed his hope for "one big commercial hit and then I'd come down here to live and drink some rum."

After some carefree days as "James Hughes" in Grenada, Martinique, and Puerto Rico, Langston returned on the day before Thanksgiving to New York, where he found good news and bad. The producer David Suskind intended to feature *Simply Heavenly* on his "Play of the Week" program on New York's Channel 13, and the show was already in rehearsal. On the other hand, *Tambourines to Glory* was stalled indefinitely, with Lawrence Langner of the Theatre Guild now seriously ill in a Manhattan hospital.

Disappointed, Langston returned to his smaller projects. By mid-December, deep in African material for his "African Treasury" anthology, he also prepared to help ship the books and art objects donated to the "Gifts for Ghana" project. The drive had been a success. Among the many black writers solicited for contributions, "All but 4 writers (3 of whom are abroad) sent Gifts for Ghana. Even Baldwin from Paris. Our greatest one here didn't. Maybe might will yet. (Guess who?)" Responding to an appeal from Martin Luther King, Jr., he composed and sent "Poem for a Man" to be read at a Carnegie Hall tribute to the veteran labor leader A. Philip Randolph and also seized the opportunity to express again to King his "greatest admiration for you and your work." When publicity on television, including the showing of *Simply Heavenly*, generated too many calls, Langston cut off his phone and posted "OUT OF TOWN" notices all over the house while he closed out work on his African anthology. On Christmas day, he was on the screen again, appearing live on CBS Television's "Christmas, USA" to send holiday greetings on behalf of Harlem.

A bad cold ruined a visit early in the new year, 1960, to his Uncle John and his cousin Flora Coates in Los Angeles. When he returned home, the prospect of a reading tour in February added to his sense of tiredness and depression. At fifty-eight, Langston was sick of the road, if he had to earn his keep there; sick, too—at least for the moment—of his typewriter. No respite was in sight. At the invitation of the Ford Foundation, he had applied for a fellowship to study the latest trends in popular theater in Paris, but in January he learned that he had been turned down. He finished "An African Treasury" and turned it in to Crown Publishers. Then, unwillingly, he faced the road. Making hay was wearying business, especially in the autumn of one's life. "Like Pearl Bailey," he moaned, " 'Ah'm taired'."

The tour lived up to his fears. In the years since 1953 and his appearance before Senator Joseph McCarthy, right-wing attacks on Langston had never ceased entirely, although the U.S. State Department itself had invited him to lecture overseas and regularly asked him to receive various foreign visitors to New York. But his rising popularity had revived his enemies. An article called "Langston Hughes: Malevolent Force" in the anti-communist magazine *American Mercury* had declared: "The record of this writer is plain, for all to see. From the first, it was and is pro-Communist." Specifically, the author pointed to Braziller's thick *Langston Hughes Reader* and the inclusion by the Methodist Church ("strong arm of the National Council of Churches") of Hughes's work on a reading list recommended for study by church groups. Such events "justify definitive research on Langston Hughes." The current mode in literature was to load the text, "to varying degrees, with depravities, obscenities, and miscellaneous, malodorous barnyard dirt. Hughes goes far beyond the call of duty in piling filth on filth." Most of the article, in fact, was a reprisal of the charges against Hughes as compiled up to 1953 by various investigating bodies.

He was not long on the road when trouble flared. In Buffalo, a bomb threat brought a squad of policemen to his reading. When no explosive device was found, Langston read his poems, but nervously. Recently, he joked, the same thing had happened at the same place to Robert Frost, "so we figure somebody in town just doesn't like poets." However, when some white churchmen in Grand Rapids, Michigan, provoked by conservative forces, objected to his coming, Langston abruptly cancelled his visit. Blaming influenza, he also showed an unusual degree of irritability. "I thought such stupid attacks had ceased," he wrote to a sponsor about the right-wingers behind the trouble. "I haven't got the energy (nor patience) right now to battle their thickheadedness." Then, with an effort, he recovered his sense of humor. "If I were feeling O.K. I wouldn't mind battling it out," but in his present state, he "might cuss them out instead (smile)."

Soon, having met his other speaking obligations, including a major visit to Detroit, he sent out the word that he wanted no more engagements outside of New York City for at least a year. Ironically, the opposition to his visit by churchmen had come after weeks in which Langston's interest in religion had appeared to deepen. Starting the previous year on November 22, he had devoted almost a dozen of his *Defender* columns to outlining the tenets of various religions. "Understanding is necessary for respect and tolerance toward other faiths," he explained. "And the meanings of religious differences is a fascinating study in itself." In January, he had proposed a "First Book of Prayer" to Franklin Watt. When the idea was rejected, he compiled an international collection of prayers to offer to other publishers. And on January 31, after several rehearsals with a church choir, he had presented the first program in what he hoped would be a series on religious songs and poems at the black Antioch Baptist Church in Brooklyn.

At times, Langston's deepening involvement in religion seems to have been more a gambit than the mark of a new personal piety. Perhaps it was also strategic, as he sought to counter, as best he could, his almost ineradicable reputation as an atheist. However, he made no effort to appear pious in public, and attached himself to no church. His deepening involvement was professional and cautious but probably, at the same time, also genuine. In the last column in his *Defender* series on religion, "The Meaning of Faith: Personal," he gave some indication of his beliefs. "Were I asked to preach a sermon about God," he wrote, "I would have to begin by saying that I don't know very much about God—but I have a feeling that God is related to everything and everybody on earth." God was everywhere, in all countries and among all people.

Can I say that there is no God in Georgia simply because Jim Crow makes more headlines? God may keep silent for a long time, but when He speaks the map of history is changed. When He speaks, the slate is wiped clean. When He speaks, sorrow runs like a river to the sea and the land is cleansed again. Do you think that God is gone just because He is banned somewhere? Who can ban God? Or you, His child? Or me, the least of his children? Try to step between me and God—and you will be thinner than a shadow and less of a wall than the evening fog. So I would end my sermon on God.

Back in Manhattan after his troubled reading tour, Langston found his and Robert Glenn's *Shakespeare in Harlem* uneasily installed at the 41st Street Theatre on a budget of only $15,000. Godfrey Cambridge and Isabel Sanford sparkled in the cast, but attendance was sparse. This was curious, since the reviews had been fine. Adding *Shakespeare in Harlem* to *Simply Heavenly,* the veteran critic Brooks Atkinson pronounced, "Langston Hughes begins to cast a long shadow." Although *Shakespeare in Harlem* was hardly a play, "the delicacy of feeling it discloses, the idiomatic music of the lines and the immaculate taste of the performance endow it with thoughtful beauty." This delicacy of feeling and taste without a sacrifice of the exuberant aspect of black American culture was exactly Langston's goal. He hoped that the play would catch on with the public.

Early in March, however, *Shakespeare in Harlem* succumbed on Broadway after only thirty-two performances. The play closed in a tempest of bad faith. Seizing the box-office door and refusing to let go, one distraught woman, an investor, created at least as much dramatic tension in the lobby as on the stage. Bad faith seemed to Langston, at the moment, epidemic. At the first rehearsal for a concert version of *The Barrier,* held at his home in his absence, Muriel Rahn and Jan Meyerowitz exploded at one another, while a second singer wept hysterically. "I were not present," Langston intoned to Arna Bontemps, "and have shut off my phone to keep from being bothered."

Accepting another Broadway defeat, Langston consoled himself with the knowledge that, whatever its limitations as commercial theater on Broadway, *Shakespeare in Harlem* had offered its audience a fair and engaging lyric portrait of the black experience. As such, Hughes and Robert Glenn's drama contrasted particularly with the tone and spirit of certain other plays on Broadway. On February 17, for example, Langston had readily attended but only barely endured the premiere of *The Long Dream,* a dramatization by Ketti Frings of the novel with which Richard Wright, an exile for over a decade with his wife and children in Paris, had tried to recapture the spirit of the South he had fled over thirty years before. In the play, as Langston saw it, Wright's black women seemed almost all to be whores, the black men mainly brutes, "with only moments here and there real enough on stage to seem real in real life." Affronted, Sidney Poitier had stalked out of the theater after the first act. Langston himself stayed to the end, but was appalled by Wright's degrading depiction of black people. This depiction only added, he said, to the sorry record of Broadway, from O'Neill to the present, in portraying blacks. "Dear Lord! How long is the list of plays in which the Negro is defeated in the end!" he complained in the *Defender*. "We ain't no good, we got no strength, we are undone and done in long before the curtain falls."

He could not understand why a black writer would thus present his people on the stage. *The Long Dream* seemed part of the moral deterioration of the age, part of the destruction and, in some cases, the self-destructiveness, of black culture. Most appalling to him in the dramas of teenage rebellion which were increasingly in vogue on the American stage and screen was the depiction of black youths as beyond redemption. "Am I becoming oversensitive racially, and NAACP-ish?" he asked in January, recoiling from the play *The Cool World,* based on a novel of the same name by Warren Miller—"a holy horror with nobody at all sympathetic or likable." "A 14 year old strumpet and a 15 year old pimp and a 16 year old junkie whose brother goes to Fisk," he protested, "is just *un peu trop!* . . . . If I'm over sensitive, tell me. I tries to be objective." Harlem was becoming more dangerous, but his love for the people and his faith in the young were not lessened. "None are *that* bad," he insisted. "Oh, well, set back 50 years again! But the last setback—when it comes—will be the boomerang that will set back the setter-backers!" (In contrast, James Baldwin endorsed *The Cool World* as "one of the finest novels about Harlem that had ever come my way.")

As if in direct response to what he saw as the slandering of black youth, the day after seeing *The Cool World* Langston wrote to Bernard Perry at Indiana University Press to suggest an anthology of recent poetry by young black writers. Reminding Perry that no collection of black poets had been published in ten years, or since his and Arna Bontemps's *The Poetry of the Negro* in 1949, he stressed that among the writers not included in that anthology were about a dozen "quite good ones, some young." When Perry's response was favorable, Langston began at once to solicit material for "New Negro Poets."

His involvement with the younger writers and black youth in general was fortified towards the end of the winter of 1960 when Langston made two trips into the South that took him close to major theaters of the civil rights struggle. On February 1, the campaign had taken a dramatic and historic turn. On that day, four black freshmen from North Carolina A. and T. College in Greensboro had quietly claimed seats at a whites-only Woolworth lunch counter and refused to move when they were denied service. The "sit-in" tactic, enforced thereafter across the South by thousands of daring students, black and white, spread quickly to challenge segregrated beaches, libraries, churches, and other public institutions. Langston followed the news of the sit-ins with keen interest, especially the news from Nashville. In February, Arna Bontemps's youngest child, Alex, was one of seventy-six Fisk University students jailed after an attempt to desegregate a local Woolworth lunch counter. When Z. Alexander Looby, in whose law firm Arna's son-in-law Avon Williams was a partner, undertook to defend the Fisk students in court, his home was bombed.

In this new, confrontational stage of the Movement, the students across the South were supported initially by three established civil rights organizations, then began to rely almost exclusively on one that was radically new. James Farmer's Congress of Racial Equality, Martin Luther King, Jr.'s Southern Christian Leadership Conference, and the NAACP all backed the sit-ins. To facilitate the campaign, however, and with the special blessing of King's group, the Student Non-Violent Coordinating Committee was formed. With this event, the leadership of the most perilous aspect of the civil rights struggle passed largely into the hands of the young.

On Friday, March 11, the biggest local snowfall in memory thickened the skies over Atlanta as Langston prepared to read his poems to the women students in Rockefeller Hall at Spelman College. But the weather was as nothing compared to the tension nearby on the campus of Atlanta University, where black students defied the attempts of armed white police and a police dog to eject "loiterers" from a campus drugstore. Langston read his poems at dignified Spelman, but he was hungry for inside reports about the confrontation. One youth, he heard, coolly asked a red-faced policeman to define "loiterer"; another, a veteran of Korea, made a crisp promise: "I will kick that dog in the teeth if you sic him on me!" Completely unaccustomed to black defiance, the embarrassed and angry white police withdrew, but threatened to return. "Those college kids down there," Langston soon wrote to the "Beat" poet LeRoi Jones, "are *TREMENDOUS!*" The students were "GREAT," especially in their utter fearlessness: "And not being afraid, they are beginning to win."

As a series of readings in North Carolina drew near, the administrators of one black college, fearing the strength left in an old lion, begged Langston not to roar too loudly during his expected visit. "I writ back," he tittered mischievously, "I am just reading my same old 'deep like the rivers'." But many of his poems, although some were forty years old, were inspirational tracts for the present time. On the other hand, he had no intention of playing the racial demagogue. At the University of North Carolina in Chapel Hill, the scene of one of his bravest hours, when he had risked his life to defy segregation on his tour of the South in 1931, Langston carried himself with both dignity and modesty on a campus that in 1960 still had needed to debate the wisdom of inviting a Negro to speak. "White" and "Colored" signs still endorsed Jim Crow, and two local movie houses denied admission to blacks, as did all the motels. To one white observer, Hughes epitomized "gentleness and humanity" even as he reminisced about his tempestuous visit in 1931. Unlike other famous writers to visit Chapel Hill, Langston Hughes was entirely unaffected: "Indeed, he could ask directions to the men's room without an epigram.'' Neither a vaudeville entertainer nor a patrician poet in his demeanor, ''he seemed incapable of regarding himself with undue seriousness.'' As he reminisced about his life, however, Langston also managed to exude, along with his wit and humor, more than a trace of sadness at the inhumanity of American culture. ''We had intended to bring to the University a Negro spokesman under the guise of a poet but, in the end, we got a human being instead.''

For all his modesty, Langston eagerly looked to the day when the gifted young writers of his race would go beyond the clamor for civil rights and integration and take a genuine pride in being black. As he prepared his anthology for Indiana University Press, he found this latter quality starkly absent in even the best of them—poets such as LeRoi Jones, Julian Bond (the son of Horace Mann Bond, the president of Lincoln University), Oliver Pitcher, Ted Joans, Conrad Kent Rivers, Samuel Allen (also known as Paul Vesey and James B. Smith), and Calvin Hernton. Some of the poets were gifted, and some of their poems were moving, but too many seemed eager to avoid the central social fact of their lives—that they were blacks in white America—or to avoid looking for artistic inspiration in native black forms such as blues and jazz, as Langston had been advocating, with only limited success among other black writers, since the 1920s. The result was, in most cases, pallid rhythms and weakly motivated verse by otherwise vigorous young men and women. From this racial point of view, Langston's favorite among them, LeRoi Jones, was perhaps the most troubling, since he was clearly the most gifted.

Born in Newark, New Jersey, and educated at Howard University, Jones at twenty-six had emerged as a leader in the most progressive poetry circles in Greenwich Village—and the United States. With the white poet Diane DiPrima, he edited *Yugen* magazine, of which Langston was well aware (although he persisted for some time in calling it ''*Yungen*''). Being in a position to pass judgment, however marginally, on the work of some of the most adventurous younger white writers in the nation, including Allen Ginsberg, Gregory Corso, Gary Snyder, Gilbert Sorrentino, and Jack Kerouac, Jones held a place of authority virtually unprecedented among black Americans. Only William Stanley Braithwaite early in the century, with his Boston newspaper reviews and his influential annual anthologies of magazine verse, had enjoyed a similar prestige.

Langston was impressed by this involvement by a young black—but not entirely so. ''Who wants to be Beat?'' he pointedly had asked the AMSAC black writers in February, 1959. ''Not Negroes. That is what this conference is all about—how *not* to be Beat.'' More than once, perhaps snidely, he had asked if the poet and editor LeRoi Jones were indeed black. One day, Jones had telephoned Langston's home to leave a message clearing up the ''mystery.'' Jones finally met Hughes—but apparently without Langston realizing it. ''It was at the Village Vanguard, when he was appearing with Mingus and Phineas Newborn,'' Jones recalled more than twenty years later. ''I went up to him and introduced myself. But I guess he didn't catch my name, with all the

Portrait by Henri Cartier-Bresson, 1956. *Magnum Photos.*

On Broadway, 1957.

At Newport Jazz Festival, with Ralph Ellison and James Baldwin, 1958.

In Chicago, 1960. *Photo by Roy DeCarava.*

At the Spingarn Medal award ceremony, 1960. Behind Hughes, Arthur B. Spingarn.

With Sunday Osuya and Janet Osuya, Lagos, Nigeria, 1961.

At the White House, 1962. Aaron Douglas, John F. Kennedy, Charles Wesley.

With Chinua Achebe, Lagos, 1962.

With Loften Mitchell, Market Place Gallery, Harlem, 1962.

With Arna Bontemps, 1962.

noise, although he was very polite, because I heard later that he was asking about me.'' Earlier, liking one of Jones's published poems, Langston had astonished the younger man by writing to him ("He sent me a letter, and I'd never talked to him before in my life. He sent me a letter and said he liked the poem!''). Then he had dispatched a recommendation on Jones's behalf for a fellowship from the Whitney Foundation. Langston also submitted his own and other material to *Yugen,* solicited back issues of the journal, and called attention to its editor in the *Defender:* ''LEROI JONES represents color within the Beat Generation very well because his poetry is good and the little magazine he publishes in the Village, 'Yungen,' is quite worth reading. With his beard he looks like Othello. Beat—but all reet!''

For a fellowship earmarked for young black writers, Langston nominated, in descending order of importance, Jones, Julian Bond, Oliver Pitcher, and Conrad Kent Rivers. But he was not convinced that Jones, in working so far outside the race, was serving his own talent, much less black people, in the most advantageous way.

On March 23, Langston sent the first draft of his anthology of work by forty-six black poets to Bernard Perry. Obviously unsure himself about the quality of some of the poems, he asked Perry for ''your quite *frank* comments, please.'' When Perry's poetry editor, David Wagoner, found the volume unacceptable as it stood, with only twenty-three publishable poems out of a much larger number, Langston quickly agreed to cast his net again.

This task lasted most of the spring. In June, due for a vacation, Langston took it. That month, the illustrated *Holiday* magazine carried a major essay by Peter Abrahams, ''The Meaning of Harlem,'' Among its portraits of the community's leaders was a splendid study of the ''world-famous poet'' Langston Hughes in Mt. Morris Park. Behind him was Harlem's decrepit share of Fifth Avenue, which glittered only near the dividing line at Central Park North, and below it. ''Mr. Hughes has lived in Harlem for many years,'' the magazine noted; ''his affection for the district has been called a long and beautiful love affair.'' As if on cue, Langston flew south for a two-week holiday in Puerto Rico and the Virgin Islands.

He had planned to return for a celebration of Carl Van Vechten's eightieth birthday, but an airline strike kept ''James Hughes'' in San Juan past the event. He was still in Puerto Rico, at the Caribe Hilton, when a telegram from Henry Lee Moon of the NAACP informed him that the organization had chosen him to receive the forty-fifth annual Spingarn Medal. Exultant, Langston returned on June 22 to New York, where he found a telegram from Amy Spingarn: ''WARMEST CONGRATULATIONS! IT HAS LONG BEEN MY ARDENT WISH THAT YOU RECEIVE THE SPINGARN MEDAL—AND I AM DELIGHTED, AND OVERJOYED THAT IT HAS AT LONG LAST BEEN AWARDED TO YOU.''

Although Langston did not know it, his selection had hardly been unanimous. In beating out Gwendolyn Brooks, Lorraine Hansberry, and the four Greensboro, N.C., sit-in students (after Roy Wilkins, the executive secretary of the NAACP, carefully reminded the selectors that the medal was never intended to be a civil rights award), Langston had been the first choice of two of the six judges, and the second choice of another judge. He was neither the first nor the second choice of the other three judges.

On June 25 he flew to St. Paul, Minnesota, the site of the fifty-first NAACP convention. The next day, sixteen hundred delegates at Northrup Auditorium heard their executive secretary Roy Wilkins appeal passionately to frightened Southern whites and timid Northern liberals to join blacks in a new American crusade. Then Arthur B. Spingarn, introducing Langston to the convention, presented him with the award he had so long coveted.

His brief speech was as carefully sculpted as if it were for the Nobel Prize in Literature (which a Venezuelan newspaper, *El Universal,* later that year, in November, insisted he should win). Quoting "The Negro Speaks of Rivers," "Merry-Go-Round," and "I, Too, Sing America," Langston acknowledged his primal debt as a poet to the black tales and songs of his boyhood in Kansas and Ohio. He asserted the dignity of black America, the compatibility of its culture with great art, and the boundless potential of the black artist who chooses to write about his people instead of fleeing from them in confusion and shame.

His own example was clear. It would be "of the utmost conceit," Langston said, to accept the medal "in my name alone; or in the name of literature, which is my field. I can accept it only in the name of the Negro people who have given me the materials out of which my poems and stories, plays and songs, have come; and who, over the years, have given me as well their love and understanding and support.

Without them, on my part, there would have been no poems; without their hopes and fears and dreams, no stories; without their struggles, no dramas; without their music, no songs.

Had I not heard as a child in the little churches of Kansas and Missouri, "Deep river, my home is over Jordan," or "My Lord, what a morning when the stars begin to fall," I might not have come to realize the lyric beauty of *living* poetry. . . .

There is so much richness in Negro humor, so much beauty in black dreams, so much dignity in our struggle, and so much universality in our problems, in *us*—in each living human being of color—that I do not understand the tendency today that some American Negro artists have of seeking to run away from themselves, of running away from *us*, of being afraid to sing our own songs, paint our pictures, write about ourselves—when it is our music that has given America its greatest music, our humor that has enriched its entertainment media for the past 100 years, our rhythm that has guided its dancing feet from plantation days to the Charleston. . . . Yet there are some of us who say, "Why write about Negroes? Why not be *just a writer?*" And why not—if one wants to be "just a writer?" Negroes in a free world should be whatever each wants to be—even if it means being "just a writer." . . .

There is nothing to be ashamed of in the strength and dignity and laughter of the Negro people. And there is nothing to be afraid of in the use of their material.

Could you be possibly afraid that the rest of the world will not accept it? Our spirituals are sung and loved in the great concert halls of the whole world. Our blues are played from Topeka to Tokyo. Harlem's jive talk delights Hong Kong and Paris. Those of our writers who have *most* concerned themselves with our very special problems are translated and read around the world. The local, the regional can—and does—become universal. Sean O'Casey's Irishmen are an example. So I would say to young Negro writers, do not be afraid of yourself. *You* are the world. . . .

At a news conference after the ceremony Langston defended the sit-in demonstrations in the South, which some people insisted on seeing as dangerously counterproductive. Much had changed since his own attacks on Jim Crow in the early 1930s, but not the basic issue of social rights for blacks in the South, where changes had come only after bitter protest. About his role as a writer in an era of confrontation, he was less certain. No art in itself could change the world, but perhaps his writings had helped a little to blunt the force of racism.

Proud of his medal and what it signified about his place within black America, Langston returned to Harlem. A day or so later, he left on his annual visit to Newport, Rhode Island, for the Newport Jazz Festival. Recently, little of artistic significance had come out of the gathering. Loyally, however, Langston had continued to attend and to serve on its board of directors. The festival of 1960 would be different.

12

ASK YOUR MAMA!
1960 to 1961

TELL ME, TELL ME, MAMA,
ALL THAT MUSIC, ALL THAT DANCING
CONCENTRATED TO THE ESSENCE
OF THE SHADOW OF A DOLLAR
PAID AT THE BOX OFFICE
WHERE THE LIGHTER IS THE DARKER
IN THE QUARTER OF THE NEGROES
AND THE TELL ME OF THE MAMA
IS THE ANSWER TO THE CHILD . . .

Ask Your Mama, 1961

O N THE MORNING of Saturday, July 2, 1960, as Langston slept late in his room at the local Hotel Viking, a huge traffic jam began to clog the approaches to Newport, Rhode Island, and jam the city streets. The major phase of the five-day Newport Jazz Festival was clearly going to be a success. At Freebody Park, its main venue, the Festival had opened on Thursday with Cannonball Adderly, the local Newport Youth Band, and various modern small combos and old-time piano players. On Friday, as Langston later reported, "three swinging groups displayed their wares: Dizzy Gillespie, Gerry Mulligan, and Louis Armstrong. Freebody Park jumped, and the festivities seemed rolling merrily on toward a whaling [*sic*] Fourth of July."

On Saturday night, a capacity audience quickly took every seat in Freebody Park to listen to the music of an excellent collection of jazz talent—the Horace Silver Quintet, the Canadian pianist Oscar Peterson, the singer Dakota Staton, the jazz vocal trio of Lambert, Hendricks, and Ross, and Ray Charles and his group. Unfortunately, even more people were shut out. Teased by the amplified jazz music and in an increasingly vile, rebellious mood encouraged by beer-drinking, a crowd of about three thousand persons—mostly young white men—gathered outside the park. Hoping against hope for admission, some began to jeer at the puny contingent of local police between them and the seats inside. Soon, a boisterous group in the front of the crowd began to press against the gates, then decided to storm Freebody Park. Within seconds, they overran the police, burst through the gates, and proceeded to rout indignant spectators from their seats.

What the gentry of Newport had long dreaded and tried to prevent—a civic disturbance in their historic city by jazz-crazed youths—finally had happened. The local police quickly counterattacked. In recapturing the entrance, however, they also succeeded in turning the thousands outside the park into a mob. When officers tried to clear the streets using tear gas and high-pressure water hoses, the youths fought back with bottles and rocks. A battle began for control of the streets of Newport. In the next few hours, the city hospital treated about 50 persons for various cuts and bruises, and 182 persons were thrown in jail. Near midnight, with Newport still in a state of turmoil, the Governor of Rhode Island finally assumed command. He ordered into the streets three companies of National Guardsmen, turned back all ferries approaching the harbor, and shut down the main bridge on the major road from the larger city of Providence to Newport. Two hours later, calm finally settled over Newport.

The next day, to the surprise of few observers but to the despair of the musicians and organizers, the City Council voted to cancel the rest of the concerts. "It's terrible," the saxophonist Coleman Hawkins protested; "nothing worse could have happened." To the drummer Max Roach, the events were "a tragedy." When frantic efforts to overturn the decision proved futile, it was left to Langston himself to preside over the last, unhappy session of the official festival, including performances by the famed bluesmen Muddy Waters, John Lee Hooker, and Jimmy Rushing, as well as the Sammy Price Trio, before a subdued crowd of about two thousand patrons.

"No more appropriate program could have been presented to mark the end of the Newport Jazz Festival," he later observed in the *Defender*. "Jazz was born of the Blues." On the spot, as an elegy for the festival, Langston composed "Goodbye Newport Blues" ("I got the Newport Blues . . . / Those sad, bad, Goodbye Newport Blues"). His elegy was quickly set to music by the pianist Otis Spann, and sung with feeling by Muddy Waters. Then, taking up the song, the entire group of performers joined Hughes and Waters on stage. "Many of these musicians had never played or sung together before," Langston guessed. "But the Blues is everybody's river. And they all plunged into that stream whose source is deep in the heart of the people who made up, 'Trouble in mind, I'm blue—but I won't be always. The sun's gonna shine in my back-door some day'." Finally, at about twenty minutes to six in the evening, the seventh—and what seemed certain to be the last—Newport Jazz Festival ended to the mournful notes of his blues.

As an official of the festival, instead of going back to New York that night Langston remained at the Hotel Viking to take part in critical discussions about its future. Perhaps the city leaders could be placated; perhaps the festival itself should move on to another city. But its future meant much less to Langston than did the outburst of rebellion and violence by young middle-class whites. In spite of his almost playful blues composition marking the festival's premature end, the Newport riot, though modest as American riots went, seemed to him portentous. In the vented rage of these young whites he saw what a later leader, Malcolm X, would describe as chickens coming home to roost, the whirligig of American history bringing, at long last, a token of its nearing final revenge. The rioters had been like dry tinder, to which black jazz had been a lighted match. In a city of wealth and elegance built on the stinking cargoes of slave ships, and where Langston in the early days of the festival had more than once endured racist snubs, Africa had returned to haunt Europe. The descendants of masters now danced to the music of the descendants of slaves; American "civilization" had begun, in however modest a degree, a fateful slide toward revolution.

On July 4, Independence Day, Langston began by far the most ambitious single poem of his life—certainly the most ambitious since October, 1935, when, heartsick with his humiliation by the drama critics and his producer over the Broadway opening of his play *Mulatto,* he had written his anthem for the Depression, "Let America Be America Again." In 1960, Langston felt for America not the sentimental idealism that mainly had inspired his Depression plea but flaring rage and a mocking, sardonic contempt for the national history of racism and lies. Working on twenty-five sheets of six different kinds of paper—whatever was at hand—typing some lines and scribbling others, he composed the first draft of a poem that would eventually run to some eight hundred lines, by far his longest single effort in verse. He would first call this poem "Show Fare, Mama: Notes for Jazz," then publish it as a book, *Ask Your Mama: Twelve Moods For Jazz.*

IN THE
IN THE QUARTER
IN THE QUARTER OF THE NEGROES
WHERE THE DOORS ARE DOORS OF PAPER
DUST OF DINGY ATOMS
BLOWS A SCRATCHY SOUND.
AMORPHOUS JACK-O'-LANTERNS CAPER
AND THE WIND WON'T WAIT FOR MIDNIGHT
FOR FUN TO BLOW DOORS DOWN.

BY THE RIVER AND THE RAILROAD
WITH FLUID FAR-OFF GOING
BOUNDARIES BIND UNBINDING
A WHIRL OF WHISTLES BLOWING
NO TRAINS OR STEAMBOATS GOING—
YET LEONTYNE'S UNPACKING.

IN THE QUARTER OF THE NEGROES
WHERE THE DOORKNOB LETS IN LIEDER
MORE THAN GERMAN EVER BORE,
HER YESTERDAY PAST GRANDPA—
NOT OF HER OWN DOING—

IN A POT OF COLLARD GREENS
IS GENTLY STEWING . . .

At the heart of his poem was anger, but the crux of its form was insult. Specifically, the form invoked was the "Dozens," a ritual of insult, collectively played by both males and females, prominent in black culture. Sometimes "clean," the Dozens were also often "dirty," involving the most sordid accusations of incest and adultery. In some cases, the ritual of insult ended in violence; more often, a premium was placed on returning insult only with insult, and disdaining violence. As Langston knew well, the pioneering scholarly article on this social ritual had been "The Dozens: Dialectic of Insult," published in November, 1936, in the magazine *American Imago* by the psychologist John Dollard of the Institute of Human Relations at Yale University. The landmark essay, which had caught Langston's attention on its appearance—as he distinctly recalled during his revising of *Ask Your Mama*—was an important piece of work by Dollard, who was the first American social scientist to declare himself a Freudian. A year later, he published his classic study *Caste and Class in a Southern Town* and in 1939 was co-author of the influential essay "Frustration and Aggression."

In these works, Dollard laid the groundwork of virtually all future social theory about group violence by advancing for the first time the idea that frustration leads to aggression. This idea, novel at the time, would become a commonplace in explaining phenomena of violence as different as the barbaric nature of Nazi Germany and the explosions of urban violence in black communities of the U.S.A. Examining the Dozens as a cultural device to cope with frustration, Dollard had ended with a weighty observation: "The building up of aggressive responses, started sometimes from trivial causes, must be carefully studied since to know the mechanisms involved may offer means of control. What we want to know is how aggressive expression may get out of social control and become disruptive of social life. Patterns of aggressive expression, like the Dozens, are undoubtedly valuable, but if unchecked interaction teases out of individuals or nations the ultimate in repressed aggression that pattern is a dangerous one to human society."

With this formal, academic justification to inspire him as he worked and reworked the poem, Langston went through thirteen drafts of the poem over a period of seven months, ending on his birthday the following year, 1961. In the process, he completed a fusion of jazz and other music with the mocking words of an oblique but deliberate attack on American history. For each section, consciously taking his lead from Vachel Lindsay's *The Congo: A Study of the Negro Race,* he carefully fashioned musical cues integral to his poetic meaning. Each section, too, was freighted with allusions—allusions, however, that arose for the most part not from European literary sources but instinctively, naturally, out of the heart of lived black American culture, and that parodied and thus challenged the modernist poetry of the arcane as practiced by Melvin

Tolson and others. The immediate settings and the musical cues shift and alter, but the biting tone remains consistent:

> IN THE QUARTER OF THE NEGROES
> WHERE THE PALMS AND COCONUTS
> CHA-CHA LIKE CASTANETS
> IN THE WIND'S FRENETIC FISTS
> WHERE THE SAND SEEDS AND THE
> SEA GOURDS MAKE MARACAS OUT OF ME,
> ERZULIE PLAYS A TUNE
> ON THE BONGO OF THE MOON.
> THE PAPA DRUM OF SUN
> AND THE MOTHER DRUM OF EARTH
> KNOWS TOURISTS ONLY FOR
> THE MONEY THAT THEY'RE WORTH
> IN THE QUARTER OF THE NEGROES. . . .

In moving from draft to draft, Langston forged ahead toward his final arrangement of twelve sections. Each section is attended by musical cues that bring into the poem not only black American blues but also Dixieland, "bop," and even more "progressive" jazz, as well as Hispanic "cha cha," German lieder, the "Battle Hymn of the Republic," Jewish liturgy, West Indian calypsoes, and African drums. The eleventh section, "Jazztet Muted," for example, calls at one point for "bop blues into very modern jazz burning the air eerie like a neon swamp-fire cooled by dry ice":

> IN THE NEGROES OF THE QUARTER
> PRESSURE OF THE BLOOD IS SLIGHTLY HIGHER
> IN THE QUARTER OF THE NEGROES
> WHERE BLACK SHADOWS MOVE LIKE SHADOWS
> CUT FROM SHADOWS CUT FROM SHADE
> IN THE QUARTER OF THE NEGROES
> SUDDENLY CATCHING FIRE
> FROM THE WING TIP OF A MATCH TIP
> ON THE BREATH OF ORNETTE COLEMAN.
> IN NEGRO TOMBS THE MUSIC
> FROM JUKEBOX JOINTS IS LAID
> AND FREE-DELIVERY TV SETS
> ON GRAVESTONES DATES ARE PLAYED.
> EXTRA-LARGE THE *KINGS* AND *QUEENS*
> AT EITHER SIDE ARRAYED
> HAVE DOORS THAT OPEN OUTWARD
> TO THE QUARTER OF THE NEGROES
> WHERE THE PRESSURE OF THE BLOOD
> IS SLIGHTLY HIGHER—

DUE TO SMOLDERING SHADOWS
THAT SOMETIMES TURN TO FIRE.

HELP ME, YARDBIRD!
HELP ME!

The final musical cue of the poem demands music "very loud, lively, and raucous for full chorus to BIG ENDING," with a solo flute crying "alone, high, sharp, loud, and mad." No doubt in insulting parody of T. S. Eliot's celebrated notes to *The Waste Land*—and his fellow black poet Melvin Tolson's own scholarly impedimenta—Langston included brief "LINER NOTES: For the Poetically Unhep," in order to explain the basic meaning of each section to the ignorant.

First he dedicated "Ask Your Mama" jointly to the jazz pianist Randy Weston and trombonist Melba Liston, then to Weston alone, then finally to the best-known jazz musician, Louis Armstrong, "the greatest horn blower of them all." Because of its rhythmic centrality within the wide field of black jazz, Langston admired Armstrong's playing; in addition, Armstrong was almost certainly the most popular, authentically rooted jazz musician in the world. In this dedication to a black jazz horn blower, to a Joshua whose music, like all jazz music, threatened to blow down the walls of America in the battle of blacks for freedom, Langston further signified the spirit of rebellion and even of apocalypse at the core of the work.

In July, with the precious first draft of his new poem packed away, he returned to Harlem to attend to the forthcoming production of *Tambourines to Glory* by the Theatre Guild and Joel Schenker, a major real-estate developer and former actor who increasingly was turning away from his thriving business to the world of drama. Almost every aspect of the show was now encouraging. In a long session on August 1, he reached an informal agreement with the director Herbert Machiz and other key members of the production about its tempo, mood, and meaning. Eva Jessye, who had directed the choir in the original staging of *Porgy and Bess,* was now the musical director of *Tambourines to Glory,* with the jazz pianist Sammy Price as its "Minister of Music," as a gospel church pianist was often called. In the gifted cast were Joseph Attles, Anna English, Nipsey Russell (who had finally agreed to be in the show), the gospel star Clara Ward in the key role of Birdie Lee, the drummer for the choir, and—as the projected star of the entire production—the elegant pianist and singer Hazel Scott. After three successful years performing in Paris, and a highly publicized estrangement from her husband Rev. Adam Clayton Powell, Jr., Scott had just returned home to play the Apollo Theater in Harlem.

With *Tambourines to Glory* in rehearsal, Langston felt free to travel to Chicago for a few days of publicity work for Columbia Pictures on the set of the motion picture *A Raisin in the Sun.* For this effort he received $100 a day, plus expenses—a small but ripe plum tossed his way in return for his part in the title. With him on this assignment was his former collaborator on *The Sweet*

Flypaper of Life, the photographer Roy DeCarava. Together they interviewed Lorraine Hansberry, who shyly declined to have her face photographed but offered instead her hands—about which Langston deferentially wrote in a brief essay.

Back in Harlem, he stirred up publicity for his own latest work—*The First Book of Africa,* for young readers, from Franklin Watts; and his adult anthology from Crown, *An African Treasury: Articles / Essays / Stories / Poems By Black Africans.* The response to both books was positive, but Langston was especially pleased by praise for the latter, because it was "a very personal treasury—a selection gathered from several thousands of pages of writing by Africans of color I have read during the past six years." Included were pointed articles on South African life by Bloke Modisane, Peter Abrahams, Ezekiel Mphahlele, and Phyllis Ntantala, among others; more general essays, such as those on African cinema, the work songs, and Akan poetry; short stories by writers including Efua Sutherland, Amos Tutuola, Adelaide Casely-Hayford, Richard Rive, Mabel Dove-Danquah, and Peter Kumalo; verse by Wole Soyinka, Léopold Senghor, Birago Diop, Gabriel Okara, and other black poets. Hailed in one place as "a rich and timely gift," *An African Treasury* left almost all reviewers admiring it as a timely corrective to the traditional American ignorance of Africa. The South African writer Ezekiel Mphahlele, now a co-editor of the influential African journal *Black Orpheus,* heartily endorsed Hughes's effort: "What delights me is that you have captured African writing which resounds through and through like the footsteps of a giant rubbing his eyes as he walks, just from a deep sleep."

One tribute to the power of *An African Treasury* came from the white leaders of the Union of South Africa, who promptly banned the book. Anyone caught with it faced a fine of a thousand pounds, or five years in prison. In the New York *Post,* Hughes talked of the enormous expense and work involved in its preparation. Dealing with Africa was no routine effort, he attested, but was well worth the trouble. The American Bible Society had complained that Africans used leaves from the Bible to wrap items, to roll cigarettes, and as toilet paper. That's why they *need* the Bible, he mocked.

The satiric tone of his *Post* interview was perhaps part of the legacy of Newport—a mood that lingered with Langston as he quietly kept at his revisions of "Ask Your Mama." Early in August, the mood was still with him when he went north to Tanglewood, the summer home of the Boston Symphony, for the world premiere the next day of his and Jan Meyerowitz's latest effort, the one-act opera *Port Town,* directed by Boris Goldovsky. "I had always loved Langston's poem of the same name," Meyerowitz recalled, "and I made him agree to write a libretto for me based on it." The poem "Port Town" had first appeared in Hughes's *The Weary Blues* in 1926, and he had reproduced it without any change in his *Selected Poems.*

Hello, sailor boy,
In from the sea!

Hello, sailor,
Come with me!

Come on drink cognac.
Rather have wine?
Come here, I love you.
Come and be mine.

Lights, sailor boy,
Warm, white lights.
Solid land, kid.
Wild, white nights.

Come on, sailor,
Out o' the sea.
Let's go, sweetie!
Come with me.

Although the setting for *Port Town* was sublime, with soaring green trees all quiet in the breathless summer air and a sunset of mauve and gold, he was unmoved. "Country never did agree with me," he complained to Van Vechten. With "Ask Your Mama" in gestation, Langston stared with alienated eyes at the high-toned, overwhelmingly white, elitist world of American opera. This time, not surprisingly, he was ready for his clash with Jan Meyerowitz. When once again barely a word of his libretto could be heard above the score, Langston grinned his way to the stage to take his bows, but seethed inside. Hustling back to Harlem, he vowed to take "no more parts of operas or rural life ever!" His spirit was not lifted by the unenthusiastic reviews of *Port Town,* and especially not by the critic in the *Herald-Tribune* who wrote of an irreconcilable conflict between the exalted melodies and Hughes's appropriately "salty and colloquial" libretto. A few days later, Langston crisply rejected Meyerowitz's outline for a new opera. "I really am not interested in writing any more [libretti] for anyone," he announced. "As operas are done in America, the words had just as well be nonsense syllables. I see no point in spending long hours of thought, and weeks of writing seeking poetic phrases and just the right word— and then not enough of the librettist's lines are heard for anybody to know what is being sung. . . . When there is *no* artistic joy in hearing (or rather NOT hearing) one's work, and no financial income, either, why bother? . . . I wish I could write music. I'd leave words alone."

Well aware of how much and how selflessly Langston had helped to launch his career following his arrival in the United States as a refugee just after World War II, Meyerowitz now stepped gingerly around him. He thanked God that "what we have *done* already will keep me in touch with you: you remain my favoured American and an object of great affection and admiration."

Meanwhile, the rehearsals of *Tambourines to Glory* were proceeding smoothly—"*too* smoothly," Langston judged. Hazel Scott was "going to be very, VERY GOOD,'' and Clara Ward, banging artfully on her drums, was sensational. At the Theatre Guild, there was talk of taking the show directly to Broadway. On Labor Day, September 5, when the show at last tried out at the Westport Country Playhouse in Connecticut, it was a hit. In a poll, 314 out of 386 patrons liked the show ''very much,'' and many were sure that *Tambourines to Glory* was ready for Manhattan. However, two important problems loomed. By appearing at times bored and contemptuous, Hazel Scott was alienating much of the audience. Langston himself judged her ''definitely weak, beautiful, but generally unconvincing. Replacement should be considered.'' The second problem was harder to solve. On religious, moral, and political grounds, several observers found the play in appalling taste. ''Worst thing I've ever seen,'' one patron complained to the New York *Amsterdam News*. Another protested: ''I thought we'd gotten away from that kind of thing.'' According to whom one talked, a columnist concluded, *Tambourines to Glory* was either great or awful.

''People forget,'' Langston argued lamely, ''that comedy, as well as tragedy, can be used as a weapon of social criticism.'' But the reports stopped the show in its tracks. Although Hughes wanted to proceed, Lawrence Langner and the Theatre Guild would have nothing to do with pushing a play said to be Uncle Tommish and generally demeaning of blacks. Dismayed, Langston rushed to try to rescue the production. For *Tambourines to Glory* he composed a new prologue, new songs, a new opening scene, and a closing sermon to improve its final tone. He added folk idioms to the dialogue, smoothed certain transitions, and listened carefully to the advice of Langner, the producer Joel Schenker, and the young black playwright Loften Mitchell, who had voiced vigorous but helpful objections to the work. Schenker suggested moving the action from the present time to the Depression, in order to deflect criticism of its lack of political acuteness. On this point Langston held his ground, but he remained ready to make other changes as he completed a tenth draft of *Tambourines to Glory*. ''Who said, 'Plays are not written—but re-written'?'' he wearily asked Loften Mitchell.

But the production remained stalled. After Hazel Scott was quietly dropped, not one of the small circle of established black stars, including Eartha Kitt, Langston's favorite, and Pearl Bailey, who would have been ideal, wanted to replace her. Obviously they were suspicious of the gospel format and the tawdry social setting of the show. Disappointed, Langston moved on. In mid-September he offered one of his rare public reviews of a play, following the Broadway premiere of *The World of Carl Sandburg*, starring Bette Davis and Leif Ericson. Speaking on the radio station WNEW, Langston welcomed this tribute to ''the dean of American poets'' and a production that started sleepily but soon became ''gloriously alive.''

Not long afterwards, publicity of a more troubling kind came with the tumultuous arrival in Harlem of the Cuban leader Fidel Castro, whose revolution had triumphed on January 1 the previous year, 1959, with the flight of the dictator Fulgencio Batista. Since that time, Castro had steered his country steadily to the left, making in the process an enemy of the U.S. government. Castro's deliberate choice of the Hotel Theresa on Seventh Avenue at 125th Street over, say, the Waldorf-Astoria (favored by African dignitaries) delighted Harlem. Excited crowds of blacks hoping for a glimpse of a rebel beard on the ninth floor lined the streets in front of the Theresa. In 1931, disgusted by Cuba's status as an imperialist football, Langston virtually had called for a revolution, and on Marxist grounds. In 1960, however, he could not afford the slightest association with Fidel Castro. But on September 27, to his dismay and chagrin, both the *New York Times* and the popular columnist Leonard Lyons in his *Post* column "The Lyons Den" ("where, like Daniel, I have been caught," he complained) announced that Langston Hughes had dined with Castro the previous Friday in the company of Henri Cartier-Bresson, the beat poet Allen Ginsberg, and a bellboy.

Two dozen inquiring phone calls in one day shattered his peace at 20 East 127th Street. One caller was the actress Claudia McNeill of *A Raisin in the Sun,* who offered "to breathe a prayer for me in case it were true I had dined with such a 'Satanic person'." Leonard Lyons immediately corrected his story, but on October 3, *Time* magazine reported "Left-Wing Poet Langston Hughes" dropping in "to pay respects" to Castro. Soon, *Time* published his denial: "I do not know Fidel Castro and have never had any sort of contacts with him or communications with him." In fact, just after the Newport Jazz Festival, Hughes had refused to join a group of black Americans on an all-expenses-paid tour of Cuba. Ironically, the invitation had come from Richard Gibson, the young black writer who years before had haughtily dismissed Langston Hughes as an artist in an attack on protest literature in *Perspectives* magazine. (Another writer who made this visit to Cuba was LeRoi Jones. For him, it marked the beginning of the high road to radicalism. "As apolitical as I was," he wrote Langston, "I was moved.")

Avoiding radical politics, Hughes concentrated his efforts elsewhere. He continued to revise "Ask Your Mama." For the progressive publisher Lawrence Hill of Hill and Wang, he agreed to prepare a selection of the best of the Simple stories, as well as a collection of short stories. And he kept up his efforts on behalf of younger black writers. Revising his anthology "New Negro Poets" as ordered by Indiana University Press, he recreated a fresh collection which emphasized more modernist styles at the expense of poems of racial feeling. However, Langston did so unwillingly. With prophetic words, he soothed the hurt feelings of one older poet, Margaret Danner, and predicted the coming of a new racial day. "Loud and angry race cries such as you and I are accustomed to give," he conceded, "are not at the moment 'comme il faut' or 'à la mode' as a poetic style. (But don't worry, I expect they will be again in due time!)"

Through the fall, he kept close to home even as requests for appearances still poured in. After someone tried to exploit his popularity by passing as his lecture agent, he angrily placed a notice in the *Saturday Review* to the effect that he was "not represented by any lecture bureau or individual." The notice promptly brought an inquiry from his old lecture agency W. Colston Leigh, which had dropped him years before during the worst period of his baiting by the right. But Langston declined to rejoin Leigh's bureau, ''since I do not make a major career of lecturing (writing being my primary job).'' To another inquirer, he clarified his position. He now avoided white or integrated sponsors wherever possible, because they brought out the worst in the right wing. Liberal whites, not noted for their courage, then became scared if ''one single letter is written to the paper—and leave the Negroes holding the bag in the end.'' He would continue to speak before blacks, or before carefully chosen audiences of whites. Otherwise, he would stick to his typewriter.

Avoiding the lecture circuit did not mean becoming a recluse. From California in September came Matt Crawford and his daughter, Nebby Lou, now a striking young woman of twenty-three; later came Arna and Alberta Bontemps, with Arna en route to a conference in Uganda in East Africa. When a Southern admirer presented Langston with a rare regional treat, a coon packed in dry ice, Langston turned the cooking of the beast into an event, with a special invitation to the dynamic pianist-singer Nina Simone, whom he had met at Newport. Downtown he attended a smart buffet party where the Irish poet Padraic Colum recited his poetry, and he himself was guest of honor at a PEN party to mark the publication of his two African books. Uptown on Riverside Drive he dined with the poet and progressive Muriel Rukeyser, whom he had long admired, and he attended a dinner of the Teachers' Union of New York at the Hotel Commodore. The last weekend in October found him in Philadelphia, celebrating the twenty-fifth anniversary of the ministry of Frank B. Mitchell, a Lincoln schoolmate. Early in November, Langston spoke at Barnard College, where he stressed the importance of the coming elections to blacks and lamented the slowness of change in the South. Although he nowhere publicly endorsed a presidential candidate that year, he left little doubt whom he preferred in the race between John F. Kennedy, who had risen in the regard of blacks because of an exquisitely timed telephone call to Mrs. Martin Luther King, Jr., while her husband was languishing in a jail in the South, and Richard M. Nixon. Simple, on the other hand, was unimpressed by the two men. ''The only reason I would vote for either one of them,'' he declared, ''would be to keep the other one from getting in.''

As careful as he was about the lecture circuit, perhaps his oldest itch—the urge to travel—stayed alive. Arna Bontemps's trip to Uganda particularly provoked him (''AFRICA! I'm envious and jealous!''). Thus, on short notice in November, Langston leaped at an invitation from Nnamdi Azikiwe to attend, with all expenses paid by his host, the inauguration of Azikiwe as Governor General and Commander-in-Chief of Nigeria, which had gained independence from Great Britain on October 1. The invitation from ''Zik'' was not to Langston alone but to about thirty former schoolmates and at least one former professor at Lincoln University. After frantic efforts to secure visas and the other necessary papers, Langston left Idlewild Airport early in November for London, where a chartered jetliner awaited this new Lincoln Battalion on its African venture. Joining him as guests of Azikiwe were W. E. B. Du Bois and his wife Shirley Graham, who had left the United States for Ghana, Ralph Bunche, and Rev. Martin Luther King, Jr. (By this time, Hughes was on better terms with Du Bois. In recent years, he had mentioned the old warrior respectfully in several *Defender* columns and had devoted one entirely to his honor.)

Severe fog made it necessary to land in Accra and refuel. There, for the first time since June, 1923, when the *West Hesseltine* had docked at Dakar in Senegal, Langston watched the sun rise over Africa. His week in Nigeria passed in a daze. The bright, burning tropical sun, the pomp and circumstance of the ceremonies, the majesty of the moment as power passed from the imperial British into black African hands, his prestige as an honored guest ferried in limousines from the Ikeja Arms Hotel to event after event, all dazzled Langston and left him more than a little giddy. After a cocktail party in the lush gardens at the State House, Azikiwe's official residence, he attended the inaugural state luncheon and a state dinner at which he found himself seated with Azikiwe himself and his wife and son. He was placed prominently again at a Sunday thanksgiving service in Azikiwe's honor at the Cathedral Church of Christ in Lagos. Perhaps the single most intoxicating moment for Langston came when Azikiwe, after formally taking the oath of office as the personal representative of Queen Elizabeth II, closed his address with a recitation of "Poem" from Hughes's *The Weary Blues* ("We have tomorrow / Bright before us / Like a flame . . .").

The visit allowed Langston finally to meet the African "son" he had acquired via the postal service, Chuba Nweke, who presented him with an African robe and a cap but did not improve his position with Hughes. In Lagos, however, Langston acquired another "son." Before the garden party at the State House, as his car idled outside and the crowd pressed forward to catch a glimpse of the dignitaries, a young black policeman steered the curious away from Hughes, but in such a gentle, polite way that Hughes remembered him at their second encounter, at the art museum. Introducing himself to the startled policeman, Langston took down not only his name, Sunday Osuya, but also his address and the names and addresses of other policemen outside the garden of the State House. Langston and Sunday Osuya, a Kwale man from the Ibo region, who could scarcely believe his good fortune, promised to write one another.

Too soon the visit ended; Langston left Africa after "a wonderful week." In Rome for the first time in his life, he slept away his visit in a room at the imposing Excelsior Hotel, then awoke refreshed for the flight to Paris, which he had last seen in 1938. Paris, after New York, Lagos, and Rome, completely charmed him again. "Such an endearing city," he reminisced later to a friend. "I think I'll go back and stay." Looking for the Grand Duc nightclub, where he had toiled as a dishwasher in 1924 and written some of his first and best jazz poetry, he found instead the American-style Canada Bar; where Florence Embry Jones and Bricktop had sung the blues, a juke box blasted the air at the corner of rue de la Rochefoucauld and rue Pigalle. No matter—Paris was incomparable. He liked Montmartre, but he also loved sitting quietly in the Parc Monceau and the Tuilleries, riding in the *bateaux-mouches* on the Seine and strolling in the Luxembourg Gardens. "I loved Nigeria, but Paris more."

Hiding behind the name of "James L. Hughes," he loafed about the city. In the Latin Quarter he befriended a young African from Guinea, a student at the Sorbonne. Langston's generosity and style, but also his intentions even under the cloak of anonymity, may be judged from a letter sent by the grateful student to thank him for "une amitié sincere et exempte de tout vice." "Mon fils et mon frère!" "James" Hughes replied. Throwing off anonymity at least once, he paid a visit to 4, rue Regis, the home of Richard Wright. From Wright in October had come a touching appeal to Langston: "Say, guy, what with all the current sweep forward of Africa and our people in general, we ought to keep in closer touch." Wright had picked up mysterious amoebas there, but "I'm hankering to get back into Africa. The place haunts me." Answering the doorbell, Wright's teenaged daughter Julia greeted Langston, then led him to her father's bedroom. In the doorway, a shocked Hughes stopped abruptly. Dressed in a gray suit and tie, Wright lay stretched on the bed. "Man," Langston blurted, "you look like you are ready to go to glory!" The two men, who had not seen one another in many years, laughed heartily. Wright explained that he was awaiting his doctor, who would escort him to a hospital for tests. "How is Harlem?" he asked. "I'd like to see it again." As they talked about Harlem and Chicago, his spirit revived until he seemed to Langston the Richard Wright of old—charming, effervescent, modest. Before leaving with his doctor, he pressed into Langston's hands "Daddy Goodness," a play he had written. Perhaps Hughes could place it with some small theater company in the United States. "I'll write you soon," Wright promised.

A day or two later, in rainy, pleasant London, Langston attended a party at the African writer Bloke Modisane's modest flat. The talk turned to Wright's controversial African travel book, *Black Power,* which many Africans had disliked. At midnight, the news came on the radio that Richard Wright was dead. Langston could scarcely believe the report, since Wright had not seemed ill. On November 30, he sent Ellen Wright a telegram: "MY DEEPEST SYMPATHY TO YOU AND YOUR DAUGHTER."

The trip to Africa and Europe ravaged his bank balance, which soon fell below $100. But moved perhaps by his brush with death, or by the Christmas spirit, or by both, Langston plunged on his return into the holiday season. To Jan Meyerowitz he sent the libretto of a Nativity cantata, "On a Pallet of Straw." To Margaret Bonds went another, "The Ballad of the Brown King," dedicated to Martin Luther King, Jr. By mid-December, working with young helpers, Langston had also launched a mighty Christmas card operation. When the last of several hundred envelopes were mailed on December 21, he jovially awarded special scrolls of gratitude, complete with red ribbons, to his young friends. One was a namesake, Langston Hughes Mickens, who had been brought to Langston's attention some years before by a schoolteacher; the other was Luis Velez, a neighborhood child of Puerto Rican descent. He also helped to prepare two television shows. In one for the CBS series "Look Up and Live," he narrated a gospel concert with the 120-voice Abyssinian Baptist Gospel Choir ("In a gospel church, when they ride on the glory train of song, nobody is ashamed, or afraid of being carried away"). On the local ABC program, "Expedition New York," he talked about "A Poet's Harlem."

In spite of this invaluable "exposure," the new year found Langston moaning his favorite blues of the past decade. "I am nothing but a literary sharecropper," he cried one more time early in 1961. "Swing low, sweet chariot and rescue me!" Nevertheless, he stuck by his resolve to work mainly at his desk, although he had planned a tour for February. In January, for example, he went out to the Hun School in Princeton to read to students and to record poems for the National Library of Spoken Literature, but turned down about twenty other invitations to read. He vowed to avoid the podium, "which I vowed before, but this time I MEAN it. Just the art of writing from here on in." Anxious to offer "Ask Your Mama" to Knopf for publication, he revised yet another draft in the last few days of the month. He signed contracts for two new books, including one that called for extensive research—"Fight for Freedom," an official history of the NAACP. Much of this research he entrusted to his earnest young secretary George Bass.

He completed liner notes for a recording of spirtuals by the Robert Shaw Chorale, but certainly had more fun writing a poem, "African Woman," for Randy Weston's album *Uhuru, Afrika!*. This album was one of several produced by black jazz musicians in response to the independence movement in Africa; Max Roach and Sonny Rollins also wrote and recorded suites on the theme. "Langston was the only black writer writing about us in those days," Weston recalled. (Weston was president of the African-American Music Society, which had been protesting the injustice of building the huge Lincoln Center arts complex in Manhattan without even a nod to jazz or other black musical forms.) "Lots of white guys wrote about black musicians, but from our own people only Langston it seemed bothered to write about us. He was truly a musician, as far as I am concerned. I asked him to write a poem about the African woman for my suite—it had four movements—and he said sure, man, in his very calm and relaxed way. He had a beautiful way of making everything seem so simple, so easy. For a man as great as he was, his sheer ease was something to behold."

On February 6, sponsored by Adele Glasgow and Ramona Lowe at their Market Place Gallery in Harlem, and with Margaret Bonds backing him at the piano, "Ask Your Mama" made a sensational debut. Overflowing audiences, drawn by a publicity scheme in which Langston had dispatched invitations to more than one hundred and twenty people mentioned in the poem (including the arch-segregationist politicians Orval Faubus of Arkansas and James Eastland of Mississippi), cheered two readings at the gallery. The next day he began his tour. Heading west by train, he delivered the Carter G. Woodson

Memorial Lecture at Berea College, Kentucky, the alma mater of Woodson, for whom Langston had worked in 1924 in Washington, D.C. Once a school mainly for black and Native American students, Berea College was now almost exclusively white—but his visit passed without incident. A few days later, he was less fortunate. In Oakland, California, right-wing opposition marred a much heralded three-day visit to the prestigious Mills College for women. Perhaps because no recent visitor, except the U.S. Secretary of State Dean Rusk, had generated "so much excitement" on the campus, a coalition of forces passed out leaflets denouncing Hughes, and hostile callers deliberately jammed the switchboard on the morning of the talk. This time, his liberal hosts stood firm. Langston gave his address to a packed auditorium, then visited classes without further harassment. At the home of the president, C. Easton Rothwell, he dined with Grayson Kirk of the University of California, the novelist Wallace Stegner of Stanford University, and his friend from the 1930s, the poet Sarah Bard Field.

Ten pleasant days in sunny Los Angeles with his Uncle John and his cousin Flora Coates were capped by a major reading at UCLA and an elaborate performance, sponsored by the regional NAACP, of "Ask Your Mama" (the world premiere, Hughes announced) in Santa Monica, backed by Buddy Collette's jazz group.

Soon after returning home, Langston attended the first of a series of three productions of "Voice of His People," an admiring narrative based on his life and composed by his talented secretary, George Bass. The skilled *a capella* octet "Voices, Inc.," of which Bass was a leading member, offered the show to appreciative audiences at the Church of the Master in Harlem. Then, following the news of the most significant national honor of his life, Langston braced himself for further publicity. The National Institute of Arts and Letters, the honorary academy founded in 1898 and limited to two hundred and fifty American citizens of distinction in literature and the fine arts, had voted to admit him to its ranks. Also to be inducted into the Institute was Carl Van Vechten. "I see you and I are to represent the Race," Langston teased his friend, "which delights me to have such genial company therein." Undoubtedly he was pleased by the honor—but not as pleased as he once would have been. The honor was belated, and he was never to be elected to the fifty-member Academy of Arts and Letters, the inner circle of excellence drawn from the membership of the Institute. (Among blacks, only Du Bois preceded Hughes in the Institute; later, Ralph Ellison became the first Afro-American in the Academy.)

He was less than elated in April when he attended the formal welcoming dinner for new members of the National Institute. Although he had gone to many events at the imposing complex on Broadway at West 155th Street, he had never been there in as exalted a position, or one as lonely. To his dismay, or disgust, he was the only black there—unless one counted Van Vechten. It was difficult to believe that one was virtually in Harlem. The surreal quality of the evening was heightened for him by an ancient white man who sat at their table and absentmindedly combed his long white beard, as if the National Institute were a kind of Sleepy Hollow. Only the presence of Robert Frost stirred Langston's interest (recently, Hughes had contributed a poem to an anthology in his honor). As the only black present, Langston had been installed prominently at the head table with Frost, who had become virtually the poet laureate of the United States following his reading of a poem at President Kennedy's inauguration earlier that year. To Langston's astonishment, the elderly Frost recited several of his own poems from memory, "which is more than I can do at my young age." (In spite of his decades of readings and their crucial financial support, Langston knew virtually none of his poems by heart. "I do not like them well enough to learn them," he confessed, "but they are always my ace in the hole.")

His formal ascent into the glory of the National Institute of Arts and Letters came later still, in the spring, but Langston remained ambivalent about the honor. In fact, he had decided to skip the luncheon marking the event, until Van Vechten put his aged foot down. "Mr. Carl Van Vechten has told me," he let the Institute know with a hint of insolence, "it is my *bounden* duty to rise from my bed (no matter if I do work all night)" and attend the luncheon. At the ceremony on May 24 with his fellow inductees, including Leonard Bernstein, Ludwig Mies van der Rohe, Jacques Lipchitz, and Arthur M. Schlesinger, Jr., he noted sadly once again that "I was the only cullud alone on the platform amidst a sea of white folks." The exclusiveness of the honor brought him only diluted pleasure, and a haunting sense of discomfort. The speeches were "long and dull as usual," he complained to Arna Bontemps. "There ought to be a law about people reading speeches and citations." With dignity he accepted a scroll from his Institute, "with a gold seal thereon." Then, after going out for drinks with Van Vechten, Van Vechten's young biographer Bruce Kellner, and a few other friends, he made his way back to Harlem.

The first news of his recognition by the National Institute accompanied an unusual burst of interest in his work. Without any qualification, Knopf took "Ask Your Mama." It was assigned to a bright young editor, Judith Jones, who had once worked for Ivan von Auw at Harold Ober Associates. "I was completely in awe of Langston Hughes," she later remembered, "but he was definitely a most polite and gentle and helpful author. We planned something different for the book, something with more color and variety than our usual sort of poetry book, and he liked and approved all our ideas without hesitation. He saw the book as different, and he wanted it to look different. It could have been a trying experience, but it turned out to be very pleasant. He made it so. I had the greatest respect for him as a writer and a human being."

Other projects fared equally well. After the rejection by university presses at Stanford and Illinois of a volume of five of his plays edited by Webster Smalley, a white instructor at the University of Illinois, Bernard Perry quickly accepted it at Indiana University Press. For taking this initiative, Langston was grateful to Smalley—"Merci à vous!" He insisted that Smalley himself write an introduction.

Two doctoral dissertations brought students to his Harlem home. James

Emanuel, a diligent black graduate student and poet at Columbia University, was working on Hughes's short stories; and Donald Dickinson of the University of Kansas was preparing a Langston Hughes "bio-bibliography." Apparently diffident, but in truth charmed by such projects, Langston laughed at the idea that "the academics think I've suddenly become an authority or something on how to write."

"Langston Hughes was a better man than I imagined he or anyone so famous could be," James Emanuel recollected. "I hadn't met him before, but he set me down at his desk, and although some drawers were locked, I was free to look at anything I wanted, without any surveillance. He was a giving person, who wanted to help you, but he also felt neglected and underestimated by the critics. On the other hand, I don't think I ever saw a sign of irritation cross his face, ever. He was philosophical about what life had done to him. He had made his choices. I respected him as someone who had given his whole life to exposing the realities of his people, where so many other black writers aimed to please and impress whites. His key mode was not anger and rage—he did not publish in the age when black anger and rage paid well—but irony. And he was a true professional, in the best sense of the word. I felt privileged to be writing about him and his work."

Although a big, red-inked "NO" in his appointment book underscored his resolve to work, Langston remained as sociable as ever. For the visiting Jamaican writer Andrew Salkey he gave a pleasant little cocktail party. The gala premiere of the movie *A Raisin in the Sun* allowed him to mix with various movie stars and reflect in the glory of its title. Less enjoyable was a preview he caught of Jean Genet's play *The Blacks,* with perhaps the finest cast of black actors ever assembled, including James Earl Jones (the son of the star of Langston's Harlem Suitcase Theatre in 1938), Cicely Tyson, Raymond St. Jacques, Godfrey Cambridge, Louis Gossett, Maya Angelou, Charles Gordone, and Roscoe Lee Browne. Unfortunately, Langston found the play (he had enjoyed Genet's *The Balcony*) "a 33rd degree bore," more outrageous than Samuel Beckett's *Waiting for Godot* "and even less amusing." The production needed "lightness and a humorous approach to its fantasy—which is extreme, grotesque and long-winded." (Hughes would never venture, as a reviewer, to put such shrewd, trenchant observations in print.) He fled after the first act to catch earthy Nina Simone at the Village Gate, and pledged to see "NO MORE ART SHOWS this, or any other, season. NO!" Willing to aid an unpretentious community venture, he attended the awards ceremony of the Police Athletic League's Essay Contest, for which he and Bennett Cerf were judges.

He wanted nothing to do with art shows, and nothing to do with politics. When the disastrous Bay of Pigs of Cuba invasion by anti-Castro forces backed by the United States brought an imploring plea from his old friend Nicolás Guillén, the president of the Cuban Association of Writers and Artists, for Langston to stand up against "estos vandálicos hechos," he did not budge. Believing (incorrectly) that both LeRoi Jones and Richard Gibson had lost their jobs following their visit to Cuba the previous summer, he declined to assist a rally planned by the Fair Play for Cuba Committee. George Bass wrote the committee that Mr. Hughes would be in California most of March, which was not so. When the committee sought his signature to a newspaper notice, Langston did not reply. In red pencil he scribbled "not signed" on the letter, and secured it in his files. For his various actions, or inactions, Hughes earned the gratitude of the U.S. Senate Subcommittee on Internal Security. Later, it would mention him favorably in noting that American blacks had shrewdly resisted Cuban schemes "to popularize Cuba among Negroes."

However, Langston could be counted on to support civil rights groups at home, if mainly by his writing. Aided by George Bass's research in the NAACP archives, he worked on its official history. To a fund-raising auction sponsored by the Congress of Racial Equality, he donated a manuscript. He still relied on the newspapers, and occasional letters from the South, to keep him informed about events and important shifts in strategy on the various civil rights fronts. Atlanta, for example, which he had visited the previous March, was gripped by a black boycott of white merchants. "The cold war we're in the midst of now would make last March seem cozy and warm," he had learned from Millicent Dobbs Jordan, a prominent Atlantan and the sister of the singer Mattiwilda Dobbs. "These are great times." In the spring, the headlines about boycotts and sit-ins gave way to news of the Freedom Rides. On May 4, an integrated group of bus riders set out for the South from Washington to test compliance with integration orders. Far from being protected, at various stops riders were brutally beaten and arrested. To protect them, the U.S. Attorney General, Robert Kennedy, ordered six hundred Federal marshalls into Alabama. In Jackson, Mississippi, local authorities arrested twenty-seven Freedom Riders.

Against this backdrop of violence, Langston wondered at the fact that so many of the younger writers still seemed unwilling to seize on race as a topic or as inspiration. His appeals for contributions to "New Negro Poets" were bringing him into touch with exciting new voices—Jay Wright, Sarah Webster Fabio, A. B. Spellman, Calvin Hernton, Raymond Patterson, Julian Mayfield, and Lindsay Patterson, for example; and Mari Evans, whose work excited Langston, and who once thanked him, in a sense, for all of them: "I can never articulate all your interest has meant to me." Raymond Patterson remembered Hughes's help and encouragement when Patterson organized a poetry series for Adele Glasgow at the Market Place Gallery. "It was the list of names and addresses of poets, furnished by Langston Hughes, that put me in touch with most of the poets who attended or participated in the series," Patterson later recalled. "I neglected to invite him, thinking he would be too busy, but he let word get back to me that he was disappointed at not being invited. I was very much in awe of Hughes, although he was always, in my presence, unassuming, friendly, sociable. My impression is that Langston Hughes had a hand in the careers of most black poets who have distinguished themselves during the last quarter century."

In the first year or two of the sixties, what the youngsters were writing was another matter. When Indiana complained that some new poems seemed "slapped out and apparently not worked over,'' Langston shook the tree again. To him, many of the poets lacked true motivation. When the German translator and anthologist Eva Hesse complained about the imitativeness of the new black poets, he replied that integration was going too far. The poets were often "good in an inconsequential fashion—like most white poets with no social base." Although he liked some of the poems, Langston had little to cheer about on this score later in the year when the most gifted of the younger writers, LeRoi Jones, published his first book of verse, *Preface to a Twenty Volume Suicide Note*.

Still, to some people Hughes's own writing was short of power. In San Francisco, the Beat poet Lawrence Ferlinghetti rejected an excerpt from "Ask Your Mama" sent as "a polite protest" for a proposed journal of protest: "Perhaps we are looking for something a lot more impolite!"

Langston was not prepared to be very impolite. Early in June, he decorously helped to judge a creative writing contest sponsored jointly by *Readers' Digest* and the United Negro College Fund, spoke at a testimonial dinner for a Lincoln University professor in Philadelphia, then generously attended the premiere of the Jan Meyerowitz opera for which he had bluntly refused to write a libretto. Praising the music, he encouraged Meyerowitz in his efforts—although Langston could not resist noting tartly that the show was "even partially audible lyrically." To raise money for a revival of their greatest success, *The Barrier,* proposed by the conductor Maurice Peress of New York University and avidly desired by Meyerowitz, Langston personally sent several letters of appeal for money to friends. From the production itself, in which he was only mildly interested, he kept a respectful distance. As usual, Jan Meyerowitz was not so easily contained—until one day, prancing about the stage and making something of a nuisance of himself with opinions and demands, he tumbled into the orchestra pit and broke a leg. Peering down at his stricken form, Maurice Peress murmured a consolation: "God's will is sometimes best." Or so Langston heard, and took pleasure in repeating.

His basic message, seasoned realistically by his hatred of racism and his zeal for civil rights, was about joy and peace and justice for all. Under bitter attack, Langston responded not in kind but with kindness. The latest public test of his spirit had occurred on June 20, when an invitation to narrate a blues section as part of a concert on the Boston Common during the city's annual arts festival was denounced. Langston Hughes, according to a story in the Boston *Globe*, was "a Communist sympathizer and a danger to the children of Boston." But he made no attempt to engage his enemies directly. Instead, with hostile pickets and extra policemen in place, about twenty thousand patrons heard him genially deliver "an exceptionally well-knit program" on the blues. "So far as the children of Boston were concerned," the music critic Robert Taylor concluded, "the most incendiary statement made was the poet's conviction that life is fun."

Dignified himself, Langston was impatient with those who thought that cruder language and vulgar actions would be more effective in the long run. Later that year—but with distinct distaste—he acceded to an appeal from LeRoi Jones after he and Diane DiPrima, co-editors of the magazine *The Floating Bear*, were arrested (Jones was jailed briefly) for sending allegedly obscene material through the mail. The June, 1961 number of *The Floating Bear*, which included a section from Jones's novel-in-progress *The Systems of Dante's Hell* and an equally lively piece by William Burroughs, had been mailed to an inmate at Rahway State Prison in New Jersey. To have the case dropped, Jones needed testimonials to his integrity as an artist and to the seriousness of *The Floating Bear*. "What I'll never understand," Langston scolded Jones, "is *why* did you-all send that particular BEAR to a guy in jail." But he sent a testimonial: "LeRoi Jones is one of the most talented of America's younger poets, a serious and dedicated writer intent on exploring the many varied facets of the emotional life of our times, and one whose work seems to me of interest and value." Of *The Floating Bear* he said nothing.

With obscenity, Langston wanted nothing to do. On the other hand, at about this time he seemed to become more and more fascinated by the liberal spirit sweeping through American fiction and American life concerning the discussion and depiction of human sexuality. The previous fall, Hughes had started "L'Amour à Trois," later called "Family of Three," a short story about a white couple and a dominant black man, in which the white woman relates their adventures—or misfortunes—to an Austrian doctor. "If we had both been a little less putty in that black man's hand, my husband and I," the wife declares. "If we had both been a little less fire in his forge." Hughes seemed unable to go much further. The first draft lasted only a page, and the second died after two pages. In some respects, this story was a throwback for Langston as a venture in fiction—a continuation of "Slave on the Block," the first story Hughes had written, under the influence of D. H. Lawrence, of those that went in 1934 to form his finest collection of short fiction, *The Ways of White Folks*. The basic image is similar in both stories: a potent black man commanding, by the force of his sexuality, a socially superior white man and woman who are little more, in fact, than emotional dilettantes.

At some point, almost certainly around this time, Langston began a more adventurous story, "Seven People Dancing." This tale is set in the Harlem apartment of Marcel Smith, who makes money by giving parties at which he sells liquor, and by renting out rooms to couples for trysts. Marcel, who calls himself "Marcel de la Smith," used to call himself "de la Smythe," until his friends ridiculed him. Marcel "was a fairy. . . . His dancing was too fanciful to be masculine and too grotesque to be feminine. But everything that he did was like that so it was very easy to tell he was a fairy." The people dance to a Dizzy Gillespie record. "The music was uranium, and those seven people, had they been super-duper spies, could not have known more about atomic energy." One of the women dancing is wealthy, and the only white there. Her escort is golden-skinned. When she seems to offer herself to a "very dark very handsome hard-rubber-ball man," the black women there become angry. But little in the story is certain. "I do not know the ultimate 'why' of anything," the narrator concedes, and the tale is hardly more definitive. All vaguely decadent in atmosphere, mood, and tone, it ends inconclusively. If the author gives away a sexual preference through the story, it may be that of the voyeur—with a fondness for heterosexual scenes. The "old fairy" Marcel seems ridiculous.

Hughes's body of work, extremely large and varied as it is, is virtually devoid of pieces that even hint at an interest in homosexuality. However, in the summer of 1961, he started the first draft of "Blessed Assurance," the only story he ever published explicitly on the theme of homosexuality. Finished two years later, after fourteen revisions, the tale is about Delmar, an effeminate young black man with an excellent mind and an exquisite voice. Delmar's effeminacy baffles and enrages his insensitive father, who takes no comfort in the fact that his son is "a brilliant queer." On the other hand, to Dr. Manley Jaxon, the effusive male organist of his church, Delmar is an utter delight. Writing an anthem ("*Entreat me not to leave thee*") based on the Biblical story of Ruth, Dr. Jaxon not only dedicates it to Delmar but assigns it to him to sing before the congregation, because "the girls in the ensemble really have *no* projection." At the performance—to the mortification of Delmar's father—"as the organ wept and Delmar's voice soared above the Choir with all the sweetness of Sam Cooke's *tessitura,* backwards off the organ stool in a dead faint fell Dr. Manley Jaxon." As the father seethes with rage, the choir tries to cover with song the ensuing confusion.

"Blessed Assurance" aims at satire all around. All three males are, to varying degrees, ridiculous. The narrator is amused by them, in almost a heartless way. The story attempts no psychological questing into the sexual condition, offers no hints about the possibility of sexual ambivalence in the father, and neither criticizes nor endorses the son or his organist-admirer. Again, as in "Seven People Dancing," the author is not a scientist or anatomist of the human scene. Rather is he something of a sophisticated voyeur, taking a clandestine, esoteric delight in the absurdities of the human condition.

Hughes's interest in the theme of sex in literature in the early 1960s apparently led to one other work, which was also never finished. In 1963, on a train going to Cleveland, he began to scribble notes for "a book about sex," which he expected to call "Sex Silly Season." The few notes recount the sexual initiation of a black boy by a slightly older, more experienced white girl. Although written in the first person and perhaps autobiographical—but reported to Arna Bontemps simply as the start of "a new novel"—the fragment appears to be as devoid of sentimental or neurotic self-involvement on Hughes's part as any of his other pieces on sex.

Behind this stab at writing a novel of sex could have been the huge success of James Baldwin's best-selling *Another Country,* on its appearance in June, 1962. This work was unprecedented in Afro-American fiction in its sexual frankness, with graphic depictions of heterosexual, homosexual, and interracial sex, including rape and sodomy. Reporting on it anonymously for the influential Kirkus review service, Langston deplored what he saw as the absence in it of emotional and intellectual depth. *Another Country* was a novel about love that "will probably be widely read. Its subject is tormented love: love between men and women, homosexuals, whites and Negroes. . . . All these people are hopelessly involved in each other, and with themselves, and search for love in each other generally in physical ways. . . . The ending is a tragic and inconclusive general dissolution in which truth destroys love. It is a curiously juvenile book for a man who has done so much writing. Neither the style nor the thought is particularly brilliant. Yet it has a certain emotional power. As the characters talk endlessly about their passion and the pain, they reveal a staggering collection of the less commonplace griefs of our time. And this relentless insistence, despite a certain banality and naïveté, ends by conveying [an] honest and despairing conviction of reality."

To Langston, there was little that was truly creative, much less visionary, about *Another Country*. Privately to Arna Bontemps, he described Baldwin as aiming for a best-seller in "trying to out-Henry Henry Miller in the use of bad BAD *bad* words, or run [Harold Robbins's] *The Carpetbaggers* one better on sex in bed and out, left and right, plus a description of a latrine with all the little-boy words reproduced in the telling." In the same letter, Langston linked what he saw as Baldwin's excesses to the trend of integration sapping the strength of black youth. Paying a stiff price for the modicum of integration allowed them, young blacks were abandoning the old values and practices in the rush to be like whites. "Cullud is doing everything white folks are doing these days!" Langston mocked. Flocking now to white barbershops, blacks were beginning to ignore parlors owned by members of their own race. Some blacks were seeking to bury their dead with Park Avenue undertakers and were even insisting on white pallbearers. "Integration is going to RUIN Negro business," he predicted—as it apparently threatened to ruin the finest young writer of fiction in the race. (The previous year, however, Langston had praised Baldwin's new collection of "brilliantly written" essays, *Nobody Knows My Name*, as "a book more colored in a racial sense than any other volume on the market this year.")

Langston's reticence in facing the sexual complexity of *Another Country* and his apparent inability to develop his own stories of sex contrasted sharply with assumptions about his sexuality at this point of his life. To some people, that he was aging, unmarried, and often in the company of various handsome, sensitive, artistic young men, meant that he was homosexual. His secretaries and helpers frequently heard these accusations about their employer, and their denials hardly mattered. Once, horrified, a secretary listened as a woman reported to him the crude way Hughes had been dismissed by one of her acquaintances: "Ain't nothing over there but a fat old homosexual!" Other people, without sharing the scorn in the remark, more or less endorsed its substance. "Around the streets of Harlem in the sixties," one man later insisted, "everyone knew that Langston Hughes was gay. We just took it for granted, as a fact. He was gay, and there was no two ways about it."

Twenty years after Hughes's death, although many people approached for information confirmed that he was thought to be gay, no one could recall any concrete evidence for his reputation. No one could offer the name of a man who had been involved with Hughes, or recall an incident, even at secondhand, involving Langston's presumed homosexuality. By choice, he lived in a situation—with the vigilant Toy Harper and her husband Emerson, and various roomers—that certainly did not lend itself to a gay life. Yet for some people the idea was fixed: Langston Hughes was a homosexual. For the greater part of his life, Hughes made almost a fetish of the secrecy about his sexual interests, so that from the start of his adulthood even close friends of liberated sexuality, such as Countee Cullen, Wallace Thurman, Carl Van Vechten, and Bruce Nugent, vouched privately not for the nature or relative strength of his sexuality but for its maddening elusiveness. In choosing to live like a son with the Harpers, rather than have his own home, he compounded that elusiveness. But had he in fact changed by the 1960s, as the nation and the world entered a period of more relaxed morality than he had ever known, so that what he may have once concealed he was now ready to show? Or was Langston's relationship to his young men in fact, as the African student in Paris had put it the previous year, "exempte de tout vice?"

The truth about his sexuality will probably never be discovered. If Hughes indeed had homosexual lovers, what may be asserted incontrovertibly is that he did so with almost fanatical discretion. On this question, every person curious about him and also apparently in a position to know the truth was left finally in the dark. He laughed and joked and gossiped with apparent abandon, but somehow contrived to remain a mystery on this score even to his intimates. His ability to appear to be at ease and defenseless, and at the same time to deny certain kinds of knowledge to those with him, was extraordinary. All his life he prized control far too highly for him to surrender it in his most mature years. Control above all meant to him the preservation of his position as the most admired and beloved poet of his race. That position, which he saw as a moral trust, and which intimately connected his deepest emotional needs to his function as an artist, may have meant too much for him to risk it for illicit sex.

What also seems clear, however, is that Hughes found some young men, especially dark-skinned men, appealing and sexually fascinating. (Both in his various artistic representations, in fiction especially, and in his life, he appears to have found young white men of little sexual appeal.) Virile young men of very dark complexion fascinated him. One such person, for example, was his young namesake Langston Hughes Mickens, who had been brought to his attention late in the 1950s by David Edelstein, a teacher, when Mickens was a little boy in public school, and who remained a friend well into his young adulthood. Mickens's jet-black skin endlessly intrigued Langston. The boy was dark—"darker than Canada Lee and Clarence Muse *combined*." "He is so dark," Langston once explained in a letter about Mickens as a truant, "none of the teachers could see him in classes." His fascination with young Mickens evidently derived from some combination of the effect of the boy's skin color, his lack of sophistication, and the way in which his difficult family situation touchingly reminded Langston of his own loneliness as a child. Sometimes, after roaming the streets at night looking for his father, Mickens would turn up at two or three o'clock at Langston's door, where he was welcome. Hughes would set his work aside. Together they broke into Mrs. Harper's pantry to look for food, such as cans of spaghetti, and listened to records chosen by Langston—the classic Billie Holiday rendition of "God Bless the Child That's Got His Own"; or Oscar Brown, Jr.'s "Nothing But a Plain Black Boy," his setting of Gwendolyn Brooks's "Of De Witt Williams on his way to Lincoln Cemetery."

There were those who wondered why a man of Hughes's years and station could be so close to a plain black boy, unless some form of homosexual attraction was involved. For his part, however, far from being furtive or clandestine about their relationship, Langston behaved in public like a man completely above such a charge. Well known to Mickens's teachers, who encouraged his interest in Mickens, he made no attempt whatsoever to hide his affection for him—even if he also found the boy amusing: "I am proud of that boy, getting through school and cannot read a lick." Now and then he bought Mickens clothes, sometimes gave him money, and consoled him when he was lonely or confused. Mickens was "My favorite godchild! *Regardless.*" The mixture of incredulity and affection with which he viewed the boy and his world comes through in an excerpt from a letter to Arna Bontemps: "4 A.M. now. My full-name godson just this minute phoned. 16—but a nightowl like me. His boon buddy, barely 16, is the proud father of a bouncing baby girl by a 15-year-old white girl. Present at the birthing, when the nurses asked, 'Who's the father,' and this little 4 foot colored boy stepped forward, they like to fainted. (Life is at least amusing.) My godson was looking at my TV LATE-LATE-LATE Show in the front room last week. I went in and didn't see anything but the screen. In the dark I couldn't see him at all. He is THAT dark! He quit school to go to work. Home problems. He claims nobody likes him. I used to feel that way myself, so I understand. 'Lonely house, lonely me. . . .' "

Hughes's reputation as a homosexual is based almost exclusively on rumor and suspicion, very much like his reputation as a communist, which he denied and denied for almost thirty years without quieting his accusers or stamping out the rumors that he had once belonged to the Communist Party and perhaps still did. Hughes never won this nasty battle with the right wing; he only kept his opponents at bay. In his lifetime, he was never called upon to assert or deny that he was a homosexual, but it is clear that—whatever the truth—he did not want to be considered gay. Whether this attitude derived from a personal aversion to homosexuality, or only from shame or fear, is impossible to say.

Far more pressing than this question of sexuality—although doubtless related to it, as well as to his lonely childhood—was a certain emptiness deep in his affections that a few highly sensitive people claimed to see. The heartiest of men in the public eye, at a more intimate level Hughes had become almost— heartless, as if too much loneliness and pain had scorched him and made him incapable of raw feeling. The serious, reflective Roy DeCarava, Langston's collaborator on *The Sweet Flypaper of Life,* recalled becoming angry with him again and again when Langston reacted to suffering with not simply a brittle laugh, which might have been excusable, but a guffaw. "I remember once he was telling me about a man who had beaten his woman and dragged her down a flight of stairs," DeCarava said. "I was appalled by the story, but even more appalled by the fact that Langston was telling it as a big joke, complete with howls of laughter. I think his laughter had nothing to do with laughter, and everything to do with impotence. If I ever spoke of pain to Langston, he would become uncomfortable and turn away in embarrassment. It was obvious to me that he had been hurt a great deal but refused to face the fact in a way that might, just might, have resulted in healing. He was serious sometimes but his seriousness was oblique. Mostly he laughed. You could not get to him."

DeCarava also remembered photographing Hughes for *I Wonder as I Wander.* "I ended up shooting between twenty and thirty rolls of film. But very few of the exposures were any good. He showed two sides—one looking at the camera, the other smiling that smile. I could never get past those two. I kept waiting for his real character to come through, but I couldn't see it. Maybe I should have shot one roll and just taken what was there. Whatever was underneath he either couldn't, or wouldn't, reveal."

One person who was even more privileged than DeCarava in getting close enough to Langston was Lindsay Patterson, a young black writer befriended by him in the sixties. Patterson never worked for Hughes, but stayed off and on at 127th Street as he tried to nurture a career that took him at least once to the prestigious McDowell writing colony. Patterson later recalled a masked but intrinsically tortured Langston Hughes, whose memory of childhood hurt was intense—"he hated his mother and father as if they were still alive"—and who freely indulged expressions of rage as long as he could hide them behind the plastic mask of his smile. "Many people who thought he liked them," Patterson said, "Langston hated. He didn't hesitate to use the word 'hate'." The house at 127th Street was less a home than "a burden," something that Toy Harper had talked him into buying, to his later regret. As for whites in general, Hughes did not like them—except for the blind producer Stella Holt, with whom he talked almost every night. "He felt he had been exploited and humiliated by them," Patterson insisted. "He was cynical about his editors, because few challenged him, or tried to guide him. They simply used him—and never encouraged him with the kind of advance they lavished on white writers of far less ability."

As for his sexuality, "Langston knew at the end that he was being snickered at behind his back because of the young men about him. But he didn't care. He cultivated the people he felt he had to cultivate—white or black—and he kept on with his writing. His smile made everything possible. He hid many things. He hid the fact that he was very well read, and had strong ideas. He would see a play, dissect it, but refuse to put his critical ideas in print. He *mastered* the smile, the grin, the surface pleasantness."

"Conceit and egotism is cold and dangerous. It will destroy anyone and leave you lonely in the declining years." So wrote one woman to Hughes, on the strength of having read some of his work and visited his home two or three times. "You have never loved anyone dearly. This element was left out of your life from the very beginning of your childhood. . . . You were a lonely cold child."

Against such analyses of Langston's personality and psychology is the memory of him preserved by people such as Phil Petrie, later a writer and an editor, who roomed at 20 East 127th Street from 1960. The house was "hardly a rooming house, because it was such an open house, where people lived in a very pleasant relationship to one another. It was truly a home. I never saw any tension between Mr. Hughes and the Harpers. Mr. Hughes was always gracious. We were aware that it was his home, but he was a kind man. If he had a play going, he sent you a ticket. If you yourself did something kind, he sent you a note of thanks, or a gift. He remembered your birthday, he gave you little jobs when he thought you needed money. And he didn't ask for anything in return—except a certain degree of respect, I think."

Ruth Jett, a leader in the Commitee for the Negro in the Arts and, later, an employee of the Carnegie Endowment for International Peace, offered an even more enchanted view of Langston. In turn, he clearly thought of her as a loving friend, and often sent her Valentine greetings. "I am not very objective about Langston, because I was very fond of him," she admitted. "He was like a brother to me and to many people. The house was a warm, loving place, where he wanted to be and where he did things he wanted to do—like entertain his friends, or the neighborhood children. He would gather them and Aunt Toy made lemonade for them and entertained them in the back yard. One could feel the love he felt for her, and them. He was generous. Now and then he might be angry, but only about something specific that had happened, something unfortunate—and he was never bitter. He laughed a lot, and sometimes I felt that a part of that was laughing to keep from crying. There was a certain point you couldn't cross. But long before you got to that point, you were satisfied to have known him."

In an even better position to know Hughes was Adele Glasgow of the Negro Book Society and the Market Place Gallery in Harlem. Glasgow had first met him in 1938, through the Harlem Suitcase Theatre. Working on and off for him as a typist through the 1950s—even when he could not pay her—she became a close friend, who saw him in a wide variety of situations. Well read and intelligent, Glasgow was quietly assertive, even commanding (she was "sweet, but earthy and very strong," DeCarava judged). Yet her sense of Langston was all benign. "He was a wonderful person, entirely without vindictiveness," she insisted. "If he was not always cheerful, what was incredible about him was his inability to be mean-spirited. He was the most wonderful human being I have ever known." Hughes turned out an awful amount of work, "and perhaps some of it isn't very good. But what he accomplished was extraordinary." As for his home, "it was a happy house, a beautiful place in its furnishings and its spirit. He was loved by many people, and he knew and appreciated it. Any other basic picture of Langston and how he lived simply isn't true."

The 1960s was a time of change for the nation as a whole, and for Langston Hughes perhaps no less. In a few notes scribbled after his death, his best friend Arna Bontemps would reflect on the last stage of Hughes's life as finding him "trapped between two powerful impulses—his passionate love of people and his compelling need for isolation." These were forces, Bontemps suggested, like those of Scylla and Charybdis, that threatened destruction on either side. (Bontemps himself may have believed that Langston was homosexual, although it is highly unlikely that the men ever discussed the subject. A fragmentary and puzzling note observed that Langston had "Never betrayed the mincing or posturing offensive to the straight world.")

Turmoil and contradiction, however, were for Hughes the stuff of art. And even as he headed uncertainly toward the end, he was ready for fresh adventures as an artist. They would be linked, as always, to the lives and art of black Americans.

13

IN GOSPEL GLORY
1961 to 1963

Christ is born on earthen floor
In a stable with no lock—
Yet kingdoms tremble at the shock
Of a King in swaddling clothes
At an address no one knows , , ,

Black Nativity, 1961

WHISPERED INSINUATIONS and rumors did not lessen Langston's popularity or diminish his prestige. Few days passed without some writer or artist from Latin America, the Caribbean, Africa, or Europe, ringing the doorbell at 20 East 127th Street. So many of these visitors came now at the request of the Department of State that Langston finally protested to Washington that if he was to be "the official host of Harlem," he should have an official stipend. But without a stipend, and in a few crowded days, he welcomed at one point a group of French theater folk, a poet from Colombia, a writer from Jamaica, and two writers from Africa. Some visitors were more welcome than others. The charming Wole Soyinka ("Bright boy") enlivened the house as he learned the "twist" from George Bass and demonstrated in turn the Nigerian "JuJu." With visitors who proved to be bores, as a few did, Langston as often as not took them to the Baby Grand nightclub, where the music was usually so loud that he could ignore them. Some visitors, however, refused to be ignored. One night, an ominous-looking white man sat outside the house all night, then scurried past Mrs. Harper on the heels of another visitor who had brought a tape recording of a play which "almost put me to sleep." The mysterious white man wanted to borrow a few thousand dollars. He went quietly only after Langston, in desperation, handed him three one-dollar bills. "So my day was shot! Took me 24 hours to get my nerves together again. At the moment neither white folks nor Negroes get past the front door."

With the fall came various receptions and dinners—for Alioune Diop of the prominent magazine *Présence Africaine;* for Marvin Wachman, the new president of Lincoln University; for the British intellectual C. P. Snow, given by the National Institute of Arts and Letters (sitting together, Langston and the equally bored and restless Carson McCullers passed the time translating the menu from French into jive talk and "down home" dialect). For all his periodic discomfort, however, Langston seemed to have no real desire to decline these more formal invitations. He clearly enjoyed dressing up and stepping out in style, away from Harlem for an evening. With his gift of conversation and laughter he was an excellent dinner guest—even if he once satirized his position at otherwise all-white dinner parties in "Dinner Guest: Me."

> I know I am
> The Negro Problem
> Being wined and dined,
> Answering the usual questions
> That come to white mind
> Which seeks demurely
> To probe in polite way
> The why and wherewithal
> Of darkness U.S.A.—
> Wondering how things got this way
> In current democratic night,
> Murmuring gently
> Over *fraises du bois*,
> "I'm so ashamed of being white."
>
> The lobster is delicious,
> The wine divine,
> And center of attention
> At the damask table, mine.
> To be a Problem on
> Park Avenue at eight
> Is not so bad.
> Solutions to the Problem,
> Of course, wait.

November 3 brought the social highlight of the year—perhaps of Langston's life—when he attended a luncheon for about thirty guests in honor of Léopold Sédar Senghor, the poet and president of Senegal, at the White House. If nothing else, Langston's presence there demonstrated how far he, Africa, the United States, and John F. Kennedy himself had all come since Langston's humbling by Joseph McCarthy in 1953. His invitation had originated with Senghor, but Kennedy's White House staff had not blocked it. For this, Langston was undoubtedly grateful—although he pretended to have been far more interested in the hors d'oeuvres of smoked salmon and the "GREAT BIG" trout *aux amandes*, grilled tomatoes, and *pommes parisiennes* on his luncheon plate. He was also pleased when the spotlight fell on him briefly after dessert, as the two presidents toasted one another with champagne. Senghor specifically mentioned Langston Hughes as a major early source of inspiration. As Hughes beamed in appreciation, President Kennedy turned quizzically to see "just which poet I might be." This visit to the White House doubtless encouraged Langston's admiration for Kennedy, which had grown since the inauguration but remained tempered by Kennedy's gradualism on civil rights. "Give the new President a chance," Langston had urged in February. "Many of his words sound good. Words are the coins of education. So speak, Mr. Kennedy, speak!"

(In Nashville, Tennessee, a newspaper spoke about the presence of Langston Hughes in the White House as "an affront to every man and woman in this country, of all creeds.")

The major professional event of the fall of 1961 for Langston was the appearance from Knopf, in a text of unusual and colorful design, of *Ask Your Mama*—"the most handsome looking book I have ever had." (In fact, the design verged on the gaudy.) Knopf was anticipating a brisk Christmas gift-book sale. To publicize it, he converted the poem into a dialogue for the actors Ozzie Davis and Ruby Dee, asked the rising choreographer Alvin Ailey to compose a ballet based on the text, and pressed Randy Weston for a musical score for the entire poem. Copies of the book went to a wide array of people— from Ezra Pound, now released from his psychiatric prison in Washington and returned in peace to Rapallo, Italy, to Louis "Satchmo" Armstrong—who, to Langston's disappointment, acknowledged neither the gift of a copy nor the dedication of the book to him.

But Langston's efforts were largely in vain. The reviews of *Ask Your Mama,* with some exceptions, were mainly punitive. Although the book might attract partisans, the Kirkus review service was sure that "lovers of real poetry won't be among them"; and *Library Journal* dismissed it for being "as thin and topical as much of the beat material it resembles." In the *New York Times,* Dudley Fitts, who had crushed Hughes's Gabriela Mistral volume, declared that *Ask Your Mama* "cannot be evaluated by any canon dealing with literary right or wrong" and reported "stunt poetry, a nightclub turn." A Dallas, Texas, reviewer asked: "What does it take to get one's manuscript published?" To a North Carolina reviewer, *Ask Your Mama* was "merely curiously interesting and enjoyable because of its novelty of presentation." In some respects, and significantly so, this was the worst-received volume by Hughes since *Fine Clothes to the Jew,* in which he had achieved his finest work with the blues in poetry.

Some voices strongly disagreed. In the Chicago *Tribune,* Paul Engle found wit and conscience "and the thrust of life right now." J. Saunders Redding saw a revitalized Hughes, "more sophisticated now and—oddly—less confined." The jazz critic Rudy Blesh perceptively hailed *Ask Your Mama* as "the retort—half-derisive, half-angry—to the smug, the stupid, the bigoted, the selfish, the cruel, and the blind among us. . . . With this great theme, a talented poet finds a universal voice." And at Howard University, Owen Dodson saluted Hughes's achievement: "It is cogent, burning, hilarious, satirical, bible black and whore yellow. No one in the world could have done this with such dash and insight as you."

Langston seemed especially disturbed that "NOT A SINGLE white reviewer" had noted the roots of the poem in the black form of ritualized insult called the "Dozens," or understood "what the real meaning of the poems are." To Therman O'Daniel, the editor of the scholarly journal of the predominantly black College Language Association, he ventured that "some colored reviewer should wake them up." Langston also complained directly to John Dollard, the Yale professor of psychology whose pioneering article on the "Dozens" he had admired in 1936. "Let's see if the critics of culture know what they're reading," Hughes wrote to S. I. Hayakawa in sending him a copy of his book. "If not, you can break it to them gently." In spite of these efforts, *Ask Your Mama* sank quietly out of sight. No scholar, whether black or white, apparently was prepared to take the poem seriously. No one was challenged sufficiently by its allusions or references, or by its possible novelty as a fusion of jazz and literary language. Perhaps Hughes should not have been surprised. Even after the lavish praise heaped on Melvin Tolson by eminent whites such as Allen Tate, Selden Rodman, Karl Shapiro, and John Ciardi, Tolson's highly crafted verse had also gone almost entirely unnourished by criticism. The white academic world continued to see the work of black writers as generally beneath notice, and the black academic world more or less had no mind of its own.

Ask Your Mama had flopped, but Langston was far from finished as a writer—a fact underscored at a Negro Book Club party in Harlem, when lovers of Jesse B. Semple snapped up more than one hundred and fifty copies of Hill and Wang's *The Best of Simple,* collected from Langston's four Simple books and his abundant *Defender* columns. Almost at the same time, however, he was on the brink of something new—a dramatic concept drawn from the past but also distinctively novel in its essence. In November, Langston began a gospel play based on the theme of the Nativity. One idea above all guided him. Instead of writing a play like *Tambourines to Glory* that included gospel songs, he would attempt to make black gospel music the heart and soul of the drama, and not merely its adornment. Gospel itself had been virtually exploding in popularity, with several of its finest exponents now performing with great success in nightclubs such as the Village Vanguard, the Blue Angel, and Birdland, where jazz had ruled alone. "Jazz makes people happy on the surface," Mahalia Jackson explained. "But a gospel song lasts—it penetrates much deeper and stays with you."

The core of Langston's idea had probably come from the brief Christmas libretti written the previous year for Margaret Bonds and Jan Meyerowitz; Hughes was undoubtedly also well aware of the phenomenal success of Gian Carlo Menotti's Christmas classic *Amahl and the Night Visitors,* which had become the most frequently staged opera in the world. Specifically, however, Langston was responding to a commission from a former music scholar, Gary Kramer, in his early thirties, who had abandoned his doctoral work on Wagner and the influence of Bayreuth to work for Atlantic Records and lecture on jazz and gospel. "Convinced that gospel is poised for a breakthrough to mass popularity akin to the rock 'n roll surge of 1953–54," as the *New York Times* reported, Kramer somewhat impetuously threw over his job and helped to found a gospel management company. As an Atlantic executive, he had talked with Langston about producing a record of his poetry with the Fisk Jubilee Singers. Among Kramer's first decisions now was to commission from him a gospel drama to be staged that Christmas.

Inspired by the challenge, Langston worked so long and hard that a two-tone beard blossomed on his cheeks. As with Kurt Weill on *Street Scene* over fifteen years before, when they had taken to the New York streets in search of inspiration for lyrics and music, he went directly to the major sources of gospel music in Harlem. Haunting the store-front churches and temples, he slipped in among the faithful while the services were in full swing and the melodic and religious fervor rising to its zenith. Then he hurried back to his desk to revise and revamp his text for Gary Kramer. His hard work brought results. On December 6, he sent his drama agent not only the script of "Wasn't That a Mighty Day!", later called *Black Nativity,* but also another gospel play, *The Prodigal Son.* (He finished a third, *The Gospel Glory: A Passion Play,* on the Crucifixion, early the following year, and proposed staging the three shows in one evening as *Master of Miracles: The Life of Christ.*)

Black Nativity marked a major breakthrough in the gospel musical form. As with his evolving mastery of the blues in the 1920s, when he had moved from merely framing the black form within traditional European stanzaic patterns to a complete immersion in it—writing blues themselves, without mediation—Hughes now deliberately allowed black music and religion to overwhelm the traditional play form. Serving to link but also to liberate the vocal skills and religious emotions of a company of authentic gospel musicians, the narrator offers a few remarks here, a touching lyric invitation there:

> *Here again the Christmas story—*
> *Christ is born in all His glory.*
> *Baby laid in manger dark,*
> *Lighting ages with the spark*
> *Of innocence that is the Child,*
> *Trusting all within His smile.*
> *Tell again the Christmas story*
> *With the halo of His glory;*
> *Halo born of humbleness*
> *By the breath of cattle blest.*
> *By the poverty of stall*
> *Where a bed of straw is all,*
> *By a door closed at the Inn*

Where only men of means get in,
By a door closed to the poor.
Christ is born on earthen floor
In a stable with no lock—
Yet kingdoms tremble at the shock
Of a King in swaddling clothes
At an address no one knows
Because there is not hotel sign—
Nothing but a star divine,
Nothing but a halo bright
About His young head in the night.
Mary's son in manger born!
Music of the Angel's horn!
Mary's Son in straw and glory!
Wonder of the Christmas story!

Except for a few melodies set by Alex Bradford, an ordained minister and the musical director of the Greater Abyssianian Church of Newark, New Jersey, all the songs were in the public domain as part of the religious music tradition. The set would comprise simple platforms of various levels "and a star, a single glowing star high over a place that might be a manger." The actors and singers would wear plain smocks. With gospel singers at hand, God's altar needed no polishing. To pull the whole unprecedented effort together (like a fire chief at a five-alarm fire, Langston marvelled), on Hughes's insistence Kramer hired Vinnette Carroll, a dynamic young black director. This move proved decisive.

Currently on the faculty of the High School for the Performing Arts, Vinnette Carroll had trained first as a clinical psychologist, then taken courses in theater at the New School in Manhattan. She had toured with a one-woman show, including several Hughes poems, before turning to directing. Her first full-length effort had been an acclaimed Harlem production of Richardson and Berney's *Dark of the Moon*, which Langston had admired. Carroll had an excellent eye for talent: Alvin Ailey had been her choreographer, Ellis Haizlip her stage manager, and Cicely Tyson, James Earl Jones, Rosalind Cash, and Clarence Williams III members of the cast. Now, for *Black Nativity*, she assembled a company almost entirely of true believers—the magnificent Marion Williams and her all-woman "Stars of Faith" quartet; Rev. Alex Bradford, who would preach the sermon in down-home style and also sing with a group of four men and a woman; and a gifted soloist, Princess Stewart, blind since the age of nineteen. Ellis Haizlip would be the stage manager again.

If Carroll had a clear sense of what was vital in theater—"a dramatic fusion of words, dance, and song so that each element reinforced and explicated the others into a totality of meaning"—she found in Hughes an ideal playwright. "He was totally respectful and cooperative with everything I wanted to do," she remembered. "What I got from Langston was the freedom to do anything

I wanted. He wrote and rewrote as I asked. 'Vinnette, I don't care what you do with the material,' he told me, '—you directors do what you want to do, in any case. Do what you want—just as long as you leave my name on the play!' I took him at his word, and he was happy—and astonished, really—about the way the thing turned out.''

Black Nativity was a product of Hughes's faith in the importance of a black racial sense, and as such—in the golden age of integration—it offended some blacks. Carmen De Lavallade, a star dancer with the Metropolitan Opera, who was hired by Carroll to dance and mime the role of Mary when the play was still called "Wasn't That a Mighty Day!," balked at the new name. "The title now seems in bad taste and I don't want to be a part of it,'' De Lavallade explained when she left the cast. Departing with her, out of loyalty to his friend and colleague, was Alvin Ailey, who had been retained by Carroll to choreograph the show and dance the role of Joseph. They were replaced by the Jamaican-born Clive Thompson and Cleo Quitman of the New York Negro Ballet.

In addition, the religious spirit on stage had little effect on the producers, who fought among themselves, according to the ancient laws of Broadway, in anticipation of the profits. With Gary Kramer absent and seriously ill (he eventually committed suicide), his partners pressed Langston to scratch his name off the contract. Flatly refusing to do so, Langston instead penned his own initials next to Kramer's name in an attempt to endorse Kramer's continuing proprietorship in the show.

Against this troubled background, *Black Nativity* opened on December 11 at the 41st Street Theatre on Broadway. The response was extraordinary. The audience could hardly be restrained, nor could the performers. Aroused by the musical and religious fervor on stage, the capacity audience yelled and cooed ecstatically. One white woman sprang from her seat with a cry, then fainted dead away; and in honor of God and in defiance of Equity, the singers sang for about half-an-hour past the prescribed end of the show. Unanimously, except for remarks about its sometimes sentimental tone, the critics hailed *Black Nativity* as a major entertainment. To the *Mirror,* the show offered "an exciting blend of text, dance, spirituals and hymns,'' and the *Post* marvelled at its "spirit, zest and uninhibited joy.'' Of the unusually spare narrative, Walter Kerr cannily noted that Hughes had "neither obtruded himself nor extended himself to assert his function as playwright.''

Langston had little time to savor his triumph. Two days later, on a cold morning, he left New York by air for Africa. He left as part of a delegation of performers organized by the American Society of African Culture, or AMSAC, to take part in a festival of Afro-American and African arts in Lagos, Nigeria— a tribute from black Americans to their brothers and sisters in the Motherland, and an opportunity to examine the relationship between the cultures of Africa and Afro-America. Assembled at a cost of $45,000, the troupe included over thirty artists, musicians, dancers, and other luminaries, including Lionel Hampton, Randy Weston, the classical pianist Natalie Hinderas, Nina Simone and Odetta, the actor-singer Brock Peters, the dancer-choreographer Geoffrey Holder, the artist Hale Woodruff, the Nigerian-born drummer Michael "Baba" Olatunji, now a resident of the United States, and the president of AMSAC and former head of Lincoln University, Horace Mann Bond.

To a rousing reception by Nigerians, with radio, television, and newspapers on hand to begin coverage of the first such festival in Africa, the party descended on Lagos. A contingent of police officially escorted its motorcade to the finest hotel in the city, the Federal Palace. In addition to an art exhibition and various stimulating symposia, two major concerts were scheduled at King George V Park. The concerts were the most eagerly awaited portion of the festival, and Langston was assigned to be master of ceremonies at the first. With his customary blend of modesty and charm, he set what he thought was the ideal tone for this black American return home to Africa. The Americans had come, he assured the Nigerians, "to exchange with you our gifts, to exchange with your artists our art . . . in all humbleness and love and sincerity. In a sense, we feel we are coming *home,* to our ancestral home, back to the roots of our culture."

Despite his respectful longing for a landmark cultural exchange, the homecoming was a disaster. Denouncing the effort as "everything from 'badly organized' to 'an unqualified fiasco' and [a] 'downright insult' " to African intelligence and taste, the Nigerian press heaped scorn on its organizers. The painting and sculpture were called facile and imitative, but the music drew the harshest comments. Its subtlety lost in King George V Park, Lionel Hampton's cool, modern sound, built around his vibraphone, went over poorly. The idea of mixing jazz with Natalie Hinderas's classical piano, in a soccer stadium, was seen as a deliberate insult to Africans. Words such as "stupid," "repulsive," and "embarrassing" appeared frequently in the local press from both African and expatriate European reviewers. Apart from Langston Hughes and Geoffrey Holder, who were praised, the visitors were all patronizing and insufferable.

"What happened with Lionel Hampton," Randy Weston recalled, "was that he rehearsed a lot of good music, but once the show started he went into his 'show biz' rountine, with a lot of clowning around. I guess the Africans felt like he was insulting them. They didn't know he does that stuff all the time! Things went downhill after that."

This hostility seemed to open Langston's eyes. "In the new African countries, honest," he wrote soon after in the *Defender,* "I thought everything was roses and sunrise and dew. . . . How naive can even an ancestor-worshipper like me be?" Indeed, certain British reviewers of his *An African Treasury* had criticized his approach for ignoring the distressing realities of Africa's march to independence—graft and corruption, technological backwardness, appalling standards of service, and internecine strife. Now Lagos unfolded as part tropic paradise, part horror. The city was a big, hot, tropical Chicago of twenty-five-story buildings and three-room slum houses holding twenty-five residents each.

Sofas bore Paris labels, but beneath them poisonous snakes were known to loiter. In the rush to be like Chicago, Lagos was "a combination of the most enticing travel folders on the tropics and Dürer's impressions of Dante's *Inferno*."

Still, he recovered his senses and his morale and stayed over a month in Nigeria. Travelling to Benin City, and bearing gifts for his African "son," he visited Sunday Osuya, the polite young dark-skinned policeman he had befriended on his last visit, and Osuya's fiancée. Again, the men got along very well, with each finding something different to prize in the other. Osuya was incredulous about his stroke of good luck: "I still remember, how we met and how you treated me from then and I have, till now, begin to think the type of person you are and the God who brought me your way. . . . I am not a quarter your useless nails." In turn, Langston was more and more convinced that he had found his African son, whatever his son's hopes and intentions: "You must NOT write to me again, 'I am not a quarter of your useless nails,' or anything like that, for that is not true. You are just as much as I am." Sunday Osuya was not convinced by all this democracy. "If I am given any cause to describe you," he wrote Hughes, "I would do so in only two [words]—A 'perfect man'."

Christmas in Lagos turned out to be one long celebration that took Langston from one end of the city to the other, and ended with a thoroughly enjoyable turkey dinner. On New Year's Day, repeating this happy tour, he feted his way "from bootleg palm wine joints to holiness churches with tom-toms instead of organs." Then, on January 7, he left Nigeria. Not surprisingly, the visit to Africa ended in confusion, with Langston broke and owing over $500 in hotel, chauffeur, and other bills. He was forced to telegram to the United States for a loan. The money reached Lagos promptly enough, but was then forwarded at a leisurely—and maddening—pace to him.

But the inconveniences of Lagos hardly mattered in the end. Tremendously stimulated by his visit, Langston soon approached Franklin Watts about doing a "First Book of Nigeria." After a week in Paris, "lovely even in the rain, rain, rain," he returned to New York.

Two days later, coyly bearing vials of French perfume for the women in the show, Langston attended a rousing performance of *Black Nativity*, which had moved to the York Theatre on First Avenue at 64th Street. The show was still playing at capacity when it closed near the end of January for the lack of a theater. But it was hardly dead. One enthusiastic visitor had been Gian Carlo Menotti, the main force behind the internationally famous Festival of Two Worlds at Spoleto, Italy, founded in 1957. At the theater, a young man had tapped Menotti on the shoulder and quietly assured him that the youth's father, a Swiss banker, could be persuaded to finance the production at Spoleto. *Black Nativity* was soon set for the festival.

The success of *Black Nativity* now stirred interest in *Tambourines to Glory*. However, when the Theatre Guild proposed a similar staging, with minimal sets and costumes, Langston was disappointed. "Lo, the poor Negro," he noted mordantly, "—always reduced to simplicity." In one sense, his response was curious. To several people, the trouble with his script for *Tambourines to Glory* was precisely that it reduced black life to simple passions and appetites. Eager to capitalize on the success of *Black Nativity,* Lawrence Langner and his associates still pushed for a more politically progressive script for the older show. "You cannot deal with this vital subject in America today," Hughes was warned, "and then completely ignore . . . the issues of our times." Somewhat unwillingly, he agreed to upgrade the status of the young hero of the play to make him more expressive of contemporary black thinking.

Gospel seemed to be the music of the moment, poised on the brink of international recognition. And with mounting concern he watched the influx of white gospel groups into a field pioneered and perfected by blacks. The oldest, saddest story in American entertainment was about to be repeated. On *Black Nativity,* his own producers started acting as if *"they* discovered the format of dramatizing the gospel format *themselves."* In six months, he predicted, white entertainers "will claim to have originated the idiom—and maybe get away with it in the public prints." Before the year was out, in fact, his backers listed *Black Nativity* in the *New York Times* as having a "narrative by Langston Hughes." Livid, he demanded that his creation be acknowledged as being " 'by Langston Hughes' *without any other qualification."*

Later in the year, he would move to gain greater control of his gospel material by signing an agreement with an apparently promising but inexperienced young black producer, Alfred Duckett. Among their projects was a television series called "Gospel TV Time," a long-playing record of Christmas gospel music, and the world premiere of *The Gospel Glory: From the Manger to the Mountain,* billed as the first Negro passion play, which took place late in October in the Bedford-Stuyvesant district of Brooklyn at the Temple of the Church of God in Christ.

Unfortunately, after a dreadful production in Westport, Connecticut—Langston had never seen "a more amateurishly and carelessly presented performance"—he angrily ended the agreement. He demanded that Duckett relinquish all rights to produce or present the show "in any form whatsoever anywhere in this world or the other from this date on." Thereafter, he left professional productions of his works to professionals—even if he had to watch his pocket, and theirs, at the same time.

His sixtieth birthday slipped quietly by, with telegrams and gifts from a few close friends, including champagne from Van Vechten. Perhaps Langston discouraged a public celebration, unwilling to be reminded of the passage of time. The previous year, 1961, had seen the death of at least four old friends, including his true "discoverer" in 1921, the writer and editor Jessie Fauset, the elegant Harlem boulevardier Harold Jackman, and the singer Muriel Rahn, who in 1950 had beautifully created the role of the mother in *The Barrier.* The serious illness of other friends (in Carmel, California, Marie Short had been struck by a massive coronary attack) made him nervous. The sudden death of his Lincoln schoolmate Frank B. Mitchell's mother in Philadelphia, while Langston was staying overnight at her home, absolutely chilled him. He was "still here," but for how long?

These intimations of mortality mocked his pride in knowing that he was the main subject of five books now in preparation, including James Emanuel's study of his short fiction, Donald Dickinson's bio-bibliography, and a full-scale biography (which Langston adamantly refused to authorize, although he was willing to grant interviews) by a white free-lance writer, Constance Maxon. "*Explain* this to me, if you can," he demanded of Arna Bontemps, "*all within a month*, I get word from 5 separate people that each intends to do a *book* about ME, or some aspect of my work. What's happening, this sudden and simultaneous interest bookwise??????" He offered an explanation: "Do you reckon they all think I'm dead? And me still intending to write my third auto-biography??????? One or two books, I can see, maybe—but 5 and all getting underway at once!!! Coincidence, or what??????" Such was part of the price, Bontemps gallantly responded, "for becoming an institution, a part of the culture," a classic in his own time. To which Langston bashfully quoted his favorite line by Emily Dickinson: "How public like a frog. . . ."

In cheerier moments, however, life seemed fine. Blacks were gaining in the South. On Broadway, "things theatrical for Negroes seem on the upgrade." Diahann Carroll was a star in Richard Rodgers's *No Strings,* and Ruby Dee and Ossie Davis's *Purlie Victorious* seemed destined to run forever. Jean Genet's *The Blacks,* Errol John's *Moon on a Rainbow Shawl,* and *Fly, Blackbird* with Avon Long were going strong off Broadway. To *Moon On A Rainbow Shawl* he escorted Mari Evans, an "excellent new poet" from the Midwest. He welcomed Henri Cartier-Bresson from Paris, and took Arthur Spingarn to the fashionable Lüchow's Restaurant to celebrate his eighty-fourth birthday. Langston made progress on one new book, and defaulted on another. For Hill and Wang, he completed a new collection of his short stories, to appear as *Something in Common.* With a third autobiography in mind—he soon gave up work on it—he admitted to his home a talented young Harvard graduate with a brilliant first novel, *A Different Drummer,* expected soon from Doubleday. William B. Kelley was to assist his research. (Ironically, Kelley's father, then an influential editor of the *Amsterdam News,* had scorched Hughes once in the nineteen twenties for writing blues poetry.)

For Kelley, in flight from an alienating education first as a boy at the Ethical Culture and Fieldston schools in New York and then at Harvard, this chance to be close to a major black writer was a rare gift. Later, he would hail Langston Hughes as "my spiritual and literary father." But he also quickly sensed something of an incongruity in the whirl of activity about Langston, who seemed oddly removed from it all. "There wasn't a high sexual energy coming off of Langston," Kelley judged. "It was almost like he was a celibate. He gave off the aura of a Catholic priest, more than anything else." For all his love of fun, he seemed almost monkish, "as opposed to somebody with some kind of sexual appetite whether heterosexual or homosexual." Langston was a man apart.

"There was loneliness there," according to Kelley. "I often wondered whether Langston had somebody to love him, whether there was a woman out there, whether there was a man out there, whether there was *somebody* who really cared about Langston. There were people around him, but I didn't know whether or not there was somebody special for him. I always had the sense that he was there alone."

In mid-April, Langston flew to Los Angeles for a brief visit to his uncle John Hughes and discovered, to his astonishment, that the irascible eighty-six-year-old man had savings of over $30,000 in the bank, in addition to other holdings. Returning home, he finished for Cyril Clemens's *Mark Twain's Journal* a brief tribute to Ernest Hemingway, whom Hughes had known and admired in Madrid during the Spanish Civil War, and who had shot himself to death the previous year, 1961. Towards another literary titan, Langston was less charitable. At a luncheon of the National Institute of Arts and Letters on May 24, he barely concealed his disgust when William Faulkner received the 1962 Gold Medal for Literature. The previous year, at an Institute dinner, Langston had opposed awarding the medal to Faulkner, whom he despised. As he explained it, he told the Institute "why I wouldn't give it to the leading Southern cracker novelist if it were left to me, great 'writer' though he may be." A pained silence had greeted his remarks, but afterwards more than one person had sidled up to whisper, " 'Langston, I think you're right'." As for the decision: "No wonder the Negro problem is what it is in America."

In his most notorious interview on the civil rights struggle, on February 21, 1956, Faulkner had been reported as saying: "I don't like enforced integration any more than I like enforced segregation. If I have to choose between the United States government and Mississippi, then I'll choose Mississippi. What I'm trying to do now is not have to make that decision. As long as there's a middle road, all right, I'll be on it. But if it came to fighting I'd fight for Mississippi against the United States even if it meant going out into the street and shooting Negroes. After all, I'm not going out to shoot Mississippians." Faulkner explained that by "Mississippians" he meant both blacks and whites, because in Mississippi, "Ninety per cent of the Negroes are on one side with the whites, against a handful like me who believe that equality is important." At another point he had insisted to the interviewer: "The Negroes are right—make sure you've got that—they're right." Later that year, he described people in the "middle" as Southern whites who were "present yet detached, committed and attainted neither by [white] citizens' council nor NAACP."

The same year, in the *Defender,* Langston had devoted an entire column to Faulkner's remarks. Since Faulkner had declared his willingness to take up arms against the Federal government, what would happen to him the next time he applied for a passport? Would he be treated as Paul Robeson was being treated for making statements weaker than Faulkner's against the government? "Personally, I respect genius, and I respect sincerity. I believe Mr. Faulkner is an excellent writer and a sincere citizen. He is not a political demagogue talking for votes. So when he says what he says, he really means what he says. But WHY he says what he says is not clear.'' Faulkner's remarks, Langston insisted, showed a deep hostility to blacks. But the National Institute had either disagreed with him, or considered the question irrelevant.

The end of spring brought no respite from his busy schedule. In New Haven, Langston attended a Yale Little Theatre awards ceremony at which the Trinidadian dramatist Errol Hill was honored. Soon after, he was at home to the anthropologist Oscar Lewis, the author of the famed study of Mexican life, *Children of Sanchez*. Lewis was thinking of doing a similar study of Harlem. Welcoming the plan, Langston pledged to help as best he could.

A week later, he achieved another milestone when the *New York Post* hired him to write a weekly column much like that in the *Chicago Defender,* including the opinions and exploits of Simple. By this time, his relationship with the *Defender* was almost dead. Over the years, he had been irked by its indifferent editing, consistent inefficiency, and grudging payments. With white syndicated columnists available at $5 a week, the newspaper executives wondered why they should pay Langston Hughes a penny more. At one point, the *Defender* had owed him six months of pay, then sent checks for six weeks and curtly demanded a column. But age had made Langston less accommodating. The previous December, after his checks stopped coming without explanation, he quit sending material: "No word, no money—no writeeee!" (His column would resume in September.)

Early in June, he again left the United States for Africa, his third visit there in two years. This time he would attend a conference of writers at Makerere University College in Kampala, Uganda, and speak at the dedication of a new United States Information Service Center and Library in Ghana. On Saturday, June 9, Langston reached Entebbe, Uganda, on his first visit to East Africa. Two days later, the M'bari Writers Conference opened in Kampala, with about forty-five writers, editors, scholars, and journalists from nine African countries, Great Britain, the United States, and the Caribbean in attendance. (''M'bari'' referred to an Ibo custom of building a special hut, or ''m'bari,'' in ceremonial homage to a deity.) Langston had accepted this invitation at once. The rise of the new African nations, as he explained to a Soviet writer, ''inspires me poetically, as it is inspiring other Afro-American poets who see in their ancestral homeland a sunrise tomorrow. . . . Poetry has a new subject to explore, a new theme to celebrate.''

With sessions scheduled from morning to dusk on five consecutive days, he found the pace of the conference gruelling. But he enjoyed the company of most of the younger writers, among whom were Chinua Achebe, Wole Soyinka, Ezekiel Mphahlele, Bloke Modisane, and Cyprian Ekwensi of Africa, and Arthur Drayton and Barry Reckord of Jamaica; also there was the Afro-American critic J. Saunders Redding. In a spontaneous move that surprised and moved Langston, the conference declared him its guest of honor. ''Someone proposed it quietly and just about everyone agreed at once,'' Redding recalled. ''With Bloke Modisane in the chair, Mphahlele delivered a five-minute tribute that seemed to stun and embarrass Langston. I joined in by reading a few of his poems. At the end Langston half-rose, bowed quickly, sat down, and gave a long sigh.''

Respectfully he listened to the sometimes heated debate on the great literary questions of the hour, posed against the backdrop of sweeping political changes from colonialism to independence. What was African literature? Writing by black Africans only? Was there a distinctly African literary sensibility? What role could the white readership, and the white publisher, play? The presence of the publisher Andre Deutsch from London and representatives of Northwestern University Press and the *Kenyon Review* in the United States prompted sarcastic remarks about a new, sordid scramble for the spoils of Africa. As the first black in the United States, and perhaps in the world, to live by his writings, Langston heard these points of debate as so many clamorous echoes of moments of concussion in his own long career. Negritudinous far in advance of the doctrine of *Négritude,* he had long ago faced for the first time these fundamental questions of art and identity, of the conflict of cultures, of the future of blacks in a world ruled by Europe. To the younger writers, he held up the ideal of a racial basis to black art, even as it moved at the same time toward universality. African writing, he said, should reflect "Negro emotions." In at least one quarter his counsel was brushed off. "There are no such things," a white South African journalist scolded Hughes, who was only a "genial, sentimental public entertainer."

Perhaps the journalist's attitude was shared by some of the younger blacks. Langston's friend Mercer Cook, later U.S. Ambassador to Senegal, recalled Langston telling him of a painful incident in Uganda. "A young black man apparently came up to him and said, 'I have never thought the day would come when the great Langston Hughes would be an Uncle Tom.' Langston laughed when he related the story, but I could see that he was hurt." On the other hand, in a published report, one black African later emphasized Langston's "beautiful readings from his own poems."

From Uganda, Langston flew to Cairo, on his first visit to Egypt, then to Rome to see a successful production of *Shakepeare in Harlem* at the Teatro Goldoni, the oldest theater in the city. Dropping in without notice, he delighted the black American cast, which had been stocked mainly with castaways from the shooting of the motion picture *Cleopatra.* However, his main destination in Italy was the small town of Spoleto, in the Umbrian district, and Gian Carlo Menotti's Festival of Two Worlds. There, in an eighteenth-century theater packed at each performance, *Black Nativity* was the undisputed critical and popular hit of the season. Hughes's black gospel drama had been hailed as the most electrifying event in the history of Spoleto, rivalled only by Jerome Robbins's "Ballets: U.S.A." five years before. "It was a fantastic hit," Vinnette Carroll recalled (she had acted as narrator). "We could hardly walk the streets of the town without people stopping us to shake our hands and touch us and offer congratulations."

With a European tour of *Black Nativity* set, he returned to Africa. In Nigeria, he travelled to Ibadan to visit his African "son," Sunday Osuya, who was enrolled there in a refresher course in police work, and with whom Langston had kept corresponding. Then, near the last day of June, he reached Accra, Ghana. He had agreed to speak at the formal opening of the new U.S. library there after the famed reporter Edward R. Murrow, now the director of the United States Information Agency, had advised him that Washington attached "rather special significance to this event." Murrow did not have to say much more. With the recent murder of Patrice Lumumba in the Congo, probably at the hands of CIA-backed forces, and the growing pro-Marxism of Kwame Nkrumah, the presence of Langston Hughes at the ceremony would be a fine thing for the U.S. effort in Ghana. If Langston had misgivings about performing what Murrow called "this little chore," he probably shelved them when he learned that the new ambassador to Ghana was the liberal Democratic lawyer William P. Mahoney of Arizona. "Ghana will be fortunate to have him in residence," he wrote Murrow. Bill Mahoney was married to Noël Sullivan's niece Alice Doyle. Langston had not only known her as a young girl, but had stayed with the Mahoneys once as a houseguest in Phoenix.

The Mahoneys had been only two weeks in Ghana, and had barely un-packed, when Langston arrived for the opening. For him and Alice Mahoney, it was a special moment. They had first met twenty-eight years before, in 1934, on the beach at Carmel, when he had lived there on the generous patronage of her uncle. She was celebrating her eleventh birthday, and he had given her a collapsible camp stool, bright red in color. "And here we were now, thirty years later, and in Ghana of all places," Alice Mahoney recalled. "Langston and I hugged and laughed and pretty soon we were talking about Uncle Noël and saying, 'Isn't this really great? Wouldn't Uncle Noël have really loved it?' "

The next day, at the opening, Langston said the right things. Africa and America depended on one another. "Today, when America comes to Africa," he declared, "as through these library shelves, to offer an *exchange* of knowledge (not merely to *give* in the old patronizing sense), America is bolstering her own basic dreams, and finding here in Africa a new strengthening of the old concept of freedom in your liberated lands. Black Africa today is sending rejuvenating currents of liberty over all the earth reaching even as far as Little Rock, Birmingham and Jackson, Mississippi." Once thought of by many in the outside world as the 'Dark Continent,' today:

> Africa, sleepy giant,
> You've been resting awhile
> Now I see the thunder and the lightning
> In your smile
> Now I see the storm clouds
> In your waking eyes,
> The thunder, the wonder, and the young surprise,
> Your every step reveals the new stride in your thighs—
> Uhuru, Africa!

Africa deserved a better poem (he read others, and closed with "We Have Tomorrow"), but few black Africans could hear these lines delivered by an American of any color and be unmoved. He was powerful again when he and Alice Mahoney visited Ghana's leading high school, Achimota College, to read to the students. "They received Langston so beautifully," she remembered. "They loved him right away, and he had them absolutely in the palm of his hand."

Enjoying the company of another house guest, Father Theodore Hesburgh, the president of the University of Notre Dame, where he and Bill Mahoney had been classmates, Langston stayed on through the Fourth of July. During this time, he made no other appearances in Ghana, and he did not meet Kwame Nkrumah. Perhaps there was nothing sinister to this fact. "The only reason Nkrumah did not receive Langston," Bill Mahoney later affirmed, "was because I did not have enough sense at the time to ask him."

Back in the United States, he helped to launch his history of the NAACP, *Fight for Freedom*. A draft had been greeted warmly by Jack Greenberg of the NAACP Legal Defense and Education Fund, who called it "the most exciting telling of the N.A.A.C.P. story that I have seen." To Thurgood Marshall, who had left the leadership of the Fund to take a U.S. Circuit Court judgeship, Hughes had done "a wonderful job." Apart from the communist press, most reviews praised the liveliness of his chronicle. "Somebody ought to put it in every library in the country!" the *Saturday Review* advised. With its complex organization and many branches, the NAACP set Hughes a trying publicity schedule. Faithfully he tried to make as many engagements as possible—although not all were as much fun for Langston as a "Twist for Freedom" book-party-and-dance sponsored at Small's Paradise in Harlem.

Late in October, news of the Cuban missile crisis broke while he was in Washington, D.C., where he had come to take part in the first national poetry festival in the history of the United States. Organized by Louis Untermeyer, the poetry consultant to the Library of Congress, the event brought together thirty-three major American poets to mark the fiftieth anniversary of *Poetry* magazine by celebrating American verse. Although the omission of certain writers, such as Allen Ginsberg, William Carlos Williams, Archibald Mac-Leish, Carl Sandburg, and Ezra Pound, brought charges of a conservative bias, Langston joined Gwendolyn Brooks in representing The Race at an extraordinary gathering of poetic accomplishment. Among the poets present were Robert Frost, R. P. Blackmur, John Berryman, Robert Lowell, Randall Jarrell, John Crowe Ransom, Kenneth Rexroth, Delmore Schwartz, Muriel Rukeyser, Mark Van Doren, Louise Bogan, Richard Eberhart, and Robert Penn Warren. Langston attended a reception for the group at the White House, hosted by Mrs. Kennedy.

He was proud to be in such company but especially happy to greet Gwendolyn Brooks and her daughter, Nora. Among the writers gathered for the festival, at least one other poet touched him with her presence—Katherine Garrison Chapin, whose inclusion in this elite group of writers drew snide remarks about her social prominence in Washington. To Langston, however, she brought back painful memories. Katherine Chapin Biddle and her sister, Cornelia Chapin, had been the two young women closest to "Godmother," Mrs. Rufus Osgood Mason, during his years of luxury and, in the end, heartbreak under her patronage between 1927 and 1931. In Washington, Langston and Katherine Chapin had a pleasant talk. She remembered the young Langston Hughes, she later wrote him; "But I am glad you stand where you do."

At a morning panel on "The Poet and the Public," where much of the talk was about the alleged chasm between poet and audience, Langston declared flatly that he wrote with the public in mind and yet had enjoyed a long career, even if it meant being constantly a "performer and reading in a loud voice." The next day, as the U.S. Navy prepared to halt Soviet ships, he read in an afternoon session with R. P. Blackmur, Katherine Chapin, and Babette Deutsch (who had flayed him in the *New York Times* some years before for *Montage of a Dream Deferred*). He took the occasion seriously. Although each reader had only ten minutes, he had made seven drafts of his text. From his various volumes dating back to 1926, he selected nine poems. First came "Still Here," the defiant anthem of the second half of his life ("I been scarred and battered . . ."). Then he read "American Heartbreak," about the denial of black freedom; the nihilistic "Distance Nowhere"; the first blues verse he had ever heard; his benchmark poem, first published in 1921, "The Negro Speaks of Rivers"; one of the witty "Madam to You" verse pieces; "Negro," which had been the first poem printed in his first book, as he pointed out; "Poem" ("We have tomorrow . . ."); and "Merry-Go-Round." Finally, with a quip about himself and Kenneth Rexroth being "the only beatniks here, except for Randall Jarrell, who has a beard," he closed with the first eighty-four lines of *Ask Your Mama*.

In deference to the current crisis, however, Langston cannily dropped several lines, including references to "THE PAPERS / THAT HAVE NO NEWS THAT DAY OF MOSCOW." Probably no one at the festival had given more public readings than Langston Hughes. One of the longest and loudest ovations of the entire event rewarded his expert performance.

In mid-November, after attending a seventy-fifth birthday dinner for Marianne Moore, he left for Cleveland for a major book party for *Fight for Freedom* at which he sold almost five hundred copies. Then he flew to Los Angeles for a brief visit with his uncle. Returning on Thanksgiving to New York, he found more bad news waiting about *Tambourines to Glory*. Earlier, replacing Herbert Machiz as director, Nikos Psacharopoulos of the Yale University Drama School had opened auditions for the show at the Broadhurst Theatre in Manhattan. However, the parade of talent had barely started before Lawrence Langner fell ill again and entered a hospital. *Tambourines to Glory* reentered limbo.

Two days before Christmas, however, and after wonderful receptions on its extended tour of Europe, *Black Nativity* swept into town to begin a week of shows in Philharmonic Hall at Lincoln Center. Again the Nativity gospel show was a sensation. By the end of the week, the enormous hall was almost sold out. In high spirits, Langston telephoned Lawrence Langner at his hospital to suggest it for the Theatre Guild's cross-country series. Promising to see *Black Nativity* the next night, Langner agreed to make a quick decision about its inclusion in the series. Hours later, he dropped dead. The news shook Langston, who had known Langner since the 1920s. To his widow Armina Marshall, Hughes wired his condolences on the loss of not only an associate in the theater but "also to me a wonderful adviser and friend."

He put *Tambourines to Glory* out of his mind; the show seemed hopelessly star-crossed. Besides, as 1963 opened, and the Civil Rights Movement and the backlash against it plunged deeper into violence and confusion, even as preparations for the Emancipation Centennial began, the play's political wisdom never seemed more questionable. The pressure on leading blacks to comment forcefully on the struggle had increased. Before an overflowing hall at Michigan State University in East Lansing on January 8, and the next evening at Wayne State University in Detroit, when he was forced to move to a larger room in the middle of his reading, he chose fighting words. "In the hard-core states of the South we have learned that you can't work these problems out piece-meal," he insisted. Six hundred soldiers had been sent to protect one black man, James Meredith, seeking an education at a state school, the University of Mississippi, but the government hesitated and vacillated almost everywhere else in the South. Langston called for "a sweeping overall announcement once and for all that we intend to integrate and go in with an army if necessary."

At the same time, he showed his dismay at the first, ominous signs of a new emphasis in black activism. In the Detroit *Free Press,* defending the NAACP's legalistic approach, Hughes also attacked what he saw as a "wave of pessimism" sweeping over blacks even as social conditions improved generally. In Detroit, he argued, blacks enjoyed better economic conditions than ever and should build on that improvement. With writers such as Margaret Danner, Oliver LaGrone, Powell Lindsay, and Dudley Randall, a true renaissance was unfolding in the city. Langston greeted the first signals of the new black ultranationalism with a disapproval that would grow steadily in the following years. Although he had always been proud to be a "race man," the central tenet of his pride in belonging to the race was that blackness was a normal aspect of world humanity. He claimed very little more. "I've never felt," he asserted to a black friend in 1961, "that my 'me' was any less or any more than anybody else. Nor have I ever felt very race-conscious in the ingrown sense—which is maybe why I have an objectivity of sorts in my writing which is not as 'colored' as it seems to be on the surface."

One of Langston's favorite jokes, according to the playwright Alice Childress, poked fun at Negro chauvinism. Some students at a strife-torn college were offered money to do summer research on a topic carefully chosen to avoid controversy. The topic was the elephant. Asked about his planned approach, a

German student responded: "I will write a ten-volume introduction to the study of the elephant." Next, a French student spoke of writing on "the romance in the ways of the elephant, and the poetry of the elephant." Then a white American student ventured: "Oh, well, like you got to be something, man, like, so what's wrong with elephants?" The last student was a black American. "I will write about the elephant," he vowed, "and its relationship to racism in the United States of America."

Langston's broad-minded attitude would soon be out of favor among the most vocal black spokesmen. Before the year was half over, Martin Luther King, Jr., who previously had been stabbed by an alleged madwoman in Harlem, would be pelted with eggs when he arrived to preach an evening sermon at Salem Methodist Episcopal in Harlem. Much of the blame for the incident would be placed on a powerful rising force in the black world the uncompromising Black Muslim leader Malcolm X, who had often denounced nonviolence as a bankrupt philosophy. Civil rights organizations were beginning to turn on one another, as when Roy Wilkins of the NAACP openly accused other groups of wantonly stealing credit for social changes from the Association. The gap between the charismatic Kennedy leadership and black spokesmen widened after a meeting between some blacks, including artists, and Attorney General Robert Kennedy, arranged in New York by James Baldwin (and to which Langston was not invited), ended in confusion and distrust.

Psychologically, Hughes was in trouble even before the surfacing of the Black Power movement two years later. He was disturbed not so much by the chasm between liberal approaches, such as that of the NAACP, and the pessimism that would sanction counterviolence, as by his own relative inaction as the movement grew. A note of weariness and foreboding had begun to creep into his utterances about integration, civil rights, politics, and the nation's future. In a discussion on January 28 sponsored by PEN, Langston reflected sadly on Faulkner's remarks about shooting blacks. "If he did say it," he hazarded, "maybe he was a little drunk. Maybe we are all a little drunk, intoxicated on the moonshine of history." Instead of optimism, "we find ourselves relying on the aspirin of a Supreme Court edict when, in some parts of our country, we are suffering the cancer of death." And yet he continued to view the civil rights struggle from a distance, with only token gestures of involvement. He agreed to be a co-sponsor, with Leonard Bernstein and other prominent figures, of a reception for the Southern Christian Leadership Conference at which Martin Luther King, Jr. would speak. But when the eighty-four-year-old Arthur Spingarn gallantly shuffled south to Greenwood, Mississippi, "to prove he is with the freedom riders," as Langston put it, he made no plans to join him. Instead, he sent along only his best wishes and the detritus of his growing fatness—a bundle of old clothes for the poor—two woolen shirts, three pairs of slacks, five suits, six sport coats, and twenty-one outmoded neckties.

He was tired to the bone. His promised speech at a testimonial dinner in April for Lloyd K. Garrison, the veteran legal advisor to the NAACP and a past president of the National Urban League, as well as a key counsellor in

Langston's struggle with Joseph McCarthy, would "POSITIVELY be my LAST public appearance of the century," he swore. "I started out to be a writer, not a public speaker, and a writer I intends to be!" Weary of platform speaking, he was almost as tired of writing itself, after more than forty years of diligent labor. Although he perhaps did not recognize his exhaustion, and certainly never admitted it, there was an element of resigned self-criticism in his humorous response to a young Detroit writer, Ron Milner, who had sought his advice: "I told him not to try to write like me. We need a few writers who also think."

Ironically, his energy sagged even as opportunities grew for him and other blacks to speak and publish. To Indiana University Press, the delayed "New Negro Poets" project suddenly became urgent, and in February he sent off the final manuscript. In March, his collection of short stories *Something In Common* appeared from Hill and Wang, which was dedicated to "Gwendolyn." (Gwendolyn Brooks was "SO SHOCKED I WAS ON THE BRINK OF COLLAPSE," but Hughes may have had additionally in mind his stepbrother's daughter Gwendolyn, of whom he was also very fond.) In April, the first copies of Webster Smalley's *Five Plays by Langston Hughes* arrived.

Interest in his work continued to mount. The longest scholarly study of his poetry, running almost one hundred pages in *Les Poètes Negres des Etats-Unis* by the French academic Jean Wagner, who had been welcomed at Langston's home, underscored his prominent place in the pantheon of black writers. From Leningrad came news of a new edition of his *Selected Poems* there, and a request for a revised foreword and new poems. The drama editor of the *Massachusetts Review,* Doris Abramson, preparing a dissertation on black drama, inquired about his plays. Bruce Kellner, at work on his authorized biography of Carl Van Vechten, came for the first of several conversations. For books on Richard Wright, the French scholar Michel Fabre and an American counterpart, Edward Margolies, sought information and opinion. In these honors and inquiries Langston saw his own end approaching. When Pierre Seghers selected him as the fourth American (after Whitman, Poe, and Dickinson) in his *Poètes d'Aujourd'hui* series, he was impressed but wary: "Comme je ne suis pas encore mort, c'est un honneur, non?"

Langston now saw such interest in him as funereally tinged, as if he had died already and become his papers. The Yale University Library truck, dispatched punctually from New Haven to Harlem by the curator in American literature, Donald Gallup, began to assume a slightly sinister aspect. In a letter, he gave Arna Bontemps formal permission to write "my officially authorized biography," and to edit his *Collected Poems,* presumably after Hughes's death.

On February 16, at the invitation of the photographer Richard Avedon, he and Carl Van Vechten posed for a joint portrait. At the time, according to Avedon, he was requesting sittings by persons whose life and work he respected. The forty-year friendship of Langston Hughes and Carl Van Vechten seemed to him admirable, even noble, and he wanted to memorialize it. Both men quickly agreed to sit for him. The result was a somewhat macabre but revealing portrait, in which Avedon draped one of Van Vechten's arms like a withered bough (he was then eighty-three years old) over Langston's bloated shoulder.

In April, casting a backward glance with a small essay, "My Early Days in Harlem," the sixty-one-year-old Langston seemed on the brink of saying farewell. The winter had been marred by three bad colds, doubtless encouraged by his chain-smoking, his increased imbibing of gin, and the beginning of obesity—he was now over 180 pounds.

And yet a tired Langston Hughes had more energy than many ordinary men. For the NAACP, he continued his *Fight for Freedom* publicity with a script for a "Sing for Freedom" show, with the actress Diana Sands, at a Baptist church in Brooklyn. He went to the White House for a reception marking the Emancipation Centennial. To honor Russell and Rowena Jelliffe, whom he had known for forty-seven years, he visited Cleveland to read a special poem, "And So the Seed," at a gala dinner for a thousand people. And he remained as accessible as ever to visitors. Bloke Modisane came in March and Chinua Achebe in May, when Achebe, Langston, and his namesake Langston Mickens attended a revival of *Street Scene* at City Center in Manhattan.

In March, he provoked a squall of criticism among some Jewish readers of the *Post* when, in the course of a column about crime among blacks, Simple drawled that "the Jewish peoples can change their names from Levine or Levinsky to Lewis or Lee or whatever else they want to, and nobody knows they are Jewish until they die. Then you read in the papers where they was buried by a rabbi." The same was true of Italians and other groups, but a picture of a black criminal not only held up all blacks to scorn, but fostered a sense of shame about being black. One reader accused Langston of no doubt "chuckling with delight" during the Holocaust. "Your tirades against the Caucasian race," another insisted, "are quite absurd." To both letters, and to others similarly hostile, Langston sent soothing replies.

But the unjustified accusations of anti-Semitism wounded him. They were further signs of the toxic racial climate in America, which became worse with every new clash in the South or, increasingly, the North. In Alabama, where Governor George Wallace vowed in his inaugural speech that year to have "segregation now, segregation tomorrow, segregation forever," Dr. Martin Luther King, Jr., was arrested once again when he launched a campaign against discrimination in Birmingham. In Savannah, Georgia, thousands of demonstrators demanded the end of segregation, and in Cambridge, Maryland, a similar campaign led to violent clashes between blacks and whites that resulted in the imposition of martial law. Demonstrations in various parts of Mississippi were galvanized in June when the personable local NAACP leader Medgar Evers was shot and killed outside his home in Jackson. Boycotts protesting *de facto* segregation rocked the Boston and Chicago school systems, and in New York there were what Langston called "minor riots" in Harlem in June.

He wrote of these "minor riots" in an anguished essay not about civil rights but on the devastating spread of drugs in Harlem. At two o'clock in the morning on 125th Street, the main artery across Harlem, only policemen and junkies could be seen in the aftermath of the disturbances. Curiously untroubled by the police, the junkies "drooped and dozed and leaned or slept on their feet all the way from Lexington Avenue to Broadway. In front of broken windows, over-turned garbage cans and other evidences of minor vandalism, sat or stood the addicts like zombies. They leaned in a daze over undrunk coffee in the few cafes still open. Like robots they went through the motions of living in drug-dreams on corners where policemen kept post-mortem." "The teenagers of Harlem are my teenagers," he wrote in the *Post*. "I would think the President, our Congress, our State Legislature and our City Council would care, too—enough to help them. How can decent men anywhere not care about kids, black or white, who can buy marijuana and heroin without trouble almost any time in any of our major American cities? I refuse to believe the powers of government do not care."

Tired and dispirited in spite of his brave, busy front, Langston dreamed of taking a freighter out of New York, just as he had done forty years before, in 1923, on his way to Africa. He went further, and booked passage on a slow old boat due to leave about the first day of June. When word came that the departure was delayed until July, he moved decisively. He made preparations for a trip to Europe and the Mediterranean that would take him away from home for most of the summer.

He also revised his will. ("If Mr. Hughes was depressed at this time," George Bass later remarked, "it is news to me. He read me portions of the will and the related material and was laughing uproariously most of the time. He had fun with it. I was under the impression that Arthur Spingarn had sug-gested strongly that a new will was in order.") Lincoln University remained his ultimate legatee, but Arna Bontemps and young George Bass became his new executor-trustees. Langston also made explicit provision for Bontemps to be his official biographer, as if he knew beyond a doubt that he would die before his friend. He made generous financial provision for the family of his stepbrother, and for Sunday Osuya of Nigeria. Then, drawing up arrangements for his own memorial service, Langston blended decorum with his offbeat sense of humor—"one might as well have a little fun at one's own finalization." There was to be no public display of his body, but a swift cremation. Any memorial service must consist "*entirely* of music, with no speaking whatso-ever."

He specified the pieces and their order of presentation. First would come Thomas Dorsey's *Precious Lord, Take My Hand,* sung by a soloist or small gospel group. Next, "Nothing But a Plain Black Boy," by Oscar Brown, Jr., based on Gwendolyn Brooks's poem "Of De Witt Williams on His Way to Lincoln Cemetery." Then, W. C. Handy's *St. Louis Blues,* played by a jazz group but *without* a singer. Duke Ellington's *Caravan,* or "Blue Sands" by Buddy Collette, or both, played by the same group, would follow. The last piece, also played without a singer, would be Ellington's *Do Nothing Till You Hear from Me*.

"The names of the performing artists may be printed on a card or program, as there should be no Master of Ceremonies. The artists are to be paid union scale or above. And the entire occasion should have the air of an enjoyable concert. My ashes after the memorial may then go to the James Weldon Johnson Collection at Yale University, New Haven, Connecticut, to be catalogued with my other memorabilia, or disposed of as considered fitting and desirable by Yale. Perhaps they might be integrated with the wind."

14

BLUES FOR MISTER BACKLASH
1963 to 1965

. . . Mister Backlash, Mister Backlash,
What do you think I got to lose?
Tell me, Mister Backlash,
What you think I got to lose?
I'm gonna leave you, Mister Backlash,
Singing your mean old backlash blues.

You're the one,
Yes, you're the one
Will have the blues.

"The Backlash Blues," 1966

"YOUR LAUGHTER and your song, your pity for the human condition, your poetic prophecy, the deep seriousness that pulses through your poems exemplify the ancient Grecian concept of the poet as the shaper and maker of our destinies, pointing the way to that one divine event toward which the whole creation moves: the brotherhood of man." With this citation, on June 7, Howard University awarded Langston his second honorary doctorate. The fulsome appeal to the concept of "the brotherhood of man" could hardly have been more timely. At a party given in his honor by Owen Dodson, his friend on the theater faculty, most of the talk was about the violence sweeping the nation as a result of the Civil Rights Movement—and about the astoundingly concurrent epidemic of crime by blacks in Washington, D.C., in the face of apparent racial progress. Listening, Langston looked forward to a summer spent far from the United States.

Before leaving, he finished work on a new gospel play. After a man at a party suggested casually that the civil rights struggle should be excellent inspiration for such a show, Langston swiftly drafted the outline of *Jericho-Jim Crow,* a serious but entertaining and optimistic play about the freedom movement. Ironically, just about the same time, and in spite of the charges of political irresponsibility leveled against it and Hughes, *Tambourines to Glory* found a sponsor. The "angel" was Louis Hexter, a sixty-three-year-old Texas real es-

364

tate millionaire once active as an actor and a director in the Dallas Little Theatre, which he had helped to found. To the delight of Langston and the producer Joel Schenker, Hexter offered to advance most of the $100,000 needed. The only sour note now was struck by the composer, Jobe Huntley. Seeking a bigger share of the royalties, Huntley demanded a renegotiation of their agreement. Langston was outraged. Perhaps Huntley was "a bit confused, and/or misinformed," he wrote Marian Searchinger, his drama agent. "Or, like so many others I have encountered in show business, just plain greedy."

This was not the first time Huntley had complained. In fact, he had become deeply suspicious of his collaborator. Just before the Westport production in 1960, on the advice of a friend, he had protested to Langston that their contract assigned him only twenty-five percent of the royalties, and not the fifty percent that he believed they had agreed on verbally from the start. Langston had refused to budge. "He told me that 'Lorenz Hart didn't give Richard Rodgers that much'," Huntley recalled years later. "And besides, the agent had worked out the percentage." Unfortunately for Huntley's peace of mind, Langston's drama agent represented both men. "I thought about this for a long time," Huntley wrote of Hughes, "then concluded that he was getting the agent to do his dirty work. . . . I was very angry because I had trusted him."

The composer was furious again when a sign for the show outside the Westport Playhouse did not mention his name (although the playbill gave him credit for the music). He went directly to confront Langston, who calmly explained the omission as "an oversight on the printer's part," as Huntley recalled, and promised to have the name added. Apparently it never was. But what Huntley really wanted was both equal pay with Langston and equal billing as creator of the entire show. This concession Langston was not prepared to make; Huntley had been a part of the enterprise from the start, but Langston had conceived and written the musical play. However, just before rehearsals started for the Broadway run, he agreed to have Huntley's name printed on the playbill in the same size as his own, and to increase the composer's share by five percent, to thirty percent. Beyond that point he would not move. But Huntley was not satisfied. "I thought to myself," he later wrote, " 'gypped again, Jobe'."

Leaving the production in Joel Schenker's charge, on July 2 "James L. Hughes" boarded an Air France jet for Europe. With him, toting a new portable typewriter and a bag of books, was his secretary George Bass. The Fourth of July found the men comfortably installed in Paris at the Hotel Grand et de Noailles, the old, gracious establishment near the Opéra in Paris. Comfort was very much on Langston's mind as he began what was in effect a Grand Tour. Although the French newspapers were full of news about the civil rights struggle in the United States, including the massive March on Washington planned for late August, Langston was determined to enjoy his first true vacation in several years. "Mr. Hughes obviously had decided that he wanted to make the tour in style," George Bass recalled. "All the accommodations were first class, and we ate and drank very well, very well indeed. I think he had been looking forward to this trip for a long time. Maybe he thought it might be his last grand vacation, and he was determined to do it right. We had fun!''

After a few quiet days in Paris, the men travelled by train south to Marseilles. Then, leisurely, they moved on to the Riviera. In Nice, they shared an excellent room at the Hotel Negresco, overlooking the Mediterranean. A few days later, on June 10, they reached Venice, which Langston had last visited in 1924, at the age of twenty-two. Then, his companion had been Alain Locke, who had divided his time between pedantically murmuring to Langston about the artistic treasures of the city (when Langston wished to see its poor) and attempting to seduce him. After a night at the Hotel Bauer Grunewald, Hughes and Bass boarded the tourist ship *Athinai* for what Langston had planned as the highlight of his vacation: a two-week cruise of the Adriatic and the Mediterranean.

Sailing in splendid weather, the *Athinai* took its complement of travellers as far west as Dubrovnik in Yugoslavia, then on to Athens, the island of Rhodes, and the port of Haifa in Israel. Langston enjoyed the restful days at sea. He had always loved the ocean, and his last voyage, returning to New York from Europe, had been almost exactly twenty-five years before, in 1938. Moreover, as much as he had roved in his lifetime, every port on the itinerary of the *Athinai* was new to him. He particularly wanted to see the ruins of Athens and the Holy City of Jerusalem, and to visit Israel. "I've always wanted to go to Israel," he had written to someone two years before, "and have the greatest admiration for that gallant little country. (Someday I shall go.)"

The cruise was wonderful, but the land portions of the tour took their toll on the rotund Langston. At five feet, four inches, he strained to carry his weight of 185 pounds. "After three or four of the escorted tours," George Bass recalled, "Mr. Hughes began to select a place in the midst of each of the ruins or monuments where he might sit and view the environs without taking another step." Once, when Bass urged him to move closer to the base of some celebrated site, Langston continued to sit. "A rock," he declared, "is a rock." Returning to Venice, the men left two days later for a few days in Florence before going on to the Excelsior Hotel in Rome, where they were entertained by members of the small black American colony, including the singer Bricktop.

In early August, they returned to Paris. The weather was rainy and unseasonably cool, but Langston was as charmed as ever by the city. Making no attempt to get in touch with his many friends there, he instead enjoyed a week of peace and comfort at the deluxe Hotel Westminster in the rue de la Paix. Then, leaving George Bass behind, he crossed the Channel for a brief visit to England mainly to see a production of *Black Nativity*. On his return to France, he moved to the Boulevard St. Michel and a cheaper hotel full of African students, where he could relax and feel almost at home. Paris had changed over the years, but mainly for the better. The city was now far more mixed racially, and more tolerant. When Parisians celebrated on August 24 the anniversary of its liberation from the Nazis, the star of the evening, dressed in a

French military uniform and singing her most stirring songs, "Mon Paris" and "J'ai Deux Amours," was his countrywoman Josephine Baker. "She had all her medals on," he reported home to Arna Bontemps about her performance before "what looked like a half million people" in front of the Paris Town Hall, "and without makeup—quite thrilling. And the crowd was made up of all the races of this now very cosmopolitan (more than ever) city."

Across the Atlantic, in Washington, D.C., a mightier crowd was gathering, but Langston made no move to return for the highly controversial March on Washington led by the civil rights veterans A. Philip Randolph and Bayard Rustin. He seemed content to read in the Paris newspapers about the assembly of 250,000 people and the spellbinding "I Have a Dream" oration (with overtones of some of his own various "dream" poems, as several friends pointed out) delivered by Dr. Martin Luther King, Jr. Langston was also in Paris when word came of the death in Ghana on August 27 of W. E. B. Du Bois. "MY DEEPEST SYMPATHY TO YOU AND TO THE WORLD IN ITS LOSS," he wired Shirley Graham Du Bois. The death of the greatest of Afro-American intellectuals touched Langston. As a boy in Kansas, his grandmother had read to him from Du Bois's *Crisis*. One of the first books he had read on his own was *The Souls of Black Folk*. The *Crisis* had published "my earliest poems. . . . It seems as if, one way or another, I knew Dr. Du Bois all my life. Through his work, he became a part of my life."

Late on Sunday, September 1, Langston returned to the United States after two months abroad. The next day, Labor Day, brought a stream of guests to 20 East 127th Street to welcome him home and paint thrilling pictures of the March on Washington (some days later, even the quiet Arna Bontemps remained exhilarated: "I'm still vibrating!"). Langston was both fascinated by the event and oddly detached. Perhaps he was more than a little guilty for having been away at such a time, but he did not regret his—in some ways—perfectly timed tour. And he had something to offer to the hour: the first copies of his latest book, *Poems From Black Africa, Ethiopia and Other Countries*, from Indiana University Press, launched with a remarkable, free publicity boost—a full-page spread of selections from it in the current issue of *Time* magazine, in further testimony to Africa's new significance.

The day after Labor Day, Langston was in touch with the *Tambourines to Glory* company. Once again, he faced questions about the political message of the play. An urgent letter late in August from the producer Joel Schenker, written against the backdrop of the March on Washington, asked a pertinent question: "In these trying days, what does Langston Hughes think? How can we not be accused of being frivolous or of Langston Hughes fiddling while Rome burns?" Schenker wanted a small addition to the script, perhaps only a minute in length, in which a character would speak Hughes's mind in support of the freedom movement. To reporters, however, Langston spoke only of how much he liked *Tambourines to Glory* and saw it as pure entertainment, without messages or lectures. Nothing altered his attitude about the show—not even his horror at the ghastly events of Sunday, September 15, when the bombing of the black Sixteenth Street Baptist Church in Birmingham, Alabama, killed four small children.

Langston was not against militance either within or outside the theater. He did not dream of objecting when perhaps the most inflexible of the black leaders, Malcolm X, spoke at the opening of a revival in Los Angeles of Hughes's radical play of 1938, *Don't You Want to Be Free?* Nor was he much intimidated by two acts of censorship against him that fall, when a Chicago production of *Black Nativity* was crippled by an anti-communist smear campaign ("Foes Seek to Bar Negro Poet's Play," the *New York Times* reported), and when a Nashville, Tennessee, television station operated by the local Board of Education, calling Hughes an atheist and a communist, refused to air a film of an old, entirely harmless interview with the New York *Herald-Tribune* drama critic Walter Kerr. "Beaming Hughes as a 'celebrity' to the public," the local *Banner* declared, "would be an affront to decency."

In offering *Tambourines to Glory,* Langston simply believed that he was entitled to present a drama of black life without explicit reference to political problems, and that such a show had a better chance of success with a public presumably weary of politics and race. The fact that he was also determined to avoid confrontation did not mean that Langston lacked passion. George Bass, whose distrust of whites ("I learned to distrust whites in New York City; before, except for sheltered encounters and broad Southern attitudes, I had little knowledge of them") had led Langston to call him "his resident mau-mau," caught a rare glimpse one evening of the rage of which his employer was capable. One of the *Tambourines* producers, impatient with Langston's rewriting of a scene, suggested that he should let Bass try his hand at it. Quietly, Hughes declined to do so. Later, an enraged Bass ("The producer had boldly insulted the man I looked up to as my mentor, and he had simply turned the other cheek") openly accused Hughes of an unseemly passivity. As Bass went on, Langston only smiled and smiled. Then: "Suddenly, his calm manner harnessed a fierceness and a rage that I had never seen in him. He exploded at me, releasing his anger in an intense and startling pound[ing] on the table. 'Do you think I love white people?' he asked. 'Yes, I love them. I love them so much I wish God would take them all to his bosom, right now!' "

"The anger amazed me," Bass recalled, "but also the form it took: benevolence, ultimately, for the very people who were tormenting him." Hughes's apparent passivity was deliberate and complex. Vinnette Carroll remembered his advice on how to deal with racists: "Always be polite to them, Vinnette. In fact, be over-polite. Kill them with kindness." But he insisted on recognizing that all whites are not racist, and definitely enjoyed the company of those who sought him out in friendship and with respect. Later that year, for example, in December, he was quite pleased to attend a dinner at the Essex House Hotel of the Missouri Society of New York, founded in 1960. Hughes hardly knew Missouri, but he appreciated this literary association with Mark Twain, T. S. Eliot, Marianne Moore, and other well-known writers, and became a trustee of the group. Unquestionably he enjoyed the sophisticated social tone of the dinner—at which he was most likely the only black present. More and more, he seemed to need such respites from Harlem. "Langston was always complaining about groups such as the National Institute of Arts and Letters not having more blacks," Raoul Abdul remembered, "and he did try to have more admitted. But I know for a fact that he actually came to *like* certain social situations in which he was the only black present. As Harlem became more and more difficult, he liked going downtown by himself or maybe with one friend to dinner in a restaurant where the food was fine and the service what one should expect—which is not what one got in Harlem, unless you were lucky. Of course, he still loved Harlem, but he also needed to get away."

Certainly he still loved Harlem. One visitor to 20 East 127th Street about this time was the author Gay Talese, then a reporter for the *New York Times*. "I remember how eager he was to show me as much of Harlem as he could in a short time," he recalled. "We took a walking tour of about three hours, a wonderful afternoon that made me forget I was a reporter. He exuded a sense of proprietorship about Harlem that no Rockefeller could have had about their vast real-estate holdings. He gave off a sense that all he saw was his. There was warmth and cordiality. He loved Harlem and was proud of it, and he exuded a sense of peace and contentment about living there."

In October, he attended Josephine Baker's show at Carnegie Hall and visited backstage with her afterwards. He also saw the premiere of Edward Albee's adaptation of his friend Carson McCullers's novella *Ballad of the Sad Cafe*. But most of Langston's time was taken by *Tambourines to Glory*, in which he had invested $2000 of his own money. The versatile cast included Clara Ward, Joseph Attles, and Anna English in their old parts from the Westport production, as well as Louis Gosset and Hilda Simms in the leading roles, and Brother John Sellers and Rosetta LeNoire. Without the benefit of a trial run, the show prepared to open at the six-hundred-seat Little Theater on 44th Street near Broadway. Its director, in charge of his first Broadway show, was Nikos Psacharopoulos of the Yale School of Drama. For blacks, there were two "firsts." Dick Campbell, who had produced and managed almost all the USO shows at black camps in World War II, became the first black company manager in Broadway history, and Otis Edwin Young became the first black stage manager.

But almost everything else went badly. The youthful owner of the newly refurbished Little Theater clashed first with the stagehands' union, then with the producers. At a dress rehearsal, a fist fight almost erupted. The next night, at a preview, a scuffle broke out in full view of the audience. Threats of suits and countersuits tainted the air. "Cullud behaving (on the whole) beautifully," Langston reported. "But the white folks!!!!! . . . Me, still smiling through."

The union troubles cut deeply into the rehearsal schedule, but the producers stuck to the announced opening date early in November. This decision proved costly. Inadequately prepared, *Tambourines to Glory* pleased virtually no one, although Jobe Huntley's music was applauded. "As drama it is embarrassing,"

Howard Taubman wrote in the *New York Times* of a production that looked "slapped together"; worse, "it cannot make up its mind to a point of view, and it shifts carelessly from comedy to satire to melodrama to piety. Its characterization is as casual as a comic strip's. And the story drags foolishly and gets in the way of the singing." Walter Kerr of the *Herald-Tribune* was more succinct. *Tambourines to Glory* was "almost a musical and almost a straight play, and almost is the worst word I know."

A wave of criticism of another kind, aimed squarely at Langston, also rolled in. At St. Mark's Church, the respected black leader Anna Arnold Hedgeman of the YWCA and the National Council of Churches severely criticized *Tambourines to Glory*. "You are part of the talent of our time," she wrote Hughes; it seemed "tragic irony" that he should present such a dreadful picture of the black church "when we so much need the truly significant religious story of the Negro to be presented." A white patron denounced its "miserable clichés" about black life, as well as the shabby staging. "WHAT A PRODUCTION! What pathetic staging—it looks like a high-school production." "That show made me so mad!" Roy DeCarava recalled. "I was deeply disappointed by Langston after all the great work he had done, and I told him to his face how I felt. I could see that he was startled, surprised. I don't know what he expected after that disgraceful presentation."

A rumor spread that a picket line would oppose the show. According to Jobe Huntley, Langston was determined to counter-picket, and even prepared a sign that read "YOUR MAMA LIKES GOSPEL SONGS." Huntley would trail him with another sign: "AND I WRITE THEM."

Ingeniously, the *Tambourines* producers cut and pasted a curious pastiche of favorable critical comment. Ed Sullivan, the host of a nationally popular television variety show, was persuaded to present an excerpt from the play on his Sunday night broadcast. The owner of the Little Theater did his part by offering free alcoholic drinks to patrons. But the end came quickly, on November 23, before the Ed Sullivan broadcast and within three weeks of the opening. *Tambourines to Glory* lost $125,000. This was the major setback in what Langston would call "my bad-luck-in-theatre season."

To the playwright Loften Mitchell, the failure of the show had little to do with Langston's competence. "The attack on the black storefront church was not only justifiable, it badly needed to be made. But I'm not sure that whites were interested in such a matter, so the theater patrons stayed away. But there wasn't anything superficial about the play. Religion meant a lot to Langston. He and Richard Wright had been victims of the same kind of religious fundamentalism in their childhood, so they had expectations about religion that religion could not deliver, and they hated dishonesty in the church. In so many of Langston's productions, I don't know if the audience knew half the time what they were looking at. *Tambourines to Glory* was like that." Its failure coincided with the disaster of the Broadway musical play *Ballad for Bimshire*, for which Mitchell had written the book. To Mitchell's amazement, Langston seemed more concerned with his friend's failure than his own. "Langston was the senior writer, but he made time to come over and see me and console me. I thought that was poetic. I thought that was a very fine thing for him to do.''

In contrast, Langston's professional relationship with Jobe Huntley was just about finished, in spite of his warm telegram to Huntley on opening night— "IT HAS BEEN WONDERFUL WORKING WITH YOU AND I WISH US BOTH SUCCESS BUT ESPECIALLY YOU TONIGHT.'' This telegram, Huntley later revealed, "made me feel that he was cutting me loose now that all the music was written and the show was opening.'' A second and even more generous telegram after the reviews—"JOBIE YOU ARE THE STAR OF TAMBOURINES ALL YOUR REVIEWS WERE WONDERFUL AND I AM DELIGHTED CONGRATULATIONS ON BEING BROADWAYS FIRST GOSPEL COMPOSER''—did nothing to lessen Huntley's chronic suspicions about the motives of his collaborator.

The closing of *Tambourines to Glory* was hastened and overshadowed by the assassination of President Kennedy. Langston was in midtown at the Manhattan Hotel on Eighth Avenue, working in a rented room there, as he sometimes did, when he heard the unbelievable news about the shooting during a motorcade in Dallas. Deeply upset by the death of a man who had three times admitted him to the White House, at three o'clock that afternoon he sent a telegram of condolence from the hotel to Mrs. Jacqueline Kennedy. Langston mourned the loss of "A GREAT AND BELOVED AMERICAN FOR WHOM I AMONG MILLIONS GRIEVE.''

The failure of *Tambourines to Glory* was an expensive lesson for Langston. For the production of *Jericho-Jim Crow*, his new gospel musical of the freedom movement, he returned to Stella Holt, the dauntless champion of *Simply Heavenly,* and "the sweetest, nicest, most honest producer in the business.'' When she set a tight little budget of $2500 for a production at the Greenwich Mews Theater on West 13th Street in Greenwich Village, he put up $1500 of his own money. Langston also wanted no repeat of the criticism of his politics. Accordingly, the script of *Jericho-Jim Crow,* which was "dedicated to the young people of all racial and religious backgrounds who are meeting, working, canvassing, petitioning, marching, picketing, sitting-in, singing and praying today to help make a better America for all, and especially for citizens of color,'' received the imprimatur of the Congress of Racial Equality, the Student Non-Violent Coordinating Committee, and the NAACP. In addition, the three groups would jointly share the proceeds from a benefit performance, and Langston would waive royalty payments by nonprofit groups "whose ticket sales, collections, or donations received go toward the freedom movement.'' At a rehearsal, some ministers inspected the show and confirmed that it was respectful of religion.

Jericho-Jim Crow would not rush, like *Tambourines to Glory,* to its premiere. The day after Christmas, following nervous conferences with Langston and the co-directors of the play, Alvin Ailey and William Hairston, Stella Holt postponed the official opening by a few days. The players, including the veterans Rosalie King and Joseph Attles, the more youthful Hilda Harris and the baritone Gilbert Price, and a white actor, Willian Cane, who enacted various roles, were thus in full stride when *Jericho-Jim Crow* opened on January 12, 1964, at the Sanctuary, the church that housed in its basement Holt's Greenwich Mews Theater.

No production of any kind by Hughes ever received more extravagant praise than *Jericho-Jim Crow*. One reviewer wrote of its "incredible heights of poetry and pathos." *Variety* blessed a "happy entertainment." Another journal hailed "a major landmark in the history of American theatre." If you could sit unmoved by the gospel singer Dorothy Drake, the *Post* warned, "you'd better see an undertaker." But the star of the production was young Gilbert Price, acclaimed especially for his singing of "Freedom Land," for which Langston proudly claimed to have written both the words and the music. The *Times* found Price "stirring and prophetic." In the *Morning Telegraph,* Whitney Bolton praised "the best Negro voice I have heard" since the heyday of Paul Robeson. "It has golden assurance and it soars into the songs, whether old or new." To the *Post* reviewer, the song itself seemed "destined to take its place in the great canon of Negro music."

Exactly how Langston had written "Freedom Land" is a mystery, since he could not write music, play an instrument, or carry a tune past his lips. In his determination to be a songwriter, however, he regarded none of these handicaps as insuperable. George Bass or Raoul Abdul (who had returned to Langston's employ) would listen intently to his moaning, then pick out a tune on the piano. "Is this it, Mr. Hughes?" "That's it!" Langston would assert, impounding the melody. Whatever its origins, he was beside himself with pride over "Freedom Land" (according to Raoul Abdul, George Bass composed it.) At one point, after begging Stella Holt for three weeks to have it repeated in the course of the show, he threatened her: "Unless it is done, I have no intention of darkening the door of the Sanctuary again."

"Langston was exceptionally proud of having written that song," Gilbert Price remembered. " 'Just sing my song, Gilbert,' he would say, 'you just sing my song!' He was like a little kid to me, the joy he got from having written that song!" Fond of the song, he was evidently at least as fond of its singer, to whom he had introduced himself backstage one night after Price's performance in the off-Broadway show *Fly, Blackbird*. Price was twenty-two years old, a former student at Erasmus Hall High School, from which he had graduated as Class Actor and the recognized star in a choral group that included Barbra Streisand. After training at the American Theatre Wing, he had toured with Harry Belafonte and the Leonard de Paur chorus and also played in two off-Broadway shows. His personality had been deepened by a serious diabetic condition that had almost killed him as a teenager. As shy as he was handsome and gifted, the Harlem-born singer made a tremendous impression on Langston.

The two became fast friends. When Langston went to Hampton Institute in early February to help open its new Communications Center, he took Price along to sing on the program. A few weeks later, when he flew for a reading to St. Croix, the birthplace of Price's mother, the youngster again went along to perform. Missing their plane, they returned via Puerto Rico and a pleasant two-day stay at El Convento Hotel in the historic district of Old San Juan. Not long after, when Hughes went out to Lincoln University to read, he was pleased by his reception but wanted Price nearer. "I miss you as a travelling companion," he scribbled. "Wish you were on this trip, too. We had the most fun."

Of all Langston's many friendships with young men in his last years, none seemed more heartfelt than that with Price, with whom he seemed to fall in love. His feeling was reciprocated. "He was a very caring man," according to Price. "When he met my mother and grandmother, the rapport was beautiful. I loved my father, but I had never really known him; he had his own family. I found in Langston a father, a theater father, just when I needed an older man to help me. I would visit him at home and just sit in his room, comfortable, while he worked. He'd get me a ginger beer and rap to me off and on. To listen to him was like listening to great prose. He was a teacher and a father and a guide. He would tell me about all the great people he knew, like Josephine Baker and Dorothy Maynor and James Baldwin, and urge me to be like them, develop my talent. When we walked in the street he would point out old buildings and tell me who had lived there, and what the buildings meant to Harlem, and *could* mean if we all put our minds to it and worked for the community, for the people."

Price was aware that some people speculated about his relationship with Langston, but he insisted that "there was nothing more to it than a deep friendship, and nothing less. At least one member of my family asked me flat out about Langston, because he had a certain reputation. But he did nothing with me to deserve one, and I never saw him approach anyone else in that way." He would always treasure the memory of Langston Hughes. "I was grateful and blessed to be with him. I got joy from him, and a great deal of understanding, and I know he got joy from me. I saw his loneliness, but he never let it come between us. In those days I was very young, and I had a great deal of expectation and hope, and I think he liked me because he saw *himself* in me. He had a smile like a little child, a smile that came out of his eyes. Langston was very beautiful. I don't think of him as being dead at all. I love him very much."

Perhaps because of the striking success of *Jericho-Jim Crow* and the ripening of his relationship with Price, Langston seemed to become a happier, even revitalized man. He appeared to recover completely not only from the drastic failure of his Broadway show but also from the brooding on death that had led him the previous year to rewrite his will and devise his own funeral service. Where previously he had shied away from various honors, seeing them haunted by the specter of death, he now seemed to crave them. In January, sitting proudly on the dais, he enjoyed his place of prominence at the fifty-fourth annual dinner of the Poetry Society of America at the Hotel Astor. A week later, publicly celebrating his birthday for the first time in many years, he greeted one hundred and twenty-five personally invited guests at a performance on February 1 of *Jericho-Jim Crow*. In Detroit, a police escort with flashing lights and wailing sirens sped "the Poet Laureate of the American Negro" in a motorcade from the airport to City Hall, where he received the key to the city. February 9 was proclaimed "Langston Hughes Day" by Mayor Jerome Cavanaugh, and an autograph party at the prominent J. L. Hudson department store was the best-attended in its history. Behind the honors were his Detroit admirers Dudley Randall, Oliver LaGrone, Powell Lindsay, Ron Milner, and Margaret Danner, the director of the Boone House cultural center and a poet with whom Langston had been preparing a recording, "Writers on the Revolution," for Motown Records of Detroit. At a testimonial banquet at the Park Shelton hotel, a bust sculpted by LaGrone was presented to Langston. A montage of some of his poems was dramatized in his honor at the Institute of Arts.

The next week, it was New York's turn to honor Hughes. Governor Nelson Rockefeller issued a proclamation, and the Brooklyn Museum of Art prepared a series of events. The highlight of the series was a concert on Sunday, February 16, of music by Hughes and his various collaborators, from Kurt Weill and Jan Meyerowitz to Dave Martin and Toy Harper, organized mainly by Margaret Bonds. Gilbert Price sang "Freedom Land," and the Lincoln University Glee Club, led by Professor Orrin Suthern II, performed the world premiere of Bonds's cycle of songs, "Fields of Wonder." The next day, Langston celebrated again at a PEN cocktail party for himself, Muriel Spark, and other writers at the Hotel Pierre. Here, Langston was being honored for *Jericho-Jim Crow* and the reprint of his second autobiography *I Wonder as I Wander* by Hill and Wang, which had also reissued *The Big Sea*.

He was clearly happier than at any time in recent years. In February, touched by the ceremony, he attended the wedding of his stepbrother Kit Clark's daughter, Gwendolyn, who seemed to him "the most beautiful bride I have ever seen." His sense of family was still strong. Although his relationship with Kit was strained at best, Langston kept in touch with Kit's wife, Norma, and his five children, Carroll, Langston, Calvin, Maceo, and Gwendolyn, who were all listed in his will as beneficiaries. On February 25, he and millions of other people found a new hero. Passing up a concert by the singer Jennie Tourel, he listened with fascination to a radio broadcast of the fight in Miami between the heavyweight champion Sonny Liston and the handsome braggart—and rank underdog—from Louisville, Kentucky, Cassius ("I Am The Greatest!") Clay, who often boasted in rhyme. Stopping Liston in the seventh round, Clay took the title. In celebration, Langston propped up a big picture of Clay's head and upper body in his study and sent him a suitably inscribed copy of his and Milton Meltzer's *Pictorial History of the Negro:* "I hear you are interested in History. / Well, History is no mystery. . . ."

Emotionally more content, Langston also spoke now with a clearer voice on politics. Attending a Carnegie Hall memorial to W. E. B. Du Bois, undeterred by the fact that Du Bois had died a communist, he also published a tribute to him in the New York *Post* and in black newspapers through the Associated Negro Press. To interviewers from Italian television and the Voice of America, and in an appearance for CORE at Barnard College, he spoke confidently, but in the interests of moderation, about the freedom movement. The present turmoil was a good thing, because it was making people think. Those who did not think, but wailed apocalyptically, were doing little good. Here, James Baldwin was again on Langston's mind. In a *Post* essay following a series of articles by another writer on Baldwin, whose new collection of essays *The Fire Next Time* captured the bitterness and fatalism that was overwhelming the honeyed promises of integration, Hughes challenged Baldwin for allowing a personal sense of desperation and abandonment—his "don't-care-ness"—to overwhelm his political judgment. "If Baldwin did not care just a bit more," Hughes argued, "in fact, if he did not care at all, *at all*, perhaps he might suggest a solution to the problems he so vividly and powerfully poses. Or does he have a solution to suggest for the current race situation? The solution he now leaves up to white America. Maybe Baldwin can just cry, 'Fire,' and not have the least idea how to put it out. Or maybe he knows what to do, but will not tell us. Maybe he does not wish to face the next McCarthy."

At the end of April, *Jericho-Jim Crow* closed at the Sanctuary but was hardly dead. Rather than risk its righteous exuberance on jaded Broadway, Stella Holt and Hughes decided to offer it to theaters in the greater metropolitan area. Almost everywhere on the "subway" circuit, the show won praise. Less flattering was the reaction to Langston's anthology *New Negro Poets USA* (with an introduction by Gwendolyn Brooks that he had requested and offered to subsidize, because "I . . . respect her intelligence so much"). More important, it showed how strange were some of the sudden changes overtaking the nation. Three years before, while Langston had sought a greater emphasis on race, Indiana University Press had asked him for more modernist verse. Now the book was so out of step with the times that the important *Publishers Weekly* erroneously proclaimed it "a turning point from total preoccupation with protest literature to more universal themes" in black writing. The trend in black writing was, of course, exactly the opposite. One result of this confusion was unusually scornful reviews. Dubbing the collection of thirty-seven black poets "The Sepia Deb Ball of American 'Verse'," the *Nation* reviewer asked: "Why does an anthology like this get published? Certainly not for the poems." Denouncing the book as "a mistake in conception and a failure in execution," *Saturday Review* reported that "all the faults of adolescent poetry are here: trite sentiment, fake simplicity, self-pity, punch lines." Even before these two reviews appeared, however, the course of Afro-American literature was drastically altered—and by one of the poets in the ridiculed anthology.

On May 1, at the Cherry Lane Theater, Langston attended a play and knew at once that he had witnessed something historic. "I saw a most hair-raising play last night," he wrote the next day, "—with all the bad words in the book in it"—LeRoi Jones's *Dutchman*. "Only a half hour long," the drama was "worth seeing for a battering ram treatment of the race problem that outdoes Baldwin 50 x 50 times." In *Dutchman,* which would catapult him to overnight fame, Jones used a confrontation on a train between a stuffy middle-class black man, Clay, and a seductive but murderous white woman, Lula, to open some of the ugliest wounds of racism. In *Baptism,* another play that year, 1964 ("The Jones Year," Langston later called it), set in a Baptist church and featuring a chronic masturbator who just might be the Son of God, Jones kept up his furious assault on bourgeois propriety. To the poet and editor Dudley Randall, Langston wrote that *Baptism,* compared to *Dutchman,* was "almost as good, and even more shocking. Both packed with the dirtiest words you ever heard— but used in a highly dramatic way." As for Jones, "He's a real theatre poet." As much as Langston disliked obscenity, he understood that Jones was a seri- ous, possibly profound interpreter of American culture. To an old friend, he soon dubbed LeRoi Jones "the cullud Eugene O'Neill." Later in the year, after seeing James Baldwin's play *Blues for Mr. Charlie,* which he disliked, he confirmed his opinion that *Dutchman* was "the most."

With the success of *Dutchman,* however, Jones began a new phase in his change from an interracial Bohemian into the most implacable reviler of whites in the Afro-American literary world. So gifted and energetic was he that this drastic personal shift would affect, in one way or another, and at the same time, almost every contemporary black writer of the slightest importance, as well as almost the entire generation of younger black writers. Langston Hughes did not have to wait long to be touched by the accusatory finger of black ultra- nationalism. The same month he attended *Dutchman,* he read in the Harlem *Liberator* (subtitled "the voice of the Afro-American protest movement in the United States and the liberation movement of Africa") a belated review of an edition of his autobiography *The Big Sea,* which had been reissued two years before. In this review, for the first time in his life, he came under attack for showing an inadequate racial sense. Lamenting that Hughes "tells us about himself but not of his self," the writer concluded that Langston had been un- able "to communicate his 'negroness'. It is as if he is saying to 'make it' in this white man's world one has to sacrifice one's blackness."

However this attack first affected him, Langston refused to be intimidated by the new, radical definitions of blackness. In any event, his many poems about the beauty of blackness and the necessity of justice for blacks, composed before most of the militants were born, still stood up well to new tests of racial con- sciousness. But as if to prove his relevance to the age, he now offered Knopf "Words Like Freedom," a selection of his more aggressive poems on racism and freedom, and virtually insisted that the book be printed in a cheap, paper- back edition to ensure a wide readership. But Knopf balked. "I liked the book, and other people here also liked it," his editor Judith Jones recalled later, "but the way he wanted it done, I told him that we would have to sell an enormous amount for us to break even."

Langston shelved "Words Like Freedom." Then, to help in the struggle as best he could, he sent twenty-five copies of *Pictorial History of the Negro* to a

SNCC official in Mississippi for its freedom schools there, agreed to serve on the board of sponsors of the New Orleans-based Free Southern Theatre, and composed a poem-anthem at the request of CORE's Southern Education Project. For the NAACP, he joined a host of entertainers and actors, including Elizabeth Taylor, Lena Horne, Jackie Gleason, and Sammy Davis, Jr., on a broadcast on closed circuit television to forty-nine cities from Madison Square Garden, marking the tenth anniversary of *Brown vs. the Board of Education of Topeka, Kansas.* Also for the NAACP, he composed an anthem, "Dream of Freedom," of startling ineptness ("There is a dream in the land / With its back against the wall. / By muddled names and strange / Sometimes the dream is called . . .).

Helping in the struggle did not rule out fun. As an honored—and proud—guest on Africa Day at the New York World's Fair, he was present when His Majesty Mwambutsa IV, king of Burundi, dedicated the African pavilion. Returning with the aged Amy Spingarn, he camped near the vendors of African food and enjoyed a performance by the Zulu dancers. At the Community Church of New York, before a performance there of *Jericho-Jim Crow,* he made certain he arrived in time for a Strawberry Shortcake Festival ("what a wonderful means of fellowship!"). To promote *New Negro Poets USA,* in spite of its reviews, he organized a successful reading by twelve poets at Adele Glasgow's Market Place Gallery. And visitors from overseas continued to climb the steps at 20 East 127th Street: the African writer Cyprian Ekwensi, the German folklorist and Africanist Janheinz Jahn, and various young people seeking assistance, including at least two Africans formally sponsored by Langston as students in the United States.

He kept his projects as simple as possible. For a recording by Nina Simone for Mercury Records, Langston wrote a dazzling promotional essay. At one point, he converted his macabre little play from the thirties, *Soul Gone Home,* about a mother and her dead son, into a short story. For a Harlem bank, the Carver Federal Savings and Loan, he supervised the preparation by George Bass ("Mr. Hughes made the commitment, then got bored with the idea, so he turned it over to me") of a calendar based on the Civil Rights Movement. In a step that suggested how much he was moving against the ultra-nationalistic grain, he offered a huge old manuscript, "Book of Negro Humor" (part of which had gone to make the *Book of Negro Folklore*), to Indiana University Press as "the *first* definitive well-rounded collection of American Negro humor." Indiana rejected it at once. Too often, the press insisted, the jokes were not only stale but also insulting to blacks. Langston was not dismayed. "By this point in his career," George Bass remembered, "Mr. Hughes had an almost cynical attitude to publishing. If anything was rejected, he didn't seem to care. 'Don't worry,' he would say. 'Somebody will take it.' And somebody usually did. Nothing was so bad that someone wouldn't want it." Dodd, Mead took "Book of Negro Humor."

This altogether cheery spring ended appropriately with a landmark honor in Cleveland, the city of his youth. On June 10, at stately Severance Hall, Langston Hughes, "poet, writer and powerful advocate of the cause of freedom," received his third honorary degree. For the first time, however, the donor was a white institution, Western Reserve University, to which many of Langston's fellow high school graduates in 1920 had gone as undergraduates. To the new graduates of Adelbert College, the oldest unit of Reserve, Langston tried to blend a spirit of affirmation with criticism of American racism and poverty. "Mississippi aligns us with South Africa," he warned the students, "more closely than Ohio aligns us with the free world of Europe whose people see in their newspapers more pictures of fire hoses trained on students than they see of Adelbert College." The situation must be reversed, and people of good will break the ties that bind America to the past of slavery and Jim Crow.

On July 1, George Bass, who had just won a $1000 prize for film writing, and was determined to be an artist in spite of Langston's dire warnings and prophecies, worked his last day. Raoul Abdul promised to help with the typing chores (and soon returned as Hughes's full-time secretary) but wanted to concentrate on his own career in music. From Fisk University, Arna Bontemps offered a replacement for Bass. ("L.H. wants to know what [he] looks like," Bass wrote Bontemps. "No ill-will, but please not like Jimmy Baldwin.") The new young man arrived, but did not last long. Within a day or two, he and Langston were forced to duck into a doorway to avoid being killed by gunfire on the corner of Lenox Avenue and 126th Street. His heart had barely stopped pounding from this incident when a thug placed a gun to his head and relieved him of his wallet and watch outside Langston's home. He fled New York.

The gunfire had come during the worst riot in Harlem since 1943. On July 16, in predominantly white Yorkville on the Upper East Side of Manhattan, an off-duty white policeman shot to death a 15-year-old black boy, Jimmy Powell, who apparently had been armed with a knife. The shooting horrified Harlem, and Hughes. In ninety-degree heat and oppressive humidity, he went down to a funeral parlor on Seventh Avenue to take his place in a long line of blacks filing past Powell's body—"I saw him lying in his coffin looking very small and dead." The night of the funeral, July 19, Langston heard gunfire within a hundred yards of his home. "What fire *next* time?" he asked. "It's here, I thought." He heard "cries sharper than any words speakers speak or committees formulate or typewriters take down on paper." From Harlem rooftops, bottles began to rain on the police below. Blacks attacked businesses with firebombs, then attacked the white firemen who arrived to put out the fires. Before the disturbances ended, one person was killed, one hundred and forty were injured, and five hundred arrested.

The following Sunday, Langston joined various Harlem parents and school-teachers on the local CBS television station to talk about the events of the past few days. Calm and deliberate on the air, he was otherwise inside. ("How many bullets does it take / To kill a fifteen-year-old kid?" he asked in his poem "Death in Yorkville." "How many bullets does it take / To kill me?") In the *New York Post,* he saw the rioting in Harlem as completely predictable, caused by the racism that still kept blacks tied down in neo-slavery in the North as well as the South. ''Harlem's feet, through no fault of its own, are mired in Dixie,'' he wrote. Comparing the black community to a starving, snarling dog, he heaped scorn on those who denied it food and drink but tried to pacify it with promises. '' 'Be nice, Harlem! Lie down, Harlem! Now, behave, Harlem,' coming from voices that formally never even said a friendly 'Hello' to Harlem, is hardly conducive to calming an emotionally upset psyche, or downing a bristling tail and causing it to wag again. Harlem has been wagging its tail so long in thanks for the bones that have come its way that it is time now for somebody to throw Harlem, not a bone, but some meat.''

Harlem slowly returned to normal, but the rioting left Langston more eager than ever to spend time outside the United States. When an invitation came to attend the Berlin Folk Festival early in the fall, he accepted it promptly. For the third consecutive year, Langston planned to be out of the country for about two months. In the meantime, to lift his spirits, and perhaps in retaliation against an enterprising neighbor who had opened an odorous barbecue stand, ''The Garden of Eden,'' in his backyard, Langston threw a Harlem Renaissance-style ''rent party.'' Aiming for authenticity, he supplied his guests with pickled pig's feet, cheap gin, endless piano playing, fast women, hustling men, and the obligatory wealthy white interloper from downtown—Carl Van Vechten, in an arthritic reprise of his classic role.

With pleasure, he finished liner notes for a new album by the folksinger Joan Baez, whose vibrato, heard unexpectedly on a summer night in Newport during one of the jazz festivals, had reminded him of snowcapped mountains and pure white clouds seen as a child in Colorado. Baez was ''a peak alone'' among singers. Taking most of Langston's time towards the end of the summer, however, was an ambitious eighteen-part BBC radio series, ''The Negro in America,'' scheduled to be broadcast in the fall. Langston helped the BBC producer Geoffrey Bridson to supervise recordings by a cross-section of black poets, including Arna Bontemps (whose first book of verse had just appeared in Britain), Sterling Brown, Gwendolyn Brooks, LeRoi Jones, Mari Evans, Margaret Danner, Jay Wright, Oliver Pitcher, and James Emanuel. Also in the series was Langston's *Jericho-Jim Crow,* some songs by Odetta, and plays by Alice Childress and Adrienne Kennedy. Broadcast on the BBC starting on September 28, at year's end the series would be hailed by the authoritative *Listener* magazine as ''the most important radio event'' of the year in Britain.

Also in September, preparing for Europe, he successfully applied for a loan of $1200 from Manufacturers Hanover Trust. The bank had no difficulty handing over the money, since 20 East 127th Street was now free of mortgage and brought in $3,860 a year from its roomers. Langston should not have needed a loan. *Black Nativity* had been drawing well in Chicago, but the producers had suddenly shut down the show and responded quizzically to his inquiries about unpaid royalties amounting to nearly $10,000. Livid, Hughes hired a black law firm in Chicago to challenge the producers. When the firm fumbled the matter, he impatiently dismissed it and turned the matter over to a veteran New York lawyer, Maxwell T. Cohen of Cohen, Kirschenbaum and Taubman. Cohen was Stella Holt's lawyer at the Greenwich Mews and represented some prominent entertainers. At last, with two companies of the show set to leave the United States, the producers conceded that they owed Langston $6900. With this victory, Max Cohen became Hughes's lawyer.

Near the end of September, just in time for a special, five-day gathering of poets, he reached Berlin for the Folk Festival. Berlin was hardly his favorite city. Langston had last been there in 1932, en route to Russia. Then, he had deplored the wholesale traffic in sex in the economically depressed city. Now he could not put aside feelings of revulsion at the Holocaust and World War II. "On the flight from New York, try as I did," he wrote in the *Post* and the *Defender*, "I could not forget the gas ovens of Buchenwald, Auschwitz and Dachau, and the millions of Jews put to death, and the other millions of human beings killed in [the] senseless war, and my own friends who died fighting the Nazis." Although the Germans were kind to him, he remained uneasy: "Did the very name *Berlin* bear a kind of poison in its sound?"

Certainly he had admirers in the country. His first foreign publication had been in a German newspaper, and German interest in his work had been steady, if relatively modest. He met at least three of his translators—Roswith Reise, Herbert Roch, and Paridem von dem Knesebeck, who had translated *First Book of Jazz* and helped produce the superb German edition of *The Sweet Flypaper of Life*. Everywhere, Germans treated him with great courtesy. A crowd of fourteen hundred people heard him read at the University of Hamburg, when the Free Academy of the Arts awarded him a medal and a laurel wreath. The theme of the Berlin festival—the impact of black Africa on art and culture in the twentieth century—guaranteeing Langston's rapt attention, he enjoyed sessions with writers such as Wole Soyinka, Jorge Luis Borges, and Aimé Césaire, and attended productions of his *Black Nativity*, Jean Genet's *The Blacks* (including Cicely Tyson, Roscoe Lee Browne, and James Earl Jones), and Aimé Césaire's *La Tragédie du Roi Christophe*. Ensembles from Nigeria, the Cameroons, and Dahomey also helped to make the festival the most exciting international gathering of black artists in memory. In the absence of Alioune Diop, the founder of *Présence Africaine*, Langston chaired a session of the festival organized by the Paris-based magazine. In East Berlin, he visited an old friend, the black American cartoonist Ollie "Bootsie" Harrington, now a resident there.

The entire visit to Germany was memorable, but mainly for the wrong reason. He could not forget the Nazis and the war. "And not forgetting, I could not forgive. When my plane took off to Paris, I felt like singing."

After about a week in London, where *Black Nativity* was also playing, Langston went to Paris for a much longer stay. He took a room at the modest Hotel California in the Latin Quarter, with a tiny balcony opening on rue des Ecoles, and began a round of events to promote two recent books: François Dodat's translations of his poems in the series *Poètes d'Aujourd'hui* from Editions Seghers ("C'est beau et très bien fait," Langston thanked Pierre Seghers); and—published in Brussels—Raymond Quinot's *Langston Hughes, ou l'Étoile Noire* ("Je suis enchanté d'être le sujet d'une livre si poétique et charmant écrit"). He was the guest of honor at a reception at the elegant Hotel Lutétia on Boulevard Raspail given by the leftist National Writers Committee. The American Cultural Center organized a program featuring him at its popular library on rue du Dragon. And in early November, after Langston returned from a quiet trip to Tangier for a vacation, he spoke to a *Présence Africaine* gathering in a room at the Palais de la Mutualité. Later, he dined privately with Louis Aragon and Elsa Triolet.

Out of this visit to Paris came Hughes's eager acceptance of three challenging French projects—and an awakened interest in returning to Paris for a long stay. For Editions Seghers, which had published a translation of *An African Treasury* in 1962, he promised a three-hundred-page anthology of Afro American poetry and a condensation of his two autobiographies. For the publisher Robert Laffont, he agreed to help in "L'Ingénu d'Harlem," a translation of selected Simple stories. These volumes, in addition to the two recent books, would make an excellent basis for a stay of a year or so, or even longer, in Paris. On the other hand, he turned aside an invitation from the scholar Jean Wagner to take a visiting professorship at the University of Grenoble, at the foot of the French Alps, and refused similar offers from universities in Colorado and Nigeria. If he could not have Paris, he would stay in New York.

"White folks thrive on vacations, but they almost kill Negroes!" Quoting Simple's axiom to one and all, he returned home on November 8 after what he called eight wonderful weeks away. Almost at once, with Paris on his mind, he plunged into work on the promised French books. Other offers soon arrived. One proposal Langston turned down flat—the chance to share with James Baldwin the writing of Josephine Baker's life story. Baker had asked Langston to do the American or "the real home side" of her life, while Baldwin would chronicle "the revolutionary side." But he accepted a fee of $500 to compose the lyrics of a cantata for the next biennial meeting of the Union of American Hebrew Congregations, which would feature a concert of modern Jewish music. Perhaps the organizers had thought of him because the previous June his old poem "Freedom Train," set by Charles Davidson, had won an annual award of the American Conference of Cantors. At the Concord Hotel in the Catskills, Langston had heard a seventy-voice choir from Temple Sinai in Brooklyn sing the piece. For the new cantata, which would be based on the "Yizkor," a prayer of remembrance, the composer would be the versatile David Amram, at home in both classical music and jazz, and with several film and play scores to his credit although still a young man.

"When I heard that Langston was to be approached to write the text, I was thrilled at the chance to work with a person of such stature," Amram recalled. "The better the text, the better the music, and I knew he would leave his imprint as a great poet on the words." Elsewhere, Amram wrote of an early meeting with Langston and a rabbi who seemed worried that Hughes might not be able to capture "this particular Jewish feeling that we're after." Langston "very casually" replied, " 'I understand, Rabbi, and I think I know the kind of feeling because it's something that's part of me. You see, my grandfather was Jewish.' This really blew the rabbi's mind and after this he left us alone to work on the cantata by ourselves." (Actually, one of Langston's great-grandfathers had been Jewish.) Collaborating on the piece, "Let Us Remember," was a pleasure. "Because Langston was such a consummate lyric artist and had written so much for voice, he was familiar with the problems that composers have. He presented me with many beautiful poems and allowed me to use whichever parts of them I wished."

Away in Europe, Langston had missed Carl Van Vechten and Fania Marinoff's fiftieth wedding anniversary celebration. On his return he had immediately written Van Vechten to say he was back: "I'd love to come down and show you and Fania my Akademie medal and laurel wreath and all whenever you all will receive me, maybe next week if you're free. It's been much too long since I've seen you." But on December 21, a telegram from the National Institute of Arts and Letters announced sad news: "HAVE YOU HEARD THAT CARL VAN VECHTEN DIED THIS MORNING IN HIS SLEEP?" Two days before Christmas, Langston attended the memorial service for his friend of forty years. Van Vechten's body was cremated, and his ashes scattered in the Shakespeare Gardens in Central Park, across from his home. For the National Institute, Langston composed its official tribute, but a letter about a month later showed deeper emotion. "That you blessed *us* for coming to your house the other day," he wrote Fania Marinoff, "was the sweetest thing you could have done because we didn't know what to say—except that we wanted to bless you and Carlo for blessing us all through so many wonderful years of knowing you both. Your sorrow radiated love. And you know that all your friends are at your command if there is anything helpful that we can do." For Langston, as philosophical as he now was about death, the passing of the single most important figure in the launching of his long career inevitably cast a shadow over Christmas, 1964.

Yet the presence of no fewer than twenty-three brightly wrapped presents for him under Mrs. Harper's Christmas tree assured Langston that he was wanted and needed and loved. Both to strangers and to friends, he exuded an unusual sense of benevolence, compassion, and inner peace. After a visit to a school on 128th Street, for example, the obviously moved principal wrote to marvel how "all felt, as something tangible, the aura of calm, wisdom, humanity, and love of beauty which you exude. We were all a little better for having met you." Following an Easter program on CBS-Television starring the folksinger Odetta, with William Shatner reading Hughes's script, his cousin Flora Coates sent a tribute from California: "God placed a special star in the elements for you."

In that serene mood, so unlike the nervous quavering of recent years, he faced the harvest of death in the coming months—his former secretary Nate White's first wife, Dupree, after a long illness; Charlie, the man who regularly cleaned Langston's suite at home; Nancy Cunard, whose gallant, controversial life had ended in despair; Marie Short of Carmel, after "a long, hard and unhappy struggle" in her last years, as her son John Short wrote to Langston. And, at 20 East 127th Street, a roomer known only as "Mr. Poole," a hearty, virile fellow, died of asphyxiation after a fire started accidentally in his room on Langston's floor. Only a sprinkler system and an alert young neighbor, Luis Velez, prevented a total disaster. "This is the DYING season," Langston sighed.

In the first days of 1965, Hughes was so confident that he deliberately stirred controversy. "Taxi, Anyone," a column in the *New York Post* on white cab-drivers who systematically refuse to pick up black passengers—a bitter point with many blacks—drew the most abusive letters of all the essays he had ever written. Passing through Harlem, white taxi drivers regularly displayed "OFF DUTY" signs. "It would be better for the OFF DUTY cabbies not to come through Harlem at all," Hughes ended. "Better to bypass Harlem than to insult Harlem." "I think you belong with that other moron Malcolm X," one reader admonished him. "I never read your column," said another; "I find you *un-bearable*." "Get a hack license," advised a third, "and pick up your animal friends in your beautiful hometown, Harlem." The wife of a black cabdriver, lamenting the prevalence of black crime, defended the drivers: "I am ashamed of my race." In a taxi one day, a black driver begged Langston to autograph a copy of the column, then took the side of the white drivers. Privately, Langston defended stirring up such a tempest. First, "adverse (and particularly controversial) comment which arouses discussion does more GOOD than harm." Secondly, every episode of controversy had made his own public stock rise. "Result: book sales grew, lecture audiences increased, folks wanted to see for themselves what the excitement was all about."

In another column, "That Boy LeRoi," he turned his sights on LeRoi Jones and other black writers who seemed clearly to be exposing the freedom movement to possibly crippling counterattack by, as Arna Bontemps put it, "making pornography their symbol and image." Hughes's initial admiration for Jones's *Dutchman* and *Baptism* had turned to dismay: "Mr. Jones might become America's new Eugene O'Neill—provided he does not knock himself out with pure manure. His current offering, 'The Toilet,' [is] full of verbal excrement." He believed that the gains achieved after great sacrifice by organizations such as the NAACP, CORE, and SCLC were being sabotaged by the new generation of foul-mouthed militants. (The same month, January, he became a life member of the NAACP.) Unquestionably, a chasm had opened between black ultra-nationalists and people like himself. In a symposium in April in Hoyt Fuller's *Negro Digest,* Hughes—as did most of the thirty-six writers quoted—defended a moderate position: "The Negro image deserves objective well-rounded (rather than one-sided) treatment, particularly in the decade of a tremendous freedom movement in which all of us can take pride. The last thing Negroes need now are black imitators of neurotic white writers who themselves have nothing of which to be proud. We possess within ourselves a great reservoir of physical and spiritual strength to which poetry, fiction and the stage should give voice."

But LeRoi Jones had taken a radically different approach: "The Black Artist's role in America is to aid in the destruction of America as he knows it." The artist must make the readers, "if they are white men, tremble, curse, and go mad, because they will be drenched with the filth of their evil."

The fact that Langston had attacked Jones publicly did not mean that he disliked the younger writer. "Langston was definitely taken with LeRoi," George Bass recalled. "He thought he was very gifted and he also simply liked him as a person." Jones himself felt kindly towards Hughes as an individual—but he did not have much respect for him as a writer. In time, his view would change. More than twenty years later, he spoke of what he had missed: "See, what I thought about Langston was that Langston was very glib and facile, that he could write, you know, as easily as breathing, and it's true. What I didn't understand is the consistently high quality of all that he did write."

Censorious of LeRoi Jones, Langston was also critical of aspiring writers who kept entirely out of the fray, or who even at this late stage of the racial conflict disdained a democratic aesthetic. He laughed at the zeal with which the poet Robert Hayden disavowed any connection to a black aesthetic, and he ridiculed the verboseness and pedantry of Melvin B. Tolson. Befuddled by some typically allusive lines in Tolson's latest opus ("O Cleobulus, / Othales, Solon, Periander, Bias, Chilo, / O Pittacus, / unriddle the phoenix riddle of this?"), Langston privately mocked the black poet: "I say, MORE POWER TO YOU, MELVIN B., GO, JACK, GO! That Negro not only reads, but *has read!*" But Langston believed that the greater danger was posed by the excesses of the black ultra-nationalists. This belief led him to revise his understanding of one of the key figures of black history, Booker T. Washington, the powerful antagonist of Du Bois at the dawn of the century. In an essay for a new edition of Washington's autobiography, *Up from Slavery,* Langston described the accommodationist leader as a man who "lived his life with his head in the lion's mouth," someone who "knew in his heart that most men can do only one thing well." He had chosen to build Tuskegee Institute—a splendid accomplishment—and done so against tremendous odds.

In the *Defender,* Langston compared Washington and contemporary moderate leaders such as Martin Luther King, Jr. and Roy Wilkins of the NAACP, on one side, to the highly vocal young militants, including LeRoi Jones. Scornfully he noted a major change in the nation since Washington's day: "In 1965 it is the Negro who raises the most hell who gets the most attention and admiration, plus sizable sums of money." (On the other hand, writing the previous year in support of an initiative by the uncompromising Malcolm X to bring the plight of black Americans to the attention of the Conference of African States, Hughes made the point that while whites saw Malcolm as "vulgar, rude and impudent in speech," to Malcolm the whites were "themselves not only vulgar, rude and impudent in speech, but in almost everything else they do in relation to their black compatriots he thinks their behavior is execrable.")

The question of the place of the artist in society, of the function of poetry, now preoccupied Langston. In his long career as a black American poet, one who not only had wrestled with racism but also had dared at one time to believe openly in the efficacy of radical socialism, what had he learned about the interplay between poetry and ethnicity, and between poetry and politics? How is a poet to act in the face of naked power? What wisdom could he pass on now to the new generation—if anyone in that generation would listen to an aging, gentle, smiling poet?

The previous December, writing a brief piece called only "Draft ideas," he had quietly laid out a manifesto he made no attempt to advertise, but in which he deeply believed.

Politics in any country in the world is dangerous. For the poet, politics in any country in the world had better be disguised as poetry. . . . Politics can be the graveyard of the poet. And only poetry can be his resurrection.

What is poetry? It is the human soul entire, squeezed like a lemon or a lime, drop by drop, into atomic words. The ethnic language does not matter. Ask Aimé Césaire. He knows. Perhaps not consciously—but in the soul of his writing, he knows. Of all of the poets of African blood, he most unconsciously knows. The Negritudinous Senghor, the Caribbean-esque Guillén, the American me, are regional poets of genuine realities and authentic values. Césaire . . . takes all that we have, Senghor, Guillén and Hughes, and flings it at the moon, to make of it a space-ship of the dreams of all the dreamers in the world.

As a footnote I must add that, concerning Césaire, all I have said I deeply feel is for me true. Concerning politics, nothing I have said is true. A poet is a human being. Each human being must live within his time, with and for his people, and within the boundaries of his country. Therefore, how can a poet keep out of politics?

Hang yourself, poet, in your own words. Otherwise, you are dead.

15

FINAL CALL
1965 to 1966

Our grief, transmitted everywhere,
tel-starred in the cosmic air ———
Ah, Kiddush Hashem! Ah, Kiddush Hashem!
  Ah, Kiddush Hashem!
Our tears flow in the heart of God . . .

"Let Us Remember," 1965

T HE WINTER OF 1965 brought the freedom movement to a new level of intensity. Late in February, Malcolm X was shot to death at the Audubon Ballroom in upper Manhattan. On March 7, in Selma, Alabama, after the killing of a civil rights worker and the arrest of about a thousand demonstrators in the voter registration drive there, Martin Luther King, Jr. and John Lewis of SNCC led a march of some five hundred people out of the city, heading towards Montgomery. At the Edmund Pettus bridge, in one of the most galvanizing actions of the entire era, the marchers were met and driven back by two hundred state troopers and deputies using whips, clubs, and tear gas. Television images of the brutal police action shocked the country and moved President Lyndon Johnson to take an unprecedented step. A week later, addressing a joint session of Congress on behalf of an historic Civil Rights Act, he dramatically proclaimed a link between presidential power and the Civil Rights Movement by closing with words taken from the anthem of the movement—"We Shall Overcome."

In Harlem, Langston watched this astonishing moment on televison and immediately sent Johnson a telegram: "YOU HAVE MADE A GREAT AND HISTORIC SPEECH TONIGHT FOR WHICH ALL AMERICA MUST THANK YOU." Three days later, however, when a telegram from Martin Luther King, Jr. summoned Langston to join a defiant second march out of Selma toward Montgomery, he did not leave New York—he probably did not even answer the telegram. Thousands of citizens, many of them prominent personalities, responded to King's call. But when the second march began Langston was ensconced in a room, which he had been using for some time as a working studio, on the sixth floor of the Hotel Wellington on Seventh Avenue in midtown Manhattan. Specifically, he was cutting and pasting his way through his 1949 anthology with Arna Bontemps, *The Poetry of the Negro,* which Double-day was now "eager" to have updated. Unwilling or unable to join the march, he consoled himself by listening to stirring recordings of folk songs by Odetta spun on a phonograph lent to him by a neighbor on the floor, the actress Cicely Tyson. No doubt he also consoled himself with the knowledge that his work over the decades had contributed to developing in younger blacks the pride and positive self-consciousness behind the current drive for freedom. But his acts of support remained largely token—as when he agreed to write a brief intro-duction to *Freedom School Poetry,* published by SNCC in Atlanta. On the other hand, he had not retired from public service. He joined the advisory board of the Museum of African Art in Washington, D.C., at the request of sponsors S. I. Hayakawa and Jacob Lawrence. And he agreed with alacrity to a request by the State Department for a series of readings and lectures in Eu-rope.

He was also careful to avoid being caught in the gathering maelstrom over American involvement in Vietnam. To an appeal for help from the poet Denise Levertov and her husband Mitchell Goodman in publishing a statement in the *New York Times* against the war, Langston was deaf. For a person of his check-ered background, he believed, opposition to the Vietnam War, which still en-joyed widespread public support, threatened to raise the specter of new accu-sations of pro-communism—and Langston was still being hounded by the old. An appearance late in April at Wichita State University in Kansas was protested in identical telegrams from four white ministers who, urged on by the right-wing John Birch Society, accused him of being a communist. In Oakland, California, conservatives threatened to file a law suit if copies of *Pictorial History of the Negro,* denounced as communist propaganda, were not removed from school libraries. "I have never been a Communist," Langston pleaded one more time, "am not now a Communist, and don't intend to be a Commu-nist in my natural life."

He was more concerned, however, with what he saw as the clear drift of the Civil Rights Movement toward separatism. His emotions unusually tender dur-ing a homecoming before a large crowd in Lawrence, Kansas, on April 28, he came closer than ever to revealing his sorrow at the racial hatred being de-manded by many militant young blacks. Talking about the troubled times, he defended the tradition of white activism in support of blacks. He spoke of John Brown (without mentioning his grandmother's death-link to Harpers Ferry), the white teachers who had gone south to teach the former slaves in the postbellum South, and Viola Liuzzo, the white civil rights sympathizer from Detroit, who had been shot to death a month earlier after a rally in Montgomery, Alabama. A white Unitarian minister, James Reeb, had also been killed at Selma. Yet now, Langston noted sadly, all whites were being called racists. At this point— "and now look at the faces in the march"—his voice quavered, and he seemed close to tears. The problem was not one of blacks and whites, he insisted, but of "people of good will" against the rest.

To Hughes, economics—capitalist greed—was even more powerful than racism in marring America, and especially in the steady destruction of the black world. What was behind the soaring black crime rate? His bitter answer came the following month in "America's Casbah" in the *New York Post*. What the newspapers and magazines all screamed about blacks was true. "We are America's Casbah," he conceded. "Our crime rate is the highest. Negroes fill the jails. We mug the taxicab drivers, rape old ladies, snatch pocketbooks." The violent black criminal had become a staple of literature even in the work of black writers like James Baldwin and LeRoi Jones. "So we might as well be what it is said we are." But who was responsible for America's Casbah, and what could blacks do? His answer was sardonic. "Admit the Casbah, yes. Negroes *are* backed into a corner. Take the blows and there is no way not to bleed. Sign the confession. You did it! . . . The detectives who beat you and the detectives who grilled you and the district attorneys who accepted your confession of complicity in all the isms of the Casbah, will be promoted, will rise on the political ladder, will slide on your blood to their $30,000-a-year jobs. There are so many dollars in the Casbah. Heroin produces many many more dollars. There are millions in the Casbah. Narcotics should begin its spelling with two strokes through it—$-$-$-$—dollars, dollars, dollars! Nice old lady, *who* raped you in the elevator? The answer, which you will not at the moment comprehend, is $$$$$ dollars."

Returning home from Kansas, he found a letter from Jones inviting him to a benefit, within a few days, at Jones's Black Arts Theater in Harlem, to which the playwright had moved at long last. The theater barred whites. "I . . . would love to see your place," Langston cordially replied—two months later. About this time, a mimeographed magazine published in Oakland, California, reprinted Hughes's essay "That Boy LeRoi" but denounced its author: "Let Langston and his ilk keep silent in the face of real artists. Theatre 1965 is not for left-over Lazaruses from the so-called 'Negro Renaissance,' nor is it for prissy puritans. Jesse B. Simple should take his well-deserved place along side the Brontosaurus and the Dodo bird!!"

Rosetta LeNoire, the veteran black actress and singer who would later found in Manhattan the specifically integrated AMAS Repertory Theatre, recalled Langston's attitude to the new theater and her own: "We talked about LeRoi Jones and I told him that I thought LeRoi was going too far, that those ultrablack nationalists were really no different from the Ku Klux Klan, no different at all. Langston didn't quite agree. He said, 'Miss Rosie, I understand why you're saying that, but you must remember that sometimes we need the pendulum to swing way over in order to get things right. There are people who just have to be shaken up. The important thing, though, is to know when to stop.' I believe he wasn't so sure that Jones and his friends knew when to stop." But Langston harbored no anger toward Jones. "He was such a gentleman, such a kind human being. There was no bitterness in him. He tried to open your eyes and your mind with humor."

Langston's latest play, *The Prodigal Son,* was now in rehearsal at Stella Holt's Greenwich Mews Theater, where it would share a bill with *The Exception and the Rule,* Bertolt Brecht's argumentative Marxist drama about a merchant and his servant, translated and adapted by Eric Bentley, with a score by Stefan Wolpe, and directed by Isaiah Sheffer. "Eric Bentley and I had put on the show at Columbia University in 1961," Sheffer recalled, "and it had received very nice press notices. We raised some money for a professional production, but not enough to go it alone. Somehow we got to the Greenwich Mews and a double billing with the great Langston Hughes. For the most part, everything went smoothly. We shared some members of the cast, and the set was designed to serve both productions without much trouble. Hughes was not deeply involved in staging his show, but I remember him telling me once how much he admired Bertolt Brecht, and that although the twin bill was a marriage of convenience, he was truly delighted to be a part of it."

Langston barely had time to look in at rehearsals before he was off to Europe for the State Department. With him on this series of talks on Afro-American writing were his one-time helper William M. Kelley, author of the novel *A Different Drummer* and the collection of stories *Dancers on the Shore,* and Paule Marshall, whose novel *Brown Girl, Brownstones* had been hailed in 1959 as a moving tale of a black child's passage to maturity. "Langston was given *carte blanche* by the State Department to pick anyone to go with him," Paule Marshall believed. "He hardly knew me then, but it was just like him to choose two younger writers instead of those better known. He was always aware of what we youngsters were doing, always very giving of himself to us."

The tour turned out to be a mixture of the pleasant and the poor. "We were overworked, constantly kept on the move, kept hungry by the State Department people," according to Marshall. "Langston did not complain much, but he definitely complained about the lack of food!" After a demanding roundtable discussion at the American Cultural Center on rue du Dragon in Paris, the trio went by bus sixty kilometers north to Royaumont Abbey, an ancient, partially restored structure of great charm, for the ninth annual seminar on American literature sponsored by the Cercle Culturel de Royaumont. At Royaumont, they were joined by the preeminent French scholar of Afro-American literature, Jean Wagner of the University of Grenoble, author of the massive study *Black Poets of the United States.* Among the other scholars was Michel Fabre, still at work on his biography of Richard Wright.

For Fabre, Hughes was a revelation. "His ability to take material he must have given hundreds of times before, and make it sound new and fresh, was amazing. His rapport with everyone was also astonishing. Whenever students approached him with questions, he was always patient and helpful and kind, apparently without any effort." Although Hughes drank heavily at times, he always seemed in control of himself. Late one evening, after Fabre sought him out in his room for a few quiet words about books, he began to talk. "For two or three hours," Fabre recalled, "Hughes talked about everything. He talked about the twenties when he was young, about Jean Toomer and Wallace Thurman and Countee Cullen and about how he and his friends had produced *Fire!!* magazine, through the thirties and forties, about Richard Wright and Ralph Ellison, and everything else, just going on and on, effortlessly but with intensity, until his face took on a luminous look, with a sort of glow, a fire." Finally it was Fabre who, exhausted, ended their session and went to bed.

Hughes's warmth and gentleness struck other people. William Kelley never forgot the trip out to Royaumont, when the bus was so crowded that he and Hughes, boarding last, were forced to crouch in the back stairwell. Langston seemed completely unaware of any inconvenience, much less of an indignity. "I remember my impression of him was, 'Gee, this man really has humility, that he wouldn't assert himself and say, *I demand a seat!* I mean, after all, this was the sixties." But he refused to pull rank, and talked and laughed with Kelley all the way to Royaumont.

To Jean Wagner, who had visited Hughes in Harlem while researching his book on black poetry, "Langston was like a father figure to all of us there. He was comfortable and at ease with himself. He said some sharp things about LeRoi Jones, but even then he seemed to speak as a father might, with a mixture of severity and compassion." Hughes had "a deep confidence about his work, and it was justified. I know what others thought of him—Melvin Tolson had told me scornfully that Hughes was not a serious poet, just a folk poet—but that was really a poor judgment. Especially coming from the learned circus-monkey in the Battle Royal of Afro-American literature, with his ridiculous Allen Tate connections. Langston was a real poet, a great poet."

Accompanied by Paule Marshall (after William Kelley returned home), Hughes travelled to Britain. This stage of the tour included a discussion in London sponsored by the Council of African Organizations, a speech at Leeds University, and a reading for the Oxford Poetry Society. The event in London was unpleasant. "Certain of the young people apparently decided to take him to task for what they considered his conservatism," Marshall recalled. "Langston became quite annoyed and reminded those people that he had been on the firing line before they were born. It was the first time I had seen him become so cutting. Obviously it affected him deeply, and annoyed him deeply." He was disturbed again when Marshall herself, during a discussion of race relations in the U.S., rebuked his eighty-seven-year-old friend Arthur Spingarn, who was visiting from New York. Perhaps Hughes believed that Spingarn, the president since 1940 of the NAACP, deserved gentler treatment. But when Spingarn had suggested that the civil rights situation was improving, even if "prejudice exists in all American states," Marshall had shot back that "whether you string up a man on a rope . . . or refuse him admittance to a job as the case is in New York, is to me only two different kinds of brutality." The times called for tough talk. "I remember Langston was a good bit disturbed by Paule and me," Kelley recalled of the Paris leg, "how hard we jumped on America. But I don't think it affected us personally. I think he was aware of the ferment and at the same time aware of the powers that were against progress. He had been around a long time."

Copenhagen provided a respite from the intense pace of the tour, and from tension in general. "This was a lovely, laid-back part of the trip," according to Marshall, "and the time I got to know Langston best. Because of the white nights he couldn't fall asleep, and we stayed up all night talking. I sat at his feet and he told marvellous stories. All he needed was a little glass of gin by his side and a cigarette in the middle of his mouth, with ashes dripping down onto his chest, and he could go on talking forever, and in the most fascinating, engaging way. When we got back to Paris, he took me out for a night on the town, rode with me back to the hotel at midnight in a cab, said goodnight at the door, and stepped back into the cab and took off into the night! For him, apparently, the fun was just about to start!"

Alone, he went on to Germany for engagements arranged by the U.S. Department of State in Cologne, Bonn, and Munich. With a sense of relief, he ended the tour and headed for Tunis and the sun. After a few days there early in June, he flew back to Paris and the comfort of the Hotel California on the rue des Ecoles, before ending a two-month stay outside the United States.

He returned to New York to find his name at the center of a controversy in Boston, where the school board, long under fire for *de facto* segregation ("racial imbalance," the board called it), had summarily fired a temporary teacher for reading an old poem by Langston Hughes to a classroom of black children. In the largely comic poem, "Ballad of the Landlord" ("Landlord, landlord, / My roof has sprung a leak"), a tenant threatens violence unless his rights are honored. The teacher was Jonathan Kozol, a *summa cum laude* graduate of Harvard and a Rhodes scholar. The news of his firing reached newpapers all around the country after Senator Edward Kennedy of Massachusetts, in an address in Illinois, strongly criticized the firing. In Boston, the chairman of the School Committee, Louise Day Hicks, a dogged segregationist, blasted him for interfering with the board. In Harlem, Langston stayed out of the crossfire.

He also returned to find *The Prodigal Son* a hit at the Greenwich Mews, with Brecht's *The Exception and the Rule.* After a fumbling start with another director, he and Stella Holt had summoned Vinnette Carroll to rescue the production. Again, as with *Black Nativity,* she moved boldly. "Langston and I were such good friends," she recalled, "he understood that whatever I did, I meant it to be in the best interests of his play. He had only one request—that I keep the leading actor, Joseph Attles, which I did. But music and dance were going to be more important than dialogue, so I brought in Ben Vereen, in his first professional role, to dance the title role." Tearing the script apart, and aided by the choreography of Syvilla Forte, she turned Hughes's gospel drama into "a swinging dance pantomime," as he marvelled, "a novel concoction I never dreamed of—but a delightful one." To *Cue* magazine, *The Prodigal Son* was "a major theatre event." Joseph Attles and Glory Van Scott, the leading actors, won praise for their performances. Unfortunately, *The Exception and the Rule* was not nearly as well received. *Newsday* dismissed it as a "ponderous Germanic trifle," and *The New Yorker* quipped that it was stylized to the point of rigor mortis. However, the show had its admirers, and the twin bill drew crowds to Stella Holt's theater in Greenwich Village.

Encouraged by this success, Langston turned his attention to two main tasks— the preparation of an anthology, "The Best Short Stories by Negro Writers," for Little, Brown, and the drafting of a television script for the influential folk-singer and actor Harry Belafonte. The television script was the greater challenge. Troubled, as Langston was, by the painfully recurring image of blacks as violent and embittered, Belafonte had come up with the idea of a variety show to be set in Harlem in its most glamorous period, the 1920s. He had picked the subject after reading Hughes's autobiography *The Big Sea,* which still remained the liveliest firsthand account of the era. Race-proud but principled in a way like Langston, he envisioned an entertainment that would accent the positive side of "the Negro face, not the angry face reflecting the difficulties of current struggles. We've had enough of that." In turn, Langston had long admired Belafonte for his careful and yet inspired use of folk songs—"the way he transforms the material and gives it a meaningful life for the American public."

Performing in the show would be top black entertainers, including Sammy Davis, Jr., Duke Ellington, Diahann Carroll, and Sidney Poitier, but the real star was to be Harlem. The community would be seen from street level, as it were, poor and pressured, but also warm, loving, and creative. In a major challenge to Langston as scriptwriter, Sidney Poitier was to narrate the show, but would do so with a difference. He would be the "stroller," a Harlem dandy dressed up and stepping out in the grandest twenties style, but also a poetic presence speaking in jingling rhymes. This idea amused and intrigued Langston. Early in August, he submitted a draft to Belafonte. He would revise the material after conferences in Los Angeles later in the month.

This effort to show something other than "the angry face" of blacks was timely. Just as Langston was handing over his draft, the predominantly black district of Watts in Los Angeles exploded into the worst rioting of the decade after an unemployed black youth was arrested for drunken driving. In five days, thirty-four persons were killed, over a thousand injured, and about four thousand arrested. Hundreds of businesses were destroyed or badly damaged. Looting and arson ceased only after 13,000 National Guardsmen regained control of the streets.

By comparison, Harlem was quiet. But Langston was hardly fooled. To the composer David Amram, with whom he was collaborating on the cantata "Let Us Remember" for the Union of American Hebrew Congregations, he talked of a changed Harlem. "All those hundreds of years of bitterness and frustrations are beginning to overflow," Amram recalled him saying. "We've been promised so much for so long and now there's so much to be had, a lot of the young people figure if they don't get it they're going to go out and *take* it. I'm a different generation. You see, I love Harlem. I've lived all over the world and I still find it's one of the most beautiful places I know. But the younger people don't feel this way. History is finally catching up with America. Still, I hate to see the anger in the young faces all the time—it's even hard for me to write my Simple stories anymore. There's so much bitterness and anger that they don't seem to be as funny as they used to.''

The Prodigal Son was still running smoothly when Stella Holt proposed an abrupt end to the production. Her aim was to detach the play from its companion piece, Brecht's *The Exception and the Rule,* and send it on a tour of Europe. Her action was challenged at once by an indignant Isaiah Sheffer, the director of the Brecht play. He accused Holt, Maxwell T. Cohen (Hughes's lawyer), and finally Hughes himself of improper behavior. Since two-thirds of the original production money had come from supporters of the Brecht play, Sheffer asked, was the proposed move "fair, decent, or moral?" After more than a hundred performances, the bill was still drawing well. A meeting on September 20 turned nasty. The Brecht backers accused Max Cohen of threatening them, and one of Langston's assistants apparently hurled racist epithets against the opposition. Langston, who had not attended the meeting—"nor was I aware of it, and do not know who was there"—insisted that he had had little to do with the production, especially with its business aspects, and that his own royalty payments were behind schedule (Holt had insisted that Hughes, Sheffer, and Bentley defer their royalties until the fall). But an insinuation that Hughes and Holt were acting in collusion also came in an open letter from a disgruntled member of the *Prodigal Son* ensemble, who questioned the terms set for the players in Europe. "Stella, have you *really* been honest?" she asked. "And Mr. Hughes, 'What happens to a dream deferred?' ''

Were Hughes and Holt in collusion? "Stella was very devoted to Langston," Vinnette Carroll recalled, "and Langston absolutely loved her. There were two sides to Stella—she was sweet, but she was something of a maniac where money was concerned. Just try to get a dollar out of her, and you saw the other side!" Also looking back, Isaiah Sheffer was even more critical: "Stella Holt played the role of the sainted blind lady very well, but some of her business practices were, to put it mildly, highly questionable. You could never get her to produce her books. In my own financial dealings with her, I saw enough hanky-panky and cutting of corners to wonder about her ethics." But Sheffer doubted that Hughes was implicated. "He was too distant from everything, including even the box-office. We kept waiting for the great man to step in and settle the matter, but he kept his distance and refused to be drawn into the mess. I think he believed in Stella Holt and hoped that she would be ethical. She wasn't. But by no means was he engaged in anything corrupt."

Wittingly or unwittingly, Langston aided Holt's obvious goal of floating a European production—free of the Brechtian anchor—by leaving to her the decision whether or not to tour and by accepting without question the closing of the New York production. Also, he prepared another show, "Tell It to Telstar," a poetry-play blending excerpts from Walt Whitman with songs and spirituals, "written as a companion piece for *The Prodigal Son.*" The "author's copy" was dated August 9, or some months after the opening of the twin bill of Hughes and Brecht. In any event, on October 8, in spite of dire threats by the Brecht group of litigation against Hughes and Holt for "an outright attempt to cheat us and our investors," a company of *The Prodigal Son,* escorted by Stella Holt, left for Europe.

Langston's passivity struck many of his friends as almost unseemly. "If I had to find fault with Langston," Vinnette Carroll judged, "it is that he wasn't aggressive enough. He was laid-back. You could see passion in his writing, but you never saw it in him. I have *never* seen him angry." "He was really far too meek for his own good," the lawyer Max Cohen judged, "and far too trusting. Some people in show business probably thought Langston was sly, that he couldn't possibly be so almost lackadaisical about money and business matters, but that is exactly the way he was. He was *not* competitive. I would say that he was wordly without being sophisticated, in a sense. I always thought he should have stood up more for himself. In fact, about the only time I saw him really angry and determined to take action was when a Harlem bookselling enterprise featured his picture and an enthusiastic endorsement by him— a total fake—in its advertisemensts without even so much as consulting him." On October 11, 1965, Cohen filed suit on Hughes's behalf in the New York State Supreme Court against *The Encyclopedia of Black Culture* and three of its principals, one of whom was a prominent Harlem clergyman whose lubricious letters of reconciliation particularly irritated Hughes. Eventually, the matter was settled out of court to his satisfaction.

Through the fall of 1965, Langston kept in close touch with Harry Belafonte as they polished the script of "The Strollin' Twenties." Its jaunty image of Harlem in the 1920s contrasted with the reality of present-day life there. In two weeks, four of Hughes's friends were viciously mugged. Out of town, he protested that Harlem was not nearly as bad as people made out, but he was forced to agree that many blacks as well as whites now feared to walk its celebrated streets. When the expatriated musician Jimmy Davis wrote from France about returning home, Langston was blunt: "My advice, STAY in Paris." More and more, Hughes enjoyed his trips downtown—to Lüchow's with Arthur Spingarn; attending the Broadway musical play *Pickwick* with Amy Spingarn; attending the fiftieth anniversary dinner of the first Borzoi book from Knopf's at the Hotel Astor.

He also looked eagerly for any chance to travel free of charge. After the successful appearance of his latest Simple book, *Simple's Uncle Sam,* from Hill and Wang, he went to Cleveland for celebrations to mark the fiftieth year of service by Russell and Rowena Jelliffe of Karamu House in Cleveland. Then, for the premiere of his cantata with David Amram, "Let Us Remember," as part of a program of modern Jewish music, he travelled on to San Francisco for the concert on November 15 at the Opera House. There, before some 3,000 delegates attending the biennial convention of Reformed Judaism, the Oakland Symphony orchestra led by Gerhard Samuel, and a 150-voice chorus conducted by Robert Commanday, performed the cantata, which was dedicated "to those who have given their life for freedom at all times in all countries." With Jennie

Tourel as soloist and Edward G. Robinson the narrator, the event was a distinct success. While Amram's composition drew both praise and sarcasm from the critics (one reviewer jibed that the music could have served any text, "—Zen Buddhism or Florsheim shoes"), the libretto was lauded for its simple, direct, and yet evocative nature. Not without stock phrases, but lyric and ecumenical in spirit, the six-part libretto probed the theme of martyrdom in all countries at all times.

> Ah, Kiddush Hashem! Ah, Kiddush Hashem!
> Ah, Kiddush Hashem!
> To sanctify the name of God————
> echoed! echoed! echoed! echoed!
> For the martyred names in history's sod
> our tears flow in the heart of God.
> Our grief, transmitted everywhere,
> tel-starred in the cosmic air————
> Ah, Kiddush Hashem! Ah, Kiddush Hashem!
> Ah, Kiddush Hashem!
> Our tears flow in the heart of God. . . .

The third section stressed a subtle moral theme, but one of some importance now to Langston—oppression by the formerly oppressed. "Let not the oppressed become oppressors" is a prayer from the "Yizkor," the basis of the cantata. His text invokes the memory of many acts of oppression in Jewish and world history, but perhaps he was also thinking of one possible black reaction to oppression. "Oh, remember———— / Montgomery, Selma, and Savannah, / let not the oppressed become oppressors."

Returning home to attend a book fair at the Choate school in Connecticut, Hughes found puzzling reports about *The Prodigal Son* in Europe. While Stella Holt had written him about large, "wildly crazy" audiences in Amsterdam, Brussels, and Antwerp, the British producer Michael Dorfman, to whom Stella Holt had sold the European rights, had described the box office in the same cities as poor, and sent no royalties. Only a big week at Christmas in Paris, he said, would keep the show alive. The thought of Paris at Christmas was too much for Langston. He immediately reserved a seat on an Air France flight.

Again he intended to stay away as long as he could. To this end, he worked hard in the days before leaving. He declined an invitation to work with the soprano Leontyne Price on her life story, but completed work on his anthology of black poetry for Pierre Seghers. Looking for quick money, he hazarded a proposal for another anthology, "White on Black," stories by white writers about black life, from Poe to Reynolds Price ("50 powerful and unusual stories distinguished in themselves, regardless of the uniqueness—for some—of their subject matter"). Langston also made a fateful decision about one of the major creations of his career. After twenty-three years, he ended his column in the *Chicago Defender* and, more important, the adventures of Jesse B. Semple. In recent years, most of the columns had been about Simple, as if the times were too demanding for Langston to risk speaking with his own voice. Simple, on the other hand, could say anything—and often did. ("I keep telling him," Hughes complained, "to take those chips off his shoulders—but he won't and don't!") But the Associated Negro Press, which syndicated the column, was at least $1,000 in arrears to Langston, who was equally fed up with the management of the *Defender*.

On January 8, 1966, with the announcement that "Creator Hughes has decided to put Simple to sleep," the newspaper printed the first Simple column, that of January 19, 1943, alongside the last. Why Langston decided to end the character is not clear. Certainly he had heard the calls for its demise. In the *Post* of August 16, 1963, he had even published a caustic denunciation of Simple—and himself—by a reader: "I am a Negro and I can find no one who talks in his idiom although I live in Harlem and go to the usual places. . . . Jess Semple projects the image of the Negro as being stupid, ignorant, simple-minded, the happy-go-lucky darky type that the readers of the so-called liberal New York Post like to visualize as all Negroes. . . . Jess Semple is dead, why don't you bury him?"

Simple was not dying. Worse, perhaps, he was moving to the suburbs. His relentlessly respectable wife, Joyce, had saved enough money to buy a house on a tree-lined street among white folks and was quitting their old neighborhood. Simple was going along, but he saw a bleak future: "I will be shoveling snow, stoking the furnace and putting washers in sinks for the rest of my natural life." There would be no neighborhood bar with a juke box and someone to talk to. Since they would be the first blacks on the block, Joyce would work him to death just "to show white folks we can keep a house up as well as anybody else."

> Why leave the place where life is—to go live with birds, bees, and caterpillars and bats? Life to me is where peoples is at—not just nature and snow and trees with falling leaves to rake all by yourself, and furnaces to stoke, and no landlords downstairs to holler at to keep the heat up, and no next door neighbors across the hall to raise a ruckus Saturday nights, and no bad children drawing pictures on the walls in the halls, and nobody to drink a beer with at the corner bar—because the corner in the suburbans has nothing on it but a dim old lonesome street light on a cold old lonesome pole.
>
> And to get to Woodlawn, from where you live you have to walk to a bus line, then ride to a subway line then change at Monroe for the A train to Woodlawn. Friends, when I move to the suburbans, I am gone. So bye - bye - bye - bye! Goodbye! Jesse B. Simple is gone.

In one of the last days of December, 1965, Paris had just endured a blizzard when Langston, accompanied by his friend Jimmy Davis, arrived at the Champs Elysées theater for a performance of *The Prodigal Son*. To his annoyance, with the producer Michael Dorfman nowhere to be found, he was forced to buy tickets, which proved to be surprisingly expensive. He soon discovered that *The Prodigal Son,* so creatively mounted at first by Vinnette Carroll, was now mostly vaudeville. Afterwards, the actors were sullen and rebellious. In over two months, they had been paid only one week's wages. Two days later, when Langston stopped by the theater at intermission, expecting to meet his Argentinian translator Julio Galer, he was dismayed to find police on the premises. Nonchalantly walking by them, he entered an empty auditorium. Backstage, sitting on a box in a corner, as pale as a ghost, was Michael Dorfman. "They attacked me!" he whimpered to Langston. After arguing with him about their wages, the players had revolted in full view of the assembling audience. "The stage was in a turmoil," Julio Galer later recalled; "a group of artists (negro men and women) were angrily shouting revolutionary slogans against management and loudly declared that they would 'occupy' the Theatre." One woman, according to another report, had Michael Dorfman by the throat, religiously choking him, when gendarmes burst in to haul her away.

Distressed by the players' revolt, because it not only killed the hope of a profitable Paris run but threatened to bring a conservative backlash, Langston flew the next morning to Tunis. He passed five warm days at the Hilton Hotel there before returning to Paris on January 9. Almost at once he ran into his old California friends Matt and Evelyn Crawford, with their daughter Nebby Lou, on vacation. But there was no pleasant surprise concerning *The Prodigal Son.* Two of the players had been jailed following the disturbance. Conceding that he owed the nineteen-member cast at least $4,000, Michael Dorfman now declared the tour a financial disaster. The players had tickets to return to the United States, but were broke. The American embassy secured the release of those in jail, and Marion Williams agreed to sing a benefit concert at the American Church on the Quai d'Orsay.

Back in New York, Langston met with Stella Holt over dinner, then put the show out of his mind. (Later, Max Cohen pursued Michael Dorfman to Scotland, and with the help of a British lawyer recovered some money for Langston.) Auspiciously, on his sixty-fourth birthday, February 1, his *Book of Negro Humor* appeared from Dodd, Mead. But although the *Library Journal* recommended the volume, most reviewers yawned. The Cleveland *Plain Dealer* thought that it proved that black and white humor were alike in being "good, bad and indifferent." Shrugging off such responses, Langston again took a room at the Hotel Wellington and busied himself with other challenges in editing—"now that Negro books are in vogue again." He blew dust from his old "Battle of Harlem" manuscript and offered it, in vain, to the prosperous Johnson Publishing Company, the owner of *Ebony* magazine. The same fate befell "A Caribbean Sampler," including poems by Derek Walcott, Léon Damas, and Nicolás Guillén. But he also worked on what would be his second book with Milton Meltzer, "Black Magic: A Pictorial History of the Negro in Entertainment." And he continued his revision with Arna Bontemps of their *Poetry of the Negro,* which Langston was determined to make a "DEFINITIVE anthology, for the sake of future scholars." To make room for recent Afro-

American poetry, they abandoned the special Caribbean section. The white or "tributary" section was preserved.

February also brought a revival by the New York City Opera of *Street Scene*, now hailed as a classic example of Kurt Weill's genius; the lyricist proudly attended the show twice. In the same month, too, came Harry Belafonte's lavish television production of *The Strollin' Twenties*. But in spite of handsome sets and superb individual performances, the show was judged a failure by the critics. The *News* reported "a tiresome, boring hour." Harlem in the twenties, according to the *Times,* could not have been "as primly starched or as lifeless." Recited gallantly by Sidney Poitier, Langston's narrative paid a lyrical but not always convincing tribute to Harlem—that "dusky sash across the middle of Manhattan—I like it! I love it!" "Sure," one skeptic drawled, envisioning "an appreciative audience of absentee landlords." Also, Hughes's rhyming speech for the narrator, Sidney Poitier, generally was misunderstood—although in Hollywood the veteran actor Clarence Muse hailed it as "an innovation. It made your characters coherent and added a new dimension to the Negro idiom." (Some reviewers thought Hughes was imitating the boxer Cassius Clay, although rhymed speech had been a Harlem feature since the twenties, and later would be revived as "rap" talk.)

Defending the show, Langston pointed to the grave danger of stressing only the terrible aspects of the community, as so many writers and artists were doing—and thus encouraging mainly cynicism and despair. "There has been little balance in the Harlem picture lately," he protested, "the liberal and well meant intent seemingly being to present the worst aspects in order to arouse sympathy and action. It sometimes boomerangs and makes folks think all is hopeless." Drafting an introduction to his anthology "The Best Stories by Negro Writers" for Little, Brown, he made a similar point. Many Americans think today, Langston argued, "that all Negroes are primitive, dirty and dangerous," a notion he attributed to exposure to works by James Baldwin, LeRoi Jones, and similar writers. There was a fine line between criticizing degraded social conditions and describing a community of beasts. However, artists and intellectuals, and in particular those who genuinely wished to advance the race, needed to preserve that distinction.

To some observers, such talk bespoke a man lacking in courage. The revolutionary hour had come, whites were to be accused and condemned. In 1966, the doctrine of Black Power had just begun to be enunciated, and the emphasis on Black Beauty and Black Pride were not far behind. Far more than any other major Afro-American writer, Langston had always been in favor of blacks achieving the greatest power, and few people could teach him anything about the beauty and the heritage of his race. But he believed that certain spokesmen—Baldwin and Jones especially—were recklessly undermining the black world, no matter how stirring and inspirational their rhetoric sounded. Langston also believed that the volatility of their writing came less from a genuine, pragmatic evaluation of the Afro-American condition, energized by a love of the black race, than from narcissism, neuroses, and other private compulsions. The art that resulted from such compulsions might be sensational, but probably also was a lie. It was one thing to apply these personal compulsions to a depiction of human nature and psychology in general; it was quite another to apply them to racial and political theory and practice.

On March 24, when he delivered the Mabel Williams Lecture before a youthful audience at the Donnell Library in Manhattan, he emphasized the need for naturalness, integrity, and calm judgment in an artist. "To be a good writer," he told his young listeners, "you have to learn to be yourself—natural and undeceived as to who you are and, in so far as writing goes, calmly and surely you. Be as insecure as you might be in other things, if you can't help yourself, but *not* in writing, which must be your very own, and in which you trust, and which you don't have to share with anyone—until you share it with the world."

Langston faced the world very much like a man at peace with himself. With the arrival of his *Anthologie de la Poésie Negro-Américaine* from Editions Seghers, he had now published as author, editor, translator, or major collaborator almost as many books as he had years—including about fifty in English. But his accomplishments seemed to make him only more gracious. Alex Haley, whose *The Autobiography of Malcolm X* had appeared the previous year, was moved by their first encounter, at the Hotel Wellington, to offer a tribute: "The thing was, is, you're a veteran in this business, you've venerableness, plus weight, you could throw around, but you don't, not one whit. That's, in my book, class." Langston was also loyal. Although he no longer needed her support, he never forgot Amy Spingarn, now over eighty years old. After dinner and a showing of *Fiddler on the Roof,* with precious tickets sent to Hughes by its author, she offered her thanks: "You are a thoughtful friend and I treasure our friendship."

Even skeptics were often finally convinced of his genuine gifts of character. In February that year, 1966, at the popular Frank's Restaurant on 125th Street in Harlem, Langston, Arna Bontemps, and Langston's guest the "colored" Johannesburg writer Richard Rive ate shrimp and scallops and drank South African wine ordered by Hughes in honor of Rive. As Bontemps sipped and listened, gently amused—"half a century of poetry written on his face, on his grey-sleeked hair, on the quiet of his manner"—Hughes smoked and tried to respond to the younger writer's probing, even presumptuous questions. "Cigarette-smoking, fluttering hands toying with paper-napkin, frowning owl-eyed through horn-rimmed glasses chewing the question," Langston Hughes "talks and talks and talks, parrying questions." Rive, no doubt probing Hughes's own sexuality, asked about Countee Cullen and "the tragedy of his personal life." "I do not know," Hughes replied. Rive persisted: "Did it influence his writings?" "I do not know. Have a cigarette, Dick." In the article he published about the dinner, Rive sneered at his host's home—"'Slum exterior in a slum district, up broken steps"—but finally was in awe of Hughes: "Humility characterises the truly great."

Langston's "venerableness, plus weight," was recognized publicly soon after when President Lyndon Johnson appointed him an official American representative to the First World Festival of Negro Arts, scheduled for Dakar, Senegal, in the month of April. This appointment made Langston a leader of the American contingent of over one hundred black artists, performers, and scholars. Conceived by the poet Léopold Sédar Senghor, president of Senegal, the festival was endorsed by the United Nations and attracted delegations from about fifty countries. The United States, eager to be well represented at what would be an unparalleled opportunity for propaganda (the Soviet Union sent not only a delegation, but also a cruise ship to serve as a floating hotel), had contributed at least $150,000 to help fund the American delegation to Dakar—where the U.S. Ambassador was none other than Mercer Cook, Langston's friend since the twenties and his collaborator in translating Jacques Roumain's *Masters of the Dew*.

Late in March, after agreeing to undertake an extensive official reading tour of Africa following the festival, Langston left the United States for Senegal. This would be his fourth trip to Africa in the decade, and his longest stay out of the country in almost thirty years.

On a note of excitement that hardly dwindled in the following days, the festival opened on April 1 in Dakar with over two thousand visitors in attendance. Over more than three weeks of scheduled cultural events, the most sensational performances were almost certainly those of Duke Ellington and his orchestra, the Alvin Ailey dance troupe, Marion Williams and her gospel singers, and the bare-breasted dancers of Mali. Nevertheless, Langston left a mark probably unmatched by any single presence other than the president of Senegal himself. As the most revered literary spokesmen for black racial pride, the two poets together formed the center of the gathering—"the true spirits of a grand festival in the tradition of 'blood brothers'," as one observer later reflected. "Senghor symbolized *Négritude* while Hughes epitomized its American counterpart, *Soul*." At an audience, Senghor paid homage to Langston when he recited in English and in French two obscure poems by Langston from the twenties. Speaking years later about the American influence on *Négritude*, Senghor affirmed that "we considered Langston to be the greatest black American poet because it was Langston Hughes who best answered to our definition" of the term in verse, rooted in an African sense of artistic values—"an image or a group of images, analogical, melodious, and rhythmical."

As the president of the republic, Senghor could mix with the delegates only discreetly. Langston, under no such restriction, gave himself to the festival. "In his own way," the *New York Times* judged, he "emerged as one of the festival's most conspicuous celebrities; young writers from all over Africa followed him about the city and haunted his hotel the way American youngsters dog favorite baseball players." For him, this widespread recognition and acceptance, even adulation, by young Africa made his appointment to the Dakar festival perhaps the third great honor of his life. With the Spingarn Medal, black America had honored him. With his election to the National Institute of

Arts and Letters, white America had bestowed its laurels. At the First World Festival in Dakar, he basked in the recognition by the international African community, and their many white guests, of his extraordinary, lifelong service to the race in its quest for power and authority in the modern world. For Langston, this recognition almost certainly eclipsed all other honors.

Incompetent management plagued the festival, but he brushed aside such criticism. "In the end," he mused, "nobody is going to remember the troublesome sideshows." Dressed casually in loose shirts of local calico, spurning a collar, he took both his venerability and his official status in easy stride. He seemed to have time for everyone. Sim Copans, a white American jazz-lover who had taken part the previous year in the colloquium with Hughes, William Kelley, and Paule Marshall at the American Cultural Center in Paris, where he lived, remembered how Langston had reached out to him: "I was lonely in Dakar and I guess I was feeling out of place. I don't know how he knew it, but Langston sought me out just to find out if I was all right. He was going off for drinks with some members from the Ellington orchestra. To my amazement, he insisted that I come with them. I loved their music, but I certainly didn't know them. He introduced me to everybody, and it made all the difference in the world. It was a very kind thing for him to do." Jean Blackwell Hutson of the Schomburg Collection in Harlem was an old friend, "but Langston turned me into an instant celebrity in Dakar by telling everyone that I was his 'sweetheart.' All the doors sprung open from that moment on! And I think Langston knew exactly what he was doing!" Millicent Dobbs Jordan from Atlanta missed an impromptu visit to her hotel by "the Great One, Langston Hughes, himself!" but found a genial note on her return: "Dropped by to invite you for a 'cool one' on a hot day—Langston (né Hughes)."

The Russians had rushed in their international star, Yevgeny Yevtushenko, the anti-Stalinist poet who allegedly had outdrawn even the Beatles on a recent tour of Australia. Forbidden by Senghor to read publicly during the festival (he could read once it was over), Yevtushenko passed several days sulking in his tent—the Russian cruise ship. To draw him out, the *New York Times* correspondent Lloyd M. Garrison turned to Hughes. "I asked Langston if I could use him as bait. He said, 'Go right ahead! I'd like to meet the guy myself'. So I told Yevtushenko that I would like to visit him on the ship and bring along Langston Hughes. It worked." (Garrison's father, Lloyd K. Garrison, had advised Langston in his 1953 bout with Senator Joseph McCarthy.) "We had dinner on the ship, with an endless supply of Georgian champagne. After that, for about a week, we went out drinking every night." One companion in their revels was the Harlem-born filmmaker William Greaves, who had written a screenplay of *The Sweet Flypaper of Life* and was making a documentary movie about the festival. "We used to ride around in Yevtushenko's limousine," Bill Greaves recalled, "drinking pretty heavily and having a lot of fun." "Whatever the Russians expected in the way of rivalry," U.S. Ambassador Mercer Cook recalled, "never developed. Langston wouldn't allow it. He and Yevtushenko seemed to be arm in arm every time I saw them together."

Yevtushenko's prodigious imbibing, far in excess of what Hughes, Garrison, and Greaves could manage, led to an amusing incident late one night on board the ship. "Yevtushenko was drunk and thrashing about the cabin when suddenly these two Russian amazons burst in. Langston excused himself and went to the bathroom. I was trying to get Yevtushenko up from the floor when I heard a scream from the bathroom. 'Garrison, Garrison, help! Get me out of here!' It was Langston. One of the women had cornered him in the bathroom and was attacking him. We left that ship in a hurry. Langston couldn't stop laughing."

Garrison remembered him finally as "an unbelievably serene, bright, friendly, sweet man." Conscious of his position as a goodwill ambassador, Langston took his official duties seriously. In addition to readings at the local USIS library, which "deeply moved his largely African audience," he served as head of the jury for the Grand Prize in the field of English literature. In spite of his dislike of Robert Hayden's elitism and avoidance of racial identification, he was instrumental in having the award given to him. But Langston's major single contribution came during a special one-week colloquium on the place of art in the lives of black people. In electing to speak on "Black Writers in a Troubled World," with the emphasis on Afro-American writers in the age of the freedom movement, he boldly—and perhaps dangerously—created for himself an opportunity to articulate, before an international gathering of blacks, his basic beliefs about the function of the artist.

Langston emphasized his sense that, for the black artist, loyalty to historic Afro-American and African values forbade the excesses of obscenity and racial hatred that had become epidemic in black American writing. A true love of blackness, and confidence in it, Langston declared, would not countenance the neurotic reflexiveness that made so many young black writers see America as doomed and their own artistic purpose, therefore, as Satanic. He himself believed in a flawed but redeemable America, but the consensus among many blacks "is that American society is falling to pieces, going to the dogs, stewing in its own iniquity, and bogged down in the gutters of Saigon." Tragically, many books by these same younger blacks "are about as near the gutter as—in their opinion—America seems to be." Mentioning by name LeRoi Jones, James Baldwin, and Charles Wright, author of the novels *The Wig* and *The Messenger,* Langston marvelled at the bizarre relationship between abusive black writers who "talk about whites badly *right in the middle of the whites*' own parlors, lecture halls and libraries," and whites who seemed to adore this abuse. In this relationship lay a perversion of the function of art: "The most talented of the young Negro writers have become America's prophets of doom, black ravens cawing over carrion."

Unlike Jones and Baldwin, other black writers (he mentioned Ralph Ellison, John O. Killens, Julian Mayfield, and Paule Marshall) had criticized America "but without finger-painting in excrement on America's lily white canvas." An even older generation—Richard Wright, Bontemps, Anne Petry, and Hughes himself, for example—"never dreamed of revealing the Negro people to themselves in terms of motherfuckers; or of shocking white readers with bad words rather than with bad facts." At the root of the situation was the oldest tension in black writing: the existence of a double audience, black and white, exerting a potentially disastrous force on the writer unless resisted by racial and personal confidence. "The best writers," Langston insisted, "are those who possess enough self-integrity to wish first and foremost to please themselves, only themselves, and nobody else. But this, when one is young and one's thinking is unclear—and one's ability to analyze this world about one is not uncertain—is not easy."

In what should the black writer believe? Hughes offered first an ethnic, then a universal principle, both of which he saw as intimately related. The first principle concerned *Négritude,* which was the same as American "soul." "*Soul* is a synthesis of the essence of Negro folk art redistilled," he explained, "particularly the old music and its flavor, the ancient basic beat out of Africa, the folk rhymes and Ashanti stories—expressed in contemporary ways so definitely and emotionally colored with the old, that it gives a distinctly 'Negro' flavor to today's music, painting or writing—or even to merely personal attitudes and daily conversation. *Soul* is contemporary Harlem's *négritude,* revealing to the Negro people and the world the beauty within themselves."

He identified the universal principle: "If one may ascribe a prime function to any creative writing, it is I think, to affirm life, to yea-say the excitement of living in relation to the vast rhythms of the universe of which we are a part, to untie the riddles of the gutter in order to closer tie the knot between man and God. As to Negro writing and writers, one of our aims, it seems to me, should be to gather the strengths of our people in Africa and the Americas into a tapestry of words as strong as the bronzes of Benin, the memories of Songhay and Mele, the war cry of Chaka, the beat of the blues, and the *Uhuru* of African freedom, and give it to the world with pride and love, and . . . humanity and affection."

"What Langston has left us," Senghor insisted twenty years later, "is that he will always be a model not only for the United States but for the world" in the poetic invocation of melody and rhythm, in the perfection of "images, analogical, melodious, and rhythmical, with assonance and alliteration." This sense of perfection in art was based on African values of art but shared with other cultures, including the European. "You will find this rhythm in French poetry; you will find it in Péguy, you will find it in Claudel, you will find this rhythm in St. John Perse. . . . And it is this that Langston Hughes has left us with, this model of the perfect work of art."

16

DO NOTHING TILL YOU
HEAR FROM ME
1966 to 1967

. . . and here is
old Picasso and the dove
and dreams as fragile
as pottery with dove
in white on clay
dark brown as
earth is brown
from our old
battle ground . . .

"The Dove," 1962

A FTER A triumphant month in Dakar, Langston left Senegal to begin his grand tour of Africa for the U.S. State Department. Like the United States, Africa was changing at a swift, disturbing pace. To his disappointment, he found Lagos, Nigeria, his first stop, gripped by a crime wave of unprecedented violence and variety. "Lagos," he wrote home in awe, "is more like the old Chicago of gangster days than ever." Worse, Nigeria itself was in the grasp of a military dictatorship following a coup in mid-January by army officers that had led to several deaths, the overthrow of his friend Benjamin Azikiwe as Governor General, and the eventual start of the Biafran civil war. "The swift change," his protegé Sunday Osuya, himself an Ibo, had informed him illogically about the coup, "is believed to be the beginning of democracy in Nigeria."

In a sour epilogue to the independence movement that had transformed the former European colonies into a growing array of new black nations, *coups d'état* now seemed to threaten the dream of democratic progress for Africa. In Ghana later that year would come the most decisive blow—the overthrow of the most ambitious leader of the African independence movement, Kwame Nkrumah. Such events did not touch Langston's faith in the African peoples. Unwilling to sit in moral judgment of so vast a group of people, he also understood that behind the collapse of many black governments, including the uranium-rich Congo, where the defiant leader Patrice Lumumba had been murdered in 1961 by forces aided by the CIA, were the greedy forces of European neocolonialism. A poem written shortly after Lumumba's death had vented Langston's outrage at the murder:

> Lumumba was black
> And he didn't trust
> The whores all powdered
> With uranium dust.
>
> Lumumba was black
> And he didn't believe
> The lies thieves shook
> Through their "freedom" sieve.
>
> Lumumba was black.
> His blood was red—
> And for being a man
> They killed him dead.
>
> They buried Lumumba
> In an unmarked grave.
> But he needs no marker—
> For air is his grave.
>
> Sun is his grave,
> Moon is, stars are,
> Space is his grave.
>
> My heart's his grave
> And it's marked there.
> *Tomorrow will mark*
> *It everywhere.*

This bitterness at neocolonialism tempered Langston's enjoyment of his U.S.-sponsored tour but did not kill it. Nor was all his anger directed at the imperialist powers. In fact, the low point of the tour probably came in Ethiopia, after a visit to the Sudan (where Langston committed a gaffe at a party: "I mistook the Speaker of the Assembly for a waiter and asked him for a plate!"). Loving the land and its handsome peoples, he left the country hating Haile Selassie even as Ethiopia celebrated the twenty-fifth anniversary of its liberation from the Italians, in which Selassie had figured as an almost legendary symbol of African pride. At the request of the USIS, Langston had composed a poem in tribute to the emperor ("a symbol of our negritude," and "the symbol of a dream / That will not die"), which he was to present personally. Arriving at the appointed time and sweating profusely in European formal wear, which Selassie demanded, Langston was made to wait in a depressingly long line of

cowed supplicants. When at last he entered the imperial presence, the Lion of
Judea impassively accepted from him a scroll with the poem, then handed him
a bronze medal and waved him on without a word. This piece of African
medievalism infuriated Langston. He loved Ethiopia, he wrote home, but
"*LOATHED*" Addis Ababa.

Later, among close friends at home, he unabashedly conceded the truth of a
suggestion that he would have been more indulgent of the Queen of England.
"Haile Selassie," Langston snapped, "wasn't born European!"

Tanzania provided yet another lesson. After a visit to Kenya, on May 19
Langston reached Julius Nyerere's republic, a nation ruled according to principles directly opposite to the feudalism of Ethiopia. Tanzania had been hailed
as the pioneer of a new brand of socialism, one humanely adapted to the ancient communalism of Africa. Langston's days in Dar-es-Salaam and elsewhere
were indeed pleasant and stimulating—especially when he basked in the regard
of a group of young black foreigners who had come "home" to help build
Africa. Among them were Lebert "Sandy" Bethune, a charming, talented Jamaican-born poet and a graduate of New York University, whom Langston had
met earlier in Paris; the poet and dramatist Lindsay Barrett, also Jamaican; and
John Taylor, an American filmmaker. To them, Tanzania epitomized the new
Africa—democratic, moderate, enlightened, and open to outsiders of good will,
especially if they were black.

Langston lingered with them for a few days, then went on to a vacation in
Tangier by way of Madrid and Casablanca. Late in June, he reached Paris. At
the Hotel California, he was surveying the rue des Ecoles from his tiny balcony
when he spied a familiar but unlikely figure below—Sandy Bethune. "I just
left you in Tanzania!" Langston shouted down. "What are you doing here?"
Disconsolately, Bethune explained that without warning, and without the sem-
blance of a legal process, he and his friends had been booted out of Tanzania
for no other crime, apparently, than being foreigners. The new African socialism was not so different, after all, from other arrangements. Langston was
dismayed by the news, Bethune recalled, but philosophic. "I've been kicked
out of far better places than Tanzania," he told Bethune, "so don't even think
about it. It just isn't worth it." He talked about his skirmishes with the police
in Japan in 1933, when he had been shadowed and interrogated by them.
"Langston also tried to convince me that I shouldn't be hard on Tanzania, or
Africa, or take it personally. What had happened was simply one of those
things that happen in life. You had to take such setbacks in stride and move
on, without bitterness." Realizing that Bethune was now broke, Langston invented odd secretarial jobs and paid him for doing them. On July 18, on a page
torn from a notebook, he even composed and presented to Bethune an appropriate poem, "For You":

> It *is* wise
> To suffer illusions,
> Delusion,
> Even dreams—

Langston Hughes and Carl Van Vechten. *Photo by Richard Avedon, February 16, 1963.* © *1963 by Richard Avedon Inc. All rights reserved.*

With Emerson Harper, in the backyard at 20 East 127th Street, 1963. *Photo by George H. Bass.*

With George Bass, on board the *Athens* in the Mediterranean, 1963. *Courtesy of George H. Bass.*

On vacation in Greece, July 14, 1963. *Photo by George H. Bass.*

Jericho-Jim Crow, 1964. Behind Jim Crow, Gilbert Price.

With Stella Holt, c. 1964. *Schomburg Collection, New York Public Library.*

Merry Christmas from Langston Hughes, 1965.

With some stars of *Strollin' Twenties*, 1966.

Amiri Baraka (LeRoi Jones) and Amina Baraka, outside the Newark, New Jersey courthouse, 1967.

On the shores of Senegal, 1966. *Photo by Bracher Dakar.*

> To believe that in this life
> What is real
> May also be what it *seems*.
> What is not true
> May be—
> For you.

With money from the tour in his pocket, Langston passed a soothing month in Paris. Particularly happy to see him were Henri and Eli Cartier-Bresson, to whom Hughes had dedicated *Simple's Uncle Sam*. "It was like a seal put on our long friendship," Henri Cartier-Bresson had responded. "In each story there is your strength . . . wrapped up in your smile." The dedication was sincere but perhaps another sign of Langston's interest in moving to Paris to live. In frequent visits to the Librairie des Amis des Livres, which was virtually the headquarters of the *Présence Africaine* group, he strengthened his ties to various black writers in the city, including Alioune Diop and Léon Damas, and entertained some of them and Sandy Bethune at Le Baobob, a Senegalese restaurant on rue de la Université, as well as at inexpensive Italian and Balkan establishments on the rue de la Harpe.

"Langston was seen by some of the younger folk as being not militant enough," Bethune recollected, "but he was great company at night in places like La Cupole in Montparnasse, with his chuckling and laughing and his cigarette, always a cigarette, dangling from his lips with a good half-inch of ash suspended, while we waited for it to fall." More than once he visited Josephine Baker, her husband, and their remarkable rainbow-hued band of fourteen children, idealistically adopted from a variety of races and nationalities. On an excursion to Normandy, he made a pilgrimage to Mont-Saint-Michel, the rocky islet on the French coast celebrated as the site of an eighth-century Benedictine abbey and a masterpiece of medieval Gothic architecture.

His sometime companion about town, in addition to Sandy Bethune, was the much-travelled black American poet and artist Ted Joans, an original Greenwich Village "hipster" and a devotee of the French surrealist André Breton, but at the same time an exuberant admirer of Langston Hughes. "It was hard to believe that Langston was in his sixties," Joans recalled. "He was relaxed and smooth and easy wherever we went. He loved Paris, he really did. He should have come here to live; he would have been happy. He was open to people, to parties, to anything new and different and exciting. In fact, the only time I ever heard him say 'no' was at a little thing, a party at the Beat Hotel. (We called it that because of the crowd that hung out there, and because it didn't have a name of its own). People were smoking marijuana and some guys were stoned and I saw somebody pass a lighted joint to Langston. 'No, man!' he said. He didn't make a fuss, but he was firm. He told me afterwards that he hated drugs of any kind." (Elsewhere, Joans recalled that Hughes "added that he'd rather encounter several hundred reefer smokers in Central Park than run into three drunks, especially if they were white.")

A reading by Langston at the Shakespeare and Company bookshop, which had moved in 1951 to the rue de la Bucherie, opposite Notre Dame, drew such a huge crowd that he himself could not get in the door when he arrived with Ted Joans, who had arranged the event. "Excuse me, I'm Langston Hughes," he quietly explained to someone at the front door. "Yeah, sure," came the reply. "And I'm Richard Wright." By 1966, Shakespeare and Company had become notorious in Paris as a center of protest against the Vietnam War (not long afterwards, the government shut down the bookshop for an extended period). The crowd waiting to hear Langston Hughes seemed unusually restive, ready for anything—perhaps even a little American-style, anti-American insurrection. Reading to Ted Joans's accompaniment on the trumpet (at Langston's absolute insistence), he took control of the situation. "Hughes was very good," the proprietor, George Whitman, judged. "He easily and skillfully defused the tension that we all felt. At the same time, he managed somehow to build a mood of elation, of positive good will. He had a gracious way of reading his poems and reminiscing about his travels, and he answered questions from the attentive audience with great politeness, but also with warmth, as if he was genuinely interested in the questioner. I don't think he disappointed anyone. It was all quite remarkable."

On July 28, after four months abroad, he returned to New York. Awaiting him was a hill of projects in various stages of completion. He resolutely cancelled a reading that would have taken him to California, and once again pledged to stay off the lecture circuit and stick to writing. "One's words don't go in one ear and out the other so quickly," he reasoned. "Besides, on paper, you can be heard around the world."

By mid-September he had finished a draft of his text for the pictorial history of black entertainers with Milton Meltzer, "Black Magic." Then, for a book of tributes to Nancy Cunard compiled by Hugh Ford, aided by Walter Lowenfels and Kay Boyle, Langston sent a graceful little essay, "A Piñata In Memoriam." His most time-consuming and stimulating effort, however, was the revision with Arna Bontemps of their *Poetry of the Negro*. The biographical notes kept him aware of the passage of time, and the death of old friends. In May, the beloved Georgia Douglas Johnson, who had opened her house to Langston in 1925, when he badly needed friends in unfriendly Washington, had died. In August, Melvin Tolson had died of cancer; and so had the fiction writer Eric Walrond, one of the most brilliant members of the Harlem Renaissance, after a heart attack on a street in England. Some stars of old were still alive but sadly faded in the sky. Jean Toomer, long lost to black literature following his defection to the white world, was discovered by Arna Bontemps living but broken and infirm in a Pennsylvania nursing home. With pleasure Langston added to the white or "tributary" section of the book some poems by the beatnik Jack Kerouac, the patrician Robert Lowell, the veteran Mississippi liberal Hodding Carter, and Allen Tate, once Hughes's *bête noire* among the former "Fugitives," now repentant about his old segregationist ways. For Langston, however, the most thrilling part of his revision was the work of the latest generation of poets to keep Afro-American verse alive—gifted young writers such as Mari Evans, Sarah Webster Fabio, Audre Lorde, Ishmael Reed, Raymond Patterson, and Lucille Clifton.

By letter, telephone call, or in person, he lost few chances to encourage the younger writers. Paule Marshall recalled later how he kept in touch. "He would call me around eleven at night. He always wanted to know how much I had written that day, how much I had done. He wanted me to write more, and faster! 'Paulee, Paulee,' he asked me once, 'Do you know that I have a book out for every year that you've been alive?' His whole aim was to encourage me, to encourage us. . . . He wanted no part of the cuss-words, as he used to call them, that some of the young people were writing. He thought LeRoi Jones a fine writer, but he would fret, 'Oh those cuss-words, Paulee! Those cuss-words! Why does he have to use so many cusswords!' I think he was at peace with himself. Langston had a sense that he had done his part and his best and that the standard was now being passed on." To Loften Mitchell, "Langston set a tone, a standard of brotherhood and friendship and cooperation, for all of us to follow. You never got from him, 'I am *the* Negro writer,' but only 'I am *a* Negro writer.' He never stopped thinking about the rest of us."

When in the last days of November, with various projects out of the way, he turned to new proposals for books, he placed the emphasis again on the young. He suggested "That Is a Moon," an anthology of contemporary black poetry for young readers; "Cats, Crickets and Stars," nonracial poems by black writers; "Poems That Just Grew," a similar book, but for even younger children; "Spread My Wings and Fly," which would offer lyrics from the major black spirituals. None of these projects went anywhere, but Knopf now decided that the times demanded the book of poems about racial wrongs and civil rights it had rejected in 1964 as too risky because of Langston's insistence on a cheap edition. The new book would be composed mainly of old poems, including some going back to the 1920s, but would include new verse, such as Hughes's poem to Lumumba. Aware that a paperback edition still would be a risk, Judith Jones agreed with Langston nevertheless that it would be "very important to have a lower priced book available." Augmented by some pieces written in Africa, his new volume would be called "The Panther and the Lash." The title almost certainly came from the founding in Oakland, California, that year, 1966, by Huey Newton and Bobby Seale, of the most militant black organization to date—the Black Panther Party. The "lash" alluded perhaps to both the historical goad that had driven blacks toward a policy of revolutionary violence, and the backlash from white conservatism, of which Langston was keenly sensitive. Hughes's "Black Panther":

> Pushed into the corner
> Of the hobnailed boot,
> Pushed into the corner of the
> "I-don't-want-to-die" cry,
> Pushed into the corner of

"I don't want to study war no more,"
Changed into "Eye for eye,"
The Panther in his desperate boldness
Wears no disguise,
Motivated by the truest
Of the oldest
Lies.

This book would be his tract for the stormy times. "There is no poem in *The Panther and the Lash*," he asserted in an unpublished note written for the volume, "with which Langston Hughes does not have some direct or indirect, personal and emotional connection. They are not purely imaginary or contrived poems for the sake of form or word music. They are poems that come out of his own memories and his own life, and the lives of people he has known, loved, and cried for, and the continual pall of racial smog that envelopes America. As a contemporary creative writer living in Harlem, the world's largest Negro city within a city, it is impossible for him to be 'above the struggle' or for his art to fail to reflect the vibrant circumstances of his life."

At least one poem was over thirty years old; many were from the forties; others were fresh and unpublished. The titles of the seven sections indicate the sweep of the volume: "Words on Fire"; "American Heartbreak"; "The Bible Belt"; "The Face of War"; "African Question Mark"; "Dinner Guest: Me"; and "Daybreak in Alabama." Lacking the fuel of obscenity that increasingly powered the new black poetry, the entire book nevertheless vibrates with a sense of mission, as in "Final Call":

. . . SEND FOR LAFAYETTE AND TELL HIM, "HELP! HELP ME!"
SEND FOR DENMARK VESEY CRYING, "FREE!"
FOR CINQUE SAYING, "RUN A NEW FLAG UP THE MAST."
FOR OLD JOHN BROWN WHO KNEW SLAVERY COULDN'T LAST.
SEND FOR LENIN! (DON'T YOU DARE!—HE CAN'T COME HERE!)
SEND FOR TROTSKY! (WHAT? DON'T CONFUSE THE ISSUE,
    PLEASE!)
SEND FOR UNCLE TOM ON HIS MIGHTY KNEES.
. . . .
DuBOIS (WHEN?) MALCOLM (OH!) SEND FOR STOKELY.
    (NO?) THEN
SEND FOR ADAM POWELL ON A NON-SUBPOENA DAY.
SEND FOR THE PIED PIPER TO PIPE OUR RATS AWAY.

(And if nobody comes, "send for me.")

But *The Panther and the Lash* would have difficulty affecting a struggle that had taken yet another dramatic turn. Assuming command of the Student Non-Violent Coordinating Committee, Stokely Carmichael had electrifyingly proclaimed the doctrine of Black Power. In this total break with the old integrationist ideal, he was soon joined by Floyd McKissick, who had replaced James Farmer as director of the Congress of Racial Equality. The effect was to fracture the Civil Rights Movement. In July, at the annual convention of the NAACP, its executive secretary Roy Wilkins denounced Black Power as "the ranging of race against race on the irrelevant basis of skin color. It is the father of hatred and the mother of violence." Meanwhile, CORE denied that Black Power meant hatred, and Whitney Young, the leader of the conservative, business-oriented National Urban League, threw the great prestige of his organization behind the slogan when he declared his belief that Black Power was a proper rallying cry for black pride and black self-sufficiency.

The reaction of LeRoi Jones, however, had been swift and savage—and in verse beside which Hughes's book would seem sickly pale. "Roywilkins [*sic*] is an eternal faggot," Jones wrote. "His spirit is a faggot." The speaker of the poem promises, should he ever meet "roywilkins," to "stick half my sandal / up his / ass."

With a mixture of incredulity and amusement, Langston read Jones's poem. Late in the year, at a gathering of moderate civil rights leaders, he teased the ultra-dignified Wilkins, an old friend, by reciting lines of the poem to him. But nothing in *The Panther and the Lash* even vaguely approached the level of Jones's invective, of which Hughes did not approve but which would soon become the coin of the realm for young black poets. The following year, *The Panther and the Lash* would offer as perhaps the sole possible remark on Black Power a puzzling poem, composed in parody of the mock-beatnik style (as Langston saw it) favored by many of the new poets, called "Stokcly Malcolm Me":

> i have been seeking
> what i have never found
> what i don't know what i want
> but it must be around
> i been upset
> since the day before last
> but that day was so long
> i done forgot when it passed
> yes almost forgot
> what i have not found
> but i know it must be
> *somewhere* around.
>
> you live in the Bronx
> so folks say.
>
> Stokely,
> did i ever live
> up your

way?
???
??
?

Whatever its precise meaning, the poem was surely not a militant endorsement of Carmichael, or the new poetry. It suggests, rather, bafflement and dissociation. Langston had spoken and would continue to speak out against racism and for black pride, but not on the only terms now acceptable to LeRoi Jones or Stokely Carmichael. His note for *The Panther and the Lash* denied that he was "above the struggle." The truth is that the fray was in perpetual motion. Now, considering poetry of the kind written by Jones and his growing band of disciples, and what Langston saw as the worst excesses in the name of Black Power, the fray was somewhere beneath him.

"There was in Langston Hughes's face," the civil rights strategist Bayard Rustin recalled, "a resemblance to the character of his work. His face had a warm, dreamlike, and sardonic quality. It was full of secret and secure wisdom: the face of a man who knew the score and who, rather than shouting it, would whisper it with a smile that made you feel that the secrets he knew about himself were exactly the secrets he knew about you. . . . He was not a political thinker. He did well enough what he had to do, or lived well enough what he had to be. He looked at life, not with piousness or didacticism, but with eyes that caught experience in all its dimensions, suffering in all its ambiguities, without ever reducing in his own mind the particularity of Negro identity and experience."

"In these rather dreary times," as he pronounced them that fall, which was his last, Langston tried to keep his days and nights bright and busy. He welcomed the usual variety of overseas visitors, including Takao Kitamura, who had directed a staging of *Mulatto* in Japan. Twice Langston attended receptions for President Léopold Senghor of Senegal. With Stella Holt he discussed a revival of *Mulatto*. With the black producer-director Woodie King, he conferred about a production called "The Weary Blues," based on a selection of Hughes's poems, by the Equity Library Theatre at Lincoln Center. Introduced by Marianne Moore ("I adore Marianne Moore!"), he joined Léonie Adams in a festive opening of the season of the Academy of American Poets at the Guggenheim Museum. To a group of blind women he talked about the boundless energy of Stella Holt and the late W. C. Handy. For a reunion with Yevgeny Yevtushenko, he visited the United Nations. At Lincoln Center, after the premiere of a production of García Lorca's *Yerma,* he bluntly dismissed the staging as cloying and artificial: "It's Art with a capital 'A' (more posturing and posing than poetry). Americans have no flair for the poetic on stage."

And, as always, he found time for the young—this time, "the astounding Miss Alice Walker," an unknown Georgia-born writer barely twenty-one years old, who had already begun to perfect her literary skills as a gifted student at

Sarah Lawrence College in New York. Turning recently from poetry to fiction, she had produced a moving story, "To Hell with Dying," about the bond of admiration and affection between a sensitive young girl of decent background and a hard-drinking, fun-loving, guitar-playing old man. The story startled Langston both by its tender lyricism and its affirmation of values he had always cherished. He not only included the story in *The Best Short Stories by Negro Writers: An Anthology from 1899 to the Present,* the first copies of which reached him just after Christmas, but also boosted it in his introduction. "Neither you nor I have read a story like [hers] before," he asserted. "At least, I don't think you have." He was proud of his discovery. "Mine is her first important publication (and her first story in print)," he informed Arna Bontemps after meeting her, "so I can claim her discovery, too, I reckon." Alice Walker was " 'cute as a button' and real bright."

As so often was the case, his enthusiasm more than touched the person involved. "Langston Hughes published my first short story," Alice Walker recalled with wonder twenty years later, "and his support of me in other ways meant more to me than I can say." His disinterested kindness and unfailing courtesy were something of a revelation. "Who was this man? I wondered. That he should care so much about a young and unknown writer? That he should write to me; that he would take for granted that, yes, of course, I was a writer, and should be respected as one. How could he be so kind, so generous? How much had he suffered?" Meeting him, "I was struck by how alone Langston seemed," she wrote elsewhere, "& by the intensity of love he evoked."

How much Langston had suffered, and the effect of that suffering on his character and his art in the midst of the present social turbulence, was a question posed by other observers. In December, an article by William J. Weatherby in a British newspaper, the Manchester *Guardian,* dubbed Hughes "a sort of present-day G. K. Chesterton in burnt cork." Langston Hughes was as prolific as the genteel, Roman Catholic, British man of letters—and apparently no more profound. Hughes was "very much a hit-or-miss spontaneous writer like GKC, and free of the deepest commitments of anger, passion, or bitterness." "He speaks benignly, happily, tolerantly, even when he is speaking words of protest himself." Hughes knows nothing, or pretends to know nothing, of words like "paranoia," so often applied to black writers. "Explain youself, brother," the journalist imagined Langston saying, "and maybe we can help you: he is clearly out to help if he can, an avuncular figure spanning the worlds of Harlem and Africa, with white America somewhere in between. . . . It may be a deficiency in him as an artist, a lack of passion that sometimes draws him back from the depths instead of plunging him into them; or it could just be the effects of living through the First World War, the twenties (there must have been two lynchings a week in the South), the Depression, the Second World War, the Korean War, the Cold War, and the always pressing racial conflict, and reaching the age of 64 and knowing that nothing anybody can do will work miracles and that a little acceptance is necessary unless you don't want to go gentle into that good night."

The reality was somewhat more complex. Langston's color was real, not a theatrical daubing, and thus forbade him in America anything remotely like the settled identity of a British man of letters. Also real was his suffering; and genuine, too, was the integrity he had brought to the end of his life. His poem "Not What Was," published the previous year, echoed his sense of an impending end, but also his reconciliation to it.

> By then the poetry is written
> and the wild rose of the world
> blooms to last so short a time
> before its petals fall.
> The air is music
> and its melody a spiral
> until it widens
> beyond the tip of time
> and so is lost
> to poetry and the rose—
> belongs instead to vastness beyond form,
> to universe that nothing can contain,
> to unexplored space
> which sends no answers back
> to fill the vase unfilled
> or spread in lines
> upon another page—
> that anyhow was never written
> because the thought could not escape
> the place in which it bloomed
> before the rose had gone.

In the last days of 1966, a wave of misfortune swept over 20 East 127th Street. For the first time in her eighty years, the apparently indestructible Mrs. Harper fell seriously ill and entered a hospital for treatment. She was no sooner admitted than her condition improved. A holiday visit from two old friends, one from Salt Lake City, Utah, the other from Saratoga, New York, cheered her so much that she returned home just after Christmas. Then she and her friend from Saratoga, Rosana Vodery, the widow of the composer and bandleader Will Vodery, both collapsed. Rushed to the Harlem Hospital, Mrs. Vodery, to Langston's consternation, was promptly lost in the vast, overcrowded wards. Finally her friend from Salt Lake City, Mignon Richmond, secured permission to search the floors and found her. Meanwhile, at Sydenham Hospital, also in Harlem, the suddenly very frail Mrs. Harper, sedated and on oxygen, slipped into and out of a coma. Able to gasp out only a few words at a time, she whispered a confession to Langston that she did not think she would "ever see 20 East again."

A few days later, her husband, Emerson Harper, also fell ill. His ailments were not as severe as Mrs. Harper's, but it was left to Langston to run the fourteen-room house. In the best of times he would have flinched before the job; now the task seemed impossible. To satisfy city regulations, contracts had already been signed, at a cost of over $7000, for workmen to tear apart the structure in order to add two new bathrooms and a new furnace and to install copper plumbing throughout the house. The crowbars and hammers would arrive in the first days of the new year. Meanwhile, as he tried to work in spite of all the distractions, his assistants seemed bent on pursuing their own projects. "NO MORE AID to Cullud in 1967," he fumed. "One has to keep 5 Ethiopes to have one on hand (maybe) when needed!"

The holiday season was a dead loss. Looking forward to a late supper with the poet Muriel Rukeyser at her home on the West Side, Langston was forced to cancel the engagement. He was also compelled to break a date at the opera with Amy Spingarn. As if illness were not enough, the husband of a niece of Emerson Harper's, who lived around the corner, dropped dead. He was buried on the last day of the year.

When the workmen arrived to begin their assault on the house, Langston moved into a room at the Hotel Wellington in mid-Manhattan. He thought of going even further away, to Paris, and for a much longer time. Friends there offered him an apartment; after a while, when they sent word that it was no longer available, he made his intention clear. He wanted to know at once "if you hear of anything else for [rent] or lease." He needed a change. At this point in his life, Langston felt "kind of used and depleted," his secretary Raoul Abdul later judged. "He just wanted to go off . . . go back to France, renew his acquaintances in Paris, and with Paris, not so much people but the place itself, and just live there. I think he had a dream of that. . . ."

Three days into 1967, harried and increasingly perturbed, and helped only by his young Puerto Rican aide Luis Velez, he was still sending out his Christmas cards. On one weekend, he unplugged the telephone entirely. To Langston, the whole world seemed to be going wrong. In one week in early January, he noted five demoralizing events. On January 10, by a vote of 307 to 64, the House of Representatives voted to unseat Reverend Adam Clayton Powell, Jr., the political darling of Harlem, until his qualifications to hold office were tested. Powell, who had used his office to challenge racism and segregation from the moment he was elected in 1945, had been accused repeatedly of corruption and financial impropriety. At about the same time as his dismissal, the archsegregationist Lester Maddox took the oath of office as Governor of Georgia, and an equally rabid segregationist, George Wallace, legally unable to serve another term, was succeeded by his wife as Governor of Alabama. In New York, a high-ranking Puerto Rican city official was convicted of a crime. A black man's home was bombed in Brooklyn.

To add to Langston's troubles, his cousin Flora Coates sent an urgent message from Los Angeles that his uncle John Hughes had gone over the top, past the comforts of cigars and bourbon, and needed to be put into a nursing home. Could Langston come at once? He wanted to go, but with Toy Harper requiring special blood transfusions and other medical aid, as he wrote Arna Bontemps, "right now money is of the essence—$$$$$$." Langston was so distracted that he brusquely killed a plan by a group, including Roy DeCarava, for a public celebration of his sixty-fifth birthday. "I do NOT *now* want *NO* testimonial," he begged. "Help! Wait a little while, till I'm 75 anyhow, and the days are less hectic."

With such discouragement, his birthday passed virtually unnoticed, except for a telegram from the Writers Union of the Soviet Union. Then, on February 13, his passage paid by the student body at UCLA, he reached Los Angeles for a lecture-reading during Negro History Week. Langston visited his uncle and was relieved to find the resilient old man much improved and in no urgent need of being committed to a nursing home. Before the students at UCLA, Langston ventured to make one of his rare remarks about the Vietnam War, but his comments were hardly clear and authoritative. In rough notes for the lecture, he declared his willingness to be controversial—"since black men and women per se are controversial." As for the war against North Vietnam, "I personally cannot understand why anybody in his right mind would want to be a captive of the Americans." The conflict in Asia was connected to the experience of blacks in America: "None of us ever *liked* being captives. Why anyone would be surprised at what happened in Watts, I'll never know. It began in 1619—not at Plymouth Rock, but on a symbolic rock in Virginia," where the first African slaves landed in North America.

Whether Langston ever uttered these words, or seemed controversial to anyone, is unclear. Two days later, on the campus, he definitely appeared harmless enough when he introduced a jazz band to a packed auditorium in historic Royce Hall. Tellingly, the musical group was the New Orleans Preservation Hall Jazz Band, a group of ancients who performed in the oldtime Dixieland style. Being old did not mean being conservative, Langston insisted. "Some people," he complained to the audience, "seem to think that any musician who came along before Dizzy Gillespie or Thelonious Monk was just an Uncle Tom." But young blacks at UCLA evidently did not care for the old music. Although the hall was packed, according to the Los Angeles *Times* critic Leonard Feather, the number of blacks was "astonishingly low"; moreover, the whites were enthusiastic but seemed to know little about jazz. Privately, Langston brushed aside Feather's criticism. What did it matter that most of the audience was white? Feather was a "dope."

At Douglass House in Watts, he presented fifteen books to the writing project founded there by the novelist and screenwriter Budd Schulberg out of the ashes of the 1965 riot. Then he returned home by way of Washington, D.C. Near the city, in Greenway, Virginia, he passed two days as the guest of the exclusive Madeira Girls School. At Madeira, which drew heavily on the South for its pupils, no black had ever taught or lectured. Breaking the Jim Crow tradition there as he had done elsewhere so many times before, Langston conferred informally with various teachers of English, mingled smoothly at a buffet party at the headmistress's home, where he stayed overnight, and generally charmed the girls and women. For this task, he got $500. The unprecedented visit was a success. "Our first thought of you was as a writer who would talk about writing," a school official later wrote him, "but we also got the writer as a human being who spoke with compassion, detachment and even gentle humor about the deep tragic division that currently baffles all men of good will—and men of bad will, too, I suppose. Your visit was a revelation to our many southern students, and there was an interest and enthusiasm among them that was very heartening."

In Washington, an interviewer from the *Post* noted Hughes's "roly poly" figure, which was hardly concealed by a loose-fitting black shirt, and the endless dribble of cigarette ash from his lips. As he answered questions, Hughes "puffs acrid fumes in a kind of smoggy staccato." Not surprisingly, his breathing was labored, and his sentences punctuated by a "noisy, rasping cough." His responses, which were mostly about racism and riots and crime, showed him again and again on the defensive. In spite of the plays and novels of so many black writers, he insisted, most blacks are not criminals, prostitutes, or drug addicts. "But who's going to believe that?"

Returning to New York and the Hotel Wellington, he found Mrs. Harper's health unchanged and their Harlem home unmended. The building had been torn apart by the contractors, but work had come to a frustrating stop with the demand for still more money for renovations. Anxious about where this cash would come from, and with no patron or wealthy friend to appeal to as in days of old, Langston was touched when the actor Frederick O'Neal sent $10 as a token royalty after reading some of his poems publicly. Peevishly he noted that Dr. Martin Luther King, Jr. often used a Hughes poem or two in his speeches, but never even acknowledged the source. (At a dinner party, nevertheless, Langston refused to join in criticism of King, who had come out against the Vietnam War, by other black guests: "Me, no! I love him!")

Then he landed three small jobs. He was asked to write a pamphlet for a big collection of songs sung by Harry Belafonte, and to prepare folio notes for a Victor disc by Ethel Waters. Also, Caedmon Records, which specialized in poetry, signed a contract with him for an album of his verse. These tasks brought small advances that added up to the difference between staying in comfort at the Wellington or choking on dust at 20 East 127th Street. Other small sums came in. A reading at Brandeis University in Waltham, Massachusetts, netted him $300. As an advance on royalties from a Hungarian translation of his 1930 novel *Not Without Laughter,* Knopf sent $250.

Ironically, given Langston's scrambling for money to meet his basic expenses, *The Best Short Stories by Negro Writers* appeared from Little, Brown to a stern rebuke in the *New York Times* about his commercialism. With forty-seven stories, the collection inevitably was uneven, although there were excellent pieces by a wide range of writers from Paul Laurence Dunbar and Jean Toomer, from earlier generations, to Ralph Ellison, Paule Marshall, John A. Williams, Alice Walker, and others on the contemporary scene. "He has told us elsewhere of his youthful rebellion against his businessman-father," the scholar

Robert Bone criticized Hughes, "but he reveals . . . how much of his father remains in him. He is *merchandising* these stories; to him they are commodities. As a result, he systematically blurs the distinctions between slick or sentimental magazine fiction and the genuine, hand-tooled article."

Shrugging off this criticism, Langston took on the additional jobs he needed to keep financially solvent. Still involved in revising *Poetry of the Negro*, he agreed to write two more children's books for Franklin Watts, and—for Dodd, Mead—a book on Harlem. Bending now under the weight of more than two years' worth of promised work, he struggled to keep his spirits high, and to remind himself that there was a purpose loftier than commercialism behind his incessant writing. This purpose he summed up in March in response to a request from *Who's Who in America* for a one-sentence summary of his life's goal: "My seeking has been to explain and illuminate the Negro condition in America and obliquely that of all human kind."

Never was there a greater need to explain and illuminate the Negro condition, and to link the race to all of humanity. On March 1, to the sorrow and indignation of Harlem, Adam Clayton Powell, Jr., who previously had been stripped of his chairmanship of the House Committee on Education and Labor, was denied a seat in the 90th Congress by a vote of 307 to 116. (In a special election in April, Harlem would reelect Powell by an overwhelming majority—although he had campaigned not at all, but spent his days in balmy Bimini, out of reach of a New York court judgment against him for defamation.) Elsewhere, across the South, the Civil Rights Movement had begun to lose its momentum. Subverting its influence above all was the enraged rhetoric of the Black Power movement, which now isolated the various civil rights organizations and cut them off from the flow of volunteers and financial support that had built them. Across the nation, often in places previously untouched by urban violence, various urban communities headed toward the most destructive season of civil disorder in their history. The summer of 1967 would see major rioting in more than a dozen important American cities, including Atlanta, Newark, Toledo, Buffalo, and Minneapolis.

The threat of violence now seemed to charge almost every exchange between blacks and whites. On March 20, Langston was on the subway with Sandy Bethune, who had recently returned from Paris, on their way to a midtown hotel where Langston was to attend a gala dinner. "Langston was all dressed up, in a tuxedo," Bethune recalled, "and we were going on about our days in Paris." The tuxedo and the easy talk about Paris was too much for a white man, who was probably drunk, sitting next to Bethune. The man jostled Bethune, smirked in mock apology, then mumbled a word that sounded like "niggers." Bethune slapped him, twice: "Don't you ever do that again!" Shocked, Langston stood up swiftly. "Let's get out of here," he whispered to Bethune. Then, loud enough for everyone to hear: "People going around calling other people all kinds of names!" Bethune understood that Hughes was apologizing for him to the other passengers, who included two wide-eyed nuns. Outside the station, they searched for a taxi, but none would stop for two black men, even if one was dressed in a tuxedo; "one driver even went through a red light rather than pick us up." As the taxis passed them, Bethune felt vindicated, but at the elegant hotel, Langston insisted that he come inside—"as if to say, see, we can do *this*." Courteously served, Bethune calmed down with an ice cream sundae. Langston sipped coffee and pondered the meaning of the times.

A few days later, in an interview, the *Post* carried his explanation of why he was no longer writing about Simple: "The racial climate has gotten so complicated and bitter that cheerful and ironic humor is less and less understandable to many people. A plain, gentle kind of humor can so easily turn people cantankerous, and you get so many ugly letters."

His world seemed hopelessly stained by distrust, illness, violence, and death. "The house is still ALL torn up, and Emerson is going around in circles," Langston reported in April to Arna Bontemps. Mrs. Harper was "wasting away by the hour to [a] wisp of her former self, now too weak to sit up, but wants to come home—which would really put an end to her if she saw the house as it is now—and full of paint fumes, dust and debris. You never saw the like." Terrified by the crime rate, Emerson Harper now refused to leave the house after dark. But the most horrible news of all, and yet so typical of the age, came about Carroll Clark, one of Kit Clark's sons. Once a carefree teenager who often dropped in with friends at Langston's home, Carroll had been snatched up by the revolutionary whirlwind. Transformed by black radicalism into a hater of whites, he had changed his name to Carroll X. From California in mid-February, just out of jail and without a job, he had written Langston for a loan of $200—which he almost certainly did not get. Later, Carroll had found a job. Then he was reported missing. Several days later, the police discovered his abandoned car. Inside its trunk was his body.

Forays by Langston into the white world downtown became more and more difficult, even as they perhaps also became more necessary as a respite from the stresses of Harlem. Of course, the community was hardly all stress. In some circles he felt the certain knowledge of being absolutely appreciated and respected and loved by the people who mattered to him most. Certainly he thoroughly enjoyed a birthday party he attended on April 15 for his friend Ruth Jett at her home at 10 West 135th Street, in the Lenox Terrace complex in Harlem. "Langston was his usual self," she recalled, "warm, bubbling, full of stories, reaching out to everyone. He was the dearest of men."

But the underlying tension of the age was no doubt behind his spontaneous venture into black humor when he spoke in April at the Plaza Hotel at the fifty-seventh annual dinner of the Poetry Society of America. The guest of honor was the Missouri-born Marianne Moore, who received the Gold Medal for Distinguished Achievement from the society. The event was also an early celebration of her eightieth birthday. Following tributes by Mayor John Lindsay and by Robert Lowell before four hundred guests, Langston first praised "a wonderful and lovely lady," then—"in a burst of exuberance that evoked delighted laughter," according to the *New York Times*—delivered a richer and yet a bizarre compliment: "I consider her the most famous Negro woman poet in

America!'' *Time* magazine enjoyed the jest sufficiently to publish it, but perhaps not even Langston understood exactly what he had meant to convey in making this manic remark. Almost certainly, he intended to show his scorn at the needless and specious distinctions of race and gender in American society. Speaking before him, Robert Lowell had praised Moore as the leading woman poet in America, then saved himself by adding that the best poetry in America was now being written by women. With a joke that was no joke at all in America, Langston sardonically revealed his contempt for the divisions that set even poets apart from one another.

He longed to get away. When the first copies of *L'Ingénu de Harlem,* his Simple book from Editions Robert Laffont in Paris, arrived along with an invitation for him to visit, he was ready: "I'd LOVE to come to Paris—always do.'' Planning to leave by Air France on May 19 or 20, he drew up a long list of people in France who were to receive complimentary copies, from the black Americans Jimmy Davis and Josephine Baker to Louis Aragon, Aimé Césaire, and the Holocaust survivor Fania Fenelon. But as the day of departure drew near, Langston began to hesitate. Perhaps, with Toy and Emerson Harper's condition, and the devastation of their house, he should not go to Europe until July. Clearly he wanted to go to Paris now. "But not for just a week, not for just a year. . . . . as the song says . . . but—.''

"If you go to Paris for always, as you say, we will visit you there every now and then,'' Arna Bontemps promised. "In any case, I think one whose career in writing has reached the point of warm reflection and the reading of biographies about himself has earned residence in Paris, prior to residence in glory.'' Suddenly, with Paris in the offing, life began to seem better. Roy DeCarava called with the news that a wealthy patron had decided to support a reprint of their *Sweet Flypaper of Life.* From the Theatre Guild, Joel Schenker, who had produced *Tambourines to Glory,* telephoned to say that the actor Lou Gosset had assembled a fine cast and was anxious to stage the play at the Montreal Expo, in Paris, and maybe in Germany. Schenker also reported that he was looking into possible backing by the State Department. For Suzanne Heller's witty little "Misery'' children's book series, Langston tossed off one with a black theme ("Misery is when you are not supposed to like watermelon but you do''). For the Caedmon company, he completed the recording of a selection of his poems.

Early in May, a few days after attending the annual dinner of the Missouri Society, and just after a lively dinner party for six or seven friends at his agent Ivan von Auw's apartment, Langston was hurrying to complete his pamphlet for Harry Belafonte before leaving for Paris when he began to feel a severe pain in his lower abdomen. For the previous two months, he had been trying to ignore difficult, painful urination and frequent bouts of diarrhea. At some point within twelve to fifteen hours after his stomach pain started, he could stand it no longer. On May 6, he telephoned the nearby New York Polyclinic

Hospital on West 50th Street. Dr. J. A. Pincus, a physician there, advised him to come to the emergency room. Soon after, still in intense pain, Langston was admitted and placed in the care of Dr. A. Jacob Begner, a urologist. He had met neither man previously, and he appears to have made no attempt to reach a doctor known to him. Why he had suffered for two months without consulting a doctor is unclear. Perhaps, like many people, he was simply afraid of what an examination would reveal.

Later, a rumor would take hold that his treatment in the hospital had been negligent. One scholar reported that Langston "registered anonymously as 'James Hughes,' and for several days was treated much like an indigent and given no special medical attention. Not until he was recognized by a black orderly, who told hospital authorities, did emergency care begin." But Hughes's secretary Raoul Abdul, who oversaw many of the arrangements for him at this time, strongly denied the charge: "He was not treated as an indigent. It was a very busy place, but no one at the hospital was treated as an indigent." Polyclinic Hospital, then almost a hundred years old, was a 350-bed facility once celebrated as a training school for surgeons. Charles and William Mayo, the developers of the Mayo Clinic in Minnesota, had trained there.

In 1967, on the other hand, its finest days were past. A few years later, it declared bankruptcy and closed its doors forever. And Langston indeed did not sign the consent form for admission as "Langston Hughes." Instead, as he had done from time to time at least since 1922, he signed as "James L. Hughes," and offered only that he was an employee of Harry Belafonte Productions. The "face sheet" of his chart, prepared by the admitting office, listed his name as "James Langston Hughes," but almost all other documents of his stay referred to him as "James Hughes." Neither Dr. Begner nor any other hospital official appeared to know exactly who he was. Whether his anonymity—or his skin color—affected the quality of his treatment is impossible to say. But both factors were overshadowed by something more important. He had no health insurance, and probably could not assure the hospital of payment for its services.

Nevertheless, treatment began promptly. Initial tests indicated the presence of a rounded mass at the lower end of his abdomen—his bladder, distended by urine he could not pass. A rectal examination showed that his prostate gland was not only enlarged and tender but also contained a hard nodule, possibly cancerous. His blood pressure was high, 200 over 120, and his pulse rate 100 beats per minute. He was suffering from infections of the urinary tract and of the upper respiratory system. His enlarged prostate, pressing against his bladder, had painfully prevented the flow of urine. His diarrhea remained a puzzle; perhaps it was caused by a low-grade infection.

Dr. Begner ordered a catheter, which drained about 500 cc's of clear urine. Then, on May 8, he performed a needle biopsy, through the rectum, of the hard nodule in the prostate. Tissue analysis showed no trace of cancer, but he decided to go ahead with a prostatectomy if further tests showed that Langston was capable of withstanding such an operation. On May 10, an electrocardiogram revealed distinct though not alarming cardiovascular disease. Not suprisingly, X-rays showed a significant increase in the size of Langston's heart chambers.

By this time, however, his blood pressure had dropped to 145 over 80. Deciding that Hughes could withstand the stress of prostate surgery, Dr. Begner scheduled the operation for May 12. Langston immediately scrawled the text of a message to be sent to Paris: "Unfortunately suddenly in hospital for operation therefore cannot come to Paris this month." Hurrying to set his affairs in order as he prepared for the first operation of his life, apart from a tonsillectomy in 1931, he gave Raoul Abdul a long list of tasks, including various banking transactions. He also insisted on no visitors to the hospital. "I was to notify Arna Bontemps," Abdul recalled, "but no one else. And no one was to be admitted to the hospital to see him."

But his hospitalization could not be kept a secret. One telephone caller was Ivan von Auw, his host at dinner some days before. "I asked him, 'What are you doing in the hospital, Langston?' He laughed out loud, his usual big laugh. Then he said, 'Ivan, I'm laughing to keep from dying. I think you poisoned me at your dinner party.' I promised to come and see him soon."

Just before the operation, Sandy Bethune and Lindsay Patterson slipped through the cordon on the heels of Raoul Abdul. "I had come to the hospital thinking the worst," Bethune remembered. "I don't know why, but I had assumed that Langston was gay, and I just imagined that he had been injured in some homosexual encounter, and that prostate trouble was a euphemism. But I also remembered how one day in Paris, walking from Montparnasse to the Latin Quarter, how Langston had huffed and puffed so much that, to make him feel better, I had lied and said, 'Man, this walk really did me in!' In fact, I hadn't felt tired at all, but he was wiped out."

Langston received Bethune and Patterson warmly, but he was obviously tense. He was fidgeting with a tray of papers on his lap, Bethune recalled, when Raoul Abdul began to explain that the bank had closed before he could get to it that day. "Suddenly, Langston got so angry that he let out a shout, picked up the tray of papers on his lap, and dashed it to the floor." High strung, and equally unnerved by the coming operation, Raoul screamed back. Then the room fell silent. Bethune was visibly shocked. "I guess I lost my cool, Sandy," Langston sheepishly confessed.

About this time, without explanation, Abdul recalled, "he asked me to bring him a copy of *One-Way Ticket*. I don't know why, but that was the one he wanted."

At 8:05 in the morning on May 12, Dr. Begner began the surgery. Because the prostate gland was so enlarged, the procedure called for cutting above the pubic bone to provide easy access to it. Begner found no evidence of cancer. In addition to the prostatectomy, he cleared the neck of the bladder of obstructions to the flow of urine, and he also performed a vasectomy as a safeguard against further infection. Langston apparently endured the operation well, although he began to hiccough soon after it ended. With his condition listed as "good," rather than "fair" or "poor," he was taken to room 821, on the eighth floor of the hospital.

"His first day of recuperation was fine," Raoul Abdul later stated. "Physically he felt great, and he was in very good spirits." But almost at once he began to deteriorate. With his heart racing, he was started on digitalis, a drug used since the seventeenth century to lower the heart rate and cause a stronger beat. By May 15, three days after the operation, he was continually restless, complaining about pain, and still suffering from hiccoughs. In response to symptoms of pneumonia, a course of penicillin was begun.

The next day, with his temperature climbing, he was given ampicillin, an antibiotic with a range different from penicillin. His condition stabilized briefly, but congestive heart failure had begun. Toxins were also spreading through his body, perhaps from bacteria that entered the bloodstream as a result of the surgery. The toxins soon affected his kidneys, which began to fail. With fluids entering his lungs and depriving his blood of oxygen, he sank deeper into distress. His temperature, a normal 98.6 degrees at his admission, rose to 101. He was now suffering from acute bronchopneumonia.

To this point after surgery, Langston's physicians had been mainly inexperienced residents. His nurses were capable people, according to Raoul Abdul. "I hired two wonderful women, both black Americans, to look after him around the clock," Abdul later stated. "They were marvellous." But deterioration continued. On May 20, when a resident deemed him "acutely ill," Langston signed a release allowing the use of an experimental antibiotic. His condition was now so ravaged that he badly misspelled his own name. At six o'clock that evening, he was barely conscious, and his temperature reached 103 degrees. The experimental drug was never given; perhaps it was unavailable.

On May 22, Dr. Julian Bennett Hyman, an experienced internist, declared Langston "critically ill." His potassium level was now dangerously high (high or low potassium can cause severe cardiac dysfunction). He was rushed into the Intensive Care Unit and placed on peritoneal dialysis: in a desperate effort to save him, a tube was inserted into his abdominal cavity to flush out toxins and give his kidneys a chance to recover. Monitors kept close track of his heart function and his fluid balance, but both were failing. By this time he had developed severe pulmonary edema, or an abnormal accumulation of fluids in his lungs. At seven that evening he was "slightly improved," but two hours later he was comatose and in septic shock. Hydrocortisone was injected to counter the septic toxin, but to no effect. His pulse rate raced to 120 beats per minute while his blood pressure fell to 80 over 60. At 10:40 he stopped breathing.

On his Certificate of Death, prepared and signed by Dr. Alfredo Hernandez, the cause was listed as "Septic Shock," due to "Bacteremia—followed surgical procedure," in other words, the spread of toxins through his body following the operation. The need for surgery was stated as "Benign Prostatic Hypertrophy." The major finding of the operation was "Fibromuscular Hyperplasia," or an actual enlargement of the tissue of the prostate rather than a mere swelling. No autopsy was performed.

George Bass, who had been named as executor-trustee of Hughes's estate along with Arna Bontemps, joined Raoul Abdul in making the last arrangements. "We didn't find his will with the instructions for his funeral rites until later," Bass later explained, "so I had to go by my memory of what Mr. Hughes had read to me from the document in 1963." They decided on a service at Benta's funeral home in Harlem, which could seat about two hundred and seventy-five mourners in two rooms. Bass and Abdul sent out identical telegrams to at least two hundred people, taking names from an address book that Hughes had kept beside his telephone, with a mark for particular friends:

YOU ARE REQUESTED TO ATTEND A PRIVATE MEMORIAL SERVICE FOR LANGSTON HUGHES ON THURSDAY, MAY 25TH AT 2:30 P.M. AT BENTA FUNERAL CHAPEL, 630 ST. NICHOLAS AVENUE CORNER OF 141ST STREET, NEW YORK CITY. PLEASE USE THIS MESSAGE FOR YOUR ADMISSION TO THE SERVICE.

THE FAMILY OF LANGSTON HUGHES

Although Hughes had not wanted it done, Benta's placed his body on display on May 24 from noon until 8:30 in the evening. The next day, it was on show again from 10 in the morning until 1 p.m. The service was scheduled for an hour later.

"Raoul or George had called me the day before and asked me to play," the jazz pianist Randy Weston remembered. "I said, yes, man, yes, anything for Langston. They asked me to prepare Duke Ellington's 'Do Nothing Till You Hear from Me,' which I figured Langston must have liked, although it was strange for a funeral. I called up Ed Blackwell, the drummer, and Bill 'Vishnu' Wood—he played bass—and they said yes, man. That night, I wrote a blues for Langston, because he loved the blues. So we went to the funeral home. A whole lot of famous people were there, Lena Horne, Ralph Bunche, a whole lot of people, sitting or standing against the wall. And more people in another room waiting to listen to the service on a loudspeaker. So there we were, setting up the drums and stuff like that. Meanwhile, Langston is in the other room, where everybody'd go look at him. He's laying in the coffin with his arms crossed, you know, laughing at us, I'm sure, cracking up. . . ."

Weston mentioned to Raoul Abdul or George Bass that he had written a blues for Langston. For a while he didn't see either man; then one or the other came up and told him it was time for him to start. "I said, 'Start? Well, where's the minister? Where's the preacher? Who's going to start it off?' He says, '*You* start it off.' I said, '*What?*' I said, '*Me?*' He says, 'Yes, *you!*' 'Man,' I said, 'What do I talk about?' He says, 'You just tell the people about the blues you wrote last night for Langston.' I said, 'And what am I supposed to play?' He said, 'You just play anything you want to play. Just remember to end with 'Do Nothing Till You Hear from Me'.' So the whole concert was blues, because Langston loved the blues. I mean, this was the wildest funeral I've ever been to in my life!"

Arna Bontemps spoke a few solemn words about "the death wish which had haunted this gentle man all his life"—or so a journalist reported. He also read a few of Hughes's several poems about death, including "Night Funeral in Harlem," "Beat the Drums for Me," and "Dear Lovely Death." Then Randy Weston started playing again. His trio ended with "Do Nothing Till You Hear from Me."

Afterwards, as the mourners gathered outside Benta's, many were not sure what to make of the jazz and blues funeral. "O Lord, Randy, I was so confused," Lena Horne confessed. "There I was, tapping my toes and humming while y'all played, and I didn't know whether to cry for Langston or clap my hands and laugh!" Langston, Weston decided, has just been putting them on. "It was funny, it was really funny, it was comical, there is no other way I can describe it. And I went back into the room and looked at Langston laying there in that coffin with his arms crossed and I laughed and said, 'Man, you gotta stop putting us on like this!' Everybody was totally *out,* you know, *totally out!!"*

Later that day, a small group of mourners led by George Bass gathered in a room at the Ferncliff Crematory in Hartsdale, New York, just north of Manhattan. In front of them was the coffin containing Hughes's body. At Bass's request, they joined hands, bowed their heads, and recited the words of "The Negro Speaks of Rivers." Then they watched as attendants rolled away the body, toward the flames.

AFTERWORD

IN MY AFTERWORD to Volume I of this biography, I wrote about the origins of the project in a chance meeting one evening in Cambridge, Massachusetts, in 1979 between myself and George and Ramona Bass. Not long after this meeting, I discovered the existence of a huge amount of correspondence and other material pertinent to a biography that Langston Hughes had left behind him. This archive was mainly in the James Weldon Johnson Collection founded by Carl Van Vechten, in the Beinecke Rare Book and Manuscript Library at Yale University. I wrote of the invitation extended to me by George Bass, a professor of drama at Brown University who had been Hughes's secretary for some years and was now the executor-trustee of his estate, to write the story of Hughes's life. I wrote of my typical experiences as I made my way through the voluminous correspondence and other material, and also as I sought out individuals who had known Hughes personally or in other ways had acquired a vital knowledge of him or aspects of his life. Although I was familiar with some of his published work, I had never met Langston Hughes. I wrote, too, of my travels to places around the world that he had visited, as I searched for more evidence of his past. And I wrote about my search for models of biography that I considered appropriate to this particular life.

This was, after all, to be the story of an African-American born near the dawn of the century into relative poverty but with a stirring sense of historic obligation to the cause of social justice, especially for black Americans (an ancestor had died fighting alongside John Brown at Harpers Ferry). This young man, against the urging of his mercenary father, had decided to try to make his living as a writer, and thus become the first African-American to do so. Moreover, he would make central to his art the depiction of the features of black American culture and black Americans in general. Embracing his identity as a black man, he would also wor-

426

ship the ideal of universal, interracial harmony and social justice for all. He would respond bravely, especially during the Great Depression of the 1930s, to the call for a socialist revolution in America and around the world. He would pay dearly for that commitment. The first volume comes to an end in January 1941 with Hughes dispirited and depressed. As war rages in Europe, his spirit is almost broken by assaults on his reputation first from the right, then from the left. His body taxed by disease as he lies in a hospital in Carmel, California, Hughes is in full and public retreat from radical politics and deep in a crisis that demands the most radical reassessment of both his life and his art.

In my afterword to Volume I, I wrote also about my determination to tell this story, for as long as I could, from Langston Hughes's point of view. I wanted to avoid the kind of authorial intervention and dominating commentary that might deprive the reader of experiencing the drama of his life, but especially his early life (in so far as I could recapture it). No specific theory of biography was behind my decision; in some respects, I was feeling my way in the dark. I came to my particular approach only after I had acquired a fairly deep familiarity with Hughes's voluminous correspondence. My approach then seemed to me the most appropriate way, almost the inevitable way, to render his life as it unfolded for this sensitive, often romantic, but also tough-minded young man.

However, when Volume II opened early in 1941, Hughes was not nearly as romantic and intuitive as he had once been. Now almost thirty-nine years of age, he was a substantially different person from the youth who had walked away at the age of twenty from the prestigious heights of Columbia University to deliver flowers in New York City, toil in a vegetable garden on Staten Island, and sweat in the galleys of freighters sailing to and from Africa and Europe—even as he steadily wrote and published moving poems that illuminated the face of black America as never before in verse. Now, in 1941, Hughes was in full flight from important aspects of his past. Repudiating as a youthful indiscretion his icono-clastic poem "Goodbye Christ," in which religious zealots and charlatans were denounced and Marx exalted, he had banned its reprinting. In his autobiography *The Big Sea*, published the previous year, 1940, Hughes had avoided almost any reference that could link him to the radical socialist enthusiasms of the previous decade. For these and other sins, he had become a pariah to his former comrades on the left.

This turning away from the past, as I surveyed it as a biographer, certainly could be the stuff of drama. And yet I knew that it more likely signaled for me, and for my potential readers, the end of the most provocative and compelling era of Hughes's life. As people grow older, I was beginning to see, they may become better, richer, and wiser—but they seldom become more interesting. Still, there was a span of twenty-six years before me as a biographer, as well as a standard or a style of biographical writing fully established in Volume I that had to be maintained in Volume II. By this remark I mean in particular the close, chrono-logical tracking of Hughes's life that marks the first volume. For better or for worse, I had decided that if the central strength of biography resides ultimately in the power of the narrative, that narrative is best reinforced, especially if the biographer is an academic, by the scrupulous and abundant provision of historic details about the subject of the biography. From the start, I had wanted to know where Hughes had been on every day of his life—indeed, if possible, at every moment of his life. Mercifully, such knowledge is impossible to come by for anyone, and certainly it is impossible in the case of Hughes despite the extent of his archive. Nevertheless, as I began to write Volume II, I knew that I was committed to providing a strict chronology and a plenitude of details even as I was becoming increasingly troubled by my suspicion or fear that the life before me was losing or had lost most of its charm.

However, if the wondrous charm was going or gone, I still had a story to tell. On reflection, this volume was to be about a man politically compromised but quietly coming to grips with a crisis that threatened all he had accomplished in his former life. Hughes was now aware, as never before, of the power to break him that the forces of conservatism and reaction fully possessed. Before this troubled passage in his life he could dream of the full possibility of radical social change. Now, as his nation went to war to preserve a way of life that made victims of virtually all black Americans, he no longer thought or wrote in such hallucinatory terms. Instead, Hughes turned the focus of his expressed indignation away from radical socialism to the safer cause of civil rights for African-Americans. Abandoning the communists and the other leaders of the left, he cast his lot with the NAACP and its courageous lawyers who challenged Jim Crow in the recalcitrant South. Immersing himself once again in black urban life after more than a year living comfortably with a white patron in rural California, he created in his newly acquired weekly column for the Chicago *Defender* the memorable literary character Jesse B. Semple, or Simple. Simple's often mordant wit and blues-inflected life, his domestic trials and his philosophical musings, captivated Hughes's black readers across the country.

Past forty, Hughes also now looked more anxiously than in the past for a modicum of financial stability and security. Maintaining his ability to earn money through public readings had been a major factor in his decisive capitulation to the religious right. For most of his life he had depended on, in addition to the fairly meager sums his writing commanded, the good will and largesse of educational foundations, patrons, and wealthy friends (almost all of them white). In 1947, his political maneuverings and realignments finally paid off. Hughes's reputation as a writer, together with an unusually liberal gesture of inclusion by the musician Kurt Weill and the playwright Elmer Rice, gave Hughes a job as lyricist on the Broadway musical play *Street Scene*. With his share of the profits, he bought a townhouse, the first home he had ever owned. The following year, at the age of forty-six, he settled down to live the rest of his life as a successful burgher in the heart of Harlem.

In and of itself, however, none of these details seemed very compelling. Indeed, they seemed mundane. For a biographer, it was more than a little disheartening to see the man who once had glowed with radical, romantic fire call himself repeatedly, even if in jest, "a literary sharecropper." Hughes was a literary sharecropper in that he was compelled to toil in fields owned by other folks—

white folks. He was a sharecropper because he had begun to seek out and accept, almost indiscriminately, writing jobs, because of the financial advances they brought. He needed money now as he had never needed it before, when he was young. With some pleasure at the challenge, but also because of the money involved, he branched out into an ever-widening range of literary forms. He wrote children's books and a history of the NAACP commissioned by the same organization that he had scorned in the 1930s. He labored on writing an autobiography of Harlem's first black policeman, but finally gave up the project in boredom and frustration. He wrote popular songs and opera libretti. However, none of the songs clicked with the public, and the operas, when they succeeded, seldom paid off in any form except critical praise. He toiled on musical plays usually devoid of even the slightest political or moral purpose. For twenty years, he hammered away at the weekly column in the Chicago *Defender* that typically glowed with distinction only when Simple was its star (unfortunately, Simple appeared in only about one-quarter of the columns).

Toward the end of Hughes's life, still profoundly fascinated by black urban life and intimately attuned as always to the moods and styles and rhythms of black music, which he regarded as the most profoundly rooted of black expressive forms, he practically invented the genre of gospel plays. These productions typically fused a terse dramatic story line with popular songs from the gospel world sung by gifted performers. In general, his efforts brought much applause and a little money, but at what cost? Probably suffering the most was Hughes's achievement as a poet. Throughout his life, even in the 1930s when he exchanged his old allegiance to blues and jazz for the strident tones of radical socialism, he held his identity as a poet close to his heart. In the 1940s, although he continued to compose and publish verse, his loss of poetic power was clear. However, twice in the two decades that followed a combination of events inspired in him distinct revivals of his original gift, as he published first *Montage of a Dream Deferred* (1951), then *Ask You Mama: 12 Moods for Jazz* (1961).

These volumes, although they were received unenthusiastically by the major critics, black and white, attest to Hughes's will to prevail, and to prevail with honor, in the second half of his life. Here, needless to say, was the biographer's challenge and his opportunity. When Hughes knuckled under in the face of Senator McCarthy's infamous Senate subcommittee, the biographer measured outrage at Hughes against outrage at his persecutors, and pity for him against admiration for his poised and successful determination to continue to function as a writer in America. When he wrote books about black heroes for younger readers and failed to mention Paul Robeson and W.E.B. Du Bois although his texts clearly called out for them (but his publishers did not), one went through this exercise in cool judgment, censure, and compassion again. It was clear that Hughes himself regretted his role in these omissions; however, he would not countenance giving up his identity as a writer, and one intimately involved with black America, for the glory of communist martyrdom. "The colored children ceased to hear my name," Du Bois wrote of his last years, when his radical activity made him *persona non grata* in most black organizations. It is hard to imagine Langston Hughes living under such a condition, because his need for the approval of black folks was perhaps the central craving of his life.

Perceived by leftists as a turncoat, Hughes consoled himself putting to good use the freedom and dignity—such as they were—left to him. In a variety of ways, his art continued to challenge boldly and imaginatively the place of Jim Crow in America. He reached out to blacks in Africa, including South Africa. His travels to Africa and his championing of its writers, largely unknown in the United States, including gifted artists such as Chinua Achebe and Richard Rive, helped to pave the way for their later success and recognition by Americans black and white. As always, he especially encouraged younger writers both abroad and at home, including talents such as Alice Walker and Paule Marshall, and went out of his way to help them. And, of course, there was, if nothing else, his continuing commitment to Harlem. With enormous pride he at one point early in the 1960s declared himself to be the only major African-American writer still living in the midst of a typical African-American urban community. (Gwendolyn Brooks had fled the South Side of Chicago, Hughes claimed, and Ralph Ellison had his back to Harlem as he lived in his elegant apartment overlooking the Hudson River.) Practically every other major black writer, or so it seemed, had fled to the suburbs to taste the sweet new fruit of racial integration.

Whatever his sense of living his life with his head in the lion's jaws, Hughes went about his business with joyful intensity to its premature end in 1967, when he died, essentially from an infection contracted in a hospital after an operation. In the years before his death, despite the disapproval of the old left and of the more exacting literary critics, the masses of black Americans who read books and were interested in poetry only increased their love for and reverence of an almost legendary figure. Hughes basked in their approval. By the end, he was also clearly satisfied with what he had accomplished in his lifetime, although no one was more aware of what he had endured because of his convictions and his choices than Langston Hughes himself.

Since the publication of *The Life of Langston Hughes: Volume I* in 1986 and of Volume II in 1988, this biography of Langston Hughes has remained in print. Especially in its paperback editions and if only in a small corner of the academic world, it continues to attract some attention. For those seeking to explore a fresh interest in the poet, it seems fair to say, *The Life of Langston Hughes* has remained to this point the primary point of reference apart from Hughes's work itself. This is a common function of biography. This is also perhaps the least that might be expected of a study that benefited from the generous access I was granted to the Langston Hughes Papers at Yale.

In recent years, however, one repeated criticism of my work has been that it represents a severe misreading of Hughes on the question of his sexuality. In general, various critics have asserted that Hughes was an active homosexual. They argue further that in shying away from such a conclusion, my biography willfully misrepresents the scholarly evidence and suggests that I am a homophobe. At one point not long ago, as I was evaluating an essay for possible acceptance by the prestigious journal *American Literature*, I was bemused by a reference to the "notorious" treatment of the subject in my books on Hughes. In addition, although the essay clearly depended to a major extent on information found only or first in my biography, it included no acknowledgment of such indebtedness, much less a suggestion that my biography has any value. This is typical behavior. Virtually all of the critics have been dependent almost entirely on material I myself unearthed and presented in my biography. Virtually none of them, as far as I can tell, has taken the trouble to work in the Hughes papers at Yale or else-where, although the papers at Yale have been open to scholars for many years now. Unless a more aggressive search for evidence is mounted by my critics on this subject, the debate will continue to be truly academic.

I believe that it is certainly possible that Hughes was gay. I also believe that it is highly unlikely that he, as some have claimed, frequented places where he would place at risk his personal reputation and his special relationship to African-Americans, many of whom would surely have seen his arrest for "indecent" behavior as a betrayal of them and their children and a blow to their own self-esteem. However, in the course of my research, I found no evidence acceptable to me to support the idea that he was gay. In fact, I found much evidence, espe-cially in my interviews with individuals who knew him well, including openly gay men such as Bruce Nugent, to suggest that he was not. I concluded then that I was dealing with something of a genuine mystery that could not be resolved simply by declaring him to have been either a homosexual or an unambiguous heterosexual. (If one believes the record, he had several intimate experiences, including love affairs, with women—but I was not prepared to accept the record without question.)

Homophobia is a serious charge, and some of my critics have been intem-perate. One published article, bristling with hostility and perhaps as a result poorly argued, mounts a frontal assault not only on my treatment of the matter but on my basic competence as a scholar. Somewhere I had declared the opinion that while a precise recovery of the past is impossible, we as human beings must not be intimidated by that fact but must continue to try to interpret the past. On the basic of this surely incontestable, even trite, observation, the author of this screed denounced my basic approach to history as "cavalier." Surely no one (at least, not since Jay Gatsby) has thought that we can actually recover the past, just as surely no one thinks that as a result we must give up on trying to interpret it. In truth, my approach to history has never been "cavalier." For example, if I wrote, as I did in Volume I, that Hughes's freighter dropped anchor in deep water off a port in Africa one day in 1923, or that the day was blustery, I did so only because I had consulted the captain's and chief engineer's logs for the ship in the Federal maritime records in Suitland, Maryland. There I had ascertained the soundings and the weather as recorded in those logs, as most conscientious biog-raphers would have done. I would never dream of suggesting, as some popular biographers do, what my subject or anyone else was thinking or feeling at any moment, unless that person had left a specific record in some form (a reference in a letter, perhaps) of such thoughts or feelings. And I certainly would not treat so important a matter as Hughes's sexuality without a similarly strict regard for the rules of evidence. I may or may not have misread the evidence, and I may have been too restrained in reviewing it, but I certainly aimed at all times to be scrupulous.

When I set out in 1979 to begin searching for material about Langston Hughes, I knew virtually nothing about his sexual history or his reputation. I can say with confidence, however, that I had no interest whatsoever in suppressing the fact that Hughes was homosexual if such turned out to be the case. I was determined to reveal any fact, no matter how controversial, that would lead to a sharper understanding of Hughes—and a livelier story. I certainly believed from the outset that sexuality was of major importance to an understanding of any artist. I also meant to be thorough. As far as I can remember, I saw no shame in homosexuality.

However, in revealing my interest in Hughes's sexuality, I knew—or soon found out—that I was disappointing a number of his admirers. Hughes had been and still was a beloved hero to many people—for example, to Adele Glasgow, the intelligent, sensitive, and upstanding Harlem leader in the arts whose Market Place Gallery had been a favorite meeting place for the poet in the 1960s. Ms. Glasgow—and I use her only as an example of several of Hughes's friends—quietly made it clear to me that she regarded any probing of Langston's sexual life as unacceptable. She, as do many people, regarded a biographer's probing of the sex life of his or her subject as on the whole unseemly, perhaps indecent, and at last irrelevant. I myself thought then, and think now, the opposite. I was also prepared to risk her disapproval by pursuing the matter. Once the first volume appeared, and despite its reticence on the subject, she had nothing further to do with me.

As much as I was troubled by her reaction, I was far more concerned with the reaction of Professor George Bass of Brown University. As I have pointed out, as the sole administrator-trustee of the Hughes estate, he had invited me to take on the project, opened all the papers at Yale to me (other scholars had enjoyed only partial access to them), and been generous in other ways in his support. In addition, he had served for some years as Hughes's secretary and had traveled abroad with him. Bass, too, believed that probing into Hughes's sex life was inappropriate for his biographer. However, we discussed the subject and he assured me, as did every other person as close to Hughes, that he had seen nothing to suggest, much less confirm, that Hughes was gay. While I considered the possibility that he and others were protecting their own reputations, their virtual unanimity had to be taken into account. At the very least, whatever Hughes did elsewhere, away from his home and office, he must have kept his employees at a distinct professional distance. While many of my critics apparently cannot imagine such restraint, I had seen too much evidence of Hughes's self-control under trying circumstances to believe that he could not control himself around younger people who worked for him.

One powerful force behind the accusations about Hughes's alleged homosexuality and the alleged urge to hide it has been the notoriety of the short "art" film *Looking for Langston* by the black British filmmaker Isaac Julien. (In our modern culture, of course, a still picture may be worth a thousand words, but a motion picture is worth many, many more.) The ostensible subject of the film is black gay life in the Harlem Renaissance. The film mainly comprises lyric and surrealistic scenes meant to capture the supposedly sophisticated styles of black male gay desire in that period. Later in the film, Julien includes stock footage from the 1950s or 1960s of Hughes reading poetry accompanied by jazz musicians. Even then, it is not at all clear why the film is called *Looking for Langston*, or why Julien believed, if he so believed, that his vision reflected in any way the reality of the Harlem Renaissance. Nevertheless, controversy surrounding the film has helped to bolster the idea that Hughes was gay. In charge of Hughes's estate, George Bass objected strenuously to Julien's presumptive use of Hughes's name in this way. When Julien flatly refused to change anything in his film, Bass retaliated by denying him the right to broadcast Hughes's words in his film. An injunction was granted against Julien, who initially complied with the law but since then has simply ignored the injunction, according to Hughes's agents.

This dispute has led to a certain amount of misinformation. In his book *Walking on Water* (1999), the talented African-American writer Randall Kenan praises Julien and writes rather strangely of *Looking for Langston* as having been "inspired by Langston Hughes's unpublished poems to a male lover, known only as 'Beauty'." (For all of my work on Hughes, I had never heard of these poems until I read about them in Kenan's book.) Siding with Julien, Kenan attacks not only the late George Bass but also the current administrators of the Hughes estate, although they have had nothing to do with the *Looking for Langston* dispute. "It seems," Kenan writes, "that though it has become common knowledge that Langston Hughes had a penchant to fall in love with men—and was moved to write about it—the people who control his estate apparently would like that information to disappear" (p. 188). This accusation is of some interest to me, since I am now, along with George's widow, Ramona Bass, one of the two administrators of the Hughes estate.

I had played no part in Bass's decision to try to stop *Looking for Langston*. In fact, before its debut in the United States, I had met Julien and sympathized with his desire for what I took to be an expression of artistic freedom. I also was present at the film festival at Lincoln Center in Manhattan when the sound was turned off at certain points in the showing of *Looking for Langston* in order to prevent Hughes's words from being heard. I considered this act of censure unfortunate, as did many people in the audience. Now I'm not so sure that Bass acted improperly. I haven't changed my attitude to artistic freedom but I now have a different sense of the obligations of the trustees of an estate. Clearly Hughes never wanted to be known publicly as gay. In the absence of clear evidence that he was, how could Bass do otherwise than oppose Julien's willful, even flagrant abuse of Hughes's name and of the wishes of his estate?

As for Mr. Kenan's most sweeping charge, I think I can speak for Ramona Bass in declaring that we do not want any information of any kind about Langston Hughes to "disappear." But what Mr. Kenan calls "common knowledge" is not "information," although in a rhetorical sleight of hand he tries to make the two one and the same. We should know that "common knowledge," especially about the sex life of a celebrity, cannot properly constitute evidence for a serious scholar, and certainly not when an array of persons close to Hughes, including persons openly homosexual, declared their opinion that he was not one.

What is meant by Hughes's homosexuality in this debate is not always clear. The most radical position, clearly held by some critics—although it is hard to count or estimate them—is that Hughes was a practicing homosexual. According to one senior academic at a prestigious university, who has spoken only informally about the subject, Hughes was known to frequent some of the more notorious outlets for gay male life in a repressed society, including public rest rooms and the like. This academic has even identified the rest rooms of Grand Central Station in New York City as one of Hughes's stamping grounds. According to the late Jim Kepner, a stern but fair critic of my biography on this subject, a young black composer he knew spoke about seeing Hughes having sex in a public bath in Harlem. Only one person has claimed intimate personal knowledge of Hughes's alleged homosexuality. In 1991, Malcolm Boyd, a controversial Episcopalian priest and the author of a book of prayers called *Are You Running With Me, Jesus?*, announced publicly that he and Hughes had once been lovers. According to Boyd, they had met in 1964, when Hughes was sixty-two and three years before his death.

In *The Life of Langston Hughes* I wrestled with this question and came up with the tentative conclusion that Hughes probably had been asexual. This may well have been weak reasoning on my part. Perhaps it was owing to homophobia (a charge, like that of racism, against which there is no defense, because the terms homophobe and racist are very hard to define). Perhaps it was owing to naivete, or to both homophobia and naivete. However, "asexual" was a word that came up spontaneously several times in talking to people who had known Hughes very well, and asexuality seems the best explanation of his condition as I was able to discover it. I am aware that to many people it is probably a bogus argument, and I myself have sometimes thought of it mainly as a metaphor for something else that is ever more difficult to pin down. After all, there is a fairly wide range of possibilities, including various fetishisms, for explaining a sexual profile as murky as Hughes's. I have concluded that he might have been asexual—but I also think that we will probably never know the truth.

There remains, after this controversy over sex has been aired and discussed, the more astonishing and rewarding and complicated matter of Hughes's art, the most valuable stuff of his lifetime and his enduring legacy to us. My biography of the writer sought to build on and also serve that legacy. I hope I have done so. In concluding my afterword to Volume I, I mentioned in passing Harold Bloom's generous but finally unacceptable (to me) praise of my books—unacceptable because the praise is quite squarely at Hughes's expense. "Reading Rampersad's *Life*," Professor Bloom has written, "is simply a more vivid and valuable aesthetic and human experience than reading the rather faded verse and prose of Hughes himself." As brilliant a critic as Professor Bloom is, I hope that time does not finally endorse this particular judgment. His errors notwithstanding, Langston Hughes led a life of uncommon courage, grace, and richness; he also left a body of art of uncommon beauty and consequence. I was fortunate to have been given the opportunity to tell the story of his life so that it could better illuminate his art.

ARNOLD RAMPERSAD
Stanford University

ABBREVIATIONS

ABSP	Arthur B. Spingarn Papers
ALLP	Alain Leroy Locke Papers
APC	American Play Company Papers, Berg Collection
ARC	Amistad Research Center, New Orleans
Bancroft	Bancroft Library, University of California, Berkeley
Berg	Berg Collection, New York Public Library
CCP	Countee Porter Cullen Papers
CMP	Claude McKay Papers
CVVP, Yale	Carl Van Vechten Papers
CVVP, NYPL	Carl Van Vechten Papers, Manuscripts Division
FPGP, UNC	Frank Porter Graham Papers, Southern Historical Collection, University of North Carolina
JESP, NYPL	Joel Elias Spingarn Papers, Manuscripts Division
JTP, Fisk	Jean Toomer Papers, Fisk University
JWJ	James Weldon Johnson Collection, Beinecke Rare Book and Manuscript Library, Yale University
LHP	Langston Hughes Papers, James Weldon Johnson Collection, Beinecke, comprising mainly Correspondence (General, Family, Fan Mail, Miscellanous, etc.) and Manuscripts (numbered)
MSP	Marie Short Papers
MSRC	Moorland-Spingarn Research Center, Howard University
NSP	Noël Sullivan Papers
NYPL	New York Public Library, Astor, Lenox and Tilden Foundations
WEBDP, UM(A)	W.E.B. Du Bois Papers, University of Massachusetts at Amherst
WTP	Wallace Thurman Papers
WWP, LC	Walter White Papers, Library of Congress

NOTES

1. Still Here

page 3

"with tenderness & caution!!'": Files of the Peninsula Community Hospital of Monterey; courtesy of the Medical Records Department. I am indebted to Dr. Howard M. Spiro of the Yale University School of Medicine for assistance in securing and interpreting this material.

"a kind of glowing little tree": LH to Carl Van Vechten, Feb. 5, 1941, CVVP, Yale.

page 4

"The very lovely gay and joyous plant": LH to Mary Blanchard, Mar. 7, 1941, Countee Cullen-Harold Jackman Papers, Atlanta University.

"Pour la vie": LH to Carl Van Vechten, Feb. 5, 1941, CVVP, Yale.

"Goodbye, / Christ Jesus Lord God Jehova": LH, "Goodbye Christ," *The Negro Worker* 2 (Nov.-Dec. 1932): 32.

"Lots of wires," "a Mountain of mail": LH to Arna Bontemps, Feb. 4, 1941, Arna Bontemps Papers. I am indebted to Arna Alexander Bontemps for generously making available to me copies of correspondence to and from his father still in his family's possession.

page 5

"Having left the terrain of the 'radical at twenty' ": LH, "Statement Concerning 'Goodbye Christ'," Jan. 1, 1941, LHP 262.

"to support the efforts of the Soviet Union": *Daily Worker*, Aug. 28, 1938.

"This Hughes is a long way": *People's World* (San Francisco), Jan. 15, 1941.

"Chicago," he muttered darkly: LH to Noël Sullivan, July 19, 1940, NSP, Bancroft.

"broke and remorseful as usual": LH to Arna Bontemps, n.d. [Jan. 1941], in Charles H. Nichols, ed., *Arna Bontemps-Langston Hughes Letters: 1925-1967* (New York: Dodd, Mead, 1980), p. 64.

page 6

"moaning and groaning" and groggy: LH to Arna Bontemps, n.d. [Jan. 1941], in Nichols, *Letters*, p. 72.

"at this curious thing": Countee Cullen, "Yet Do I Marvel," *Color* (New York: Harper & Brothers, 1925), p. 3.

"I don't think Mr. Sullivan": Eulah Pharr to author, interview, June 20, 1980.

page 7

his "purity of heart and goodness": Noël Sullivan to "Peter" [Ella Winter], copy in Sullivan to LH, Feb. 21, 1940, LHP.

"to whom life owes nothing": Noël Sullivan to LH, Dec. 2, 1941, LHP.

"I love to know you are near": Elsie Arden to LH, May 26, 1941, LHP.

"To say what your friendship has meant": LH to Noël Sullivan, Dec. 15, 1941, NSP, Bancroft.

page 8

They "seem to put me to sleep": LH to Arna Bontemps, n.d. [Feb. 7, 1941], in Nichols, *Letters*, p. 73.

"You have already given too much": Thyra Edwards to LH, Jan. 31, 1941, LHP.

"a few narrow minded religionists": Beverly C. Ransom to LH, Jan. 16, 1941, LHP.

lauded Hughes for "his bigness of spirit": *Pittsburgh Courier,* Feb. 1, 1941.

"You have so much fine work": Melvin B. Tolson to LH, Feb. 8, 1941, LHP.

page 9

"a slander on the Negro people!": LH to Arna Bontemps, Feb. 4, 1941, ABP.

"They tell me Zora laid me low": LH to William Grant Still, May 27, 1941, LHP.

"the sudden boom and abrupt decline": Arna Bontemps to LH, Jan. 26, 194[1] ("1940"), LHP.

page 10

Kauffer seemed "not well acquainted": LH to Alfred A. Knopf, Inc. (Sidney Jacobs), Feb. 6, 1941, Alfred A. Knopf, Inc. files, New York.

"I hope colored folks will like": LH to Arna Bontemps, Mar. 22, 1941; in Nichols, *Letters,* p. 78.

the "enormous amount of bookkeeping involved": Alfred A. Knopf, Inc. (Joseph C. Lesser) to LH, Feb. 14, 1941, LHP.

"the outright purchase of the earlier books": Blanche Knopf to LH, Mar. 20, 1942, LHP.

"Let's do no more about the poem": LH to Arthur B. Spingarn, Jan. 30, 1941, ABSP, MSRC.

page 11

"Me," he solemnly vowed, "I have retired": LH to Arna Bontemps, Feb. 14, 1941, LHP.

"I bought a big note book": LH to Arna Bontemps, n.d., in Nichols, *Letters,* p. 73.

"I was unhappy for a long time": LH, *The Big Sea* (New York: Knopf, 1940), pp. 16–17.

"When the program was over": LH, *The Big Sea,* p. 25.

page 12

"I hated my father": *The Big Sea,* p. 49.

"This is a song for the genius child": LH, "Genius Child," *Opportunity* 15 (Aug. 1937): 239.

page 13

"I used to take her flowers at the Ritz": LH to Arna Bontemps, Feb. 18, 1941, Arna Bontemps Papers; courtesy of Arna A. Bontemps.

who seemed "truthfully represented": Willa Cather to LH, Apr. 15, 1941, LHP.

"I couldn't put it down": LH to Carl Van Vechten, Apr. 8, 1941, CVVP, Yale.

"What he says about the Negroes": LH to Roy Wilkins, Mar. 22, 1941, LHP.

what he called "a very nice letter": LH to Alfred A. Knopf, Inc. (J. R. de la Torre Bueno, Jr.), Mar. 22, 1941, LHP.

"personally, I regard him as . . . a great poet": LH to Frank R. Bohnhorst, Jan. 6, 1942, LHP.

influenza "and general disgustedness": LH to Richard Wright, Feb. 15, 1941; courtesy of Michel Fabre.

"the highest and noblest achievement": Bruce Kellner, ed., *The Harlem Renaissance: A Historical Dictionary for the Era* (Westport, Ct.: Greenwood Press, 1984), p. 339.

page 14

"swell" about Wright's "triumph, isn't it?": LH to Powell Lindsay, Mar. 30, 1941, LHP.

"The written word is the only record": LH, "The Need For Heroes," *Crisis* 48 (June 1941): 184–185, 206.

page 15

"of a protest nature depicting horror": LH, "Proposed Project for Rosenwald Fellowship," n.d. [Dec. 1940], Rosenwald Fund Papers (microfilm), ARC.

"To read it . . . you would almost think": LH to Louise Thompson Patterson, Mar. 10, 1941; courtesy of Louise Thompson Patterson.

"rail and sweat and frown in anger": LH, "What the Negro Wants," *Common Ground* 2 (Autumn 1941): 52–54.

page 16

"too easy, too trivial and too unchallenging": Rowena Woodham Jelliffe to the Rosenwald Fund, Jan. 25, 1941, Rosenwald Fund Papers (microfilm), ARC.

"a sort of Amos and Andy sequence": Maxim Lieber to LH, Oct. 31, 1940, LHP.

would "cover Harlem like a book from Sunday": LH to Moe Gale, Mar. 12, 1941, LHP.

"very definite financial promise": Maxim Lieber to LH, Mar. 17, 1941, LHP.

"I don't think that Gale is a marijuana addict": Maxim Lieber to LH, Apr. 21, 1941, LHP.

"All aboard for the Radio Special!": Maxim Lieber to LH, May 1, 1941, LHP.

page 17

"Thus armoured . . . I return to the struggle": LH to Louise Thompson Patterson, n.d.; courtesy of Louise Thompson Patterson.

"a simple jolly plump little soul": LH to Carl Van Vechten, Apr. 4, 1941, CVVP, Yale.

"prima donna busts": LH to Arna Bontemps, Mar. 22, 1941, in Nichols, *Letters,* p. 78.

"I've known rivers": LH, "The Negro Speaks of Rivers," *Crisis* 22 (June 1921): 71.

"MY FIRST PUBLISHED POEM": Copy courtesy of Thomas H. Wirth, *Fire!!* Press, Metuchen, New Jersey.

"Twenty years of Writing and Publishing": *Ibid.*

page 18

had been "more propaganda than art": Frank Marshall Davis to LH, Apr. 15, 1941, LHP.

"a good Negro patriotic song": LH to W.C. Handy, Mar. 28, 1941, LHP.

"Bird in hand worth ten in bush": LH to Charles Leonard, June 12, 1941, LHP.

page 19

"You are like a warm dark dusk": LH, "Young Negro Girl," *Pine Cone,* July 18, 1941; the other poems were "Refugee," "One," "Silence", "Snail," "Gypsy Melodies," and "Big Sur."

"Where is the Jim Crow section": LH, "Merry-Go-Round," *Shakespeare in Harlem* (New York: Knopf, 1942), p. 80.

page 20

"I've been scarred and battered": LH, *Jim Crow's Last Stand* (New York: Negro Publication Society, 1943), p. 19.

"might as well be 42nd Street and Fifth Avenue": LH to Arna Bontemps, July 24, 1941, in Nichols, *Letters,* p. 86.

page 21

"My uncle's style of entertaining": From the transcript of an interview concerning Robinson and Una Jeffers, n.d.; courtesy of Alice Doyle Mahoney.

A buffet . . . "for 180!": LH to Leslie Roos, Aug. 9, 1941; courtesy of Thomas H. Wirth.

"a little Heaven": LH to Noël Sullivan, May 16, 1940, NSP, Bancroft.

"Langston was terribly broken up by the killing": Eulah Pharr to author, interview.

"The bride, a young lady whose mama breathed": LH to Arna Bontemps, Feb. 14, 1941; in Nichols, *Letters,* p. 76.

page 22

"Someone would be talking softly": Leander Crowe to author, interview, May 22, 1980.

He liked "*Tristan,* goat's milk, short novels": S.J. Kunitz and H. Haycraft, *Twentieth Century Authors* (New York: H.W. Wilson, 1942), p. 684.

"the kind of Texas crackers": LH to Arna Bontemps, July 4, 1941, ABP.

"he donated a pint of blood to the British": LH to Arna Bontemps, Mar. 22, 1941, LHP.

page 23

"a common hussy in death mask": LH, "War and Peace," n.d, LHP 3821.

"Let us kill off youth": LH, "Comment on War," *Crisis* 47 (June 1940): 190.

"bitten with the war bug": *People's World,* Jan. 15, 1941.

page 24

"a paradox, full of contradictions": LH, "Democracy, Negroes, and Writers," May 3, 1941, LHP 286.

"But at least under Democracy": LH to Carl Van Vechten, Oct. 8, 1941, CVVP, Yale.

"should set the stage handsomely": Arna Bontemps to LH, June 22, 1941, in Nichols, *Letters,* p. 83.

"We shall fight him by land": *New York Times,* June 23, 1941.

"And I do declare!": LH to Carl Van Vechten, June 21 [*sic*], 1941, CVVP, Yale.

page 25

"Today the deliberate increase": W.H. Auden, *Spain, 1937* (London: Faber and Faber, 1937), n.p.

"I dream a world where man": LH, "I Dream a World," from "Troubled Island: An Opera," n.d., LHP 3792.

page 26

"After long last . . . he lays an egg": Maxim Lieber to LH, Sept. 24, 1941, LHP.

"Folks like that": LH to Arna Bontemps, July 4, 1941, in Nichols, *Letters,* p. 85.

"That . . . is how sly": Maxim Lieber to LH, Aug. 7, 1941, LHP.

"in the FLESH": LH to Toy Harper, Aug. 6, 1941, LHP.

"pretty good, and most beautifully set": LH to Arna Bontemps, July 16, 1941, ABP.

"The struggle is terrific!": LH and Charles Leonard, "Mad Scene from Woolworth's," from "Run, Ghost, Run (A Negro Revue)," 1941, LHP 3434.

"A peculiar misfortune certainly dogs": Maxim Lieber to LH, Mar. 11, 1941, LHP.

page 27

"I noticed with pleasure": LH to Eleanor Roosevelt, Aug. 12, 1941, LHP.

"I am delighted . . . to NOT have to dress": LH to Arna Bontemps, August 27, 1941, in Nichols, *Letters,* p. 88.

"When I take you back": LH to Carl Van Vechten, Sept. 13, 1941, CVVP, Yale.

"Maybe that is where we should": LH to Toy Harper, Sept. 9, 1941, LHP.

page 28

"so I bought a new suit, grey tweed": LH to Arna Bontemps, Sept. 28, 1941; Nichols, p. 89.

"the great truth and beauty of your art": LH to Paul Robeson, Oct. 11, 1927, Paul Robeson Papers. I am indebted to Martin Duberman for allowing me to see relevant documents in the Robeson papers.

"a little nervous" about the porter idea: Essie Robeson to LH, Oct. 6, 1941, LHP.

page 29

"All of Langston's work so far": Essie Robeson to Paul Robeson, June 25, 1939, Paul Robeson Papers.

"As long as the picture industry": Maxim Lieber to LH, Oct. 14, 1941, LHP.

"I think only a subsidized Negro Film Institute": LH to Arna Bontemps, Sept. 28, 1941, in Nichols, *Letters,* p. 89.

"Hollywood's favorite Negro character": LH, "The Negro in American Entertainment," June 25, 1951, LHP 757.

"The lamentations of Jeremiah are mild": Maxim Lieber to LH, Oct. 14, 1941, LHP.
then "boogied on Northward": LH to Carl Van Vechten, Oct. 14, 1941, CVVP, Yale.
"If I ever *did* have a son": LH, "Sailor Ashore," *Laughing to Keep from Crying* (New York: Henry Holt, 1952), p. 57.
page 30
"Thanks a lot for the plug, pal": Chester Himes to LH, Oct. 20, 1941, LHP.
the university would "play this up": Carl Van Vechten to LH, June 8, 1941, LHP.
page 31
"If the Schomburg collection is famous": Carl Van Vechten to LH, Oct. 27, 1941, LHP.
"What a wonderful title you have given": LH to Carl Van Vechten, June 21, 1941, CVVP, Yale.
"I will now become self-conscious": LH to Carl Van Vechten, Oct. 30, 1941, CVVP, Yale.
"As a spokesman for the Negro": Carl Van Vechten to LH, Nov. 4, 1941, LHP.
"If ever you need me": LH to Noël Sullivan, Dec. 15, 1941, NSP, Bancroft.

2. Jim Crow's Last Stand

page 32
"Tell Horace I'll take him up": LH to Arna Bontemps, Oct. 10, 1941, in Nichols, *Letters*, p. 92.
page 33
"the focal point for life in the south side": *Chicago Sunday Tribune*, Jan. 11, 1942.
"Langston was charming and boyish": Horace R. Cayton, *Long Old Road* (New York: Trident, 1965), p. 247.
"I had known Langston since I was eighteen": Irma Cayton Wertz to author, interview, Dec. 19, 1987.
"In you I feel one whose life": Louise Thompson to LH, Jan. 18, 1940, LHP.
page 34
"He had done so much": Louise Thompson Patterson to author, interview, May 23, 1984.
"You uttered all the idol-shattering truths": Jacob Weinstein to LH, Dec. 2, 1941, LHP.
"They keep writing me how beautiful": LH to Arna Bontemps, Nov. 8, 1941, in Nichols, *Letters*, p. 96.
"EVERYBODY will be having nappy hair": Carl Van Vechten to LH, Nov. 17, 1941, LHP.
"*I will catch hell!!*": LH to Carl Van Vechten, Nov. 8, 1941, CVVP, Yale.
page 35
"the best possible man for the job": LH to Dr. Walter G. Alexander, June 19, 1941, LHP.
he called the book "swell" in a letter: LH to Alfred A. Knopf, Inc. (Sidney R. Jacobs), Dec. 8, 1941, LHP.
"forget our special grievances" and join: W. E. B. Du Bois, "Close Ranks," *Crisis* 16 (July 1918): 111.
page 36
"The Angel of Mercy's / Got her wings in mud": LH, *Jim Crow's Last Stand*, p. 8.
"the settlement of vexing racial problems": Peter M. Bergman, *The Chronological History of the Negro in America* (New York: Harper and Row, 1969), p. 494.
"Pearl Harbor put Jim Crow on the run": LH, "Jim Crow's Last Stand," *Jim Crow's Last Stand*, pp. 29–30.

page 37

"How I hated to leave Hollow Hills!": LH to Noël Sullivan, Dec. 15, 1941, NSP, Bancroft.

"Langston said he wanted to write": Irma Cayton Wertz to author, interview, Dec. 19, 1987.

page 38

"It could be gay, funny, sad, glamourous": LH to Carl Van Vechten, Nov. 4, 1941, CVVP, Yale.

"The janitor said, very calmly": LH to Arna Bontemps, Jan. 27, 1942, in Nichols, *Letters,* p.97.

"They think it's charming": LH to Arna Bontemps, Jan. 27, 1942, in Nichols, *Letters,* p. 97.

"anything but dice and wishbones": LH to Alfred A. Knopf, Inc., Oct. 24, 1942; Alfred A. Knopf, Inc. files, New York.

"Those-Awful-Gilpins-That-Do-Those": Rowena Woodham Jelliffe to LH, Apr. 22, 1942, LHP.

page 39

"It's going to be *good!*": LH to Noël Sullivan, Feb. 5, 1942, NSP, Bancroft.

"that furthermore Negroes were never asked": LH to Maxim Lieber, Jan. 27, 1942, LHP.

"I need not tell you what to write": Office of Emergency Management (Bernard C. Schoenfeld) to LH, Dec. 31, 1941, LHP.

"so far the programs seeming aimed": LH to Office of Emergency Management (Bernard C. Schoenfeld), Jan. 27, 1942, LHP.

"a most reactionary and difficult medium": LH to Office of Civilian Defense (William Alexander), Jan. 31, 1942, LHP.

"God knows we better win": LH to Maxim Lieber, Jan. 27, 1942, LHP.

page 40

"to overcome intolerance and discrimination": *Common Ground* 2 (Autumn 1941): 1.

the jacket had been "an error": Blanche Knopf to Rowena Jelliffe, Feb. 16, 1942, copy in LHP.

"I think it is my most beautiful book": LH to Carl Van Vechten, Feb. 17, 1942, CVVP, Yale.

"concerned overmuch with the most uprooted": *Opportunity* 20 (July 1942): 219.

"a soldier for human rights": *Journal of Negro History* 27 (Apr. 1942): 236–237.

page 41

"slanted particularly for the Caucasian": Chicago *Bee,* Apr. 5, 1942.

"The thing that hurts is the laughter": *Christian Science Monitor,* Apr. 1, 1942.

"The careless reader might easily fall": *Saturday Review of Literature* 25 (Apr. 25, 1942): 9.

"so sure a touch and an insight": New York *Herald-Tribune,* May 3, 1942.

"neither his imagination nor his intelligence": *New York Times Book Review,* Mar. 22, 1942.

"Various reviewers have accused me": LH, note in "The Dark People of the Soviet" (later "I Wonder As I Wander"), n.d. [1942], LHP 519.

"My old mule, / He's got a grin": LH, *Shakespeare in Harlem,* p. 29.

page 43

"You see," he laughed self-deprecatingly: Chicago *Sun,* Apr. 19, 1942.

"I look ahead—and I see my race": LH, "The Sun Do Move" (1942), LHP 3705.

"I could summon more enthusiasm": Carl Van Vechten to Rosenwald Fund, Mar. 2, 1942, Rosenwald Fund Papers (microfilm), ARC.

"There is an ever enriching of character": Rowena Woodham Jelliffe to Rosenwald Fund, Apr. 14, 1942; Rosenwald Fund Papers (microfilm), ARC.

page 44

"All the women around here": Margaret Taylor Goss to LH, Nov. 5, 1942, LHP.

"Remember us young cullud writers": Margaret Taylor Goss to LH, Feb. 7, 1943, LHP.

"my baby's destruction of the dignity": Gwendolyn Brooks to LH, Mar. 11, 1942, LHP.

"I greatly want to discuss": Gwendolyn Brooks to LH, Mar. 11, 1942, LHP.

"He was intent, he was careful": Gwendolyn Brooks, *Report from Part One* (Detroit: Broadside Press, 1972), p. 71.

"You have never ceased to encourage": Margaret [Walker] to LH, July 15, 1942, in *Common Ground* correspondence (with M. Margaret Anderson), LHP.

"Yale feels like it is": LH to Carl Van Vechten, May 17, 1942, CVVP, Yale.

page 45

"Everybody seems so rich up here!": LH to Arna Bontemps, May 17, 1942, in Nichols, *Letters,* p. 99.

Knollenberg . . . was "a splendid fellow": LH to Arna Bontemps, May 23, 1942, LHP.

painfully "jejune. . . . I once were nuts": LH to Carl Van Vechten, May 17, 1942, CVVP, Yale.

"Don't chuck out a thing": Norman Holmes Pearson to LH, Oct. 29, 1942, LHP.

"to awaken and inspire liberty-loving Americans": Treasury Department (Shirley Burke) to LH, Mar. 24, 1942, LHP.

page 46

"It seems the radio is like many": LH to Noël Sullivan, June 20, 1942, NSP, Bancroft.

"Hitler he may rant": LH and Emerson Harper, "Freedom Road," June, 1942, LHP + 3868.

"Negro Composer Has Hit": LH to Levia Friedberg, Aug. 14, 1942, LHP.

"for which I once wrote an ad": LH to Carl Van Vechten, Oct. 11, 1942, CVVP, Yale.

"When my gal writes a letter": LH, "Go-and-Get-the-Enemy Blues," July 30, 1942, LHP + 3871.

The song "tried to echo the hope": Publicity material, LHP + 3870.

page 47

"It was TERRIFIC!!!!": LH to Arna Bontemps, June 18, 1942, in Nichols, *Letters,* p. 100.

decided to return . . . to "MI CASA": LH to Noël Sullivan, June 20, 1942, NSP, Bancroft.

"New York is so nice and hot": LH to Carl Van Vechten, Aug. 10, 1942, CVVP, Yale.

"She is certainly the current Harriet Beecher Stowe": LH to Noël Sullivan, June 20, 1942, NSP, Bancroft.

"You know, I started all this": *Ibid.*

page 48

"This is really a delightful place": LH to Arna Bontemps, Aug. 9, 1942, in Nichols, *Letters,* p. 103.

it was "wonderful" to have: LH to Carl Van Vechten, Aug. 10, 1942, CVVP, Yale.

"forcefully bringing home to us": LH to Noël Sullivan, Aug. 11, 1942, NSP, Bancroft.

"their hind brains don't work": LH to Carl Van Vechten, Aug. 22, 1942, CVVP, Yale.

page 49
"I've always wanted to be a songwriter": LH to Tom Rutherford, Sept. 11, 1942, LHP.

"The Lord has blessed me with ASCAP": LH to Maxim Lieber, Oct. 16, 1941, LHP.

"I shall have four, possibly six": LH to Arna Bontemps, Aug. 16, 1942, in Nichols, *Letters,* p. 106.

"But my *determination* is to keep on!": LH to Arna Bontemps, Sept. 10, 1942, LHP.

page 50
"The Axis is out to crush": LH, "Negro Writers and the War," Aug. 24, 1942, LHP 772.

"Jim Crow Army, / And Navy, too": LH, "The Black Man Speaks," *Jim Crow's Last Stand,* p. 5.

"Negroes, / Sweet and docile": LH, "Roland Hayes Beaten (Georgia: 1942)," *Selected Poems* (New York: Knopf, 1959), p. 167.

page 51
"Oh, tragic bitter river": LH, "The Bitter River," *Jim Crow's Last Stand,* p. 13.

"Some folks think / By imprisoning Nehru": LH, "Freedom," *Jim Crow's Last Stand,* p. 7.

"There are the inactive ones who": LH, "Stalingrad: 1942," in Joy Davidman, ed., *War Poems of the United Nation: Three Hundred Poems, One Hundred Poets from Twenty Countries* (New York: Dial, 1943), pp. 321–324.

page 53
"I wish to register herewith": LH to Selective Service, Sept. 28, 1942, LHP.

"even when it is sunny": LH to Levia Friedberg, n.d. [1942], LHP.

"not object to Langston Hughes": Edward C. Sweeny to Elizabeth Ames, Oct. 16, 1942; Yaddo files, with thanks to Billie Allen.

pleased by Hughes's "magnificent piece": *Chicago Defender* (Metz T. P. Lochard) to LH, Oct. 26, 1942, LHP.

"specific incidents and stories": *Chicago Defender* (Metz T. P. Lochard) to LH, Oct. 26, 1942, LHP.

Yaddo—"a grand place": LH to Carl Van Vechten, Nov. 26, 1942, CVVP, Yale.

"the best, the greatest, and the finest": *Kansas City Call,* Nov. 27, 1942.

"His personal magnetism and the boyish air": *Ibid.*

the "internationally beloved apostle of freedom": Indiana *Recorder,* Nov. 28, 1942.

"You are so without bitterness": Caroline Slade (Mrs. John A. Slade) to LH, Oct. 5, 1942, LHP.

"I am heartbroken that I shall have": LH to Carl Van Vechten, Oct. 26, 1942, CVVP, Yale.

page 55
"Hey now! / Some skin, gate!": LH, poem to Carl Van Vechten; text courtesy of Bruce Kellner.

"was like a Christmas tree": Carl Van Vechten to LH, Nov. 25, 1942, LHP.

"the dean of popular American Negro musicians": *Chicago Defender,* Nov. 28, 1942.

page 56
"Dangerous / Are the western waters now": LH, "To Captain Mulzac," *Jim Crow's Last Stand,* p. 16.

"Thus do the outlaws . . . of one generation": Carl Van Vechten to LH, Feb. 1, 1943, LHP.

"As long as I have a place": Toy Harper to LH, n.d. [c. 1934], LHP.

page 57
"so he can see his way through life": LH to Emerson Harper, Nov. 9, 1939, LHP.

"This is my land America": LH, "My America," *Journal of Educational Sociology* 16 (Feb. 1943): 334–336.

a long "prose poem": National Urban League (Lester B. Granger) to LH, Jan. 26, 1943, LHP.

page 58

"I do remember that Langston brought": Ann Tanneyhill to author, Jan. 14, 1982.

"When a man starts out with nothing": LH, "Freedom's Plow," *Selected Poems*, pp. 291–297. First published in *Opportunity* 21 (Apr. 1943): 66–69.

page 59

"The reason Dixie / Is so mean today": LH to William L. Patterson, Oct. 26, 1942; courtesy of Louise Thompson Patterson.

"I swear to the Lord": LH, "The Black Man Speaks," *Jim Crow's Last Stand*, p. 5.

page 60

"Goodmorning, Stalingrad!": LH, "Good Morning, Stalingrad," *Jim Crow's Last Stand*, p. 27.

"I would wear it": LH, "Color," *Jim Crow's Last Stand*, p. 7. For "Note on Commercial Theatre" and "Daybreak in Alabama," see pp. 24 and 25.

3. Simple Speaks His Mind

page 61

"What kind of cranks?": New York *Herald-Tribune*, Aug. 18, 1957. See also LH, "Simple and Me," *Phylon* 6 (Oct.-Dec. 1945): 349–352. Quotations from the *Herald-Tribune* and *Phylon* accounts of this meeting, obviously given fictional treatment by Hughes, are here intermingled.

page 62

"a foil for patriotic propaganda": New York *Herald-Tribune*, Aug. 18, 1957.

"My Simple Minded Friend said": LH, "Here to Yonder," *Chicago Defender*, Feb. 13, 1943.

page 65

"really very simple. It is just myself": LH, "Simple and Me," p. 349.

Simple "simply started talking to me": New York *Daily Compass*, Oct. 15, 1951.

pronouncing Simple "a very happy creation": Arna Bontemps to LH, Feb. 22, 1943, LHP.

"You have a good ear for speech": Loren Miller to LH, n.d. [c. 1944], LHP.

page 66

Simple was "killing me": Richard Durham to LH, Dec. 2, 1944, LHP.

"much less 'simple' and much more psychopathic": Thelma Braithwaite to LH, Jan. 31, 1945, LHP.

"But, look here! You musn't have too much": LH to Maggie Treadwell, Jan. 11, 1945, LHP.

"I do not recall ever in my column": LH to Zella Selance, Sept. 13, 1945, LHP.

declared himself "very pleased": *Chicago Defender* (Metz T. P. Lochard) to LH, Sept. 22, 1943, LHP.

page 67

The essay "should be framed and placed": J. T. Wardlaw to LH, Sept. 22, 1945, LHP.

"You are a voice speaking": Mabel H. Spearman to LH, Sept. 4, 1945, LHP.

"If now is not the time": *Chicago Defender*, Jan. 30, 1943.

"the insides of my body seemed to do": Mayron Crenshaw to LH, Feb. 4, 1944, LHP.

"Continue your fight Mr. Hughes": Bert Berbaro to LH, n.d., LHP.

"The wheels of the Jim Crow car": LH, "What Shall We Do About the South?" *Common Ground* 3 (Winter 1943): 3–6.

"Why do you harp on racial equality?": Alice P. Ware to LH, Dec. 16, 1942, LHP.

"loaded with dynamite": *Common Ground* (M. Margaret Anderson) to LH, Dec. 12, 1943, LHP.

page 68

"with a kind of horrified fascination": *Common Ground* (M. Margaret Anderson) to LH, Jan. 6, 1944, LHP.

"One smart-alect negro," a white man warned: M. Margaret Anderson, "Letter to the Reader," *Common Ground* 4 (Spring 1944): 92.

"the way you keep hammering": *Common Ground* (M. Margaret Anderson) to LH, July 4, 1943, LHP.

"Millions of darker peoples": LH to *India News* (R. Lal Singh), Oct. 7, 1944, LHP. See also LH, [Public Appearances], LHP 3074.

"Folk know what I can do": LH to Arna Bontemps, Mar. 17, 1943, LHP (dated Apr. 17, 1943 in Nichols, *Letters*, p. 126).

page 69

"There are words like 'Freedom' ": LH, "Refugee in America," *Saturday Evening Post* 215 (Feb. 6, 1943): 64.

"an atheistic communist, a self-confessed communist": *Chicago Defender*, Apr. 24, 1943.

"I am for the Christianity that fights": *Ibid.*

page 70

as a fight for "freedom—the preservation of freedom": LH, [Public Appearances], LHP 2994–3400, box 2.

"You cannot imagine the great impression": Margaret Wyke to LH, Apr. 22, 1943, LHP.

"He was timed by several watches": Horace Mann Bond, *Education for Freedom: A History of Lincoln University, Pennsylvania* (Lincoln, Pa.: Lincoln University, 1976), p. 428.

"more than anyone could expect": *Lincoln University Bulletin* 48 (July 1943): 1.

"I was sitting on the platform": LH to Arna Bontemps, May 23, 1943, LHP.

"explode in the face of democracy": *Atlanta Daily World*, Apr. 8, 1945.

page 71

"Hitler could hardly desire more": LH to Carl Van Doren, Mar. 18, 1943, LHP.

blacks "are made to feel ourselves": *The Saratogian*, Sept. 25, 1943.

"Don't let nobody tell you": LH, "For This We Fight: Sailor Ashore," June 1, 1943, LHP +3858.

"Blitz the Fritz": LH, "Third War Loan Campaign," [1943], LHP 3776.

page 72

"on whom we have come to depend": Writers' War Board to LH, Feb. 12, 1943, LHP.

"top authors and composers": American Theatre Wing Music War Committee (Oscar Hammerstein II) to LH, Sept. 22, 1943, LHP.

"The muse of black-face comedy": Arna Bontemps to LH, n.d. [c. Mar. 4, 1943], LHP.

"Langston encouraged me but he also": Margaret Walker Alexander to author, interview, Dec. 20, 1981.

page 74

"We all agreed that it was": Claude McKay to LH, Aug. 9, 1943, LHP.

"The two . . . don't mix very well": LH to Countee Cullen, July 23, 1944, LHP.

page 75

would show "what New York is": Fiorello La Guardia to LH, July 1, 1943, LHP.

"so that there will be no danger": Writers' War Board to LH, July 15, 1943, LHP.

"(at least in my experience)": LH to Writers' War Board, July 29, 1943, LHP.

"Personally, I DO NOT LIKE RADIO": LH to Eric Barnouw, Mar. 27, 1945, LHP.

"You know I'm sorry I missed": LH to Arna Bontemps, Aug. 5, 1943, in Nichols, *Letters*, p. 135.

"I am dying to go to Harlem": LH to Noël Sullivan, Aug. 5, 1943, NSP, Bancroft.

"I reckon I lost my watch in the riots": LH to Arna Bontemps, Aug. 5, 1943.

page 76

"All the best colored people": LH to Carl Van Vechten, Aug. 13, 1943, CVVP, Yale.

"I know WHY the riots": Carl Van Vechten to LH, Sept. 12, 1943, LHP.

"Cullud folks, who are terribly ashamed": Arna Bontemps to LH, Sept. 16, 1943, LHP.

"I do not know why [the looting] tickles me": LH to Arna Bontemps, Aug. 5, 1943, LHP.

"If Margie Polite / Had of been white": LH, "Ballad of Margie Polite," *One-Way Ticket* (New York: Knopf, 1949), p. 78.

page 77

"the finest job that has been done": Writers' War Board to LH, Aug. 19, 1943, LHP.

"only the most typical and daily kinds": LH to Writers' War Board, Aug. 16, 1943, LHP.

"Delicate nuance of the color line": LH, "Private Jim Crow," Aug. 16, 1943, LHP 2974.

page 78

"among Dr. Du Bois's 'talented tenth' ": LH, "Down Under in Harlem," *The New Republic* 110 (Mar. 20, 1944): 405.

"You say I O.K.ed / LONG DISTANCE?": LH, "Madam and the Phone Bill," *One-Way Ticket*, p. 13. For the first pieces, see LH, "Madam to You!: Four Poems Concerning the Life and Times of Alberta K.," *Common Ground* 3 (Summer 1943): 88–90. These poems are "Madam's Past History," "Madam and Her Madam," "Madam and the Army," and "Madam and the Movies."

page 79

"THE lyric for THE war song!": LH to Arna Bontemps, Aug. 31, 1943, LHP.

"It's almost exactly like a fellow": Arna Bontemps to LH, Oct. 1, 1943, LHP.

"I'm walking on air": Arna Bontemps to LH, Aug. 23, 1943, LHP.

"Back in town, thank God!": LH to Carl Van Vechten, Oct. 4, 1943, LHP.

page 80

but "*dis-and-dat* dialect to speak and sing": LH to Arna Bontemps, n.d. [c. Oct. 19, 1943], LHP.

"with colored boys in the Navy": Charles Leonard to LH, Labor Day, 1943, LHP.

"I am personally not interested": LH to Arna Bontemps, n.d. [Sept. 1943], LHP.

"when a wave of democracy swept over": LH to Nancy Cunard, June 2, 1954, LHP.

("I like this environment of books"): Arna Bontemps to LH, Sept. 6, 1943, LHP.

page 81

"You left Fisk and Meharry humming": Arna Bontemps to LH, Nov. 24, 1943, LHP.

"They groan aloud in school": Arna Bontemps to LH, Oct. 13, 1943, LHP.

"The Jim Crow car seems to me": LH to Arna Bontemps, Sept. 14, 1943, in Nichols, *Letters*, p. 142.

"You and I, living today": LH, "The Slave Trade" [Public Appearances], Dec. 12, 1943, LHP 2994–3400, box 2.

"then what he [the Negro] needs": William T. Couch to Rayford W. Logan, Nov. 7, 1943, copy, LHP.

"at all! I do not understand how": LH to William T. Couch, Dec. 21, 1943, LHP.

from "your Negro allies in the U.S.A.": LH, "The Ballad of the Man Who Went to War," Feb. 11, 1944, LHP 84.

page 83

"Come here, hell!": LH to Russell and Rowena Jelliffe, Mar. 21, 1943, LHP.

but "me remaining triumphant with weapon!": LH to *Common Ground* (M. Margaret Anderson), Jan. 30, 1944, LHP.

"Just be yourself at Town Hall": Arna Bontemps to LH, Feb. 15, 1944, LHP.

"how bankrupt southern white leaders are": *Common Ground* (M. Margaret Anderson) to LH, Feb. 10, 1944, LHP.

"Some people bring up the dog-gonest arguments": LH, "Let's Face The Race Question" [Public Appearances], Feb. 17, 1944, LHP 2994.

page 84

"I could hear your shy little stammer": Essie Robeson to LH, Feb. 28, 1944, LHP.

at Hughes's "truly genuine simplicity": *Baltimore Afro-American,* Mar. 4, 1944.

"the excellent manner you represented the cause": Herman M. Sweatt to LH, n.d, LHP.

"Go on back to Russia": Unsigned, n.d., LHP.

"Dear old hunk of Asafoetida": "Grant Lincoln" to LH, Mar. 5, 1944, LHP.

page 85

"Langston had strongly opposed": Irma Cayton Wertz to author, interview, Dec. 19, 1987.

"I wonder why anybody lives anywhere": *Chicago Defender,* Apr. 15, 1944.

"To help me with my work!": LH to Noël Sullivan, Apr. 28, 1944, NSP, Bancroft.

"I reckon the war has done": LH to Arna Bontemps, Apr. 29, 1944, LHP.

page 86

"As I told you that night": LH to Frank Lin, June 1, 1944, LHP.

"My first one thousand dollars!": LH, [Personal Papers], n.d., LHP 863.

"the most I have ever had": LH to Carl Van Vechten, Apr. 23, 1944, CVVP, Yale.

"the most loved of any": LH to Noël Sullivan, Jan. 30, 1944, NSP, Bancroft.

page 87

"He's had some bad bumps": Edwin R. Embree, *13 Against the Odds* (New York: Viking, 1944), p. 117.

"The good qualities he attributes to me": LH, [Review of Edwin R. Embree's *13 Against the Odds*], Jan. 30, 1944, LHP 3425.

"sulfa drugs—which makes a person": LH to Blanche Knopf, June 28, 1944, LHP.

"and without payment of any further sums": Joseph C. Lesser to LH, June 21, 1944.

"I told you on the phone": Blanche Knopf to LH, June 22, 1944, LHP.

4. Third Degree

page 88

"an ALL STAR million dollar show!": LH to Arna Bontemps, July 10, 1944, in Nichols, *Letters,* p. 168.

page 89

"the Negroes are paying and I am getting": *Ibid.*

for "all the fine little things": W. C. Handy to LH, Aug. 30, 1944, LHP.

"I am a colored West Indian": Roger Mais to LH, June 3, 1944, LHP.

page 90

to "interpret Negroes as human beings": *Pittsburgh Courier,* Dec. 23, 1944.

He was "an avowed Communist": *Hearings Before A Special Committee on Un-American Activities, House of Representatives, 78th Congress* 17 (Sept. 27–29, Oct. 3–5, 1944): 10336–10337. Washington, D.C.: U.S. Government Printing Office, 1944.

the "extent, character, and objects of un-American": *Hearings* 17 (Sept. 27–29, Oct. 3–5, 1944), n.p.

that Langston was "a Communist poet": *Hearings Before A Special Committee on Un-American Activities, House of Representatives* 4 (Dec. 9, 1938): 3008.

"run for office on the Communist Party ticket": *Hearings Before a Special Committee on Un-American Activities,* House of Representatives 14 (Aug. 29, Oct. 1, 2, 4, 1940; May 21, 22, 26, 27, 29, 1941; June 10, 12, Aug. 11, 1941): 8474.

"the leading Communist front organization in the United States": *Hearings* 17 (Sept. 27–29, Oct. 3–5, 1944): 10304.

page 91

he had "a perfect score": *Hearings* 17 (1944): 10332.

"His name is so well known": *Hearings* 17 (1944): 10336.

"He has written a number of volumes": *Hearings* 17 (1944): 10337.

"meant to be a kind of ironic satire": LH to *Common Ground* (M. Margaret Anderson), quoted in Anderson to editor, *Citizen and Chronicle* (Cranford, N.J), Oct. 31, 1944, LHP.

page 92

"So I figure it isn't just the poem": *Ibid.*

the "International Association for the Preservation": Federal Bureau of Investigation report, Feb. 19, 1944; in LH files, FBI 100–15139 (section 1, serials 1–55).

page 93

"You are the leading poet of your people": William L. Patterson to LH, Apr. 12, 1943, LHP.

"So often I have tried": William L. Patterson to LH, Jan. 16, 1943, LHP.

"What I think is missing from your poem": Louise Thompson Patterson to LH, Nov. 5, 1942, LHP.

page 94

"a people's institute in our community": Max Yergan to LH, Feb. 19, 1943, LHP.

page 95

One group "got hot because I wouldn't": LH to Arna Bontemps, n.d., in Nichols, *Letters,* p. 177.

"Lenin walks around the world": LH, "Lenin," *New Masses* 58 (Jan. 22, 1946): 5.

page 96

"You are reelected as the People's artist": Margaret T. Goss to LH, Aug. 9, 1944, LHP.

"a ruthless egomaniac, utterly unscrupulous": Theodore Ward to LH, Jan. 24, 1944, LHP.

page 97

"We have a fight on our hands": New Brunswick *Daily Home News,* Oct. 7, 1944.

to rise at "ungodly morning hours": LH to Colston Leigh, Inc., Oct. 12, 1946, LHP.

"delighted and thrilled" by his success: *Common Ground* (Read Lewis) to LH, Nov. 16, 1944, LHP.

"Hughes had a fantastic time": M. Margaret Anderson to author, interview, Nov. 19, 1981.

and "put 'on the rack' ": Louise Kirschner to *Common Ground* (M. Margaret Anderson), Nov. 6, 1944, copy, LHP.

"It is impossible to estimate": Louise Kirschner to *Common Ground* (M. Margaret Anderson), Oct. 27, 1944, copy, LHP.

"His day with us did more": Elizabeth A. Ditzell to *Common Ground* (Arthur C. Sides), Nov. 1, 1944, copy, LHP.

"It is too bad you do not have": C.R. Hopkins to *Common Ground* (M. Margaret Anderson), Oct. 28, 1944, copy, LHP.

"A better lesson in true American democracy": Arthur E. Storer to *Common Ground* (M. Margaret Anderson), Nov. 3, 1944, copy, LHP.

"The question now is, when can we": Clarence Dumm to *Common Ground* (M. Margaret Anderson), Nov. 10, 1944, copy, LHP.

"Not in years have we had": Principal of Barringer High School to *Common Ground* (M. Margaret Anderson), Nov. 13, 1944, copy, LHP.

"The whole business made me a bit sore": LH to Arna Bontemps, Dec. 8, 1944, LHP.

page 98

"the National Organization for the Association": *Chicago Defender,* June 16, 1945.

"It will be the biggest thing": William Grant Still to LH, Sept. 13, 1944, LHP.

page 99

"I had a very pleasant visit": LH to William Grant Still, Nov. 30, 1944, William Grant Still Papers, University of Arkansas (Fayetteville).

page 100

"The room is pleasantly dark": LH, "Saratoga Rain," *Negro Story* 1 (Mar.-Apr. 1945): 6.

"*I do not wish under any*": LH to Feakins, Inc., Dec. 9, 1944, LHP.

"you will have no difficulties": National Conference of Christians and Jews (Maurice H. Terry) to LH, Jan. 3, 1945, LHP.

page 101

"but won't let him drink it": LH, "Here to Yonder," *Chicago Defender,* Aug. 4, 1945.

"Are you a Puerto Rican?": LH to Arna Bontemps, Mar. 2, 1945, in Nichols, *Letters,* p. 178.

"Chef want to see you in kitchen": LH, "Here to Yonder," *Chicago Defender,* June 2, 1945.

"I would advise Negro travellers": *Ibid.*

"Have spent my life buying tickets": LH to Arna Bontemps, n.d. [Mar. 1945], in Nichols, *Letters,* p. 179.

"a very bad, rainy, foggy afternoon": LH to Joseph F. Makel, Mar. 19, 1945, LHP.

page 102

"the nuances of color in Europe": LH to Feakins, Inc., Dec. 9, 1944, LHP.

"Pay attention to the labor field": *Atlanta Daily World,* Apr. 8, 1945.

"a dramatic or interpretative reader": *Michigan Chronicle,* May 19, 1945.

"I don't think a tour provides": Arna Bontemps to LH, Mar. 23, 1944, LHP.

"your increased stature, physically": Melvin B. Tolson to LH, July 29, 1944, LHP.

page 103

"The interest . . . will have to be": LH to Carl Van Vechten, June 26, 1945, CVVP, Yale.

"From most relatives, some of my friends": Noël Sullivan to LH, Sept. 4, 1945, LHP.

"I was riding in a Jim Crow car": LH, "Here to Yonder," *Chicago Defender,* May 12, 1945.

"Plenty of people are dead": LH, "Here to Yonder," *Chicago Defender,* Aug. 18, 1945.

"running on any Atom Bomb ticket": *Chicago Defender,* Aug. 18, 1945.

page 104

"For wounds received in action": LH, "Here to Yonder," *Chicago Defender,* Mar. 24, 1945.

"As an American I am deeply sorry": LH, "Here to Yonder," *Chicago Defender,* June 23, 1945.

page 105

"That is the thought that will eventually shake": LH, "Here to Yonder," *Chicago Defender*, Jan. 27, 1945.

"What a grand time was the war!" LH, "World War," *Harlem Quarterly* 1 (Winter 1949–1950): 9.

it was "preparing to close up": Writers' War Board (Rex Stout) to LH, July 10, 1945, LHP.

page 106

"the finest Haitian novel yet published": Mercer Cook to LH, Feb. 26, 1945, LHP.

"When did you learn to say": LH, "A Poem for Jacques Roumain (Late Poet of Haiti)," Mar. 25, 1945, LHP 1621.

"It just seems to me": LH to Arna Bontemps, July 27, 1945, LHP.

"Glad you colored up the story": Arna Bontemps to LH, ["V-J Day plus 1"], 1945, LHP.

page 107

"I was fresh out of the Army": Nathaniel V. White to author, interview, Aug. 12, 1980.

"THERE IS SOMETHING I WOULD LIKE": Elmer Rice to LH, Aug. 23, 1945, LHP.

5. Street Scene

page 108

he "had thought of it many times": Ronald Sanders, *The Days Grow Short: The Life and Music of Kurt Weill* (New York: Holt, Rinehart and Winston, 1980), p. 352.

page 109

"That I, an American Negro": LH, "My Collaborator: Kurt Weill," Oct. 27, 1955, LHP 729.

The lyrics . . . "should attempt to lift": Kurt Weill, "Score for a Play," *New York Times*, Jan. 5, 1947.

"We asked Langston Hughes": Clipping by "Shanger Anger," n.d., *Street Scene* scrapbook, LHP.

"men without intellect, perception": *Philadelphia Evening Bulletin*, Dec. 10, 1946.

"a trivial pastime, devised by grown-up children": *Ibid.*

page 110

"fine in quality and very right": Elmer Rice to LH, Sept. 6, 1945, LHP.

page 111

"I am delighted, of course": LH to Elmer Rice, Oct. 23, 1945, LHP.

"our democracy is so big": Marquette, Michigan *Daily Mining Journal*, Oct. 29, 1945.

the best hotel "in this former Klan territory!": LH to Arna Bontemps, Nov. 9, 1945, LHP.

"raw, cold, and prejudiced": LH to Arna Bontemps, Nov. 14, 1945, LHP.

"Art must be like religion": *Chicago Defender*, Apr. 6, 1946.

"To tell the truth," he wrote: *Chicago Defender*, Apr. 20, 1946.

"a wonderful surprise": LH to Ethel Welch, Nov. 2, 1945, LHP.

page 112

"I must make this a city": Olive Lindsay Wakefield, "Vachel Lindsay, Prophet of God," 1950, in LHP 81.

tales "about his travels over most": *Ibid.*

"Come again soon, won't you?": Olive Lindsay Wakefield to LH, Nov. 5, 1945, LHP.

"I was never so glad": LH to Arna Bontemps, Nov. 14, 1945, LHP.

"one of the greatest 'I' poets": LH, "The Ceaseless Rings of Walt Whitman," Nov. 30, 1945, LHP 553.

page 113

this "amazing character": Ira de A. Reid to LH, Oct. 18, 1945, LHP.

"the only new humorous creation": Arna Bontemps to LH, Jan. 30, 1945, LHP.

"I personally like this idea": LH to Maxim Lieber, Nov. 24, 1945, LHP.

page 114

"I have bought two fine suits": LH to Arna Bontemps, Nov. 14, 1945.

"Brecht would have left": LH, "My Collaborator: Kurt Weill" [earlier draft and notes], LHP 729.

"I had no theatrical precedents": *Ibid.*

"a swell guy to work with": LH to Arna Bontemps, Oct. 19, 1945, LHP.

"a great folk artist": LH, "My Collaborator: Kurt Weill" [final draft], LHP 729.

"music in an American Negro national idiom": *Ibid.*

page 115

"Instead (nigger-like), they quoted": Arna Bontemps to LH, n.d., LHP.

"We do not have any other poet": *Chicago Defender*, Feb. 2, 1946.

page 116

"Not a Negro in town!": LH to Arna Bontemps, Jan. 28, 1946, LHP.

"I have lectured more lectures": LH to Arna Bontemps, Apr. 30, 1946, LHP.

Things were "getting pretty hot": Kurt Weill to LH, Jan. 22, 1946, LHP.

"You see there is quite a lot": *Ibid.*

"I cannot be worried with anything": LH to Arna Bontemps, Apr. 23, 1946, LHP.

page 117

"most of all—you were just you": Mrs. Frank J. Civiletto to LH, May 11, 1946, LHP.

"YOU ARE A VERY GENEROUS MAN": Gwendolyn Brooks to LH, Aug. 24, 1945, LHP.

"This book is just about": *Chicago Defender*, Sept. 1, 1946.

page 118

"You can imagine how happy I was": Gwendolyn Brooks to LH, Mar. 28, 1944.

"I do not consider myself": LH, [Review of Gwendolyn Brooks, *A Street in Bronzeville*], Sept. 17, 1945, LHP 3418; published in *Opportunity* 23 (Fall 1945): 222.

"which would be ok with me": Ralph Ellison to Richard Wright, Feb. 1, 1948; copy courtesy of Michel Fabre.

page 119

"a good novel about *good* Negroes": LH, "It's About Time," May 22, 1946, LHP 554.

"Some people contend that when": LH, "My Collaborator: Kurt Weill," LHP 729.

"This is indeed a labor": Maxim Lieber to LH, Apr. 25, 1946, LHP.

"I have also tried": LH to Mercer Cook, Sept. 26, 1946, LHP.

page 120

"When Wallace Stevens visited the office": William R. Cole to author, interview, Nov. 8, 1981.

"my first more or less completely": LH to Blanche Knopf, Sept. 25, 1946, LHP.

"I do not believe there were ever": LH, "My Poems and Myself," July 12, 1945, LHP 735.

"Dictatorship of the Proletariat is too rigid": Loren Miller to LH, n.d. [c. 1941], LHP.

"an acquired surface knowledge may lead": *Chicago Defender*, Oct. 20, 1945.

page 121

"I already belong to more": LH to Max Yergan, Mar. 2, 1947, LHP.

page 122

"As if such freedom existed in Arkansas": *Chicago Defender*, June 1, 1946.

committees with "fine sounding names": Maxim Lieber to LH, Oct. 1, 1946, LHP.

"All of us think you have done": Elmer Rice to LH, July 26, 1946, LHP.
"The only way for colored to do": LH to Arna Bontemps, July 20, 1946, LHP.
"Shows, I do believe," he mourned: LH to Carl Van Vechten, Aug. 15, 1946, CVVP, Yale.
Jeffreys "looks like a junior Mae West": LH to Arna Bontemps, Jan. 2, 1947 [misdated 1946], LHP.

page 124
"an outspoken, militant, and atheistic communist": Andrew Simzak to Roscoe L. West, Jan. 28, 1947, copy in LHP ("Goodbye Christ" files).
"an extraordinary and engrossing evening": *Philadelphia Recorder*, Dec. 17, 1946.
"grotesquely disproportionate" to the action: *Philadelphia Inquirer*, Dec. 17, 1946.
they were decidedly "something else": Philadelphia *Daily News*, Dec. 17, 1946.
"an avalanche of Langston Hughes poetry": *Billboard*, Dec. 18, 1946.
"uneven and sometimes silly and banal": *Variety*, Dec. 18, 1946.
The Philadelphia run was "cataclysmic": Elmer Rice, *Minority Report: An Autobiography* (New York: Simon and Schuster, 1963), p. 412.
"changing and rechanging, yowling and howling": LH to Arna Bontemps, Dec. 22, 1946, LHP.

page 125
to find a room "miles away": Elmer Rice, *Minority Report*, p. 413.
"were all bent, bound, and determined to sing": LH to Amy Spingarn, Mar. 8, 1947, LHP.
"As yet nobody is big and bad and bold": LH to Arna Bontemps, Dec. 22, 1946, LHP.
"every play sells out": Elmer Rice, *Minority Report*, p. 412.
"I loved the show so much": *Ibid*.
"Me, I am resolved NOT to die": LH to Arna Bontemps, Dec. 22, 1946, LHP.
"as though I were on my way": Elmer Rice, *Minority Report*, p. 413.

page 126
"Believe it or not I even prayed": Clarence Muse to LH, Jan. 16, 1947, LHP.
a musical play "of magnificence and glory": *New York Times*, Jan. 10, 1947.
"an approach to American folk opera": *New York Journal-American*, Jan. 20, 1947.
"the most important step toward significantly": *New York Times*, Jan. 26, 1947.
"The Lord . . . does not intend": LH to Arna Bontemps, Jan. 2, 1947 [misdated 1946], LHP.
to "have long known and admired": LH to Oscar Emmett Williams, Mar. 8, 1947, LHP.

page 127
"The customers are rolling in and making": Elmer Rice to LH, Jan. 23, 1947, LHP.
"Into what slow, safe, solid": LH to Carl Van Vechten, n.d., CVVP, Yale.

6. Heart on the Wall

page 128
"the troubador, the people's poet": Atlanta *Daily World*, Feb. 9, 1947.
"a roly-poly guy with slick hair": Griffith J. Davis, "On Cockroaches and a Langston Hughes Class," 1947, LHP 75. Courtesy of Griffith J. Davis.
"there to observe the star shine": Juanita Toomer, "An Adventure in Star-Gazing," 1947, LHP 75.
"it would be occupied by at least seven": LH to Owen Dodson, Jan. 28, 1947, Countee Cullen-Harold Jackman Papers, Atlanta University.

"a rolling green sloping down": *Chicago Defender*, May 3, 1947.

"playing records from his collection": Harry Murphy to author, Dec. 21, 1982.

"not only has a soul that grows": Linwood Stevenson, "Chatting With Langston Hughes," Morehouse College *Maroon Tiger* (Jan.-Feb. 1947): 17–18.

"I am continually amazed at some": LH to Elizabeth Ames, Mar. 14, 1947, LHP.

page 130

"but the rest of Georgia": LH to Mary L. Shank, Apr. 2, 1947, LHP.

"if a white person and a colored person": *Chicago Defender*, Mar. 29, 1947.

"the discourteous and uncivilized treatment": LH to Robert K. Carr, Mar. 13, 1947, LHP.

"a poet of great promise": LH to Rosenwald Fund, n.d. (1947), LHP.

Hughes had "rediscovered himself": *Baltimore Afro-American*, Apr. 12, 1947.

Hughes had "matured in his talents": New York *Amsterdam News*, Apr. 5, 1947.

"penetrating, compassionate, mellow in his cynicism": *Christian Science Monitor*, May 10, 1947.

"the brevity and leanness" of many poems: *New York Times*, May 4, 1947.

page 131

"shallow, or false and contrived": New York *Herald-Tribune Weekly Book Review*, Aug. 31, 1947.

"the empty lyricisms of a man": *People's World*, Apr. 10, 1947.

"the poet's deep sense of reality": *New Masses* 63 (June 10, 1947): 26.

"me as well / Like stroke / Of lightning": LH, "Birth," *Fields of Wonder* (New York: Knopf, 1947), p. 9.

"There are / No clocks on the wall": LH, "End," *Fields of Wonder*, p. 28.

page 132

"I used to wonder / About living and dying": LH, "Border Line," *Fields of Wonder*, p. 13.

"Rocks and the firm roots of trees": LH, "Spirituals," *Fields of Wonder*, p. 113.

"The Negro / With the trumpet at his lips": LH, "Trumpet Player: 52nd Street," *Fields of Wonder*, p. 93.

page 133

"I think that with the publication": Arna Alexander Bontemps to author, interview, June 16, 1984.

"This week I'm hog-tied again": Arna Bontemps to LH, Oct. 15, 1945, LHP.

"once you contract in advance": Arna Bontemps to LH, Dec. 27 ("Xmas plus 2"), 1946, LHP.

page 134

"I think that there is little chance": Blanche Knopf to LH, Oct. 2, 1946, LHP.

"if he wishes . . . I will help him": LH to Blanche Knopf, Mar. 2, 1947, LHP.

became "apparently kinder mad" at losing: LH to Arna Bontemps, July 4, 1947, LHP.

"Most of the people in it": LH to Blanche Knopf, Aug. 26, 1947, LHP.

"I am sorry that you feel": Blanche Knopf to LH, Sept. 3, 1947, LHP.

"just about the *last* thing": LH to Maxim Lieber, Mar. 2, 1947, LHP.

"I do not see why a firm": LH to Arna Bontemps, Mar. 8, 1947, LHP.

page 135

"*Don't* be mad at ME": LH to Kurt Weill, Apr. 21, 1947, LHP.

"Like Pearl Bailey in *St. Louis Woman*": LH to Colston Leigh, Inc. (Beatrice R. Grant), Feb. 21, 1947, LHP.

"*I DO NOT WANT* any speaking": LH to Colston Leigh, Mar. 27, 1947, LHP.

"one of the richest and most interesting": LH to Rufus E. Clement, May 1947, LHP.

"a vivid, simple, lyric English": *New York Times Book Review*, June 15, 1947.

"a marvellously close rendering": New York *Herald-Tribune,* Aug. 3, 1947.

"Is it not a little soon for us": Blanche Knopf to LH, Sept. 3, 1947, LHP.

page 136

"Who's the engineer on the Freedom Train": LH, "Ballad of the Freedom Train," *The New Republic* (Sept. 1947): 27.

"I was wonderfully welcomed by Emerson Harper": Jan Meyerowitz to author, interview, Apr. 20, 1983.

page 137

"Musically it is my and my people's story": Jan Meyerowitz, "Why I Wrote 'The Barrier'," Oct. 1953, essay for Radio Hilversum, Holland, LHP 3681.

"Aunt Toy looked at the pages": Jan Meyerowitz to author, interview.

"I like what you've done": LH to Jan Meyerowitz, Sept. 4, 1947, LHP.

"quite good and genuinely moving": LH to Maxim Lieber, Sept. 7, 1947, LHP.

"The opera sounds like nothing": LH to Carl Van Vechten, Sept. 22, 1947, CVVP, Yale.

"While many of the lyrics": Elmer Rice to LH, July 26, 1946, LHP.

page 138

"CERTAINLY we stick by our guns": LH to Maxim Lieber, Sept. 20, 1947, LHP.

"Do you think Elmer has lost his mind?": LH to Maxim Lieber, Sept. 27, 1947, LHP.

"it no drunk me yet": LH to Toy Harper, Oct. 3, 1947, LHP.

page 139

sat at ease "with a strongly repressed twinkle": Edna Manley to LH, June 25 [1948?], LHP.

"MY NEW LOVE IS JAMAICA!": *Chicago Defender,* Nov. 29, 1947.

"I believe it's gigantic": Jan Meyerowitz to LH, Nov. 14, 1947, LHP.

"We *must do* efficient and urgent work": Jan Meyerowitz to LH, Dec. 12, 1947, LHP.

page 140

"the blasphemous utterances of one who sought": J. Edgar Hoover, "Secularism— Breeder of Crime," as cited in J. Richard Spann to LH, May 13, 1948, LHP.

"of a legally admissible character": J. Edgar Hoover to "SAC, New York City," Nov. 26, 1946, LH files, FBI.

"I am not a member of the Communist Party": *Suffolk County News,* Jan. 23, 1948.

"I am a writer," he insisted: Associated Negro Press dispatch, Feb. 13, 1948, LHP.

page 141

"If I were a loud speaking gentleman": LH to Urban League, Springfield, Ill. (George B. Winston), Feb. 18, 1948, LHP.

"Publicity is what has made me": LH to Garnett Ingram, Feb. 18, 1948, LHP.

"several references reflecting Hughes": J. Edgar Hoover to Urban League, Springfield, Ill. (George B. Winston), Dec. 31, 1947, LH files, FBI.

"one of the most notorious propagandists": " 'HATE CHRIST'is the Slogan of the Communists," Gerald L.K. Smith circular, in Sen. Joseph H. Ball to J. Edgar Hoover, May 10, 1947, LH files, FBI.

"It is definitely a race war": Olive Lindsay Wakefield to "Mrs. Hoerter" in Olive Wakefield to LH, Feb. 23, 1948, LHP.

"It is heart-warming to know": LH to Olive Wakefield Lindsay Feb. 21, 1948.

page 142

"stand up for the traditional": LH to Urban League, Springfield, Ill. (George B. Winston), Mar. 3, 1948, LHP.

"really an agent of a foreign power": Akron *Beacon Journal,* Mar. 6, 1948.

"I was amazed to see a Communist": *Congressional Record: Proceedings and Debates of the 80th Congress, 2nd Session,* Apr. 1, 1948, p. 2.

"an unmitigated liar" and a "dope": LH to Horace Mann Bond, Apr. 30, 1948, LHP.

"a direct attack on the Negro people": *Palo Alto Times,* Apr. 17, 1948.

page 143

"a twinkling, goodhumored man in his early forties": *Palo Alto Times,* Apr. 22, 1948.

"a very bewildered man at the moment": *Monterey Peninsula Herald,* May 3, 1948.

"If the elderly radio commentators": *Los Angeles Tribune,* Apr. 10, 1948.

"I don't think it is I": *Palo Alto Times,* Apr. 22, 1948.

"Certainly I have no especially timely": LH to M.D. Babcock, Apr. 25, 1948, LHP.

"I am sure you could not have done it": Roger N. Baldwin to LH, Apr. 28, 1948, LHP.

"the great Negro poet whom I met": LH to Noël Sullivan, Apr. 10, 1948, NSP, Bancroft.

"My LAST engagement—Thank God A-Mighty!": LH to Toy Harper, May 16, 1948, LHP.

"Gerald L.K. Smith, the Klan and others": *Chicago Defender,* May 15, 1948.

page 144

"Certainly I agree with you": LH to Colston Leigh, Inc. (Anna D. McNeil), May 24, 1948, LHP.

7. On Solid Ground

page 146

"I would rather have a kitchenette": Cited in Constance Maxon, "Lang: A Biography," ms, n.d., Langston Hughes Memorial Library, Lincoln University, Pa.

I am indebted to Mr. Kenneth P. Neilsen for several of the details concerning the purchase of the property at 20 East 127th Street by Langston Hughes and Emerson and Toy Harper.

"there is even a beautiful lawn": LH to W.G. Still, June 14, 1948, William Grant Still Papers, University of Arkansas, Fayetteville.

page 147

"She was almost fanatical about cleanliness": Nathaniel White to author, interview, Dec. 5, 1980.

"Langston's suite was pleasant": *Ibid.*

"No children ever lived in the house": Griffith J. Davis to Akiba Sullivan Harper, Apr. 3, 1987. Courtesy of Griffith J. Davis and Akiba Sullivan Harper.

page 148

"Dear Mr. Hughes," one lady wrote: [Name withheld] to LH, June 18, 1948, LHP.

"Thank you so much for your nice note": LH to [name withheld], n.d. [1949], LHP.

"Toy was like a tigress with a cub": Frances Wills Thorpe to author, interview, June 19, 1986.

"Once we were at the table": Butler Henderson to author, interview, Nov. 2, 1987.

page 149

"Never married, but once reported engaged": LH to Arna Bontemps, May 2, 1946, LHP.

"He was certainly very friendly": Harry Murphy to author, Dec. 21, 1982.

"He was definitely curious about what": Bruce Nugent to author, interview, June 10, 1984.

"Langston may have been bisexual": Frances Wills Thorpe to author, interview.

"Mr. Poole, I see that you got her": Raoul Abdul to author, interview.

page 150

"The little hound lit out": LH to Arna Bontemps, Dec. 16, 1948, LHP.

"I needed treatments for alcoholism": Gwyn Clark to LH, n.d. [Aug. 5, 1947], LHP.

"Kit was often drunk and very ugly": Nathaniel White to author, interview.

"You may see me holler": LH, "Life is Fine," *One-Way Ticket*, p. 39.

page 151

"I have completed a new book": LH to Arna Bontemps, Sept. 14, 1948, LHP.

page 152

"Good morning daddy! / Ain't you heard": LH, "Dream Boogie," *Montage of a Dream Deferred* (New York: Henry Holt, 1951), p. 3.

page 153

"What happens to a dream deferred?": LH, "Harlem," *Montage*, p. 71.

"This poem on contemporary Harlem": LH, *Montage*, n.p.

"That is where Bop comes from": *Chicago Defender*, Nov. 19, 1949.

"With mounting excitement and interest": Carl Van Vechten to LH, Oct. 11, 1948, LHP.

it was "super—perhaps your strongest . . . expression": Arna Bontemps to LH, Oct. 2, 1948, LHP.

"a re-flowering of the Renaissance": Arna Bontemps to LH, Oct. 13, 1948, LHP.

page 154

"Looks kinder hopeless," he confessed: LH to Arna Bontemps, July 9, 1948, LHP.

"Home of happy feet! / Harlem's Hall of Joy": See LH, "Swing Time at the Savoy," July 9–28, 1948, LHP 3717–3723.

"there were many which I had finished": John F. Matheus, "Langston Hughes as Translator," *College Language Association Journal* 9 (June 1968): 325–326.

page 155

"a labor of art and love": LH to Maxim Lieber, July 10, 1948, LHP.

"We ought to be smart and make use": LH to *Chicago Defender* (Charles Browning), Oct. 6, 1948, LHP.

"My temperament at this moment": LH to Maxim Lieber, Nov. 7, 1948, LHP.

"I DO NOT BELIEVE THIS HERE ANTHOLOGY": LH to Arna Bontemps, Sept. 14, 1948, LHP.

"whom one drop of white blood": LH to Arna Bontemps, Aug. 21, 1948, LHP.

the book would be, "in short, exclusive": Louis Simpson to LH, Oct. 18, 1948, LHP.

"setting forth very clearly": LH to Arna Bontemps, Aug. 21, 1948, LHP.

"neither are we and that we are using": LH to Arna Bontemps, Aug. 5, 1948, LHP.

It was "thrilling to receive mail": Harold M. Telemaque to LH, July 8, 1948, LHP.

"you are my favorite American . . . poet": LH to Carl Sandburg, Aug. 2, 1948, LHP.

"Your letter," he wrote Hughes: Carl Sandburg to LH, Aug. 3, 1948, LHP.

page 156

"flabbergasted and amazed at the richness": LH to Arna Bontemps, Feb. 26, 1949, LHP.

"We are all so broke here": LH to Arna Bontemps, Jan. 9, 1949, LHP.

page 157

"We all admired Kurt Weill": Joe Sherman to author, interview, Nov. 13, 1987.

"I WARN YOU ONE MORE TIME": LH to Arna Bontemps, Dec. 17, 1948, LHP.

"the U.S.'s leading Negro composer": *Time* 51 (June 7, 1948): 55.

"The recognized opera companies in America": W.G. Still to LH, Feb. 19, 1947, William Grant Still Papers, University of Arkansas.

page 158

"It must, of course, be as integrated as possible": LH to W.G. Still, Jan. 18, 1937, William Grant Still Papers.

"this seems a very *small* sum": LH to W.G. Still, Oct. 29, 1946, William Grant Still Papers.

"They never heard of make-up": *Time* 51 (June 7, 1948): 55.

"Really, you are unique among collaborators": W.G. Still to LH, Mar. 15, 1945, LHP.

"I am not prepared to compromise": W.G. Still to LH, Nov. 27, 1948, LHP.

"As I remember," Hughes agreed: LH to W.G. Still, July 7, 1948, William Grant Still Papers.

"This problem is further evidence": LH to Maxim Lieber, July 10, 1948, LHP.

"Before Langston Hughes left for war-torn Madrid": Verna Arvey, "New American Opera," *New York Times,* Jan. 23, 1938.

"a major change had to be made": Verna Arvey, *In One Lifetime* (Fayetteville: Univ. of Arkansas Press, 1984), p. 97.

page 159

"It is the most beautiful aria": LH to Herbert Small, n.d., LHP.

"Max, why don't you take": Jan Meyerowitz to author, interview, Apr. 15, 1983.

"Both of my opera people": LH to Arna Bontemps, Dec. 2, 1948, LHP.

"a very beautiful job of bookmaking": LH to Blanche Knopf, Dec. 1, 1948, LHP.

"a very fine looking book": LH to Arna Bontemps, Dec. 17, 1948, LHP.

for "una edición espléndida": Nicolás Guillén to LH, Jan. 28, 1949, LHP.

"a fine and rewarding anthology": *New York Times,* Jan. 8, 1949.

page 160

"My feeling is that they are still": LH to Arna Bontemps, Jan. 28, 1949, LHP.

"one wonders if this was a gesture": *Saturday Review of Literature* 32 (Mar. 19, 1949): 16.

"I think Jean Starr has done lost": LH to Arna Bontemps, Mar. 28, 1949, LHP.

"whether for or against us": Arna Bontemps to LH, note on copy of Bontemps to *Saturday Review of Literature,* Mar. 3, 1949, LHP.

"Never before . . . had literature been so alive": A.J. Seymour to LH, *British Guiana Chronicle,* May 1, 1950.

"It is a waste of postage": Effie Lee Newsome to LH, Aug. 4, 1948, LHP.

"I've suffered a good deal": Jessie Fauset to LH, June 9, 1949, LHP.

"You have been the Dean": Bruce McM. Wright to LH, July 4, 1948, LHP.

"I wasn't writing poetry anymore": James Baldwin to author, interview, Dec. 12, 1985.

page 161

"With so many fine poets among your race": *Voices: Quarterly of Poetry* (Harold Vinal) to LH, Feb. 2, 1949, LHP.

"stale, flat, and spiritless": *Baltimore Afro-American,* Jan. 15, 1949. See also J. Saunders Redding, "Old Forms, Old Rhythms, Old Words," *Saturday Review of Literature* 32 (Jan. 22, 1949): 24.

Deploring this "so-called poetry": *Pittsburgh Courier,* Feb. 5, 1949.

"I for one should like to see": *Nation* 168 (Jan. 15, 1949): 80.

"Mr. Hughes is a highly sophisticated individual": *The New Yorker* 24 (Jan. 29, 1949): 72.

"The ultimate meaning, the subtler vision": New York *Herald-Tribune,* Jan. 9, 1949.

"faults same as mine at times": LH to Associated Negro Press (Frank Marshall Davis), Aug. 9, 1948, LHP.

page 162

"Here I sit / With my shoes mismated": LH, "Bad Morning," *One-Way Ticket,* p. 98.

"Who can purge my heart": LH, "Song for Billie Holiday," *One-Way Ticket,* pp. 47–48.

"I could've died for love": LH, "Life is Fine," *One-Way Ticket,* p. 39.

page 163

"a flashback to the twenties": LH to Arna Bontemps, Jan. 9, 1949, LHP.

"just about the most amazing campus": LH to Carl Van Vechten, Feb. 1949, CVVP, Yale.

"Have you heard the awful story": LH to Arna Bontemps, Sept. 21, 1948, LHP.

page 164

"I was amazed": LH to Dorothy Porter, Feb. 19, 1949, LHP.

"All that I have ever tried to do": Robert Hemenway, *Zora Neale Hurston: A Literary Biography* (Urbana, Ill.: Univ. of Illinois Press, 1977), p. 322.

"He was a hit," one teacher later remembered: Robert Ericson to author, interview, June 22, 1981.

"Mr. Hughes seemed perfectly at ease": "Excerpts from 10th Grade English Papers," Univ. of Chicago Laboratory School, 1949, LHP 237.

page 165

"people who recite poetry in a far-away voice": LH to Arna Bontemps, May 2, 1946, LHP.

"He was an easy man": Gwendolyn Brooks, *Report from Part One* (Detroit: Broadside Press, 1972), p. 70.

"Children are not nearly so resistant": LH, "Children and Poetry," July, 1946, LHP 239.

"a psycho-therapeutic value in that": LH, "Three Months at the Lab School," May 23, 1949, LHP 3778.

"He must have been nearly fifty": Cathline Iatser Ericson to author, interview, June 22, 1981.

page 166

"Seven o'clock in the morning": LH to Arna Bontemps, May 27, 1949, LHP.

"The race is a-rising!": LH to Johnson Publishing Co. (Ben Burns), Mar. 15, 1949, LHP.

"an idiom personal to the composer": *New York Sun,* Apr. 1, 1949.

"When I saw that bathrobe": Nathaniel White to LH, Apr. 11, 1949, LHP.

"Composers and librettists usually fall out": LH to William Worthy, May 27, 1952, LHP.

"a great success . . . but the New York critics": W.G. Still, "Communism in Music," typescript of lecture at San Jose, Calif., 1953, William Grant Still Papers.

"a man listed in 'Red Channels' ": W.G. Still to Sen. Richard M. Nixon, Jan. 3, 1951, William Grant Still Papers.

page 167

"RED VISITORS CAUSE RUMPUS": *Life* 26 (Apr. 4, 1949): 39–42.

page 168

"I am a bit weary of six months": LH to Olive Lindsay Wakefield, July 19, 1948, LHP.

Deploring the "anti-Negro, anti-Jewish": LH to Moe Gale, Inc. (Mitchell Benson), July 26, 1948, LHP.

"in breaking up the growing unity": LH to Young Women's Christian Association, Dec. 2, 1948, LHP.

"Make certain we furnish this outfit": "Director's Notation," n.d., LH files, FBI.

page 169

a "new report" on Hughes: J. Edgar Hoover to "SAC, New York," Dec. 7, 1948, LH files, FBI.

"I got a good view of the man": *Chicago Defender,* Sept. 20, 1947.

The liberal is "a nice man who acts decently": *Chicago Defender,* May 21, 1949.

page 170

"I cannot conceive of a Conference": National Council of the Arts, Sciences and Professions (Maxine Wood) to LH, Jan. 4, 1949, LHP.

"KNOW YOU ARE WITH US": National Council of the Arts, Sciences and Professions to LH, Oct. 13, 1948, LHP.

"KINDLY DO NOT USE HIS NAME": Nathaniel White to National Council of the Arts, Sciences and Professions, Oct. 14 [1948], LHP.

"Your help was invaluable": Kappo Phelan *et al.* to LH, Mar. 30, 1949, LHP.

"The strangest things are happening": LH to Elizabeth Ames, June 26, 1950, LHP.

"members of the American Politburo": *New York Times*, Oct. 15, 1949.

page 171

"my feelings being more emotional than scientific": LH to Benjamin J. Davis, Jr., Nov. 9, 1948, LHP.

"the most important thing happening in America": *Chicago Defender*, Feb. 5, 1949.

this "very moving and splendid column": Communist Party of New York State (Sam Coleman) to LH, Feb. 9, 1949, LHP.

"Your support of the Spanish Refugee Appeal": Spanish Refugee Appeal (Olin Downes) to LH, Feb. 23, 1949, LHP.

"the greatest concert attraction in the world": *Chicago Defender*, Sept. 24, 1949.

"TO ME AS TO MILLIONS OF OTHERS": LH to W.E.B. Du Bois, Feb. 23, 1948, WEBDP, UM(A).

page 172

"We squeezed perhaps a hundred people": Gwendolyn Brooks, *Report from Part One*, p. 70.

"Meshing Langston's lyric, poetic style": Joe Sherman to author, interview, June 17, 1986.

"To my mind . . . Hughes was the most musical": Elie Siegmeister to author, interview, Mar. 22, 1984.

page 173

"to enjoy your eminence": Bruce McM. Wright to LH, Jan. 19, 1950, LHP.

"Nobody knows what an *orchestrina* is": LH to Melvin B. Tolson, June 18, 1949, LHP.

the first one to arrive . . . was "God awful!": LH to *Voices* (Howard Vinal), Sept. 24, 1949, LHP.

"most intelligent and very helpful": LH to Maxim Lieber, June 22, 1949, LHP.

"a really fine office to deal with": LH to Arna Bontemps, Dec. 9, 1949, LHP.

"You are a model among authors": Simon and Schuster, Inc. (Maria Leiper) to LH, Nov. 29, 1949, LHP.

"Some of the Simple touches": LH to Arna Bontemps, Dec. 2, LHP.

"It seems to me," Langston wrote: LH to Arna Bontemps, Sept. 7, 1949, LHP.

page 174

"It's all so familiar": LH to Maxim Lieber, Aug. 29, 1949, LHP.

"I would be delighted to remain": LH to Colston Leigh, Inc., Dec. 3, 1949, LHP.

" 'hot' for stories with Negro . . . themes": LH to Blanche Knopf, Oct. 17, 1949, LHP.

"our keen—and unanimous—interest": Maria Leiper to LH, Oct. 17, 1949, LHP.

page 175

his "first full-length sustained poem": LH to Blanche Knopf, Oct. 31, 1949, LHP.

"Now that we've settled in a big house": LH to Blanche Knopf, Nov. 6, 1949, LHP.

"I don't think we should do": Blanche Knopf to LH, Nov. 10, 1949, LHP.

"and devote himself to writing": *Baltimore Afro-American*, Jan. 21, 1950.

page 176

hardly "an 'artistic' success" on Broadway: LH to Felix Brentano, n.d. (1949), LHP.

"I had sworn never to have anything": LH, "From the Blues to an Opera Libretto," *New York Times*, Jan. 15, 1950.

"the first white American to interpret": *New York Times*, Jan. 7, 1950.

"one of the strongest" in a long time: *New York Times,* Jan. 19, 1950.

it was "a distinguished production": New York *Herald-Tribune,* Jan. 20, 1950.

"it would be difficult to imagine": *The New Yorker,* Jan. 28, 1950.

"Langston told me," Meyerowitz remembered: Jan Meyerowitz to author, interview, Apr. 15, 1983.

page 178

followed by "my record spring!": LH to Simon and Schuster, Inc. (Maria Leiper), Mar. 23, 1950, LHP.

"You've written a masterpiece": Carl Van Vechten to LH, quoted in LH to Simon and Schuster, Inc. (Maria Leiper), Mar. 30, 1950, LHP.

called the revision . . . "a miracle": *Ibid.*

"Our difficulty has been": Simon and Schuster, Inc. (Maria Leiper) to LH, Nov. 2, 1949, LHP.

"We have been entirely convinced": Simon and Schuster, Inc. (Maria Leiper) to LH, Apr. 10, 1950, LHP.

it was "better than a dozen . . . studies": *New York Times,* Apr. 20, 1950.

"I don't know anything that is so candid": Prentiss Taylor to LH, May 15, 1950, LHP.

page 179

Simple was "the voice of the American Negro": *The New Republic* 123 (Sept. 4, 1950): 20.

"a literature of ideas, and ideals": Bernard Rucker to LH, May 9, 1950, LHP.

"this gentleman of color, who can't get a cup": *Chicago Defender,* Apr. 15, 1950.

"—or at all": Maria Leiper to Simon and Schuster, Inc., July 5, 1950, LHP.

a "terribly disturbed" Leiper: Maria Leiper to Simon and Schuster, Nov. 28, 1950, LHP.

"WONDERFUL about Gwendolyn Brooks": LH to Arna Bontemps, May 1, 1950, LHP.

"a very accomplished poet indeed": LH, "Name, Race, and Gift in Common," *Voices* (Winter 1950): 55–56.

then penned a "glowing tribute": Gwendolyn Brooks to LH, May 15, 1950, LHP.

"For almost ten years now": *Chicago Defender,* May 13, 1950.

page 180

"You did a fine job here": LH to John W. Parker, Aug. 2, 1949, LHP.

"I'd rather like to see": LH to Alfred A. Knopf, Inc. (William Koshland), Mar. 15, 1949, LHP.

"ALL MY LOVE AND SYMPATHY": LH to Mrs. Kurt Weill (Lotte Lenya), Apr. 3, 1950, LHP.

"There is money for hate": *Common Ground* (M. Margaret Anderson) to LII, Apr. 20, 1950, LHP.

"the stature it gave the magazine": *Common Ground* (M. Margaret Anderson) to LH, Apr. 24, 1950, LHP.

page 182

"The social high point of my summer": LH to Mrs. E.R. Alexander, Sept. 18, 1950, LHP.

only to be "THUNDERSTRUCK" to realize: LH to New York *Amsterdam News* (S.W. Garlington), July 23, 1950, LHP.

"in the sense that I was looking": Liska March Cracovaner to author, interview, Feb. 14, 1987.

"sock" score and . . . Hughes's "thoughtful lyrics": *Variety,* Aug. 1, 1950.

"One show is enough!": LH to Noël Sullivan, Sept. 3, 1950, NSP, Bancroft.

"My whole creative output has been": LH to NAACP, Baltimore Branch (Daniel E. Byrd), Sept. 20, 1950, LHP.

"FOR NEGRO ACTORS TO PERFORM IN THEATRES": LH to NAACP, Baltimore Branch (Lillian M. Jackson), Sept. 29, 1950, LHP.

a "BOMB SHELL OPERA": Associated Negro Press release, "The Barrier," n.d., LHP 121.

page 184

called the show "altogether disappointing": *Washington Post,* Sept. 27, 1950.

its "simplicity and directness" had been lost: LH to Michael Meyerberg and Joel Spector, Sept. 27, 1950, LHP 121.

"Musically, it was very bad": Jan Meyerowitz to author, interview.

"Muriel and I thought Tibbett fine": Dick Campbell to author, interview, Oct. 29, 1987.

his supporters . . . were "a sick lot": Arna Bontemps to LH, June 8, 1949, LHP.

page 185

"I can lean on this bar": LH, *Simple Speaks His Mind* (New York: Simon and Schuster, 1950), p. 178.

"Dazz L.H.'s musical sense buttin' in": Ezra Pound to LH, Oct. 2, 1950, LHP.

"I have found through many years": LH to Dorothy Porter, Jan. 13, 1949, LHP.

"overcivilized and as remote from lynching": *New York Times,* Nov. 3, 1950.

"little poignancy, little heartbreak": *New York Daily News,* Nov. 3, 1950.

"There is magnificence in it": *Daily Compass,* Nov. 3, 1950.

"Such is show business": LH to Lillian Hughes, Nov. 8, 1950, LHP.

page 186

"These Broadway producers are born blackmailers": Jan Meyerowitz to author, interview.

"a charming little thing of a sort": *Daily Compass,* Sept. 22, 1950.

page 187

"too 'atmospheric' " and like an oratorio: Marginalia, "Pennsylvania Stars," 2nd draft, Sept. 1950, LHP 848.

"I can see now," Siegmeister reasoned: Elie Siegmeister to author, interview.

"I am a literary sharecropper": LH to Arna Bontemps, Dec. 27, 1950, LHP.

"If he can take that long": *Ibid.*

page 188

"Do some more like that": Arna Bontemps to LH, Dec. 30, 1949, LHP.

"This Here / Is A Lean Year": LH to Robert and Cathline Ericson, Dec. 16, 1950; courtesy of Robert and Cathline Ericson.

"Langston's Lamenting / Loud an' Long": Ezra Pound to LH, Dec. 20, 1950, LHP.

"I hope I'm not electrocuted": LH to Arna Bontemps, Dec. 27, 1950, LHP.

8. In Warm Manure

page 189

"I'm still a literary sharecropper": LH to Arna Bontemps, Aug. 17, 1952, LHP.

"Poetry is rhythm—and, through rhythm": LH, "Ten Ways To Use Poetry In Teaching," *College Language Association Journal* 11 (June 1968): 275.

page 190

"certain unfortunate state wide publicity": John W. Davis to LH, Feb. 13, 1951, LHP.

"YOUR BOOK DARKWATER GREATLY INFLUENCED MY YOUTH": LH to W.E.B. Du Bois, Feb. 23, 1951, WEBDP, UM(A).

"the colored children ceased to hear my name": *The Autobiography of W.E.B. Du Bois,* ed. Herbert Aptheker (New York: International Publishers, 1968), p. 395.

"since I do not like to assume responsibilities": LH to National Council of the Arts, Sciences and Professions, Mar. 16, 1951, LHP.

page 191

"I am ashamed that it was my letter": Philadelphia Fellowship Commission (William Gardner Smith) to LH, Mar. 7, 1951, LHP.

"If my little book, *The First Book of Negroes*": Franklin Watts and Helen Hoke Watts, "Publisher's Note about *The First Book of Negroes* and Langston Hughes, its author," n.d., LHP 397.

"That we have merited the scourge": Noël Sullivan to LH, Sept. 20, 1950, LHP.

"I will NEVER take another advance": LH to Arna Bontemps, May 1, 1951, LHP.

"A piece of the pure gold of literature": *British Weekly,* Mar. 8, 1951.

the book "enlists sympathy for the whole": *Times Literary Supplement* (London), Mar. 23, 1951.

page 192

"should really be a novel in overall form": LH to Simon and Schuster (Maria Leiper), Apr. 9, 1951, LHP.

"the new novel—and NOVEL it will be": LH to Maxim Lieber, Apr. 16, 1951, LHP.

that he "has FINISHED his novel!": LH to Arna Bontemps, May 1, 1951, LHP.

"His images are again quick": New York *Herald-Tribune,* Mar. 11, 1951.

"a melange of self-pity, grief and defeatism": *Pittsburgh Courier,* Mar. 10, 1951.

to lapse "into a facile sentimentality": *New York Times Book Review,* May 6, 1951.

"will be as dead as the Egyptian mummies": Maxim Lieber to LH, May 7, 1951, LHP.

"Am glad to git some po'try": Ezra Pound to LH, Mar. 13, 1951, LHP.

page 193

"*The Collected Poems* make a dune-like mass": William Carlos Williams, "Carl Sandburg's Complete Poems," *Poetry* 17 (Sept. 1951): 351.

"Your dedication to poetry": Arna Bontemps to LH, June 11, 1951, LHP.

"though we meet seldom": LH to Marianne Moore, Jan. 19, 1951, LHP.

"The poems are really beautiful": LH to Arna Bontemps, June 9, 1951, LHP.

"Your hero is as charming as ever": Simon and Schuster (Maria Leiper) to LH, June 6, 1951, LHP.

page 194

"Why, Ah can not believe ma ears!": LH to Arna Bontemps, June 9, 1951, LHP.

"I am as happy in the city": *Chicago Defender,* Sept. 1, 1951.

"I know the poem says": *Chicago Defender,* July 5, 1952.

page 195

joined Hughes "in renouncing literary sharecropping": Arna Bontemps to LH, May 6, 1951, LHP.

"I'd love to do it with you": LH to Arna Bontemps, Dec. 3, 1951, LHP.

"The contracts Max got for me": LH to Arna Bontemps, Oct. 11, 1951, LHP.

"Langston and I got along well": Ivan von Auw, Jr. to author, interview, Mar. 21, 1987.

page 196

"Somebody in Washington wants to put": *Chicago Defender,* Oct. 6, 1951.

"It was of the stuff that contributed": National Committee to Defend Dr. W.E.B. Du Bois (Alice Citron) to LH, Nov. 21, 1951, LHP.

page 197

the "traitorous and corrosive quality": Charles A. Willoughby, *Shanghai Conspiracy* (New York: E.P. Dutton, 1952), p. 256.

"Since it is an ironic poem": LH to E.P. Dutton (Sherman Baker), Dec. 29, 1951, LHP.

"It looks as if reactionary whites": LH to Mrs. L.B. Smith, Mar. 9, 1952, LHP.

page 198

"A major portion of my income": LH to National Council of American-Soviet Friendship (Richard Morford), May 27, 1952, LHP.

"Negro writers, being black, have always": LH to Authors League of America, Feb. 6, 1952, LHP.

"I would like to see every Negro": *Chicago Defender*, Mar. 31, 1951.

page 199

"What the NAACP is doing benefits": *Chicago Defender*, Dec. 8, 1951.

"When I said that I was not used": *Chicago Defender*, Apr. 26, 1952.

"We are delighted to have you": *Chicago Defender*, Dec. 6, 1952.

page 200

"Every colored college I visited": LH to Randolph Edmonds, Mar. 9, 1952, LHP.

"There is nothing wrong in Negro groups": *Chicago Defender*, Jan. 20, 1951.

"We have a rich folk heritage": Cleveland *Plain Dealer*, Feb. 9, 1952.

above all his "economy of words": *New York Times Book Review*, Mar. 23, 1952.

found Hughes "very very good": *Nation* 174 (Apr. 26, 1952): 408.

"something more, something deeper and darker": Washington, D.C. *Afro-American*, Apr. 22, 1952.

Ellison was "a protégé of mine": LH to Ulysses Boykin, Apr. 17, 1952, LHP.

"We feel these days": Fanny and Ralph Ellison to LH, Apr. 2, 1952, LHP.

page 201

"DEAR FANNY (AND RALPH)": LH to Ralph and Fanny Ellison, n.d., LHP.

"I've given it some thought": LH to Arthur B. Spingarn, June 20, 1951, LHP.

"but few of his friends do": Ralph Ellison to Richard Wright, Jan. 21, 1953; copy courtesy of Michel Fabre.

"but it is my determination": LH to Wesley Collier, Apr. 17, 1953, LHP.

a novel "that will make you shake": *Chicago Defender*, Mar. 29, 1952.

"deep, beautifully written, provocative and moving": *Chicago Defender*, Feb. 28, 1953.

page 202

"Langston was a lot of fun": Ralph Ellison to author, interview, Apr. 30, 1983.

"folks who want a parole": LH to Arna Bontemps, July 16, 1952, LHP.

"Where, whence, and how come": LH to Harold Ober, Inc. (Ivan von Auw, Jr.), July 1, 1952, LHP.

page 203

"the most cussed and discussed book": LH, "Introduction" to Harriet Beecher Stowe, *Uncle Tom's Cabin* (New York: Dodd, Mead, 1952), n.p.

"I am terribly distressed about what": Elie Siegmeister to LH, Jan. 3, 1952, LHP.

"Apparently . . . you are quite content": Elie Siegmeister to LH, July 17, 1952, LHP.

Hughes "triumphed in his portion": *New York Times*, Sept. 19, 1952.

"a kind of Negro success story": LH to Harold Ober, Inc. (Ivan von Auw, Jr.), Aug. 20, 1952, LHP.

"White folks (and Ralph)," he boasted: LH to Arna Bontemps, Sept. 17, 1952, LHP.

"I wish it was a novel!": LH to Harold Ober, Inc. (Ivan von Auw, Jr.), Nov. 10, 1952, LHP.

page 204

"the largest and most appreciative . . . audiences": LH to Robert C. Weaver, Nov. 1, 1952, LHP.

"truly the finest book of its kind": Mary Elizabeth Vroman to LH, Nov. 11, 1952, LHP.

"rather appalling in some respects": Harold Ober, Inc. (Ivan von Auw, Jr.) to LH, July 3, 1952, LHP.

page 205

"the sad fact is that for most people": Alfred A. Knopf, Inc. (Herbert Weinstock) to LH, Sept. 25, 1952, LHP.

"mildly interesting," dull really: LH to Arna Bontemps, Feb. 8, 1953, LHP.

"with her feeling for the folk idiom": LH to Arna Bontemps, Feb. 18, 1953, in Nichols, *Letters*, p. 302.

page 206

his "disgust for the black hands": Richard Gibson and James Baldwin, "Two Protests Against Protest," *Perspectives USA* 2 (Winter 1953): 89–100.

"which must be one of the books": LH to Arna Bontemps, Mar. 7, 1953, in Nichols, *Letters*, p. 305.

"I didn't expect you to write": LH to James Baldwin, July 25, 1953, LHP.

"trying to leap fences and get out": LH to Arna Bontemps, Mar. 7, 1953, LHP.

page 207

"If you are a Negro": LH, "How to Be a Bad Writer (In Ten Easy Lessons)," *Harlem Quarterly* 1 (Spring 1950): 13.

"This man disgusts": Michel Fabre, *The Unfinished Quest of Richard Wright* (New York: Morrow, 1973), p. 602.

"an average, succesful business man": (Brandeis University) *Justice*, Feb. 12, 1953.

page 209

"in the field of literary-race relations": LH to Johnson Publications (*Ebony* magazine), Nov. 27, 1949, LHP.

"The victory is not his alone": LH to Johnson Publications (Dale Murphy), Nov. 12, 1952, LHP.

"After I talked with Langston": Lloyd K. Garrison to author, interview, Oct. 7, 1987.

page 210

"AS AN AMERICAN CITIZEN": LH to Sen. Joseph R. McCarthy, Mar. 22, 1953, copy, "[Autobiographical and biographical notes. 'Red-baiting']," (material pertaining to Hughes's alleged communist and atheist activities, 1941–1963), LHP 81.

"YOU ARE DIRECTED TO APPEAR": Roy Cohn to LH, Mar. 23, 1953, LHP 81.

"No words—and certainly no money": LH to Frank D. Reeves, Mar. 29, 1953, LHP. I am indebted to Faith Berry, author of *Langston Hughes: Before and Beyond Harlem* (Westport, Connecticut: Lawrence Hill, 1984) for allowing me to listen to a tape-recording of an interview between her and Frank D. Reeves (since deceased) concerning this episode.

page 212

"You see . . . once the dogs are set": Thomas C. Reeves, *The Life and Times of Joe McCarthy: A Biography* (New York: Stein and Day, 1982), p. 485.

page 213

"I refuse to answer on the grounds": LH, "[Autobiographical and biographical notes]," LHP 81.

"Poets who write mostly about love": LH, "Statement to the Senate Permanent Subcommittee on Investigations," n.d., LHP 81.

page 215

[Was there] "ever a period of time": "Copy of Transcript: State Department Information Program (Information Centers). Senate Permanent Subcommittee on Investigation of the Subcommittee on Government Operation," Washington, D.C., Mar. 26, 1953. Additional dialogue taken from "Closing Testimony of Langston Hughes . . . with Senators McCarthy and McClellan, as taken from a radio broadcast," in LHP 81.

page 217
" 'Your honery'," Simple elsewhere had threatened: LH, *Simple Speaks His Mind*, p. 211.
page 218
"When he got back to New York": John Horton to author, interview, Nov. 29, 1986.
page 219
"and every other amendment": *New York Times*, Mar. 27, 1953.
"I am a Jew": *New York Times*, Mar. 25, 1953.
page 220
"The committee's fat / Smug, almost secure": LH, "Un-American Investigators," *The Panther and the Lash: Poems of Our Times* (New York: Alfred A. Knopf, 1967), p. 76.
page 221
"Your handling of yourself": Lloyd K. Garrison to LH, Apr. 24, 1953, LHP.
"their purpose in such a discussion": *Worker*, Apr. 26, 1953.
"managed to speak something of his mind": New York *Amsterdam News*, Apr. 4, 1953.
"a more cooperative witness": *Time* 61 (Apr. 6, 1953): 29.
"We want to help in any way": Simon and Schuster (Maria Leiper) to LH, Apr. 7, 1953, LHP.
"clear cut and convincing": Charles S. Johnson to LH, Apr. 18, 1953, LHP.
to aid "your gallant fight": Amy Spingarn to LH, Apr. 2, 1953, LHP.
"I would appreciate it very much": LH to Spanish Refugee Appeal of the Joint Anti-Fascist Committee (Pauline Royce), Dec. 30, 1953, LHP.
page 222
"I have been accused of such membership": LH to William J. McWilliams, Jan. 28, 1954, LHP.

9. Out From Under

page 223
"I'm homesick for your valley": LH to Noël Sullivan, n.d. [Dec. 1952], NSP, Bancroft.
as "an informal masterpiece worthy": *Book-of-the-Month News* (June 1953): 7.
"more brilliant, more skillfully written": *New York Times Book Review*, May 31, 1953.
"I'd not thought of it before myself": LH to Benjamin Lehman, July 27, 1953, LHP.
page 224
"The relaxed, witty prose of a matured . . . Hughes": *St. Louis Post Dispatch*, June 16, 1953.
"I know of no anthropological monograph": Mozell C. Hill to LH, Feb. 18, 1954, LHP.
"the 'arty' degeneracy of writers like Richard Wright": *Masses and Mainstream* 6 (Sept. 1953): 58.
"and it is about time": *Chicago Defender*, Oct. 10, 1953.
"My stomach is actually aching": Loften Mitchell to LH, Sept. 7, 1953, LHP.
"but from long experience": LH to Columbia University (Russell Potter), May 17, 1953, LHP.
"most studios won't touch it": Harold Ober, Inc. (Ivan von Auw) to LH, May 12, 1953, LHP.
"I only wish it weren't as controversial": Lewis F. Lengfeld to Simon and Schuster (Richard Simon), July 8, 1953, LHP.

page 225

"How public—like a Frog": Emily Dickinson, ["I'm Nobody! Who are you?"], no. 288, in Thomas H. Johnson, ed., *The Poems of Emily Dickinson* (Cambridge, Mass: Harvard University Press, 1955), vol. 1, p. 206.

"We passed their graves": LH, "Peace," *The Panther and the Lash,* p. 56.

"contains the greatest poetic statements": *Chicago Defender,* July 4, 1953.

"Whitman wrote, 'Not till the sun denies you": *Chicago Defender,* Aug. 1, 1953.

page 226

"I know what had gone on with him": Matt Crawford to author, interview, May 28, 1980.

"I've been to more concerts, shows, and dinners": LH to Arna Bontemps, n.d. [1953], LHP.

In "a wonderful ten days": LH to Ben Lehman, July 27, 1953, LHP.

page 227

"the very good publicity you have been getting": William A. Robinson to LH, May 4, 1953, LHP.

a few days "of real summer sun": LH to Noël Sullivan, June 13, 1953, NSP, Bancroft.

"such *gone* (be-bop) Mahoneys!": LH to Noël Sullivan, June 4, 1953, NSP, Bancroft.

"MY HAPPINESS IN HAVING KNOWN YOU": LH to Noël Sullivan, June 16, 1953, NSP, Bancroft.

"Get out the lunch-box of your dreams": LH, "Jim Crow Car," *The Panther and the Lash,* p. 99.

in his "upholstered doghouse": LH to Eulah Pharr, July 27, 1953, LHP.

page 228

"Me standing at hot dog stand": LH to Arna Bontemps, July 13, 1953, LHP.

"I was in New York for the summer": Zeppelin Wong to author, interview, Oct. 24, 1980.

"a wonderful fellow," Langston soon agreed: LH to Franklin Watts, Inc. (Helen Hoke Watts), Aug. 27, 1953, LHP.

"the wonderful summer I spent with you": Zeppelin Wong to LH, n.d., LHP.

page 229

"Langston laughed and told me": Jan Meyerowitz to author, interview, Apr. 20, 1983.

"Miracle before God to come": LH to Arna Bontemps, Sept. 22, 1953, LHP.

page 230

"references to racial discrimination": See LH, "Famous American Negroes," Oct. 1953, LHP 346.

"That Texas oil money suddenly found them": LH to Maxim Lieber, July 11, 1954, LHP.

"Certainly Japan shook the white world": *Chicago Defender,* Aug. 15, 1953.

"It was at the height of the McCarthy . . . era": LH to William G. Horne, Oct. 25, 1965; copy courtesy of Martin Duberman.

page 231

"It was fun": LH to Dodd, Mead, Inc. (Edward Dodd, Jr.), Sept. 12, 1953, LHP.

"Those Negroes *were* tough": Marginal comment on LH, "Here to Stay," 5th draft, Aug. 26, 1953. Presentation copy to Arna Bontemps, courtesy of Mrs. Alberta Bontemps.

"Another year of starvation," he sighed: LH to Arna Bontemps, Sept. 22, 1953, LHP.

"I am running a literary factory": LH to Arna Bontemps, Oct. 21, 1953, LHP.

"Langston bought boxes of paper in different colors": Alice Childress, ["Langston

Hughes as Dramatist''], address, Feb. 21, 1987, Harlem School of the Arts, New York City.

page 232

a ''deceptively profound little book'': James Emanuel, *Langston Hughes* (New York: Twayne, 1967), p. 48.

rejected as ''too abstract'': Franklin Watts, Inc. (Helen Hoke Watts) to LH, Oct. 28, 1954.

''just about the toughest *little* job'': LH to Franklin Watts Inc. (Helen Hoke Watts), Jan. 26, 1954, LHP.

''what I really know about Jazz'': LH to Arna Bontemps, Sept. 29, 1956, LHP.

''Have to be SO careful'': LH to Arna Bontemps, July 4, 1954, Arna Bontemps Papers; courtesy of Mrs. Alberta Bontemps.

it was ''really different and human'': LH to Arna Bontemps, Oct. 19, 1953, LHP.

''Arnold Perl had seen the show'': Ruth Jett to author, interview, Oct. 12, 1987.

page 233

Perl was ''very excited'': Arnold Perl to LH, May 28, 1954, LHP.

''full of the clichés of twentieth-century instrumentation'': *New York Times,* Feb. 12, 1954.

''We produced some fragments'': Jan Meyerowitz to author, interview.

''The sun do move!'': LH to Carl Van Vechten, Mar. 6, 1954, CVVP, Yale.

''No lie! I'm telling you'': LH to Arna Bontemps, Mar. 30, 1954, LHP.

''a kind of West Indian-British Carmel'': *Ibid.*

page 234

''fortifying my resolution to accept'': LH to Henry Pratt Fairchild, Mar. 28, 1954, LHP.

he giggled—''We's rising plus!'': LH to Arna Bontemps, Feb. 10, 1954, LHP.

''Langston had traveled more than anyone'': Ralph Ellison to author, interview, Apr. 30, 1983.

page 235

who ''has assimilated completely the full poetic language'': Allen Tate, in Melvin B. Tolson, *Libretto For The Republic Of Liberia* (New York: Collier Books, 1970), p. 11.

''*Tolson writes in Negro*'': Karl Shapiro, in M.B. Tolson, *Harlem Gallery: Book 1, The Curator* (New York: Collier Books, 1969), p. 12.

''More power to tongue-in-cheek Tolson!'': LH to Arna Bontemps, Feb. 10, 1954, LHP.

''Nobody but Tolson could talk his way'': LH to Ina Qualls, Feb. 19, 1954, LHP.

''resigned pathos,'' then of ''tragic aggressiveness'': Selden Rodman, ''On Vistas Undreamt,'' *New York Times Book Review,* Jan. 24, 1954.

(''Nasty boy!''): Arna Bontemps to LH, Feb. 9, 1954, LHP.

''I've read all your latest'': Melvin B. Tolson to LH, May 2, 1956, LHP.

page 236

''iggurance like A. Tate's'': Ezra Pound to LH, June 18, 1956, LHP.

''most of it is bad, illiterate, or dull'': LH to Ray Durem, Feb. 27, 1954, LHP.

''your articles influenced me a great deal'': Andrew Salkey to LH, Aug. 9, 1953, LHP.

''Now if you will just get on a plane'': LH to Paul Breman, May 8, 1954, LHP.

''I hardly expected a reply'': Paul Breman to LH, n.d. [1954], LHP.

page 237

''Africa on the whole, and the Gold Coast'': Kwame Nkrumah to LH, Sept. 2, 1953, LHP.

''a very good book indeed'': LH to Alfred A. Knopf, Inc. (Harold Strauss), May 16, 1954, LHP.

page 238

"a spirit of 'New Africa' awakening": Richard Rive to LH, n.d. [June, 1954], LHP.

"which is calculated to enslave": Ezekiel Mphahlele to LH, Nov. 1, 1954, LHP.

"It is indeed very flattering": Ezekiel Mphahlele to LH, June 18, 1954, LHP.

"what great fellow would be writing": G.A. Addopleh to LH, July 13, 1954, LHP.

"dreaming Nigeria in my sleep": LH to Arna Bontemps, Mar. 2, 1955, LHP.

page 239

"Paul dines with us ever so often": LH to Arna Bontemps, Nov. 1, 1954, LHP.

"Nobody would have called Langston 'uncle' ": Paul Bontemps to author, interview, Dec. 24, 1984.

"What I would really like to know": LH to Youra Qualls, Feb. 27, 1956, LHP.

"Your thoughtful poem infused a new life": Chuba Nweke to LH, June 4, 1954, LHP.

page 240

"I know you are a big man": P.S.U. Asoegwa to LH, June 19, 1953, LHP.

"Dear son Chuba," Hughes soon replied: LH to Chuba Nweke, July 25, 1954, LHP.

"May God endorse our dear dreams": Chuba Nweke to LH, June 26, 1956, LHP.

"My anxiety turns to madness": Chuba Nweke to LH, Feb. 13, 1955, LHP.

"I'm becoming a children's writer": LH to Maxim Lieber, July 11, 1954, LHP.

page 241

"his affection for and kindness to children": Ellen Tarry to author, interview, Oct. 21, 1987.

"an amazing new talent": LH to Arna Bontemps, May 27, 1954, Langston Hughes Papers, Fisk University.

"I loved the library as a child": Toni Cade Bambara, ["Langston Hughes"], address, Apr. 13, 1986, Langston Hughes Festival, City College of New York.

"In those days Yellow Cabs still came": David Givens to author, interview, Feb. 1, 1986.

page 242

"The garden's in full bloom": *New York Times*, Aug. 27, 1954.

"What to do with them was another matter": Roy DeCarava to author, interview, Nov. 11, 1981.

page 243

to "write it from memory": LH to Arna Bontemps, July 17, 1954, LHP.

"I hope it reads as easily": *Ibid.*

"New York . . . is impossible": LH to Arna Bontemps, Sept. 25, 1954, LHP.

"I am currently behind a three-way": LH to Arna Bontemps, Nov. 1, 1954, LHP.

an exhibition of the "quite marvellous" photographs: LH to Aaron Douglas, July 16, 1954, LHP.

page 244

"a Rembrandt of the camera": Doubleday and Co. (Ken McCormick) to LH, Oct. 12, 1954, LHP.

Trying "one more long shot": LH to Doubleday and Co. (Ken McCormick), Oct. 15, 1954, LHP.

Simon called it "really heartbreaking": Richard Simon to Maria Leiper, Nov. 8, 1954, LHP.

"We've had so many books": LH to Simon and Schuster (Maria Leiper), Jan. 4, 195[5], LHP.

"We agreed to a contract at once": Roy DeCarava to author, interview.

"in spite of visiting foreigners and Africans": LH to Arna Bontemps, Dec. 18, 1954, LHP.

"where we got together and howled": LH to Arna Bontemps, Dec. 27, 1954, LHP.
what was "bound to be an historical evening": LH to Cornelia Otis Skinner, Dec. 12, 1954, LHP.
"one of the most memorable": LH to Cornelia Otis Skinner, Jan. 16, 1955, LHP.

page 246
"So, you see," he punned to a friend: LH to Nancy Cunard, Mar. 30, 1955, LHP.
"don't tell anybody," he begged: LH to Noël Sullivan, Apr. 8, 1955, NSP, Bancroft.
"but if you aren't, and want to help": LH to Carl Van Vechten, Apr. 3, 1955, CVVP, Yale.
"There is practically no race prejudice": LH to Alvenice H. Bryan, Nov. 9, 1956, LHP.
"I am continually trying to make publishers": LH to Associated Negro Press (Gladys Graham), Oct. 17, 1956, LHP.
"See what happens to white!": LH to Arna Bontemps, Jan. 28, 1955, LHP.

page 247
"After this one," he fumed: LH to Arna Bontemps, Feb. 16, 1955, LHP.
"an arresting score, packed with tell-tale flashes": *New York Times,* Apr. 15, 1955.
touched on the "poignant, childlike simplicity": *New York Post,* Apr. 15, 1955.
"This was probably the most important": Jan Meyerowitz to author, interview.
"I've always loved the book": LH to Noël Sullivan, n.d., [1955], NSP, Bancroft.
"I *never* owned a Sophie Tucker record!": LH to Walter A. Weiss, Nov. 11, 1954, LHP.
"are all with a jaundiced eye": LH to Arna Bontemps, n.d., LHP.
the "absolutely thrilling" photographs: LH to Arna Bontemps, Apr. 23, 1955, LHP.

page 248
"I was overjoyed when Arna": Milton Meltzer to author, interview, Dec. 1, 1980.
to "provoke, shock, amuse, or otherwise intrigue": LH to Simon and Schuster (Maria Leiper), Sept. 28, 1955, LHP.
"Nicest thing about going away": LH to Arna Bontemps, Sept. 2, 1955, LHP.

page 249
Monroe was "awfully pretty and awfully nice": LH to Arna Bontemps, Nov. 8, 1955, LHP.
"I knew that it was not supposed to be": Roy DeCarava to author, interview.
"a harmony which is more than poetry": New York *Herald-Tribune,* Dec. 13, 1955.
"a delicate and lovely fiction-document": *New York Times Magazine,* Nov. 27, 1955.
"the subtle, the almost exquisite interplay": *Image: Journal of Photography* 4 (Dec. 1955): 71.
"a mixture of the warm and the stark": *Village Voice,* Dec. 14, 1955.
"the sensitivity of the photographs": Henri Cartier-Bresson to LH, Jan. 14, 1956, LHP.

page 250
"He swoons each time he plays": LH to Arna Bontemps, Aug. 18, 1955, LHP.
"I beg of you," he wrote despairingly: LH to Jan Meyerowitz, July 30, 1955, LHP.
"Your threateningly witty letter worries": Jan Meyerowitz to LH, Aug. 4, 1955, LHP.

page 251
"I trust you realize that this": LH to Jan Meyerowitz, n.d., LHP.
"*Hughes:* Hello": LH, [Personal Papers], Jan. 23, 1956, LHP.
"The finest living American author": Jan Meyerowitz to LH, Jan. 23, 1956, LHP.
"Art thou Ahasuerus? A mere piece": LH to Jan Meyerowitz, Jan. 23, 1956, LHP.
"The stuff I received this morning": Jan Meyerowitz to LH, Jan. 24, 1956, LHP.
"you will not permit art": LH to Jan Meyerowitz, Jan. 25, 1956, LHP.
"If you want to die, be disturbed": LH to James Baldwin, July 25, 1953, LHP.

"I remember once being with him": Alice Childress to author, interview, Feb. 21, 1987.

page 252

("Left, oh, left me!" Meyerowitz mourned): Jan Meyerowitz to LH, Feb. 17, 1956, LHP.

"My 65 year old heart": Noël Sullivan to LH, May 3, 1955, LHP.

"If you need me," Langston had replied: LH to Noël Sullivan, Nov. 14, 1955, NSP, Bancroft.

"I hadn't had a leisurely quiet . . . week": LH to Noël Sullivan, Feb. 18, 1956, NSP, Bancroft.

"I think you were the best 'medicine' ": Marie Short to LH, Feb. 15, 1956, LHP.

"I'm dying!" he groaned: LH to Arna Bontemps, Feb. 15, 1956, LHP.

page 253

"if there are enough poems": LH to Indiana University Press (Bernard B. Perry), Feb. 20, 1956, LHP.

and found "some very beautiful indeed": LH to Indiana University Press (Bernard B. Perry), Feb. 27, 1956, LHP.

"Esther reads better that I'd thought": LH to Jan Meyerowitz, May 29, 1956, LHP.

"a heroic and *very* American historical subject": *Ibid.*

"or composition with orchestra, singers, and . . . Narrator": LH to Dr. Vincent T. Williams, Sept. 25, 1955, LHP.

page 254

"You told me to be careful": Elaine Guthrie Lorillard, "Time in Old Newport," *Collier's* 138 (July 20, 1956): 52.

"Duke made the cool night hot": *Chicago Defender,* July 21, 1956.

page 255

"an urban-folk-Harlem-*genre*-melodrama": LH to Walter Weiss, Sept. 14, 1956, LHP.

"Some gospel singers these days": *Chicago Defender,* Dec. 12, 1953.

"about the last refuge of Negro folk music": LH to Walter Weiss, Sept. 14, 1956, LHP.

"It's a singing, shouting, wailing drama": LH to Arna Bontemps, July 26, 1956, LHP.

page 256

"His lyrics were so easy to set": Jobe Huntley, *I Remember Langston Hughes* (New York: Jobe Huntley, 1983), p. 16.

"So now I had some gospel songs": Jobe Huntley, *I Remember Langston Hughes,* p. 77.

"thus killing two birds with one stone": LH to Elmer Rice, Oct. 5, 1956, LHP.

"so I reckon I have to explore": LH to Arna Bontemps, Sept. 6, 1956, LHP.

page 257

"GOD CALLED NOEL SULLIVAN TO HIMSELF": Brenda Doyle Ferrari to LH, Sept. 16, 1956, LHP.

"California (indeed the whole world)": LH to Alice Doyle Mahoney, Nov. 4, 1956, LHP.

"We who had the good fortune": *Carmel Pine Cone-Cymbal,* Sept. 20, 1956.

"Are there enough people who would be": Elmer Rice to LH, Oct. 3, 1956, LHP.

page 258

"depuis bien longtemps j'aime": Editions Seghers (Pierre Seghers) to LH, Nov. 30, 1955.

"If all authors," Franklin Watts attested: Franklin Watts Inc. (Franklin Watts) to LH, Nov. 23, 1956, LHP.

"It was really *your* party": Ina Qualls to LH, n.d. [Nov. 1956], LHP.

"kept right up to date": LH to Simon and Schuster (Maria Leiper), Sept. 21, 1955, LHP.

"had hardly expected to live": *Pittsburgh Courier,* Nov. 14, 1956.

"a kind of majestic sweep to a story": New York *Herald-Tribune,* Nov. 18, 1956.

"Few of its pages can be read": *Saturday Review* 39 (Dec. 1, 1956): 46.

page 259

"more wandering than wondering": New York *Herald-Tribune,* Dec. 23, 1956.

"Your own buoyant heart emerges": Nancy Cunard to LH, Apr. 25, 1957, LHP.

"I've now cut out all the impersonal stuff": LH to Arna Bontemps, Apr. 26, 1956, LHP.

"in a sense betray your race": Theodore Webs to LH, Jan. 27, 1956, LHP.

page 260

called his act "both disgusting and cowardly": Karol Fahnestock to LH, July 16, 1956, LHP.

"but you are a *wise* person": Marie Short to LH, Jan. 25, 1957, LHP.

"not only a readable tale": *Daily Worker,* Nov. 29, 1956.

"for perhaps the tenth time": LH to W.E.B. Du Bois, May 22, 1956, WEBDP, UM(A).

"even men like Langston Hughes": W.E.B. Du Bois, "Tribute to Paul Robeson," in Philip S. Foner, ed., *W.E.B. Du Bois Speaks: Speeches and Addresses 1920-1963* (New York: Pathfinder Press, 1970), p. 296.

"Personally, I found the book fascinating": LH to W.E.B. Du Bois, Oct. 28, 1959, Du WEBDP, UM(A).

page 261

"Delighted! I figured I photographed as well": LH to Maxim Lieber, Sept. 17, 1956, LHP.

"into 50-11 languages": LH to Simon and Schuster (Maria Leiper), Nov. 1. 1955, LHP.

with others of "your great verses": Albert Christ-Janer to LH, Sept. 16, 1955, LHP.

page 262

"just about the most moving pieces": LH to Simon and Schuster (Maria Leiper), Mar. 10, 1956, LHP.

"Have these things been changed": LH to Roy Hofheinz, Aug. 24, 1955, LHP.

"the guys in the corner bars are saying": LH to Arna Bontemps, Feb. 15, 1956, LHP.

"If Miss Lucy wanted to go to bed": *Chicago Defender,* Mar. 24, 1956.

"Which means," Langston reckoned: LH to Arna Bontemps, Feb. 15, 1956, LHP.

10. Making Hay

page 263

"I am ready to retire to an ivory tower": LH to Arna Bontemps, Jan. 9, 1957, LHP.

"about the busiest of my life": LH to Earl Hague, Aug. 14, 1957, LHP.

page 264

"my favorite reading": LH, "Humor and the Negro Press," Jan. 10, 1957, LHP 515.

"a double entendre out of P-P": *Ibid.*

"What Rev. King lacks in years": *Chicago Defender,* June 8, 1957.

"essentially a topical book": LH to Carl Van Vechten, Jan. 9, 1957, CVVP, Yale.

a consistency of "mood and meaning": LH to Indiana University Press, Feb. 26, 1957, LHP.

a foreword by . . . "an American poet": *Ibid.*

"Trying to run a major career": LH to Amy Spingarn, Apr. 18, 1960, LHP.

to ensure "a *socially slanted* book": LH to Arna Bontemps, Jan. 31, 1957, LHP.

page 265

("a wonderful collaborator"): LH to Dave Martin, May 21, 1957, LHP.

"I felt there was so little": *New York Times,* Aug. 29, 1967.

"Stella Holt was very important to us": Loften Mitchell to author, interview, Oct. 26, 1987.

"What Broadway needs," he decided: LH to Arna Bontemps, Jan. 25, 1957, LHP.

page 266

"I do believe cullud liberals": LH to Arna Bontemps, Nov. 2, 1955, LHP.

"I neither sing, play—nor care much for": LH to Arna Bontemps, Jan. 28, 1957, in Nichols, *Letters,* p. 357.

"You've taken my blues and gone": LH, "Note on Commercial Art" [later, "Note on Commercial Theatre"], *Crisis* 47 (Mar. 1940): 79.

page 267

"Made in U.S.A. / And it rocks from pole to pole!": LH to Dave Martin, Aug. 29, 1955, LHP.

"I see no reason," he informed: *Ibid.*

"Jewish theme, Gentile cast": LH to Elie Siegmeister, Feb. 28, 1957, LHP.

heard "a powerful libretto": *Daily Illini,* Mar. 20, 1957.

called Langston's words "intelligent and beautiful": *News-Gazette* (Champaign-Urbana), Mar. 18, 1957.

"I note you are *just like a composer*": LH to Jan Meyerowitz, Apr. 2, 1957, LHP.

"Frommochai, the Jew" and his "obscene" denial: Jan Meyerowitz to LH, Apr. 20, 1957, LHP.

page 268

"He claimed the whole black race": George Houston Bass to St. Clair Bourne, interview, n.d. [1985]; courtesy of the New York Center for Visual History.

"THANK YOU FOR THE NEW STORY": LH to John A. Williams, Nov. 24, 1965; courtesy of John A. Williams.

"Langston had sent it": John A. Williams to author, interview, Nov. 14, 1987.

"I had never met him": Doris Abramson, address at symposium, "Langston Hughes and the American Theatre," Feb. 21, 1987, Harlem School of the Arts. Courtesy of James Bartow and the Harlem School of the Arts.

page 269

"Each time we are together": Flora D. Coates to LH, Sept. 29, 1957, LHP.

"the Marian Anderson of the Night Clubs": LH to David Lipsky, May 27, 1957, LHP.

"I dressed casually and loosened my tie": Melvin Stewart to author, interview, Dec. 29, 1987.

"We are skating on thin ice": LH to Stella Holt, Apr. 10, 1957, LHP.

"You know show business in the U.S.A.": LH to Claudia McNeill, Apr. 14, 1957, LHP.

page 270

Langston seemed "calm, collected, reasonable": Simon and Schuster (Maria Leiper) to LH, May 9, 1957, LHP.

"Negro writers, just by being black": LH, "The Writer's Position in America," May 7, 1957, LHP 3251.

one white woman "wept unashamedly": Alice Childress to LH, June 3, 1957, LHP.

page 271

"What I suggest now is that": LH to Melvin Stewart, May 15, 1957, LHP.

"a trifle ramshackle in structure": *New York Post,* May 22, 1957.

"Mr. Hughes loves Harlem": *New York Times,* May 22, 1957.

a "rambling, sometimes ramshackle": *New York Journal-American,* May 23, 1957.

openly "disturbed and bewildered": Alice Childress to LH, June 3, 1957, LHP.

"I cannot say that I liked it": William L. Patterson to LH, June 7, 1957, LHP.

page 272

"it's the old story—and the problem": LH to William L. Patterson, June 8, 1957, LHP.

"Bitterness is not a part of me": LH to Helen E. Brown, June 9, 1957, LHP.

"Always something, as Simple says": LH to Arna Bontemps, June 2, 1957, in Nichols, *Letters,* p. 359.

page 273

"God, when will I ever": LH to Arna Bontemps, June 20, 1957, LHP.

("such beautiful poems!"): *Ibid.*

"You have made Miss Mistral's poetry": Indiana University Press (Bernard B. Perry) to LH, May 14, 1957, LHP.

"gracias a dios! Although it was": LH to Arna Bontemps, July 20, 1957, in Nichols, *Letters,* p. 361.

"The gloom was so thick": *New York Post,* July 12, 1957.

"Something is always happening": New York *Herald-Tribune,* Aug. 18, 1957.

into a "bore and a flop": LH to Stella Holt, July 9, 1957, LHP.

Goldwyn of Hollywood ("his *own* self"): LH to Arna Bontemps, July 5, 1957, in Nichols, *Letters,* p. 360.

page 274

"So we're internationally known!": LH to Dave Martin, July 8, 1957, LHP.

"the amiable little show . . . rather frail": *New York World Telegram and Sun,* Aug. 21, 1957.

"warming but not overwhelming": *New York Daily News,* Aug. 21, 1957.

to "capture you as an alert, pleasant": Walter Brough to LH, June 3, 1957, LHP.

"One of the things which still brightens": LH to Walter Brough, Sept. 27, 1957, LHP.

page 275

Simple "looms in and over the life": *Baltimore Afro-American,* Oct. 19, 1957.

"who cease being fictional": *New York Times,* Sept. 17, 1957.

"a plump pixy of a man": *New York Post,* Nov. 24, 1957.

"For most of my life I have been": *Chicago Defender,* Apr. 11, 1959.

page 276

"Langston forgot his tie and I wore it": William M. Kunstler to author, Dec. 24, 1982.

"me, I'm somewhat weary of it": LH to Arna Bontemps, Nov. 6, 1957, in Nichols, *Letters,* p. 363.

"very comfortable and pretty": LH to Arna Bontemps, Nov. 16, 1957, LHP.

from the "feudin' and fightin' ": LH to Arna Bontemps, Dec. 28, 1957, LHP.

There were "charges and countercharges": LH to Arna Bontemps, Dec. 28, 1957, LHP.

page 277

"good paper that will not turn yellow": LH to Rinehart amd Co. (Dudley Frasier), Oct. 5, 1957, LHP.

"I guess you know *who*": LH to Carl Van Vechten, Nov. 30, 1957, CVVP, Yale.

"so we would have come full circle": LH to Carl Van Vechten, Dec. 3, 1957, CVVP, Yale.

"I certainly do not think": Alfred A. Knopf, Inc. (Herbert Weinstock) to LH, Dec. 17, 1957, LHP.

for the "perpetuation of the fame": Carl Van Vechten to LH, Oct. 11, 1959, LHP.

"I despised his photography": Ralph Ellison to author, interview, Apr. 30, 1983.

page 278

"Usually, Mr. Hughes was still sleeping": Raoul Abdul to St. Clair Bourne, interview, Oct. 18, 1985. Courtesy of St. Clair Bourne and the New York Center for Visual History.

page 279

"a memorable evening": *New York Age,* Mar. 8, 1958.

"You cats know what the big thing is": *New York Daily News,* Mar. 6, 1958.

page 280

the "original jazz poet": LH to Alfred A. Knopf, Inc. (Herbert Weinstock), June 3, 1958, LHP.

"I don't know the beatniks": Toronto *Star,* Apr. 4, 1959.

"Jazz gives poetry a much wider": *Ibid.*

"but with more beat to my ear": LH to Ralph Ellison, Aug. 23, 1956, LHP.

page 281

"Me, no more do anything": LH to Arna Bontemps, Mar. 14, 1958, LHP.

"Some of those *Ways of White Folks*": ibid.

thought his translations "excellent": *Spirit* 24 (Jan. 1958): 178.

called the book "useful and moving": *Chicago Sun,* Jan. 12, 1958.

as "a *fracaso* of good intentions": *New York Times,* Dec. 1, 1957.

"Shouldn't Mr. Hughes have called in": Edwin Honig, "Poet of Womanhood," *Saturday Review of Literature* 41 (Mar. 22, 1958): 22.

"I can only say that": LH to *Saturday Review of Literature* (Norman Cousins), Mar. 21, 1958, LHP.

page 282

"almost stomped down the chapel". LH to Dave Martin, Apr. 28, 1958, LHP.

"What are you reading about Negroes": LH to Arna Bontemps, May 24, 1958, LHP.

"not a sensation or presumptuous novelty": Ruth Berges, "Esther in Boston," *Opera News* 23 (Oct. 10, 1958): 17.

page 283

"To hell with the message": Dave Martin to LH, May 7, 1958, LHP.

"a score that harks back": *London Observer,* May 25, 1958.

"the most undistinguished score": *London Evening News,* May 20, 1958.

"raucous, tasteless, humorless hotch-potch": *London Evening News,* May 21, 1958.

"in being restaged, Simple's original simplicity": LH to Dave Martin, May 31, 1958, LHP.

"your name and books are known": *Foreign Literature* (A. Chakovsky) to LH, Mar. 24, 1959, LIIP.

page 284

"most grateful . . . for introducing": LH to Paridem von dem Knesebeck, Apr. 8, 1958, LHP.

"in the name of Humanity": Freie Akademie der Künste to LH, July 6, 1954, LHP.

"Japanese people, especially teen-agers": Shozo Kojima to LH, July 10, 1955, LHP.

"When headed for the pit": LH to Arna Bontemps, June 4, 1958, LHP.

"Colored literature in these days": *Washington Afro-American,* May 24, 1958.

page 285

"You are, as the expression used to be": Arna Bontemps to LH, June 6, 1958, LHP.

"extraordinary on every one": *Berkshire Eagle,* July 12, 1958.

ban this "blasphemous creature": *Ottawa Citizen,* July 17, 1958.

"How times do change!": LH to Arna Bontemps, Sept 10, 1958, LHP.

page 286

"for Adults or Teenagers": LH, "The Nine O"Clock Bell," May 27, 1958, LHP 791.

"I could tell you about writing": LH to Robert Hayden, Mar. 5, 1958, LHP.

"Ralphie is getting real baldheaded": LH to Arna Bontemps, July 9, 1958, LHP.

"Langston was always genial to me": Ralph Ellison to author, interview.

page 287

"It must be hard to keep": LH to Arna Bontemps, July 9, 1958, in Nichols, *Letters,* p. 374.

11. *You* Are the World

page 288

"Mr. Hughes conveyed not merely poetry": *University Daily Kansan,* Oct. 8. 1958.

page 289

a "world-renowned poet and author": Joplin *Globe,* Oct. 12, 1958.

"They even had an *interracial* cocktail party": LH to Arna Bontemps, n.d. [Oct. 1958], LHP.

"stuck in a corner" at a party: Philip Jones to Henry Harder, Jan. 21, 1981; courtesy of Prof. Henry Harder.

page 290

"the mild-mannered, soft-spoken poet-author": Joplin *Globe,* Oct. 12, 1958.

"I now have a warm spot": LH to Max Baird, Oct. 20, 1958, LHP.

"one of the greatest folk poets": *Saturday Review* 41 (Nov. 22, 1958): 19.

"the consistently high quality": *New York Times Book Review,* Nov. 23, 1958.

"one of the best anthologies": *The New Republic* 140 (Feb. 16, 1959): 19-20.

"a limp and pallid recommendation": *Library Journal* 84 (Jan. 1, 1959): 119.

"a wonderfully funny yet touching book": *New York Post,* Jan. 11, 1959.

"We made lots of money": Rachelle Marshall to author, interview, Apr. 24, 1988.

page 291

"your masterful poem": Aaron Douglas to LH, Jan. 8, 1959, LHP.

page 292

"the closing of the ring": Arna Bontemps to LH, Dec. 30, 1958, LHP.

"It looks like your last will": LH to Alfred A. Knopf, Inc. (Herbert Weinstock), Nov. 19, 1958, LHP.

another step "to crown my career": LH to Arna Bontemps, Jan. 31, 1959, in Nichols, *Letters,* p. 379.

"who shall have made the highest": *American Society of African Culture Newsletter* 2 (June 30, 1960): 1.

"Have lived longer than any . . . Negro": LH to Arna Bontemps, Aug. 30, 1958, LHP.

"so you might send it on": LH to Arna Bontemps, Jan. 31, 1959, LHP.

"Was this what you wanted?": Dorothy Peterson to LH, Feb. 12, 1959, LHP.

"Pride rose within me": LH to Kwame Nkrumah, Feb. 28, 1958, LHP.

page 293

"If I could find out what it were": *Chicago Defender,* Feb. 7, 1959.

"with an *integrated* (God help us) threesome": LH to Arna Bontemps, Feb. 16, 1959, LHP.

"it being hard to make irony clear": LH to Arna Bontemps, Jan. 31, 1959, LHP.

page 294

"Even to sell *bad* writing": LH, "Speech on Selling Writing," Feb. 27, 1959, LHP 3283.

"Langston's speech just tore up the place": Loften Mitchell to author, interview, Oct. 26, 1987.

"I am the author of a . . . play": Lorraine Hansberry to LH, Feb. 8, 1958, LHP.

regarded by him as "my discovery": LH to Arna Bontemps, Mar. 8, 1959, LHP.

"bids fair to become a milestone": *Chicago Defender* Mar. 14, 1959.

"I intend to holler": LH to Arna Bontemps, Mar. 8, 1959, LHP.

page 295

"because you were the first one": LH to Carl Van Vechten, Jan. 18, 1959, CVVP, Yale.

"familiar poems and new-to-me ones": Ben Lehman to LH, Mar. 23, 1959, LHP.

the "voice of pain and isolation": *St. Louis Post-Dispatch,* Mar. 22, 1959.

"some of the saddest, most humorous": *San Francisco Chronicle,* Apr. 5, 1959.

"Every time I read Langston Hughes": *New York Times Book Review,* Mar. 29, 1959.

page 296

"thought-provoking, tantalizing, irritating": *New York Times Book Review,* Feb. 26, 1956. See also LHP 3413 (Nov. 19, 1955).

"fat, fine, and worried . . . as usual": LH to Arna Bontemps, June 23, 1959, in Nichols, *Letters,* p. 385.

"With all this talking about the Free World": *Chicago Defender,* Jan. 12, 1957.

"our white folks will never get through": *Chicago Defender,* June 11, 1960.

page 297

"It is. Congested with people": LH, "A Poet's Harlem," Dec. 27, 1960, LHP 2998.

"the silent, accumulating contempt and hatred": James Baldwin, "Fifth Avenue Uptown," *Esquire* 54 (July 1960): 70.

"Oh if the muse would let me": Conrad Kent Rivers to LH, Mar. 5, 1959, LHP.

"changed my outlook toward myself": Conrad Kent Rivers to LH, Aug. 25, 1962, LHP.

page 298

"not only as my mentor": Lorraine Hansberry to LH, n.d., LHP.

"Jimmy shows Langston no *respect*": William J. Weatherby, *Squaring Off: Mailer vs. Baldwin* (New York: Mason/Charter, 1977), p. 128.

"because they were *about* something": Robert Hayden to LH, n.d., LHP.

"Some things in his deepest nature": Raoul Abdul to author, interview, Nov. 22, 1981.

"Langston and I were sitting there": *ibid.*

"Baldwin, who was usually relaxed": William J. Weatherby, *Squaring Off,* pp. 129-130.

page 299

"I hadn't really read the book": James Baldwin to author, interview, Dec. 12, 1985.

"I suppose it's not too much": James Baldwin to Clayton Riley, interview, Feb. 14, 1986. Courtesy of the New York Center for Visual History.

"He made so many friends": Raoul Abdul to author, interview.

page 300

by "a pick-pocket thug": LH to Arna Bontemps, June 11, 1956, LHP.

"It was almost a sudden kind of thing": Randy Weston to author, interview, June 20, 1986.

"a basically nice kid": LH to Arna Bontemps, Oct. 26, 1957, LHP.

"but young ones who can't make art": *Ibid.*

"Folks treated me so nice": LH to Arna Bontemps, May 28, 1959, in Nichols, *Letters,* pp. 382-83.

page 301

to allow "the lack of bitterness": LH to CBS (Richard Ellison), Aug. 17, 1959, LHP.

"ironic little novel" of miscegenation: LH, Introduction to Mark Twain, *Pudd'nhead Wilson* (New York: Bantam Books, 1959), p. vii.

"head and shoulders above the other": *Pudd'nhead Wilson,* p. xi.

"the cullud dope-taking servant-whore": LH to Arna Bontemps, Jan. 31, 1959, in Nichols, *Letters,* p. 378.

a "quiet and unconspicuous" new graduate: Arna Bontemps to LH, Mar. 5, 1959, Arna Bontemps Papers, Fisk University.

page 302

"not TOO energetic": LH to Arna Bontemps, Mar. 19, 1959, LHP.

"I wouldn't care if he was a Mau Mau": LH to Arna Bontemps, Mar. 8, 1959, LHP.

"By that time, I had long given up": George Houston Bass to author, interview, June 4, 1987.

page 303

"about the loveliest show": LH to Lucille Lortel, Oct. 28, 1961, LHP.

"a lusty Harlem sideshow": *Variety,* Sept. 9, 1959.

"a small masterpiece": *The Scotsman,* Oct. 10, 1959.

"a minor classic of its kind": *Manchester Evening News,* Sept. 10, 1959.

"brilliantly executed, excruciatingly funny": *Oxford Mail,* Sept. 17, 1959.

"There has not been a bang-up . . . show": LH to Lawrence Langner, Mar. 22, 1959, LHP.

"a top-notch play-doctor": LH to Folkways Records Inc. (Moses Asch), Nov. 1, 1959, LHP.

page 304

after "a glittering affair": LH to Flora D. Coates, Nov. 4, 1959, LHP.

She had "a wonderful husband": Anne Marie Coussey Wooding to LH, Oct. 18, 1959, LHP.

the "very good" poet: LH to [unidentified, n.d.], LHP.

"What I remember most about Langston": Derek Walcott to author, interview, Nov. 14, 1987.

page 305

his hope "for one big commercial hit": Trinidad *Guardian,* Nov. 13, 1959.

"All but 4 writers": LH to Arna Bontemps, Dec. 17, 1959, LHP.

his "greatest admiration for you": LH to Martin Luther King, Jr., Dec. 12, 1959, LHP.

"Like Pearl Bailey," Langston moaned: LH to Arna Bontemps, Feb. 15, 1960, LHP.

page 306

"The record of this writer": Elizabeth Staples, "Langston Hughes: Malevolent Force," *American Mercury* 88 (Jan. 1959): 46–47.

"so we figure somebody in town": LH to Carter Smith, Oct. 10, 1960, LHP.

"I thought such stupid attacks": LH to Ethel B. Coe, Feb. 9, 1960, LHP.

"Understanding is necessary for respect": *Chicago Defender,* Nov. 22, 1959.

page 307

"Were I asked to preach a sermon": *Chicago Defender,* Jan. 23, 1960.

"Langston Hughes begins to cast": *New York Times,* Feb. 10, 1960.

"I were not present": LH to Arna Bontemps, Mar. 7, 1960, LHP.

page 308

"with only moments here and there": LH to Arna Bontemps, Feb. 18, 1960, Arna Bontemps Papers, Fisk University.

"Dear Lord! How long is the list": *Chicago Defender,* Mar. 3, 1960.

"Am I becoming oversensitive": LH to Arna Bontemps, Jan. 21, 1960, LHP.

"one of the finest novels": Quoted on dust jacket, Warren Miller, *The Cool World* (London: Secker & Warburg, 1959).

a dozen "quite good ones, some young": LH to Indiana University Press (Bernard B. Perry), Jan. 22, 1960, LHP.

page 309

"I will kick that dog": LH to Nancy Cunard, Mar. 21, 1960, LHP.

"Those college kids down there": LH to LeRoi Jones, Mar. 17, 1960, LHP.

The students were "GREAT": LH to Nancy Cunard, Mar. 21, 1960, LHP.

"I writ back," he tittered: LH to Arna Bontemps, Mar. 7, 1960, LHP.

Hughes epitomized "gentleness and humanity": Francis E. Kearns, "The Un-angry Langston Hughes," *Yale Review* 60 (Autumn 1970): 158–60.

"Who wants to be Beat?": LH, "Speech on Selling Writing."

"It was at the Village Vanguard": Amiri Baraka (LeRoi Jones) to author, interview, Apr. 25, 1983.

page 311

"he sent me a letter": Amiri Baraka (LeRoi Jones) to St. Clair Bourne, Oct. 17, 1985. Courtesy of St. Clair Bourne and the New York Center for Visual History.

"LEROI JONES represents color": *Chicago Defender,* Mar. 28, 1959.

"your quite *frank* comments, please": LH to Indiana University Press (Bernard B. Perry), Mar. 23, 1960, LHP.

the "world-famous poet" Langston Hughes: Peter Abrahams, "The Meaning of Harlem," *Holiday* 27 (June 1960): 74.

"WARMEST CONGRATULATIONS!": Amy Spingarn to LH, June 15, 1960, LHP.

page 312

It would be "of the utmost conceit": LH, "Langston Hughes's Acceptance of the Spingarn Medal, NAACP Convention, St. Paul, Minnesota," June 26, 1960, LHP 3304.

12. Ask Your Mama!

page 314

"three swinging groups displayed their wares: *Chicago Defender,* July 23, 1960.

page 315

"It's terrible," . . . Coleman Hawkins protested: *Providence Journal,* July 4, 1960

the events were "a tragedy": *Ibid.*

"No more appropriate program": *Chicago Defender,* July 23, 1960.

"I got the Newport Blues": LH, "Goodbye Newport Blues," July 3, 1960, LHP 2271.

"Many of these musicians": *Chicago Defender,* July 23, 1960.

page 316

"IN THE / IN THE QUARTER": LH, *Ask Your Mama: Twelve Moods For Jazz* (New York: Knopf, 1961), pp. 3–4.

page 317

"The building up of aggressive responses": John Dollard, "The Dozens: Dialectic of Insult," *American Imago* 1 (Nov. 1939): 25.

page 318

"IN THE QUARTER OF THE NEGROES": LH, *Ask Your Mama* (New York: Knopf, 1961), pp. 49–50. This section, "Gospel Cha-Cha," was published (with a few minor changes) as "Haiti (Mood For Maracas)," *The New Republic* 145 (Sept. 25, 1961): 22. For "Jazztet Muted," see *Ask Your Mama,* pp. 75–78.

page 320

"a very personal treasury": LH, *An African Treasury: Articles / Essays / Stories / Poems By Black Africans* (New York: Crown, 1960), p. ix.

"a rich and timely gift": *Virginia Kirkus Service Bulletin* 28 (May 15, 1960): 398.

"What delights me is that you have": Ezekiel Mphahlele to LH, July 27, 1960, LHP.

"I had always loved Langston's poem": Jan Meyerowitz to author, interview, Apr. 20, 1983.

"Hello, sailor boy, / In from the sea!": LH, "Port Town," *The Weary Blues* (New York: Knopf, 1926), p. 74.

page 321

"Country never did agree with me": LH to Carl Van Vechten, August 8, 1960, CVVP, Yale.

"no more parts of operas": *Ibid.*

"I really am not interested": LH to Jan Meyerowitz, Aug. 27, 1960, LHP.

"what we have *done* already: Jan Meyerowitz to LH, Aug. 30, 1960, LHP.

"*too* smoothly," Langston judged: LH to Arna Bontemps, Aug. 2, 1960, LHP.

page 322

"definitely weak, beautiful, but . . . unconvincing": LH, ["Confidential Notes" to Lawrence Langner, Joel Schenker, Herbert Machiz, *et al.*], n.d., LHP 3761.

"Worst thing I've ever seen," New York *Amsterdam News,* Sept. 17, 1960.

"People forget," Langston argued lamely: *Sunday Herald* (Connecticut), Sept. 4, 1960.

"Who said, 'Plays are not written—'": LH to Loften Mitchell, Sept. 26, 1960, LHP.

"the dean of American poets": LH, "The World of Carl Sandburg," Sept. 14, 1960, LHP 3433.

page 323

"where, like Daniel, I have been caught": LH to Leonard Lyons, Sept. 27, 1960, LHP.

"to breathe a prayer for me": *Ibid.*

"Left-Wing Poet Langston Hughes": *Time* 76 (Oct. 3, 1960): 16.

"I do not know Fidel Castro": *Time* 76 (Oct. 24, 1960): 10.

"As apolitical as I was": LeRoi Jones to LH, Jan. 30, 1961, LHP.

"Loud and angry race cries": LH to Margaret Danner, Oct. 7, 1960, LHP.

"not represented by any lecture bureau": LH to *Saturday Review of Literature,* Oct. 15, 1960, LHP.

page 324

"since I do not make a major career": LH to W. Colston Leigh, Inc., Oct. 20, 1960, LHP.

if "one single letter is written": LH to Frank G. Greenwood, Oct. 27, 1960, LHP.

"The only reason I would vote": *Chicago Defender,* Nov. 5, 1960.

"AFRICA! I'm envious and jealous": LH to Arna Bontemps, Aug. 26, 1960, LHP.

page 325

"We have tomorrow": LH, "Poem," *The Weary Blues,* p. 108.

after "a wonderful week": LH to Hill and Wang, Inc. (Lawrence Hill), Dec. 12, 1960, LHP.

"Such an endearing city": LH to Jan Meyerowitz, Dec. 8, 1960, LHP.

page 326

"I loved Nigeria, but Paris more": LH to Jan Meyerowitz, Dec. 15, 1960, LHP.

for "une amitié sincere et exempte": Diallo Alpha to LH, n.d., LHP.

"Mon fils et mon frère!" LH to Diallo Alpha, Dec. 2, 1960, LHP.

"Say, guy, what with all the current sweep": Richard Wright to LH, Oct. 8, 1960, LHP.

"Man," Langston blurted: LH, "Richard Wright's Last Guest," Dec. 15, 1960, LHP 3443.

"MY DEEPEST SYMPATHY TO YOU": LH to Ellen Wright, Nov. 30, 1960, LHP.

page 327

"In a gospel church, when they ride": LH, "That Glory Train," Dec. 21, 1960, LHP 3767.

"I am . . . a literary sharecropper": LH to Arna Bontemps, Jan. 28, 1961, LHP.

"which I vowed before": LH to Arna Bontemps, Jan. 20, 1961, LHP.

"Langston was the only black writer": Randy Weston to author, interview, June 20, 1986.

page 328

"so much excitement" on the campus: Bette B. Bauer, "A Spokesman Speaks," *Mills Quarterly* (May 1961): 25.

"I see you and I": LH to Carl Van Vechten, in Bruce Kellner, *Carl Van Vechten and the Irreverent Decades* (Norman: Univ. of Oklahoma Press, 1968), p. 309.

page 329

"which is more than I can do": LH to Arna Bontemps, Apr. 12, 1961, in Nichols, *Letters,* p. 415.

"I do not like them well enough": See LH, "My Adventures as a Social Poet," *Phylon* (Fall 1947): 205–212.

"Mr. Carl Van Vechten has told me": LH to National Institute of Arts and Letters, May 5, 1961, LHP.

"I was the only cullud": LH to Arna Bontemps, May 25, 1961, in Nichols, *Letters,* pp. 417–18.

"I was completely in awe": Judith Jones to author, interview, Dec. 12, 1986.

"Merci à vous!": LH to Webster Smalley, Mar. 24, 1961, LHP.

page 330

"the academics think I've suddenly become": LH to Arna Bontemps, Mar. 24, 1961, LHP.

"Langston Hughes was a better man": James A. Emanuel to author, interview, Sept. 18, 1981.

"a 33rd degree bore": LH to Arna Bontemps, Apr. 30, 1961, LHP.

against "estos vandálicos hechos": Nicolás Guillén to LH, Apr. 18, 1961, LHP.

page 331

he scribbled "not signed": Note on William Worthy (Fair Play for Cuba Committee) to LH, Apr. 10, 1961, LHP.

"to popularize Cuba among Negroes": *New York Times,* Aug. 26, 1961.

"The cold war we're in": Millicent Dobbs Jordan to LH, Jan. 16, 1961, LHP.

"I can never articulate": Mari Evans to LH, May 5, 1961, LHP.

"It was the list of names": Raymond R. Patterson to author, July 9, 1987.

page 332

"slapped out and apparently": Indiana Univ. Press to LH, Apr. 17, 1961, LHP.

"good in an inconsequential fashion": LH to Eva Hesse, Feb. 16, 1961, LHP.

sent as "a polite protest": LH to Lawrence Ferlinghetti, May 30, 1961, LHP.

"Perhaps we are looking for something": Lawrence Ferlinghetti to LH, n.d., LHP.

"even partially audible lyrically": LH to Jan Meyerowitz, June 8, 1961, LHP.

"God's will is sometimes best": LH to Richard Beals, July 12, 1961.

"a Communist sympathizer and a danger": *Boston Globe,* June 19, 1961.

"an exceptionally well-knit program": *Boston Herald,* June 21, 1961.

page 333

"What I'll never understand": LH to LeRoi Jones, Nov. 1, 1961, LHP.

"LeRoi Jones is one of the most talented": *Ibid.*

"If we had both been a little less putty": LH, "Family of Three," Oct. 26, 1960, LHP 345.

"Marcel de la Smith": LH, "Seven People Dancing," n.d., LHP 3485.

page 334

his son is "a brilliant queer": LH, *Something in Common* (New York: Hill and Wang, 1963), p. 227.

notes for "a book about sex": LH, "Sex Silly Season," Mar. 25, 1963, LHP 3486.

the start of "a new novel": LH to Arna Bontemps, Mar. 29, 1963, LHP.

"will probably be widely read": *Virginia Kirkus Service Bulletin* 30 (June 1, 1962): 478.

page 335

"trying to out-Henry Henry Miller": LH to Arna Bontemps, May 28, 1962, LHP.

"Integration is going to RUIN": *Ibid.*

collection of "brilliantly written" essays: *Chicago Defender,* Aug. 26, 1961.

"Ain't nothing over there": [Name withheld] to author, interview, June 10, 1983.

"Around the streets of Harlem": [Name withheld] to author, interview, Oct. 12, 1984.

page 336

"darker than Canada Lee": LH to Arna Bontemps, Mar. 29, 1963, LHP.

"He is so dark": LH to Arna Bontemps, Mar. 16, 1963, LHP.

page 337

"I am proud of that boy": LH to Arna Bontemps, Apr. 23, 1963, in Nichols, *Letters,* p. 461.

"4 A.M. now. My full-name godson": LH to Arna Bontemps, Jan. 25, 1964, LHP.

page 338

"I remember once he was telling me": Roy DeCarava to author, interview, Nov. 14, 1981.

"he hated his mother and father": Lindsay Patterson to author, interview, Dec. 5, 1980.

page 339
"Conceit and egotism is cold and dangerous": Mabel D. Bass to LH, Nov. 31, 1962, LHP.

"hardly a rooming house": Phil W. Petrie to author, interview, Oct. 26, 1987.

"I am not very objective about Langston": Ruth Jett to author, interview, Oct. 12, 1987.

"sweet, but earthy and very strong": Roy DeCarava to author, interview.

"He was a wonderful person": Adele Glasgow to author, interview, Apr. 26, 1983.

page 340
"trapped between two powerful impulses": Notes by Arna Bontemps, Mar. 5, 1971. I am indebted to Arna Alexander Bontemps for access to this material.

13. In Gospel Glory

page 341
"the official host of Harlem": LH to Arna Bontemps, Nov. 21, 1961, LHP.

("Bright boy"): LH to Arna Bontemps, Nov. 21, 1961, LHP.

"almost put me to sleep": *Ibid.*

page 342
"I know I am / The Negro Problem": LH, "Dinner Guest: Me," *The Panther and the Lash*, p. 73.

the "GREAT BIG" trout *aux amandes*": LH to Indiana University Press (Bernard Perry), Nov. 10, 1961, LHP.

page 343
"Give the new President a chance": *Chicago Defender*, Feb. 18, 1961.

"an affront to every man": *Nashville Banner*, Feb. 2, 1962.

"the most handsome looking book": LH to Alfred and Blanche Knopf, Oct. 16, 1961, LHP.

"lovers of real poetry": *Virginia Kirkus Service Bulletin*, Oct. 16, 1961.

"as thin and topical as much of the beat material": *Library Journal*, Dec. 1, 1961.

"cannot be evaluated by any canon": *New York Times Book Review*, Oct. 29, 1961.

"What does it take": *Dallas Times-Herald*, Oct. 22, 1961.

"merely curiously interesting and enjoyable": *Greensboro, N.C. News*, Dec. 24, 1961.

"and the thrust of life right now": Chicago *Tribune*, Oct. 29, 1961.

"more sophisticated now and . . . less confined": *Baltimore Afro-American*, Dec. 2, 1961.

"the retort, half-derisive, half-angry": New York *Herald-Tribune*, Nov. 26, 1961.

page 344
"It is cogent, burning, hilarious": Owen Dodson to LH, Oct. 3, 1961, LHP.

"NOT A SINGLE white reviewer": LH to Therman B. O'Daniel, May 18, 1962, LHP.

"Let's see if the critics": LH to S.I. Hayakawa, Aug. 14, 1961, LHP.

"Jazz makes people happy": New York *Herald-Tribune*, June 2, 1963.

page 345
"Convinced that gospel is poised": *New York Times*, Feb. 18, 1962.

"*Here again the Christmas story*": LH, "Black Nativity," Mar. 1962, LHP 173.

"and a star, a single glowing star": *Ibid.*

page 346
"a dramatic fusion of words, dance, and song": Vinnette Carroll to author, interview, Aug. 21, 1987.

page 347

"The title now seems in bad taste": *New York Post,* Dec. 3, 1961.

"an exciting blend of text, dance, spirituals and hymns": *New York Mirror,* Dec. 12, 1961.

"spirit, zest and uninhibited joy": *New York Post,* Dec. 12, 1961.

"neither obtruded himself nor extended himself": New York *Herald-Tribune,* Dec. 12, 1961.

page 348

"to exchange with you our gifts": LH, [Public Appearances], Dec. 18, 1961 (fragment, unsigned), LHP 3334.

"everything from 'badly organized' ": *Pittsburgh Courier,* Jan. 27, 1962.

"What happened with Lionel Hampton": Randy Weston to author, interview, June 20, 1986.

"In the new African countries, honest": LH, "Return to Africa," June 6, 1962, LHP 3411.

page 349

"a combination of the most enticing travel folders": *Ibid.*

"I still remember, how we met": Sunday Osuya to LH, Dec. 13, 1960, LHP.

"You must NOT write to me": LH to Sunday Osuya, Dec. 20, 1960, LHP.

"If I am given any cause": Sunday Osuya to LH, July 4, 1962, LHP.

"from bootleg palm wine joints": LH to Willard Motley, Mar. 24, 1962, LHP.

"lovely even in the rain, rain, rain": LH to Arna Bontemps, Jan. 18, 1962, LHP.

page 350

"Lo, the poor Negro": LH to Arna Bontemps, Jan. 27, 196[2], LHP.

"You cannot deal with this vital subject": Lawrence Langner to LH, Nov. 23. 1962, LHP.

as if "*they* discovered the format": LH to Arna Bontemps, Feb. 16, 1962, LHP.

"a narrative by Langston Hughes": LH to Marian Searchinger, Nov. 24, 1962, LHP.

"a more amateurishly and carelessly presented": LH to Alfred Duckett, Dec. 11, 1962, LHP.

page 351

"*Explain* this to me, if you can": LH to Arna Bontemps, Mar. 4, 1962, LHP.

"for becoming an institution": Arna Bontemps to LH, Mar. 6, 1962, LHP.

"things theatrical for Negroes": LH to Billy Banks, Apr. 10, 1962, LHP.

"an excellent new poet": LH to Arna Bontemps, Apr. 29, 1961, LHP.

"my spiritual and literary father": William M. Kelley to author, interview, Oct. 22, 1987.

page 352

"why I wouldn't give it": LH to Arna Bontemps, Nov. 7, 1961, LHP.

"Langston, I think you're right": LH to Arna Bontemps, May 23, 1962, LHP.

"I don't like enforced integration any more": William Faulkner to Russell Warren Howe, interview, Feb. 21, 1956, published in *Sunday Times* (London), Mar. 4, 1956. See also Charles D. Peavy, *Go Slow Now: Faulkner and the Race Question* (Eugene: Univ. of Oregon, 1971), pp. 69–70.

"Personally, I respect genius": *Chicago Defender,* May 16, 1956.

page 353

"No word, no money—no writeeee!": LH to Arna Bontemps, Feb. 9, 1962, LHP.

"inspires me poetically, as it is inspiring": LH to Mary Becker, May 1, 1963, LHP.

"Someone proposed it quietly": J. Saunders Redding to author, interview, Nov. 13, 1981.

page 354

should reflect "Negro emotions": Philip Segal, "African Writers' Conference," *Cape Times* (Cape Town, South Africa), July 2, 1962.

"There are no such things": *Ibid.*

"A young black man apparently came": Mercer Cook to author, interview, Aug. 5, 1981.

"beautiful readings from his own poems": Bloke Modisane, "Literary Scramble for Africa," *West Africa* (London), June 30, 1962.

"It was a fantastic hit": Vinnette Carroll to author, interview.

page 355

"rather special significance to this event": United States Information Agency (Edward R. Murrow) to LH, May 10, 1962, LHP.

"Ghana will be fortunate": LH to United States Information Agency (Edward R. Murrow), May 12, 1962, LHP.

"And here we were now, thirty years later": Alice Doyle Mahoney to author, interview, June 21, 1980.

"Today, when America comes to Africa": LH, "American Interest in African Culture," June 29, 1962, LHP 3341.

"They received Langston so beautifully": Alice Doyle Mahoney to author, interview.

page 356

"The only reason Nkrumah did not receive": William P. Mahoney to author, interview, June 21, 1980.

"the most exciting telling": NAACP Legal Defense and Education Fund (Jack Greenberg) to LH, Nov. 14, 1961, LHP.

"a wonderful job": Thurgood Marshall to LH, Nov. 20, 1961, LHP.

"Somebody ought to put it in every library": *Saturday Review* 45 (Sept. 29, 1962): 33.

page 357

"But I am glad you stand": Katherine Garrison Biddle to LH, Nov. 14, 1962, LHP.

a "performer and reading in a loud voice": *Washington Post*, Oct. 24, 1962.

"the only beatniks here": *Washington Star*, Oct. 25, 1962.

page 358

"also to me a wonderful adviser": LH to Armina Marshall, Dec. 26, 1962, LHP.

"In the hard-core states of the South": *Michigan Daily*, Jan. 9, 1963.

a "wave of pessimism": Detroit *Free Press*, Jan. 10, 1963.

"I've never felt," he asserted: LH to Faith Wilson, July 30, 1961, LHP.

page 359

"I will write a ten-volume introduction": Alice Childress, address, symposium on "Langston Hughes and the Theatre," Feb. 21, 1987, Harlem School of the Arts. Courtesy of James Bartow and the Harlem School of the Arts.

"If he did say it": LH, "The Problems of the Negro Writer," Feb. 4, 1963, LHP 3349.

"to prove he is with the freedom riders": LH to Nancy Cunard, Apr. 28, 1963, LHP.

page 360

"POSITIVELY be my LAST public appearance": LH to Arna Bontemps, Mar. 29, 1963, LHP.

"I told him not to try": LH to Arna Bontemps, Apr. 15, 1963, LHP.

"SO SHOCKED I WAS ON THE BRINK": Gwendolyn Brooks to LH, Mar. 25, 1963, LHP.

"Comme je ne suis pas encore mort": LH to Pierre Seghers, June 20, 1963, LHP.

"my officially authorized biography": LH to Arna Bontemps, Mar. 11, 1963, in Nichols, *Letters*, p. 455.

page 361

"the Jewish peoples can change their names": *New York Post*, Mar. 22, 1963.

"chuckling with delight" during the Holocaust: [Name withheld] to LH, Mar. 22, 1963, LHP.

"Your tirades against the Caucasian race": [Name withheld] to LH, n.d., LHP.

page 362

the junkies "drooped and dozed and leaned": *Chicago Defender,* Aug. 3, 1963.

"The teenagers of Harlem are my teenagers": *New York Post,* Aug. 2, 1963.

"If Mr. Hughes was depressed": George H. Bass to author, interview, Aug. 17, 1987.

"one might as well have a little fun": LH to Alan L. Dingle, in "Last Will and Testament," June 6, 1963, LHP 612.

14. Blues for Mister Backlash

page 364

"Your laughter and your song": Citation on award of honorary doctorate, Howard University, June 7, 1963, LHP.

page 365

"a bit confused, and/or misinformed": LH to Marian Searchinger, June 22, 1963, LHP.

"He told me that 'Lorenz Hart'": Jobe Huntley, *I Remember Langston Hughes,* p. 51.

"I thought to myself": Jobe Huntley, *I Remember Langston Hughes,* p. 74.

"Mr. Hughes obviously had decided": George H. Bass to author, interview, June 1, 1986.

page 366

"I've always wanted to go": LH to Florence Castleman, May 23, 1961, LHP.

"After three or four of the escorted tours": George H. Bass, "Five Stories About A Man Named Hughes: A Critical Reflection," *Langston Hughes Review* 1 (Spring 1982): 3.

page 367

"She had all her medals on": LH to Arna Bontemps, Aug. 25, 1963, LHP.

"MY DEEPEST SYMPATHY TO YOU": LH to Shirley Graham Du Bois, Aug. 28, 1963, LHP.

had published "my earliest poems": *Freedomways* 5 (1st Quarter 1965): 11.

"I'm still vibrating!": Arna Bontemps to LH, Aug. 29, 1963, LHP.

"In these trying days": Joel W. Schenker to LH, Aug. 26, 1963, LHP.

page 368

"Foes Seek to Bar": *New York Times,* Oct. 28, 1963.

"Beaming Hughes as a 'celebrity' ": *Nashville Banner,* Oct. 12, 1963.

"his resident mau-mau": George H. Bass, "Five Stories," p. 4.

"Always be polite to them, Vinnette": Vinnette Carroll to author, interview, Aug. 21, 1987.

page 369

"Langston was always complaining": Raoul Abdul to author, interview, Nov. 22, 1981.

"I remember how eager he was": Gay Talese to author, interview, June 13, 1987.

"Cullud behaving (on the whole) beautifully": LH to Arna Bontemps, Oct. 28, 1963, LHP.

"As drama it is embarrassing": *New York Times,* Nov. 4, 1963.

page 370

"almost a musical and almost a straight play": New York *Herald-Tribune,* Nov. 4, 1963.

"You are part of the talent": Anna Arnold Hedgeman to LH, Nov. 4, 1963, LHP.

its "miserable clichés" about black life: Murray D. Morrison to LH, Nov. 1, 1963, LHP.

"That show made me so mad": Roy DeCarava to author, interview, Nov. 14, 1981.

"YOUR MAMA LIKES GOSPEL SONGS": Jobe Huntley, *I Remember Langston Hughes*, p. 82.

"my bad-luck-in-theatre season": LH to James E. ("Jimmy") Davis, Apr. 28, 1964, LHP.

"The attack on the black storefront church": Loften Mitchell to author, interview.

page 371

"IT HAS BEEN WONDERFUL": *I Remember Langston Hughes*, p. 79.

"JOBIE YOU ARE THE STAR": *I Remember Langston Hughes*, p. 80.

"A GREAT AND BELOVED AMERICAN": LH to Mrs. John F. Kennedy, Nov. 22, 1963, LHP.

"the sweetest, nicest, most honest": LH to Arna Bontemps, Jan. 25, 1964, LHP.

"dedicated to the young people": LH, "Dedication," in "Jericho-Jim-Crow-Jericho" (draft title), June 9, 1963, LHP 560.

page 372

"incredible heights of poetry and pathos": New York *Herald-Tribune*, Jan. 13, 1964.

a "happy entertainment": *Variety*, Jan. 29, 1964.

"a major landmark": *Town and Village*, Jan. 16, 1964.

"you'd better see an undertaker": *New York Post*, Jan. 13, 1964.

"stirring and prophetic": *New York Times*, Jan. 13, 1964.

"the best Negro voice": *Morning Telegraph*, Jan. 14, 1964.

"Is this it, Mr. Hughes?": Raoul Abdul to author, interview.

"Unless it is done": LH to Stella Holt, Jan. 20, 1964, LHP.

"Langston was exceptionally proud": Gilbert Price to author, interview, Nov. 5, 1987.

page 373

"I miss you as a . . . companion": LH to Gilbert Price, Apr. 3, 1964, LHP.

"He was a very caring man": Gilbert Price to author, interview.

page 374

"the most beautiful bride": LH to Gwendolyn Clark Watson, Feb. 23, 1964, LHP.

"I hear you are interested": LH to Muhammad Ali (Cassius Clay), Mar. 3, 1964, LHP.

page 375

"If Baldwin did not care": LH, "Fire and James Baldwin," Jan. 28, 1964, LHP.

"I . . . respect her intelligence": LH to Indiana University Press, Sept. 23, 1963, LHP.

proclaimed it "a turning point": *Publishers Weekly*, Dec. 9, 1963.

"The Sepia Deb Ball": *Nation* 198 (June 29, 1964): 666.

"all the faults of adolescent poetry": *Saturday Review* 47 (May 30, 1964): 42.

"I saw a most hair-raising play": LH to Frost [Wilkinson], May 2, 1964, LHP.

page 376

("The Jones Year"): LH and Milton Meltzer, *Black Magic: A Pictorial History of the Negro in American Entertainment* (Englewood Cliffs, New Jersey: Prentice Hall, 1971), p. 251.

was "almost as good": LH to Dudley Randall, May 6, 1964, LHP.

"the cullud Eugene O'Neill": LH to Ina Qualls, "Memorial Day," 1964, LHP.

Dutchman was "the most": LH to John Horton, Aug. 14, 1964, LHP.

Hughes "tells us about himself": *Liberator* 4 (May 1964): 22.

"I liked the book, and other people": Judith Jones to author, interview, Dec. 12, 1986.

page 377

"There is a dream": LH, "Dream of Freedom," Apr. 1, 1964; Arna Bontemps Papers, courtesy of Arna Alexander Bontemps.

"what a wonderful means": LH to Ida Cullen (Cooper), June 15, 1964, LHP.

"the *first* definitive . . . collection": LH to Indiana University Press, July 2, 1964, LHP.

"By this point in his career": George H. Bass to author, interview.

page 378

"poet, writer and powerful advocate": [Public Appearances: Western Reserve University], June 10, 1964, LHP 3364.

"Mississippi aligns us": *Ibid.*

"L.H. wants to know": George H. Bass to Arna Bontemps, Apr. 8, 1964; Arna Bontemps Papers, courtesy of Arna A. Bontemps.

"I saw him lying in his coffin": LH, "The Harlem Riot—1964," in John Henrik Clarke, ed., *Harlem: A Community In Transition* (New York: Citadel Press, 1970), pp. 214–220.

"How many bullets does it take": LH, "Death in Yorkville," *The Panther and the Lash*, p. 15.

page 379

"Harlem's feet, through no fault": LH, "The Harlem Riot—1964," p. 215.

Baez was "a peak alone": LH, [Recommendations, Tributes, etc.], n.d., LHP 3408.

"the most important radio event": *Listener* (Great Britain), Dec. 31, 1964.

page 380

"On the flight from New York": *New York Post,* Feb. 5, 1965.

"And not forgetting": *Ibid.*

"C'est beau et très bien fait": LH to Pierre Seghers, Aug. 16, 1964, LHP.

page 381

"Je suis enchanté d'être le sujet": LH to Raymond Quinot, Aug. 16, 1964, LHP.

"White folks thrive on vacations": LH to Carl Van Vechten, Dec. 8, 1964, CVVP, Yale.

"the real home side": Josephine Baker to LH, Dec. 23, 1964, LHP.

"When I heard that Langston": David Amram to author, interview, Dec. 11, 1987.

"this particular Jewish feeling that we're after": David Amram, *Vibrations* (New York: Macmillan), p. 443.

page 382

"I'd love to come down": LH to Carl Van Vechten, Dec. 8, 1964, CVVP, Yale.

"HAVE YOU HEARD THAT CARL": National Institute of Arts and Letters to LH, Dec. 21, 1964, LHP.

"That you blessed *us*": LH to Fania Marinoff (Mrs. Carl Van Vechten), Jan. 27, 1965, LHP.

"all felt, as something tangible": Isidore Platt to LH, Feb. 15, 1965, LHP.

"God placed a special star": Flora D. Coates to LH, Apr. 18, 1965, LHP.

page 383

"a long, hard and unhappy struggle": John D. Short, Jr., to LH, June 10, 1965, LHP.

"This is the DYING season": LH to Arna Bontemps, Mar. 20, 1965, LHP.

"It would be better for the OFF DUTY cabbies": *New York Post,* Jan. 8, 1965.

"I think you belong": "A Cab Driver" to LH, n.d., LHP.

"I never read your column": Unsigned to LH, n.d., LHP.

"Get a hack license": Warren J. Russo to LH, Jan. 8, 1965, LHP.

"I am ashamed of my race": Unsigned to LH, n.d., LHP.

"adverse (and particularly controversial) comment": LH to Bobb J. Hamilton, Jan. 18, 1965, LHP.

"making pornography their symbol": Arna Bontemps to LH, Jan. 7, 1965, LHP.

"Mr. Jones might become America's new": *New York Post,* Jan. 15, 1965.

"The Negro image deserves": *Negro Digest* 14 (Apr. 1965): 75.

page 384

"The Black Artist's role": *Negro Digest* 14 (Apr. 1965): 65.

"Langston was definitely taken": Raoul Abdul to author, interview, Nov. 22, 1981.

"See, what I thought about Langston": Amiri Baraka (LeRoi Jones) to St. Clair Bourne, interview, Feb. 14, 1986. Courtesy of the New York Center for Visual History.

"O Cleobulus, / Othales, Solon": LH to Arna Bontemps, Mar. 20, 1965, LHP.

"lived his life with his head": LH, [Introductions: Booker T. Washington, *Up From Slavery*], Mar.-Apr., 1965, LHP 552.

"In 1965 it is the Negro": *Chicago Defender,* May 15, 1965.

"vulgar, rude and impudent in speech": *New York Post,* July 17, 1964.

page 385

"Politics in any country in the world": LH, "Draft ideas," Dec. 3, 1964, LHP.

15. Final Call

page 386

"YOU HAVE MADE A GREAT": LH to Lyndon Baines Johnson, Mar. 15, 1965, LHP.

page 387

now "eager" to have updated: Doubleday, Inc. (Charles Harris) to LH, Jan. 8, 1965, LHP.

"I have never been a Communist": *Wichita Beacon,* Apr. 26, 1965.

"and now look at the faces": LH, "Life Makes Poetry," tape recording of speech, Apr. 28, 1965; Langston Hughes Papers, Kenneth Spencer Research Library, University of Kansas, Lawrence, Kansas.

page 388

"We are America's Casbah" he conceded: *New York Post,* May 21, 1965.

"I . . . would love to see": LH to LeRoi Jones, July 27, 1965, LHP.

"Let Langston and his ilk": Bobb Hamilton, "A Reply," *Soulbook* 1 (Spring 1965): 114.

"We talked about LeRoi Jones": Rosetta LeNoire to author, interview, Oct. 9, 1987.

page 389

"Eric Bentley and I had put on": Isaiah Sheffer to author, interview, Sept. 23, 1987.

"Langston was given *carte blanche:* Paule Marshall to author, interview, Oct. 22, 1987.

"His ability to take material": Michel Fabre to author, interview, Oct. 12, 1981.

"I remember my impression": William M. Kelley to author, interview, Oct. 22, 1987.

page 390

"Langston was like a father figure": Jean Wagner to author, interview, Oct. 11, 1981.

"prejudice exists in all American states": *Pittsburgh Courier,* July 31, 1965.

page 391

"Landlord, Landlord / My roof": LH, "Ballad of the Landlord," *Selected Poems,* pp. 238–239.

"Langston and I were such good friends": Vinnette Carroll to author, interview.

"a swinging dance pantomime": *New York Post,* Sept. 3, 1965.

"a major theatre event": *Cue,* May 29, 1965.

a "ponderous Germanic trifle": *Newsday,* May 21, 1965.

page 392

the positive side of "the Negro face": *Sunday News,* Feb. 20, 1966.

"the way he transforms the material": LH to Gilbert Price, Oct. 15, 1963, LHP.

"All those hundred of years": David Amram, *Vibrations,* p. 442.

page 393

"fair, decent, or moral?": Isaiah Sheffer to LH, Sept. 29, 1965, Langston Hughes Papers, Fisk University.

"nor was I aware of it": LH to Isaiah Sheffer, Oct. 21, 1965, LHP.

"Stella, have you *really* been honest": G. Jeannette Hodge, "Open Letter to the Producers of the Production of 'The Prodigal Son' and 'The Exception and the Rule'," Sept. 3, 1965, LHP.

"Stella was very devoted to Langston": Vinnette Carroll to author, interview.

"Stella Holt played the role": Isaiah Sheffer to author, interview.

"written as a companion piece": LH, "Tell It to Telstar," Aug. 9, 1965, LHP 3762.

page 394

"an outright attempt to cheat us": Isaiah Sheffer to LH, Oct. 19, 1965, LHP.

"If I had to find fault with Langston": Vinnette Carroll to author, interview.

"He was really far too meek": Maxwell T. Cohen to author, interview, June 26, 1984.

"My advice, STAY in Paris": LH to James E. Davis, Oct. 9, 1965, LHP.

"to those who have given": LH, "Let Us Remember," Nov. 15, 1965, LHP 628

page 395

"—Zen Buddhism or Florsheim shoes": Alan Rich, "American Judaism looks at the living arts: Sing unto the Lord," *American Judaism* 15 (Winter 1965–66): 27.

"wildly crazy" audiences: Stella Holt to LH, Oct. 29, 1965, LHP.

"50 powerful and unusual stories": LH, "White On Black," Dec. 15, 1965, LHP 3839.

page 396

"I keep telling him . . . to take those chips": LH to Jack Golden, Apr. 4, 1963, LHP.

"Creator Hughes has decided": *Chicago Defender,* Jan. 8, 1966.

"I am a Negro and I can find": *New York Post,* Aug. 16, 1963.

page 397

"They attacked me!": LH to Pat Belcher, n.d. [Jan. 1966], LHP.

"The stage was in a turmoil": Julio Galer to author, June 5, 1987.

"good, bad and indifferent": Cleveland *Plain Dealer,* Feb. 22, 1966.

"now that Negro books": LH to Johnson Publishing Co. (Doris Saunders), Feb. 24, 1966, LHP.

a "DEFINITIVE anthology": LH to Arna Bontemps, Nov. 26, 1966, LHP.

page 398

"a tiresome, boring hour": *Daily News,* Feb. 22, 1966.

"as primly starched or as lifeless": *New York Times,* Feb. 22, 1966.

that "dusky sash across the middle": *Variety,* Feb. 23, 1966.

hailed it as "an innovation": Clarence Muse to LH, Feb. 28, 1966, LHP.

"There has been little balance": LH to Milton Larkin, Feb. 25, 1966, LHP.

"that all Negroes are primitive": LH, ed., *The Best Short Stories by Negro Writers* (Boston: Little, Brown, 1967), p. ix.

page 399

"To be a good writer": LH, "On Being A Writer," Mar. 24, 1966, LHP 3389.

"The thing was, is, you're a veteran": Alex Haley to LH, Jan. 25, 1966, LHP.

"You are a thoughtful friend": Amy Spingarn to LH, Jan. 29, 1966, LHP.

"Half a century of poetry": Richard Rive, "Taos in Harlem: An Interview with Langston Hughes," *Contrast* (South Africa) 4 (Nov. 1966): 36.

page 400

"the true spirits of a grand festival": Millicent Dobbs Jordan, "Personal Reminiscences of Langston Hughes," *Langston Hughes Review* 1 (Fall 1982): 12.

"We considered Langston Hughes to be": Léopold Sédar Senghor to René Tavernier, interview, Dec. 12, 1985. Transcribed and translated by Sarah Arvio. Courtesy of the New York Center for Visual History.

"In his own way": *New York Times,* May 1, 1966.

page 401

"In the end . . . nobody is going to remember": *New York Times,* Apr. 24, 1966.

"I was lonely in Dakar": Sim Copans to author, interview, Sept. 22, 1981.

"but Langston turned me": Jean Blackwell Hutson to author, interview, June 18, 1984.

"the Great One, Langston Hughes": Millicent Dobbs Jordan, "Personal Reminiscences of Langston Hughes," p. 12.

"I asked Langston if I could use": Lloyd M. Garrison to author, interview, Oct. 5, 1987.

"We used to ride around": William Greaves to author, interview, Feb. 25, 1987.

"Whatever the Russians expected": Mercer Cook to author, interview, Aug. 5, 1981.

page 402

"deeply moved his largely African audience": *New York Times,* May 1, 1966.

"is that American society": LH, "Black Writers In A Troubled World," Mar. 26, 1966, LHP 3390.

"What Langston has left us": Léopold Sédar Senghor to René Tavernier, interview.

16. Do Nothing Till You Hear From Me

page 404

"Lagos . . . is more like the old Chicago": LH to Arna Bontemps, May 1, 1966, in Nichols, *Letters,* p. 473.

"The swift change": Sunday Osuya to LH, Feb. 2, 1966, LHP.

page 405

"Lumumba was black / And he didn't trust": LH, "Lumumba's Grave," *The Panther and the Lash,* pp. 65–66.

"I mistook the Speaker of the Assembly": LH to Arna Bontemps, May 1, 1966, LHP.

"a symbol of our negritude": LH, "To Emperor Haile Selassie," [Public Appearances], 1966, LHP 3392.

page 406

but "*LOATHED*" Addis Ababa: LH to Raoul Abdul, June 8, 1966, LHP.

"Haile Selassie," Hughes snapped: George H. Bass, "Five Stories," p. 5.

"I just left you in Tanzania!": Lebert "Sandy" Bethune to author, interview, Nov. 16, 1981.

page 407

"It was like a seal": Henri Cartier-Bresson to LH, June 24, 1966, LHP.

"It was hard to believe": Ted Joans to author, interview, Oct. 7, 1981.

Hughes "added that he'd rather encounter": Ted Joans, "The Langston Hughes I Knew," *Black World* 21 (Sept. 1972): 18.

page 408

"Excuse me, I'm Langston Hughes": *Ibid.*

"Hughes was very good": George Whitman to author, interview, Oct. 6, 1981.

"One's words don't go in one ear": LH to Arna Bontemps, Aug. 5, 1966, LHP.

"He would call me": Paule Marshall to author, interview.

page 409

"very important to have a lower priced book": Alfred A. Knopf, Inc. (Judith Jones) to LH, Nov. 18, 1966, LHP.

"Pushed into the corner": LH, "Black Panther," *The Panther and the Lash,* p. 19.

page 410

"There is no poem": LH, "A Note On Prejudices," Nov. 26, 1966, LHP 838.

"SEND FOR LAFAYETTE AND TELL HIM": LH, "Final Call," *The Panther and the Lash,* p. 21. Previously, "Harlem Call (After the 1964 riots)," *American Dialog* (Oct.-Nov. 1964): 37.

page 411

"the ranging of race against race": Peter M. Bergman, *Chronological History of the Negro in America* (New York: Harper and Row, 1969), p. 596.

"Roywilkins is an eternal faggot": LeRoi Jones, "Civil Rights Poem," *Black Magic: Collected Poetry, 1961–1967* (New York: Bobbs-Merrill Co.), p. 140.

"i have been seeking / what i have never found": LH, "Stokely Malcolm Me," *The Panther and the Lash,* p. 94.

page 412

"There was in Langston Hughes's face": Bayard Rustin, "On Langston Hughes." Transcript of remarks at Langston Hughes Memorial Evening, Columbia University, 1967. Courtesy of Milton Meltzer.

"In these rather dreary times": LH to Academy of American Poets (Elizabeth Kray), Aug. 22, 1966, LHP.

("I adore Marianne Moore!"): *Ibid.*

"It's Art with a capital 'A' ": LH to Arna Bontemps, Dec. 9, 1966, LHP.

"the astounding Miss Alice Walker": LH, *The Best Short Stories by Negro Writers,* p. xii.

page 413

"Mine is her first important publication": LH to Arna Bontemps, Dec. 22, 1966, LHP.

"Langston Hughes published my first short story": Alice Walker to Oxford Univ. Press (Jeffrey Seroy), May 19, 1986, OUP files. Courtesy of Alice Walker.

"I was struck by how alone Langston seemed": Alice Walker to author, Oct. 13, 1986. Courtesy of Alice Walker.

"a sort of present-day G.K. Chesterton": W.J. Weatherby, "Chesterton in burnt cork," *The Guardian* (Manchester), Dec. 5, 1966, p.6.

page 414

"By then the poetry is written": LH, "Not What Was," *Massachusetts Review* 6 (Winter-Spring 1965): 305.

page 415

"NO MORE AID to Cullud": LH to Arna Bontemps, Dec. 28, 1966, LHP.

"if you hear of anything": LH to Ermaline Lebeer, Dec. 26, 1966, LHP.

He felt "kind of used and depleted": Raoul Abdul to St. Clair Bourne, interview, Oct. 18, 1985. Courtesy of the New York Center for Visual History.

page 416

"right now money is of the essence": LH to Arna Bontemps, Apr. 19, 1967, LHP.

"I do NOT *now* want": LH to Arna Bontemps, Jan. 5, 1967, LHP.

"since black men and women": LH, "Notes For A Poetry Reading," n.d. [1967?], LHP 3395.

"Some people," he complained to the audience: *Los Angeles Times,* Feb 20, 1967.

Feather was a "dope": LH to Marian Palfi, Feb. 22, 1967, LHP.

page 417

"Our first thought of you": Margaret C. Gates to LH, Mar. 14, 1967, LHP.

Hughes's "roly poly" figure: *Washington Post,* Feb. 22, 1967.

"Me, no! I love him": LH to Arna Bontemps, Apr. 19, 1967, LHP.

page 418

"He has told us elsewhere": *New York Times Book Review,* Mar. 5, 1967.

"My seeking has been to explain": LH to *Who's Who in America,* n.d. [1967], LHP.

"Langston was all dressed up": Lebert Bethune to author, interview, Nov. 16, 1981.

"The racial climate has gotten so complicated": Martha MacGregor, "The Week in Books," *New York Post,* Mar. 25, 1967.

"The house is still ALL torn up": LH to Arna Bontemps, Apr. 22, 1967, LHP.

"Langston was his usual self": Ruth Jett to author, interview, Oct. 12, 1987.

page 420

"a wonderful and lovely lady": *New York Times,* Apr. 14, 1967.

"I'd LOVE to come to Paris": LH to Editions Robert Laffont (Françoise Lebert), Apr. 25, 1967, LHP.

"But not for just a week": LH to Arna Bontemps, Apr. 22, 1967, LHP.

"If you go to Paris": Arna Bontemps to LH, Apr. 22, 1967, LHP.

"Misery is when you are not supposed": LH, "Black Misery," Apr. 28, 1967, LHP 173.

page 421

"registered anonymously as James Hughes": Faith Berry, *Langston Hughes: Before and Beyond Harlem,* p. 328.

"He was not treated as an indigent": Raoul Abdul to author, interview, Oct. 29, 1987.

he signed as "James L. Hughes": Records of New York Polyclinic Medical School and Hospital, Chart No. 100475 (James Langston Hughes). Declaring bankruptcy, the hospital closed in 1977. Its records are in the possession of Mr. Augustine Rodriguez, Court Appointed Procurator of Medical Records, Long Island City, New York.

For an analysis of the medical records I am indebted to Dr. Julian Bennett Hyman of St. Clare's Hospital and Health Center. Dr. Hyman was one of Hughes's attending physicians in his last illness. For further analysis of the records, I am additionally indebted to Dr. Sarah Horton Kelly of the Columbia College of Physicians and Surgeons, Columbia University, New York.

page 422

"Unfortunately suddenly in hospital": LH to Editions Robert Laffont (Françoise Lebert), n.d. [May 1967], LHP.

"I asked him, 'What are you doing": Ivan von Auw, Jr. to author, interview, Mar. 21, 1987.

"I had come to the hospital": Lebert Bethune to author, interview.

"I guess I lost my cool": *Ibid.*

"he asked me to bring him": Raoul Abdul to author, interview, Oct. 29, 1987.

"His first day of recuperation": *Ibid.*

page 424

"We didn't find his will": George H. Bass to author, interview, Sept. 2, 1986.

"YOU ARE REQUESTED TO ATTEND": Jobe Huntley, *I Remember Langston Hughes,* p. 98.

"Raoul or George had called me the day before": Randy Weston to author, interview, June 20, 1986.

page 425

"the death wish which had haunted this gentle man": *New York Post,* May 26, 1967.

ACKNOWLEDGMENTS

IN THE SUMMER of 1979, at the request of Professor George Houston Bass of Brown University, the surviving executor-trustee of the Langston Hughes estate, I began the task of writing a biography of Hughes. With the appearance of my second volume, the job is done. I am indebted to Professor Bass for his kindness and encouragement at every point, as well as for sharing with me his knowledge of Langston Hughes. Above all, I thank him for allowing me to express, without hindrance, my own version and vision of Hughes's life.

Among institutions, I am grateful to the National Endowment for the Humanities, the Rockefeller Foundation, the Center for Advanced Study in the Behavioral Sciences, the John Simon Guggenheim Foundation, and the American Council of Learned Societies, as well as to Stanford University and Rutgers University. At Stanford, I thank in particular Bliss Carnochan, William Chace, Diane Middlebrook, Albert Gelpi, Robert Polhemus, and Jay Fliegelman. At Rutgers, I have been indebted to many people, including George Levine, Richard Poirier, Thomas Van Laan, Donald Gibson, and Cheryl Wall of the Department of English, as well as to Tilden Edelstein and Kenneth Wheeler.

Among librarians, I would like to acknowledge my debt above all to the administrators and staff of the Beinecke Rare Book and Manuscript Library at Yale University, where the Langston Hughes Papers, donated by Hughes himself, may be found in the James Weldon Johnson Memorial Collection of Negro Arts and Letters founded by Carl Van Vechten. I am grateful to Donald Gallup and David Schoonover, former curators of the Collection in American Literature, as well as to Patricia Cannon Willis, the present curator. I also thank Lisa Browar, Joan Hofmann, Steve Jones, and many others on the staff, past and present, for their unfailing skill and courtesy. All researchers in the Langston Hughes Papers are particularly indebted to George P. Cunningham who, with Patricia Gaskins and Martha Schall, organized the Langston Hughes correspondence at the Beinecke.

I also thank members of the staff at the Amistad Research Center (New Orleans); the Archives Department of the Atlanta University Center Woodruff Library; Special Collections at the University of Arkansas, Fayetteville; the Bancroft Library of the University of California; the Bibliothèque Nationale; the Harrison Memorial Library of Carmel, California; the Library of Congress; the Columbiana Collection and the Butler Library at Columbia University; the archives of the Federal Bureau of Investigation; the Fisk University Library;

the Civica Biblioteca Berio of Genoa, Italy; the Hatch-Billops Collection, New York; the Hoover Institution; the Huntington Library; the Carl Sandburg Collection of the University of Illinois; the Lenin Library in Moscow; the Lincoln, Illinois Public Library; Lincoln University (Pennsylvania) Library; the Kenneth Spencer Research Library, the University of Kansas; the University of Massachusetts, Amherst; the Moorland-Spingarn Research Center, Howard University; the National Archives, Washington, D.C.; the New York Historical Society; the Bobst Library, New York University; the New York Public Library, Astor, Lenox and Tilden Foundations, including the Schomburg Center for Research in Black Culture, the Library and Museum of the Performing Arts at Lincoln Center, the Berg Collection in English and American Literature, and the Manuscripts and Archives Division; the New York Center for Visual History; the Southern Historical Collection of the University of North Carolina; the Oklahoma Department of Libraries; the Oberlin College Archives; Rutgers University Library; Stanford University Library; the George Arents Research Library of Syracuse University; the library of the University of Texas, Austin; the Western Reserve Historical Society; and the Vivian Harsh Collection at the Carter G. Woodson Regional Library Center of the Chicago Public Library. For collections of material still in private hands, I would like to thank especially Alberta Bontemps, Louise Thompson Patterson, and Gladys Mahoney.

For generously sending me important pieces of information over the years, as well as encouraging me in other ways, I am indebted to Kenneth P. Neilson, the author of *The World of Langston Hughes Music* (1982), as well as to other friends such as Katie Armitage of Lawrence, Kansas, and Thomas A. Webster of Kansas City, Missouri. In the past decade, I have also benefited from the brilliance and hard work of various research assistants, including Peter Gibian and Marcia Ellis at Stanford, and Garrett White at Rutgers.

In preparing the biography, I have spoken to countless people who have shared with me their personal knowledge of Langston Hughes. These include M. Margaret Anderson, Ivan von Auw, Jr., Raoul Abdul, David Amram, Gonzales Austen, Louis Aschille, Margaret Walker Alexander, Billie Allen, George Houston Bass, Alberta Bontemps, Arna Alexander Bontemps, Paul Bontemps, Gwendolyn Brooks, Amiri Baraka (LeRoi Jones), Roy Blackburn, the late James Baldwin, Richmond Barthé, Lebert Bethune, Eugene Bone, the late Marguerite Cartwright, Matt N. Crawford, John Henrik Clarke, Maxwell T. Cohen, the late Mercer Cook, Dick Campbell, Vinnette Carroll, Alice Childress, Liska March Cracovaner, Lee Crowe, Sim Copans, Henri Cartier-Bresson, William R. Cole, St. Clair Drake, Robert Dudley, Griffith J. Davis, Arthur P. Davis, Ann Dufaux-Rhodes, Jimmy "Lover Man" Davis, Roy DeCarava, Toye Davis, Robert D. Ericson, Cathline Iatser Ericson, Ralph Ellison, James A. Emanuel, Albert A. Edwards, Michel Fabre, Elton Fax, W. Edward Farrison, Howard Fenton, Julio Galer, Lloyd K. Garrison, Lloyd M. Garrison, Adele Glasgow, David Givens, the late Paul Green, Eugene Grigsby, Thomasena Grigsby, William Greaves, Harold L. Gaines, John Horton, Alex Haley, Dr. Julian Bennett Hyman, Jean Blackwell Hutson, Butler Henderson, Blyden Jackson, Ruth Jett,

Grace Johnson, Judith Jones, Rowena Woodham Jelliffe, Millicent Dobbs Jordan, Ted Joans, Leroy D. Johnson, John Henry Jones, Bruce Kellner, the late George Kent, William M. Kelley, the late Jay Leyda, Si-lan Chen Leyda, Maxim Lieber, Minna Lieber, Rosetta LeNoire, David Leeming, the late Rayford W. Logan, Paule Marshall, the late Henry Lee Moon, Rachelle Marshall, Harry Murphy, Milton Meltzer, William P. Mahoney, Alice Doyle Mahoney, Gladys Mahoney, Jan Meyerowitz, Loften Mitchell, the late Richard Bruce Nugent, the late Therman B. O'Daniel, Louise Thompson Patterson, Lindsay Patterson, Raymond Patterson, Phil W. Petrie, Gilbert Price, Eulah Pharr, Paul Peters, George N. Redd, the late Jay Saunders Redding, Mary Savage, the late John D. Short, Jr., Joe Sherman, Elie Siegmeister, Isaiah Sheffer, Melvin Stewart, Gay Talese, Ellen Tarry, Frances Wills Thorpe, Sue Bailey Thurman, Prentiss Taylor, Nate V. White, Irma Cayton Wertz, Randy Weston, Derek Walcott, Thomas A. Webster, the late Jean Wagner, John A. Williams, William J. Weatherby, Zeppelin Wong, George Whitman, and Bruce M. Wright.

Many people contributed in a variety of ways also indispensable to my research—by responding to requests for information, expediting my research in libraries, reading portions of the manuscript, or in other tangible and intangible ways aiding me in my project over the past nine years. I thank Katie Armitage, Richard Avedon, Michel Auffray of the Institut Francophone de Paris, M. Margaret Anderson, Sam Allen, Ivan von Auw, Nancy Abrams, Jervis Anderson, Lois Bloom, Florence E. Borders, Ursula Berg-Lunk, Faith Berry, St. Clair Bourne, Jean-Claude Boffard, Esme Bhan, Richard Brophy, Phyllis Bischof, E. Randolph Biddle, A'lelia Bundles, William E. Bigglestone, Thomas H. Bresson, William C. Beyer, Richard Barksdale, Marcellus Blount, Rae Linda Brown, Rudolph Byrd, Dottie Berryman, Harold W. Billings, Schuyler Chapin, Brigitte Carnochan, Jack Chen, Leslie Collins, Wayne Cooper, Michael Clegg, Charles Cooney, Jackie Coogan, Sophy Cornwell, Catherina Caldwell, Marina Castañeda, James Casey, the late Ida Cullen Cooper, Dean Crawford, Gail Cohen, Walter Daniel, Michael Dabrishus, the late Charles T. Davis, Ann Dufaux-Rhodes, Carolyn Davis, Martin Duberman, Ruth Donaldson, Mari Evans, Katherine Emerson, Dolores Elliott, Lillie Johnson Edwards, Grace Frankowsky, Wendell Foster, Robert Farnsworth, Geneviève Fabre, Darra Goldstein, Mary Green-Cohen, Sandra Govan, Christine Gilson, J. Lee Greene, Zelma George, Chryss Galassi, James Geiwetz, Richard Green, Henry Harder, Nathan Irvin Huggins, Ken Hall, Louis R. Harlan, Kathleen Hauke, Paul Horgan, Melvin Hinton, Robert Hemenway, Akiba Sullivan Harper, Michael Wesley Harris, James Hatch, Gary Imhoff, Donald Joyce, Eloise McKinney Johnson, Steve Jansen, Philip L. Jones, Howard M. Jason, Ivy Jackman, Charles H. Johnson, the late Arthur Koestler, William Koshland, Roberta Klatzsky, Allen Klots, Phyllis R. Klotman, Jamie Katz, William Kunstler, the late Alfred A. Knopf, Vera Kubitskaya, Hilja Kukk, Dr. Sarah Horton Kelly, Werner Lange, Gardner Lindzey, Diana Lachatanere, Vaughn C. Love, Kenneth Lohf, Susan Lardner, Cliff Lashley, David Levin, David Levering Lewis, Edward Lyon, Richard A. Long, Paule Marshall, Marlene Merrill, Robert W. McDonnell,

John H. Mackey, Harry Murphy, Alice Clarke McClanahan, Henry G. Morgan, James Murray, Penelope Niven McJunkin, Michael Miller, Daphne Muse, Edward J. Mullen, Mark Naison, Minda Novek, Olivia Martin, Kenneth P. Neilson, Richard Powell, Paul R. Palmer, Zella J. Black Patterson, Bernard Perry, LeRoy Percy, Youra Qualls, Virginia Rust, Natasha Russell, Sylvia Lyons Render, Daniel and Florence Ryan, Leslie Sanders, Everett Sims, Richard Schrader, Mark Scott, Jessie Carney Smith, Warren Smith, Ann Allen Shockley, Deborah Willis-Ryan, Paulette Sutton, Reuben Silver, Eloise Spicer, Sandra Solimano, Kaethe Schick, Murray Sperber, John Stinson, Marian and Howard M. Spiro, James Spady, G. Thomas Tanselle, Arthur L. Tolson, John Edgar Tidwell, Antoine Tissier, A. Morgan Tabb, Ann Tanneyhill, Joy Thompson, Roy Thomas, Robert Thomas, William M. Tuttle, Jr., Honor Tranum, Lenora Vance-Robinson, Kraig S. Weston, Beatrice White, Grace Walker, Emery Wimbish, Jr., Emily Woudenberg, H. A. Selby Wooding, William H. Waddell, Kenneth Warren, R. B. Wellington, Sheryl K. Williams, Allen Wright, Thomas Weir, Ella Wolfe, Richmond B. Williams, Craig Werner, Mary Jane Welch, Rhoda Wynn, Michael R. Winston, Thomas H. Wirth, Irving and Marilyn Yalom, and Andrea Lerner Young.

I have probably failed to mention some of the many people on whom I depended over the years in researching and writing these two volumes. If so, I am sorry.

As in the case of the first volume, Bruce Kellner, Arna Alexander Bontemps, and my wife Marvina White read various versions of this book and provided advice and encouragement. At Oxford University Press, I again thank William Sisler for his early and lasting confidence in my story, and Susan Meigs for her splendid efforts to improve it. My thanks again, also, to Quitman Marshall, and to Patricia Powell of Harold Ober Associates for her advice and counsel.

For permission to quote excerpts from previously unpublished material written by Langston Hughes, I thank George Houston Bass, executor-trustee of the Langston Hughes Estate. For permission to quote this material, as well as material in the Carl Van Vechten Papers, I also thank the Collection of American Literature, Beinecke Rare Book and Manuscript Library, Yale University. I am also indebted to the Beinecke Library for permission to reproduce certain photographs from the Langston Hughes Papers.

For other photographs, I thank Richard Avedon; Raoul Abdul; Bill Fitzgerald and AP/Wide World Photos; George Houston Bass; Photo Bracher Dakar; Henri Cartier-Bresson and Magnum Photos; Griffith J. Davis; Roy DeCarava; Ralph and Fanny Ellison; A. Hansen Studio; Don Hunstein; Karsh of Ottawa, Woodfin Camp Associates, and the Billy Rose Collection, Library and Museum of the Performing Arts at Lincoln Center, New York Public Library; Bruce Kellner; the late Marian Palfi; Joe Sherman; the William Grant Still Papers, Special Collections, University of Arkansas Libraries, Fayetteville; and the Schomburg Center for Research in Black Culture, New York Public Library, Astor, Lenox and Tilden Foundations.

For both volumes of this biography, I also gratefully acknowledge permission from Amistad Research Center (Clifton H. Johnson, curator), for quotations from the Countee Cullen Papers; the Special Collections Department of the University of Arkansas Libraries, Fayetteville; Atlanta University Center Woodruff Library, Archives Department, for quotations from the Countee Cullen-Harold Jackman Collection; Bancroft Library, University of California, Berkeley, for letters from LH to Noël Sullivan and Marie Short; Carl Cowl and the Claude McKay Estate, for letters from Claude McKay; the late Ida M. Cullen-Cooper, for unpublished letters by Countee Porter Cullen; Clive E. Driver and the Marianne C. Moore Estate for a letter from Marianne Moore; Ralph Ellison, for letters to LH and to Richard Wright; Dr. C. J. Hurston, for letters from Zora Neale Hurston; Rowena Woodham Jelliffe, for correspondence with the Rosenwald Foundation; Maxim Lieber, for letters to LH; Alfred A. Knopf, Inc., for excerpts from various books by Langston Hughes, including *I Wonder as I Wander, Shakespeare in Harlem, Fields of Wonder, One-Way Ticket, Selected Poems, Ask Your Mama,* and *The Panther and the Lash.;* Alfred A. Knopf, Inc., again, for letters from Blanche Knopf, Alfred Knopf, and other Knopf officials to LH; the Moorland-Spingarn Research Center (Thomas C. Battle, director); the New York Center for Visual History, for excerpts from certain interviews in connection with the "Voices and Visions" television series on major American poets; the New York Public Library, Astor, Lenox and Tilden Foundations; Louise Thompson Patterson, for letters to LH from her and from the late Mr. William L. Patterson; the Schomburg Center for Research in Black Culture; Simon and Schuster, for quotations from letters from their officials to LH; Judith Anne Still, for letters from William Grant Still; the Carl Van Vechten Estate, for excerpts from letters from Van Vechten. For quotations from the letters of Arna Wendell Bontemps to Langston Hughes, I am grateful to Mrs. Alberta Bontemps and to Harold Ober Associates.

INDEX